W9-CMR-689

INTRODUCTION TO LOGIC

INTRODUCTION TO LOGIC

FOURTH EDITION

Irving M. Copi University of Hawaii

MACMILLAN PUBLISHING CO., INC.
New York
COLLIER MACMILLAN PUBLISHERS
London

Printed in the United States of America

Macmillan Publishing Co., Inc.
866 Third Avenue, New York, New York 10022

Collier-Macmillan Canada, Ltd.

Library of Congress catalog card number: 70–171565

Printing: 8 9 Year: 6 7 8 9

This book is dedicated to
my mother and father

Preface

There are obvious benefits to be gained from the study of logic: heightened ability to express ideas clearly and concisely; increased skill in defining one's terms; enlarged capacity to formulate arguments rigorously and to scrutinize them critically. But the greatest benefit, in my judgment, is the recognition that reason can be applied in every aspect of human affairs.

Democratic institutions are under attack today from all directions. They can best be defended by being made to work. And this can be accomplished only by each citizen thinking for himself, discussing issues freely with his fellows, deliberating, weighing evidence, and acknowledging that with effort we can tell the difference between good and bad arguments. If we are to govern ourselves well and responsibly, we must be reasonable. The study of logic can give us not only practice in reasoning but respect for reason.

To help achieve these goals a textbook of logic should contain illustrations and exercises that are of human, scientific, and philosophical interest, and that have been published by serious writers as significant attempts to solve real problems. Ideally these should include fallacies as well as paradigms of demonstration. This new edition contains over 600 new exercises, many of which were selected specifically to fulfill this requirement. Others were introduced to provide a more gradual transition from easier to more difficult and challenging exercises that the student must master if he is to emerge from the course with logical skills as well as logical understanding.

Some new materials have been inserted in this edition to help the student translate arguments from ordinary English to the logical symbolism in which they are more readily appraised. And some additional helpful hints or rules of thumb are supplied for the construction of proofs of validity for extended arguments. Thanks largely to the useful criticisms by Professor C. L. Hamblin in his book *Fallacies,* some corrections have been made in Chapter 3.

Since the appearance of the third edition, many readers have written to suggest changes in the book, and in many cases I have gratefully accepted their recommendations. Among those whose correspondence was particularly helpful are: Professor Bernard Adelman of Bentley College, Mr. Dale E. Baker of the University of Nebraska at Omaha, Mr. David Bradley of the University of Connecticut, Professor James I. Campbell of Eisenhower College, Mr. Walter Charen of Rutgers University, Professor George Chatalian of Franklin Pierce College, Professor Carl Cohen of the University of Michigan, Mrs. Beatrice E. Cseplo of the University of Cincinnati, Professor John J. Dillon of Villanova University, Miss Joan Gallagher of the State University of New York at New Paltz, Miss Mary Ann Leonard of Montclair State College, Dr. Jakob Levy-Zaks of Tel Aviv, Professor Charles R. Magel of Moorehead State College, Professor C. Mason Myers of Northern Illinois University, and Professor Marsha Rockey of Ohio State University. I have also been fortunate in receiving some very good advice from my colleague Professor Edward Harter. Mrs. Karuna Ramashanker and Miss Heide Miller kindly helped with some of the proofreading.

Again, most of all I am deeply grateful to my wife for her help and encouragement in preparing this new edition.

I. M. C.

Contents

PART ONE LANGUAGE

Part One Language

Chapter 1
Introduction

. . . this we do affirm—that if truth is to be sought in every division of Philosophy, we must, before all else, possess trustworthy principles and methods for the discernment of truth. Now the Logical branch is that which includes the theory of criteria and of proofs; so it is with this that we ought to make our beginnings.

—*Sextus Empiricus*

1.1 What Is Logic?

Logic is the study of the methods and principles used to distinguish good (correct) from bad (incorrect) reasoning. This definition must not be taken to imply that only the student of logic can reason well or correctly. To say so would be as mistaken as to say that one can run well only if he has studied the physics and physiology involved in describing that activity. Some excellent athletes are quite ignorant of the complex processes that go on inside themselves when they perform. And, needless to say, the somewhat elderly professors who know most about such things would perform very poorly were they to risk their dignity on the athletic field. Even given the same basic muscular and nervous apparatus, the person who knows might not surpass the "natural athlete."

But given the same native keenness of intellect, a person who has studied logic is more likely to reason correctly than one who has never thought about the general principles involved in that activity. There are several reasons for this. First of all, the proper study of logic will approach it as an art as well as a science, and the student will do exercises in all parts of the theory being learned. Here, as anywhere else, practice will help to make perfect. In the second place, a traditional part of the study of logic has been the examination and analysis of fallacies, or mistakes in reasoning. Not only does this part of the subject give increased insight into the principles of reasoning in general, but an acquaintance with these pitfalls helps to keep us from stumbling into them. Finally, the study of logic will give the student certain techniques, certain easily applied methods for testing the correctness of many different kinds of reasoning, including his own; and when errors are easily detected they are less likely to be made.

Logic has frequently been defined as the science of the laws of thought. But this definition, although it gives a clue to the nature of logic, is not accurate. In the first place, thinking is one of the processes studied by psychologists. Logic cannot be "the" science of the laws of thought, because psychology is also a science which deals with laws of thought (among other things). And logic is not a branch of psychology; it is a separate and distinct field of study.

In the second place, if "thought" refers to *any* process that occurs in people's minds, not all thought is an object of study for the logician. All reasoning is thinking, but not all thinking is reasoning. Thus one may "think" of a number between one and ten, as in a parlor game, without doing any "reasoning" about it. There are many mental processes or kinds of thought that are different from reasoning. One may remember something, or imagine it, or regret it, without doing any reasoning about it. Or one may let his thoughts "drift along" in a daydream or reverie, building castles in the air, or following what psychologists call free association, in which one image is replaced by another in an order that is anything but logical. There is often great significance to the sequence of thoughts in such free association, and some psychiatric techniques make use of it. One need not be a psychiatrist, of course, to gain insight into a person's character by observing the flow of his stream of consciousness. It is the basis of a very effective literary technique pioneered by James Joyce in his novel *Ulysses*. Conversely, if a person's character is sufficiently well known beforehand, the flow of his stream of consciousness can be traced or even anticipated. We all remember how Sherlock Holmes used to break in on his friend Watson's silences, to answer the very question to which Dr. Watson had been "led" in his musings. There seem to be certain laws governing reverie, but they are studied not by logicians but by psychologists; the laws which describe the movements of the mind in reverie are psychological laws rather than logical principles. To define "logic" as the science of the laws of thought is to make it include too much.

Another common definition of logic calls it the science of reasoning. This definition is better, but it still will not do. Reasoning is a special kind of thinking in which inference takes place, in which conclusions are drawn from premisses. It is still a kind of thinking, however, and therefore still part of the psychologist's subject matter. As psychologists examine the reasoning process they find it to be extremely complex, highly emotional, consisting of awkward trial-and-error procedures illuminated by sudden—and sometimes apparently irrelevant—flashes of insight. These are all of importance to psychology. But the logician is not in the least concerned with the dark ways by which the mind arrives at its conclusions during the actual process of reasoning. He is concerned only with the correctness of the completed process. His question is always: does the conclusion reached follow from the premisses used or assumed? If the premisses provide adequate grounds for accepting the conclusion, if asserting the premisses to be true warrants asserting the conclusion to be true also, then the reasoning is correct. Otherwise it is incorrect.

The distinction between correct and incorrect reasoning is the central problem with which logic deals. The logician's methods and techniques have been developed primarily for the purpose of making this distinction clear. The logician is interested in all reasoning, regardless of its subject matter, but only from this special point of view.

1.2 Premisses and Conclusions

To clarify the explanation of logic offered in the preceding section, it will help to set forth and discuss some of the special terms used by the logician in his work. *Inference* is a process by which one proposition is reached and affirmed on the basis of one or more other propositions accepted as the starting point of the process. The logician is not concerned with the process of inference, but with the propositions that are the initial and end points of that process, and the relationships between them.

Propositions are either true or false, and in this they differ from questions, commands, and exclamations. Only propositions can be either asserted or denied: questions may be asked and commands given and exclamations uttered, but none of them can be affirmed or denied, or judged to be either true or false.

It is necessary to distinguish between sentences and the propositions they may be used to assert. Two sentences, which are clearly two because they consist of different words differently arranged, may in the same context have the same meaning and express the same proposition. For example:

John loves Mary.
Mary is loved by John.

are two different sentences, for the first contains three words, whereas the second contains five, the first begins with the word "John," whereas the second begins with the word "Mary," and so on. Yet the two sentences have exactly the same meaning. It is customary to use the term "proposition" to refer to what such sentences as these may be used to assert.

The difference between sentences and propositions is brought out by remarking that a sentence is always a part of a language, the language in which it is enunciated, whereas propositions are not peculiar to any of the languages in which they may be expressed. The three sentences:

It is raining.
Il pleut.
Es regnet.

are certainly different, for the first is in English, the second in French, the third in German. Yet they have but a single meaning, and in appropriate contexts may be used to assert the proposition of which each of them is a different formulation.

In different contexts one and the same sentence can be used to make very different *statements*. For example:

The present President of the United States is a former Senator.

would be uttered in 1968 to make a statement about L. B. Johnson, but would be uttered in 1972 to make a statement about R. M. Nixon. In those different temporal contexts the sentence in question would be used to assert different propositions or to make different statements. The terms "proposition" and "statement" are not exact synonyms, but in the context of logical investigation they are used in much the same sense. Some writers on logic prefer "statement" to "proposition"; however, the term "proposition" has been more common in the history of logic. In this book both terms will be used.

Although the *process* of inference is not of interest to logicians, corresponding to every possible inference is an *argument,* and it is with these arguments that logic is chiefly concerned. An argument, in this sense, is any group of propositions of which one is claimed to follow from the others, which are regarded as providing grounds for the truth of that one. Of course the word "argument" is often used to refer to the process itself, but in logic it has the technical sense explained. An argument is not a mere collection of propositions, but has a structure. In describing this structure, the terms "premiss" and "conclusion" are usually employed. The *conclusion* of an argument is that proposition which is affirmed on the basis of the other propositions of the argument, and these other propositions which are affirmed as providing grounds or reasons for accepting the conclusion are the *premisses* of that argument.

It should be noted that "premiss" and "conclusion" are relative terms: one and the same proposition can be a premiss in one argument and a conclusion in another. Consider, for example, the following argument:

> All that is predetermined is necessary.
> Every event is predetermined.
> Therefore every event is necessary.[1]

Here the proposition *every event is necessary* is the conclusion, and the other two propositions are the premisses. But the second premiss in this argument, *every event is predetermined,* is the conclusion in the following (different) argument:

> Every event caused by other events is predetermined.
> Every event is caused by other events.
> Therefore every event is predetermined.

No proposition by itself, in isolation, is either a premiss or a conclusion. It is a premiss only when it occurs as an assumption in an argument. It is a conclusion only when it occurs in an argument in which it is claimed to follow from propositions assumed in that argument. Thus "premiss" and "conclusion" are relative terms, like "employer" and "employee." A man by himself is neither employer nor employee, but may be either in different contexts: employer to his gardener, employee of the firm for which he works.

In some arguments, such as the two foregoing, the premisses are stated first and the conclusion last. But not all arguments are so arranged. Often the conclusion is stated first, followed by whatever premisses are offered in its support, as in the following argument in Aristotle's *Politics:*

[1] This argument and the following one are discussed by Gottfried Leibniz in *The Theodicy: Abridgment of the Argument Reduced to Syllogistic Form.*

> In a democracy the poor have more power than the rich, because there are more of them, and the will of the majority is supreme.

Incidentally, we have here a further distinction between sentences and propositions. As in this example, a single sentence may formulate an entire argument, whereas an argument always involves at least two propositions—a conclusion plus one or more premisses.

The conclusion of an argument need not be stated either at its end or at its beginning. It can be, and often is, sandwiched in between different premisses offered in its support. For example, in *A Treatise of Human Nature* David Hume argues:

> Since morals . . . have an influence on the actions and affections, it follows that they cannot be deriv'd from reason; and that because reason alone as we have already prov'd, can never have any such influence.

Here the conclusion that *morals cannot be derived from reason* is claimed to follow from the propositions that precede and follow it in Hume's formulation.

To carry out the logician's task of distinguishing correct from incorrect arguments, one must first be able to recognize arguments when they occur, and to identify their premisses and conclusions. We shall consider the second of these problems first. Given an argument, how can we tell what its conclusion is, and what are its premisses? We have already seen that an argument can be stated with its conclusion first, or last, or in between its several premisses. Hence the conclusion of an argument cannot be identified in terms of its position in the formulation of the argument. How, then, can it be recognized? There are certain words or phrases that typically serve to introduce the conclusion of an argument. Among the most common of these *conclusion-indicators* are "therefore," "hence," "thus," "so," "consequently," "it follows that," "we may infer," and "we may conclude." Other words or phrases typically serve to mark the premisses of an argument. Among the most common of these *premiss-indicators* are "since," "because," "for," "as," "inasmuch as," and "for the reason that." Once an argument has been recognized, these words and phrases help us to identify its premisses and conclusion.

But not every passage that contains an argument need contain these special logical terms. Consider, for example, the following passage from a fairly recent decision of the United States Supreme Court:

> It takes obtuse reasoning to inject any issue of the "free exercise" of religion into the present case. No one is forced to go to the religious classroom and no religious exercise or instruction is brought to the classrooms of the public

schools. A student need not take religious instruction. He is left to his own desires as to the manner or time of his religious devotions, if any.[2]

Here the conclusion, which might be paraphrased as "the present case has no connection with the 'free exercise' of religion," is stated in the first sentence. The last three sentences offer grounds or reasons in support of that conclusion. How can we know that the first sentence formulates the conclusion and that the other three formulate premisses? Context is enormously helpful here, as indeed it usually is. Also helpful are some of the phrasings used in expressing the various different propositions involved. The phrase "it takes obtuse reasoning to inject . . ." suggests that the question of whether or not the issue of "free exercise" of religion is involved in the present case is precisely the point of contention, about which the disagreement centers. The other propositions are formulated in matter-of-fact terms, as though there is no dispute about them, and thus no question of their being accepted as premisses.

It should be remarked that not everything said in the course of an argument is either premiss or conclusion of that argument. A passage containing an argument may also contain other material, which is sometimes irrelevant but often supplies important background information that enables the reader or hearer to understand what the argument is about. For example, in his *Studies in Pessimism* Schopenhauer writes:

If the criminal law forbids suicide, that is not an argument valid in the Church; and besides, the prohibition is ridiculous; for what penalty can frighten a man who is not afraid of death itself?

Here the material before the first semicolon is neither premiss nor conclusion. But without some such information we should not know what "prohibition" is referred to in the conclusion. Here the conclusion is that *the criminal law's prohibition of suicide is ridiculous.* The premiss offered in its support is that *no penalty can frighten a man who is not afraid of death itself.* This example shows also that propositions can be asserted in the form of "rhetorical questions," which are used to make statements rather than to ask questions, even though they are interrogative in form.

Some passages may contain two or more arguments, either in succession, or intertwined. For example, in *Concerning Civil Government* John Locke writes:

It is not necessary—no, nor so much as convenient—that the legislative should be always in being; but absolutely necessary that the executive power

[2] Mr. Justice Douglas, for the Court. *Zorach* vs. *Clauson* 343 US 306 (1952).

should, because there is not always need of new laws to be made, but always need of execution of the laws that are made.

This passage can be analyzed in various different ways, but one perfectly straightforward way is to regard it as containing two different arguments. In one the conclusion that *it is not necessary that the legislative power should be in continuous session* is supported on the grounds that *there is not always need of new laws to be made.* In the other the conclusion that *it is absolutely necessary that the executive power should continue in being* is supported on the grounds that *there is always need of execution of the laws that are made.* In some passages containing more than one argument their connection is even closer, as when the conclusion of one argument is a premiss of another. Consider, for example, the following passage:

Since there is no electrical resistance in the current-carrying coils of a superconducting magnet, no power is dissipated as heat, and strong fields can be maintained with practically no expenditure of power.[3]

In it we have the premiss *there is no electrical resistance in the current-carrying coils of a superconducting magnet,* from which *no power is dissipated as heat* [*from a superconducting magnet*] is inferred as conclusion in the first argument. Then in the second argument, the conclusion of the first argument serves as premiss from which the further conclusion is inferred that *strong fields can be maintained* [*in a superconducting magnet*] *with practically no expenditure of power.*

EXERCISES[4]

I. Identify the premisses and conclusions in the following passages, each of which contains just one argument:

★ 1. But, they maintain, man wishes to live in society; he must therefore forego a portion of his private good for the sake of public good.

—THE MARQUIS DE SADE, *Juliette*

2. There must be simple substances because there are composites; for a composite is nothing else than a collection or *aggregation* of simple substances.

—GOTTFRIED LEIBNIZ, *The Monadology*

[3] W. B. Sampson, P. O. Craig, and M. Strongin, "Advances in Superconducting Magnets," *Scientific American,* Vol. 216, No. 3, March 1967.

[4] Solutions to starred exercises will be found at the back of the book on pages 489–526.

3. . . . when a man sees a mirage in the desert, he is not thereby perceiving any material thing; for the oasis which he thinks he is perceiving does not exist.

—ALFRED J. AYER, *The Foundations of Empirical Knowledge*

4. Since most faculty feel that order and quietude are basic requirements for research and the making of their names, they are natural allies of the university *status quo.*

—MICHAEL MILES, "Whose University?" *The New Republic,* April 1969

★ 5. Every art and every inquiry, and similarly every action and pursuit, is thought to aim at some good; and for this reason the good has rightly been declared to be that at which all things aim.

—ARISTOTLE, *Nicomachean Ethics*

6. As good almost kill a man as kill a good book: who kills a man kills a reasonable creature, God's image; but he who destroys a good book kills reason itself.

—JOHN MILTON, *Areopagitica*

7. Because logic is one of the principal means which assures intellectual discipline and integrity, it can, if properly applied, only promote the achievement of desirable social ends.

—ILMAR TAMMELO, *Outlines of Modern Legal Logic*

8. To safeguard one's happiness is a duty, at least indirectly; for discontent with one's condition amidst the press of worries and unsatisfied wants may easily become a great *temptation to the transgression of duties.*

—IMMANUEL KANT, *The Fundamental Principles of the Metaphysics of Ethics*

9. Good sense is of all things in the world the most equally distributed, for everybody thinks himself so abundantly provided with it, that even those most difficult to please in all other matters do not commonly desire more of it than they already possess.

—RENÉ DESCARTES, *A Discourse on Method*

★ 10. During the school period the student has been mentally bending over his desk; at the University he should stand up and look around. For this reason it is fatal if the first year at the University be frittered away in going over the old work in the old spirit.

—A. N. WHITEHEAD, *The Aims of Education*

11. God created the Universe from nothing; . . . time did not exist previously, but was created; for it depends on the motion of the sphere, and the sphere has been created.

—MOSES MAIMONIDES, *The Guide for the Perplexed*

12. Since political philosophy is a branch of philosophy, even the most provisional explanation of what political philosophy is cannot dispense with an explanation, however provisional, of what philosophy is.

—LEO STRAUSS, *What Is Political Philosophy? and Other Studies*

13. Whether our argument concerns public affairs or some other subject we must know some, if not all, of the facts about the subject on which we are to speak and argue. Otherwise, we can have no materials out of which to construct arguments.

—ARISTOTLE, *Rhetoric*

14. No man will take counsel, but every man will take money: therefore money is better than counsel.

—JONATHAN SWIFT

★ 15. The conscientious objector . . . has no place in a republic like ours, and should be expelled from it, for no man who won't pull his weight in the boat has a right in the boat.

—THEODORE ROOSEVELT

16. The fence around a cemetery is foolish, for those inside can't get out and those outside don't want to get in.

—ARTHUR BRISBANE, *The Book of Today*

17. The citizen who so values his "independence" that he will not enroll in a political party is really forfeiting independence, because he abandons a share in decision-making at the primary level: the choice of the candidate.

—BRUCE L. FELKNOR, *Dirty Politics*

18. Since happiness consists in peace of mind, and since durable peace of mind depends on the confidence we have in the future, and since that confidence is based on the science we should have of the nature of God and the soul, it follows that science is necessary for true happiness.

—GOTTFRIED LEIBNIZ, *Preface to the General Science*

19. He that accepts protection, stipulates obedience. We have always protected the Americans; we may therefore subject them to government.

—SAMUEL JOHNSON, *Address to the Electors of Great Britain*

★ 20. Venus and Mercury must revolve around the sun, because of their never moving far away from it, and because of their being seen now beyond it and now on this side of it . . .

—GALILEO GALILEI, "Dialogue Concerning the Two Chief World Systems"

21. A tiger has a natural right to eat a man; but if he may eat one man he may eat another, so that a tiger has a right of property in all men, as potential tiger-meat.

—THOMAS HENRY HUXLEY, *Natural Rights and Political Rights*

22. Tourism [in Egypt] should normally earn $100 million a year with such attractions as the pyramids, the Sphinx, and other pharaonic tombs and temples. But earnings this year will be only about $40 million, because Britain has imposed tight currency controls on its tourists, West Germany discourages its vacationers from going to Egypt because Cairo broke diplomatic relations over Bonn's recognition of Israel, and big-spending Americans are fed up with second-class hotels, shoddy service, and foul food.

—LEE GRIGGS, "Business Around the Globe: Egypt's Broken-down Economy," *Fortune,* May, 1967, page 70

23. Poetry is finer and more philosophical than history; for poetry expresses the universal and history only the particular.

—ARISTOTLE, *Poetics*

24. The western window through which he had stared so intently has, I noticed, one peculiarity above all other windows in the house—it commands the nearest outlook on to the moor. There is an opening between two trees which enables one from this point of view to look right down upon it, while from all the other windows it is only a distant glimpse which can be obtained. It follows, therefore, that Barrymore, since only this window would serve his purpose, must have been looking out for something or somebody upon the moor.

—A. CONAN DOYLE, *The Hound of the Baskervilles*

25. All censorships exist to prevent anyone from challenging current conceptions and existing institutions. All progress is initiated by challenging current conceptions, and executed by supplanting existing institutions. Consequently the first condition of progress is the removal of censorships. There is the whole case against censorships in a nutshell.

—G. BERNARD SHAW, Preface to *Mrs. Warren's Profession*

II. Each of the following passages contains more than one argument. Distinguish them and identify their premisses and conclusions:

★ 1. Matter is activity, and therefore a body is where it acts; and because every particle of matter acts all over the universe, every body is everywhere.

—R. G. COLLINGWOOD, *The Idea of Nature*

2. We cannot compare a process with 'the passage of time'—there is no such thing—but only with another process (such as the working of a chronometer).
Hence we can describe the lapse of time only by relying on some other process.

—LUDWIG WITTGENSTEIN, *Tractatus Logico-Philosophicus*

3. Since an individual left to himself cannot realize all the good things that he might otherwise obtain, therefore he must live and work with others. But society is not possible without sympathy and love; therefore the primary virtue which it is the duty of every one to develop is love for mankind.

—M. M. SHARIF, *Muslim Thought*

4. Liberty, indeed, though among the greatest of blessings, is not so great as that of protection, inasmuch as the end of the former is the progress and improvement of the race, while that of the latter is its preservation and perpetuation. And hence, when the two come into conflict, liberty must, and ever ought, to yield to protection, as the existence of the race is of greater moment than its improvement.

—JOHN C. CALHOUN, *A Disquisition on Government*

★ 5. . . . we are told that this God, who prescribes forbearance and forgiveness of every fault, exercises none himself, but does the exact opposite; for a punishment which comes at the end of all things, when the world is over and done with, cannot have for its object either to improve or deter, and is therefore pure vengeance.

—ARTHUR SCHOPENHAUER, "The Christian System"

6. The true distinction between these forms . . . is, that in a democracy, the people meet and exercise the government in person: in a republic, they assemble and administer it by their representatives and agents. A democracy, consequently, must be confined to a small spot. A republic may be extended over a large region.

—JAMES MADISON, *The Federalist,* Number XIV

7. On examining the apparently solid shell of a hen's egg, one may wonder how the egg can absorb the oxygen necessary to sustain the life and development of the embryo inside it. Obviously the shell must be permeable to oxygen; it must therefore have holes that are large enough to allow oxygen molecules to enter.

—H. E. HINTON, "Insect Eggshells"[5]

[5] Reprinted from "Insect Eggshells" by H. E. Hinton in *Scientific American,* Vol. 223, No. 2, August 1970.

8. Because Hindu villagers will never slaughter a cow, the only cattle available for eating are those that die a natural death; eating beef therefore amounts to eating carrion.[6]

9. "... You have been at your club all day, I perceive."

"My dear Holmes!"

"Am I right?"

"Certainly, but how—?"

He laughed at my bewildered expression.

"There is a delightful freshness about you, Watson, which makes it a pleasure to exercise any small powers which I possess at your expense. A gentleman goes forth on a showery and miry day. He returns immaculate in the evening with the gloss still on his hat and his boots. He has been a fixture, therefore, all day. He is not a man with intimate friends. Where, then, could he have been? Is it not obvious?"

—A. CONAN DOYLE, *The Hound of the Baskervilles*

★ 10. The institution of long apprenticeships has no tendency to form young people to industry. A journeyman who works by the piece is likely to be industrious, because he derives a benefit by every exertion of his industry. An apprentice is likely to be idle, and almost always is so, because he has no immediate interest to be otherwise.

—ADAM SMITH, *The Wealth of Nations*

11. The evidence of the senses further corroborates this. How else would eclipses of the moon show segments shaped as we see them? As it is, the shapes which the moon itself each month shows are of every kind—straight, gibbous, and concave—but in eclipses the outline is always curved: and, since it is the interposition of the earth that makes the eclipse, the form of this line will be caused by the form of the earth's surface, which is therefore spherical.

—ARISTOTLE, *On the Heavens*

12. . . . if Materialism is true, all our thoughts are produced by purely material antecedents. These are quite blind, and are just as likely to produce falsehood as truth. We have thus no reason for believing any of our conclusions—including the truth of Materialism, which is therefore a self-contradictory hypothesis.

—JOHN MCTAGGART ELLIS MCTAGGART, *Philosophical Studies*

13. Perhaps you may think that the whole question of the creation of the Universe could be avoided in some way. But this is not so. To avoid the issue of creation it would be necessary for all the material of the Universe to be infinitely old, and this it cannot be for a very practical reason.

[6] Reprinted from "The 'Untouchables' of India" by M. N. Srinivas and Andre Beteille in *Scientific American,* Vol. 213, No. 6, December 1965.

For if this were so, there could be no hydrogen left in the Universe. . . . Hydrogen is being steadily converted into helium throughout the Universe and this conversion is a one-way process—that is to say, hydrogen cannot be produced in any appreciable quantity through the breakdown of the other elements. How comes it then that the Universe consists almost entirely of hydrogen? If matter were infinitely old this would be quite impossible. So we see that the Universe being what it is, the creation issue simply cannot be dodged.

—FRED HOYLE, "Continuous Creation and the Expanding Universe"

14. All our ideas owe their origin to physical and material causes which operate upon us independently of our will, because these causes result from our intimate organization and from the impact external objects have upon us; motives are in turn the results of these causes, and as a consequence our will is not free.

—THE MARQUIS DE SADE, *Juliette*

★ 15. A teacher who asks a question is tuned to the right answer, ready to hear it, eager to hear it, since it will tell him that his teaching is good and that he can go on to the next topic. He will assume that anything that sounds close to the right answer is meant to be the right answer. So, for a student who is not sure of the answer, a mumble may be his best bet.

—JOHN HOLT, *How Children Fail*

16. It seems clear first of all that the Russians have only begun to test MIRV's. Since U.S. surveillance systems for monitoring missile tests can discriminate tests of MIRV's, and since the Russians are hardly likely to manufacture and emplace an untested system, the U.S. can in effect monitor compliance with the ban on production and deployment by verifying the cessation of testing; therefore no on-site inspection is necessary.

—"Science and the Citizen," *Scientific American*[7]

17. If objective, a relation must exist in something. It cannot however exist in either of the two things it brings together. It must therefore be in a third thing. But to bring this third thing and the first two together, other relations must be needed, and these other relations must require still other things in which to exist, and so on till infinity. This would lead to an infinite regress which is inadmissible. Relations therefore have no existence.

—M. M. SHARIF, *Muslim Thought*

18. Our determinism leads us to call our judgments of regret wrong, because they are pessimistic in implying that what is impossible yet ought

[7] Reprinted from "Science and the Citizen" in *Scientific American,* Vol. 224, No. 3, March 1971.

to be. But how then about the judgments of regret themselves? If they are wrong, other judgments, judgments of approval presumably, ought to be in their place. But as they are necessitated, nothing else *can* be in their place; and the universe is just what it was before—namely, a place in which what ought to be appears impossible.

—WILLIAM JAMES, "The Dilemma of Determinism"

19. . . . if a man says that most of the students in the university like sport and that most of them work hard, and that therefore most of the students both like sport and work hard, we refute him by pointing out that inference does not hold, perhaps by citing an example of an inference which is of the same form and which has true premises but a false conclusion. (For example: most of the positive integers less than ten are greater than four, and most of the positive integers less than ten are less than six, but it is not the case that most of the positive integers less than ten are both greater than four and less than six.)

—J. J. C. SMART, *Philosophy and Scientific Realism*

20. It will not be possible to apply exactly the same teaching process to the machine as to a normal child. It will not, for instance, be provided with legs, so that it could not be asked to go out and fill the coal scuttle. Possibly it might not have eyes. But however well these deficiencies might be overcome by clever engineering, one could not send the creature to school without the other children making excessive fun of it. It must be given some tuition. We need not be too concerned about the legs, eyes, etc. The example of Miss Helen Keller shows that education can take place provided that communication in both directions between teacher and pupil can take place by some means or other.

—A. M. TURING, "Computing Machinery and Intelligence," *Mind,* LIX (1950)

1.3 Recognizing Arguments

We turn now to the problem of recognizing arguments. In every argument one or more premisses and a conclusion are asserted. But not every assertion of several propositions constitutes an argument. Newspapers, magazines, and history books abound in assertions, though they tend to contain relatively few arguments. Containing several assertions is a necessary condition for discourse to express an argument, but it is not a sufficient condition. Nevertheless that necessary condition distinguishes arguments from several kinds of nonarguments with which they are sometimes confused.

Consider the statement:

If objects of art are expressive, they are a language.

Such a proposition is called a "conditional." Its component proposition *objects of art are expressive* is not asserted, nor is its other component proposition *they are a language*. It asserts only that the former implies the latter, but both could be false for all the statement in question asserts. No premiss is asserted, no inference is made, no conclusion is claimed to be true: there is no argument here. But consider the following quotation from John Dewey's *Art as Experience:*

> Because objects of art are expressive, they are a language.

Here we do have an argument. The proposition *objects of art are expressive* is asserted as premiss, and the proposition *they are a language* is claimed to follow from that premiss and is therefore asserted to be true. A conditional statement may look like an argument, but it is not an argument; and the two should not be confused.

Consider another passage that looks—at first glance—even more like an argument. In the preface to Roget's *Thesaurus* we find:

> Synonyms are good servants but bad masters; therefore select them with care.

In spite of the presence of the standard conclusion-indicator "therefore" in the above passage, we do not generally regard such utterances as expressing arguments. What follows the "therefore" is a command rather than a proposition, and since a command is neither true nor false, it cannot be claimed to be true on the basis of what is asserted in the rest of the passage. Wherever a command rather than an assertion occupies the place appropriate to a conclusion, we do not have an argument. Premisses and conclusions must be asserted in an argument, and that is why such passages as these do not express arguments.

We have already remarked that although every passage expressing an argument contains several propositions asserted in it, not every passage in which several propositions are asserted need contain an argument. For an argument to be present, one of those asserted propositions must be claimed to follow from other propositions asserted to be true, which are presented as grounds for, or reasons for believing, the conclusion. This claim may be either explicit or implicit. It may be made explicit by the use of premiss-indicators or conclusion-indicators, or by the occurrence of such words as "must," "should," "ought," or "necessarily" in the conclusion. But the presence of these argument-indicators is not always decisive. We have already seen how "therefore" may introduce a command instead of a conclusion. Quite a few of these argument-indicators have other functions as well. For example, if we compare

> Since Henry graduated from medical school his probable income is very high.

with

> Since Henry graduated from medical school there have been many changes in medical techniques.

we see that although the first is an argument in which the word "since" indicates the premiss, the second is not an argument at all. In the second, the word "since" has temporal rather than logical significance.

The words "because" and "for" also have other than strictly logical uses. Compare the following two passages:

> No system can exist half matter and half antimatter, because the two forms of matter annihilate each other.[8]

and

> The Roman Empire crumbled to dust because it lacked the spirit of liberalism and free enterprise.[9]

In the first we have an argument, in which the term "because" indicates the premiss. It is known that *the two forms of matter annihilate each other,* and from this it is inferred that *no system can exist half matter and half antimatter.* But in the second there is no argument. We do not infer that *the Roman Empire crumbled to dust.* The assertion that *the Roman Empire lacked the spirit of liberalism and free enterprise* is not offered as evidence, grounds, or reason for believing that *the Roman Empire crumbled to dust.* The latter proposition is much better known and well attested than the former. What we have here is von Mises' proposed explanation of why the Roman Empire crumbled to dust. What is asserted is a causal connection between the Roman Empire's lack of the spirit of liberalism and free enterprise and its crumbling into dust. Both propositions are asserted, and a connection is asserted to hold between them. But

[8] H. Alfvén, "Antimatter and Cosmology," *Scientific American,* Vol. 216, No. 4, April 1967.

[9] Ludwig von Mises, *Human Action, A Treatise on Economics.*

there the resemblance ends, even though the formulations of these nonarguments may be exactly like those of arguments.

The difference between these arguments and nonarguments is primarily one of purpose or interest. Either can be formulated in the pattern

$$Q \text{ because } P.$$

If we are interested in establishing the truth of Q, and P is offered as evidence for it, then "Q because P" formulates an argument. However, if we regard the truth of Q as being unproblematic, as being at least as well established as the truth of P, but are interested in explaining why Q is the case, then "Q because P" is not an argument but an explanation. The two examples discussed are fairly easy to distinguish, the first being an argument and the second an explanation. But not all examples are so easily classified. In each case the context may help to make clear the intention of the writer or speaker. If his purpose is to establish the truth of one of his propositions, he formulates an argument. If his purpose is to explain, then he formulates an explanation. Explanations will be discussed in greater detail later in this book, in Chapter 13.

EXERCISES

Only some of the following passages contain arguments. Indicate those with arguments and identify their premisses and conclusions:

★ 1. And friends have all things in common, so that one of you can be no richer than the other, if you say truly that you are friends.

—PLATO, *Lysis*

2. Ask the same for me, for friends should have all things in common.

—PLATO, *Phaedrus*

3. If thine enemy hunger, feed him; if he thirst, give him drink: for in doing so thou shalt heap coals of fire on his head.

—*Romans,* 12:20

4. Where all other circumstances are equal, wages are generally higher in new than in old trades. When a projector attempts to establish a new manufacture, he must at first entice his workmen from other employments by higher wages than they can either earn in their own trades, or than the nature of his work would otherwise require, and a considerable time must pass away before he can venture to reduce them to the common level.

—ADAM SMITH, *The Wealth of Nations*

★ 5. If you want to find out your real opinion of anyone, observe the impression made upon you by the first sight of a letter from him.

—ARTHUR SCHOPENHAUER, *Psychological Observations*

6. Few would deny that a license tax laid specifically on the privilege of disseminating ideas would infringe the right of free speech. For one reason among others, if the state may tax the privilege it may fix the rate of tax and, through the tax, control or suppress the activity which it taxes.

—MR. CHIEF JUSTICE STONE, dissenting. *Jones* v. *City of Opelika* 316 US 584 (1942)

7. If we take eternity to mean not infinite temporal duration but timelessness, then eternal life belongs to those who live in the present.

—LUDWIG WITTGENSTEIN, *Tractatus Logico-Philosophicus*

8. Sedatives do not merely induce sleep, and indeed people who suffer from a transient insomnia are ill advised to take several drinks and then sleeping pills, particularly if they are over fifty. In combination the drug effects are enhanced, and the doses a person may consider moderate can even prove fatal.[10]

9. The mason employed on the building of a house may be quite ignorant of its general design; or at any rate, he may not keep it constantly in mind. So it is with man: in working through the days and hours of his life, he takes little thought of its character as a whole.

—ARTHUR SCHOPENHAUER, *Counsels and Maxims*

★ 10. "Universities are full of knowledge. The freshmen bring a little in, and the seniors take none away, and knowledge accumulates."

—HARVARD PRESIDENT A. L. LOWELL

11. Since it is impossible for every individual, as for every nation, simultaneously to be stronger than his neighbors, it is a truism that liberty, as distinct from the liberties of special persons and classes, can exist only in so far as it is limited by rules, which secure that freedom for some is not slavery for others.

—R. H. TAWNEY, *Equality*

12. Take therefore no thought for the morrow; for the morrow shall take thought for the things of itself. Sufficient unto the day is the evil thereof.

—*Matthew*, 6:34

[10] By permission from *Sleep*, by Gay Gaer Luce and Julius Segal. Copyright, 1966. Coward-McCann, Inc. New York.

13. If it came to the point where we had the means of knowing what was going on in a person's brain and could use this as a basis for predicting what he would do, and if this knowledge extended to our own future conduct, it is unlikely that our present view of life would remain the same.

—ALFRED J. AYER, *The Concept of a Person*

14. It is bad to be oppressed by a minority, but it is worse to be oppressed by a majority. For there is a reserve of latent power in the masses which, if it is called into play, the minority can seldom resist. But from the absolute will of an entire people there is no appeal, no redemption, no refuge but treason.

—LORD ACTON, "The History of Freedom in Ancient and Modern Europe"

★ 15. If I am mobilized in a war, this war is *my* war; it is in my image and I deserve it. I deserve it first because I could always get out of it by suicide or by desertion; these ultimate possibles are those which must always be present for us when there is a question of envisaging a situation. For lack of getting out of it, I have *chosen* it.

—JEAN-PAUL SARTRE, *Being and Nothingness*

16. Yes, and if oxen and horses or lions had hands, and could paint with their hands, and produce works of art as men do, horses would paint the forms of the gods like horses, and oxen like oxen, and make their bodies in the image of their several kinds.

—XENOPHANES, Fragment 15 in John Burnet, *Early Greek Philosophy*

17. For he whom evil is to befal, must in his own person exist at the very time it comes, if the misery and suffering are haply to have any place at all; but since death precludes this, and forbids him to be, upon whom the ills can be brought, you may be sure that we have nothing to fear after death, and that he who exists not, cannot become miserable. . . .

—LUCRETIUS, *On the Nature of Things*

18. The notion that individuals might be free, en masse, to continue their psychological, intellectual, moral and cognitive development through their teens and into their 20's would have been laughed out of court in any century other than our own; today, that opportunity is open to millions of young Americans. Student unrest is a reflection not only of the failures, but of the extraordinary successes of the liberal-industrial revolution. It therefore occurs in the nations and in the colleges where, according to traditional standards, conditions are best.

—KENNETH KENISTON, "You Have to Grow Up in Scarsdale to Know How Bad Things Really Are," *The New York Times,* April 27, 1969

19. It is true that most trustees tend to be preoccupied with other matters than education, that they are inaccessible to teachers and students, and that a dispiriting number of them have reached an age and station in life calculated to protect them against fresh ideas. It is not surprising, therefore, that professors and students are sparing in the confidence they lavish on trustees.

—CHARLES FRANKEL, *Education and the Barricades*

20. Everyone who deals with children these days has heard the dictum that children need to be loved, must be loved. But even to those who like them most, children are not always a joy and delight to be with. Often they are much like older people, and often they are exasperating and irritating. It is not surprising that there are many adults who do not like children much, if at all. But they feel that they ought to like them, have a duty to like them, and they try to discharge this duty by acting, particularly by talking, as if they liked them. Hence the continual and meaningless use of words like *honey, dearie,* etc. Hence, the dreadful, syrupy voice that so many adults use when they speak to children.

—JOHN HOLT, *How Children Fail*

1.4 Deduction and Induction

Arguments are traditionally divided into two different types, *deductive* and *inductive*. Although every argument involves the claim that its premisses provide some grounds for the truth of its conclusion, only a *deductive* argument involves the claim that its premisses provide *conclusive* grounds. In the case of deductive arguments the technical terms "valid" and "invalid" are used in place of "correct" and "incorrect." A deductive argument is *valid* when its premisses, if true, do provide conclusive grounds for its conclusion, that is, when premisses and conclusion are so related that it is absolutely impossible for the premisses to be true unless the conclusion is true also. Every deductive argument is either valid or invalid; the task of deductive logic is to clarify the nature of the relation between premisses and conclusion in valid arguments, and thus to allow us to discriminate valid from invalid arguments. The theory of deduction, including both traditional and symbolic logic, occupies Part Two of this book.

An inductive argument, on the other hand, involves the claim, not that its premisses give conclusive grounds for the truth of its conclusion, but only that they provide *some* grounds for it. Inductive arguments are neither "valid" nor "invalid" in the sense in which those terms are applied to deductive arguments. Inductive arguments may, of course, be evaluated as better or worse, according to the degree of likelihood or probability which their premisses confer upon their conclusions. Our discussion of probability and the theory of induction is presented in Part Three.

Deductive and inductive arguments are sometimes characterized and distinguished from one another in terms of the relative generality of their premisses and conclusions. William Whewell wrote in *The Philosophy of the Inductive Sciences* that ". . . in Deduction we infer particular from general truths; while in Induction we infer general from particular. . . ." Thus the classical example of deductive argument

All men are mortal.
Socrates is a man.
Therefore Socrates is mortal.

indeed has a *particular* conclusion inferred (validly) from premisses the first of which is a general or universal proposition. By contrast, a fairly standard form of inductive argument is illustrated by

Socrates is a man and is mortal.
Plato is a man and is mortal.
Aristotle is a man and is mortal.
Therefore probably all men are mortal.

in which a general or universal conclusion is inferred from premisses all of which are particular propositions. There is some merit to this method of distinguishing between deduction and induction, but it is not universally applicable. For valid deductive arguments may have universal propositions for conclusions as well as for premisses, as in

All men are animals.
All animals are mortal.
Therefore all men are mortal.

and they may have particular propositions for their premisses as well as for their conclusions, as in

If Socrates is a man then Socrates is mortal.
Socrates is a man.
Therefore Socrates is mortal.

And inductive arguments may have universal propositions for premisses as well as for conclusions, as in

All cows are mammals and have lungs.
All horses are mammals and have lungs.
All men are mammals and have lungs.
Therefore probably all mammals have lungs.

and they may have particular propositions for their conclusions, as in

Hitler was a dictator and was ruthless.
Stalin was a dictator and was ruthless.
Castro is a dictator.
Therefore Castro is probably ruthless.

So it is not altogether satisfactory to characterize deductive arguments as those which derive particular conclusions from general premisses, or inductive arguments as those which infer general conclusions from particular premisses.

A more adequate insight into the difference between deduction and induction is suggested by the following. If a deductive argument is valid, then its conclusion follows with equal necessity from its premisses no matter what else may be the case. From the two premisses *All men are mortal* and *Socrates is a man* the conclusion *Socrates is mortal* follows necessarily, no matter what else may be true. The argument remains valid no matter what additional premisses may be added to the original pair. Whether we add information that Socrates is ugly, or that angels are immortal, or that cows give milk, the conclusion follows strictly from the enlarged set of premisses because it follows strictly from the two original premisses initially given. And if the argument is valid, nothing can make it *more* valid: if the conclusion follows validly from a given set of premisses it cannot follow from an enlarged set any *more* validly or strictly or logically.

But the case is different for inductive arguments. Consider the following inductive argument:

Most corporation lawyers are Conservatives.
Roderick Malcolm is a corporation lawyer.
Therefore Roderick Malcolm is probably a Conservative.

This is a pretty good inductive argument: if its premisses are true, its conclusion is more likely true than false. But adding new premisses to the original pair can serve either to weaken or to strengthen the resulting argument. If we enlarge the premisses by adding that

Roderick Malcolm is an officer of Americans for Democratic Action.

and

No officers of Americans for Democratic Action are Conservatives.

the conclusion no longer even seems to follow, and in fact the opposite conclusion now follows deductively, that is, validly. On the other hand, if we enlarge the original set of premisses by adding the following additional premisses:

Roderick Malcolm campaigned vigorously for Goldwater for president.

and

Roderick Malcolm is a member of President Nixon's cabinet.

then the original conclusion follows with much greater likelihood from the enlarged set of premisses.

Accordingly, we characterize a deductive argument as one whose conclusion is claimed to follow from its premisses with absolute necessity, this necessity not being a matter of degree and not depending in any way upon whatever else may be the case. And in sharp contrast we characterize an inductive argument as one whose conclusion is claimed to follow from its premisses only with probability, this probability being a matter of degree and dependent upon what else may be the case.

EXERCISES

Distinguish between the deductive and inductive arguments contained in the following passages:

★ 1. Since tests proved that it took at least 2.3 seconds to operate the bolt on Oswald's rifle, Oswald obviously could not have fired three times—hitting Kennedy twice and Connally once—in 5.6 seconds or less.[11]

2. None of us is oriented to external objects quite like anyone else, for we occupy different positions, and while we exchange positions the objects age.

—W. V. O. QUINE, "On Mental Entities"

[11] "Autopsy on the Warren Commission," *Time*, Vol. 88, No. 12, September 16, 1966.

3. That Hamilton ever held any considerable sum in securities seems highly improbable, for he was at no time a rich man, and at his death left a small estate.

—CHARLES A. BEARD, *An Economic Interpretation of the Constitution of the United States*

4. Since man is essentially rational, the constant recurrence of metaphysics in the history of human knowledge must have its explanation in the very structure of reason itself.

—ETIENNE GILSON, *The Unity of Philosophical Experience*

★ 5. A gardener who cultivates his own garden with his own hands, unites in his own person the three different characters, of landlord, farmer, and labourer. His produce, therefore, should pay him the rent of the first, the profit of the second, and the wages of the third.

—ADAM SMITH, *The Wealth of Nations*

6. At an underprivileged school in Harlem, they used to test the intelligence of all the children at two-year intervals. They found that every two years each advancing class came out ten points lower in "native intelligence." That is, the combined efforts of home influencing and school education, a powerful combination, succeeded in making the children significantly stupider year by year; if they had a few more years of compulsory home ties and compulsory education, all would end up as gibbering idiots.

—PAUL GOODMAN, *Growing Up Absurd*

7. In attempting to understand the elements out of which mental phenomena are compounded, it is of the greatest importance to remember that from the protozoa to man there is nowhere a very wide gap either in structure or in behavior. From this fact it is a highly probable inference that there is also nowhere a very wide mental gap.

—BERTRAND RUSSELL, *The Analysis of Mind*

8. One may go so far as to say that if there were no lack or stint of food, then those animals that are now afraid of man or are wild by nature would be tame and familiar with him, and in like manner with one another. This is shown by the way animals are treated in Egypt, for owing to the fact that food is constantly supplied to them the very fiercest creatures live peaceably together. The fact is they are tamed by kindness, and in some places crocodiles are tame to their priestly keeper from being fed by him. And elsewhere also the same phenomenon is to be observed.

—ARISTOTLE, *History of Animals*

9. It seems that the will of God is changeable. For the Lord says (*Gen.* vi. 7): *It repenteth Me that I have made man.* But whoever repents of

what he has done, has a changeable will. Therefore God has a changeable will.

—THOMAS AQUINAS, *Summa Theologica*, I, Question 29, Article 7

★ 10. It is evident from the state of the country, from the habits of the people, from the experience we have had on the point itself, that it is impracticable to raise any very considerable sums by direct taxation. Tax laws have in vain been multiplied; new methods to enforce the collection have in vain been tried; the public expectation has been uniformly disappointed, and the treasuries of the states have remained empty.

—ALEXANDER HAMILTON, *The Federalist*, Number XII

11. ". . . I've always reckoned that looking at the new moon over your left shoulder is one of the carelessest and foolishest things a body can do. Old Hank Bunker done it once, and bragged about it; and in less than two years he got drunk and fell off of the shot tower, and spread himself out so that he was just a kind of a layer, as you may say; and they slid him edgeways between two barn doors for a coffin, and buried him so, so they say, but I didn't see it. Pap told me. But anyway it all come of looking at the moon that way, like a fool."

—MARK TWAIN, *The Adventures of Huckleberry Finn*

12. Induction presupposes metaphysics. In other words, it rests upon an antecedent rationalism. You cannot have a rational justification for your appeal to history till your metaphysics has assured you that there *is* a history to appeal to; and likewise your conjectures as to the future presuppose some basis of knowledge that there *is* a future already subjected to some determinations.

—ALFRED NORTH WHITEHEAD, *Science and the Modern World*

13. . . . at bottom I did not believe I had touched that man. The law of probabilities decreed me guiltless of his blood for in all my small experience with guns I had never hit anything I had tried to hit and I knew I had done my best to hit him.

—MARK TWAIN's *Notebook*

14. Sir: Your Essay includes the following statement: "Since tests proved that it took at least 2.3 seconds to operate the bolt action on Oswald's rifle, Oswald obviously could not have fired three times—hitting Kennedy twice and Connally once—in 5.6 seconds or less." This argument, which has appeared in many publications since the assassination,

is faulty, and I am surprised that I haven't seen it refuted before this. Assuming that the bolt of Oswald's rifle can, in fact, be operated in 2.3 seconds, then Oswald definitely could fire 3 shots in less than 5.6 seconds, for a stop watch would be started when the first shot was fired; the second shot would be fired when the stop watch read 2.3 seconds, and the third shot would be fired when the stop watch read 4.6 seconds. You have apparently overlooked the fact that, in the time it takes to fire 3 shots, it is only necessary to operate the bolt twice.

—FREDERICK T. WEHR[12]

★ 15. A plentiful subsistence increases the bodily strength of the labourer, and the comfortable hope of bettering his condition, and of ending his days perhaps in ease and plenty, animates him to exert that strength to the utmost. Where wages are high, accordingly, we shall always find the workmen more active, diligent, and expeditious, than where they are low. . . .

—ADAM SMITH, *The Wealth of Nations*

16. It is also easy, I consider, to set aside the method of induction. For, when they propose to establish the universal from the particulars by means of induction, they will effect this by a review either of all or of some of the particular instances. But if they review some, the induction will be insecure, since some of the particulars omitted in the induction may contravene the universal; while if they are to review all, they will be toiling at the impossible, since the particulars are infinite and indefinite. Thus on both grounds, as I think, the consequence is that induction is invalidated.

—SEXTUS EMPIRICUS, *Outlines of Pyrrhonism*

17. Any illiterate peasant can talk perfectly well about his after-images, or how things look or feel to him, or about his aches and pains, and yet he may know nothing whatever about neurophysiology. A man may, like Aristotle, believe that the brain is an organ for cooling the body without any impairment of his ability to make true statements about his sensations. Hence the things we are talking about when we describe our sensations cannot be processes in the brain.

—J. J. C. SMART, "Sensations and Brain Processes,"
Philosophical Review, April 1959

18. . . . the simplest form of the theological argument from design, once well known under the name of "Paley's watch." Paley's form of it was just this: "If we found by chance a watch or other piece of intricate

[12] Letters, *Time,* Vol. 88, No. 14, September 30, 1966, p. 16.

mechanism we should infer that it had been made by someone. But all around us we do find intricate pieces of natural mechanism, and the processes of the universe are seen to move together in complex relations; we should therefore infer that these too have a Maker."

—B. A. O. WILLIAMS, "Metaphysical Arguments," *The Nature of Metaphysics,* D. F. Pears, ed.

19. . . . natural science as a form of thought exists and always has existed in a context of history, and depends on historical thought for its existence. From this I venture to infer that no one can understand natural science unless he understands history: and that no one can answer the question what nature is unless he knows what history is.

—R. G. COLLINGWOOD, *The Idea of Nature*

★ 20. First of all, it is doubtful what the Philosopher really held on this point, for he speaks differently in different places and has different principles, from some of which one thing seems to follow whereas from others the very opposite can be inferred. Wherefore, it is probable that he was always doubtful about this conclusion and at one time seems to be drawn to one side and at other times to the other depending on whether the subject matter he was treating at the moment was more in accord with the one or with the other.

—DUNS SCOTUS, *Oxford Commentary on the Sentences of Peter Lombard*

21. . . . since there are more people on the earth than hairs on any one person's head, I know that there must be at least two people with the same number of hairs. . . .

—F. P. RAMSEY, *The Foundations of Mathematics*

22. Even if all mercury dumping is stopped now, the methyl mercury problem will be with us for a long time because for many years it has been standard practice to dump mercury in the nearest body of water, in the mistaken beliefs that mercury is chemically inert and that this was a safe disposal method.

—DR. SELINA BENDIX, *Science News,* Vol. 99, No. 9, February 27, 1971

23. . . . there can be but one universe, since anything outside, by being outside, would be related to it and collateral, and so after all would form a part of it.

—GEORGE SANTAYANA, *The Realm of Matter*

24. A remarkable feature of malaria is the precise timing of its recurrent attacks, which are always at some multiple of 24 hours. Since the cause of malaria is a small protozoan (single-celled) parasite that grows

in the red blood corpuscle, the attacks show that this rather simple organism has a highly accurate biological clock.

—FRANK HAWKING, "The Clock of the Malaria Parasite"[13]

★ 25. There is, of course, no filament or heating element in the transistor to burn out. Consequently, transistors should last almost indefinitely, subject only to the limitations of abuse, deterioration through diffusion of water vapor through the casing, and so on.

—LEONARD ENGEL, "Little Gadget with a Large Future"

26. And indeed since the Planets are seen at varying distances from the Earth, the centre of Earth is surely not the centre of their orbits.

—NICOLAUS COPERNICUS, "On the Revolutions of the Heavenly Spheres"

27. The life of every civilized community is governed by rules. Neither peace of mind for the present nor intelligent planning for the future is possible for men who either live without rules or cannot abide by the rules they have. Making rules for the community, and enforcing them, is the job of government. No community can be truly civilized, therefore, without an effective and reasonably stable government.

—CARL COHEN, *Civil Disobedience: Conscience, Tactics, and the Law*

28. There is no such thing as free will. The mind is induced to wish this or that by some cause, and that cause is determined by another cause, and so on back to infinity.

—BARUCH SPINOZA, *Ethics*

29. When we see that the three classes of modern society, the feudal aristocracy, the bourgeoisie and the proletariat, each have their special morality, we can only draw one conclusion, that men consciously or unconsciously, derive their moral ideas in the last resort from the practical relations on which their class position is based—from the economic relations in which they carry on production and exchange.

—FRIEDRICH ENGELS, *Anti-Dühring*

30. Over the last quarter-century, as this is written, the average work week in industry has increased moderately. The standard work week has declined but this has been more than offset by increased demand for overtime work and the companion willingness to supply it. During this period average weekly earnings, adjusted for price increases, have nearly

[13] Reprinted from "The Clock of the Malaria Parasite" by Frank Hawking in *Scientific American*, Vol. 222, No. 6, June 1970.

doubled. On the evidence, one must conclude that, as their incomes rise, men will work longer hours and seek less leisure.

—JOHN KENNETH GALBRAITH, *The New Industrial State*

1.5 Truth and Validity

Truth and falsehood may be predicated of propositions, but never of arguments. And the properties of validity and invalidity can belong only to deductive arguments, never to propositions. There is a connection between the validity or invalidity of an argument and the truth or falsehood of its premisses and conclusion, but the connection is by no means a simple one. Some valid arguments contain only true propositions, as, for example:

All whales are mammals.
All mammals have lungs.
Therefore all whales have lungs.

But an argument may contain false propositions exclusively, and be valid nevertheless, as, for example:

All spiders have six legs.
All six-legged creatures have wings.
Therefore all spiders have wings.

This argument is valid because if its premisses were true its conclusion would have to be true also, even though in fact they are all false. On the other hand, if we reflect upon the argument:

If I owned all the gold in Fort Knox, then I would be wealthy.
I do not own all the gold in Fort Knox.
Therefore I am not wealthy.

we see that although its premisses and conclusion are true, the argument is invalid. That the premisses could be true and the conclusion false, if not immediately apparent, may be made clear by considering that if I were to inherit a million dollars, the premisses would remain true while the conclusion would become false. This point is further illustrated by the following argument, which is of the same form as the preceding one:

If Rockefeller owned all the gold in Fort Knox, then Rockefeller would be wealthy.
Rockefeller does not own all the gold in Fort Knox.
Therefore Rockefeller is not wealthy.

The premisses of this argument are true, and its conclusion is false. Such an argument cannot be valid, because it is impossible for the premisses of a valid argument to be true while its conclusion is false.

The preceding examples show that there are valid arguments with false conclusions, as well as invalid arguments with true conclusions. Hence the truth or falsehood of its conclusion does not determine the validity or invalidity of an argument. Nor does the validity of an argument guarantee the truth of its conclusion. There are perfectly valid arguments which have false conclusions—but any such argument must have at least one false premiss. The term "sound" is introduced to characterize a valid argument all of whose premisses are true. Clearly the conclusion of a sound argument is true. A deductive argument fails to establish the truth of its conclusion if it is unsound, which means either that it is not valid or that not all of its premisses are true. To test the truth or falsehood of premisses is the task of science in general, since premisses may deal with any subject matter at all. The logician is not so much interested in the truth or falsehood of propositions as in the logical relations between them, where by the "logical" relations between propositions we mean those which determine the correctness or incorrectness of arguments in which they may occur. Determining the correctness or incorrectness of arguments falls squarely within the province of logic. The logician is interested in the correctness even of arguments whose premisses might be false.

A question might be raised about the value of this last point. It might be suggested that we ought to confine ourselves to arguments which have true premisses, ignoring all others. But as a matter of fact we are interested in, and must often depend upon, the correctness of arguments whose premisses are not known to be true. Examples of such situations suggest themselves readily. When a scientist is interested in verifying his theories by deducing testable consequences from them, he does not know beforehand which theories are true. If he did, there would be no need for verification. In our everyday affairs, we are often confronted with alternative courses of action. Where these courses are genuine alternatives which cannot all be adopted, we may try to reason about which should be chosen. Such reasoning generally involves figuring out the consequences of each of the different actions among which we must choose. One might argue: suppose I choose the first alternative, then such and such will be the case. On the other hand, assuming that I choose the second alternative, then something else will follow. In general, we are inclined to choose among alternative courses of action on the basis of which set of consequences we prefer to have realized. In each case, we are interested in reasoning correctly, lest we deceive ourselves. Were we interested only in arguments which have true premisses, we should not know which line of argument to consider until we knew which of the alternative premisses was true. And if we knew which premiss was true, we should not be interested in the arguments at all, because our purpose in considering the arguments was to help us decide which alternative premiss to make true. To confine our attention to arguments with true premisses alone would be self-defeating and stultifying.

So far we have been speaking only about propositions and the arguments which contain them as premisses and conclusion. As has been explained, these are not linguistic entities such as sentences, but what sentences can be used to assert. Whether the actual process of thinking or reasoning requires language or not is an open question. It may be that thinking requires the use of symbols of some sort, words or images or what not. We all feel a certain sympathy with the girl who was told to think before she spoke, and replied, "But how can I know what I think until I hear what I say?" Perhaps all thinking does require words or some other kind of symbols, but that is not a question that concerns us here. It is obvious that the communication of any proposition or any argument requires symbols, and involves language. In the rest of this book we shall be concerned with stated arguments, whose propositions are formulated in language.

The use of language, however, complicates our problem. Certain accidental or misleading features of their formulations in language may make more difficult the task of investigating the logical relations between propositions. It is part of the task of the logician, therefore, to examine language itself, primarily from the point of view of discovering and describing those aspects of it which tend to obscure the difference between correct and incorrect argument. It is for this reason that Part One of this book is devoted to language.

EXERCISES

Indicate the premisses and conclusions of the arguments contained in the following passages. (Some contain more than one argument.)

★ 1. It is illogical to reason thus, "I am richer than you, therefore I am superior to you," "I am more eloquent than you, therefore I am superior to you." It is more logical to reason, "I am richer than you, therefore my property is superior to yours," "I am more eloquent than you, therefore my speech is superior to yours." You are something more than property or speech.

—EPICTETUS, *Enchiridion*

2. Every state is a community of some kind, and every community is established with a view to some good; for mankind always act in order to obtain that which they think good. But, if all communities aim at some good, the state or political community, which is the highest of all, and which embraces all the rest, aims at good in a greater degree than any other, and at the highest good.

—ARISTOTLE, *Politics*

3. With regard to good and evil, these terms indicate nothing positive in things considered in themselves, nor are they anything else than modes of thought, or notions which we form from the comparison of one thing with another. For one and the same thing may at the same time be both good and evil or indifferent. Music, for example, is good to a melancholy person, bad to one mourning, while to a deaf man it is neither good nor bad.

—BARUCH SPINOZA, *Ethics*

4. Whensoever a man transferreth his right, or renounceth it; it is either in consideration of some right reciprocally transferred to himself, or for some other good he hopeth for thereby. For it is a voluntary act; and of the voluntary acts of every man, the object is some *good to himself*. And therefore there be some rights which no man can be understood by any words or other signs, to have abandoned or transferred. As first a man cannot lay down the right of resisting them that assault him by force, to take away his life; because he cannot be understood to aim thereby, at any good to himself.

—THOMAS HOBBES, *Leviathan*

★ 5. Even though there may be a deceiver of some sort, very powerful and very tricky, who bends all his efforts to keep me perpetually deceived, there can be no slightest doubt that I exist, since he deceives me; and let him deceive me as much as he will, he can never make me be nothing as long as I think that I am something. Thus, after having thought well on this matter, and after examining all things with care, I must finally conclude and maintain that this proposition: *I am, I exist,* is necessarily true every time that I pronounce it or conceive it in my mind.

—RENÉ DESCARTES, *Meditations*

6. It is indeed an opinion strangely prevailing amongst men, that houses, mountains, rivers, and in a word all sensible objects, have an existence, natural or real, distinct from their being perceived by the understanding. But with how great an assurance and acquiescence soever this principle may be entertained in the world, yet whoever shall find in his heart to call it in question may, if I mistake not, perceive it to involve a manifest contradiction. For what are the forementioned objects but the things we perceive by sense? and what do we perceive *besides our own*

ideas or sensations? and is it not plainly repugnant that any one of these, or any combination of them, should exist unperceived?

—GEORGE BERKELEY, *A Treatise Concerning the Principles of Human Knowledge*

7. Let us consider the red and white colors in porphyry; hinder light but from striking on it, and its colors vanish; it no longer produces any such ideas in us. Upon the return of light, it produces these appearances on us again. Can anyone think any real alterations are made in the porphyry by the presence or absence of light, and that those idea of whiteness and redness are really in porphyry in the light, when it is plain it has no color in the dark? It has indeed such a configuration of particles, both night and day, as are apt, by the rays of light rebounding from some parts of that hard stone, to produce in us the idea of redness, and from others the idea of whiteness. But whiteness or redness are not in it at any time, but such a texture that hath the power to produce such a sensation in us.

—JOHN LOCKE, *An Essay Concerning Human Understanding*

8. Nothing can possibly be conceived in the world, or even out of it, which can be called good without qualification, except a *good will.* Intelligence, wit, judgment, and the other *talents* of the mind, however they may be named, or courage, resolution, perseverance, as qualities of temperament, are undoubtedly good and desirable in many respects; but these gifts of nature may also become extremely bad and mischievous if the will which is to make use of them, and which, therefore, constitutes what is called *character,* is not good. It is the same with the *gifts of fortune.* Power, riches, honor, even health, and the general well-being and contentment with one's condition which is called *happiness,* inspire pride, and often presumption, if there is not a good will to correct the influence of these on the mind, and with this also to rectify the whole principle of acting, and adapt it to its end.

—IMMANUEL KANT, *Fundamental Principles of the Metaphysics of Morals*

9. The object of reasoning is to find out, from the consideration of what we already know, something else which we do not know. Consequently, reasoning is good if it be such as to give a true conclusion from true premisses, and not otherwise. Thus the question of its validity is purely one of fact and not of thinking. *A* being the premisses and *B* the conclusion, the question is, whether these facts are really so related that if *A* is *B* is. If so, the inference is valid; if not, not. It is not in the least the question whether, when the premisses are accepted by the mind, we feel an impulse to accept the conclusion also. It is true that we do gen-

erally reason correctly by nature. But that is an accident; the true conclusion would remain true if we had no impulse to accept it; and the false one would remain false, though we could not resist the tendency to believe in it.

—CHARLES SANDERS PEIRCE, *"The Fixation of Belief"*

10. The problem is, in a broad sense, political: given that the bulk of mankind are certain to commit fallacies, is it better that they should deduce false conclusions from true premisses or true conclusions from false premisses? A question of this sort is insoluble. The only true solution seems to be that ordinary men and women should be taught logic, so as to be able to refrain from drawing conclusions which only *seem* to follow. When it is said, for example, that the French are "logical," what is meant is that, when they accept a premiss, they also accept everything that a person totally destitute of logical subtlety would erroneously suppose to follow from the premiss. This is a most undesirable quality, from which, on the whole, the English-speaking nations have, in the past, been more free than any others. But there are signs that, if they are to remain free in this respect, they will require more philosophy and logic than they have had in the past. Logic was, formerly, the art of drawing inferences; it has now become the art of abstaining from inferences, since it has appeared that the inferences we naturally feel inclined to make are hardly ever valid. I conclude, therefore, that logic ought to be taught in schools with a view to teaching people not to reason. For, if they reason, they will almost certainly reason wrongly.

—BERTRAND RUSSELL, *Sceptical Essays*[14]

EXERCISES IN REASONING

The following problems require reasoning for their solution. To prove that an answer is correct, once it is achieved, requires an argument whose premisses are contained in the statement of the problem, and whose conclusion is the answer to it. If the answer is correct, a valid argument can be constructed. In working at these problems, the reader is urged to concern himself not merely with discovering the answers, but also with formulating arguments to prove those answers correct.[15]

★ 1. In a certain mythical community, politicians always lie, and non-politicians always tell the truth. A stranger meets three natives, and asks the first of them if he is a politician. The first native answers the question. The second native then reports that the first native denied being a

[14] By permission from *Sceptical Essays* by Bertrand Russell. Copyright, 1928, by Bertrand Russell. Published by W. W. Norton and Company, Inc., and by George Allen and Unwin, Ltd.

[15] Hints at the solutions to some of these exercises can be found in Section 7.6.

politician. The third native says that the first native *is* a politician.

How many of these three natives are politicians?

2. Of three prisoners in a certain jail, one had normal vision, the second had only one eye, and the third was totally blind. All were of at least average intelligence. The jailer told the prisoners that from three white hats and two red hats he would select three and put them on the prisoners' heads. Each was prevented from seeing what color hat was placed on his own head. They were brought together, and the jailer offered freedom to the prisoner with normal vision if he could tell what color hat was on his head. The prisoner confessed that he couldn't tell. Next the jailer offered freedom to the prisoner with only one eye if he could tell what color hat was on his head. The second prisoner confessed that he couldn't tell. The jailer did not bother making the offer to the blind prisoner, but agreed to extend the same terms to him when he made the request. The blind prisoner then smiled broadly and said:

> "I do not need to have my sight;
> From what my friends with eyes have said,
> I clearly see my hat is ———!"

3. On a certain train, the crew consists of three men, the brakeman, the fireman, and the engineer. Their names listed alphabetically are Jones, Robinson, and Smith. On the train are also three passengers with corresponding names, Mr. Jones, Mr. Robinson, and Mr. Smith. The following facts are known:

a. Mr. Robinson lives in Detroit.

b. The brakeman lives halfway between Detroit and Chicago.

c. Mr. Jones earns exactly $20,000 a year.

d. Smith once beat the fireman at billiards.

e. The brakeman's next-door neighbor, one of the three passengers mentioned, earns exactly three times as much as the brakeman.

f. The passenger living in Chicago has the same name as the brakeman.

What was the engineer's name?

4. The members of a small loan company are Mr. Black, Mr. White, Mrs. Coffee, Miss Ambrose, Mr. Kelly, and Miss Earnshaw. The positions they occupy are manager, assistant manager, cashier, stenographer, teller, and clerk, though not necessarily in that order. The assistant manager is the manager's grandson; the cashier is the stenographer's son-in-law; Mr. Black is a bachelor. Mr. White is twenty-two years old; Miss Ambrose is the teller's step-sister; and Mr. Kelly is the manager's neighbor.

Who holds each position?

★ 5. Benno Torelli, genial host at Hamtramck's most exclusive nightclub, was shot and killed by a racketeer gang because he fell behind in his protection payments. After considerable effort on the part of the police, five men were brought before the District Attorney, who asked them what they had to say for themselves. Each of the men made three statements, two true and one false. Their statements were:

LEFTY: I did not kill Torelli. I never owned a revolver in all my life. Spike did it.

RED: I did not kill Torelli. I never owned a revolver. The other guys are all passing the buck.

DOPEY: I am innocent. I never saw Butch before. Spike is guilty.

SPIKE: I am innocent. Butch is the guilty man. Lefty lied when he said I did it.

BUTCH: I did not kill Torelli. Red is the guilty man. Dopey and I are old pals.

Whodunnit?

6. Mrs. Adams, Mrs. Baker, Mrs. Catt, Mrs. Dodge, Mrs. Ennis, and that dowdy Mrs. Fisk all went shopping one morning at the Emporium. Each woman went directly to the floor carrying the article which she wanted to buy, and each woman bought only one article. They bought a book, a dress, a handbag, a necktie, a hat, and a lamp.

All the women except Mrs. Adams entered the elevator on the main floor. Two men also entered the elevator. Two women, Mrs. Catt and the one who bought the necktie got off at the second floor. Dresses were sold on the third floor. The two men got off at the fourth floor. The woman who bought the lamp got off at the fifth floor, leaving that dowdy Mrs. Fisk all alone to get off at the sixth floor.

The next day Mrs. Baker, who received the handbag as a surprise gift from one of the women who got off at the second floor, met her husband returning the necktie which one of the other women had given him. If books are sold on the main floor, and Mrs. Ennis was the sixth person to get out of the elevator, what did each of these women buy?

7. Five men who were buddies in the late war are having a reunion. They are White, Brown, Peters, Harper, and Nash, who by occupation are printer, writer, barber, neurologist, and heating-contractor. By coincidence, they live in the cities of White Plains, Brownsville, Petersburg, Harper's Ferry, and Nashville, but no man lives in the city having a name similar to his, nor does the name of his occupation have the same initial as his name or the name of the city in which he lives.

The barber doesn't live in Petersburg, and Brown is neither heating-contractor nor printer—nor does he live in Petersburg or Harper's Ferry.

Mr. Harper lives in Nashville and is neither barber nor writer. White is not a resident of Brownsville, nor is Nash, who is not a barber, nor a heating-contractor.

If you have only the information given above, can you determine the name of the city in which Nash resides?

8. Daniel Kilraine was killed on a lonely road, two miles from Pontiac, at 3:30 A.M., March 17, 1952. Otto, Curly, Slim, Mickey, and the Kid were arrested a week later in Detroit and questioned. Each of the five made four statements, three of which were true and one of which was false. One of these men killed Kilraine. Whodunnit? Their statements were:

OTTO: I was in Chicago when Kilraine was murdered. I never killed anyone. The Kid is the guilty man. Mickey and I are pals.

CURLY: I did not kill Kilraine. I never owned a revolver in my life. The Kid knows me. I was in Detroit the night of March 17th.

SLIM: Curly lied when he said he never owned a revolver. The murder was committed on St. Patrick's day. Otto was in Chicago at this time. One of us is guilty.

MICKEY: I did not kill Kilraine. The Kid has never been in Pontiac. I never saw Otto before. Curly was in Detroit with me on the night of March 17th.

THE KID: I did not kill Kilraine. I have never been in Pontiac. I never saw Curly before. Otto lied when he said I am guilty.

9. A woman recently gave a tea party to which she invited five guests. The names of the six women who sat down at the circular table were Mrs. Abrams, Mrs. Banjo, Mrs. Clive, Mrs. Dumont, Mrs. Ekwall, and Mrs. Fish. One of them was deaf, one was very talkative, one was terribly fat, one simply hated Mrs. Dumont, one had a vitamin deficiency, and one was the hostess.

The woman who hated Mrs. Dumont sat directly opposite Mrs. Banjo. The deaf woman sat opposite Mrs. Clive, who sat between the woman who had a vitamin deficiency and the woman who hated Mrs. Dumont. The fat woman sat opposite Mrs. Abrams, next to the deaf woman and to the left of the woman who hated Mrs. Dumont. The woman who had a vitamin deficiency sat between Mrs. Clive and the woman who sat opposite the woman who hated Mrs. Dumont. Mrs. Fish, who was a good friend of everyone, sat next to the fat woman and opposite the hostess.

Can you identify each of these lovely women?

★ 10. Nine men—Brown, White, Adams, Miller, Green, Hunter, Knight, Jones, and Smith—play the several positions on a baseball team. (The battery consists of the pitcher and the catcher; the infield consists of the first, second, and third basemen and the shortstop; the outfield consists of the right, left, and center fielders.) Determine, from the following data, the position played by each man.

a. Smith and Brown each won $10 playing poker with the pitcher.

b. Hunter was taller than Knight and shorter than White, but each of these weighed more than the first baseman.

c. The third baseman lives across the corridor from Jones in the same apartment house.

d. Miller and the outfielders play bridge in their spare time.

e. White, Miller, Brown, the right fielder, and the center fielder were bachelors; the rest were married.

f. Of Adams and Knight, one played outfielder position.

g. The right fielder was shorter than the center fielder.

h. The third baseman was brother to the pitcher's wife.

i. Green was taller than the infielders and the battery, except for Jones, Smith, and Adams.

j. The third baseman, the shortstop, and Hunter made $150 each speculating in U.S. Steel.

k. The second baseman was engaged to Miller's sister.

l. The second baseman beat Jones, Brown, Hunter, and the catcher at cards.

m. Adams lives in the same house as his own sister but dislikes the catcher.

n. Adams, Brown, and the shortstop lost $200 each speculating in copper.

o. The catcher had three daughters, the third baseman had two sons, but Green was being sued for divorce.

11. In a certain bank there were eleven distinct positions, namely, in decreasing rank, President, First Vice-President, Second Vice-President, Third Vice-President, Cashier, Teller, Assistant Teller, Bookkeeper, First Stenographer, Second Stenographer, and Janitor. These eleven positions are occupied by the following, here listed alphabetically: Mr. Adams, Mrs. Brown, Mr. Camp, Miss Dale, Mr. Evans, Mrs. Ford, Mr. Grant, Miss Hill, Mr. Jones, Mrs. Kane, and Mr. Long. Concerning them, only the following facts are known:

a. The Third Vice-President is the pampered grandson of the President, but is disliked by both Mrs. Brown and the Assistant Teller.

b. The Assistant Teller and the Second Stenographer shared equally in their father's estate.

c. The Second Vice-President and the Assistant Teller wear the same style of hats.

d. Mr. Grant told Miss Hill to send him a stenographer at once.

e. The President's nearest neighbors are Mrs. Kane, Mr. Grant, and Mr. Long.

f. The First Vice-President and the Cashier live at the exclusive Bachelor's Club.

g. The Janitor, a miser, has occupied the same garret room since boyhood.

h. Mr. Adams and the Second Stenographer are leaders in the social life of the younger unmarried set.

i. The Second Vice-President and the Bookkeeper were once engaged to be married to each other.

j. The fashionable Teller is the son-in-law of the First Stenographer.

k. Mr. Jones regularly gives Mr. Evans his discarded clothing to wear, without the elderly Bookkeeper knowing about the gift.

Show how to match correctly the eleven names against the eleven positions occupied.

12. Five terminal cancer patients are in a poker game: Brown, Perkins, Turner, Jones, and Reilly. Their brands of cigarettes are Luckies, Camels, Kools, Old Golds, and Chesterfields, but not necessarily in that order. At the beginning of the game, the number of cigarettes possessed by each of the players was 20, 15, 8, 6, and 3, but not necessarily in that order.

During the game, at a certain time when no one was smoking, the following conditions obtained:

a. Perkins asked for three cards.

b. Reilly had smoked half of his original supply, or one less than Turner smoked.

c. The Chesterfield man originally had as many more, plus half as many more, plus $2\frac{1}{2}$ more cigarettes than he now has.

d. The man who was drawing to an inside straight could taste only the menthol in his fifth cigarette, the last one he smoked.

e. The man who smokes Luckies had smoked at least two more than anyone else, including Perkins.

f. Brown drew as many aces as he originally had cigarettes.

g. No one had smoked all his cigarettes.

h. The Camel man asks Jones to pass Brown's matches.

How many cigarettes did each player have to begin with, and of what brand?

13. Alice, Betty, Carol, and Dorothy were either a lifeguard, a housewife, a pilot, or a professor. Each wore either a white, yellow, pink, or blue dress.

The lifeguard beat Betty at canasta, and Carol and the pilot often played bridge with the women in pink and blue dresses. Alice and the professor envied the woman in the blue dress, but this was not the housewife, as she always wore a white dress.

What was each woman's occupation and dress color?

14. In the same mythical community described in Exercise 1, a traveler on his way to the capital comes to a fork in the road. He knows that only one of the two branches leads to the capital but he does not know which. A native is present who will answer just one question, and that with only a "yes" or "no." What question should the traveler ask to learn which road leads to the capital?

Chapter 2
The Uses of Language

It is indeed not the least of the logician's tasks to indicate the pitfalls laid by language in the way of the thinker.

—*Gottlob Frege*

2.1 Three Basic Functions of Language

Language is so subtle and complicated an instrument that we often lose sight of the multiplicity of its uses. Here, as in many other situations, there is danger in our tendency to oversimplify.

A not uncommon complaint of those who take too narrow a view of the legitimate uses of language concerns the way in which words are "wasted" at social functions. "So much talk, and so little said!" sums up this kind of criticism. And more than one person has been heard to remark, "So and so always asks me how I am. What a hypocrite! He doesn't care in the least how I am!" Such remarks reveal a failure to understand the complex purposes for which language is used. It is shown also in the deplorable conduct of the bore, who, when asked how he is, actually proceeds to tell about the state of his health—usually at great length and in much detail. But people do not usually talk at parties to instruct each other. And ordinarily "How are you?" is a friendly greeting, not a request for a medical report.

The philosopher George Berkeley remarked long ago in his *Treatise Concerning the Principles of Human Knowledge* that

> . . . the communicating of ideas . . . is not the chief and only end of language, as is commonly supposed. There are other ends, as the raising of some passion, the exciting to or deterring from an action, the putting the mind in some particular disposition; to which the former is in many cases barely subservient, and sometimes entirely omitted, when these can be obtained without it, as I think does not infrequently happen in the familiar use of language.

More recent philosophers have elaborated in great detail the variety of uses to which language can be put. In his *Philosophical Investigations* Ludwig Wittgenstein insisted rightly that there are "countless different kinds of use of what we call 'symbols,' 'words,' 'sentences.' " Among the examples suggested by Wittgenstein are: giving orders, describing the appearance of an object or giving its measurements, reporting an event, speculating about an event, forming and testing a hypothesis, presenting the results of an experiment in tables and diagrams, making up a story, play-acting, singing catches, guessing riddles, making a joke and telling it, solving a problem in practical arithmetic, translating from one language into another, asking, thanking, cursing, greeting, and praying.

Some order can be imposed on the staggering variety of language uses by dividing them into three very general categories. The threefold division of the functions of language here proposed is admittedly a simplification, possibly even an oversimplification, but it has been found useful by many writers on logic and language.

The first of these three uses of language is to communicate information. Ordinarily this is accomplished by formulating and affirming (or denying) propositions. Language used to affirm or deny propositions, or to present arguments, is said to be serving the *informative* function. In this context we use the word "information" to include misinformation: false as well as true propositions, incorrect as well as correct arguments. Informative discourse is used to describe the world, and to reason about it. Whether the alleged facts are important or unimportant, general or particular, does not matter; in any case the language used to describe or report them is being used informatively.

We distinguish two other basic uses or functions of language in addition to the informative, and refer to them as the *expressive* and the *directive*. Just as science provides us with the clearest examples of informative discourse, so poetry furnishes us the best examples of language serving an expressive function. The following lines of Burns,

> O my Luve's like a red, red rose
> That's newly sprung in June:
> O my Luve's like the melodie
> That's sweetly play'd in tune!

are definitely not intended to inform us of any facts or theories concerning the world. The poet's concern is not with knowledge but with feelings and attitudes. The passage was not written to report any information but to express certain emotions that the poet felt very keenly and to evoke similar feelings in the reader. Language serves the expressive function whenever it is used to vent or to arouse feelings or emotions.

Not all expressive language is poetry, however. We express sorrow by saying "That's too bad," or "Oh my," and enthusiasm by shouting "Wow!" or "Right on!" The lover expresses his delicate passion by murmuring "Darling!" or "Oh baby!" The poet expresses his complex and concentrated emotions in a sonnet or some other verse form. A worshipper may express his feeling of wonder and awe at the vastness and mystery of the universe by reciting the Lord's Prayer or the twenty-third Psalm of David. All these uses of language are not intended to communicate information but to express emotions, feelings, or attitudes. Expressive discourse *as expressive* is neither true nor false. For a person to apply only the criteria of truth or falsehood, correctness or incorrectness, to expressive discourse like a poem is to miss its point and to lose much of its value. The student whose enjoyment of Keats' sonnet "On first looking into Chapman's Homer" is marred by his historical knowledge that Balboa rather than Cortez discovered the Pacific Ocean is a "poor reader" of poetry. The purpose of the poem is not to teach history, but something else entirely. This is not to say that poetry can have no literal significance. Some poems do have an informative content which may be an important ingredient in their total effect. Some poetry may well be "criticism of life," in the words of a great poet. But such poems are more than merely expressive, as we are using the term here. Such poetry may be said to have a "mixed usage," or to serve a multiple function. This notion will be discussed further in the following section.

Expression may be analyzed into two components. When a man curses to himself when he is alone, or a poet writes poems which he shows to no one, or a man prays in solitude, his language functions to express his own attitude but does not serve to evoke a similar attitude in anyone else. On the other hand, when an orator seeks to inspire his audience—not to action, but to share enthusiasm; when a lover courts his beloved in poetic language; when the crowd cheers its athletic team; the language used not only expresses the attitudes of the speakers but is intended to evoke the same attitudes in the hearers. Expressive discourse, then, is used either to *express* the speaker's feelings or to *evoke* certain feelings on the part of the auditor. Of course it may do both.

Language serves the *directive* function when it is used for the purpose of causing (or preventing) overt action. The clearest examples of directive discourse are commands and requests. When a mother tells her little boy to wash his hands before supper, she does not intend to communicate any information to him or to express or evoke any particular emotion. Her language is intended to get results, to cause action of the indicated kind. When the same mother asks a shopkeeper to deliver certain goods to her house, she is again using language directively, to produce *action*. To ask a question is ordinarily to request an answer, and is also to be classified as directive discourse. The difference between a command and a request is a rather subtle one, for almost any command can be translated into a request by adding the word "please," or by suitable changes in tone or voice or in facial expression.

In its nakedly imperative form, directive discourse is neither true nor false. A command such as "Close the window" cannot be either true or false in any literal sense. Whether the command is obeyed or disobeyed does not affect or determine its truth value, for it has none. We may disagree about whether a command has been obeyed or not: we may disagree about whether a command *should* be obeyed or not; but we never disagree about whether a command is true or false, for it cannot be either. However, the reasonableness or propriety, the unreasonableness or impropriety of commands are properties somewhat analogous to the truth or falsehood of informative discourse. Some efforts have been made to develop a "logic of imperatives," but not very much systematic work has been devoted to the subject as yet. Because of the tentative nature of these attempts, they will not be discussed in the present text.[1]

2.2 Discourse Serving Multiple Functions

In the preceding section the examples presented were chemically pure specimens, so to speak, of the three basic kinds of communication. The threefold division proposed is illuminating and valuable, but it cannot be applied mechanically, because almost any ordinary communication will probably exemplify, to a greater or lesser extent, all three uses of language. Thus a poem, which is primarily expressive discourse, may have a moral and be in effect a command to the reader (or hearer) to lead a certain kind of life, and may also convey a certain amount of information. On the other hand, although

[1] For an introduction to this topic the interested reader can consult Part Eight of *Contemporary Readings in Logical Theory* by I. M. Copi and J. A. Gould (New York: The Macmillan Company, 1967).

a sermon may be predominantly directive, seeking to cause certain appropriate action by members of the congregation (whether to abandon their evil ways, or to contribute money to the church, or what not), it may express and evoke sentiments, thus serving the expressive function, and may also include some information, communicating some factual material. And a scientific treatise, essentially informative, may express something of the writer's own enthusiasm, thus serving an expressive function, and may also, at least implicitly, serve some directive function or other, perhaps bidding the reader to verify independently the author's conclusion. Most ordinary uses of language are mixed.

It is not always the result of any confusion on the part of the speaker when his language serves mixed or multiple functions. It is rather the case that effective communication demands certain combinations of functions. Few of us stand to each other in the relation of parent to child or employer to employee. And outside the context of such formal relationships as these, one cannot simply issue an order with any expectation of having it obeyed. Consequently a certain indirection must be employed: a bald command would arouse antagonism or resentment and be self-defeating. Ordinarily one cannot cause action merely by voicing an imperative; it is necessary to use a more subtle method of stimulating the desired action.

Action may be said to have very complex causes. Motivation is more properly to be discussed by a psychologist than a logician, but it is common knowledge that actions usually involve both desires and beliefs. A man who desires to eat food will not touch what is on his plate unless he believes it to be food; and even though he believes it to be food he will not touch it unless he desires to eat. This fact is relevant to our present discussion because desires are a special type of what we have been calling attitudes.

Consequently actions may be caused by evoking appropriate attitudes and communicating relevant information. Assuming your listeners to be benevolent, you may cause them to contribute to a given charity by informing them of its effectiveness in accomplishing benevolent results. In such a case your use of language is ultimately directive, since its purpose is to cause action. But a naked command would be far less effective in this situation than the informative discourse used. Suppose, on the other hand, that your listeners are already persuaded that the charity in question does accomplish benevolent results. Here again you cannot simply command with any great hope of being obeyed, but you may succeed in causing them to act in the desired fashion by somehow arousing a sufficiently benevolent feeling or emotion in them. The discourse you use to realize your end is expressive discourse; you must make a "moving appeal." Thus your language will have a mixed use, functioning both expressively and directively. Or finally, let us suppose that you are seeking a donation from people who have neither a benevolent attitude nor a belief that the charity serves a benevolent purpose. Here you must use both informative and expressive language. In such a case the language used serves all three functions, being directive, informative, and expressive all at once, not accidentally as a mere mixture that just happens to occur, but essentially, as necessary to successful communication.

Another interesting and important mixed use of language is that which has often been called the *ceremonial.* Included within this category are many different kinds of phrases, ranging from relatively trivial words of greeting to the more portentous discourse of the marriage ceremony, phrasings of state documents, and the verbal rituals performed on holy days in houses of worship. These can all be regarded as mixtures of expressive and directive discourse, rather than some altogether different and unique kind. For example, the usual ceremonial greetings and chitchat at social gatherings serve the purpose of expressing and evoking goodwill and sociability. Perhaps for some speakers they are intended also to serve the directive purpose of causing their hearers to act in certain definite ways, to patronize the speaker's business, to offer him employment, or to invite him to dinner. At the other extreme, the impressive language of the marriage ceremony is intended to emphasize the solemnity of the occasion (its expressive function), and also to cause the bride and groom to perform in their new roles with heightened appreciation of the seriousness of the marriage contract (its directive function).

Some ceremonial uses of language are not always recognized as such. Thus John Kenneth Galbraith in *The Affluent Society* wrote,

> In some measure the articulation of the conventional wisdom is a religious rite. It is an act of affirmation like reading aloud from the Scriptures or going to church. The business executive listening to a luncheon address on the virtues of free enterprise and the evils of Washington is already persuaded, and so are his fellow listeners, and all are secure in their convictions. Indeed, although a display of rapt attention is required, the executive may not feel it necessary to listen. But he does placate the gods by participating in the ritual. Having been present, maintained attention, and having applauded, he can depart feeling that the economic system is a little more secure. Scholars gather in scholarly assemblages to hear in elegant statement what all have heard before. Yet it is not a negligible rite, for its purpose is not to convey knowledge but to beatify learning and the learned.

There is still another use of language that is somewhat akin to the ceremonial. When the minister or justice of the peace says at the end of the marriage ceremony, "I now pronounce you man and wife," though his words may seem merely to report what he is doing, their utterance actually constitutes the doing of it. Here is an instance of the performative use of language. A *performative utterance* is one that is uttered in appropriate circumstances to do what it appears to report. Such performative utterances involve what may be called performative verbs, where a *performative verb* is one that denotes an action that in appropriate circumstances is typically accomplished by using that verb in the first person. Obvious examples of performative verbs are "accept," "advise," "apologize," "christen," "congratulate," "offer," "promise," and "suggest." The performative function of language is only one among others, but perhaps it merits special mention because it seems to fit less well than the others into our threefold division of language functions.[2]

2.3 The Forms of Discourse

Textbooks of grammar commonly define a sentence as the unit of language that expresses a complete thought, and divide sentences into four categories, usually called declarative, interrogative, imperative, and exclamatory. These four grammatical categories do not coincide with those of assertions, questions, commands, and exclamations. We may be tempted to identify form with function—to think that declarative sentences and informative discourse coincide, and that exclamatory sentences are suitable only for expressive discourse. Regarding questions as requests for answers, we may be led further to think that directive discourse consists exclusively of sentences in the interrogative and imperative moods. Were such identifications possible, it would immensely simplify the problem of communication, for then we should be able to tell the intended use or function of a passage by its form, which is open to direct inspection. Some people apparently do identify form with function, but these are not sensitive readers, for the identification often makes them misunderstand what is said, and they "miss the point" of much that is to be communicated.

It is a mistake to believe that everything in the form of a declarative sentence is informative discourse, to be valued if true and rejected if false. "I had a very nice time at your party" is a declarative sentence, but its function need not be informative at all, but rather ceremonial or expressive, expressing a feeling of friendliness and appreciation. Many poems and prayers are in the form of declarative

[2] The notion of performative utterance was first developed by the late Professor John Austin of Oxford University; that of performative verb was first suggested to me by my friend Professor Richard L. Cartwright of M.I.T.

sentences, despite the fact that their functions are not informative. To regard them as such and to attempt to evaluate them by the criteria of truth or falsehood is to shut oneself off from aesthetic and religious satisfactions. Again, many requests and commands are stated indirectly—perhaps more gently—by means of declarative sentences. The declarative sentence "I would like some coffee" should not be taken by a waitress to be a mere report of the psychological fact it apparently asserts about her customer, but as an order or request for action. Were we invariably to judge the truth or falsehood of declarative sentences such as "I'd appreciate some help with this" or "I hope you'll be able to meet me after class at the library," and do no more than register them as information received, we should soon be without friends. These examples should suffice to show that the declarative form is no certain indication of the informative function. Declarative sentences lend themselves to the formulation of every kind of discourse.

It is the same with other forms of sentences. The interrogative sentence "Do you realize that we're almost late?" is not necessarily a request for information but may be a command to hurry. The interrogative sentence "Isn't it true that Russia and Germany signed a pact in 1939 which precipitated the Second World War?" may not be a question at all but either an oblique way of communicating information or an attempt to express and evoke a feeling of hostility toward Russia, functioning informatively in the first instance and expressively in the second. Even a grammatical imperative, as in official documents beginning "Know all men by these presents that . . . ," may not be a command, but rather informative discourse in what it asserts and expressive discourse in its use of language to evoke the appropriate feelings of solemnity and respect. In spite of its close affinity to the expressive, an exclamatory sentence may serve a quite different function. The exclamation "Good Lord it's late!" may really communicate a command to hurry. And the exclamation "What a beautiful ring!" uttered by a young lady to her gentleman friend as they pass a jeweler's window, may function much more directively than expressively.

It should be remembered that some discourse is intended to serve two or possibly all three functions of language at once. In such cases each aspect or function of a given passage is subject to its own proper criteria. One having an informative function may have that aspect evaluated as true or false. The same passage serving a directive function may have that aspect evaluated as proper or improper, right or wrong. And if there is also an expressive function served by the passage in question, that component of it may be evaluated as sincere or insincere, as valuable or otherwise. To evaluate a given passage properly requires knowledge of the function or functions it is intended to serve.

Truth and falsehood, and the related notions of correctness and incorrectness of argument, are more important in the study of logic than the others mentioned. Hence, as students of logic, we must be able to differentiate discourse that functions informatively from that which does not. And we must be able further to disentangle the informative function a given passage serves from whatever other functions it may also be serving. To do this "disentangling" we must know what different functions language can serve and be able to tell them apart. The grammatical structure of a passage often serves as a cue to its function, but there is no *necessary* connection between function and grammatical form. Nor is there any strict relation between the function and the content—in the sense of what might seem to be asserted by a passage. This is very clearly shown by an example of Bloomfield's in his chapter on "Meaning": "A petulant child, at bed-time, says *I'm hungry,* and his mother, who is up to his tricks, answers by packing him off to bed. This is an example of displaced speech."[3] The child's speech here is directive—even though it does not succeed in procuring the wanted diversion. By the function of a passage we mean the intended function. But, that, unfortunately, is not always easy to determine.

When a passage is quoted in isolation, it is often difficult to say what language function it is primarily intended to serve. The reason for this difficulty is that context is extremely important in determining the answer to such a question. What is an imperative or a flat statement of fact, by itself, may in its proper context function expressively, as part of a larger whole whose poetic effect is derived from all its parts in their arrangement. For example, in isolation,

Come to the window.

is an imperative serving the directive function; and

The sea is calm tonight.

is a declarative sentence serving an informative function. But both are from Matthew Arnold's poem "Dover Beach," and in that context contribute to the expressive function served by the larger whole.

It is important also to distinguish between the proposition which a sentence formulates and some fact about the speaker for which his

[3] Reprinted from *Language* by Leonard Bloomfield. Copyright, 1933, by Henry Holt and Company, Inc.

uttering that sentence is evidence. When a man remarks, "It is raining," the proposition he asserts is about the weather, not about himself. Yet his making the assertion is evidence that he believes it to be raining, which is a fact about the speaker. It also may happen that a person makes a statement which is ostensibly about his beliefs, not for the sake of giving information about himself, but simply as a way of saying something else. To say "I believe that gold is valuable" is ordinarily not to be construed as a psychological or autobiographical report on the beliefs of the speaker, but simply his way of saying that gold *is* valuable. Similarly, voicing a command is usually evidence that the speaker has certain desires; and under appropriate circumstances to assert that one has such and such a desire is to give a command. To utter an exclamation of joy gives evidence that the speaker is joyful, although the speaker makes no assertion in the process. On the other hand, to present a psychological report which affirms that the speaker is joyful is to assert a proposition, something quite different from exclaiming joyously.

In subsequent chapters we shall develop certain logical techniques that can be applied quite mechanically to the formulations of arguments for the purpose of testing their validity. But there is no mechanical technique for recognizing the *presence* of an argument. There is no mechanical method for distinguishing language that is informative and argumentative from language that serves other functions instead. This requires thought, and demands an awareness of and sensitivity to the flexibility of language and the multiplicity of its uses.

EXERCISES

I. What language functions are most probably intended to be served by each of the following passages?

★ 1. A civil war is like the heat of a fever; but a foreign war is like the heat of exercise, and serveth to keep the body in health.

—FRANCIS BACON, *Essays*

2. Next in importance to freedom and justice is popular education, without which neither freedom nor justice can be permanently maintained.

—JAMES A. GARFIELD

3. Education is fatal to anyone with a spark of artistic feeling. Education should be confined to clerks, and even them it drives to drink. Will the world learn that we never learn anything that we did not know before?

—GEORGE MOORE, *Confessions of a Young Man*

4. Language is the armory of the human mind; and at once contains the trophies of its past, and the weapons of its future conquests.

—SAMUEL TAYLOR COLERIDGE

★ 5. Language—human language—after all, is but little better than the croak and cackle of fowls, and other utterances of brute nature—sometimes not so adequate.

—NATHANIEL HAWTHORNE, *American Notebook*

6. Language! the blood of the soul, sir, into which our thoughts run, and out of which they grow.

—OLIVER WENDELL HOLMES, *The Professor at the Breakfast Table*

7. The bad workmen who form the majority of the operatives in many branches of industry are decidedly of opinion that bad workmen ought to receive the same wages as good.

—JOHN STUART MILL, *On Liberty*

8. War is the greatest plague that can afflict humanity; it destroys religion, it destroys states, it destroys families. Any scourge is preferable to it.

MARTIN LUTHER, *Table-Talk*

9. There is but one way for a newspaper man to look at a politician, and that is down.

—FRANK H. SIMONDS

★ 10. We must all hang together or assuredly we shall all hang separately.

—BENJAMIN FRANKLIN (to the other signers of the Declaration of Independence)

11. I understand well the respect of mankind for war, because war breaks up the Chinese stagnation of society, and demonstrates the personal merits of all men.

—RALPH WALDO EMERSON, *The Conservative*

12. Eternal peace is a dream, and not even a beautiful one. War is a part of God's world order. In it are developed the noblest virtues of man: courage and abnegation, dutifulness and self-sacrifice. Without war the world would sink into materialism.

—HELMUTH VON MOLTKE

13. War crushes with bloody heel all justice, all happiness, all that is God-like in man. In our age there can be no peace that is not honorable; there can be no war that is not dishonorable.

—CHARLES SUMNER

14. I believe that war is at present productive of good more than of evil.

—JOHN RUSKIN

★ 15. A little philosophy inclineth man's mind to atheism; but depth in philosophy bringeth man's mind about to religion.

—FRANCIS BACON, *Essays*

16. Belief in the existence of God is as groundless as it is useless. The world will never be happy until atheism is universal.

—J. O. LA METTRIE, *L'Homme Machine*

17. Nearly all atheists on record have been men of extremely debauched and vile conduct.

—J. P. SMITH, *Instructions on Christian Theology*

18. Man scans with scrupulous care the character and pedigree of his horses, cattle, and dogs before he matches them; but when he comes to his own marriage he rarely, or never, takes any such care.

—CHARLES DARWIN, *The Descent of Man*

19. The story of the whale swallowing Jonah, though a whale is large enough to do it, borders greatly on the marvelous; but it would have approached nearer to the idea of miracle if Jonah had swallowed the whale.

—THOMAS PAINE, *The Age of Reason*

★ 20. War has the deep meaning that by it the ethical health of the nations is preserved and their finite aims uprooted. And as the winds which sweep over the ocean prevent the decay that would result from its perpetual calm, so war protects the people from the corruption which an everlasting peace would bring upon it.

—GEORG HEGEL, *The Philosophy of Law*

21. That all particular appetites and passions are toward *external things themselves,* distinct from the *pleasure arising from them,* is manifested from hence—that there could not be this pleasure were it not for that prior suitableness between the object and the passion; there could be no enjoyment or delight from one thing more than another, from eating food more than from swallowing a stone, if there were not an affection or appetite to one thing more than another.

—JOSEPH BUTLER, Sermon "Upon the Love of Our Neighbor"

22. "An unhappy alternative is before you, Elizabeth. From this day you must be a stranger to one of your parents. Your mother will never see you again if you do *not* marry Mr. Collins, and I will never see you again if you *do*."

—JANE AUSTEN, *Pride and Prejudice*

23. "Of this man Pickwick I will say little; the subject presents but few attractions; and I, gentlemen, am not the man, nor are you, gentlemen,

the men, to delight in the contemplation of revolting heartlessness, and of systematic villainy."

—CHARLES DICKENS, *Pickwick Papers*

24. You praise the men who feasted the citizens and satisfied their desires, and people say that they have made the city great, not seeing that the swollen and ulcerated condition of the State is to be attributed to these elder statesmen; for they have filled the city full of harbors and docks and walls and revenues and all that, and have left no room for justice and temperance.

—PLATO, *Gorgias*

25. The physical difference of sex thus appears at the same time as a difference of intellectual and moral type. With their exclusive individualities these personalities combine to form a *single person:* the subjective union of hearts, becoming a "substantial" unity, makes this union an ethical tie—*Marriage.* The "substantial" union of hearts makes marriage an indivisible personal bond—monogamic marriage: the bodily conjunction is a sequel to the moral attachment. A further sequel is community of personal and private interests.

—GEORG HEGEL, *The Philosophy of Mind*

II. For the following passages, indicate what propositions they may be intended to assert, if any, what overt actions they may be intended to cause, if any, and what they may be regarded as providing evidence for about the speaker, if anything.

★ 1. He [Benjamin Disraeli] is a self-made man, and worships his creator.

—JOHN BRIGHT

2. I have sworn upon the altar of God eternal hostility against every form of tyranny over the mind of man.

—THOMAS JEFFERSON

3. If [he] does really think that there is no distinction between virtue and vice, why, sir, when he leaves our houses let us count our spoons.

—SAMUEL JOHNSON

4. I have tried sedulously not to laugh at the acts of man, nor to lament them, nor to detest them, but to understand them.

—BARUCH SPINOZA, *Tractatus Theologico-politicus*

★ 5. We hear about constitutional rights, free speech and the free press. Every time I hear these words I say to myself, "That man is a Red, that man is a Communist." You never heard a real American talk in that manner.

—FRANK HAGUE, speech before the Jersey City Chamber of Commerce, January 12, 1938

6. You'll never have a quiet world until you knock the patriotism out of the human race.

—GEORGE BERNARD SHAW, *O'Flaherty, V.C.*

7. Of what use is political liberty to those who have no bread? It is of value only to ambitious theorists and politicians.

—JEAN PAUL MARAT

8. While there is a lower class I am in it, while there is a criminal element I am of it, and while there is a soul in prison I am not free.

—EUGENE DEBS

9. If there were a nation of gods they would be governed democratically, but so perfect a government is not suitable to men.

—JEAN JACQUES ROUSSEAU, *The Social Contract*

★ 10. There are three classes of citizens. The first are the rich, who are indolent and yet always crave more. The second are the poor, who have nothing, are full of envy, hate the rich, and are easily led by demagogues. Between the two extremes lie those who make the state secure and uphold the laws.

—EURIPIDES, *The Suppliant Women*

11. I am convinced that turbulence as well as every other evil temper of this evil age belong not to the lower but to the middle classes—those middle classes of whom in our folly we are so wont to boast.

—LORD ROBERT CECIL, *Diary in Australia*

12. God will see to it that war shall always recur, as a drastic medicine for ailing humanity.

—HEINRICH VON TREITSCHKE, *Politik*

13. I would rather that the people should wonder why I wasn't President than why I am.

—SALMON P. CHASE

14. Students are not the best judges; if they were, they would not have to be students.

—CHARLES FRANKEL, *Education and the Barricades*

★ 15. Indeed I tremble for my country when I reflect that God is just.

—THOMAS JEFFERSON

16. Even a fool, when he holdeth his peace, is counted wise; And he that shutteth his lips is esteemed as a man of understanding.

—PROVERBS 17:28

17. A word fitly spoken is like apples of gold in settings of silver.

—PROVERBS 25:11

18. If there are some who are slaves by nature, the reason is that men were made slaves against nature. Force made the first slaves, and slavery, by degrading and corrupting its victims, perpetuated their bondage.

—JEAN JACQUES ROUSSEAU, *The Social Contract*

19. A free man thinks of nothing less than of death, and his wisdom is not a meditation upon death but upon life.

—BARUCH SPINOZA, *Ethics*

★ 20. I have seen, and heard, much of Cockney impudence before now; but never expected to hear a coxcomb ask two hundred guineas for flinging a pot of paint in the public's face.

—JOHN RUSKIN, on Whistler's painting "Nocturne in Black and Gold"

21. When people who are tolerably fortunate in their outward lot do not find in life sufficient enjoyment to make it valuable to them, the cause generally is, caring for nobody but themselves.

—JOHN STUART MILL, *Utilitarianism*

22. A young man is not a proper hearer of lectures on political science; for he is inexperienced in the actions that occur in life, but its discussions start from these and are about these; and, further, since he tends to follow his passions, his study will be vain and unprofitable, because the end aimed at is not knowledge but action.

—ARISTOTLE, *Nichomachean Ethics*

23. Men are never so likely to settle a question rightly as when they discuss it freely.

—THOMAS BABINGTON, Lord Macaulay

24. In a people, not conceived in a lawless and unorganized condition, but as a self-developed and truly organic totality—in such a people sovereignty is the personality of the whole, and this is represented in reality by the person of the monarch.

—GEORG HEGEL, *The Philosophy of Law*

25. But of the many falsehoods told by them, there was one which quite amazed me;—I mean when they said that you should be upon your guard and not allow yourselves to be deceived by the force of my eloquence. To say this, when they were certain to be detected as soon as I opened my lips and proved myself to be anything but a great speaker, did indeed appear to me most shameless—unless by the force of eloquence they mean the force of truth; for if such is their meaning, I admit that I am eloquent. But in how different a way from theirs!

—PLATO, *Apology*

2.4 Emotive Words

We have already observed that a single sentence can serve both an informative and an expressive function. For the sentence to formulate a proposition, its words must have literal or cognitive meaning, referring to objects or events and their properties or relations. When it expresses an attitude or feeling, however, some of its words may also have an emotional suggestiveness or impact. A word or phrase can have both a literal meaning and an emotional impact. It has become customary to speak of the latter as "emotive significance" or "emotive meaning." There is a high degree of independence between the literal and emotive meanings of a word. For example, the words "bureaucrat," "government official," and "public servant" have almost identical literal meanings. But their emotive meanings are quite different. The term "bureaucrat" definitely tends to express resentment and disapproval, while the term "public servant" is an honorific one, which tends to express favor and approval. The phrase "government official" is more nearly neutral than either of the others.

As John Kenneth Galbraith put it in *The Affluent Society:*

> The notion of a vested interest has an engaging flexibility in our social usage. In ordinary intercourse it is an improper advantage enjoyed by a political minority to which the speaker does not himself belong. When the speaker himself enjoys it, it ceases to be a vested interest and becomes a hard-won reward. When a vested interest is enjoyed not by a minority but by a majority, it is a human right.

It is important to realize that one and the same thing can be referred to by words that have very different emotive impacts. It might be thought that the emotive impact of a word is always connected with the properties possessed by its referent. In the poet's phrase: "A rose by any other name would smell as sweet." It is true that the actual fragrance of the rose would remain the same through any change of name we might assign it. But our attitude toward them would very likely change if we began to refer to roses as, say, "skunkweeds." Changes in the other direction are familiar: purveyors of canned horse mackerel sell much more of their product now that they call it tunafish. In the same vein, after denouncing the extent to which specialized vocational training has displaced humanistic studies in our colleges, William H. Whyte, Jr., in *The Organization Man,* wrote:

> It is not entirely facetious to suggest that the only way any reform could be effected would be through a subversive movement by the humanists. In what would be poetic justice to the vocationalists, humanists in disguise could

appropriate their terminology and smuggle education into the curriculum by pretending to specialize it further. Who would dare cavil at the humanities were they presented as "Mercantile Influence in the Renaissance," "Market Patterns in Pre-Industrial England," or "Communication Techniques in Elizabethan Drama"?

It has been said that language has a life of its own independent of the facts it is used to describe. In our terminology, words can have exactly the same descriptive or literal meanings and yet be either moderately or completely opposite in their emotive suggestiveness or meaning. Certain physiological activities pertaining to reproduction and elimination can be unemotionally described, using a medical vocabulary, without offending the most squeamish taste; but all of these terms have certain four-letter synonyms whose usage shocks all but the most hardened interpreters. A writer has reported

> . . . the illuminating story of a little girl who, having recently learned to read, was spelling out a political article in the newspaper. "Father," she asked, "what is Tammany Hall?" And her father replied in the voice usually reserved for the taboos of social communication, "You'll understand that when you grow up, my dear." Acceding to this adult whim of evasion, she desisted from her inquiries; but something in Daddy's tone had convinced her that Tammany Hall must be connected with illicit *amour,* and for many years she could not hear this political institution mentioned without experiencing a secret non-political thrill.[4]

The emotive meaning of a word may always be acquired by association, but these associations need not always be directly with the word's literal referent.

An instructive joke based upon the contrast between literal and emotive meaning was made by the philosopher Bertrand Russell when he "conjugated" an "irregular verb" as

> I am firm; you are obstinate;
> he is a pig-headed fool.

The London *New Statesman and Nation* subsequently ran a contest soliciting such irregular conjugations and picked among the winners the following:

> I am righteously indignant; you are annoyed;
> he is making a fuss about nothing.
> I am fastidious; you are fussy;
> he is an old woman.
> I have reconsidered it; you have changed your mind;
> he has gone back on his word.

[4] By permission from *The Gift of Tongues,* by Margaret Schlauch. Copyright, 1942, by Margaret Schlauch. Published by the Viking Press, Inc.

In his lively book entitled *How to Think Straight,* Robert Thouless made an experiment designed to show the importance of emotively colored words in poetry. There he examined two lines from Keats' "The Eve of St. Agnes":

> Full on this casement shone the wintry moon,
> And threw warm gules on Madeline's fair breast.

He proposed to show that their beauty arises primarily from the proper choice of emotionally colored words, by showing how that beauty is lost completely if those words are replaced by neutral ones. Selecting the words "casement," "gules," "Madeline," "fair," and "breast," Mr. Thouless wrote:

> *Casement* means simply a kind of window with emotional and romantic associations. *Gules* is the heraldic name for red, with the suggestion of romance which accompanies all heraldry. *Madeline* is simply a girl's name, but one calling out favorable emotions absent from a relatively plain and straightforward name. *Fair* simply means, in objective fact, that her skin was white or uncolored—a necessary condition for the colors of the window to show—but also *fair* implies warm emotional preference for an uncolored skin rather than one which is yellow, purple, black, or any of the other colors which skin might be. *Breast* also has similar emotional meanings, and the aim of scientific description might have been equally well attained if it had been replaced by such a neutral word as *chest.*
>
> Let us now try the experiment of keeping these two lines in a metrical form, but replacing all the emotionally-colored words by neutral ones, while making as few other changes as possible. We may write:
>
> "Full on this window shone the wintry moon,
> Making red marks on Jane's uncolored chest."
>
> No one will doubt that all of its poetic value has been knocked out of the passage by these changes. Yet the lines still mean the same in external fact; they still have the same objective meaning. It is only the emotional meaning which has been destroyed.[5]

To the extent that humorous impact is to be included in emotive meaning, the revised lines of "poetry" have considerable emotive meaning, though very different from that possessed by the original verses.

EXERCISES

1. Give five original "conjugations of irregular verbs," where literally the same activity is given a laudatory description in the first person, a

[5] Reprinted from *How to Think Straight* by Robert H. Thouless. Copyright, 1932, 1939, by Simon and Schuster, Inc.

fairly neutral one in the second person, and a derogatory one in the third person.

2. Select two brief passages of poetry and perform Thouless' "experiment" on them.

2.5 Kinds of Agreement and Disagreement

The "irregular verb" conjugations mentioned in the preceding section make one thing abundantly clear. The same state of affairs can be described in different words which express widely divergent attitudes toward it. And to the extent that anything can be described by means of alternative phrases—one of which expresses an attitude of approval, another an attitude of disapproval, still another a more or less neutral attitude—there are different kinds of agreement and disagreement expressible with respect to any situation or activity.

Two people may disagree as to whether or not something has happened, and when they do they may be said to have *disagreement in belief*. On the other hand, they may agree that an event has actually occurred, thus agreeing in belief, and yet they may have strongly divergent or even opposite attitudes toward it. One who approves of it will describe it in language which expresses approval, the other may choose terms that express disapproval. There is disagreement here, but it is not disagreement in belief as to what has occurred. The disagreement manifested is rather a difference in feeling about the matter, a *disagreement in attitude*.[6]

With respect to any matter, two persons may agree in belief and disagree in attitude, or they may agree in both belief and attitude. It is also possible for people to agree in attitude despite disagreeing in belief. One may believe that so-and-so has changed his mind, and praise him for "listening to the voice of reason," while the other may believe that he has *not* changed has mind and praise him for "refusing to be swayed by blandishment." This third kind of situation often occurs in politics; people may support the same candidate for different and even incompatible reasons. There is a fourth possibility also, in which the disagreement is complete. One speaker, believing that so-and-so has changed his mind, may strongly approve of him for having wisely reconsidered the matter, while the second speaker, believing that he has *not* changed his mind, may just as vigorously disapprove of him for being too pig-headed to admit his

[6] I am indebted to my friend Professor Charles L. Stevenson for the terms agreement and disagreement "in belief" and agreement and disagreement "in attitude," and also for the notion of *persuasive definition,* which will be discussed in Chapter Four. Cf. his *Ethics and Language,* Yale University Press, 1944.

mistake. Here there is disagreement in belief and also disagreement in attitude.

If we are interested in the problem of resolving disagreements, it is important to realize that agreement and disagreement may relate not only to the facts in a given case, but to attitudes toward those facts. Different methods are applicable to the resolution of different kinds of disagreement, and if we are unclear as to what kind of disagreement exists we shall be unclear as to what methods should be utilized. If the disagreement is in belief, it can be resolved by ascertaining the facts. In the preceding instance, the factual question is whether so-and-so at one time held a certain view and at a later time held a different view, or whether at the later time he still maintained the earlier view. To decide the question—were it of sufficient importance—the usual techniques for verification could be utilized: witnesses could be questioned, documents consulted, records examined, and so on. Theoretically, the facts could be established and the issue decided, and this would resolve the disagreement. The methods of scientific inquiry are available here, and it suffices to direct them squarely at the question of fact about which there is disagreement in belief.

On the other hand, if there is disagreement in attitude rather than disagreement in belief, the techniques appropriate to settling it are rather different, being more inclusive and less direct. To call witnesses, consult documents, or the like, to the end of establishing either that the man held two different views on two different occasions or that he held the same view on the two occasions, would be fruitless in the case of this type of disagreement. What may be regarded as the facts of the case are not at issue; the disagreement is not over what the facts *are* but over how these facts are to be valued. A serious attempt to resolve this disagreement in attitude may involve reference to many factual questions—but not the one mentioned so far. Instead, it may be fruitful to consider what implications or consequences are entailed by the action in question, and what would have been entailed by this or that alternative course of action. Questions of motive and of intention are of great importance here. These are all factual questions, to be sure, but none of them is identical with what would be the issue if the disagreement were in belief rather than in attitude. Still other methods are available which may resolve a disagreement in attitude. Persuasion may be attempted, with its extensive use of expressive discourse. Rhetoric may be of paramount utility in unifying the will of a group, in achieving unanimity of attitude. But of course it is wholly worthless in resolving a question of fact.

A word of warning is appropriate here. Such words as "good" and "bad," "right" and "wrong" occur frequently in the writings of moral philosophers. There is no doubt that these terms, in their strictly ethical uses, tend to have very strong emotive impacts. It could scarcely be denied that to characterize an action as *right,* or a situation as *good,* is to express an attitude of approval toward it, whereas to characterize it as *wrong* or as *bad* is to express an attitude of disapproval. Some writers on ethics deny that these terms have any literal or cognitive meaning in addition to their emotive meaning. Other writers on ethics vigorously insist that they have cognitive meaning, and refer to objective properties of whatever is being discussed. In this quarrel the student of logic need not take sides. It must be insisted, however, that not every attitude of approval or disapproval implies a moral judgment. Beside moral values there are aesthetic values, and beyond these two important categories there are surely other types, personal preferences that reflect only matters of taste. A negative attitude, say toward a particular dress or dessert, need not involve either ethical or aesthetic judgment. Yet such attitudes exist and may be given verbal expression.

Where disagreement is in attitude rather than in belief, the most vigorous—and, of course, genuine—disagreement may be expressed in statements which are all of them literally true, at least as far as their informative content is concerned. An illuminating example of this is reported by Lincoln Steffens in his *Autobiography.* Shortly after the turn of the century, Steffens, in his capacity as a muckraker, went to Milwaukee to prepare an exposé of "that demagogue," Robert La Follette, then Governor of Wisconsin. Steffens called first on a banker, who said that La Follette was "a crooked hypocrite who stirred up the people with socialist-anarchist ideas and hurt business." Steffens asked the banker for evidence, and described what ensued as follows:

> . . . the banker set out to demonstrate . . . hypocrisy, socialism-anarchism, etc., and he was going fast and hot till I realized that my witness had more feeling than facts; or if he had facts, he could not handle them. He would start with some act of La Follette and blow up in a rage. He certainly hated the man, but I could not write rage.[7]

Steffens' conversation with the banker was interrupted by the arrival of an attorney, who was prepared to present the "evidence" against La Follette. Steffens' account proceeds:

> When I told him how far we had got, the banker and I, and how I wanted first the proofs of the dishonesty alleged, he said: "Oh, no, no. You are getting

[7] By permission from *The Autobiography of Lincoln Steffens.* Copyright, 1931, by Harcourt, Brace and Company, Inc.

> off wrong. La Follette isn't dishonest. On the contrary, the man is dangerous precisely because he is so sincere. He's a fanatic."

We may remark that the third possibility mentioned previously is perfectly exemplified in the present example. There was disagreement in belief between the banker and the lawyer on the question of La Follette's honesty. But this factual question was completely overshadowed by that of attitude. Here there was vigorous agreement. Both disapproved of La Follette and his actions: curiously enough, the banker because the Governor was "crooked," the lawyer because the Governor was "so sincere." Then the lawyer got down to cases. His motive here was to achieve agreement with Steffens. The report continues:

> The attorney, with the banker sitting by frowning, impatient, presented in good order the charges against La Follette, the measures he had furthered, the legislation passed and proposed, his political methods. Horrified himself at the items on his list and alarmed over the policy and the power of this demagogue, he delivered the indictment with emotion, force, eloquence. The only hitch was that Bob La Follette's measures seemed fair to me, his methods democratic, his purposes right but moderate, and his fighting strength and spirit hopeful and heroic.

What happened here was that the lawyer's statement of the facts, which presumably Steffens agreed with the lawyer in believing, was not sufficient to produce the kind of agreement in attitude which the lawyer desired. Steffens' attitude toward those facts was altogether different from the lawyer's. Adducing more evidence that the facts were as described—literally—would not have brought the two men a hair's breadth nearer to agreement—in attitude. The lawyer's "emotion, force, eloquence" were relevant, but not sufficient. What the lawyer regarded as newfangled innovations and radical departures from established order, Steffens tended to regard as progressive improvements and the elimination of antiquated prejudice. Both would agree on the fact that change was involved. But their evaluations were different. The reverse was the case with the lawyer and the banker. Their evaluations were the same, even though they disagreed on the factual question of whether La Follette was crooked or sincere.

The lesson we may draw from these considerations is simple but important. When two parties claim to disagree and express their divergent views in statements which are logically consistent with each other, both being perhaps literally true, it would be a mistake to say that the parties do not "really" disagree, or that their disagreement is "merely verbal." They are not merely "saying the same thing in different words." They may, of course, be using their words to affirm what is literally the same fact, but they may also be using their words to express conflicting attitudes toward that fact. In such a case, their disagreement, although not "literal," is nevertheless *genuine*. It is not "merely verbal," because words function expressively as well as informatively. And if we are interested in resolving disagreements, we must be clear about their nature, since the techniques appropriate to the resolution of one kind of disagreement may be hopelessly beside the point for another.

Knowledge of the different uses of language is an aid in discerning what kinds of disagreements may be involved and is thus an aid in resolving them. Drawing the indicated distinctions does not by itself solve the problem or resolve the disagreement, of course. But it clarifies the discussion and reveals the kind and locus of the disagreement. And if it is true that questions are more easily answered when they are better understood, then the study of the different uses of language is of considerable value.

EXERCISES

Identify the kinds of agreement or disagreement exhibited by the following pairs:

★ 1. a. Mrs. Blank is a fluent conversationalist.
b. Mrs. Blank talks incessantly.

2. a. Mr. Blank is an independent thinker.
b. Mr. Blank never agrees with anybody.

3. a. Mrs. Dash generously contributed five dollars.
b. Mrs. Dash gave only five dollars.

4. a. Mr. Dash came within 2 per cent of meeting his quota.
b. Mr. Dash failed to meet his quota.

★ 5. a. Mrs. Roe served a delightful little lunch.
b. Mrs. Roe served a magnificent banquet.

6. a. Mr. Roe talked too much at the meeting.
b. Mr. Roe maintained a stupid silence at the meeting.

7. a. Mrs. Doe served a positively skimpy meal.
b. Mrs. Doe really overdid it serving such vulgarly excessive portions at her dinner.

8. a. Communists sweep ahead in five-mile advance.
b. Reds stopped cold after five-mile push.

9. a. Little Mary often attempts to win by unorthodox methods.
 b. Little Mary cheats at games.

★ 10. a. Suzy has a marvelous imagination.
 b. Suzy has no respect for facts.

11. a. I know of no pursuit in which more real and important services can be rendered to any country than by improving its agriculture, its breed of useful animals, and other branches of a husbandman's cares.

—GEORGE WASHINGTON, *Letter to John Sinclair*

b. With the introduction of agriculture mankind entered upon a long period of meanness, misery, and madness, from which they are only now being freed by the beneficent operation of the machine.

—BERTRAND RUSSELL, *The Conquest of Happiness*

12. a. Whenever there is, in any country, uncultivated land and unemployed poor, it is clear that the laws of property have been so far extended as to violate natural right.

—THOMAS JEFFERSON

b. Every man has by nature the right to possess property of his own. This is one of the chief points of distinction between man and the lower animals.

—POPE LEO XIII, *Rerum novarum*

13. a. An honest man's the noblest work of God.

—ALEXANDER POPE, *An Essay on Man*

b. An honest God is the noblest work of man.

—ROBERT G. INGERSOLL, *The Gods, and Other Lectures*

14. a. The right of revolution is an inherent one. When people are oppressed by their government, it is a natural right they enjoy to relieve themselves of the oppression, if they are strong enough, either by withdrawal from it, or by overthrowing it and substituting a government more acceptable.

—ULYSSES S. GRANT, *Personal Memoirs,* I

b. Inciting to revolution is treason, not only against man, but against God.

—POPE LEO XIII, *Immortalie Dei*

★ 15. a. History is simply a piece of paper covered with print; the main thing is still to make history, not to write it.

—OTTO VON BISMARCK

b. Anybody can make history. Only a great man can write it.

—OSCAR WILDE, *The Critic as Artist*

16. a. How does it become a man to behave towards the American

government today? I answer, that he cannot without disgrace be associated with it.

—HENRY DAVID THOREAU, *An Essay on Civil Disobedience*

b. With all the imperfections of our present government, it is without comparison the best existing, or that ever did exist.

—THOMAS JEFFERSON

17. a. Farming is a senseless pursuit, a mere laboring in a circle. You sow that you may reap, and then you reap that you may sow. Nothing ever comes of it.

—JOANNES STOBAEUS, *Florilegium*

b. No occupation is so delightful to me as the culture of the earth.

—THOMAS JEFFERSON

18. a. Our country: in her intercourse with foreign nations may she always be in the right; but our country, right or wrong!

—STEPHEN DECATUR, Toast at a dinner in Norfolk, Virginia, April 1816

b. Our country, right or wrong. When right, to be kept right; when wrong, to be put right.[8]

—CARL SCHURZ, Speech in the Senate, January 1872

19. a. A bad peace is even worse than war.

—TACITUS, *Annals*

b. The most disadvantageous peace is better than the most just war.

—DESIDERIUS ERASMUS, *Adagia*

20. a. It makes but little difference whether you are committed to a farm or a county jail.

—HENRY DAVID THOREAU, *Walden*

b. I know few things more pleasing to the eye, or more capable of affording scope and gratification to a taste for the beautiful, than a well-situated, well-cultivated farm.

—EDWARD EVERETT

2.6 Emotively Neutral Language

In the preceding discussion it has been insisted that the expressive use of language is just as legitimate as the informative. There is nothing wrong with emotive language; and there is nothing wrong with language that is nonemotive, or neutral. Similarly, we can say that there is nothing wrong with pillows and nothing wrong with

[8] On this kind of disagreement G. K. Chesterton commented in *The Defendant* that, "'My country, right or wrong' is like saying, 'My mother, drunk or sober'."

hammers. True enough, but it does not mean that we should be successful in attempting to drive nails with pillows or comfortable in trying to sleep with our heads resting on hammers. A great deal of value was lost in Thouless' translation of Keats' lines into neutral language—although the literal meaning was preserved. Here is a case in which emotively colored language is preferable to neutral language. Are there any circumstances in which neutral language is preferable to emotively colored language?

Clearly, when we are trying to "get at the facts," to follow an argument, or to learn the truth about something, anything which distracts us from that goal tends to frustrate us. It is a commonplace that the passions tend to cloud the reason, and this view is reflected in the usage of "dispassionate" and "objective" as near synonyms. It follows that when we are attempting to reason about facts in a cool and objective fashion, referring to them in strongly emotive language is a hindrance rather than a help.

Thus William James, in his essay "The Dilemma of Determinism," explained his "wish to get rid of the word 'freedom' " on the grounds that "its eulogistic associations have . . . overshadowed all the rest of its meaning." He rightly preferred to discuss the issue using the words "determinism" and "indeterminism," because "their cold and mathematical sound has no sentimental associations that can bribe our partiality either way in advance." We should do well to follow James' example.

If we are interested in calculating, for example, what economic consequences in terms of productivity and efficiency would follow from various degrees of government economic control, we shall find our task made more difficult if we insist upon referring to the phenomena in question by words as emotionally charged as "freedom" and "bureaucatic interference" on the one hand and "license" and "irresponsibility" on the other.

The use of such stereotypes is properly frowned upon, not merely because of their lack of literary value, but because of the way in which the hackneyed emotional reactions stirred by them get in the way of any objective appraisal of the facts they refer to. This danger is familiar to those who have studied public opinion polls, like Gallup's or Roper's. In seeking to discover people's views, interviewers must be careful not to prejudice the issue by phrasing their questions in such a way as to influence the answers. An interesting report on this problem is given by Stuart Chase in his book *The Proper Study of Mankind:*

> In 1946 Roper ran an interesting semantic test. He matched two groups of people so they were practically identical samples. He proved it by asking

various questions and getting percentage results which were very close. He then asked each group a similar series of questions except that for one group a new and ugly word was introduced, the word "propaganda."

The general topic was the usefulness of foreign broadcasts by the State Department. Group A was asked to select from three alternative positions, one of which read: "Some people say it is better to explain our point of view as well as give the news." The answer came back "yes," 42.8 percent. Group B got the following wording, *and observe it is precisely the same question:* "Some people say it is better to include some propaganda as well as give the news." The "yes" reaction was almost cut in half, to 24.7 percent! It would be hard to find a better example of what an emotion-stirring word will do to people's opinions![9]

It may be doubted whether it is "precisely the same question" which was asked the two groups. As often used today, at least part of the literal meaning of the word "propaganda" concerns the use of nonrational methods to cause acceptance of a point of view. To propagandize is surely a different thing from simply explaining our point of view. Not all emotive differences between closely related words are independent of their descriptive meanings; some are directly derived from them. The differences in our attitudes toward *education* and *indoctrination,* for example, are based on real differences between the two activities, as well as on whatever emotive differences may attach to the two words.

The point, however, is this. If our purpose is to communicate information, and if we wish to avoid being misunderstood, we shall find that language most useful which has the least emotive impact. If our interest is scientific, we shall do well to avoid emotional language and to cultivate as emotively neutral a set of terms as we can. This has been done most extensively in the physical sciences. Older and more emotively exciting terms—such as "noble" and "base" characterizing metals—have either been displaced by a special jargon or have come through the passage of time to be completely divorced from their former honorific or derogatory associations. This has been a contributing factor to scientific progress.

Thus if we are concerned to investigate the literal truth or falsity of a view and to discover its logical implications, our task will be facilitated if we translate any highly emotive formulation concerning it into as nearly neutral a description as possible. Suppose, for example, we are interested in the question of national compulsory health insurance. In the course of our investigations we shall come across certain highly emotive phraseology, as in the text of the statement by Dr. Elmer L. Henderson, Chairman of the Board of Trustees

[9] By permission from *The Proper Study of Mankind* by Stuart Chase. Copyright, 1948, by Stuart Chase. Published by Harper and Brothers.

of the American Medical Association, on President Truman's proposed national compulsory health insurance program. Dr. Henderson stated that:

> There is a great deal of double talk in the President's message, but what he actually proposes is a national compulsory health insurance system which would regiment doctors and patients alike under a vast bureaucracy of political administrators, clerks, bookkeepers and lay committees.[10]

Now, can this passage be translated into more nearly neutral language without doing violence to the informative content? No more information is presented by Dr. Henderson in the passage cited than in the following:

> There is some ambiguity in the President's message, but its intended meaning is the proposal to set up a national compulsory health insurance system in which contact between doctors and patients would be regulated by an administrative agency of large size, which would employ government officials, clerks and bookkeepers, and committees not composed exclusively of M.D.'s.

These are the facts as Dr. Henderson sees them, and his information may well be correct. But when it is formulated with such a liberal sprinkling of emotively explosive words, like "double talk," "regimentation," "vast bureaucracy," "*political* administrators," and when there is the hint that "doctors and patients alike" would be *under* clerks and bookkeepers (as though no doctor ever employed a clerk or bookkeeper to keep his own records straight), then it requires a disproportionate amount of effort to cut through to the actual information presented.

Emotive language is not in itself bad, but when it is information we are after, we shall do well to choose words whose emotive meanings do not distract and hinder us from dealing successfully with what they describe. As students of logic, we are not only concerned to work out a more adequate terminology to use in connection with argument, but also interested in critically examining the results of ignoring the preceding directive. The careless use of language in argument often results in fallacies, which will occupy our attention in the following chapter.

EXERCISE

Select a brief passage of highly emotive writing from some current periodical and translate it in such a way as to retain its informative content while reducing its expressive significance to a minimum.

[10] By permission from *The Journal of the American Medical Association,* Vol. 140, No. 1, May 7, 1949. Page 114.

Chapter 3
Informal Fallacies

. . . arguments, like men, are often pretenders.

—Plato

3.1 Classification of Fallacies

Although most textbooks of logic contain discussions of fallacies, their treatments are not all the same. There is no universally accepted classification of fallacies. This situation is not surprising: as the early modern logician De Morgan aptly said, "There *is* no such thing as a classification of the ways in which men may arrive at an error: it is much to be doubted whether there ever *can be*."

The word "fallacy" is used in various ways. One perfectly proper use of the word is to designate any mistaken idea or false belief, like the "fallacy" of believing that all men are honest. But logicians use the term in the narrower sense of an error in reasoning or in argument. A fallacy, as we shall use the term, is a type of incorrect argument. Since it is a type of incorrect argument, we can say of two different arguments that they contain or commit the same fallacy. Some arguments, of course, are so obviously incorrect as to deceive no one. It is customary in the study of logic to reserve the term "fallacy" for arguments which may be psychologically persuasive, although incorrect. We therefore define a fallacy as a type of argument that may seem to be correct but which proves, upon examination, not to be so. It is profitable to study such arguments, for familiarity and understanding will help keep us from being misled by them. To be forewarned is to be forearmed.

In spite of De Morgan's warning not to take the classification of fallacies too seriously, we shall nevertheless find it helpful to group them in the following way. First, fallacies are divided into two broad groups, formal and informal. Formal fallacies are most conveniently discussed in connection with certain patterns of valid inference to which they bear a superficial resemblance. We shall accordingly defer consideration of them to subsequent chapters. For the present, we shall be concerned with informal fallacies, errors in reasoning into which we may fall either because of carelessness and inattention to our subject matter or through being misled by some ambiguity in the language used to formulate our argument. We may divide informal fallacies into fallacies of *relevance* and fallacies of *ambiguity*. No attempt will be made at completeness; only eighteen informal fallacies will be considered, the most common and deceptive ones.

Only thirteen types of fallacies were listed by the first logician, Aristotle, in his book *Sophistical Refutations* (Vol. I of *The Works of Aristotle,* ed. W. D. Ross. Oxford University Press, 1928). Fifty-one fallacies are "named, explained, and illustrated" by W. Ward Fearnside and William B. Holther in their recent book *Fallacy: The Counterfeit of Argument* (Englewood Cliffs, N.J.: Prentice-Hall, 1959). To the best of my knowledge the most comprehensive—or at least voluminous—list of fallacies is given by David Hackett Fischer in his book *Historian's Fallacies* (New York: Harper & Row, 1970). The Index of Fallacies in Fischer's book contains 112 fallacies, but in the body of his book he discusses and names more than are listed in his index. A historical, critical, and theoretical treatment of the topic is given by C. L. Hamblin in his book *Fallacies* (London: Methuen, 1970). All of these books can be warmly recommended to readers who wish to go more deeply into the subject of fallacies.

3.2 Fallacies of Relevance

The first group of fallacies we shall consider consists of the fallacies of relevance. Common to all arguments which commit fallacies of relevance[1] is the circumstance that their premisses are logically irrelevant to, and therefore incapable of establishing the truth of, their conclusions. The irrelevance here is logical rather than psychological, of course, for unless there were some psychological

[1] Except for the fallacy of Petitio Principii, or begging the question, which is discussed on page 83.

connection, there would be no persuasiveness or seeming correctness. How psychological relevance can be confused with logical relevance is explained in some cases by reference to the fact that language can be used expressively as well as informatively, to stimulate such emotions as fear, hostility, pity, enthusiasm, or awe.

A number of particular types of irrelevant argument have traditionally been given Latin names. Some of these Latin names have become part of the English language, "ad hominem," for example. Others are less familiar. We shall consider only a few of them here. How they succeed in being persuasive despite their logical incorrectness is in some cases to be explained by their expressive function of evoking attitudes likely to cause the acceptance of, rather than supplying grounds for the truth of, the conclusions they urge.

1. ***Argumentum ad Baculum* (*appeal to force*).** The *argumentum ad baculum* is the fallacy committed when one appeals to force or the threat of force to cause acceptance of a conclusion. It is usually resorted to only when evidence or rational arguments fail. The *ad baculum* is epitomized in the saying "might makes right." The use and threat of "strong-arm" methods to coerce political opponents provide contemporary examples of this fallacy. Appeal to nonrational methods of intimidation may of course be more subtle than the open use or threat of concentration camps or "goon squads."

The lobbyist uses the *ad baculum* when he reminds a representative that he (the lobbyist) represents so many thousands of voters in the representative's constituency, or so many potential contributors to campaign funds. Logically these considerations have nothing to do with the merits of the legislation the lobbyist is attempting to influence. But they may be, unfortunately, very persuasive.

On the international scale, the *argumentum ad baculum* means war or the threat of war. An amusing, though at the same time frightening, example of *ad baculum* reasoning at the international level is told in Harry Hopkins' account of the "Big Three" meeting at Yalta toward the end of World War II. Churchill is reported to have told the others that the Pope had suggested that such and such a course of action would be right. And Stalin is supposed to have indicated his disagreement by asking, "And how many divisions did you say the Pope had available for combat duty?"

2. ***Argumentum ad Hominem* (*abusive*).** The phrase *argumentum ad hominem* translates literally as "argument directed to the man." It is susceptible to two interpretations, whose interrelationship will be explained after the two are discussed separately. We may designate this fallacy on the first interpretation as the "abusive" variety. It is committed when, instead of trying to disprove the truth of what is asserted, one attacks the man who made the assertion. Thus

it may be argued that Bacon's philosophy is untrustworthy because he was removed from his chancellorship for dishonesty. This argument is fallacious, because the personal character of a man is logically irrelevant to the truth or falsehood of what he says or the correctness or incorrectness of his argument. To argue that proposals are bad or assertions false because they are proposed or asserted by Communists (or by Hippies or by doves or by hawks or by extremists) is to argue fallaciously and to be guilty of committing an *argumentum ad hominem* (abusive). This kind of argument is sometimes said to commit the "Genetic Fallacy," for obvious reasons.

The way in which this irrelevant argument may sometimes persuade is through the psychological process of transference. Where an attitude of disapproval toward a person can be evoked, it may possibly tend to overflow the strictly emotional field and become disagreement with what that person says. But this connection is only psychological, not logical. Even the most wicked of men may sometimes tell the truth or argue correctly.

The classic example of this fallacy has to do with British law procedure. There the practice of law is divided between solicitors, who prepare the cases for trial, and barristers, who argue or "plead" the cases in court. Ordinarily their cooperation is admirable, but sometimes it leaves much to be desired. On one such latter occasion, the barrister ignored the case completely until the day it was to be presented at court, depending upon the solicitor to investigate the defendant's case and prepare the brief. He arrived at court just a moment before the trial was to begin and was handed his brief by the solicitor. Surprised at its thinness, he glanced inside to find written: "No case; abuse the plaintiff's attorney!"

3. *Argumentum ad Hominem* (*circumstantial*). The other interpretation of the fallacy of *argumentum ad hominem,* the "circumstantial" variety, pertains to the relationship between a person's beliefs and his circumstances. Where two men are disputing, one may ignore the question of whether his own contention is true or false and seek instead to prove that his opponent ought to accept it because of his opponent's special circumstances. Thus if one's adversary is a clergyman, one may argue that a certain contention must be accepted because its denial is incompatible with the Scriptures. This is not to prove it true, but to urge its acceptance by that particular individual because of his special circumstances, in this case his religious affiliation. Or if one's opponent is, say, a Republican, one may argue not that a certain proposition is true, but that he ought to assent to it because it is implied by the tenets of his party. The classical example of this fallacy is the reply of the hunter when accused of barbarism in sacrificing unoffending animals to his own amusement. His reply is to ask his critic, "Why do you feed on the flesh of harmless cattle?" The sportsman here is guilty of an *argumentum ad hominem* because he does not try to prove that it is right to sacrifice animal life for human pleasure, but merely that it cannot consistently be decried by his critic because of the critic's own special circumstances, in this case his not being a vegetarian. Arguments such as these are not really to the point; they do not present good grounds for the truth of their conclusions but are intended only to win assent to the conclusion from one's opponent because of his special circumstances. This they frequently do; they are often very persuasive.

In the preceding paragraph we described the use of the circumstantial *ad hominem* to get one's adversary to accept a conclusion. It is also used as the basis for rejecting a conclusion defended by one's adversary, as when it is argued that the conclusions arrived at by one's opponent are dictated by his special circumstances rather than based upon reason or evidence. Thus if a manufacturer's arguments in favor of tariff protection are rejected on the grounds that a manufacturer would naturally be expected to favor a protective tariff, his critic would be committing the fallacy of *argumentum ad hominem* (circumstantial). This type of argument, though often persuasive, is clearly fallacious.

The connection between the abusive and the circumstantial varieties of *argumentum ad hominem* is not difficult to see. The circumstantial variety may even be regarded as a special case of the abusive. The first use of the circumstantial *ad hominem* charges the man who disputes your conclusion with inconsistency, either among his beliefs or between his preaching and his practice, which may be regarded as a kind of reproach or abuse. The second use of the circumstantial *ad hominem* charges the adversary with being so prejudiced that his alleged reasons are mere rationalizations of conclusions dictated by self-interest. And that is certainly to abuse him. This particular kind of *ad hominem* is sometimes called "poisoning the well," for obvious reasons.

4. *Argumentum ad Ignorantiam* (*argument from ignorance*). —The fallacy of *argumentum ad ignorantiam* is illustrated by the argument that there must be ghosts because no one has ever been able to prove that there aren't any. The *argumentum ad ignorantiam* is committed whenever it is argued that a proposition is true simply on the basis that it has not been proved false, or that it is false because it has not been proved true. But our ignorance of how to prove or disprove a proposition clearly does not establish either the truth or the falsehood of that proposition. This fallacy often arises in connection with such matters as psychic phenomena, telepathy, and the like, where there is no clear-cut evidence either for or against. It is curious how many of the most enlightened people are prone to this fallacy, as witness the many students of science who affirm the falsehood of spiritualist and telepathic claims simply on the grounds that their truth has not been established.

Although this mode of argument is fallacious in most contexts, it should be pointed out that there is one special context in which it is not fallacious—namely, in a court of law; for in a court of law the guiding principle is that a person is presumed innocent until proved guilty. The defense can legitimately claim that if the prosecution has not proved guilt, this warrants a verdict of not guilty. Since this claim is based upon the special legal principle mentioned, however, it is quite consistent with the fact that the *argumentum ad ignorantiam* is a fallacy in all other contexts.

It is sometimes maintained that the *argumentum ad hominem* (abusive) is not fallacious when used in a court of law in an attempt to impeach the testimony of a witness. True enough, doubt can be cast upon a witness' testimony if it can be shown that he is a chronic liar and perjurer. Where that can be shown, it certainly reduces the credibility of the testimony offered. But if one goes on to infer that the witness' testimony establishes the falsehood of that to which he testifies, instead of concluding merely that his testimony does not establish its truth, then the reasoning is fallacious, being an *argumentum ad ignorantiam*. Such errors are more common than one might think.

A qualification should be made at this point. In some circumstances it can safely be assumed that if a certain event had occurred, evidence of it could be discovered by qualified investigators. In such circumstances it is perfectly reasonable to take the absence of proof of its occurrence as positive proof of its nonoccurrence. Of course, the proof here is not based on ignorance but on our knowledge that if it had occurred it would be known. For example, if a serious F.B.I. investigation fails to unearth any evidence that Mr. X is a communist, it would be wrong to conclude that their research has left them ignorant. It has rather established that Mr. X is not one. Failure to draw such conclusions is the other side of the bad coin of innuendo, as when one says of a man that there is "no proof" that he is a scoundrel. In some cases not to draw a conclusion is as much a breach of correct reasoning as it would be to draw a mistaken conclusion.

5. *Argumentum ad Misericordiam* (*appeal to pity*). The *argumentum ad misericordiam* is the fallacy committed when pity is appealed to for the sake of getting a conclusion accepted. This argument is frequently encountered in courts of law, when a defense attorney may disregard the facts of the case and seek to win his client's acquittal by arousing pity in the jurymen. Clarence Darrow, the celebrated trial lawyer, was a master at using this device. In defending Thomas I. Kidd, an officer of the Amalgamated Woodworkers Union, who was indicted on a charge of criminal conspiracy, Darrow spoke these words to the jury:

> I appeal to you not for Thomas Kidd, but I appeal to you for the long line—the long, long line reaching back through the ages and forward to the years to come—the long line of despoiled and downtrodden people of the earth. I appeal to you for those men who rise in the morning before daylight comes and who go home at night when the light has faded from the sky and give their life, their strength, their toil to make others rich and great. I appeal to you in the name of those women who are offering up their lives to this modern god of gold, and I appeal to you in the name of those little children, the living and the unborn.[2]

Is Thomas Kidd guilty as charged? Darrow's appeal was sufficiently moving to make the average juror want to throw questions of evidence and of law out the window. Yet, however persuasive such a plea might be, from the point of view of logic that argument is fallacious which draws from "premisses" such as these the conclusion that the accused is innocent.

The issue of what counts as relevant in matters of this kind, however, is not always quite so clear as one might wish. Thus Professor C. L. Hamblin, for example, in his book on *Fallacies,* after referring to these words of Darrow, cautions that:

> . . . more depends on a lawsuit, or a political speech, than assent to a proposition. A proposition is presented primarily as a guide to action and, where action is concerned, it is not so clear that pity and other emotions are irrelevant.

An older and considerably more subtle example of the *argumentum ad misericordiam* is reported by Plato in the *Apology,* which purports to be a record of Socrates' defense of himself during his trial.

> Perhaps there may be some one who is offended at me, when he calls to mind how he himself on a similar, or even a less serious occasion, prayed and entreated the judges with many tears, and how he produced his children in court, which was a moving spectacle, together with a host of relations and friends; whereas I, who am probably in danger of my life, will do none of these things. The contrast may occur to his mind, and he may be set against me, and vote in anger because he is displeased at me on this account. Now

[2] As quoted in *Clarence Darrow for the Defense* by Irving Stone. Copyright, 1941, by Irving Stone. Published by Garden City Publishing Company, Inc., Garden City, N.Y.

if there be such a person among you—mind, I do not say that there is—to him I may fairly reply: My friend, I am a man, and like other men, a creature of flesh and blood, and not "of wood or stone," as Homer says; and I have a family, yes, and sons, O Athenians, three in number, one almost a man, and two others who are still young; and yet I will not bring any of them hither in order to petition you for acquittal.

The *argumentum ad misericordiam* is sometimes used with ludicrous effect, as in the case of the youth who was tried for a particularly brutal crime, the murder of his mother and father with an axe. Confronted with overwhelming proof of his guilt, he pleaded for leniency on the grounds that he was an orphan.

6. *Argumentum ad Populum.* The *argumentum ad populum* is sometimes defined as the fallacy committed in directing an emotional appeal "to the people" or "to the gallery" to win their assent to a conclusion unsupported by good evidence. But this definition is so broad as to include the *ad misericordiam,* the *ad hominem* (abusive), and most of the other fallacies of relevance. We may define the *argumentum ad populum* fallacy a little more narrowly as the attempt to win popular assent to a conclusion by arousing the feelings and enthusiasms of the multitude. This is a favorite device with the propagandist, the demagogue, and the advertiser. Faced with the task of mobilizing public sentiment for or against a particular measure, the propagandist will avoid the laborious process of collecting and presenting evidence and rational argument by using the short-cut methods of the *argumentum ad populum.* Where the proposal is for a change and he is against it, he will express suspicion of "newfangled innovations" and praise the wisdom of the "existing order." If he is for it, he will be for "progress" and opposed to "antiquated prejudice." Here we have the use of invidious terms with no rational attempt made to argue for them or to justify their application. This technique may be supplemented by displaying the flag, brass bands, and whatever else might serve to stimulate and excite the public. The demagogue's use of the *argumentum ad populum* is beautifully illustrated by Shakespeare's version of Marc Antony's funeral oration over the body of Julius Caesar.

It is to the huckster, the ballyhoo artist, the twentieth-century advertiser that we may look to see the *argumentum ad populum* elevated almost to the status of a fine art. Here every attempt is made to set up associations between the product being advertised and objects of which we can be expected to approve strongly. To eat a certain brand of processed cereal is proclaimed a patriotic duty. To bathe with a certain brand of soap is described as a thrilling experience. Strains of symphonic music precede and follow the mention of a certain dentifrice on the radio and television programs sponsored by its manufacturer. In pictorial advertisements, the people using the products advertised are always pictured as wearing the kind of clothing and living in the kind of houses calculated to arouse the approval and admiration of the average consumer. The young men pictured as delightedly using the products are clear-eyed and broad-shouldered, the older men are invariably "of distinction." The women are all slim and lovely, either very well dressed or hardly dressed at all. Whether you are interested in economical transportation or in high-speed driving, you will be assured by each automobile manufacturer that his product is "best," and he will "prove" his assertion by displaying his car surrounded by pretty girls. Advertisers "glamorize" their products and sell us daydreams and delusions of grandeur with every package of pink pills or garbage disposal unit.

Here, if they are trying to prove that their products adequately serve their ostensible functions, their procedures are glorified examples of the *argumentum ad populum*. Besides the "snob appeal" already referred to, we may include under this heading the familiar "band-wagon argument." The campaigning politician "argues" that he should receive our votes because "everybody" is voting that way. We are told that such and such a breakfast food, or cigarette, or motor car is "best" because it is America's largest seller. A certain belief "must be true" because "everyone knows it." But popular acceptance of a policy does not prove it to be wise; widespread use of certain products does not prove them to be satisfactory; general assent to a claim does not prove it to be true. To argue in this way is to commit the *ad populum* fallacy.

7. *Argumentum ad Verecundiam* (*appeal to authority*). The *argumentum ad verecundiam* is the appeal to authority—that is, to the feeling of respect people have for the famous—to win assent to a conclusion. This method of argument is not always strictly fallacious, for the reference to an admitted authority in the special field of his competence may carry great weight and constitute relevant evidence. If laymen are disputing over some question of physical science and one appeals to the testimony of Einstein on the matter, that testimony is very relevant. Although it does not prove the point, it certainly tends to support it. This is a relative matter, however, for if experts rather than laymen are disputing over a question in the field in which they themselves are experts, their appeal would be only to the facts and to reason, and any appeal to the authority of another expert would be completely without value as evidence.

But when an authority is appealed to for testimony in matters outside the province of his special field, the appeal commits the fallacy of *argumentum ad verecundiam*. If in an argument over religion one of the disputants appeals to the opinions of Darwin, a great authority in biology, the appeal is fallacious. Similarly, an appeal to the opinions of a great physicist like Einstein to settle a political or economic argument would be fallacious. The claim might be made that a person brilliant enough to achieve the status of an authority in an advanced and difficult field like biology or physics must have correct opinions in fields other than his specialty. But the weakness of this claim is obvious when we realize that in this day of extreme specialization, to obtain thorough knowledge of one field requires such concentration as to restrict the possibility of achieving authoritative knowledge in others.

Advertising "testimonials" are frequent instances of this fallacy. We are urged to smoke this or that brand of cigarette because a champion swimmer or football star affirms their superiority. And we are assured that such and such a cosmetic is better because it is preferred by this opera singer or that movie star. Of course, such an advertisement may equally well be construed as snob appeal and listed as an example of an *argumentum ad populum.* But where a proposition is claimed to be literally true on the basis of its assertion by an "authority" whose competence lies in a different field, we have a fallacy of *argumentum ad verecundiam.*

8. *Accident.* The fallacy of accident consists in applying a general rule to a particular case whose "accidental" circumstances render the rule inapplicable. In Plato's *Republic,* for example, an exception is found to the general rule that one should pay one's debts: "Suppose that a friend when in his right mind has deposited weapons with me and he ask for them when he is not in his right mind, ought I to give them back to him? No one would say that I ought or that I should be right in doing so. . . ." What is true "in general" may not be true universally and without qualification, because circumstances alter cases. Many generalizations known or suspected to have exceptions are stated without qualification, either because the exact conditions restricting their applicability are not known or because the accidental circumstances that render them inapplicable occur so seldom as to be practically negligible. When such a generalization is appealed to in arguing about a particular case whose accidental circumstances prevent the general proposition from applying, the argument is said to commit the fallacy of accident.

Some examples of this fallacy are scarcely better than jokes: for example: "What you bought yesterday, you eat today; you bought raw meat yesterday; therefore, you eat raw meat today." In this argument the premiss "What you bought yesterday, you eat today" applies generally only to the substance of what is bought, rather than to its condition. It is not intended to cover every accidental circumstance, such as the raw condition of the meat. Of this example De Morgan wrote: "This piece of meat has remained uncooked, as fresh as ever, a prodigious time. It was raw when Reisch mentioned it in the *Margarita Philosophica* in 1496: and Dr. Whately found it in just the same state in 1826."[3]

In its more serious forms, however, the fallacy of *accident* is often fallen into by moralists and legalists who try to decide specific and complicated issues by appealing mechanically to general rules. As H. W. B. Joseph remarked, ". . . there is no fallacy more insidious than that of treating a statement which in many connections is not misleading as if it were true always and without qualification."[4]

9. *Converse Accident* (*hasty generalization*). In seeking to understand and characterize all cases of a certain kind, one can usually pay attention to only some of them. But those examined should be typical rather than atypical. If one considers only exceptional cases and hastily generalizes to a rule that fits them alone, the fallacy committed is that of converse accident. For example, observing the value of opiates when administered by a physician to alleviate the pains of those who are seriously ill, one may be led to propose that narcotics be made available to everyone. Or considering the effect of alcohol only on those who indulge in it to excess, one may conclude that all liquor is harmful and urge that its sale and use should be forbidden by law. Such reasoning is erroneous and illustrates the fallacy of converse accident or hasty generalization.

10. *False Cause*. The fallacy of *false cause* has been variously analyzed in the past and given alternative Latin names, such as *non causa pro causa* and *post hoc ergo propter hoc*. The first of these is more general and means to mistake what is not the cause of a given effect for its real cause. The second is the inference that one event is the cause of another from the mere fact that the first occurs earlier than the second. We shall regard any argument of either sort as an instance of the fallacy of false cause.

What actually constitutes a good argument for the presence of causal connections is perhaps the central problem of inductive logic or scientific method and will be discussed in later chapters. (The meaning of "cause" is examined in Section 12.1 of Chapter 12.) It is easy to see, however, that the mere fact of coincidence or temporal succession does not establish any causal connection. Certainly we should reject the savage's claim that beating his drums is

[3] *Formal Logic* by Augustus De Morgan, The Open Court Company, 1926. It appeared even earlier in the twelfth-century *Munich Dialectica*. See *Logica Modernorum; a Contribution to the History of Early Terminist Logic* by Lambertus Marie De Rÿk, Assen, Van Gorcum, 1962–1967. Cited by C. L. Hamblin.

[4] *An Introduction to Logic* by H. W. B. Joseph, Oxford University Press, 1906.

the cause of the sun's reappearance after an eclipse, even though he can offer as evidence the fact that every time drums have been beaten during an eclipse, the sun has reappeared! No one would be misled by this argument, but countless people are "suckers" for patent-medicine testimonials which report that Mrs. X suffered from a head cold, drank three bottles of a "secret" herb decoction, and recovered in only two weeks.

11. ***Petitio Principii* (*begging the question*).** In attempting to establish the truth of a proposition, one often casts about for acceptable premisses from which the proposition in question can be deduced as conclusion. If one assumes as a premiss for his argument the very conclusion he intends to prove, the fallacy committed is that of *petitio principii,* or begging the question. If the proposition to be established is formulated in exactly the same words both as premiss and as conclusion, the mistake would be so glaring as to deceive no one. Often, however, two formulations can be sufficiently different to obscure the fact that one and the same proposition occurs both as premiss and conclusion. This situation is illustrated by the following argument reported by Whately: "To allow every man unbounded freedom of speech must always be, on the whole, advantageous to the state; for it is highly conducive to the interests of the community that each individual should enjoy a liberty, perfectly unlimited, of expressing his sentiments."[5]

It should be noted that the premiss is not logically irrelevant to the truth of the conclusion, for if the premiss is true the conclusion must be true also—since it is the same proposition. But the premiss is logically irrelevant to the purpose of *proving* or *establishing* the conclusion. If the proposition is acceptable without argument, no argument is needed to establish it; and if the proposition is not acceptable without argument, then no argument which requires its acceptance as a premiss could possibly lead one to accept its conclusion. In any such argument the conclusion asserts only what was asserted in the premisses, and hence the argument, though perfectly valid, is utterly incapable of establishing the truth of its conclusion.

Sometimes a chain of several arguments is used in attempting to establish a conclusion. Thus one may argue that Shakespeare is a greater writer than Robbins because people with good taste in literature prefer Shakespeare. And if asked how one tells who has good taste in literature, one might reply that such persons are to be identified by their preferring Shakespeare to Robbins. Such a circular argument clearly begs the question and commits the fallacy of *petitio principii.*

[5] *Elements of Logic* by Richard Whately. London, 1826.

12. ***Complex Question.*** It is obvious that there is something "funny" about questions like "Have you given up your evil ways?" or "Have you stopped beating your wife?" These are not simple questions to which a straightforward "yes" or "no" answer is appropriate. Such questions presuppose that a definite answer has already been given to a prior question that was not even asked. Thus the first assumes that the answer "yes" has been given to the unasked question "Have you in the past followed evil ways?" and the second assumes an affirmative answer to the unasked question "Have you ever beaten your wife?" In either case, if a simple "yes" or "no" answer to the trick question is given, it has the effect of ratifying or affirming the implied answer to the unasked question. A question of this sort does not properly admit of a simple "yes" or "no" answer because it is not a simple or single question but a complex question which consists of several questions rolled into one.

Complex questions are not confined to obvious jokes like those in the first two examples. In cross-examination a lawyer may ask complex questions of a witness to confuse or even to incriminate him. He may ask, "Where did you hide the evidence?" "What did you do with the money you stole?" or the like. In propaganda, where a flat statement might be extremely difficult to prove or get accepted, the idea may be "put across" very persuasively by means of a complex question. A spokesman for utilities interests may propound the question: "Why is private development of resources so much more efficient than any public control?" A jingo may demand of his audience: "How long are we going to tolerate foreign interference with our national interests?"

In all such cases the intelligent procedure is to treat the complex question not as a simple one, but to analyze it into its component parts. It may well be the case that when the implicit or implied prior question is correctly answered, the second or explicit one simply dissolves. If I did not hide any evidence, the question of where I hid it does not make sense.

There are other kinds of complex questions. A mother may ask her youngster if he wants to be a good boy and go to bed. Here the matter is less deceptive. There are clearly two questions involved; one does not presuppose a particular answer to the other. What is wrong here is the suggestion that one and the same answer must be given to both of the questions. Are you "for" the Republicans and prosperity, or not? Answer "yes" or "no"! But here is a complex question, and it is at least conceivable that the two questions have different answers.

In parliamentary procedure the motion "to divide the question" is a privileged motion. This rule acknowledges that questions may be complex and can therefore be considered more intelligently when separated. Our practice with respect to the President's veto power is less enlightened. The President can veto a measure as a whole, but he cannot veto the part he disapproves and sign the remainder. The President cannot divide the question but must veto or approve, answer "yes" or "no," to any question no matter how complex. This restriction has led, as is well known, to the congressional practice of attaching, as "riders" to measures that the President is generally known to approve, certain additional—often completely irrelevant—clauses which he is known to oppose. When presented with such a bill, the President must either approve something he disapproves or veto something he approves.

Still another kind of complex question involves question-begging epithets, as when one asks, "Is so and so a screwball radical?" or "an unthinking conservative?" or, "Is this policy going to lead to ruinous deflation?" Here, as elsewhere, one must divide the complex question. The answers might be, "a radical, yes, but not a screwball," "a conservative, yes, but not unthinking," or, "It will lead to deflation, yes; however, that will not be ruinous but a healthy readjustment."

Thus far we have discussed complex questions in general, but have not yet specifically identified the **fallacy** of *complex question.* In its wholly explicit form the fallacy of complex question occurs in dialogue: one speaker poses a complex question, the second speaker unwarily responds with "yes" or with "no," and the first speaker then draws a fallacious inference that may seem appropriate. For example:

INVESTIGATOR: Did your sales increase as a result of your misleading advertising?
WITNESS: No.
INVESTIGATOR: Aha! So you admit that your advertising was misleading. Do you know that your unethical conduct can get you into trouble?

Less explicitly, the fallacy of complex question may involve just one speaker, who poses the complex question, answers it himself, and then goes on to draw the fallacious inference. Or still less explicitly, the speaker may simply pose the question and draw the inference, with the answer not stated at all, but merely suggested or presupposed.

13. ***Ignoratio Elenchi* (*irrelevant conclusion*).** The fallacy of *ignoratio elenchi* is committed when an argument purporting to establish a particular conclusion is directed to proving a different conclusion. For example, when a particular proposal for housing legislation is under consideration, a legislator may rise to speak in

favor of the bill and argue only that decent housing for all the people is desirable. His remarks are then logically irrelevant to the point at issue, for the question concerns the particular measure at hand. Presumably everyone agrees that decent housing for all the people is desirable (even those will pretend to agree who do not really think so). The question is: will this particular measure provide it, and if so, will it provide it better than any practical alternative? The speaker's argument is fallacious, for it commits the fallacy of *ignoratio elenchi,* or irrelevant conclusion.

In a law court, in attempting to prove that the accused is guilty of murder, the prosecution may argue at length that murder is a horrible crime. He may even succeed in proving that conclusion. But when he infers from his remarks about the horribleness of murder that the defendant is guilty of it, he is committing the fallacy of *ignoratio elenchi.*

The question naturally arises, how do such arguments ever fool anybody? Once it is seen that the conclusion is logically irrelevant, why should the argument mislead anyone? In the first place, it is not always obvious that a given argument is an instance of *ignoratio elenchi.* During the course of an extended discussion, fatigue may lead to inattention and errors, and irrelevancies may tend to pass unnoticed. That is only part of the answer, of course. The other part has to do with the fact that language may serve to evoke emotion as well as to communicate information.

Consider the first example of *ignoratio elenchi.* By urging that decent housing for all the people is desirable the speaker may succeed in evoking an attitude of approval for himself and for what he says, and this attitude may tend to get transferred to his final conclusion, by psychological association rather than by logical implication. The speaker may have succeeded in evoking such a positive sentiment for housing improvement that his hearers will vote more enthusiastically for the bill he supports than if he had really proved its passage to be in the public interest.

Again, in the second example, if the prosecution has given a sufficiently moving picture of the horribleness of murder, the jury may be so aroused, such horror and disapproval may be evoked in them, that they will bring in a verdict of guilty more swiftly than if the prosecutor had "merely" proved that the defendant had committed the crime.

Although every emotional appeal is logically irrelevant to the truth or falsehood of one's conclusion, not every case of *ignoratio elenchi* need involve an emotional appeal. An argument may be stated in cold, aseptic, neutral language and still commit the fallacy of irrelevant conclusion. It does so if its premisses are directed toward a conclusion different from the one that is supposed to be established by them. One sympathetic judge complimented a young lawyer on his excellent speech and expressed the hope that he would some day find a case to which it actually applied.

EXERCISES

Identify the fallacies of relevance in the following passages and explain how each specific passage involves that fallacy or fallacies.

★ 1. Kenneth Robinson, when he was Great Britain's minister of health, told Parliament that Scientology was "potentially harmful" and "a potential menace."

Elliott, the local minister of the Church of Scientology, was asked to comment on those criticisms. Of the remarks made before Parliament, he said: "I am afraid Mr. Robinson has since suffered two demotions and was just in the last few weeks quietly released from the Wilson Administration altogether."

—*The Honolulu Advertiser,* November 22, 1969, page B-1

2. To put it briefly, then, we can maintain that natural reason cannot prove that the resurrection is necessary, neither by way of *a priori* reasons such as those based on the notion of the intrinsic principle in man, nor by *a posteriori* arguments, for instance, by reason of some operation or perfection fitting to man. Hence we hold the resurrection to be certain on the basis of faith alone.

—DUNS SCOTUS, *Oxford Commentary on the Sentences of Peter Lombard*

3. According to R. Grunberger, author of *A Social History of the Third Reich,* published in Britain, the Nazis used to send the following notice to German readers who let their subscriptions lapse: "Our paper certainly deserves the support of every German. We shall continue to forward copies of it to you, and hope that you will not want to expose yourself to unfortunate consequences in the case of cancellation."

—*Parade,* May 9, 1971

4. In a picture by the famous French comedian Sacha Guitry some thieves are arguing over division of seven pearls worth a king's ransom. One of them hands two to the man on his right, then two to the man on his left. "I," he says, "will keep three." The man on his right says, "How come you keep three?" "Because I am the leader." "Oh. But how come you are the leader?" "Because I have more pearls."

★ 5. When Rodger Babson, whose prediction of the great stock market crash brought him renown, became ill with tuberculosis, he returned to his home in Massachusetts rather than follow his doctor's advice to remain in the West. During the freezing winter he left the windows open, wore a coat with a heating pad in back, and had his secretary wear mittens and hit the typewriter keys with rubber hammers. Babson got well and attributed his cure to fresh air. Air from pine woods, according to Babson, has chemical or electrical qualities (or both) of great medicinal value.

MARTIN GARDNER, *Fads and Fallacies in the Name of Science*

6. Like an armed warrior, like a plumed knight, James G. Blaine marched down the halls of the American Congress and threw his shining lances full and fair against the brazen foreheads of every defamer of his country and maligner of its honor.

For the Republican party to desert a gallant man now is worse than if an army should desert their general upon the field of battle.

—ROBERT G. INGERSOLL, Nominating speech at the Republican National Convention, 1876

7. On the Senate floor in 1950, Joe McCarthy announced that he had penetrated "Truman's iron curtain of secrecy." He had 81 case histories of persons whom he considered to be Communists in the State Department. Of Case 40, he said, "I do not have much information on this except the general statement of the agency that there is nothing in the files to disprove his Communist connections."

—RICHARD H. ROVERE, *Senator Joe McCarthy*

8. I testify unto every man that heareth the words of the prophecy of this book, If any man shall add unto these things, God shall add unto him the plagues that are written in this book: And if any man shall take away from the words of the book of this prophecy, God shall take away his part out of the book of life, and out of the holy city, and *from* the things which are written in this book.

—Book of Revelation 22:18–19

9. Mysticism is one of the great forces of the world's history. For religion is nearly the most important thing in the world, and religion never remains for long altogether untouched by mysticism.

—JOHN MCTAGGART ELLIS MCTAGGART, "Mysticism," *Philosophical Studies*

★ 10. "For the benefit of those representatives who have not been here before this year, it may be useful to explain that the item before the General Assembly is that hardy perennial called the 'Soviet Item.' It is purely a propaganda proposition, not introduced with a serious purpose of serious action, but solely as a peg on which to hang a number of speeches with view to getting them into the press of the world. This is considered by some to be very clever politics. Others, among whom the present speaker wishes to be included, consider it an inadequate response to the challenge of the hour."

—HENRY CABOT LODGE, Speech to the United Nations General Assembly, November 30, 1953

11. In that melancholy book *The Future of an Illusion,* Dr. Freud, himself one of the last great theorists of the European capitalist class, has stated with simple clarity the impossibility of religious belief for the educated man of today.

—JOHN STRACHEY, *The Coming Struggle for Power*

12. The Inquisition must have been justified and beneficial, if whole peoples invoked and defended it, if men of the loftiest souls founded and created it severally and impartially, and its very adversaries applied it on their own account, pyre answering to pyre.

—BENEDETTO CROCE, *Philosophy of the Practical*

13. It is too my turn to pitch today! After all, it's my ball!

14. Why do I know more than other people? Why, in general, am I so clever? I have never pondered over questions that are not really questions. I have never wasted my strength.

—FRIEDRICH NIETZSCHE, *Ecce Homo*

★ 15. Of course socialism is desirable. Look at the facts. At one time all utilities were privately owned, now more and more of them are owned by the government. The social-security laws embody many of the principles that socialists have always maintained. We are well on our way to socialism, and its complete triumph is inevitable!

16. That new student says that I am his favorite professor. And he must be telling the truth, because no student would lie to his favorite professor.

17. "But I observe," says Cleanthes, "with regard to you, Philo, and all speculative sceptics, that your doctrine and practice are as much at variance in the most abstruse points of theory as in the conduct of common life."

—DAVID HUME, *Dialogues Concerning Natural Religion*

18. The Golden Rule is basic to every system of ethics ever devised, and everyone accepts it in some form or other. It is, therefore, an undeniably sound moral principle.

19. No mathematician has ever been able to demonstrate the truth of the famous "last theorem" of Fermat, so it must be false.

★ 20. But can you doubt that air has weight when you have the clear testimony of Aristotle affirming that all the elements have weight including air, and excepting only fire?

—GALILEO GALILEI, *Dialogues Concerning Two New Sciences*

21. What the farmer sows in the spring he reaps in the fall. In the spring he sows two-dollar-a-bushel corn. Therefore in the fall the farmer reaps two-dollar-a-bushel corn.

22. Of course there is a Santa Claus. But he doesn't bring any presents to children who don't believe in him.

23. The alarmists have not succeeded in proving that radioactive fallout is dangerously harmful to human life. Therefore it is perfectly safe to continue our program of testing thermonuclear weapons.

24. I'm absolutely certain about how fast I was driving, Officer, and it was well below the speed limit. I've had tickets before, and if you give me one now it will cost me over fifty dollars. And if I have to pay a fifty-dollar fine I won't be able to afford to have my wife operated on—and she's been sick a long time and needs that operation desperately!

★ 25. There's no point in hiring a skilled worker to do the job, because many who are regarded as skilled workers are no more skilled than anybody else.

26. Nietzsche was personally more philosophical than his philosophy. His talk about power, harshness, and superb immorality was the hobby of a harmless young scholar and constitutional invalid.

—GEORGE SANTAYANA, *Egotism in German Philosophy*

27. Are you in favor of increased governmental service and higher taxes? If you are, those whose taxes are already too high will vote against you. If you are not, those who need more services from the government will vote against you. In no case can you hope to win general support.

28. In his work an attorney is always free to consult law books. And a physician often looks up cases in his medical texts. Everyone should be allowed a similar freedom of reference. So students should be permitted to use their textbooks during examinations.

29. While General Grant was winning battles in the West, President Lincoln received many complaints about Grant's being a drunkard. When a delegation told him one day that Grant was hopelessly addicted to whiskey, the President is said to have replied: "I wish General Grant would send a barrel of his whiskey to each of my other Generals!"

★ 30. The story is told about Wendell Phillips, the abolitionist, who one day found himself on the same train with a group of Southern clergymen on their way to a conference. When the Southerners learned of Phillips' presence, they decided to have some fun at his expense. One of them approached and said, "Are you Wendell Phillips?"

"Yes, sir," came the reply.

"Are you the great abolitionist?"

"I am not great, but I am an abolitionist."

"Are you not the one who makes speeches in Boston and New York against slavery?"

"Yes, I am."

"Why don't you go to Kentucky and make speeches there?"

Phillips looked at his questioner for a moment and then said, "Are you a clergyman?"

"Yes, I am," replied the other.

"Are you trying to save souls from hell?"

"Yes."

"Well—why don't you go there?"

31. You can't believe what Professor Threadbare says about the importance of higher salaries for teachers. As a teacher himself he would naturally be in favor of increasing teachers' pay.

32. I am sure that their ambassador will be reasonable about the matter. After all, man is a rational animal.

33. The wives of successful men wear expensive clothing, so the best way for a woman to help her husband become a success is to buy expensive clothing.

34. ANYTUS: "Socrates, I think that you are too ready to speak evil of men: and, if you will take my advice, I would recommend you to be careful. Perhaps there is no city in which it is not easier to do men harm than to do them good, and this is certainly the case at Athens, as I believe that you know."

—PLATO, *Meno*

★ 35. Our team is the outstanding team in the conference, because it has the best players and the best coach. We know it has the best players and the best coach because it will win the conference title. And it will win the conference title because it *deserves* to win the conference title. Of course it deserves to win the conference title, for it is the outstanding team in the conference.

36. Mr. Scrooge, my husband certainly deserves a raise in pay. I can hardly manage to feed the children on what you have been paying him. And our youngest child, Tim, needs an operation if he is ever to walk without crutches.

37. Our tests have shown that the drug in question has no medicinal value whatever, certainly none for the ailments it is claimed to cure. We conclude, therefore, that it cannot be sold successfully and will be a commercial failure.

38. During the war enemy espionage rings were exposed by tapping the telephone wires of suspects. Therefore the authorities should have the telephone wires of all suspicious persons tapped.

39. However, it matters very little now what the king of England either says or does; he hath wickedly broken through every moral and human obligation, trampled nature and conscience beneath his feet, and by a steady and constitutional spirit of insolence and cruelty procured for himself an universal hatred.

—THOMAS PAINE, *Common Sense*

40. No breath of scandal has ever touched the Senator. Therefore he must be incorruptibly honest.

3.3 Fallacies of Ambiguity

The informal fallacies to be considered next have traditionally been called "fallacies of ambiguity" or "fallacies of clearness." They occur in arguments whose formulations contain ambiguous words or phrases, whose meanings shift and change more or less subtly in the course of the argument and thus render it fallacious. The following are all fallacies of ambiguity, but it is helpful to divide and classify them according to the different ways in which their ambiguities arise.

1. ***Equivocation.*** The first fallacy of ambiguity we shall consider is that which arises through simple equivocation. Most words have more than one literal meaning, as the word "pen" may denote either an instrument for writing or an enclosure for animals. When we keep these different meanings apart, no difficulty arises. But when we confuse the different meanings a single word or phrase may have, using it in different senses in the same context, we are using it equivocally. If the context happens to be an argument, we commit the fallacy of equivocation.

A traditional example of this fallacy is the following: "The end of a thing is its perfection; death is the end of life; hence, death is the perfection of life." This argument is fallacious because two different senses of the word "end" are confused in it. The word "end" may mean either "goal" or "last event." Both these meanings are, of course, legitimate. But what is illegitimate is to confuse the two, as in this argument. The premisses are plausible only when the word "end" is interpreted differently in each of them, as: "The *goal* of a thing is its perfection," and "Death is the *last event* of life." But the conclusion that "death is the perfection of life" does not even appear to follow from these premisses. Of course the same sense of "end" could be used in both premisses, but then the argument would lose all its plausibility, for it would have either the unplausible premiss "The *last event* of a thing is its perfection" or the patently false premiss "Death is the *goal* of life." Some examples of the fallacy of equivocation are so absurd as to be a kind of joke. Such, for example, would be:

> Some dogs have fuzzy ears.
> My dog has fuzzy ears.
> Therefore my dog is some dog!

There is a special kind of equivocation that deserves special mention. This has to do with "relative" terms, which have different meanings in different contexts. For example, the word "tall" is a relative word; a tall man and a tall building are in quite different categories. A tall man is one who is taller than most men, a tall building is one which is taller than most buildings. Certain forms of argument which are valid for nonrelative terms break down when relative terms are substituted for them. The argument "an elephant is an animal; therefore a gray elephant is a gray animal," is perfectly valid. The word "gray" is a nonrelative term. But the argument "an elephant is an animal; therefore a small elephant is a small animal," is ridiculous. The point here is that "small" is a relative term: a small elephant is a very large animal. The fallacy is one of equivocation on the relative term "small." Not all equivocation on relative terms is so obvious, however. The word "good" is a relative term and is frequently equivocated on when it is argued, for example, that so and so would be a good president because he is a good general, or must be a good man because he is a good mathematician, or is a good teacher because he is a good scholar.

2. *Amphiboly.* The fallacy of amphiboly occurs in arguing from premisses whose formulations are ambiguous because of their grammatical construction. A statement is amphibolous when its meaning is indeterminate because of the loose or awkward way in which its words are combined. An amphibolous statement may be true on one interpretation and false on another. When it is stated as premiss with the interpretation which makes it true, and a conclusion is drawn from it on the interpretation which makes it false, then the fallacy of amphiboly has been committed.

The classic example of amphiboly has to do with Croesus and

the Oracle of Delphi. Amphibolous utterances were, of course, the chief stock in trade of the ancient oracles. Croesus, the king of Lydia, was contemplating war with the kingdom of Persia. Being a prudent man, he did not wish to fight unless victory was guaranteed. He consulted Delphi on the matter and received the oracular reply that, "If Croesus went to war with Cyrus, he would destroy a mighty kingdom." Delighted with this prediction, from which he inferred that he would destroy the mighty kingdom of Persia, Croesus went to war and was speedily defeated by Cyrus, king of the Persian host. Afterward, his life having been spared, Croesus wrote a bitterly complaining letter to the Oracle. His letter was answered by the priests of Delphi, who claimed that the Oracle had been right. In going to war Croesus *had* destroyed a mighty kingdom—his own! Amphibolous statements make dangerous premisses. They are, however, seldom encountered in serious discussion.

Some amphibolous sentences are not without their humorous aspects—for example, those in wartime posters urging us to "Save Soap and Waste Paper," or the definition of anthropology as "the science of man embracing woman." We should be mistaken if we inferred immodest dress on the woman described in a story: ". . . loosely wrapped in a newspaper, she carried three dresses." Amphiboly is often exhibited by newspaper headings and brief items, as in, "The farmer blew out his brains after taking affectionate farewell of his family with a shotgun."

3. ***Accent.*** Like all fallacies of ambiguity, the fallacy of accent is committed in an argument whose deceptive but invalid nature depends upon a change or shift in meaning. The way in which the meaning shifts in the fallacy of accent depends upon what parts of it may be emphasized or accented. That some statements have quite different meanings when different words are stressed is clear. Consider the different meanings that are given according to which of the italicized words is stressed in the following injunction:

We should not *speak* ill of *our friends.*

When read without any undue stresses, the injunction is perfectly sound. If the conclusion is drawn from it, however, that we should feel free to speak ill of someone who is *not* our friend, then this conclusion follows only if the premiss has the meaning it acquires when its last word is accented. But when its last word is accented, it is no longer acceptable as a moral law, it has a different meaning, and is in fact a different premiss. The argument is a case of the fallacy of accent. So too would be the argument which drew from the same premiss the conclusion that we are free to *work* ill upon our friends if only we do it silently. And similarly with the other fallacious inferences which suggest themselves. In the same light vein, depending upon how it is accented, the statement:

Woman without her man would be lost.

would be perfectly acceptable to either sex. But to infer the statement with one accent from the statement accented differently would be an instance of the fallacy of accent.

A more serious commission of this fallacy, in a slightly wider sense of the term, can occur in making a quotation, where inserting or deleting italics may change the meaning. Another kind of fallacious accenting may occur without any variation in the use of italics, when the passage quoted is torn from its context. For often a passage can be correctly understood only in the light of its context, which may make clear the *sense* in which the passage is intended, or may contain explicit qualifications without which the passage has a quite different meaning. Therefore a responsible writer who makes a direct quotation will indicate whether or not any words italicized in his quotation were italicized in the original, and will indicate any omission of words or phrases by the use of dots.

A statement which is literally true but quite uninteresting when read or written "normally" may be made quite exciting when accented in certain ways. But this accenting may change its meaning, and with its different meaning it may no longer be true. Thus truth is sacrificed to sensationalism by means of the fallacious inference produced by accenting (typographically) one part of a sentence more than another. This technique is a deliberate policy of certain tabloid newspapers to make their headlines arresting. Such a paper may run as a headline in large boldface type the words,

REVOLUTION IN FRANCE

and then below, in considerably less prominent and smaller type, may be found the words "feared by authorities." The complete statement that "Revolution in France (is) feared by authorities" may be perfectly true. But as accented in the tabloid the assertion is given an exciting but utterly false significance. The same kind of misleading accenting is found in many advertisements. Where a presumably net price is quoted for a particular commodity, closer inspection of the announcement may reveal the words, invariably in much smaller print, "plus tax" or perhaps the phrase "and up." In advertisements directed toward a presumably less literate section of the public, this kind of accenting is often quite flagrant. These are examples of misleading accenting, but they involve fallacies of accent only when they occur in the context of an argument which turns on the shift of meaning that occurs.

Even the literal truth can be a vehicle for falsehood when placed in a misleading context. Consider the following sea story. At almost the very outset of a certain ship's voyage there had been a falling-out between the captain and his first mate. The dissension was aggravated by the mate's tendency to drink, for the captain was a fanatic on temperance and seldom let an occasion go by without lecturing the mate on his failings. Needless to say, this nagging only made the mate drink more heavily. After repeated warnings, one day when the mate had imbibed even more than usual, the captain entered the fact in the ship's log book, writing, "The mate was drunk today." When next it was the mate's turn to keep the log he was horrified to find this official record of his misbehavior. The log would be read by the ship's owner, whose reaction would probably mean the mate's discharge, with a bad reference to boot. He pleaded with the captain to remove the entry, but the captain refused. The mate was unhappy until he finally hit upon a method of revenge. At the end of the regular entries he made in the log book that day he added, "The captain was sober today."

4. ***Composition.*** The term "fallacy of composition" is applied to both of two closely related types of invalid argument. The first may be described as reasoning fallaciously from the properties of the parts of a whole to the properties of the whole itself. A particularly flagrant example would be to argue that since every part of a certain machine is light in weight, the machine "as a whole" is light in weight. The error here is manifest when we consider that a very heavy machine may consist of a very large number of lightweight parts. Not all examples of this kind of fallacious composition are so obvious, however. Some are misleading. I have heard it seriously argued that since each scene of a certain play was a model of artistic perfection, the play as a whole was artistically perfect. But this is as much a fallacy of composition as it would be to argue that since every ship is ready for battle, the whole fleet must be ready for battle.

The other type of composition fallacy is strictly parallel to that just described. Here the fallacious reasoning is from properties possessed by individual elements or members of a collection to properties possessed by the collection or totality of those elements. For example, it would be fallacious to argue that because a bus uses more gasoline than an automobile, therefore all buses use more gasoline than all automobiles. This version of the fallacy of composition turns on a confusion between the "distributive" and the "collective" use of general terms. Thus although college students may enroll in no more than six different classes each semester, it is also true that college students enroll in hundreds of different classes each semester. This verbal conflict is easily resolved. It is true of college students, distributively, that they may enroll in no more than six classes each semester. This is a distributive use of the term in that we are speaking of college students taken singly, or severally. But it is true of college students, collectively, that they enroll in hundreds of different classes each semester. This is a collective use of the term in that we are speaking of college students all together, as a collection or totality. Thus buses use more gasoline than automobiles, distributively; but collectively, automobiles use more gasoline than buses, because there are so many more of them.

This second kind of composition fallacy may be defined as the invalid inference that what may truly be predicated of a term distributively may also be truly predicated of the term collectively. Thus the atomic bombs dropped during World War II did more damage than the ordinary bombs dropped—but only distributively. The matter is exactly reversed when the two kinds of bombs are considered collectively, because there were so many more bombs of the conventional type dropped than atomic ones. Ignoring this distinction in an argument would permit the fallacy of composition.

These two varieties of composition, although parallel, are really distinct, because of the difference between a mere collection of elements and a whole constructed out of those elements. Thus a mere collection of parts is no machine; a mere collection of bricks is neither a house nor a wall. A whole like a machine, a house, or a wall has its parts organized or arranged in certain definite ways. And since organized wholes and mere collections are distinct, so are the two versions of the composition fallacy, one proceeding invalidly to wholes from their parts, the other proceeding invalidly to collections from their members or elements.

5. ***Division.*** The fallacy of division is simply the reverse of the fallacy of composition. In it the same confusion is present but the inference proceeds in the opposite direction. As in the case of composition, two varieties of the fallacy of division may be distinguished. The first kind of division consists in arguing fallaciously that what is true of a whole must also be true of its parts. To argue that since a certain corporation is very important, and Mr. Doe is an official of that corporation, therefore Mr. Doe is very important, is to commit the fallacy of division. This first variety of the division fallacy would be committed in any such argument, as in going from the premiss that a certain machine is heavy, or complicated, or valuable, to the conclusion that this or any other part of the machine must be heavy, or complicated, or valuable. To argue that a girl must have

a large room because she lives in a large dormitory would be still another instance of the first kind of fallacy of division.

The second type of division fallacy is committed when one argues from the properties of a collection of elements to the properties of the elements themselves. To argue that since university students study medicine, law, engineering, dentistry, and architecture, therefore each, or even any, university student studies medicine, law, engineering, dentistry, and architecture, would be to commit the second kind of division fallacy. It is true that university students, collectively, study all these various subjects, but false that university students, distributively, do so. Instances of this variety of the fallacy of division often look like valid arguments, for what is true of a class distributively is certainly true of each and every member. Thus the argument:

Dogs are carnivorous.
Japanese Spaniels are dogs.
______
Therefore Japanese Spaniels are carnivorous.

is perfectly valid. But although it closely resembles the foregoing, the argument:

Dogs are common.
Japanese Spaniels are dogs.
______
Therefore Japanese Spaniels are common.

is invalid, committing the fallacy of division. Some instances of division are obviously jokes, as when the classical example of valid argumentation:

Men are mortal.
Socrates is a man.
______
Therefore Socrates is mortal.

is parodied by the fallacious:

American Indians are disappearing.
That man is an American Indian.
______
Therefore that man is disappearing.

The old riddle "Why do white sheep eat more than black ones?" turns on the confusion involved in the fallacy of division. For the answer, "Because there are more of them," treats collectively what seemed to be referred to distributively in the question.

The reader should try to see clearly the difference between the fallacy of composition and that of converse accident (hasty generalization). In the latter, one argues that since many or most atypical members of a class have a specified property therefore all members of the class (distributively) do also. But in the fallacy of composition one argues that since all of the members of a class have a specified property therefore the class *itself* (collectively) has that property. This is surely different.

Equally important is the difference between the fallacy of division and that of accident. In the latter one argues that since most members of a class have a specified property therefore any particular member or subclass of members, no matter how atypical, must have that property also. But in the fallacy of division one argues that since a class *itself* (collectively) has a specified property therefore any member or subclass of members of the class must have that property also. These too are clearly different.

EXERCISES

Identify the fallacies of ambiguity in the following passages and explain how each specific passage involves that fallacy or fallacies.

★ 1. Seeing that eye and hand and foot and every one of our members has some obvious function, must we not believe that in like manner a human being has a function over and above these particular functions?

—ARISTOTLE, *Nicomachean Ethics*

2. Mr. Tompkins is a poor man, and he loses whenever he plays bridge. He is, therefore, a poor loser.

3. "Who did you pass on the road?" the King went on, holding his hand out to the messenger for some hay.

"Nobody," said the messenger.

"Quite right," said the King: "this young lady saw him too. So of course Nobody walks slower than you."

—LEWIS CARROLL, *Through the Looking-Glass*

4. But space is nothing but a relation. For, in the first place, any space must consist of parts; and if the parts are not spaces, the whole is not space.

—F. H. BRADLEY, *Appearance and Reality*

★ 5. The Bible tells us to return good for evil. But Jones has never done me any evil. Hence it will be all right to play him a dirty trick or two.

6. Leaking badly, manned by a skeleton crew, one infirmity after another overtakes the little ship.

—*The Herald Tribune Books Section*

Those game little infirmities!

—*The New Yorker,* Nov. 8, 1958

7. All phenomena in the universe are saturated with moral values. And, therefore, we can come to assert that the universe for the Chinese is a moral universe.

—THOMÉ H. FANG, *The Chinese View of Life*

8. Since every third child born in New York is a Catholic, Protestant families living there should have no more than two children.

9. Her father has a very distinguished appearance, so he must be a very distinguished man.

★ 10. To press forward with a properly ordered wage structure in each industry is the first condition for curbing competitive bargaining; but there is no reason why the process should stop there. What is good for each industry can hardly be bad for the economy as a whole.

—*Twentieth Century Socialism,* p. 74. Penguin Books, 1956

11. Russian threats are no news. Therefore Russian threats are good news, since no news is good news.

12. Traffic accidents are increasing. Collisions between Model T Fords are traffic accidents. Therefore collisions between Model T Fords are increasing.

13. . . . each person's happiness is a good to that person, and the general happiness, therefore, a good to the aggregate of all persons.

—JOHN STUART MILL, *Utilitarianism*

14. Psychological testing established that Mr. Jones' concern with money was above average and that Mrs. Jones' concern with money was below average. It follows that Jones likes money more than his wife. Their marriage is not likely to last, for how can a man stand a woman to whom he prefers money?

★ 15. Each manufacturer is perfectly free to set his own price on the product he produces, so there can be nothing wrong with all manufacturers getting together to fix the prices of the articles made by all of them.

16. American buffalo are practically extinct. This animal is an American buffalo, so it must be practically extinct.

17. WHITE: I do not see any good reasons for making the trip. So I have given up my intention of going.

BLACK: Aha! You admit there are good reasons for making the trip —those are your very words! I am glad to hear of your "intention of going."

18. Improbable events happen almost every day, but what happens almost every day is a very probable event. Therefore improbable events are very probable events.

19. Good steaks are rare these days, so you shouldn't order yours well-done.

20. And to judge still better of the minute perceptions which we cannot distinguish in the crowd, I am wont to make use of the example of the roar or noise of the sea which strikes one when on its shore. To understand this noise as it is made, it would be necessary to hear the parts which compose this whole, i.e., the noise of each wave, although each of these little noises . . . would not be noticed if the wave which makes it were alone. For it must be that we are affected a little by the motion of this wave, and that we have some perception of each one of these noises, small as they are; otherwise we would not have that of a hundred thousand waves, since a hundred thousand nothings cannot make something.

—GOTTFRIED LEIBNIZ, *New Essays Concerning Human Understanding*

3.4 The Avoidance of Fallacies

Fallacies are pitfalls into which any of us may tumble in our reasoning. Just as danger signals are erected to warn travelers away from dangerous places, so the labels for fallacies presented in this chapter may be regarded as so many danger signals posted to keep us away from the quagmire of incorrect argument. Familiarity with these errors and the ability to name and analyze them may very well help to keep us from being deceived by them.

There is no sure way to avoid fallacies. To avoid the fallacies of relevance requires constant vigilance and awareness of the many ways in which irrelevance can intrude. Our study of the different uses of language should be helpful in this connection. A realization of the flexibility of language and the multiplicity of its uses will keep us from mistaking an exhortation to accept and approve a conclusion for an argument designed to prove that conclusion true.

The fallacies of ambiguity are subtle things. Words are slippery, and most of them have a variety of different senses or meanings. Where these different meanings are confused in the formulation of an argument, the reasoning is fallacious. To avoid the various fallacies of ambiguity, we must have and keep the meanings of our terms clearly in mind. One way to accomplish this is by defining the key terms that are used. Since shifts in the meanings of terms can make arguments fallacious, and since ambiguity can be avoided by careful definition of the terms involved, definition is an important matter for the student of logic. It is to the topic of definition that our next chapter is devoted.

EXERCISES

Identify the fallacies in the following passages and explain how each specific passage involves that fallacy or fallacies.

★ 1. It is necessary to confine criminals and to lock up dangerous lunatics. Therefore there is nothing wrong with depriving people of their liberties.

2. If you hold that nothing is self-evident, I will not argue with you for it is clear that you are a quibbler and are not to be convinced.

—DUNS SCOTUS, *Oxford Commentary on the Sentences of Peter Lombard*

3. The army is notoriously inefficient, so we cannot expect Major Smith to do an efficient job.

4. God exists because the Bible tells us so, and we know that what the Bible tells us must be true because it is the revealed word of God.

★ 5. Congress shouldn't bother to consult the Joint Chiefs of Staff about military appropriations. As members of the armed forces, they will naturally want as much money for military purposes as they think they can get.

6. MR. BROWN: I will give no more money to your cause next year.
SOLICITOR: That's all right, sir, we'll just put you down for the same amount that you gave this year.

7. When we had got to this point in the argument, and every one saw that the definition of justice had been completely upset, Thrasymachus, instead of replying to me, said: "Tell me, Socrates, have you got a nurse?"
"Why do you ask such a question," I said, "when you ought rather to be answering?"
"Because she leaves you to snivel, and never wipes your nose: she has not even taught you to know the shepherd from the sheep."

—PLATO, *Republic*

8. Narcotics are habit-forming. Therefore if you allow your physician to ease your pain with an opiate you will become a hopeless drug addict.

9. You can't prove that he was to blame for the misfortune, so it must actually have been someone else who was responsible.

★ 10. You can't park here. I don't care *what* the sign says. If you don't drive on I'll give you a ticket.

11. I also admit that there are people for whom even the reality of the external world and the identifications leading to it constitute a grave problem. My answer is that I do not address *them,* but that I presuppose a minimum of reason in my readers.

—PAUL FEYERABEND, "Materialism and the Mind-Body Problem," *The Review of Metaphysics,* 1963

12. All departures from law should be punished. Whatever happens by chance is a departure from law. Therefore whatever happens by chance should be punished.

13. Absolute music is perhaps the most eloquent and moving form of art, although it tells no "story." Abstract painting and sculpture are among the most magnificent products of human creativity, although neither of them has any "story" to tell. Therefore the "story" it contains contributes nothing to the excellence of a novel or a drama as a work of art.

14. Each of these sweaters is on sale at 50 per cent off. If I buy two of them, that will be 100 per cent off, so I'll really be getting them for nothing.

★ 15. During the Colonial and Revolutionary period of American history, Thomas Paine bitterly opposed reconciliation with England. In his book *Common Sense* he argued:

> Though I would carefully avoid giving unnecessary offence, yet I am inclined to believe, that all those who espouse the doctrine of reconciliation, may be included within the following descriptions.
>
> Interested men, who are not to be trusted, weak men who *cannot* see, prejudiced men who will not see, and a certain set of moderate men who think better of the European world than it deserves; and this last class, by an ill-judged deliberation, will be the cause of more calamities to this Continent than all the other three.

16. Cooks have been preparing food for generations, so our cook must be a real expert.

17. More young people are attending high schools and colleges than ever before in the history of our nation. But there is more juvenile delinquency than ever before. This makes it clear that to eliminate delinquency among the youth we must abolish the schools.

18. You say we ought to discuss whether or not to buy a new car now. All right, I agree. Let's discuss the matter. Which should we get, a Ford or a Chevy?

19. Our nation is a democracy and dedicated to the proposition that all men are created equal. We believe in equality of opportunity for everyone, so our colleges and universities should admit every applicant, regardless of his economic or educational background.

★ 20. Everything in the universe serves a function which goes beyond itself. So the universe itself must serve a function which goes beyond itself.

21. We should reject Mr. Watkins' suggestions for increasing the efficiency of our colleges. As a manufacturer he cannot be expected to realize that our aim is to educate the youth, not to make a profit. His recommendations can have no value for us.

22. Everyone said that the soup had a very distinctive taste, so they must all have found it very tasty.

23. If we want to know whether a state is brave we must look at its army, not because the soldiers are the only brave people in the community, but because it is only through their conduct that the courage or cowardice of the community can be manifested.

—R. L. NETTLESHIP, *Lectures on the Republic of Plato*

24. Once again Jesus addressed the people: "I am the light of the world. No follower of mine shall wander in the dark; he shall have the light of life." The Pharisees said to him, "You are witness in your own cause; your testimony is not valid."

—John 8:12–14

★ 25. There is no proof that the secretary "leaked" the news to the papers, so she can't have done it.

26. Diamonds are seldom found in this country, so you must be careful not to mislay your engagement ring.

27. Was it through stupidity or through deliberate dishonesty that the Administration has hopelessly botched its foreign policy? In either case, unless you are in favor of stupidity or dishonesty, you should vote against the incumbents.

28. Since all men are mortal, the human race must some day come to an end.

29. Gentlemen, I am sure that if you think it over you will see that my suggestion has real merit. It is only a suggestion of course, and not an order. As I mentioned at our last conference, I am planning to reorganize the whole business. I still hope, however, that it will not be necessary to curtail the operations of your department.

★ 30. Isn't it true that students who get all A's study hard? So if you want me to study hard, Professor, the best way to do it is to give me A's in all my courses.

31. When Bill had to go up to State with the team, the professor told him it was perfectly all right for him to miss class. So the professor doesn't care whether any of us come to class or not.

32. Old man Brown claims that he saw a flying saucer land on his farm. But old man Brown never got beyond the fourth grade in school and can hardly read or write. He is completely ignorant of what scientists have written on the subject, so his report cannot possibly be true.

33. I don't care how sick he is. He is wanted at the shop immediately. When the supervisor sends for a man, the employee is expected to make his appearance.

34. There must be lots of jobs available in physical education, because the bulletin announces that the Dean will give a talk to graduating seniors about their employment opportunities in the College Gymnasium tonight.

★ 35. A good physician cures most of his patients because he has had a sound medical education, for a man with a sound medical education is a good physician who cures most of his patients.

36. No citizen has a right to decide whether his fellow countrymen should live or die. Therefore citizens have no right to decide on the crucial issues of war or peace.

37. How much longer are you going to waste your time in school when you might be doing a man's work in the world, and contributing to society? If you had any sense of social responsibility, you would leave immediately.

38. But lest you think, that my *piety* has here got the better of my *philosophy,* I shall support my opinion, if it needs any support, by a very great authority. I might cite all the divines almost, from the foundation of Christianity, who have ever treated of this or any other theological subjects: but I shall confine myself at present, to one equally celebrated for piety and philosophy. It is Father Malebranche. . . .

—DAVID HUME, *Dialogues Concerning Natural Religion*

39. My client is the sole support of his aged parents. If he is sent to prison it will break their hearts, and they will be left homeless and penniless. You surely cannot find it in your hearts to reach any other verdict than "not guilty."

★ 40. My folks wouldn't let me go to the movies last night and they wouldn't let me stay up to watch TV either. They never want me to have any fun.

41. Anyone who deliberately strikes another person should be punished. Therefore the middleweight boxing champion should be severely punished, for he assaults all of his opponents.

42. Furthermore, all philosophers commonly assign "rational" as the difference that properly defines man, meaning by "rational" that the intellective soul is an essential part of man.

In fact, to put it briefly, no philosopher of any note can be found to deny this except that accursed Averroes in his commentary on *De anima,* BK. III, where his fantastic conception, intelligible neither to himself nor to others, assumes the intellective part of man to be a sort of separate substance united to man through the medium of sense images.

—DUNS SCOTUS, *Oxford Commentary on the Sentences of Peter Lombard*

43. . . . since it is impossible for an animal or plant to be indefinitely big or small, neither can its parts be such, or the whole will be the same.

—ARISTOTLE, *Physics*

44. It is our duty to do what is right. We have the right to disregard good advice. Hence it is our duty to disregard good advice.

★ 45. The Governor must be a good friend to the farmers of this state, because he told them so in his speech last night, and no one would lie to his friends.

46. Whether we are to live in a future state, as it is the most important question which can possibly be asked, so it is the most intelligible one which can be expressed in language.

—JOSEPH BUTLER, "Of Personal Identity"

47. "The war-mongering character of all this flood of propaganda in the United States is admitted even by the American Press. Such provocative and slanderous aims clearly inspired today's speech by the United States representative, consisting only of impudent slander against the Soviet Union, to answer which would be beneath our dignity. The heroic epic of Stalingrad is impervious to libel. The Soviet people in the battles at Stalingrad saved the world from the fascist plague and that great victory which decided the fate of the world is remembered with recognition and gratitude by all humanity. Only men dead to all shame could try to cast aspersions on the shining memory of the heroes of that battle."

—BARANOVSKY, Speech to the United Nations General Assembly, November 30, 1953

48. He who forgets most is most ignorant. He who knows most forgets most. Therefore he who knows most is most ignorant.

49. Nothing is unthinkable to me, for to think of nothing is simply not to think at all.

50. America is the wealthiest nation in the history of the world, so it is absurd to say that poverty is a problem for America.

Chapter 4
Definition

Since all terms that are defined are defined by means of other terms, it is clear that human knowledge must always be content to accept some terms as intelligible without definition, in order to have a starting-point for its definitions.

—*Bertrand Russell*

4.1 Five Purposes of Definition

1. ***To Increase Vocabulary.*** Language is a very complicated instrument. People learn to use it the same way that they learn to use other tools, such as automobiles or kitchen equipment. A boy who does much riding with his father seldom needs to be given formal instruction in driving the family car; he acquires his knowledge by observing and imitating his father. A girl who spends much time in the kitchen with her mother learns in the same way to use quite complicated kitchen appliances. It is the same with language: certainly in childhood, and for many of us throughout our lives, we learn the proper use of language by observing and imitating the linguistic behavior of the people we meet and the books we read.

There are, however, limits to this informal learning. The rising devastation of traffic accidents has made it imperative for drivers to have some formal training over and above the learning by imitation that used to suffice. The need for girls to supplement their mothers' examples has long been recognized by including courses in home economics in high school and even college curricula. The situation is similar in language study. There are occasions when the usual methods of observation and imitation do not suffice; then formal instruction, that is, deliberate explanation of the meanings of terms, is required. To explain the meaning of a term is to give a definition of it. To give a definition is not the primary method of instruction in the proper use and understanding of language; it is, rather, a supplementary device for filling the gaps left by the primary method.

In conversation or in reading, one often comes upon unfamiliar words whose meanings are not made clear by their contexts. To understand what is being said, it is necessary to find out what the words mean; here definitions are required. One purpose of definition, then, is to increase the vocabulary of the person for whom the definition is constructed.

2. ***To Eliminate Ambiguity.*** Another purpose served by definition is the elimination of ambiguity. Perhaps most words have two or more distinct meanings or senses, and usually no trouble arises from this fact. In some contexts, however, it may not be clear which sense of a given word is intended, and here its occurrence is said to be ambiguous. Fallacious arguments that result from the unwitting use of ambiguous terms have been discussed in the preceding chapter, where they were characterized as fallacies of equivocation. Such arguments are misleading only if the ambiguity passes unnoticed. When the ambiguity is resolved, the persuasiveness vanishes and the fallacy is exposed. But to resolve the ambiguity, we require definitions to explain the different meanings of the ambiguous word or phrase.

Ambiguous language can lead not only to fallacious argumentation but also to disputes which are merely verbal. Some apparent disagreements turn not on any genuine differences of opinion, but rather upon different uses of a term. Where the ambiguity of a key term has led to a merely verbal dispute, we can often resolve the dispute by pointing out the ambiguity. We do this by giving the two different definitions of the term, so the different meanings can be clearly distinguished and the confusion dispelled. A now classic example of this method of resolving merely verbal disputes by defining the ambiguous terms involved is due to William James. In the second lecture in *Pragmatism,* James wrote:

> Some years ago, being with a camping party in the mountains, I returned from a solitary ramble to find every one engaged in a ferocious metaphysical dispute. The *corpus* of the dispute was a squirrel—a live squirrel supposed to be clinging to one side of a tree-trunk; while over against the tree's opposite side a human being was imagined to stand. This human witness tries to get sight of the squirrel by moving rapidly round the tree, but no matter how fast

he goes, the squirrel moves as fast in the opposite direction, and always keeps the tree between himself and the man, so that never a glimpse of him is caught. The resultant metaphysical problem is this: *Does the man go round the squirrel or not?* He goes round the tree, sure enough, and the squirrel is on the tree; but does he go round the squirrel? In the unlimited leisure of the wilderness, discussion had been worn threadbare. Everyone had taken sides, and was obstinate; and the numbers on both sides were even. Each side, when I appeared, therefore appealed to me to make it a majority. Mindful of the scholastic adage that whenever you meet a contradiction you must make a distinction, I immediately sought and found one, as follows: "Which party is right," I said, "depends on what you *practically mean* by 'going round' the squirrel. If you mean passing from the north of him to the east, then to the south, then to the west, and then to the north of him again, obviously the man does go round him, for he occupies these successive positions. But if on the contrary you mean being first in front of him, then on the right of him, then behind him, then on his left, and finally in front again, it is quite obvious that the man fails to go round him, for by the compensating movements the squirrel makes, he keeps his belly turned towards the man all the time, and his back turned away. Make the distinction, and there is no occasion for any further dispute. You are both right and both wrong according as you conceive the verb 'go round' in one practical fashion or the other."

Although one or two of the hotter disputants called my speech a shuffling evasion, saying they wanted no quibbling or scholastic hair-splitting, but meant just plain honest English "round," the majority seemed to think that the distinction had assuaged the dispute.[1]

As James points out, no new "facts" were required to resolve the dispute; none could possibly have helped. What was needed was just what James supplied, a distinction between different meanings of the key term in the argument. This could be accomplished, of course, only by supplying alternative definitions of the term "go round." We can settle merely verbal disputes only by giving definitions of the ambiguous terms involved. The second purpose of definition, then, is to eliminate ambiguity, both for the sake of exposing fallacies of equivocation and for resolving disputes which are merely verbal.

3. *To Reduce Vagueness.* Another occasion for defining a term arises when we desire to use it but are not quite sure of the limits of its applicability, although in a sense we do know its meaning. This motive for wanting a term defined is different from the first one discussed. There the motive was to teach the meaning of an unfamiliar term. Here the purpose is to clarify the meaning of a term already known. Where the meaning of a term is in need of clarification, we say the term is vague. To clarify the meaning of a term is to reduce its vagueness, and is accomplished by giving a definition of the term which will permit a decision as to its applicability in a given situa-

[1] By permission from *Pragmatism* by William James, Longmans, Green & Company, Inc., 1907.

tion. This is sometimes confused with the second motive discussed, because vagueness is sometimes confused with ambiguity. Although the same word can be both vague and ambiguous, vagueness and ambiguity are two quite different properties. A term is *ambiguous* in a given context when it has two distinct meanings and the context does not make clear which one is intended. On the other hand, a term is *vague* when there exist "borderline cases" such that it cannot be determined whether the term applies to them or not. Most words are vague in the sense indicated. Scientists have been unable to decide whether certain viruses are "living" or "nonliving," not because they do not know whether or not the virus has the powers of locomotion, of reproduction, and so on, but because the word "living" is so vague a term. Perhaps more familiar is the difficulty in deciding whether or not a certain country is a "democracy," or whether a given work of art is "obscene."

These "difficulties" may seem trivial, but under certain circumstances they can assume great practical importance. Suppose, for example, that we had the task of administering a law which provided that financial aid be given only to countries with "democratic" governments. Here decisions on borderline cases would be fraught with the gravest moral, political, and possibly even military significance, in addition to financial implications involving millions of dollars.

The indecision attending such borderline cases may be resolved by giving a definition of the vague term which will make clear whether it is to be applied or not. Thus to decide whether a house trailer is to be taxed as a vehicle or as a dwelling, we must find out how the law defines these terms. And if the definitions on record are not sufficiently precise to determine a decision, then the court within whose jurisdiction the question arises must promulgate new definitions which will permit of clear application. For example, in 1966 the Supreme Court of the state of North Carolina ruled that a yacht was not a "motor vehicle," thus making its sale subject to the state's 3 per cent sales tax, rejecting the contention that as a motor vehicle the craft was subject only to a special 1 per cent tax.[2] A third purpose of giving definitions, then, is to reduce the vagueness of familiar terms, which is a different purpose from those previously mentioned.

4. ***To Explain Theoretically.*** Still another purpose we may have in defining a term is to formulate a theoretically adequate or scientifically useful characterization of the objects to which it is applied. For example, physical scientists have defined the term "force" as the product of mass and acceleration. This definition is not given to in-

[2] *The Wall Street Journal,* March 16, 1966, p. 1.

crease anyone's vocabulary or to eliminate ambiguity, but to embody part of Newtonian mechanics into the very meaning of the term "force" itself. Although such a definition might well reduce the vagueness of the term being defined, its primary purpose is not that but something else instead. Another example of a definition intended to serve this theoretical purpose is the chemist's definition of "acid" to mean any substance containing hydrogen as a positive radical. Everything which is correctly called an acid in ordinary usage is denoted by the term as defined by the chemist, but no pretense is made that the chemist's principle for distinguishing acids from other substances is actually applied by housewives or sheet-metal workers in their use of the term. The chemist's definition is intended to attach to the word, as meaning, that property which in the context of his theory is most useful for understanding and predicting the behavior of those substances which the word denotes. When the scientist constructs such definitions as these, his purpose is theoretical.

5. *To Influence Attitudes.* In addition to the preceding four purposes of definition, there is another, a fifth. One often defines a term with the purpose in mind of influencing the attitudes or stirring the emotions of one's readers or hearers in certain definite ways. Thus a man may rise to the defense of a friend accused of tactlessness by praising his friend's honesty, offering the definition of "honesty" as always telling the truth regardless of circumstances. Here the speaker's purpose is not to give an explanation of the literal meaning of the word "honesty," but to cause his listeners to transfer to his friend's behavior the laudatory emotive value that attaches to the term "honesty." His language is not informative; it is functioning expressively. The emotive value to be transferred need not belong initially to the term being defined but can attach to a word or phrase used in stating the definition. For example, a proponent of socialism may *define* "socialism" to mean *democracy extended to the economic field.* Here the word "socialism" is not being defined for the purpose of explaining its literal or descriptive meaning, but rather to win for it some of the approval usually aroused by the word "democracy." It may be questioned whether rhetorical devices like these should be called definitions, but the word is frequently used in this way, as in newspaper contests for the "best definitions" of various terms.

4.2 Verbal Disputes and Definition

Now that we have seen how definitions can have an expressive as well as an informative function, it may be well to qualify somewhat our previous discussion of verbal disputes. It is true, as was stated, that some disputes are merely verbal, the result of confusing two different senses of an ambiguous term, such as James' example of the squirrel. But such cases bear a superficial resemblance to other disputes which are really genuine.

Consider the prolonged disagreement between the United States and Soviet Russia following World War II. Among the points at issue have been such questions as whether or not this or that nation should be accorded certain rights and privileges, such as admission to the United Nations Organization. Some newspaper commentators and editorialists stigmatized these disputes as being merely verbal. All that was needed, the critics seemed to imply, was a well-turned definition of the key word, "democratic." After all, both of the two great powers agreed that democratic countries should have all possible rights and privileges. But the situation might better have been characterized as a "merely verbal agreement." The two powers agreed upon the emotive meaning of the word "democratic," but any definition either might have offered would have been merely rhetorical, for genuine and far-reaching disagreement separated this country and Russia. Significant moral and political issues were at stake, and to suggest that they could be settled by redefining terms would be superstitious belief in the efficacy of "word magic." In the presence of real issues separating the two nations, their agreement on the emotive meaning of the word "democracy" served to prevent agreement on any descriptively adequate definition of the term. Such a definition could be reached only as a result of having resolved the moral and political disagreement, not as a means to such resolution. Of course, agreement on the literal meaning of the word "democracy" could have been reached while the nations stood opposed, but only on condition that one or the other repudiate the honorific emotive meaning of the term.

Some disputes are merely verbal, but of course not all of them are. And where there is genuine disagreement, whether in belief or in attitude, it is not to be resolved by so simple a measure as framing new definitions of the terms involved.

Apart from explicit disagreements in attitude, as when one says "It's great!" and another replies "It's awful!", we distinguish three different kinds of disputes. The first is the obviously genuine variety, in which the parties explicitly and unambiguously disagree about a question of fact. One party may maintain that the Pacific entrance to the Panama Canal is further west than the Atlantic entrance; the other party may deny it. Or they can have an obviously genuine dispute about words, with one party maintaining that a given word is spelled, or pronounced, or used in a specified way and the other party insisting that it is spelled, or pronounced, or used in a different way. Or they can have an obviously genuine dispute about attitudes, as when two persons disagree as to whether a third person is unfriendly or only shy. There are linguistic and psychological facts as well as geographical ones. And different people can have different beliefs as to what the facts are. A dispute of this first kind always involves a disagreement in belief.

The second kind of dispute is merely verbal, where the presence of an ambiguous key term in the disputant's formulations of their beliefs conceals the fact that there is no real disagreement between them. The phrase "going round" was the ambiguous culprit in James' example. Disputes of this second kind can be resolved by revealing the ambiguity and showing that merely *different* propositions, rather than *opposing* propositions, are being maintained by the disputers.

A dispute of the third kind may be characterized as an apparently verbal dispute that is really genuine. In this third kind there is some key word or phrase used in different senses by the disputers, and here lies its resemblance to the second kind. But this third kind differs from the second in that resolving the ambiguity will not settle or end the dispute, for a dispute of this third kind reveals and is based upon a genuine disagreement in attitude between the disputers.

These three kinds of disputes can be summarily described as follows. In an obviously genuine dispute there is no ambiguity present and the disputers disagree in belief. In a merely verbal dispute there is ambiguity present but no disagreement at all. And in an apparently verbal dispute that is really genuine there is ambiguity present *and* the disputers disagree in attitude.

EXERCISES

Discuss each of the following disputes. If it is obviously genuine, indicate each of the disputers' positions with respect to the proposition at issue. If it is merely verbal, resolve it by explaining the different senses attached by the disputers to the key word or phrase that is used ambiguously. If it is an apparently verbal dispute that is really genuine, locate the ambiguity and explain the real disagreement involved.

★ 1. BLACK: Ty Cobb was the greatest hitter in the history of baseball. His lifetime batting average is higher than any other major league player's.

WHITE: No, Babe Ruth deserves that title. He hit more home runs than any other major league player.

2. BLACK: The present war must be stopped immediately. The hideous slaughter, the exorbitant cost, the dissension in our country cannot be allowed to continue.
WHITE: I cannot agree with you. Under the Constitution only Congress has the power to declare war and Congress has made no such declaration. So there is no war going on at present and hence no war to be stopped.

3. BLACK: Mrs. Jones is certainly a wonderful wife. She is a great cook, an immaculate housekeeper, and a loving mother to her children.
WHITE: I don't think so. She is so engrossed in her home that she offers very little companionship or intellectual stimulation to her husband.

4. BLACK: Amalgamated General Corporation's earnings were higher than ever last year, I see by reading their annual report.
WHITE: No, their earnings were really much lower than in the preceding year, and they have been cited by the SEC for issuing a false and misleading report.

★ 5. BLACK: Business continues to be good for National Conglomerate, Inc. Their sales so far this year are 25 per cent higher than they were at this time last year.
WHITE: No, their business is not so good now. Their profits so far this year are 30 per cent lower than they were last year at this time.

6. BLACK: Fred is an excellent student. He takes a lively interest in everything and asks very intelligent questions in class.
WHITE: Fred is one of the worst students I've ever seen. He never gets his assignments in on time.

7. BLACK: Tom did it of his own free will. No pressure was brought to bear on him, no threats were made, no inducements were offered, there was no hint of force. He deliberated about it and made up his own mind.
WHITE: That is impossible. Nobody has free will, because everything he does is inevitably determined by his heredity and his environment according to inexorable causal laws of nature.

8. BLACK: Professor Graybeard is one of the most productive scholars at the University. His bibliography of publications is longer than those of any of his colleagues.

WHITE: I wouldn't call him a productive scholar. He is a great teacher but he has never produced any new ideas or discoveries in his entire career.

9. BLACK: Harry finally got rid of that old Essex of his and bought himself a new car. He's driving a Buick now.
   WHITE: No, Harry didn't buy himself a new car. That Buick is a good three years old.

★ 10. BLACK: Dick finally got rid of that old Edsel of his and bought himself a new car. He's driving a new Pontiac now.
   WHITE: No, Dick didn't buy himself a new car. It's his roommate's new Pontiac that he's driving.

11. BLACK: Helen lives a long way from campus. I walked out to see her the other day, and it took me nearly two hours to get there.
   WHITE: No, Helen doesn't live such a long way from campus. I drove her home last night, and we reached her place in less than ten minutes.

12. BLACK: Senator Gray is a fine man and a genuine liberal. He votes for every progressive measure that comes before the legislature.
   WHITE: He is no liberal, in my opinion—the old skinflint contributes less money to worthy causes than any other man in his income bracket.

13. BLACK: The University of Winnemac overemphasizes athletics, for it has the largest college stadium in the world and has constructed new sports buildings instead of badly needed classroom space.
   WHITE: No, the University of Winnemac does not overemphasize athletics. Its academic standards are very high and it sponsors a wide range of extracurricular activities for students in addition to its athletic program.

14. BLACK: It was in bad taste to serve roast beef at the banquet, because there were Hindus present, and it is against their religion to eat beef.
   WHITE: Bad taste nothing! That was the tastiest meal I've had in a long time. I think it was delicious!

★ 15. BLACK: There are less than five million unemployed persons in this country, according to the Bureau of Labor Statistics.
   WHITE: Oh no, there are over twenty times that number of unemployed. The President's Economic Report states that there are eighty million employed in this country, and the Census Bureau reports a total population of over two hundred million. So the

government's figures reveal that there are over a hundred million unemployed persons in this country.

16. BLACK: The average intelligence of college graduates is higher than that of college freshmen, because it takes more intelligence to graduate from college than to be admitted to college.
    WHITE: No, the average intelligence of college graduates is not higher than that of college freshmen, because every college graduate was once a college freshman and a person's intelligence does not change from year to year.
17. BLACK: A tree falling in a wilderness with nobody around to hear will produce no sound. There can be no auditory sensation unless someone actually senses it.
    WHITE: No, whether anyone is there to hear it or not, the crash of a falling tree will set up vibrations in the air and will therefore produce a sound in any event.
18. BLACK: I see by the financial pages that money is much more plentiful than it was six months ago.
    WHITE: That can't be true. I read a government report just yesterday to the effect that more old currency has been destroyed at the mint during the last half year than has been replaced. Money is therefore less plentiful, not more so.
19. BLACK: Mr. Green is a real Christian. He speaks well of everyone and is never too busy to give friendly assistance to anyone who is in need.
    WHITE: I wouldn't call Green a Christian—he spends his Sundays working in his yard or playing out on the golf course, never showing his face in church from one end of the year to the other!
20. BLACK: Don't ask your wife about it. You ought to use your own judgment.
    WHITE: I will use my own judgment, and in my judgment I should ask my wife.

4.3 Five Types of Definition

Before distinguishing between different types of definition, it should be remarked that definitions are always of symbols, for only symbols have meanings for definitions to explain. We can define the word "chair," since it has a meaning; but although we can sit on it, paint it, burn it, or describe it, we cannot define a chair itself, for a chair is an article of furniture, not a symbol which has a meaning for us to explain. A definition can be expressed in either of two ways, by talking about the symbol to be defined or by talking about its referent. Thus we can equally well say either:

> The word "triangle" means a plane figure enclosed by three straight lines.

or

> A triangle is (by definition) a plane figure enclosed by three straight lines.

Two technical terms used in the theory of definition may be introduced at this point. The symbol being defined is called the *definiendum,* and the symbol or group of symbols used to explain the meaning of the definiendum is called the *definiens.* For example, in the preceding definition the word "triangle" is the definiendum, and the phrase "a plane figure enclosed by three straight lines" is the definiens. The definiens is not the meaning of the definiendum, but another symbol or group of symbols which, according to the definition, has the same meaning as the definiendum.

1. ***Stipulative Definitions.*** The first type of definition to be discussed is that given a brand-new term when it is first introduced. Anyone who introduces a new symbol has complete freedom to stipulate what meaning is to be given it. The assignment of meanings to new symbols is a matter of choice, and we may call the definitions which make the assignment *stipulative* definitions. Of course, the definiendum in a stipulative definition need not be a sound or mark or sequence of letters that is absolutely novel. It is sufficient that it be new in the context in which the defining takes place. Traditional discussions are not altogether clear, but it seems that what we are here calling stipulative definitions have sometimes been referred to as "nominal" or "verbal" definitions.

New terms may be introduced for a variety of reasons. For example, a commercial establishment with branches in foreign parts may compile a cable code in which single words are "short for" lengthy but routine messages. The advantages of introducing such new terms may include the relative secrecy their use achieves and lower costs for transmitting messages by cable. If such a code is actually to be used for communication, its maker must explain the meanings of the new terms, and to do this he will give definitions of them.

New terms are frequently introduced into the sciences. There are many advantages to introducing a new and technical symbol defined to mean what would otherwise require a long sequence of familiar words for its expression. By doing so, the scientist economizes the space required for writing out his reports or theories, and also the time involved. More importantly, he reduces the amount of attention or mental energy required, for when a sentence or equation grows too long its sense cannot easily be "taken in." Consider the economy on all counts achieved by the introduction of the exponent in mathematics. What is now written quite briefly as

$$A^{12} = B$$

would, prior to the adoption of the special symbol for exponentiation, have had to be expressed either by

$$A \times A \times A \times A \times A \times A \times A \times A \times A \times A \times A \times A = B$$

or by a sentence of ordinary language instead of a mathematical equation.

There is still another reason for the scientist's introduction of new symbols. The emotive suggestions of familiar words are often disturbing to one interested only in their literal or informative meanings. The introduction of new symbols, explicitly defined as having the same literal meanings as familiar ones, will free the investigator from the distraction of the latter's emotive associations. This advantage accounts for the presence of some curious words in modern psychology, such as Spearman's "*g* factor," for example, which is intended to convey the same descriptive meaning as the word "intelligence" but to share none of its emotional significance. And for the new terminology to be learned and used, the new symbols must have their meanings explained by definitions.

A symbol defined by a stipulative definition had no prior meaning. Hence its definition cannot be regarded as a statement or report that the definiendum and the definiens have the same meaning. They actually will have the same meaning for anyone who accepts the definition, but that is something which follows the definition rather than a fact asserted by it. A stipulative definition is neither true nor false, but should be regarded as a proposal or resolution to use the definiendum to mean what is meant by the definiens, or as a request or command. In this sense a stipulative definition is directive rather than informative. Proposals may be rejected, resolutions violated, requests refused, commands disobeyed, and stipulations ignored, but none of them are on that account either true or false. So it is with stipulative definitions.

Of course, stipulative definitions may be evaluated on other grounds. Whether or not a new term serves the purpose for which it was introduced is a question of fact. The definition may be either very obscure or so complex as to be unusable. It is not the case that any stipulative definition is as "good" as any other, but the grounds for their comparison must clearly be other than truth or falsehood, for these terms simply do not apply. Stipulative definitions are arbitrary only in the sense specified. Whether they are clear or unclear, advantageous or disadvantageous, or the like, are factual questions.

2. ***Lexical Definitions.*** Where the purpose of a definition is to eliminate ambiguity or to increase the vocabulary of the person for whom it is constructed, then if the term being defined is not new but has an established usage, the definition is *lexical* rather than stipulative. A lexical definition does not give its definiendum a meaning which it hitherto lacked, but reports a meaning it already has. It is clear that a lexical definition may be either true or false. Thus the definition:

> The word "mountain" means a large mass of earth or rock rising to a considerable height above the surrounding country.

is true; it is a true report of how English-speaking people use the word "mountain" (that is, of what they mean by it). On the other hand, the definition:

> The word "mountain" means a plane figure enclosed by three straight lines.

is false, being a false report of how English-speaking people use the word "mountain." Here is the important difference between stipulative and lexical definitions. Since a stipulative definition's definiendum has no meaning apart from or prior to the definition introducing it, that definition cannot be false (or true). But because the definiendum of a lexical definition *does* have a prior and independent meaning, its definition is either true or false, depending upon whether that meaning is correctly or incorrectly reported. Although traditional discussions are not altogether clear on this point, it seems that what we are calling lexical definitions have sometimes been referred to as "real" definitions.

One point should be made clear, however, concerning the question of "existence." Whether a definition is stipulative or lexical has nothing to do with the question of whether the definiendum names any "real" or "existent" thing. The following definition:

> The word "unicorn" means an animal like a horse but having a single straight horn projecting from its forehead.

is a "real" or lexical definition, and a true one, because the definiendum is a word with long-established usage and means exactly what is meant by the definiens. Yet the definiendum does not name or denote any existent, since there are no unicorns.

A qualification must be made at this point, for in asserting that lexical definitions of the kind illustrated were true or false, we were oversimplifying a complex situation. The fact is that many words are used in different ways, not because they have a plurality of standard meanings, but through what we should call error. Not all instances of erroneous word usage are as funny as those of Sheridan's Mrs. Malaprop when she gives the order to "illiterate him . . . from your memory," or uses the phrase "as headstrong as an allegory on the banks of the Nile." Some words are used by many people in ways that might be called erroneous or mistaken, but which are better described as unorthodox. And any definition of a word which ignores the way in which it is used by any sizable group of speakers is not true to actual usage and is, therefore, not quite correct.

Word usage is a statistical matter, and any definition of a word whose usage is subject to this kind of variation must not be a simple statement of "the meaning" of the term, but a statistical description of the various meanings of the term, as determined by the uses it has in actual speech. The need for lexical statistics cannot be evaded by reference to "correct" usage, for that too is a matter of degree, being measured by the number of "first-rate" authors whose usages of a given term are in agreement. Moreover, literary and academic vocabularies tend to lag behind the growth of living language. Unorthodox usages have a way of becoming catholic, so definitions which report only the meanings countenanced by an academic aristocracy are likely to be very misleading. Of course, the notion of statistical definitions is utopian, but dictionaries approximate it more or less by indicating which meanings are "archaic" or "obsolete" and which are "colloquial" or "slang." With the foregoing as qualification, we may repeat that lexical definitions are true or false, in the sense of being true to actual usage or failing to be true to it.

3. ***Precising Definitions.*** Neither stipulative nor lexical definitions can serve to reduce the vagueness of a term. A vague term is one for which borderline cases may arise, such that it cannot be determined whether the term should be applied to them or not. Ordinary usage cannot be appealed to for a decision, because ordinary usage is not sufficiently clear on the matter—if it were, the term would not be vague. To reach a decision, then, ordinary usage must be transcended; a definition capable of helping to decide borderline cases must go beyond what is merely lexical. Such a definition may be called a *precising definition*.

A precising definition is different from a stipulative one, because its definiendum is not a new term but one with an established, although vague, usage. Consequently, the maker of a precising definition is not free to assign any meaning he chooses to the definiendum. He must remain true to established usage so far as it goes.

Yet he must go beyond that established usage if the vagueness of the definiendum is to be reduced. Exactly how he goes beyond, just how he fills the gaps or resolves the conflicts of established usage, is partly a matter of stipulation, but not completely so. A great many legal decisions involve precising definitions in which certain statutory terms are clarified so they will specifically cover or specifically exclude the case at issue. Jurists usually present arguments intended to justify their decisions in such cases, and this practice shows that they do not regard their precising definitions as mere stipulations even in those areas not covered by precedent or established usage. Instead they seek to be guided in part by the supposed intentions of the legislators who enacted the law, and in part by what the jurist conceives to be in the public interest. The terms "true" and "false" apply only in a partial fashion to precising definitions, their application signifying that the definition conforms or fails to conform to established usage so far as it goes. In evaluating the way in which a precising definition goes beyond established usage where the latter is unclear, truth and falsehood do not apply, and we must speak instead of its convenience or inconvenience, and (especially in a legal or quasilegal context) of its wisdom or folly.

4. *Theoretical Definitions.* It is in connection with theoretical definitions that most "disputing over definitions" occurs, where a theoretical definition of a term is one which attempts to formulate a theoretically adequate characterization of the objects to which it is applied. To propose a theoretical definition is tantamount to proposing the acceptance of a theory, and, as the name suggests, theories are notoriously debatable. Here one definition is replaced by another as our knowledge and theoretical understanding increase. At one time physicists defined "heat" to mean a subtle imponderable fluid, now they define it as a form of energy possessed by a body by virtue of the irregular motion of its molecules. Physicists have given different theoretical definitions of "heat" at different times because they accepted different theories of heat at those different times.

Those who have some acquaintance with the writings of Plato will recognize that the definitions he represented Socrates as continually seeking were neither stipulative, lexical, nor precising, but theoretical. Socrates was not interested in any merely statistical account of how people use the term "justice" (or "courage," or "temperance," or "virtue"); but at the same time he insisted that any proposed definition be consonant with actual usage. Nor was he interested in giving precising definitions of these terms, for borderline cases were not emphasized. To define such terms as "good" and "true" and "beautiful" is the aim of many philosophers. That they dispute over each other's proposed definitions indicates that they are not seeking merely stipulative definitions. Nor are they after merely lexical definitions, or recourse to dictionaries or public-opinion polls on word usage could settle the matter easily. That some philosophers can agree on the application of the term "good" in all circumstances, without being bothered by any borderline cases and still disagree over how the term "good" ought to be defined indicates that they are not seeking a precising definition of the term. Philosophers as well as scientists are most interested in the construction of theoretical definitions. Theoretical definitions are sometimes referred to as "analytical" definitions, although this latter term has another sense as well.

5. ***Persuasive Definitions.*** The last type of definition to be mentioned is that whose purpose is to influence attitudes. Such definitions are called *persuasive* definitions, and their function is expressive. Persuasive definitions do not seem to be a type coordinate with the other types already discussed, however. Since the same language can function both expressively and informatively, it is plausible to suppose that a definition of any one of the other types can also be a persuasive definition if it is phrased in emotive language and is intended to influence attitudes as well as to instruct.

Entertaining and illuminating examples of persuasive definitions were published in a Honolulu newspaper during the Hawaiian State Legislature's hearings on a proposal to abolish the state's law against abortion. Under the heading "Defining Abortion a Tricky Business" appeared the following story:

> Amidst the emotional debate on the abortion issue at the State Legislature, humor still lives.
>
> Anonymous legislative staffers this week drafted and circulated to legislators a proposed "general response to constituent letters on abortion." It goes like this:
>
> "Dear Sir:
>
> "You ask me how I stand on abortion. Let me answer forthrightly and without equivocation.
>
> "If by abortion you mean the murdering of defenseless human beings; the denial of rights to the youngest of our citizens; the promotion of promiscuity among our shiftless and valueless youth and the rejection of Life, Liberty and the Pursuit of Happiness—then, Sir, be assured that I shall never waver in my opposition, so help me God.
>
> "But, Sir, if by abortion you mean the granting of equal rights to all our citizens regardless of race, color or sex; the elimination of evil and vile institu-

tions preying upon desperate and hopeless women; a chance to all our youth to be wanted and loved; and, above all, that God-given right for all citizens to act in accordance with the dictates of their own conscience—then, Sir, let me promise you as a patriot and a humanist that I shall never be persuaded to forego my pursuit of these most basic human rights.

"Thank you for asking my position on this most crucial issue and let me again assure you of the steadfastness of my stand.

"Mahalo and Aloha Nui,"[3]

In Section I we discussed five purposes of definition, and in Section III we named five types of definition. The relations between purposes and types are fairly clear. Both stipulative and lexical definitions serve the purpose of increasing the vocabulary of the person for whom the definition is constructed. Lexical definitions can also serve the purpose of eliminating ambiguity, either to expose a fallacy of equivocation or to resolve a verbal dispute. A precising definition serves the purpose of reducing the vagueness of its definiendum. A theoretical definition serves the purpose of explaining something theoretically, that is, of formulating a theoretically adequate or scientifically useful characterization of whatever it is to which the definiendum is applied. Any of these definitions can also serve the rhetorical purpose of influencing attitudes, and when they do, they are to count as persuasive definitions also.

EXERCISE

Find two examples of each type of definition and discuss the purposes they are intended to serve.

4.4 Various Kinds of Meaning

Since a definition is an explanation of the *meaning* of a term, it is important for us to have clearly in mind the different senses of the word "meaning." This topic was discussed in Chapter 2 and we need not repeat what was said there. However, a certain further distinction must be drawn in connection with what was there called descriptive or literal meaning, especially in connection with *general terms* or *class terms* applicable to more than a single object. A general term such as "planet" is applicable in the same sense equally to Mercury, Venus, Earth, Mars, etc. In a perfectly acceptable sense, these various objects to which the term "planet" is applied are meant by the word; the collection of them constitutes its meaning. Thus if I assert that all planets have elliptical orbits, part of what I

[3] "Thanks and Love," *The Honolulu Advertiser,* February 14, 1970.

may intend to assert is that Mars has an elliptical orbit, and another part that Venus has an elliptical orbit, and so on. In one sense the meaning of a term consists of the class of objects to which the term may be applied. This sense of "meaning," its referential sense, has traditionally been called *extensional* or *denotative* meaning. A general or class term *denotes* the objects to which it may correctly be applied, and the collection or class of these objects constitutes the extension or denotation of the term.

However, the foregoing is not the only sense of the word "meaning." To understand a term is to know how to apply it correctly, but for this it is not necessary to know all of the objects to which it may be correctly applied. It is required only that we have a criterion for deciding of any given object whether it falls within the extension of that term or not. All objects in the extension of a given term have some common properties or characteristics which lead us to use the same term to denote them. We explain next, in a preliminary way, the terms "intension" and "connotation," whose alternative senses will be distinguished in the following paragraphs. The collection of properties shared by all and only those objects in a term's extension is called the *intension* or *connotation* of that term. General or class terms have both an *intensional* or *connotative* meaning and an extensional or denotative one. Thus, the intension or connotation of the term "skyscraper" consists of the properties common and peculiar to all buildings over a certain height; while the extension or denotation of that term is the class containing the Empire State Building, the Chrysler Building, the Wrigley Tower, and so on.

The word "connotation" has other uses, in which it refers to the total significance of a word, emotive as well as descriptive, and sometimes to its emotive meaning alone. Thus one may say of a person that he is "not a man." Here the word "man" is used expressively, to communicate a certain attitude or feeling. This expressive function is sometimes equated with, sometimes included in, the "connotation" of a term. But logicians use the word in a narrower sense. In our usage, connotation and intension are part of the informative significance of a term.

Even with this restriction, various senses of "connotation" have yet to be distinguished. There are three different senses of the term "connotation," which have been called the *subjective*, the *objective*, and the *conventional*. The subjective connotation of a word for a particular interpreter is the set of all the properties that he believes to be possessed by the objects comprising that word's extension. It is clear that the subjective connotation of a term may vary from one individual to another. I have met New Yorkers for whom the word "skyscraper" had a subjective connotation which included the property of being located in New York City. The notion of subjective connotation is inconvenient for purposes of definition because it varies not merely from individual to individual but even from time to time for the same individual, as he acquires new beliefs or abandons old ones. We are more interested in the public meanings of words than in their private interpretations; so, having mentioned subjective connotations, we shall eliminate them from further consideration.

The objective connotation or objective intension of a term is the total set of characteristics common to all the objects that make up that term's extension. It does not vary at all from interpreter to interpreter, for if all planets do have the property of moving in elliptical orbits, for example, this will be part of the objective connotation of the word "planet" whether any user of the term knows it or not. But the concept of objective connotation is inconvenient for reasons of its own. Even in those rare cases where the complete extension of a term is known, it would require omniscience to know all the characteristics shared by the objects in that extension. And since no one has that omniscience, the objective connotation of a term is not the public meaning in whose explanation we are interested.

Since we do communicate with each other and understand the terms we use, the intensional or connotative meanings involved are neither subjective nor objective in the senses explained above. Those who attach the same meaning to a term use the same criterion for deciding of any object whether it is part of the term's extension. Thus we have agreed to use *the property of being a closed plane curve, all points of which are equidistant from a point within called the center* as our criterion for deciding of any figure whether it is to be called a "circle" or not. This agreement establishes a convention, and so this meaning of a term is known as its conventional connotation or conventional intension. The conventional connotation of a term is its most important aspect for purposes of definition and communication, since it is both public and can be known by people who are not omniscient. For the sake of brevity we shall use the words "connotation" and "intension" to mean "conventional connotation" or "conventional intension" unless otherwise specified.

The extension or denotation of a term has been explained to be the collection of all those objects to which the term applies. There are no troublesome different senses of extension comparable to those found in the case of intension. However, the notion of extension is not without interest. For one thing, the extension of a term has been alleged to change from time to time in a way that the intension does not. The extension of the term "man" has been said to change almost continually as men die and babies are born. This varying extension does not belong to the term "man" conceived as denoting *all* men, the dead as well as the yet unborn, but rather to the term "living man." But the term "living man" has the sense of "man living now," in which the word "now" refers to the fleeting present. Thus the intension of the term "living man" is different at different times. Any term with a changing extension has a changing intension also. So, in spite of the apparent difference, one is as constant as the other; when the intension of a term is fixed, the extension is fixed also.

Worth mentioning in this connection is the fact that extension is determined by intension, but not the other way around. Thus, the term "equilateral triangle" has for its intension or connotation the property of being a plane figure enclosed by three straight line segments of equal length. It has as its extension the class of all those objects and only those objects which have this property. The term "equiangular triangle" has a different intension, connoting the property of being a plane figure enclosed by three straight line segments which intersect each other to form equal angles. But the extension of the term "equiangular triangle" is exactly the same as the extension of the term "equilateral triangle." Thus terms may have different intensions but the same extension, although terms with different extensions cannot possibly have the same intension.

Consider the following sequence of terms, each of whose intensions is included within the intension of the terms following it: "man," "living man," "living man over twenty years old," "living man over twenty years old having red hair." The intension of each of these terms (except the first, of course) is greater than the intensions of those preceding it in the sequence; the terms are arranged, we may say, in order of *increasing intension*. But if we turn to the extensions of those terms, we find the reverse to be the case. The extension of the term "man" is greater than that of "living man," and so on. In other words, the terms are arranged in order of *decreasing extension*. Consideration of such sequences has led some logicians to formulate a "law of inverse variation," asserting that if a series of terms is arranged in order of increasing intension, their extensions will be in decreasing order; or in other words, that extension and intension vary inversely with each other. This alleged law may have a certain suggestive value, but it cannot be accepted without modification. The fact is shown by the following sequence of terms: "living man," "living man with a spinal column," "living man with a spinal column less than one thousand years old," "living man with a spinal column less than one thousand years old who has not read all the books in the Library of Congress." Here the terms are clearly in order of increasing intension, but the extension of all them is the same, not decreasing at all. The law has been revised to accord with such cases as these, in its amended version asserting that if terms are arranged in order of increasing intension, their extensions will be in nonincreasing order; that is, if the extensions vary at all, they will vary inversely with the intensions.

Finally, we turn to those terms which, although perfectly meaningful, do not denote any things at all. We use such terms whenever we deny the existence of things of a certain kind. When we say that there are no unicorns, we assert that the term "unicorn" does not denote, that it has an "empty" extension or denotation. Such terms show that "meaning" pertains more to intension than to extension. For although the term "unicorn" has an empty extension, this is not to say that the term "unicorn" is meaningless. It does not denote any thing because there are no unicorns; but if the term "unicorn" were meaningless, so also would be the statement "There are no unicorns." But far from being meaningless, the statement is in fact true.

Our distinction between intension and extension, and the recognition that extensions may be empty can be used to resolve the ambiguity of some occurrences of the term "meaning." Thus we can refute the following fallacy of equivocation:

> The word "God" is not meaningless and therefore has a meaning. But by definition the word "God" means a supremely good and omnipotent being. Therefore, that supremely good and omnipotent being, God, must exist.

The equivocation here is on the words "meaning" and "meaningless." The word "God" is not meaningless, and so there is an intension or connotation which is its meaning in one sense. But it does not follow simply from the fact that a term has connotation that it denotes anything. The distinction between intension and extension is an old one, but it is still valuable and important.

EXERCISES

I. Arrange each of the following groups of terms in order of increasing intension:

★ 1. animal, feline, lynx, mammal, vertebrate, wildcat.

2. alcoholic beverage, beverage, champagne, fine white wine, white wine, wine.

3. athlete, ball player, baseball player, fielder, infielder, shortstop.

4. cheese, dairy product, limburger, milk derivative, soft cheese, strong soft cheese.

5. integer, number, positive integer, prime, rational number, real number.

II. Divide the following list of terms into five groups of five terms each, arranged in order of increasing intension:

aquatic animal, beast of burden, beverage, brandy, cognac, domestic animal, filly, fish, foal, game fish, horse, instrument, liquid, liquor, musical instrument, muskellunge, parallelogram, pike, polygon, quadrilateral, rectangle, square, Stradivarius, string instrument, violin.

4.5 Techniques for Defining

1. ***Denotative Definitions.*** We may divide techniques for defining into two groups, the first centering more on denotation or extension, the second on connotation or intension. The obvious and easy way to instruct someone about the denotation of a term is to give examples of objects denoted by it. This technique is often used and is often very effective. It has certain limitations, however, which ought to be recognized.

An obvious but trivial limitation of the method of definition by example is that it cannot be used to define words which have an empty extension, such as the words "unicorn" or "centaur." Having mentioned it, however, let us go on to more serious limitations.

It was observed in the preceding section that two terms with different meanings (intensions) may have identically the same extensions. If one such term is defined by giving even a complete enumeration of the objects denoted by it, this definition will fail to distinguish it from the other term which denotes the same objects, even though the two terms are not synonyms. This limitation of the method of definition by example is a consequence of the fact that although intension determines extension, extension does not determine intension.

The preceding is a very "academic" limitation, however, because very few terms can have their extensions completely enumerated. It is impossible to enumerate all of the infinitely many numbers denoted by the term "number," and it is practically impossible to enumerate the (probably) finite but literally astronomical number of objects denoted by the term "star." In cases like these we are restricted to giving a partial enumeration of objects denoted, which involves a more serious limitation. Any given object has many,

many properties and is therefore included in the extensions of many, many different terms. Hence any example mentioned in the denotative definition of any one term will be just as appropriately mentioned in the denotative definitions of many other terms. A particular individual, John Doe, can be mentioned as an example in defining either "man" or "animal" or "husband" or "mammal" or "father." Therefore mentioning him will not help to distinguish between the meanings of any of these terms. The same is true also for two examples, or three, or for any number which falls short of the total. Thus, three obvious examples to use in defining the term "skyscraper," the Chrysler, Empire State, and Woolworth buildings, serve equally well as examples of the denotation of the terms "building," "structures completed since 1911," "objects located in Manhattan," "expensive things," and so on. Yet each of these terms denotes objects not denoted by the others, so definition by partial enumeration cannot serve even to distinguish terms which have different extensions. Of course, "negative instances" may be brought in to help specify the definiendum's meaning, as in adding to the above definition of "skyscraper" that the term does *not* denote such things as the Taj Mahal or the Pentagon Building or Central Park or the Hope diamond. But since the enumeration of these negative instances must itself be incomplete, the basic limitation remains. Definition by enumeration of examples, whether complete or partial, may have psychological reasons to recommend it, but it is logically inadequate to specify completely the meanings of the terms being defined.

The foregoing remarks have been concerned with denotative definitions in which examples are named or enumerated one at a time. Perhaps a more efficient way to give examples is not to mention the individual members of the class which is the extension of the term being defined, but to mention instead whole groups of its members. Thus to define the word "metal" as meaning gold and iron and silver and tin and the like is different from defining "skyscraper" as meaning the Chrysler and Empire State and Woolworth buildings and the like. This special kind of definition by example—definition by subclasses—also permits of complete enumeration—as when "vertebrate" is defined to mean amphibians and birds and fishes and mammals and reptiles. In spite of the indicated difference, this second kind of denotative definition has in general the same advantages and limitations as those others that have already been discussed.

A special kind of definition by example is called *ostensive* or *demonstrative* definition. Instead of naming or describing the objects denoted by the term being defined, as in the ordinary sort of denotative definition, an ostensive definition refers to the examples by means of pointing or some other gesture. An example of an ostensive or demonstrative definition would be: the word "desk" means *this,* accompanied by a gesture such as pointing a finger or nodding one's head in the direction of a desk.

It is clear that ostensive definitions have all of the limitations mentioned in the preceding discussion. In addition, ostensive definitions have some limitations peculiar to themselves. Apart from the relatively trivial geographical limitation that one cannot ostensively define the word "skyscraper" in a village or the word "mountain" on the prairie, there is the essential ambiguity of gestures to consider. To point to a desk is also to point to a part of it, and to the color of the desk, the shape, the size, the material of the desk, and also, in fact, to everything that lies in the general direction of the desk, such as the wall behind it or the garden beyond. This ambiguity can be resolved only by adding some descriptive phrase to the definiens, which results in what may be called a quasi-ostensive definition, as, for example, "The word 'desk' means this *article of furniture*" (accompanied by an appropriate gesture).

This addition, however, defeats the purposes that ostensive definitions have been claimed to serve. Ostensive definitions have sometimes been alleged to be the "first" or "primary" definitions, in the sense that all other definitions must assume that some words (those used in the definiens) are already understood, and therefore cannot be used until those words have previously been defined. It has been suggested that this difficulty can be avoided by beginning with ostensive definitions. It is by means of ostensive definitions, some writers have claimed, that we learn to understand our first words. This claim is easily seen to be mistaken, for the meaning or significance of gestures themselves must be learned. If you point with your finger to the side of a baby's crib, the baby's attention, if attracted at all, is as likely to be directed toward your finger as in the direction pointed. And surely one is in the same difficulty concerning the definition of gestures by means of other gestures. To understand the definition of *any* sign, some signs must already be understood. This bears out our earlier remark that the primary way of learning to use language is by observation and imitation, rather than definition.

It should be acknowledged that these remarks about ostensive definitions are pertinent only for the particular interpretation placed on them here. Some writers on logic have understood the phrase "ostensive definition" to include the process of "frequently hearing the word when the object it denotes is present." But such a process would not be a definition at all, as we have been using the term in the present chapter. It would rather be the primary, predefinitional way of learning to use language.

EXERCISES

I. Define the following terms by example enumerating three for each term:

★1. actor	★5. element	8. harbor
2. boxer	6. flower	9. inventor
3. composer	7. General	10. poet
4. dramatist		

II. For each of the terms in Exercise I, can you find a nonsynonymous term that your examples serve equally well to illustrate?

2. ***Connotative Definitions.*** Before turning to the topic of connotative definition proper, some mention should be made of the frequently used technique of defining a single word by giving another single word which has the same meaning. Two words which have the same meaning are called "synonyms"; so a definition of this type is called a *synonymous* definition. Many dictionaries, especially smaller ones, use this method extensively. Thus a pocket dictionary may define "adage" as meaning proverb, "bashful" as meaning shy, and so on. Synonymous definitions are almost always used in textbooks and dictionaries designed to explain the meanings of foreign words, where we have foreign words correlated in parallel columns with their English synonyms, as:

annonce	advertisement
boîte	box
chat	cat
Dieu	God
élève	pupil

The preceding is a good method of defining terms, easy and efficient. Its applicability is limited, however, by the fact that many words have no exact synonyms. And it cannot be used in the construction of *precising* or *theoretical* definitions.

A new technique for defining has recently come into prominence in the researches and writings of scientists. Early in the present century, Einstein's theory of relativity challenged the notions of absolute space and absolute time, which had been defined in abstract terms by Newton. The success and widespread acceptance of relativity theory led to the abandonment of those abstractions. It was found more fruitful to define space and time by means of the operations used in measuring distances and durations. An *operational definition* of a term states that the term is applied to a given case if and only if the performance of specified operations in that case yields a specified result. For example, the different numerical values of such a quantity as length are operationally defined by reference to the results of specified measuring operations.

An operational definition of a term has a definiens which refers only to public and repeatable operations. Some social scientists have sought to incorporate this new technique of defining into their own disciplines. They attempted to replace abstract definitions of "mind" and "sensation" by operational definitions referring exclusively to physiology and behavior. In psychology, operational definitions have tended to be associated with behaviorism. Extreme empiricists have sometimes insisted that a term is meaningful only if it is susceptible of operational definition. To evaluate the claims and counterclaims made concerning operational definitions, however, is beyond the scope of this book.[4]

Where a synonymous definition is unavailable or an operational definition inappropriate, we can often use a definition by genus and difference. This method of definition is also called definition by division, analytical definition, definition *per genus et differentia,* or simply connotative definition. It is regarded by many writers as the most important kind of definition, and by some as the only "genuine" kind. There is scarcely any justification for the latter view, but there is a certain merit to the former, since it is more generally applicable than any other technique. The possibility of defining terms by genus and difference depends upon the fact that some properties are complex, in the sense of being analyzable into two or more other properties. This complexity and analyzability can best be explained in terms of classes.

Classes having members may have their memberships divided into subclasses. For example, the class of all triangles may be divided into three nonempty subclasses: scalene triangles, isosceles triangles, and equilateral triangles. The terms "genus" and "species" are often used in this connection: the class whose membership is divided into

[4] The term "operational definition" was first used by Nobel Prize winner P. W. Bridgman in his influential book *The Logic of Modern Physics,* published in 1927. An interesting discussion of his ideas can be found in "The Present State of Operationalism," Chapter II of *The Validation of Scientific Theories,* edited by Philipp G. Frank (Boston: The Beacon Press, 1956).

subclasses is the *genus,* the various subclasses are *species.* As used here, the words "genus" and "species" are *relative* terms, like "parent" and "offspring." Just as the same person may be a parent in relation to his children and an offspring in relation to his parents, so one and the same class may be a genus in relation to its own subclasses and a species in relation to some larger class of which it is a subclass. Thus the class of all triangles is a genus relative to the species *scalene triangle,* and a species relative to the genus *polygon.* The logician's use of the words "genus" and "species" as relative terms is different from the biologist's use of them as absolute terms, and the two should not be confused.

Since a class is a collection of entities having some common property, all the members of a given genus will have some property in common. Thus all members of the genus *polygon* share the property of being closed plane figures bounded by straight line segments. This genus may be divided into different species or subclasses such that all the members of one subclass have some further property in common which is not shared by any member of any of these other subclasses. The genus *polygon* is divided into *triangles, quadrilaterals, pentagons, hexagons,* and so on. These species of the genus *polygon* are different, and the *specific* difference between members of the subclass *triangle* and members of any other subclass is that only members of the subclass *triangle* have three sides. More generally, although all members of all species of a given genus have some property in common, the members of any one species share some further property which differentiates them from the members of any other. The characteristic that serves to distinguish them is called the *specific difference.* Thus having three sides is the specific difference between the species *triangle* and all other species of the genus *polygon.*

It is in this sense that the property of being a triangle may be said to be analyzable into the property of being a polygon and the property of having three sides. To someone who did not know the meaning of the word "triangle" or of any synonym of it, but who did know the meanings of the terms "polygon," "sides," and "three," the meaning of the word "triangle" could be explained by means of a *definition by genus and difference:*

The word "triangle" means polygon having three sides.

The ancient definition of the word "man" as meaning *rational animal* is another example of definition by genus and difference. Here the species *man* is subsumed under the genus *animal* and the difference between it and other species is said to be rationality.

One defines a term by genus and difference by naming a genus of which the species designated by the definiendum is a subclass, and then naming the difference which distinguishes it from other species of that genus. Of course, in the definition of "man" just mentioned, we could regard *rational* as the genus and *animal* as the difference, as well as the other way around. The order is not absolute from the point of view of logic, although there may be extralogical reasons for considering one as genus rather than the other.

Two limitations of this technique for defining terms may be mentioned quite briefly. In the first place, the method is applicable only to words which connote *complex* properties. If there are any simple, unanalyzable properties, then the words connoting them are not susceptible of definition by genus and difference. Examples that have been suggested of such properties are the sensed qualities of specific shades of color. Whether there really are any such properties or not is an open question, but if there are, they limit the applicability of definition by genus and difference. Another limitation has to do with words connoting *universal* properties, if they may be called that, such as the words "being," "entity," "existent," "object," or the like. These cannot be defined by the method of genus and difference because the class of all *entities,* for example, is not a species of some broader genus; entities themselves constitute the very highest genus, or *summum genus,* as it is called. The same remark applies to words for ultimate metaphysical categories, such as "substance" or "property." These limitations, although worth mentioning, are of but little practical importance in appraising this method of definition.

Connotative definitions, especially definitions by genus and difference, can serve any of the purposes discussed in Section 4.1 and can be of any of the types enumerated in Section 4.3.

EXERCISES

I. Give synonymous definitions for each of the following terms:

★ 1. Absurd
2. Buffoon
3. Cemetery
4. Dictator
★ 5. Egotism
6. Feast
7. Garret
8. Hasten
9. Infant
★ 10. Jeopardy
11. Kine
12. Labyrinth
13. Mendicant
14. Novice
★ 15. Omen
16. Panacea
17. Quack
18. Rostrum
19. Scoundrel
20. Tepee

II. Construct definitions for the following terms by matching the definiendum with an appropriate genus and difference:

Definiendum	Definiens (Genus)	Definiens (Difference)
★ 1. Bachelor	1. Offspring	1. Female
2. Banquet	2. Horse	2. Male
3. Boy	3. Man	3. Married
4. Brother	4. Meal	4. Unmarried
★ 5. Child	5. Parent	5. Very large
6. Foal	6. Sheep	6. Very small
7. Daughter	7. Sibling	7. Young
8. Ewe	8. Woman	
9. Father		
★ 10. Giant		
11. Girl		
12. Husband		
13. Lamb		
14. Mare		
★ 15. Midget		
16. Mother		
17. Pony		
18. Ram		
19. Sister		
★ 20. Snack		
21. Son		
22. Spinster		
23. Stallion		
24. Wife		

4.6 Rules for Definition by Genus and Difference

Certain rules have traditionally been laid down for definition by genus and difference. They do not constitute a recipe which will enable us to construct good connotative definitions without having to think, but they are valuable as criteria for evaluating definitions once they are proposed. There are five such rules, which are intended to apply primarily to lexical definitions.

RULE 1: *A definition should state the essential attributes of the species.*

As stated, this rule is somewhat cryptic, because in itself a species has just those attributes that it has, and none is more "essential" than any other. But if we understand the rule properly, as dealing with terms, it becomes clear. We distinguished earlier between the objective connotation of a term and its conventional connotation, the latter being those properties the possession or lack of which constitutes the conventional criterion by which we decide whether an object is denoted by the term or not. Thus it is part of the objective connotation of "circle" to enclose a greater area than any other plane closed figure of equal perimeter. But to define the word "circle" by this property would be to violate the spirit or the intention of our first rule, because it is not *the* property that people have agreed to mean by that word. The conventional connotation is the property of being a closed plane curve all points of which are equidistant from a given point called the center. To define it in these terms would be to state its "essence" and thus to conform to this first rule. In our present terminology, perhaps a better way to phrase the rule would be: "A definition should state the conventional connotation of the term being defined."

It should be kept in mind that the conventional connotation of a term need not be an intrinsic characteristic of the things denoted by it, but might well have to do with the origin of those things, the relations they have to other things, or the uses to which they are put. Thus the word "Stradivarius," which denotes a number of violins, need not connote any actual physical characteristic shared by all those violins and not possessed by any other, but rather has the conventional connotation of being a violin which was made in the Cremona workshop of Antonio Stradivari. Again, governors are not physically or mentally different from all other men, they simply are related differently to their fellows. Finally, the word "shoe" cannot be defined exclusively in terms of the shapes or materials of the things denoted by it; its definition must include reference to the use to which those things are put, as outer coverings for the foot.

RULE 2: *A definition must not be circular.*

It is obvious that if the definiendum itself appears in the definiens, the definition will explain the meaning of the term being defined only to those who already understand it. In other words, if a definition is circular, it will fail in its purpose, which is to explain the meaning of its definiendum. The rule must be understood, when applied to definition by genus and difference, not merely to rule out letting the definiendum appear in the definiens, but also to rule out using any synonym of it. The reason for this interpretation is that if a synonym is assumed to be understood, one might as well give a synonymous definition instead of using the more powerful but more complicated technique of definition by genus and difference.

RULE 3: *A definition must be neither too broad nor too narrow.*

This rule asserts that the definiens should not denote more things than are denoted by the definiendum, nor fewer things either. It is clear that this consideration does not apply when we are making a stipulative definition, for in such cases the definiendum has no meaning apart from its definition, and Rule 3 could not possibly be violated. Of course, if the first rule is obeyed, the third one must be also, for if the definiens really names the conventional connotation of the definiendum, they are bound to be equivalent in denotation.

The story is told that Plato's successors in the Academy at Athens spent much time and thought on the problem of defining the word "man." Finally they decided that it meant *featherless biped*. They were much pleased with the definition, until Diogenes plucked a chicken and threw it over the wall into the Academy. Here was a featherless biped, surely, but just as surely it was not a man. The definiens was too broad, for it denoted more than the definiendum. After additional thought, the Academics added the phrase "with broad nails" to their definiens. Rule 3 is a difficult one to follow.

A violation of this rule in the other direction would be committed by defining the word "shoe" as a leather covering for the human foot, for there are wooden shoes as well as leather ones. This definition of the word "shoe" is too narrow, since there are objects denoted by the definiendum that are not denoted by the definiens.

RULE 4: *A definition must not be expressed in ambiguous, obscure, or figurative language.*

Ambiguous terms should certainly be avoided in framing definitions, because if the definiens is itself ambiguous, the definition obviously fails to perform its function of explaining the definiendum. And since the purpose of definition is to clarify meaning, the use of obscure terms defeats this purpose. Of course, obscurity is a relative matter. Words that are obscure to children are reasonably clear to most adults, and terms that are obscure to laymen are perfectly familiar to specialists in some particular field. Consider the definition of the term "dynatron oscillator" as meaning a *circuit which employs a negative-resistance volt-ampere curve to produce an alternating current*.[5] To the layman this definition is terribly obscure. But it is perfectly intelligible to the students of electrical engineering for whom it was written. This definition is not obscure,

[5] W. G. Dow, *Fundamentals of Engineering Electronics* (New York: John Wiley & Sons, 1937), p. 331.

but justifiably technical. On the other hand, in nontechnical matters, to use obscure language is to attempt to explain the unknown by the still more unknown, a futile procedure. A good example of self-defeating obscurity is found in Herbert Spencer's definition of "evolution" as "An integration of matter and concomitant dissipation of motion, during which the matter passes from an indefinite, incoherent homogenity to a definite, coherent heterogeneity, and during which the retained motion undergoes a parallel transformation." Another example of obscurity in definition often cited is Dr. Samuel Johnson's celebrated second definition of the word "net" as meaning "anything made with interstitial vacuities."

A definition which uses figurative or metaphorical language may give some feeling for the use of the term being defined, but it cannot succeed in giving a clear explanation of what the definiendum means. Thus to define "bread" as *the staff of life* gives very little explanation of the meaning of that word. Often figurative definitions are humorous, as in the definition of "wedding ring" as a *matrimonial tourniquet designed to stop circulation,* or the definition of "discretion" as *something that comes to a person after he's too old for it to do him any good.* Sometimes persuasive definitions are highly figurative, as in the liberal's definition of "prejudice" as *being down on what you aren't up on.* But any definition which contains figurative language, however entertaining or persuasive, cannot serve as a serious explanation of the precise meaning of the term to be defined.

RULE 5: *A definition should not be negative where it can be affirmative.*

The reason for this rule is that a definition is supposed to explain what a term means, not what it does not mean. It is important because for the vast majority of terms there are far too many things that they do *not* mean for any negative definition possibly to cover. To define the word "couch" as meaning *not a bed and not a chair* is to fail miserably to explain the meaning of the word, for there are infinitely many other things that are not meant by the word "couch." On the other hand, there are many terms which are essentially negative in meaning and which require negative definitions. The word "orphan" means a child who does not have parents living, the word "bald" means the state of not having hair on one's head; and so on. Often the choice between an affirmative and a negative definition is simply a matter of the choice of words. There is not much basis for preferring to define the word "drunkard" as meaning one who drinks excessively rather than as one who is *not* temperate in drink. It should be emphasized that even where a negative definition is permissible, the definiens must not be wholly negative, as in the ridiculous definition of "couch" mentioned above, but must have an "affirmative" mention of the genus and a negative characterization of the species by rejecting all other species of the genus mentioned. It is only in exceptional cases that there are few enough species of the given genus for them to be conveniently mentioned and rejected in a negative definition. Since there are only three species of triangle, when that genus is divided according to the relative lengths of the sides, a perfectly adequate definition of "scalene triangle" is a triangle which is neither equilateral nor isoceles. But we cannot define the word "quadrilateral" as a polygon which is neither a triangle nor a pentagon nor a hexagon nor . . . because there are too many alternative species of the genus polygon to be excluded. In general, affirmative definitions are preferred to negative ones.

EXERCISES

I. Construct a definition by genus and difference for each of the terms in Exercise I on page 135.

II. Criticize the following in terms of the rules for definition by genus and difference:

★ 1. "Coed" means a young woman attending a college or high school.

2. "Square" means a plane figure consisting of two isosceles right triangles having a common hypotenuse.

3. "Architecture" means frozen music.

4. "Ornament" means something not necessary for practical use.

★ 5. "Fragrance" means any odor.

6. "Lie" means a locution deliberately antithetical to a verity apprehended by the intellect.

7. "Sleep" means a dormant state of the organism.

8. "Painting" means a picture drawn on canvas with a brush.

9. "Honesty" means the habitual absence of the intent to deceive.

★ 10. "Cause" means something that produces an effect.

11. "Satisfaction" means the state of not having any unfulfilled desires.

12. "Eating" means the successive performances of the functions of mastication, humectation, and deglutination.

13. "Antidote" means a remedy to counteract the effects of arsenic.

14. "Poison" means anything that has a toxic effect.

★ 15. A bore is a person who talks when you want him to listen.

—AMBROSE BIERCE

16. Art is a human activity having for its purpose the transmission to others of the highest and best feelings to which men have risen.

—COUNT LYOF TOLSTOI, *What Is Art?*

17. Murder is when a person of sound memory and discretion unlawfully killeth any reasonable creature in being, and under the king's peace, with malice aforethought, either express or implied.

—EDWARD COKE, *Institutes*

18. A cloud is a large semi-transparent mass with a fleecy texture suspended in the atmosphere whose shape is subject to continual and kaleidoscopic change.

—U. T. PLACE, "Is Consciousness a Brain Process?" *The British Journal of Psychology,* February 1956

19. Freedom of choice: The human capacity to choose freely between two or more genuine alternatives or possibilities, such choosing being always limited both by the past and by the circumstances of the immediate present.

—CORLISS LAMONT, *Freedom of Choice Affirmed*

20. The word *body,* in the most general acceptation, signifieth that which filleth, or occupieth some certain room, or imagined place; and dependeth not on the imagination, but is a real part of that we call the universe.

—THOMAS HOBBES, *Leviathan*

III. Discuss the following definitions:

★ 1. Faith is the substance of things hoped for, the evidence of things not seen.

Hebrews, 11:1

2. "Faith is when you believe something that you know ain't true."

—Definition attributed to a schoolboy by WILLIAM JAMES in "The Will to Believe"

3. Faith may be defined briefly as an illogical belief in the occurrence of the improbable.

—H. L. MENCKEN

4. Poetry is simply the most beautiful, impressive, and widely effective mode of saying things.

—MATTHEW ARNOLD

★ 5. Poetry is the record of the best and happiest moments of the happiest and best minds.

—PERCY BYSSHE SHELLEY, *The Defence of Poetry*

6. A cynic is a man who knows the price of everything and the value of nothing.

—OSCAR WILDE, *Lady Windermere's Fan*

7. Conscience is an inner voice that warns us somebody is looking.

—H. L. MENCKEN

8. A sentimentalist is a man who sees an absurd value in everything and doesn't know the market price of a single thing.

—OSCAR WILDE, *Lady Windermere's Fan*

9. "The true," to put it very briefly, is only the expedient in the way of our thinking, just as "the right" is only the expedient in the way of our behaving.

—WILLIAM JAMES, "Pragmatism's Conception of Truth"

★ 10. To be conceited is to tend to boast of one's own excellences, to pity or ridicule the deficiencies of others, to daydream about imaginary triumphs, to reminisce about actual triumphs, to weary quickly of conversations which reflect unfavorably upon oneself, to lavish one's society upon distinguished persons and to economize in association with the undistinguished.

—GILBERT RYLE, *The Concept of Mind*

11. Economics is the science which treats of the phenomena arising out of the economic activities of men in society.

—J. N. KEYNES, *Scope and Methods of Political Economy*

12. Justice is doing one's own business, and not being a busybody.

—PLATO, *Republic*

13. What, then, is the government? An intermediate body established between the subjects and the sovereign for their mutual correspondence, charged with the execution of the laws and with the maintenance of liberty both civil and political.

—JEAN JACQUES ROUSSEAU, *The Social Contract*

14. By good, I understand that which we certainly know is useful to us.

—BARUCH SPINOZA, *Ethics*

★ 15. Political power, then, I take to be a right of making laws with penalties of death, and consequently all less penalties, for the regulating and preserving of property, and of employing the force of the community in the execution of such laws, and in defense of the commonwealth from foreign injury, and all this only for the public good.

—JOHN LOCKE, *Essay Concerning Civil Government*

16. And what, then, is belief? It is the demi-cadence which closes a musical phrase in the symphony of our intellectual life.

—CHARLES SANDERS PEIRCE, *"How to Make Our Ideas Clear"*

17. Political power, properly so called, is merely the organized power of one class for oppressing another.

—KARL MARX and FRIEDRICH ENGELS, *The Communist Manifesto*

18. Grief for the calamity of another is *pity;* and ariseth from the imagination that the like calamity may befall himself.

—THOMAS HOBBES, *Leviathan*

19. We see that all men mean by justice that kind of state of character which makes people disposed to do what is just and makes them act justly and wish for what is just.

—ARISTOTLE, *Nichomachean Ethics*

20. Inquiry is the controlled or directed transformation of an indeterminate situation into one that is so determinate in its constituent distinctions and relations as to convert the elements of the original situation into a unified whole.

—JOHN DEWEY, *Logic: The Theory of Inquiry*

Part Two Deduction

Chapter 5
Categorical Propositions

Like Molière's M. Jourdain who found that he had long been speaking prose, I found that I had long been forming propositions. I said to myself, "Yes, I form propositions when my tongue does more than wag. I form them out of terms. I say something about *something. Therefore I ought to be able, in serious talk, to pin-point those two parts of my proposition. I ought to know exactly what I am talking about, and exactly what I am saying about it."*

—*A. A. Luce*

5.1 Categorical Propositions and Classes

The preceding chapters have dealt, for the most part, with the topic of language and its influence on argumentation. We turn now to that special kind of argument called deduction. A deductive argument is one whose premisses are claimed to provide conclusive grounds for the truth of its conclusion. Every deductive argument is either valid or invalid: valid if it is impossible for its premisses to be true without its conclusion being true also, invalid otherwise. The theory of deduction is intended to explain the relationship between premisses and conclusion of a valid argument and to provide techniques for the appraisal of deductive arguments, that is, for discriminating between valid and invalid deductions.

Informal fallacies were discussed at length in Chapter 3. But even where no informal fallacy is involved, a deductive argument may be invalid rather than valid; so further techniques for appraising such arguments must be devised. The classical or Aristotelian study of deduction centered on arguments involving propositions of a special kind, called categorical propositions. In the argument:

No athletes are vegetarians.
All football players are athletes.
———————————————
Therefore no football players are vegetarians.

both premisses and conclusion are *categorical* propositions. Propositions of this kind can be analyzed as assertions about classes, affirming or denying that one class is included in another, either in whole or in part. The premisses and conclusion of the preceding argument are assertions about the class of all athletes, the class of all vegetarians, and the class of all football players.

Classes were mentioned briefly in the preceding chapter, where a class was explained to be the collection of all objects which have some specified characteristic in common. There are various ways in which classes may be related to each other. If every member of one class is also a member of a second class, then the first class is said to be included or contained in the second. If some members of one class are members of another, then the first may be said to be partially contained in the second. Of course, there are pairs of classes having no members in common, such as the class of all triangles and the class of all circles. These various different relationships between classes are affirmed or denied by categorical propositions.

There are four different standard forms of categorical propositions, which are illustrated by the four following propositions:

1. All politicians are liars.
2. No politicians are liars.
3. Some politicians are liars.
4. Some politicians are not liars.

The first is a universal affirmative proposition. It is an assertion about two classes, the class of all politicians and the class of all liars, saying that the first class is included or contained in the second, which means that every member of the first class is also a member of the second class. In the present example, the subject term "politicians" designates the class of all politicians, and the predicate term "liars" designates the class of all liars. Any universal affirmative proposition may be written schematically as:

All *S* is *P*.

where the letter *S* and *P* represent the subject and predicate terms, respectively. The name "universal affirmative" is appropriate because the proposition affirms that the relationship of class inclusion holds between the two classes, and that the inclusion is complete or universal: all members of *S* are said to be members of *P* also.

The second example:

No politicians are liars.

is a universal negative proposition. It denies of politicians universally that they are liars. Making an assertion about two classes, it says that the first class is excluded from the second—wholly excluded—which is to say that there is no member of the first class which is also a member of the second. Any universal negative proposition may be written schematically as:

No *S* is *P*.

where, again, the letters *S* and *P* represent the subject and predicate terms. The name "universal negative" is appropriate because the proposition denies that the relation of class inclusion holds between the two classes, and denies it universally: no members at all of *S* are members of *P*.

The third example:

Some politicians are liars.

is a particular affirmative proposition. Clearly what the present example affirms is that some members of the class of all politicians are (also) members of the class of all liars. But it does not affirm this of politicians universally: not all politicians universally are said to be liars, but rather some particular politician or politicians. This proposition neither affirms nor denies that *all* politicians are liars; it makes no pronouncement on the matter. It does not literally assert that some politicians are *not* liars, although in some contexts it might be taken to suggest it. The literal, minimal interpretation of the present proposition is that the class of politicians and the class of liars have some member or members in common. For definiteness, we shall adopt that minimal interpretation here.

The word "some" is indefinite. Does it mean "at least one," or "at least two," or "at least a hundred"? Or how many? For the sake of definiteness, although this may depart from ordinary usage in some cases, it is customary to regard the word "some" as meaning "at least one." Thus a particular affirmative proposition, written schematically as:

Some *S* is *P*.

is interpreted as asserting that at least one member of the class designated by the subject term *S* is also a member of the class designated by the predicate term *P*. The name "particular affirmative" is appropriate because the proposition affirms that the relationship of class inclusion holds, but does not affirm it of the first class universally, but only partially, of some particular member or members of the first class.

The fourth example:

Some politicians are not liars.

is a particular negative proposition. This example, like the one preceding it, is particular in that it does not refer to politicians universally but only to some particular member or members of that class. But unlike the former, it does not affirm that the particular members of the first class referred to are included in the second class: this is precisely what is denied. A particular negative proposition, schematically written as:

Some *S* is not *P*.

asserts that at least one member of the class designated by the subject term *S* is excluded from the whole of the class designated by the predicate term *P*.

It was traditionally held that all deductive arguments were analyzable in terms of these four standard forms of categorical propositions, and a considerable amount of theory was built up around them. Not all standard-form categorical propositions are as simple and straightforward as the examples considered thus far. Although the subject and predicate terms of a standard-form categorical proposition designate classes, they may be quite complicated expressions instead of single words. For example, the proposition:

All candidates for the position are men of honor and integrity.

has as its subject and predicate terms, respectively, the phrases "candidates for the position" and "men of honor and integrity."

EXERCISES

Identify the subject and predicate terms, and name the form of each of the following propositions:

★ 1. Some historians are extremely gifted writers whose works read like first-rate novels.

2. No athletes who have ever accepted pay for participating in sports are amateurs.

3. No dogs which are without pedigrees are candidates for blue ribbons in official dog shows which are sponsored by the American Kennel Society.

4. All satellites which are presently in orbits less than ten thousand miles high are very delicate devices that cost many thousands of dollars to manufacture.

★ 5. Some members of families that are rich and famous are not men of either wealth or distinction.

6. Some paintings produced by artists who are universally recognized as masters are not works of genuine merit that either are or deserve to be preserved in museums and made available to the public.

7. All drivers of automobiles which are not safe are desperadoes who threaten the lives of their fellow men.

8. Some politicians who could not be elected to the most minor positions are appointed officials in our government today.

9. Some drugs which are very effective when they are properly administered are not safe remedies that all medicine cabinets should contain.

10. No men who have not themselves done creative work in the arts are responsible critics on whose judgment we can rely.

5.2 Quality, Quantity, and Distribution

Every standard-form categorical proposition is said to have both a *quality* and a "*quantity*." The quality of a proposition is *affirmative* or *negative* according to whether class inclusion (complete or partial) is affirmed or denied by the proposition. Thus both universal affirmative and particular affirmative propositions are affirmative in quality, while universal negative and particular negative propositions are both negative. It is customary to use the letters ***A, E, I,*** and ***O*** as names for the four standard forms of categorical propositions, universal affirmative, universal negative, particular affirmative, and particular negative, respectively. The letter names are presumed to come from the Latin words "***A***ff***I***rmo" and "n***E***g***O***," which mean "I affirm" and "I deny," respectively.

The quantity of a proposition is universal or particular according to whether the proposition refers to all members or only to some members of the class designated by its subject term. Thus the ***A*** and ***E*** propositions are universal in quantity, whereas the ***I*** and ***O*** propositions are particular in quantity. We observe that the names "universal affirmative," "universal negative," "particular affirmative," and "particular negative" uniquely describe each of the four standard forms by mentioning first its quantity and then its quality.

Every standard-form categorical proposition begins with one of the words "all," "no," or "some." These words indicate the quantity of the proposition, and are called the "quantifiers." The first two indicate that the proposition is universal, the third that it is particular. In addition to expressing the universal quantity, the quantifier "no" serves to indicate the negative quality of the ***E*** proposition.

Between the subject and predicate terms of every standard-form categorical proposition occurs some form of the verb "to be" (accompanied by the word "not" in the case of the ***O*** proposition). This serves to connect the subject and predicate terms, and is called the "copula." In the schematic formulations given in the preceding section, only "is" and "is not" appear, but depending upon how the proposition is worded otherwise, some other form of the verb "to be" may be more appropriate. For example, in the following three propositions:

Some Roman emperors were monsters.
All communists are fanatics.
Some soldiers will not be heroes.

the symbols "were," "are," and "will not be" serve as copulas. The general skeleton or schema of a standard-form categorical proposition consists of four parts: first the quantifier, then the subject term, next the copula, and finally the predicate term. This schema may be written as:

Quantifier (subject term) copula (predicate term).

On the class interpretation, the subject and predicate terms of a standard-form categorical proposition designate classes of objects, and the proposition is regarded as being about these classes. Propositions may refer to classes in different ways, of course. A proposition may refer to *all* members of a class, or it may refer to only *some* members of that class. Thus the proposition:

All congressmen are citizens.

refers to or is about *all* congressmen, but does not refer to all citizens. It asserts that each and every member of the class of congressmen is a citizen, but it makes no assertion about all citizens. It does not affirm that each and every citizen is a congressman, but it does not deny it either. Any ***A*** proposition, of this form:

All *S* is *P*.

is thus seen to refer to *all* members of the class designated by its subject term *S*, but does not refer to all members of the class designated by its predicate term *P*.

The technical term "distribution" is introduced to characterize the ways in which terms can occur in categorical propositions. A proposition *distributes* a term if it refers to all members of the class designated by the term. As we have seen, the subject term of an ***A*** proposition is *distributed in* (or *by*) that proposition, whereas its predicate term is *undistributed in* (or *by*) it. Let us examine the other standard-form categorical propositions to see which terms are distributed or undistributed in them.

An ***E*** proposition, such as:

No athletes are vegetarians.

asserts of each and every athlete that he (or she) is not a vegetarian. The whole of the class of athletes is said to be excluded from the class of vegetarians. All members of the class designated by its subject term are referred to by an ***E*** proposition, which is therefore said to distribute its subject term. On the other hand, in asserting that the whole class of athletes is excluded from the class of vegetarians, it is also asserted that the whole class of vegetarians is excluded from the class of athletes. The given proposition clearly asserts of each and every vegetarian that he (or she) is not an athlete. An ***E*** proposition, therefore, refers to all members of the class designated by its predicate term, and is said to distribute its predicate term also. ***E*** propositions distribute both their subject and predicate terms.

The situation is different with respect to ***I*** propositions. Thus:

Some soldiers are cowards.

makes no assertion about *all* soldiers and makes no assertion about all cowards either. It says nothing about each and every soldier, nor about each and every coward. Neither class is said to be either wholly included or wholly excluded from the other. Both subject and predicate terms are undistributed in any particular affirmative proposition.

The particular negative or ***O*** proposition is similar in that it too does not distribute its subject term. Thus the proposition:

Some horses are not thoroughbreds.

says nothing about *all* horses but refers to *some* members of the class designated by the subject term. It says of this part of the class of all horses that it is excluded from the class of all thoroughbreds, that is, from the *whole* of the latter class. Given the particular horses referred to, it says that each and every member of the class of thoroughbreds is *not* one of those particular horses. When something is said to be excluded from a class, the whole of the class is referred to: when a man is excluded from a country, all parts of that country are forbidden him. The particular negative proposition does distribute its predicate term, but not its subject term.

We may summarize these remarks on distribution as follows. Universal propositions, both affirmative and negative, distribute their subject terms, while particular propositions, whether affirmative or negative, do not distribute their subject terms. Thus the *quantity* of any standard-form categorical proposition determines whether its *subject* term is distributed or undistributed. Affirmative propositions, whether universal or particular, do not distribute their predicate terms; while negative propositions, both universal and particular, do distribute their predicate terms. Thus the *quality* of any standard-form categorical proposition determines whether its predicate term is distributed or undistributed.

The following diagram summarizes this information, and may be useful in helping the student to remember which propositions distribute which of their terms.

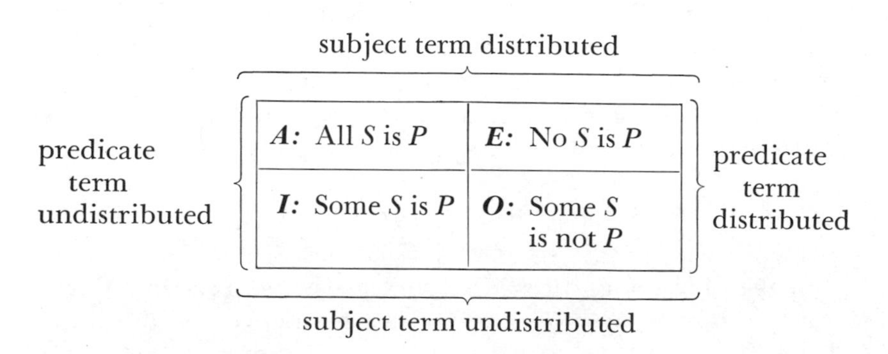

EXERCISES

Name the quality and quantity of each of the following propositions and state whether their subject and predicate terms are distributed or undistributed:

★ 1. Some presidential candidates will be sadly disappointed men.

2. All members of the Weatherman bombing squadron were sadly neglected and frustrated children.

3. Some recently identified unstable elements were not entirely accidental discoveries.

4. Some members of the military-industrial complex are mild-mannered men to whom violence is abhorrent.

★ 5. No leader of the Women's Liberation Movement is either a high government official or a major business executive.

6. All hard-line advocates of law and order at any cost will be men remembered, if at all, only for having failed to understand the major social pressures of the late twentieth century.

7. Some recent rulings of the Supreme Court were politically motivated decisions which flouted the entire history of American legal practice.

8. No harmful pesticides or chemical defoliants were genuine contributions to the long-range agricultural goals of the nation.

9. Some advocates of major political, social, and economic reforms are not responsible men and women who have a stake in maintaining the status quo.

10. All shiny new high-performance automobiles are major sources of pollution.

5.3 The Traditional Square of Opposition

Standard-form categorical propositions having the same subject and predicate terms may differ from each other in quality or in quantity or in both. This kind of differing was given the technical name "opposition" by older logicians, and certain important truth relations were correlated with the various kinds of opposition. Two propositions are *contradictories* if one is the denial of the other, that is, if they cannot both be true *and* they cannot both be false. It is clear that two standard-form categorical propositions having the same subject and predicate terms but differing from each other *both* in quantity and in quality are contradictories. Thus the ***A*** and ***O*** propositions:

All judges are lawyers.

and

Some judges are not lawyers.

which are opposed both in quantity and in quality, are obviously contradictories. Exactly one is true, and exactly one is false. Similarly, the ***E*** and ***I*** propositions:

No politicians are idealists.

and

Some politicians are idealists.

are opposed both in quantity and quality, and are contradictories. Schematically we may say that the contradictory of "All *S* is *P*" is "Some *S* is not *P*," and the contradictory of "No *S* is *P*" is "Some *S* is *P*"; ***A*** and ***O*** are contradictories, as are ***E*** and ***I***.

Two propositions are said to be *contraries* if they cannot both be true, though they might both be false. The traditional or Aristotelian account of categorical propositions held that universal propositions having the same subject and predicate terms but differing in quality were contraries.[1] Thus, it was urged, ***A*** and ***E*** propositions such as:

All poets are idlers.

and

No poets are idlers.

cannot both be true, although both might be false, and are therefore to be regarded as contraries.

Two propositions are said to be *subcontraries* if they cannot both be false, though they might both be true. The same traditional account held that particular propositions having the same subject and predicate terms but differing in quality were subcontraries. It was affirmed that ***I*** and ***O*** propositions such as:

[1] This traditional view will be examined critically in Section 5.5.

Some diamonds are precious stones.

and

Some diamonds are not precious stones.

could both be true, but could not both be false, and must therefore be regarded as subcontraries.

Thus far the examples of opposition between propositions have been such as to suggest disagreement. But "opposition" in the present context is a technical term and applies even where disagreement in the ordinary sense is not present. Thus where two propositions, again having the same subject and predicate terms, agree in quality and differ only in quantity, there is *opposition* even though there is no disagreement implied. In such cases the truth of the particular proposition was asserted to follow from or to be implied by the truth of the universal. Thus from the truth of an ***A*** proposition, such as:

All spiders are eight-legged animals.

the truth of the corresponding ***I*** proposition:

Some spiders are eight-legged animals.

was supposed to follow. And from the truth of an ***E*** proposition, such as:

No spiders are insects.

the truth of the corresponding ***O*** proposition:

Some spiders are not insects.

was supposed to follow. The opposition between a universal proposition and its corresponding particular (that is, the particular proposition having the same subject and predicate terms and the same quality as the universal) was named *subalternation*. In this situation the universal proposition is called the *superaltern*, or *subalternant*, and the particular is referred to either as the *subalternate* or simply as the *subaltern*. In subalternation, it was held, the *superaltern* implies the *subaltern*. The implication does not hold from subaltern to superaltern, for such subalterns as:

Some animals are cats.

and

Some animals are not cats.

are both true while their superalterns are clearly both false.

These various kinds of opposition were represented by a diagram called *The Square of Opposition,* which is reproduced as Figure 1.

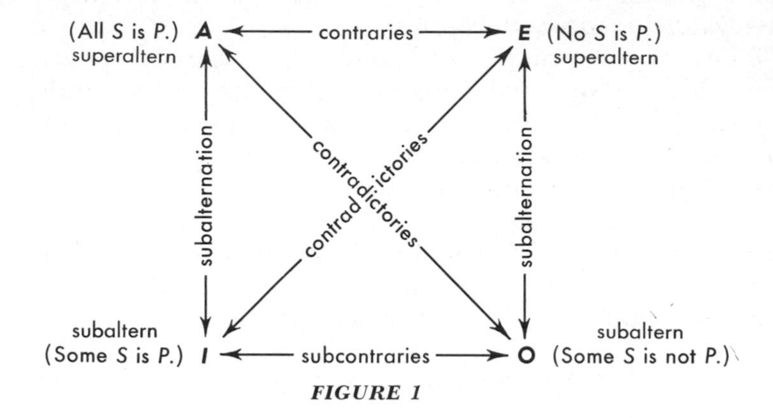

FIGURE 1

The relationships diagrammed by this Square of Opposition were believed to provide a logical basis for validating certain rather elementary forms of argument. In this connection it is customary to distinguish between *mediate* and *immediate* inference. Any inference is the drawing of a conclusion from one or more premisses. Where there is more than one premiss involved, as in a syllogism, which has two premisses, the inference is said to be mediate—presumably because the conclusion is supposed to be drawn from the first premiss through the *mediation* of the second. Where a conclusion is drawn from only one premiss, the inference is said to be *immediate.* The information embodied in the traditional Square of Opposition clearly provides a basis for a number of immediate inferences. Thus if an ***A*** proposition is taken as premiss, then according to the Square of Opposition one can validly infer that the corresponding ***O*** proposition (that is, the ***O*** proposition having the same subject and predicate terms as the ***A***) is false. And from the same premiss one can immediately infer that the corresponding ***I*** proposition is true. Of course, from the truth of an ***I*** proposition the truth of its corresponding ***A*** proposition does not follow, but the falsehood of the corresponding ***E*** proposition does. The traditional Square of Opposition provides the basis for a considerable number of such immediate inferences. Given the truth or falsehood of any one of the four standard-form categorical propositions, the truth or falsehood of some or all of the others can be inferred immediately. The immediate inferences based on the traditional Square of Opposition may be listed as follows:

A being given as true: ***E*** is false, ***I*** is true, ***O*** is false.
E being given as true: ***A*** is false, ***I*** is false, ***O*** is true.
I being given as true: ***E*** is false, while ***A*** and ***O*** are undetermined.
O being given as true. ***A*** is false, while ***E*** and ***I*** are undetermined.

A being given as false: ***O*** is true, while ***E*** and ***I*** are undetermined.
E being given as false: ***I*** is true, while ***A*** and ***O*** are undetermined.
I being given as false: ***A*** is false, ***E*** is true, ***O*** is true.
O being given as false: ***A*** is true, ***E*** is false, ***I*** is true.

EXERCISES

What can be inferred about the truth or falsehood of the remaining propositions in each of the following sets if we assume the first to be true? If we assume it to be false?

★ 1. a. All successful executives are intelligent men.
b. No successful executives are intelligent men.
c. Some successful executives are intelligent men.
d. Some successful executives are not intelligent men.

2. a. No animals with horns are carnivores.
b. Some animals with horns are carnivores.
c. Some animals with horns are not carnivores.
d. All animals with horns are carnivores.

3. a. Some uranium isotopes are highly unstable substances.
b. Some uranium isotopes are not highly unstable substances.
c. All uranium isotopes are highly unstable substances.
d. No uranium isotopes are highly unstable substances.

4. a. Some college professors are not entertaining lecturers.
b. All college professors are entertaining lecturers.
c. No college professors are entertaining lecturers.
d. Some college professors are entertaining lecturers.

5.4 Further Immediate Inferences

There are other kinds of immediate inference in addition to those associated with the traditional Square of Opposition. In this section we shall present three of these other types. The most obvious kind of immediate inference proceeds by simply interchanging the subject and predicate terms of a proposition. This is called *conversion* and is perfectly valid in the case of ***E*** and ***I*** propositions. Clearly, "No men are angels" is used to make the same assertion as "No angels are men," and either can be validly inferred from the other by the immediate inference called conversion. Just as clearly, "Some writers are women" and "Some women are writers" are logically equivalent, so that each can validly be inferred from the other by conversation. One standard-form categorical proposition is said to be the "converse" of another when it is formed by simply interchanging its subject and predicate terms. Thus "No idealists are politicians" is the converse of "No politicians are idealists," and each can validly be inferred from the other by conversion.

But the converse of an ***A*** proposition does not in general follow validly from that ***A*** proposition. Thus if our original proposition is "All dogs are animals," its converse "All animals are dogs" does not follow from the original proposition at all, the original being true while its converse is false. Traditional logic recognized this fact, of course, but asserted that something very much like conversion was valid for ***A*** propositions. This was called "conversion by limitation" (or *per accidens*). It proceeds by interchanging subject and predicate terms and changing the quantity of the proposition from universal to particular. Thus it was claimed that from the premiss "All dogs are animals" the conclusion "Some animals are dogs" could validly be inferred, the inference being a *conversion by limitation*. This type of conversion will be considered further in the next section.

Finally, it should be observed that in general an ***O*** proposition cannot validly be converted. For the true ***O*** proposition "Some animals are not dogs" would have as its converse the false proposition "Some dogs are not animals." We see, then, that an ***O*** proposition and its converse are not in general equivalent.

The term "convertend" is used to refer to the premiss of an immediate inference by conversion, and the conclusion is called the "converse." The following table was traditionally held to give a complete picture of valid conversions:

Conversions

Convertend	*Converse*
A: All *S* is *P*	***I:*** Some *P* is *S* (by limitation)
E: No *S* is *P*	***E:*** No *P* is *S*
I: Some *S* is *P*	***I:*** Some *P* is *S*
O: Some *S* is not *P*	(not, in general, equivalent)

The converse of a given proposition contains exactly the same terms as the given proposition (their order being reversed) and has the same quality.

The next type of immediate inference to be discussed is called obversion. Before explaining it, we shall find it helpful to return briefly to the notion of a "class" and to introduce some new ideas which enable us to discuss obversion more easily. A class is the collection of all objects having a certain common property which we refer to as the *class-defining characteristic*. Thus the class of all humans is the collection of all things which have the property of being human, and its class-defining characteristic is the property of being human. The class-defining characteristic need not be a "simple" property in any sense, for *any* property determines a class. Thus the complex property of being left-handed and red-headed and a student determines a class—the class of all left-handed red-headed students.

Every class has associated with it a *complementary class,* or *complement,* which is the collection of all things which do *not* belong to the original class. Thus the complement of the class of all men is the class of all things which are *not* men. The class-defining characteristic of the complementary class is the (negative) property of *not being a man*. The complement of the class of all men contains no men, but contains everything else: shoes and ships and sealing wax, and cabbages—but no kings, since kings are men. It is sometimes convenient to speak of the complement of the class of all men as "the class of all nonmen." The complement of the class designated by the term *S* is then designated by the term non-*S*, and we may speak of the term non-*S* as being the complement of the term *S*. We are using the word "complement" in two senses: one the sense of class complement, the other the sense of the complement of a term. The two senses, although different, are very closely connected. One term is the (term) complement of another just in case the first term designates the (class) complement of the class designated by the second term. It should be noted that just as a class is the (class) complement of its own complement, a term is the (term) complement of its own complement. A sort of "double negative" rule is involved here, so that we need not have strings of "non's" prefixed to a term. Thus we should write the complement of the term "voter" as "nonvoter," but we should write the complement of the latter term simply as "voter" rather than "nonnonvoter." One must be careful not to mistake contrary terms for complementary terms, as in identifying "cowards" and "nonheroes." The terms "coward" and "hero" are contraries in that no person can be both a coward and a hero, but not everyone—and certainly not everything

—need be either one or the other. Thus the complement of the term "winner" is not "loser," but "nonwinner," for although not everything—or even everyone—is either a winner or a loser, absolutely everything is either a winner or a nonwinner.

Now that we understand what is meant by the complement of a term, the process of obversion is easy to describe. In obversion, the subject term remains unchanged, and so does the quantity of the proposition being obverted. In obverting a proposition we change the quality of the proposition and replace the predicate term by its complement. Thus the ***A*** proposition:

All residents are voters.

has as its obverse the ***E*** proposition:

No residents are nonvoters.

These two propositions, it is clear, are logically equivalent, so either one can validly be inferred from the other. Obversion is a valid immediate inference when applied to *any* standard-form categorical proposition. Thus the ***E*** proposition:

No umpires are partisans.

has as its obverse the logically equivalent ***A*** proposition:

All umpires are nonpartisans.

Similarly, the obverse of the ***I*** proposition:

Some metals are conductors.

is the ***O*** proposition:

Some metals are not nonconductors.

And finally the ***O*** proposition:

Some nations were not belligerents.

has as its obverse the ***I*** proposition:

Some nations were nonbelligerents.

The term "obvertend" is used to refer to the premiss of an immediate inference by obversion, and the conclusion is called the "obverse." Every standard-form categorical proposition is logically equivalent to its obverse, so obversion is a valid form of immediate inference for any standard-form categorical proposition. To obtain the obverse of a proposition, we leave the quantity and the subject term unchanged, change the quality of the proposition, and replace the predicate term by its complement. The following table gives a complete picture of all valid obversions:

Obversions

Obvertend	*Obverse*
A: All *S* is *P*	***E:*** No *S* is non-*P*
E: No *S* is *P*	***A:*** All *S* is non-*P*
I: Some *S* is *P*	***O:*** Some *S* is not non-*P*
O: Some *S* is not *P*	***I:*** Some *S* is non-*P*

The third variety of immediate inference to be discussed introduces no new principles, for it can be reduced, in a sense, to the first two. To form the *contrapositive* of a given proposition we replace its subject term by the complement of its predicate term and replace its predicate term by the complement of its subject term. Thus the contrapositive of the ***A*** proposition:

All members are voters.

is the ***A*** proposition:

All nonvoters are nonmembers.

That these two are logically equivalent will be evident upon a moment's reflection, and from this it is clear that contraposition is a valid form of immediate inference when applied to ***A*** propositions.

It introduces nothing new, for we can get from any ***A*** proposition to its contrapositive by first obverting it, next applying conversion, and then obversion again. Thus, beginning with "All *S* is *P*" we obvert it to obtain "No *S* is non-*P*" which converts to "No non-*P* is *S*" whose obverse is "All non-*P* is non-*S*." Thus the contrapositive of any ***A*** proposition is the obverse of the converse of the obverse of that proposition.

Contraposition is most useful in working with ***A*** propositions, but it is a valid form of immediate inference when applied to ***O*** propositions also. Thus the contrapositive of the ***O*** proposition:

Some students are not idealists.

is the somewhat cumbersome ***O*** proposition:

Some nonidealists are not nonstudents.

which is logically equivalent to the first. Their logical equivalence can be shown by deriving the contrapositive a step at a time through obverting, converting, and then obverting again, as in the following schematic derivation: "Some *S* is not *P*" obverts to "Some *S* is non-*P*," which converts to "Some non-*P* is *S*," which obverts to "Some non-*P* is not non-*S*" (the contrapositive).

Contraposition is not, in general, valid for ***I*** propositions. This can be seen by noting that the true ***I*** proposition:

Some citizens are noncongressmen.

has as its contrapositive the false proposition:

Some congressmen are noncitizens.

The reason that contraposition is not generally valid when applied to ***I*** propositions can be seen when we attempt to derive the contrapositive of an ***I*** proposition by successively obverting, converting, and obverting. The obverse of the ***I*** proposition "Some *S* is *P*" is the ***O*** proposition "Some *S* is not non-*P*," whose converse does not in general follow from it.

The contrapositive of the ***E*** proposition "No *S* is *P*" is "No non-*P* is non-*S*," which does not in general follow validly from the original, as can be seen by observing that the ***E*** proposition:

No wrestlers are weaklings.

which is true, has as its contrapositive the false proposition:

No nonweaklings are nonwrestlers.

If we attempt to derive the contrapositive of an ***E*** proposition by successive obversion, conversion, and obversion, we find the reason for this invalidity. The obverse of the ***E*** proposition "No *S* is *P*" is the ***A*** proposition "All *S* is non-*P*," and in general it cannot validly be converted except *by limitation*. If we do convert it by limitation to obtain "Some non-*P* is *S*," then the latter can be obverted to obtain "Some non-*P* is not non-*S*," which we may call the contrapositive by limitation. This type of contraposition will be considered further in the next section.

Thus we see that contraposition is a valid form of immediate inference only when applied to ***A*** and ***O*** propositions. Contraposition is not valid at all for ***I*** propositions, and for ***E*** propositions only by limitation. This may also be presented in the form of a table:

Contraposition

Premiss	*Contrapositive*
A: All *S* is *P*	***A:*** All non-*P* is non-*S*
E: No *S* is *P*	***O:*** Some non-*P* is not non-*S* (by limitation)
I: Some *S* is *P*	(not, in general, equivalent)
O: Some *S* is not *P*	***O:*** Some non-*P* is not non-*S*

There are many other types of immediate inference which have been classified and given special names, but since they involve no new principles we shall not discuss them here.

EXERCISES

I. State the converses of the following propositions and indicate which of them are equivalent to the given propositions:

★ 1. No men who are considerate of other people are reckless drivers who pay no attention to traffic regulations.

2. All graduates of West Point are commissioned officers in the United States Army.

3. Some European cars are overpriced and underpowered automobiles.

4. No reptiles are warm-blooded animals.

5. Some professional wrestlers are elderly gentlemen who would be incapable of doing an honest day's work.

II. State the obverses of the following propositions:

★ 1. Some college athletes are professionals.

2. No organic compounds are metals.

3. Some clergymen are not abstainers.

4. No geniuses are conformists.

5. All objects suitable for boat anchors are objects weighing at least fifteen pounds.

III. State the contrapositives of the following propositions, and indicate which of them are equivalent to the given propositions:

★ 1. All journalists are pessimists.

2. Some soldiers are not officers.

3. All gentlemen are nondegenerates.

4. All things weighing less than fifty pounds are objects not more than four feet high.

5. Some noncitizens are not nonresidents.

IV. If "All socialists are pacifists" is true, what may be inferred about the truth or falsehood of the following propositions?

★ 1. Some nonpacifists are not nonsocialists.

2. No socialists are nonpacifists.

3. All nonsocialists are nonpacifists.

4. No nonpacifists are socialists.

★ 5. No nonsocialists are nonpacifists.

6. All nonpacifists are nonsocialists.

7. No pacifists are nonsocialists.

8. Some socialists are not pacifists.

9. All pacifists are socialists.

10. Some nonpacifists are socialists.

V. If "No scientists are philosophers" is true, what may be inferred about the truth or falsehood of the following propositions?

★ 1. No nonphilosophers are scientists.

2. Some nonphilosophers are not nonscientists.

3. All nonscientists are nonphilosophers.

4. No scientists are nonphilosophers.

★ 5. No nonscientists are nonphilosophers.

6. All philosophers are scientists.

7. Some nonphilosophers are scientists.

8. All nonphilosophers are nonscientists.

9. Some scientists are not philosophers.

10. No philosophers are nonscientists.

VI. If "Some saints were martyrs" is true, what may be inferred about the truth or falsehood of the following propositions?

★ 1. All saints were martyrs.

2. Some nonmartyrs were not nonsaints.

3. No nonsaints were martyrs.

4. Some nonmartyrs were saints.

★ 5. Some martyrs were not nonsaints.

6. No martyrs were nonsaints.

7. Some nonsaints were not nonmartyrs.

8. All martyrs were saints.

9. No saints were martyrs.

★ 10. All martyrs were nonsaints.

11. Some nonsaints were not martyrs.

12. No nonmartyrs were saints.

13. No saints were nonmartyrs.

14. Some nonmartyrs were nonsaints.

★ 15. No martyrs were saints.

16. Some nonsaints were nonmartyrs.

17. No nonmartyrs were nonsaints.

18. Some nonsaints were martyrs.

19. All nonmartyrs were saints.

★ 20. Some saints were not nonmartyrs.

21. Some martyrs were not saints.

22. No nonsaints were nonmartyrs.

23. Some martyrs were saints.

24. Some saints were nonmartyrs.

★ 25. All nonmartyrs were nonsaints.

26. All saints were nonmartyrs.

27. Some saints were not martyrs.

28. All nonsaints were nonmartyrs.

29. Some martyrs were nonsaints.

30. All nonsaints were martyrs.

31. Some nonmartyrs were not saints.

VII. If "Some merchants are not pirates" is true, what may be inferred about the truth or falsehood of the following propositions?

★ 1. Some nonpirates are not nonmerchants.

2. No nonmerchants are pirates.

3. No pirates are nonmerchants.

4. All merchants are nonpirates.

★ 5. All nonpirates are nonmerchants.

6. No merchants are pirates.

7. Some pirates are merchants.

8. No nonmerchants are nonpirates.

9. All nonpirates are merchants.

★ 10. All nonmerchants are pirates.

11. Some pirates are not nonmerchants.

12. No nonpirates are nonmerchants.

13. Some merchants are pirates.

14. Some pirates are not merchants.

★ 15. No nonpirates are merchants.

16. All pirates are nonmerchants.

17. Some merchants are not nonpirates.

18. Some nonpirates are nonmerchants.

19. Some merchants are nonpirates.

★ 20. Some nonpirates are merchants.

21. Some nonmerchants are not pirates.

22. Some nonmerchants are not nonpirates.
23. All nonmerchants are nonpirates.
24. Some nonmerchants are pirates.
★ 25. Some pirates are nonmerchants.
26. No merchants are nonpirates.
27. Some nonpirates are not merchants.
28. All merchants are pirates.
29. No pirates are merchants.
30. Some nonmerchants are nonpirates.
31. All pirates are merchants.

5.5 Existential Import

A proposition is said to have "existential import" if it asserts the existence of objects of some specified kind. For example, the proposition "There are books on my desk" has existential import, whereas the proposition *there are no unicorns* does not. It seems clear, especially in the light of our discussion of the word "some" in the first section of this chapter, that particular propositions have existential import. The ***I*** proposition "Some soldiers are heroes" asserts that there exists at least one soldier who is a hero. And the ***O*** proposition "Some soldiers are not heroes" asserts that there exists at least one soldier who is not a hero. Both particular propositions assert that the classes designated by their subject terms are not empty, that is, they do have members.

Apparent exceptions to this view are such statements as "Some ghosts appear in Shakespeare's plays" and "Some Greek gods are described in the *Iliad*." These statements are true despite the fact that there are neither ghosts nor Greek gods. But a little thought will reveal that these apparent exceptions are formulated in a misleading fashion. These statements do not really assert the existence of ghosts or of Greek gods; they assert only that certain *other* propositions are asserted or implied in Shakespeare's plays and in the *Iliad*. The propositions of Shakespeare and Homer may not be true, but it is certainly true that their writings contain or imply them. And it is only the latter that is asserted by the apparent exceptions. Outside these fairly uncommon literary or mythological contexts, ***I*** and ***O*** propositions do have existential import as explained in the preceding paragraph.

If we grant that ***I*** and ***O*** propositions have existential import, then it follows from the traditional Square of Opposition that ***A*** and ***E*** propositions have existential import also. For if ***I*** follows validly from the corresponding ***A*** by subalternation, and ***I*** asserts existence, then ***A*** must assert existence also. Similarly, ***E*** must have existential import if ***O*** does. (The existential import of ***A*** and ***E*** also follows from that of ***I*** and ***O*** if we grant the validity of conversion by limitation of ***A*** and of contraposition by limitation of ***E***.)

A difficulty arises at this point. If corresponding ***A*** and ***O*** propositions have existential import, then both could be false. If "All inhabitants of Mars are blond" and "Some inhabitants of Mars are not blond" both assert that there exist inhabitants of Mars, then they are both false if Mars is uninhabited. And if corresponding ***A*** and ***O*** propositions can both be false, then they are not contradictories. It would seem, then, that there is something wrong with the traditional Square of Opposition. It appears that if it is correct in what it says about superalterns ***A*** and ***E*** implying subalterns ***I*** and ***O***, then it is mistaken in holding corresponding ***A*** and ***O*** propositions to be contradictories. It seems also to be mistaken in holding ***I*** and ***O*** to be subcontraries.

One can defend or rehabilitate the traditional Square of Opposition, as well as conversion by limitation and contraposition by limitation, through introducing the notion of presupposition. We have already encountered this notion in discussing complex questions in Chapter 3. Some (complex) questions are properly answered "yes" or "no" only if it is presupposed that a definite answer has already been given to a prior question. Thus an answer "yes" or "no" can reasonably be given to the question "Did you spend the money you stole?" only if one grants the presupposition that you did steal some money. Similarly, the four standard-form categorical propositions may be said to presuppose that the classes to which they refer do have members. That is, questions of their truth or falsehood, and of the logical relations holding among them, are admissible only if it is presupposed that the existential question has already been answered in the affirmative. If we make the blanket presupposition that all classes designated by our terms (and their complements) do have members, then conversion and contraposition by limitation are valid, and all of the relationships set forth in the traditional Square of Opposition do hold: ***A*** and ***E*** are contraries, ***I*** and ***O*** are subcontraries, subalterns follow validly from their superalterns, and ***A*** and ***O*** are contradictories, as are ***E*** and ***I***.

The existential presupposition necessary and sufficient for the correctness of the traditional Aristotelian logic is in close accord with ordinary English usage in many cases. Suppose, for example, someone were to assert that "All the apples in the barrel are Jonathans," and we look in the barrel and find it empty. Ordinarily we should not take that to make the proposition true, nor to make it false. We would be more inclined to point out that there are no apples in the barrel, indicating that in this particular case the existential presupposition was mistaken.

There are, however, several objections to making this blanket existential presupposition. In the first place, although it preserves the traditional relations among categorical propositions, it does so at the cost of cutting down on their power to make assertions. The existential presupposition makes it impossible for any standard-form categorical proposition to deny the existence of members of the classes designated by its terms. In the second place, the existential presupposition is not in *complete* accord with ordinary usage. For example, the proposition "All trespassers will be prosecuted," far from presupposing that the class of trespassers has members, is ordinarily intended to insure that the class remain empty. And in the third place, we often wish to reason without making any presuppositions about existence. In physics, for instance, Newton's First Law of Motion asserts that every body not acted upon by external forces perseveres in its state of rest or of uniform motion in a straight line. Yet no physicist would want to presuppose that there actually are any bodies not acted upon by external forces.

On the basis of such objections as these, modern logicians decline to make this blanket existential presupposition, even though their decision forces them to give up some of the traditional Aristotelian logic. In contrast to the traditional or Aristotelian interpretation, the modern treatment of standard-form categorical propositions is called Boolean, after the English mathematician and logician George Boole (1815–1864), one of the founders of modern symbolic logic.

On the Boolean interpretation, ***I*** and ***O*** propositions have existential import, so where the class *S* is empty the propositions "Some *S* is *P*" and "Some *S* is not *P*" are both false. The universal propositions ***A*** and ***E*** are still taken to be the contradictories of the ***O*** and ***I*** propositions, respectively. Where *S* is an empty class, both particular propositions are false, and their contradictories "All *S* is *P*" and "No *S* is *P*" are both true. On the Boolean interpretation, universal propositions are understood as having no existential import. However, a universal proposition formulated in ordinary English which is intended to assert existence can be represented in Boolean terms. This is accomplished by using two propositions, the Boolean nonexistential universal and the corresponding existential particular.

We shall adopt the Boolean interpretation in all that follows. This means that ***A*** and ***E*** propositions can both be true and are therefore not contraries, and that ***I*** and ***O*** propositions can both be false and are therefore not subcontraries. Moreover, since ***A*** and ***E*** can be true while ***I*** and ***O*** are false, inferences based on subalternation are not in general valid. The diagonal (contradictory) relations are all that remain of the traditional Square of Opposition. Obversion remains valid when applied to any proposition, but conversion (and contraposition) by limitation are rejected as not generally valid. Conversion remains valid for ***E*** and ***I*** propositions, and contraposition remains valid for ***A*** and ***O*** propositions.

If it is not asserted explicitly that a class has members, it is a mistake to assume that it has. Any argument that turns on this mistake will be said to commit the Fallacy of Existential Assumption, or, more briefly, the Existential Fallacy.

EXERCISES

In the light of the preceding discussion of existential import, explain at which step (or steps) the following arguments commit the Existential Fallacy:

★ **I.** (1) No mathematician is one who has squared the circle;

therefore, (2) No one who has squared the circle is a mathematician;

therefore, (3) All who have squared the circle are nonmathematicians;

therefore, (4) Some nonmathematician is one who has squared the circle.

II. (1) No citizen is one who has succeeded in accomplishing the impossible;

therefore, (2) No one who has succeeded in accomplishing the impossible is a citizen;

therefore, (3) All who have succeeded in accomplishing the impossible are noncitizens;

therefore, (4) Some who have succeeded in accomplishing the impossible are noncitizens;

therefore, (5) Some noncitizen is one who has succeeded in accomplishing the impossible.

III. (1) No acrobat is one who can lift himself by his own bootstraps;

therefore, (2) No one who can lift himself by his own bootstraps is an acrobat;

therefore, (3) Some one who can lift himself by his own bootstraps is not an acrobat. (From which it follows that there is at least one being who can lift himself by his own bootstraps.)

IV. (1) It is true that: *No unicorns are animals found in the Bronx Zoo;*

therefore, (2) It is false that: *All unicorns are animals found in the Bronx Zoo;*

therefore, (3) It is true that: *Some unicorns are not animals found in the Bronx Zoo.* (From which it follows that there exists at least one unicorn.)

V. (1) It is false that: *Some mermaids are members of college sororities;*

therefore, (2) It is true that: *Some mermaids are not members of college sororities.* (From which it follows that there exists at least one mermaid.)

5.6 Symbolism and Diagrams for Categorical Propositions

Since the Boolean interpretation of categorical propositions depends heavily upon the notion of an empty class, it is convenient to have a special symbol to represent it. The zero symbol O is used for this purpose. To assert that the class designated by the term S has no members, we write an equals sign between S and O. Thus the equation $S = O$ asserts that there are no S's, or that S has no members.

To assert that the class designated by S does have members is to deny that S is empty. To assert that there are S's is to deny the proposition symbolized by $S = O$. We symbolize that denial by drawing a slanting line through the equality sign. Thus the inequality $S \neq O$ asserts that there are S's, by denying that S is empty.

Standard-form categorical propositions refer to two classes; so the equations which represent them are somewhat more complicated. Where each of two classes is already designated by a symbol, the class of all things which belong to both of them can be represented by juxtaposing the symbols for the two original classes. For example, if the letter *S* designates the class of all satires and the letter *P* designates the class of all poems, then the class of all things which are both satires and poems is represented by the symbol *SP*, which thus designates the class of all satiric poems (or poetic satires). The common part or common membership of two classes is called the product or intersection of the two classes. The product of two classes is the class of all things which belong to both of them. The product of the class of all Americans and the class of all composers is the class of all American composers. (One must be on guard against certain oddities of the English language here. For example, the product of the class of all Spaniards and the class of all dancers is not the class of all Spanish dancers, for a Spanish dancer is not a dancer who is Spanish, but any person who performs Spanish dances. Similarly, with abstract painters, English majors, and so on.)

This new notation permits us to symbolize ***E*** and ***I*** propositions as equations and inequalities. The ***E*** proposition "No *S* is *P*" asserts that no members of the class *S* are members of the class *P*, that is, there are no things which belong to both classes. This can be rephrased by saying that the product of the two classes is empty, which is symbolized by the equation $SP = O$. The ***I*** proposition "Some *S* is *P*" asserts that at least one member of *S* is also a member of *P*. This means that the product of the classes *S* and *P* is not empty, which is symbolized by the inequality $SP \neq O$.

To symbolize ***A*** and ***O*** propositions, it is convenient to introduce a new method of representing class complements. The complement of the class of all soldiers is the class of all things which are not soldiers, the class of all nonsoldiers. Where the letter *S* symbolizes the class of all soldiers, we symbolize the class of all nonsoldiers by $\bar{S}$ (read "*S* bar"), the symbol for the original class with a bar above it. The *A* proposition "All *S* is *P*" asserts that all members of the class *S* are also members of the class *P*, that is, that there are no members of the class *S* which are not members of *P*, or (by obversion) that "No *S* is non-*P*." This, like any other ***E*** proposition, asserts that the product of the classes designated by its subject and predicate terms is empty. It is symbolized by the equation $S\bar{P} = O$. The ***O*** proposition "Some *S* is not *P*" obverts to the logically equivalent ***I*** proposition "Some *S* is non-*P*," which is symbolized by the inequality $S\bar{P} \neq O$.

In their symbolic formulations, the interrelations among the four standard-form categorical propositions appear very clearly. It is obvious that the ***A*** and ***O*** propositions are contradictories when they are symbolized as $S\bar{P} = O$ and $S\bar{P} \neq O$, and it is equally obvious that the ***E*** and ***I*** propositions, $SP = O$ and $SP \neq O$ are contradictories. The Boolean Square of Opposition may be represented thus:

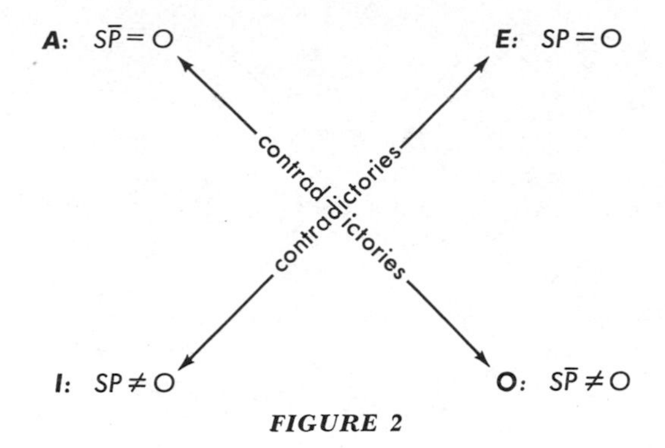

FIGURE 2

Propositions can be expressed diagrammatically by diagramming the classes to which they refer. We represent a class as a circle labeled with the term which designates that class. Thus the class *S* is diagrammed as in Figure 3.

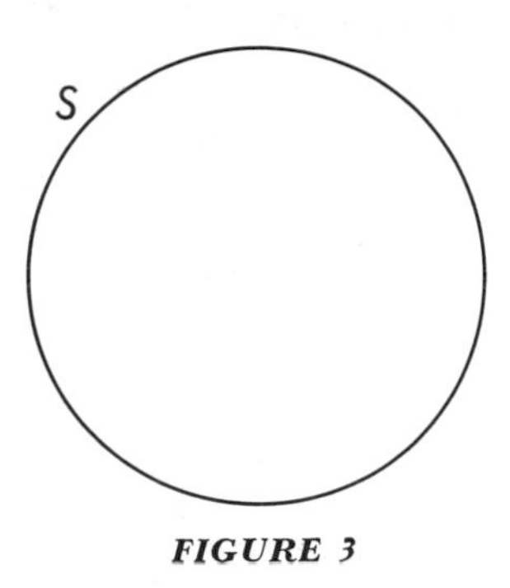

FIGURE 3

That diagram is of a class, not a proposition. It merely represents the class *S*, but makes no assertion about it. To diagram the proposition which asserts that *S* has no members, or that there are no *S*'s, we shade all of the interior of the circle representing *S*—indicating in this way that it contains nothing, but is empty. To diagram the proposition asserting that there are *S*'s, which we interpret as saying that there is at least one member of *S*, we place an *x* in the interior of the circle representing *S*—indicating in this way that there is something inside it, that it is not empty. Thus the two propositions "There are no *S*'s" and "There are *S*'s" are represented by the two diagrams in Figure 4 on page 176.

It should be noted in passing that the circle which diagrams the class *S* will also, in effect, diagram the class $\bar{S}$, for just as the interior of the circle represents all members of *S*, so the exterior of the circle represents all members of $\bar{S}$.

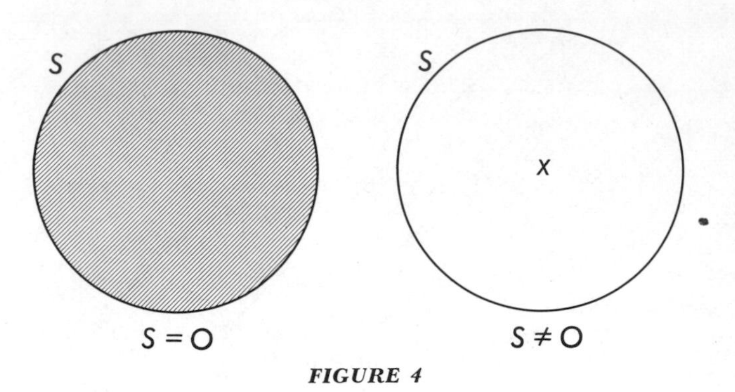

FIGURE 4

To diagram a standard-form categorical proposition, not one but two circles are required. The skeleton or framework for diagramming any standard-form proposition whose subject and predicate terms are abbreviated by *S* and *P* is constructed by drawing two intersecting circles, as in Figure 5.

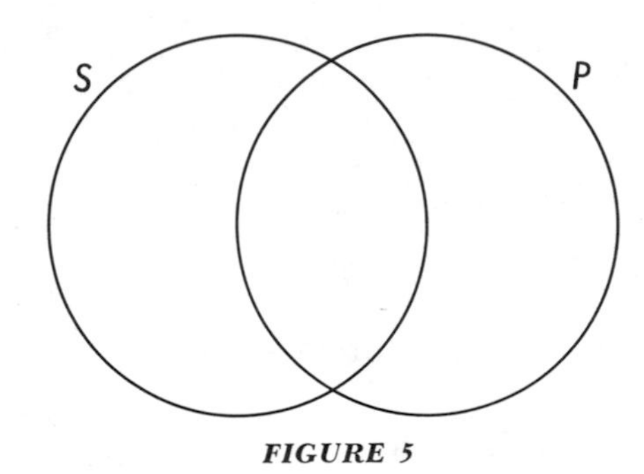

FIGURE 5

That figure diagrams the two classes *S* and *P*, but diagrams no proposition concerning them. It does not assert that either or both have members, nor does it deny that they have. As a matter of fact, there are more than two classes diagrammed by the two intersecting circles. The part of the circle labeled *S* which does not overlap the circle labeled *P* diagrams all *S*'s which are not *P*'s, and can be thought of as representing the product of the classes *S* and $\overline{P}$. We may label it $S\overline{P}$. The overlapping part of the two circles represents the product of the classes *S* and *P*, and diagrams all things belonging to both of them. It is labeled *SP*. The part of the circle labeled *P* which does not overlap the circle labeled *S* diagrams all *P*'s which are not *S*'s, and represents the product of the class $\overline{S}$ and *P*. It is labeled $\overline{S}P$.

Finally, that part of the diagram which is external to both circles represents all things which are not in *S* and not in *P* either; it diagrams the fourth class $\bar{S}\bar{P}$, so labeled. With these labels inserted, Figure 5 becomes Figure 6.

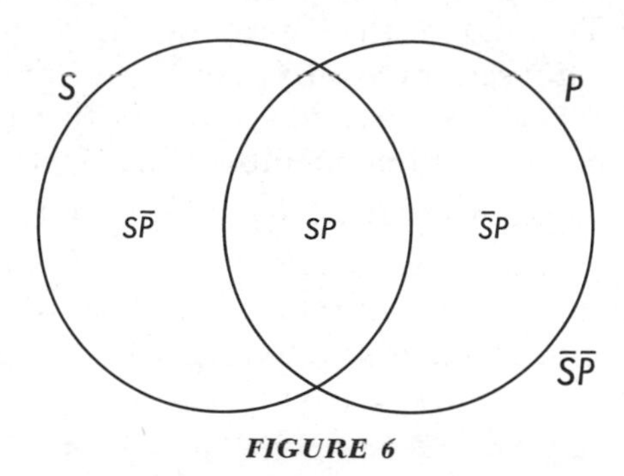

FIGURE 6

This diagram can be interpreted in terms of the various different classes determined by the class of all Spaniards (*S*) and the class of all painters (*P*). *SP* is the product of these two classes, containing all those things and only those things which belong to both of them. Every member of *SP* must be a member of both *S* and *P;* every member must be both a Spaniard and a painter. This product class *SP* is the class of all Spanish painters, which contains, among others, Velásquez and Goya. $S\bar{P}$ is the product of the first class and the complement of the second, containing all those things and only those things which belong to the class *S* but not to the class *P*. It is the class of all Spaniards who are not painters, all Spanish nonpainters, and it will contain neither Velásquez nor Goya, but it will include both the Novelist Cervantes and the dictator Franco, among many others. $\bar{S}P$ is the product of the second class and the complement of the first, and is the class of all painters who are not Spaniards. This class $\bar{S}P$ of all non-Spanish painters includes, among others, both the Dutch painter Rembrandt and the French painter Cézanne. Finally, $\bar{S}\bar{P}$ is the product of the complements of the two original classes. It contains all those things and only those things which are neither Spaniards nor painters. It is a very large class indeed, containing not merely English admirals and Swiss mountain climbers, but such things as the Mississippi River and Mount Everest. All of these classes are diagrammed in Figure 6, where the letters *S* and *P* are interpreted as in the present paragraph.

By shading or inserting *x*'s in various parts of this picture we can diagram any one of the four standard-form categorical propositions.

To diagram the ***A*** proposition "All S is P," symbolized as $S\bar{P} = O$, we simply shade out that part of the diagram which represents the class $S\bar{P}$, thus indicating that it has no members, or is empty. To diagram the ***E*** proposition "No S is P," symbolized as $SP = O$, we shade out that part of the diagram which represents the class SP, to indicate that it is empty. To diagram the ***I*** proposition "Some S is P," symbolized $SP \neq O$, we insert an x into that part of the diagram which represents the class SP. This insertion indicates that the class product is not empty but has at least one member. Finally, for the ***O*** proposition "Some S is not P," symbolized $S\bar{P} \neq O$, we insert an x into that part of the diagram which represents the class $S\bar{P}$, to indicate that it is not empty but has at least one member. Placed side by side, the diagrams for the four standard-form categorical propositions display their different meanings very clearly:

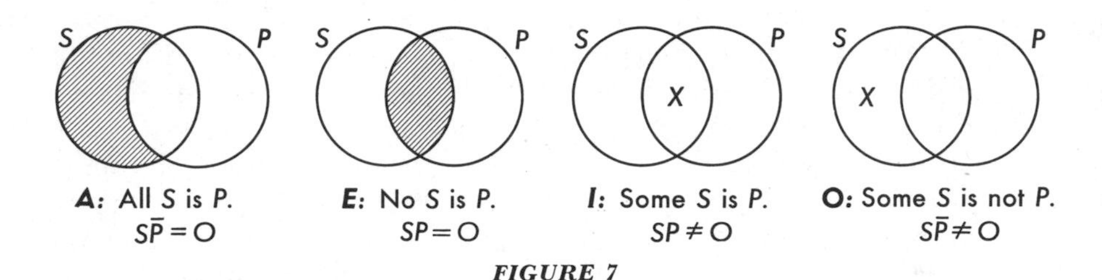

FIGURE 7

One aspect of these Venn Diagrams (named for the nineteenth-century English mathematician and logician John Venn, who first introduced them) must be emphasized. The bare two-circle diagram, labeled but not otherwise marked, represents classes but expresses no proposition. That a space is left blank signifies nothing—neither that there are nor that there are not members of the class represented by that space. Propositions are expressed only by those diagrams in which a part has been shaded out or in which an x has been inserted.

We have constructed diagrammatic representations for "No S is P" and "Some S is P," and since these are logically equivalent to their converses "No P is S" and "Some P is S," the diagrams for the latter have already been shown. To diagram the ***A*** proposition "All P is S," symbolized as $P\bar{S} = O$, within the same framework we must shade out that part of the diagram which represents the class $P\bar{S}$. It should be obvious that the class $P\bar{S}$ is the same as the class $\bar{S}P$, if not immediately, then by considering the fact that every object which belongs both to the class of all painters and the class of all non-

Spaniards must (also) belong to the class of all non-Spaniards and the class of all painters—all painting non-Spaniards are non-Spanish painters, and vice versa. And to diagram the **O** proposition "Some P is not S," symbolized by $P\bar{S} \neq O$, we insert an x into that part of the diagram which represents the class $P\bar{S}$ $(=\bar{S}P)$. The diagrams for these propositions then appear:

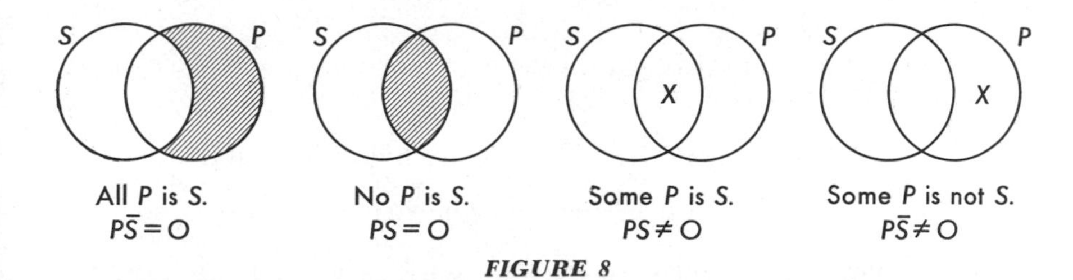

FIGURE 8

This further adequacy of the two circle diagrams is mentioned because in the following chapter it will be important to be able to use a given pair of overlapping circles with given labels, say, S and M, to diagram any standard-form categorical proposition containing S and M as its terms, regardless of the order in which they occur in it.

The Venn Diagrams constitute an *iconic* representation of the standard-form categorical propositions, in which spatial inclusions and exclusions correspond to the nonspatial inclusions and exclusions of classes. They not only provide an exceptionally clear method of notation, but also are the basis of the simplest and most direct method of testing the validity of categorical syllogisms, as will be explained in the following chapter.

EXERCISES

Express each of the following propositions as equations or inequalities, representing each class by the first letter of the English term designating it, and symbolize them by means of Venn Diagrams:

★ 1. Some sculptors are painters.

2. No peddlers are millionaires.

3. All merchants are speculators.

4. Some musicians are not pianists.

★ 5. No shopkeepers are members.

6. Some political leaders of high reputation are scoundrels.

7. All physicians licensed to practice in this state are medical college graduates who have passed special qualifying examinations.

8. Some stockbrokers who advise their customers about making investments are not partners in companies whose securities they recommend.

9. All puritans who reject all useless pleasure are strangers to much that makes life worth living.

★ 10. No modern paintings are photographic likenesses of their objects.

11. Some student activists are middle-aged men and women striving to recapture their lost youth.

12. All medieval scholars were pious monks living in monasteries.

13. Some state employees are not public-spirited citizens.

14. No magistrates subject to election and recall will be punitive tyrants.

★ 15. Some patients exhibiting all the symptoms of schizophrenia are manic-depressives.

16. Some passengers on the new large jet airplanes are not satisfied customers.

17. Some priests are militant advocates of radical social change.

18. Some stalwart defenders of the existing order are not members of political parties.

19. No pipelines laid across foreign territories are safe investments.

20. All pornographic films are menaces to civilization and decency.

Chapter 6

Categorical Syllogisms

I consider the invention of the form of syllogisms one of the most beautiful, and also one of the most important, made by the human mind.

—*Gottfried Leibniz*

6.1 Standard-Form Categorical Syllogisms

A *syllogism* is a deductive argument in which a conclusion is inferred from two premisses. A *categorical syllogism* is a deductive argument consisting of three categorical propositions which contain exactly three terms, each of which occurs in exactly two of the constituent propositions. A categorical syllogism is said to be in *standard form* when its premisses and conclusion are all standard-form categorical propositions and are arranged in a specified order. To specify that order it will be useful to explain the logician's special names for the terms and premisses of categorical syllogisms. For brevity, in this chapter we shall refer to categorical syllogisms simply as syllogisms, even though there are other kinds of syllogisms which will be discussed in later chapters.

The conclusion of a standard-form syllogism is a standard-form categorical proposition which contains two of the syllogism's three terms. The predicate term of the conclusion is called the *major* term of the syllogism, and the subject term of the conclusion is called the *minor* term of the syllogism. Thus in the standard-form syllogism:

No heroes are cowards.
Some soldiers are cowards.
Therefore some soldiers are not heroes.

the term "soldiers" is the *minor term* and the term "heroes" is the *major term*. The third term of the syllogism, which does not occur in the conclusion, appearing instead in both premisses, is called the middle term. In our example, the term "cowards" is the *middle term*.

The major and minor terms of a standard-form syllogism each occurs in a different one of the premisses. The premiss containing the major term is called the major premiss, and the premiss containing the minor term is called the minor premiss. In the syllogism stated above, the major premiss is "No heroes are cowards," and the minor premiss is "Some soldiers are cowards."

Now the other defining characteristic of a standard-form syllogism can be stated. It is that the major premiss is stated first, the minor premiss second, and the conclusion last. It should be emphasized that the major premiss is not defined in terms of its position, but as that premiss which contains the major term (which is by definition the predicate term of the conclusion). And the minor premiss is not defined in terms of its position, but is that premiss which contains the minor term (which is defined as the subject term of the conclusion).

The *mood* of a standard-form syllogism is determined by the forms and the order of the standard-form categorical propositions it contains. It is represented by three letters, the first of which names the form of the syllogism's major premiss, the second that of the minor premiss, and the third that of the conclusion. For example, in the case of the preceding syllogism, since its major premiss is an ***E*** proposition, its minor premiss an ***I*** proposition, and its conclusion an ***O*** proposition, the mood of the syllogism is ***EIO***.

But the mood of a standard-form syllogism does not completely characterize its form. Consider the two following syllogisms:

All great scientists are college graduates.
Some professional athletes are college graduates.
Therefore some professional athletes are great scientists.

and

All artists are egotists.
Some artists are paupers.
Therefore some paupers are egotists.

Both are of mood ***AII,*** but they are of different forms. We can bring out the difference in their forms most clearly by displaying their logical "skeletons," abbreviating the minor terms by S, the major terms by P, and the middle terms by M. The forms or "skeletons" of these two syllogisms are:

All P is M.	All M is P.
Some S is M.	Some M is S.
$\therefore$ Some S is P.	$\therefore$ Some S is P.

In the first the middle term is the predicate term of both premisses, while in the second the middle term is the subject term of both premisses. These examples show that although the form of a syllogism is partially described by stating its mood, syllogisms having the same mood may differ in their forms, depending upon the relative positions of their middle terms.

The form of a syllogism may be completely described, however, by stating its mood and *figure,* where the figure indicates the position of the middle term in the premisses. It is clear that there are four possible different figures that syllogisms may have. The middle term may be the subject term of the major premiss and the predicate terms of the minor premiss, or it may be the predicate term of both premisses, or it may be the subject term of both premisses, or it may be the predicate term of the major premiss and the subject term of the minor premiss. These different possible positions of the middle term constitute the First, Second, Third, and Fourth figures, respectively. They are schematized in the following array, where only the relative positions of the terms are shown, and reference to mood is suppressed by not representing either quantifiers or copulas.

$M - P$	$P - M$	$M - P$	$P - M$
$S - M$	$S - M$	$M - S$	$M - S$
$\therefore S - P$	$\therefore S - P$	$\therefore S - P$	$\therefore S - P$
First Figure	*Second Figure*	*Third Figure*	*Fourth Figure*

We give a complete description of the form of any standard-form syllogism by naming its mood and figure. Thus any syllogism of mood ***AOO*** in the Second Figure (named more briefly as ***AOO–2***) will have the form:

All P is M.
Some S is not M.
$\therefore$ Some S is not P.

Abstracting from the infinite variety of their possible subject matters, there are many different forms of standard-form syllogisms. Were the reader to list all possible different moods, beginning with ***AAA, AAE, AAI, AAO; AEA, AEE, AEI, AEO; AIA,*** . . . , and continuing through, by the time he reached ***OOO*** sixty-four different moods would have been enumerated. And since each mood can occur with each of the four different figures, there must be two hundred fifty-six distinct forms which standard-form syllogisms may assume. Only a few of them are valid, however.

EXERCISES

Rewrite each of the following syllogisms in standard form, and name its mood and figure:

★ 1. No nuclear-powered submarines are commercial vessels, so no warships are commercial vessels, since all nuclear-powered submarines are warships.

2. Some evergreens are objects of worship, because all fir trees are evergreens, and some objects of worship are fir trees.

3. All man-made satellites are important scientific achievements, therefore some important scientific achievements are not American inventions, inasmuch as some man-made satellites are not American inventions.

4. No television actors are certified public accountants, but all certified public accountants are men of good business sense; it follows that no television actors are men of good business sense.

★ 5. Some conservatives are not advocates of high tariff rates, because all advocates of high tariff rates are Republicans, and some Republicans are not conservatives.

6. All hi-fi sets are expensive and delicate mechanisms, but no expensive and delicate mechanisms are suitable toys for children, consequently no hi-fi sets are suitable toys for children.

7. All juvenile delinquents are maladjusted individuals, and some juvenile delinquents are products of broken homes, hence some maladjusted individuals are products of broken homes.

8. No stubborn individuals who never admit a mistake are good teachers, so, since some well-informed people are stubborn individuals who never admit a mistake, some good teachers are not well-informed people.

9. All proteins are organic compounds, whence all enzymes are proteins, as all enzymes are organic compounds.

10. No sports cars are vehicles intended to be driven at moderate speeds, but all automobiles designed for family use are vehicles intended to be driven at moderate speeds, from which it follows that no sports cars are automobiles designed for family use.

6.2 The Formal Nature of Syllogistic Argument

The form of a syllogism is, from the point of view of logic, its most important aspect. The validity or invalidity of a syllogism depends exclusively upon its form and is completely independent of its specific content or subject matter. Thus any syllogism of form ***AAA*–1**:

All M is P.
All S is M.
$\therefore$ All S is P.

is a valid argument, regardless of its subject matter. That is, no matter what terms are substituted in this form or skeleton for the letters S, P, and M, the resulting argument will be valid. If we substitute the terms "Athenians," "men," and "Greeks" for those letters, we obtain the valid argument:

All Greeks are men.
All Athenians are Greeks.
Therefore all Athenians are men.

And if we substitute the terms "soaps," "water-soluble substances," and "sodium salts" for the letters S, P, and M in the same form we obtain:

All sodium salts are water-soluble substances.
All soaps are sodium salts.
Therefore all soaps are water-soluble substances.

which is also valid.

A valid syllogism is a formally valid argument, valid by virtue of its form alone. This implies that if a given syllogism is valid, *any other syllogism of the same form will also be valid.* And if a syllogism is invalid, *any other syllogism of the same form will also be invalid.*[1]

[1] Here we assume that the constituent propositions are themselves neither logically true (for example, all easy chairs are chairs) nor logically false (for example, some easy chairs are not chairs). For if it contained either a logically false premiss or a logically

The common recognition of this fact is attested by the frequent use of "logical analogies" in argumentation. Suppose we were presented with the argument:

All communists are proponents of socialized medicine.
Some members of the administration are proponents of socialized medicine.
___
Therefore some members of the administration are communists.

and felt (justifiably) that regardless of the truth or falsehood of its constituent propositions, the argument was invalid. By far the best way of exposing its fallacious character would be to construct another argument having exactly the same form but whose invalidity was immediately apparent. We might seek to expose the given argument by replying, "You might as well argue that:

All rabbits are very fast runners.
Some horses are very fast runners.
___
Therefore some horses are rabbits.

And you cannot seriously defend this argument," we might continue, "because here there is no question about the facts. The premisses are known to be true and the conclusion is known to be false. Your argument is of the same pattern as this analogous one about horses and rabbits. It is invalid—so *your* argument is invalid." Here is an excellent method of arguing; the logical analogy is one of the most powerful weapons that can be used in debate.

Underlying the method of logical analogy is the fact that the validity or invalidity of such arguments as the categorical syllogism is a purely formal matter. Any fallacious argument can be proved invalid by finding a second argument which has exactly the same form and is known to be invalid by the fact that its premisses are known to be true while its conclusion is known to be false. (It should be remembered that an invalid argument may very well have a true conclusion—that an argument is invalid simply means that its conclusion is not logically implied or necessitated by its premisses.)

However, this method of testing the validity of arguments has

---

true conclusion, then the argument would be valid regardless of its syllogistic form—valid in that it would be logically impossible for its premisses to be true and its conclusion false. We also assume that the only logical relations among the terms of the syllogism are those asserted or implied by its premisses. The point of these restrictions is to limit our considerations in this chapter and the next to syllogistic arguments alone, and to exclude other kinds of arguments whose validity turns on more complex logical considerations not appropriately introduced at this place.

serious limitations. Sometimes a logical analogy is difficult to "think up" on the spur of the moment. And there are far too many invalid forms of argument for us to prepare and try to remember refuting analogies for each of them in advance. Moreover, although being able to think of a logical analogy with true premisses and false conclusion proves its form to be invalid, not being able to think of one does not prove the form valid, for it may only reflect the limitations of our thinking. There may be an invalidating analogy even though we are not able to think of it. A more effective method of establishing the formal validity or invalidity of syllogisms is required. It is to the explanation of effective methods of testing syllogisms that the remaining sections of this chapter are devoted.

EXERCISES

Refute any of the following arguments that are invalid by the method of constructing logical analogies:

★ 1. All business executives are active opponents of increased corporation taxes, for all active opponents of increased corporation taxes are members of the chamber of commerce, and all members of the chamber of commerce are business executives.

2. No medicines that can be purchased without a doctor's prescription are habit-forming drugs, so some narcotics are not habit-forming drugs, since some narcotics are medicines that can be purchased without a doctor's prescription.

3. No Republicans are Democrats, so some Democrats are wealthy men, since some wealthy men are not Republicans.

4. No college graduates are persons having an IQ of less than 70, but all persons having an IQ of less than 70 are morons, so no college graduates are morons.

★ 5. All fireproof buildings are structures that can be insured at special rates, so some structures that can be insured at special rates are not wooden houses, since no wooden houses are fireproof buildings.

6. All blue-chip securities are safe investments, so some stocks that pay a generous dividend are safe investments, since some blue chip securities are stocks that pay a generous dividend.

7. Some pediatricians are not specialists in surgery, so some general practitioners are not pediatricians, since some general practitioners are not specialists in surgery.

8. No intellectuals are successful salesmen, because no shy and retiring

men are successful salesmen, and some intellectuals are shy and retiring men.

9. All trade-union executives are labor leaders, so some labor leaders are conservatives in politics, since some conservatives in politics are trade-union executives.

10. All popular girls are good conversationalists, and all popular girls are graceful dancers, therefore some good conversationalists are graceful dancers.

6.3 Venn Diagram Technique for Testing Syllogisms

In the preceding chapter the use of two-circle Venn Diagrams for expressing standard-form categorical propositions was presented and explained. To test a syllogism by the method of Venn Diagrams it is necessary to represent both of its premisses in one diagram. Here we are required to draw *three* overlapping circles, for the two premisses of a standard-form syllogism contain three different terms, minor term, major term, and middle term, which we abbreviate as *S, P,* and *M,* respectively. We first draw two circles just as for the diagramming of a single proposition, and then draw a third circle beneath, overlapping both of the first two. We label the three circles *S, P,* and *M,* in that order. Just as one circle labeled *S* diagrammed both the class *S* and the class $\bar{S}$; and as two overlapping circles labeled *S* and *P* diagrammed four classes: SP, $S\bar{P}$, $\bar{S}P$, and $\bar{S}\bar{P}$; so three overlapping circles labeled *S, P,* and *M* diagram eight classes: $S\bar{P}\bar{M}$, $SP\bar{M}$, $\bar{S}P\bar{M}$, $S\bar{P}M$, SPM, $\bar{S}PM$, $\bar{S}\bar{P}M$, and $\bar{S}\bar{P}\bar{M}$. These are represented by the eight parts into which the three circles divide the plane:

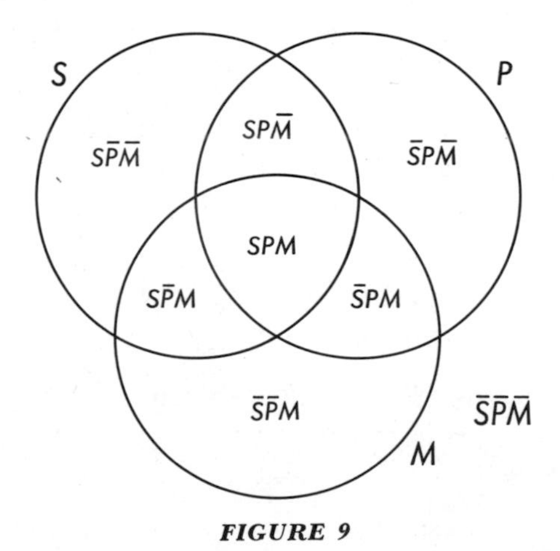

FIGURE 9

This can be interpreted in terms of the various different classes determined by the class of all Scots (S), the class of all peasants (P), and the class of all maidens (M). SPM is the product of these three classes, which is the class of all Scottish peasant maidens. $SP\bar{M}$ is the product of the first two and the complement of the third, which is the class of all Scottish peasants who are not maidens. $S\bar{P}M$ is the product of the first and third and the complement of the second: the class of all Scottish maidens who are not peasants. $S\bar{P}\bar{M}$ is the product of the first and the complement of the other two: the class of all Scots who are neither peasants nor maidens. $\bar{S}PM$ is the product of the second and third classes with the complement of the first: the class of all peasant maidens who are not Scottish. $\bar{S}P\bar{M}$ is the product of the second class with the complements of the other two: the class of all peasants who are neither Scots nor maidens. $\bar{S}\bar{P}M$ is the product of the third class and the complements of the first two: the class of all maidens who are neither Scottish nor peasants. Finally, $\bar{S}\bar{P}\bar{M}$ is the product of the complements of the three original classes: the class of all things which are neither Scots nor peasants nor maidens.

If we focus our attention on just the two circles labeled P and M, it is clear that by shading out or inserting an x we can diagram any standard-form categorical proposition whose two terms are P and M, regardless of which is the subject term and which the predicate. Thus to diagram the proposition "All M is P" ($M\bar{P} = O$) we shade out all of M that is not contained in (or overlapped by) P. This area, it is seen, includes both the portion labeled $S\bar{P}M$ and $\bar{S}\bar{P}M$. The diagram then becomes Figure 10.

And if we focus our attention on just the two circles S and M, by

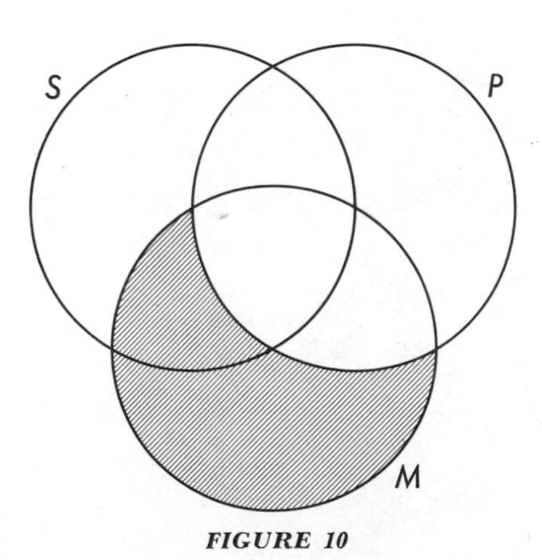

FIGURE 10

shading out or inserting an x we can diagram any standard-form categorical proposition whose two terms are S and M, regardless of the order in which they appear in it. To diagram the proposition "All S is M" ($S\overline{M} = O$) we shade out all of S that is not contained in (or overlapped by) M. This area, it is seen, includes both the portion labeled $S\overline{P}\overline{M}$ and $SP\overline{M}$. The diagram for this proposition will appear as:

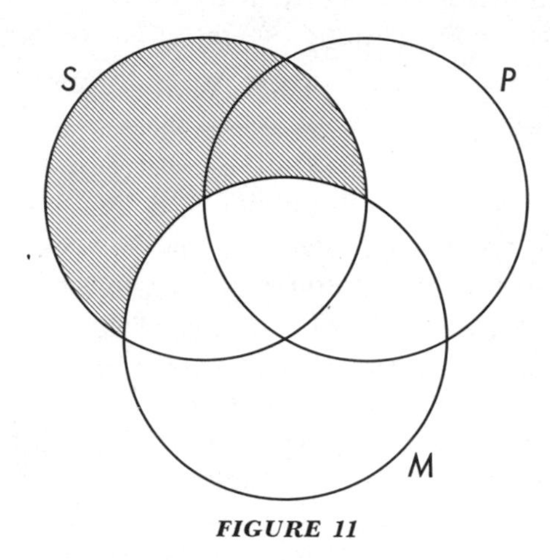

FIGURE 11

Now the advantage of having three circles overlapping is that it allows us to diagram two propositions together—on condition, of course, that only three different terms occur in them. Thus diagramming both "All M is P" and "All S is M" at the same time gives us:

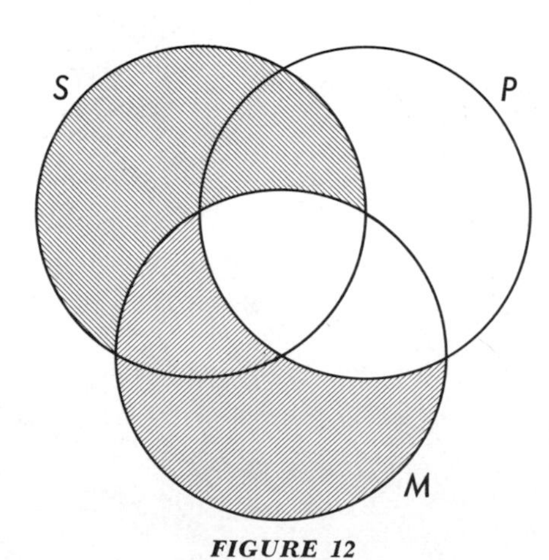

FIGURE 12

This is the diagram for both premisses of the syllogism ***AAA*–1**:

All *M* is *P*.
All *S* is *M*.
∴ All *S* is *P*.

Now the syllogism is valid if and only if the two premisses imply or entail the conclusion—that is, if together they assert what is asserted by the conclusion. Consequently, diagramming the premisses of a valid argument should suffice to diagram what its conclusion asserts also, with no further marking of the circles needed. To diagram the conclusion "All *S* is *P*" is to shade out both the portion labeled $S\bar{P}\bar{M}$ and the portion labeled $S\bar{P}M$. Inspecting the diagram which represents the two premisses, we see that it does diagram the conclusion also. And from this fact we can conclude that ***AAA*–1** is a valid syllogism.

Let us now apply the Venn Diagram test to an obviously invalid syllogism:

All dogs are mammals.
All cats are mammals.
Therefore all cats are dogs.

Diagramming both premisses gives us:

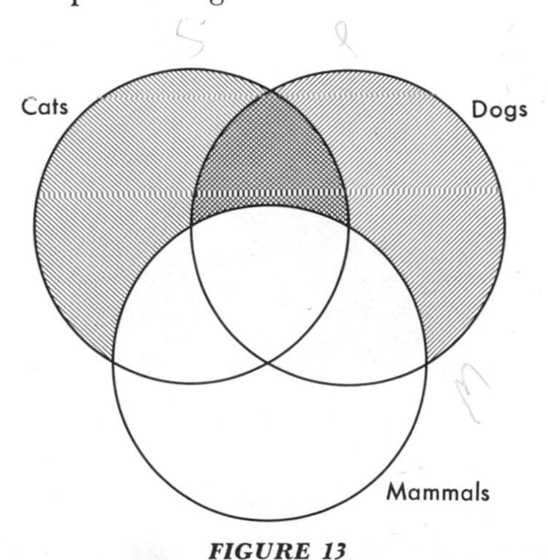

FIGURE 13

In this diagram, where *S* designates the class of all cats, *P* the class of all dogs, and *M* the class of all mammals, the portion $S\bar{P}\bar{M}$, $SP\bar{M}$, and $\bar{S}P\bar{M}$ have been shaded out. But the conclusion has not been diagrammed, because the part $S\bar{P}M$ has been left unshaded, and to diagram the conclusion *both* $S\bar{P}\bar{M}$ and $S\bar{P}M$ must be shaded out. Thus we see that diagramming the premisses of a syllogism of form ***AAA–2*** does *not* suffice to diagram its conclusion, which proves that the conclusion asserts more than is asserted by the premisses, which shows that the premisses do not imply the conclusion. But an argument whose premisses do not imply its conclusion is invalid, and so our diagram proves the given syllogism to be invalid. (It proves, in fact, that *any* syllogism of the form ***AAA–2*** is invalid.)

When we use a Venn Diagram to test a syllogism with one universal premiss and one particular premiss, it is advisable to diagram the universal premiss first. Thus in testing the ***AII–3*** syllogism:

All artists are egotists.
Some artists are paupers.
Therefore some paupers are egotists.

we should diagram the universal premiss "All artists are egotists" before inserting an *x* to diagram the particular premiss "Some artists are paupers." Properly diagrammed, the premisses appear as:

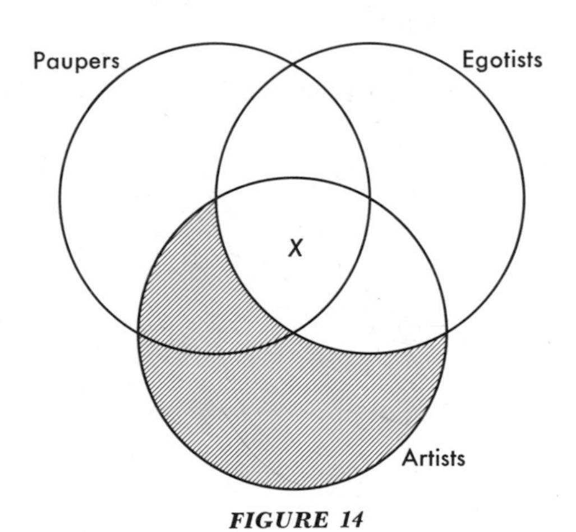

FIGURE 14

Had we tried to diagram the particular premiss first, before the region $S\bar{P}M$ was shaded out along with $\bar{S}\bar{P}M$ in diagramming the universal premiss, we should not have known whether to insert an *x* in *SPM* or in $S\bar{P}M$ or in both. And had we put it in $S\bar{P}M$ or on the line separating it from *SPM*, the subsequent shading of $S\bar{P}M$ would have obscured the information the diagram was intended to contain. Now that the information contained in the premisses has been inserted into the diagram, we examine it to see whether the conclusion has already been diagrammed. For the conclusion "Some paupers are egotists" to be diagrammed, an *x* must appear in the overlapping part of the circles labeled "paupers" and "egotists." This overlapping part consists of both of the regions $SP\overline{M}$ and SPM, which together constitute SP. There is an *x* in the region SPM, so there *is* an *x* in the overlapping part SP. What is asserted by the conclusion of the syllogism is diagrammed by the diagramming of its premisses; therefore the syllogism is valid.

Let us consider still another example, the discussion of which will bring out a further important point about the use of Venn Diagrams. In testing the argument:

> All great scientists are college graduates.
> Some professional athletes are college graduates.
> ―――――――――――――――――――――――――――――
> Therefore some professional athletes are great scientists.

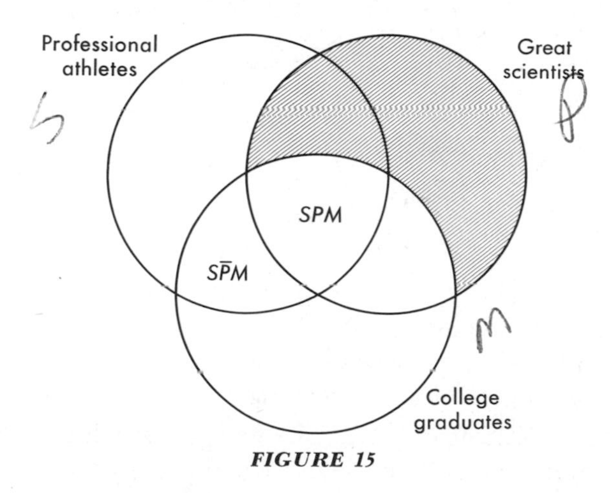

FIGURE 15

after diagramming the universal premiss first by shading out both regions $SP\overline{M}$ and $\overline{S}P\overline{M}$, we may still be puzzled about where to put the *x* required to diagram the particular premiss. That premiss is "Some professional athletes are college graduates," so an *x* must be inserted in the overlapping part of the two circles labeled "professional athletes" and "college graduates." That overlapping part, however, contains two regions: SPM and $S\overline{P}M$. In which of these should the *x* be placed? The premisses do not tell us, and if we made an arbitrary decision to place it in one rather than the other, we should be inserting more information into the diagram than the premisses warrant—which would spoil the diagram's use as a test for validity. Placing an *x* in each of them would also go beyond what the premisses assert. By placing the *x* on the line which divides the overlapping region *SM* into the two parts *SPM* and $S\bar{P}M$ we can diagram exactly what the second premiss asserts without adding anything to it. Placing an *x* on the line between two regions indicates that there is something which belongs in one of them, but does not indicate which one. The completed diagram of both premisses should be:

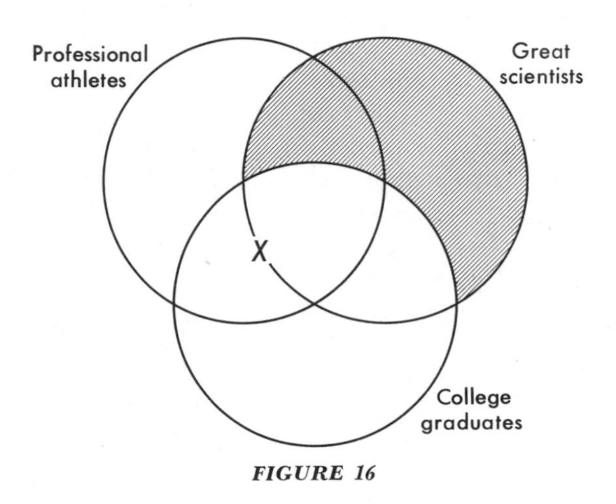

FIGURE 16

Inspecting the diagram to see whether the conclusion of the syllogism appears in it, we find that it does not. For the conclusion "Some professional athletes are great scientists" to be diagrammed, an *x* would have to occur in the overlapping part of the two upper circles, either in $SP\bar{M}$ or in *SPM*. The first of these is shaded out and certainly contains no *x*. The diagram does not show an *x* in *SPM* either. True, there must be a member of either *SPM* or $S\bar{P}M$, but the diagram does not tell us that it is in the former rather than the latter, and so for all the premisses tell us, the conclusion may be false. We do not know that the conclusion *is* false, but only that it is not asserted or implied by the premisses. The latter is enough, however, to let us know that the argument is invalid. The diagram suffices to show not merely that the given syllogism is invalid, but that all syllogisms of the form ***AII–2*** are invalid.

The general technique of using Venn Diagrams to test the validity of any standard-form syllogism may be summarily described as follows. First, label the circles of a three-circle Venn Diagram with the syllogism's three terms. Next, diagram both premisses, diagramming the universal one first if there is one universal and one particular, being careful in diagramming a particular proposition to put the *x* on a line if the premisses do not determine on which side of the line it should go. Finally, inspect the diagram to see whether or not the diagram of the premisses contains the diagram of the conclusion: if it does, the syllogism is valid, if it does not, the syllogism is invalid.

What is the theoretical basis for using Venn Diagrams to distinguish valid from invalid syllogism? The answer to this question divides into two parts. The first has to do with the formal nature of syllogistic argument as explained in Section 6.2. It was there shown that one legitimate test of the validity or invalidity of a given syllogism is to establish the validity or invalidity of a different syllogism having exactly the same form. This technique is basic to the use of Venn Diagrams. The explanation of how they serve this purpose constitutes the second part of the answer to our question.

Ordinarily a syllogism will be about classes of objects which are not all present, such as the class of all men, or great scientists, or sodium salts, or the like. The relations of inclusion or exclusion among such classes may be reasoned about and may be empirically discoverable in the course of scientific investigation. But they are certainly not open to direct inspection, since not all members of the classes involved are ever present at one time to be inspected. We can, however, examine situations of our own making in which the only classes concerned will contain by their very definitions only things which are present and directly open to inspection. And we can argue syllogistically about such situations of our own making. Venn Diagrams are devices for expressing standard-form categorical propositions, but they are also situations of our own making, patterns of graphite or ink on paper or mounds of chalk raised on blackboards. And the propositions they express can be interpreted as referring to the diagrams themselves. An example can help make this clear. Suppose we have a particular syllogism:

All successful men are men who are keenly interested in their work.
No man who is keenly interested in his work is a person whose attention is easily distracted when he is working.

Therefore no person whose attention is easily distracted when he is working is a successful man.

Its form is ***AEE*–4**, and may be schematized as:

All P is M.
No M is S.
$\therefore$ No S is P.

We may test it by constructing the following Venn Diagram, with its regions $SP\overline{M}$ and $\overline{S}P\overline{M}$ shaded out to express the first premiss, and $S\overline{P}M$ and SPM shaded out to express the second premiss.

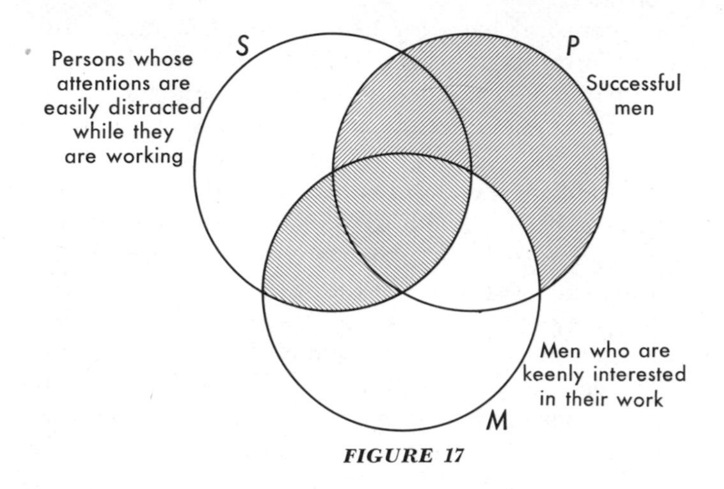

FIGURE 17

Examining the diagram, we find that SP (which consists of the regions SPM and $SP\overline{M}$) has been shaded out, so the syllogism's conclusion has already been diagrammed. Now how does this tell us that the given syllogism is valid? That syllogism concerns large classes of remote objects: there are many persons whose attentions are easily distracted while they are working, and they are scattered far and wide. However, we can construct a syllogism of the same form dealing with objects which are immediately present and directly available for our inspection. These objects are the points within the unshaded portions of the circles labeled S, P, and M in our Venn Diagram. Here is the new syllogism:

All points within the unshaded part of the circle labeled P are points within the unshaded part of the circle labeled M.
No points within the unshaded part of the circle labeled M are points within the unshaded part of the circle labeled S.

Therefore no points within the unshaded part of the circle labeled S are points within the unshaded part of the circle labeled P.

This new syllogism refers to nothing remote, but is about the parts of a situation we ourselves have created—the Venn Diagram we have drawn. All the parts and all the possibilities of inclusion and exclusion among these classes are immediately present to us and directly open to inspection. We can literally see all the possibilities here and know that since all the points of P are also points of M, and since M and S have no points in common, S and P cannot possibly have any points in common. Since it refers only to classes of points in the diagram, the new syllogism is literally seen to be valid by looking at the things it talks about. Since the original syllogism about classes of men has exactly the same form as this second one, by the formal nature of syllogistic argument the original syllogism is also seen to be valid. The explanation is exactly the same for Venn Diagram proofs of the invalidity of invalid syllogisms—there too we test the original syllogism indirectly by directly testing a second syllogism having exactly the same form but referring to the actual diagram which expresses that form.

EXERCISES

I. Test the validity of each of the following syllogistic forms by means of a Venn Diagram:

★ 1. ***AEE*–1**	6. ***OAO*–2**	11. ***AOO*–3**
2. ***EIO*–2**	7. ***AOO*–1**	12. ***EAE*–1**
3. ***OAO*–3**	8. ***EAE*–3**	13. ***IAI*–1**
4. ***AOO*–4**	9. ***EIO*–3**	14. ***OAO*–4**
★ 5. ***EIO*–4**	★ 10. ***IAI*–4**	15. ***EIO*–1**

II. Put each of the following syllogisms into standard form, name its mood and figure, and test its validity by means of a Venn Diagram:

★ 1. Some reformers are fanatics, so some idealists are fanatics, since all reformers are idealists.

2. Some philosophers are men of action, hence some soldiers are philosophers, since all soldiers are men of action.

3. Some mammals are not horses, for no horses are centaurs, and all centaurs are mammals.

4. Some neurotics are not parasites, but all criminals are parasites; it follows that some neurotics are not criminals.

★ 5. All underwater craft are submarines, therefore no submarines are pleasure vessels, since no pleasure vessels are underwater craft.

6. No criminals were pioneers, for all criminals are unsavory persons, and no pioneers were unsavory persons.

7. No musicians are active sportsmen, all musicians are baseball fans, consequently no active sportsmen are baseball fans.

8. Some Christians are not Methodists, for some Christians are not Protestants, and some Protestants are not Methodists.

9. No men whose primary interest is in winning elections are true liberals, and all active politicians are men whose primary interest is in winning elections, which entails that no true liberals are active politicians.

10. No wealthy men are labor leaders, because no wealthy men are true liberals, and all labor leaders are true liberals.

6.4 Rules and Fallacies

There are many ways in which a syllogism may fail to establish its conclusion. Just as travel is facilitated by the mapping of highways, and the labeling of otherwise tempting roads as "dead ends," so validity of argument is made easier to attain by setting forth certain rules which enable the reasoner to avoid fallacies. The advantage of having a clearly stated set of easily applied rules is manifest. Any given standard-form syllogism can be evaluated by observing whether the rules are violated or not. In the present section six rules for standard-form syllogisms are presented.

> RULE 1: *A valid standard-form categorical syllogism must contain exactly three terms, each of which is used in the same sense throughout the argument.*

The conclusion of a categorical syllogism asserts that a certain relation holds between two terms. It is clear that the conclusion is justified only if the premisses assert the relationship of each of the conclusion's terms to the same third term. Were these not asserted by the premisses, no connection between the two terms of the conclusion would be established, and the conclusion would not be implied by the premisses. Three terms must be involved in every valid categorical syllogism; no more and no less. Any categorical syllogism which contains more than three terms is invalid, and is said to commit the Fallacy of Four Terms (in Latin, *Quaternio Terminorum*).[2]

If a term is used in different senses in the argument, it is being used equivocally, and the fallacy committed is that of *equivocation*.[3] An example is the Japanese argument circulated during the late thirties, defending the "pacification" of China. It may be paraphrased as:

> All attempts to end hostilities are efforts which should be approved by all nations.
> All of Japan's present activities in China are attempts to end hostilities.
> ---
> Therefore all of Japan's present activities in China are efforts which should be approved by all nations.

This syllogism appears to have only three terms, but there are really four, since one of them, the middle term, is used in different senses in the two premisses. Only if the term "attempts to end hostilities" is interpreted as designating such activities as proposing an armistice and negotiating a treaty in good faith, can the first premiss be accepted as true. But for the second premiss to be true, the phrase "attempts to end hostilities" must have its meaning shifted to include the vigorous prosecution of war. When the term in question is interpreted in the same sense throughout the argument, one or the other premiss becomes patently false.

Arguments of this sort are more common than one might suspect. It is generally the middle term whose meaning is shifted—in one direction to connect it with the minor term, in a different direction to relate it to the major term. But this connects the two terms of the conclusion with two different terms, so the relationship asserted by the conclusion is not established. Although it is sometimes called the fallacy of the ambiguous middle, that name is not generally applicable, since one of the other terms may have its meaning shifted instead, which would involve the same error.

As we defined the term "categorical syllogism" at the beginning of this chapter, every syllogism by its very definition contains three terms. And the fallacy of equivocation was already explained and warned against in Chapter 3. But the term "syllogism" is sometimes defined more broadly than in the present book, and Rule 1 is part of the traditional logic of the syllogism. In the present context it

2 Even where it contains as many as five or six different terms, the same name is applied to the fallacy.

3 Discussed in Chapter 3, pp. 92–93.

may be regarded simply as a reminder to make sure that the argument being appraised really is a syllogism. And the "Fallacy of Four Terms" is our label for a syllogism that commits the fallacy of equivocation.

The next two rules deal with distribution. As was explained in Section 5.2 of the preceding chapter, a term is distributed in a proposition when the proposition refers to all members of the class designated by that term; otherwise the term is said to be undistributed in (or by) that proposition.

RULE 2: *In a valid standard-form categorical syllogism, the middle term must be distributed in at least one premiss.*

Consider the following standard-form categorical syllogism:

All dogs are mammals.
All cats are mammals.
Therefore all cats are dogs.

The middle term "mammals" is not distributed in either premiss, and this violates Rule 2. Any syllogism which violates Rule 2 is said to commit the Fallacy of the Undistributed Middle. It should be clear by the following considerations that any syllogism which violates this rule is invalid. The conclusion of any syllogism asserts a connection between two terms. The premisses justify asserting such a connection only if they assert that each of the two terms is connected with a third term in such a way that the first two are appropriately connected with each other through or by means of the third. For the two terms of the conclusion really to be connected through the third, at least one of them must be related to the *whole* of the class designated by the third or middle term. Otherwise each may be connected with a different part of that class, and not necessarily connected with each other at all. This is obviously what occurs in the example. Dogs are included in part of the class of mammals, and cats are also included in part of the class of mammals. But different parts of that class may be (and, in this case, are) involved, so the middle term does not connect the syllogism's major and minor terms. For it to connect them, *all* the class designated by it must be referred to in at least one premiss, which is to say that in a valid syllogism the middle term must be distributed in at least one premiss.

RULE 3: *In a valid standard-form categorical syllogism no term can be distributed in the conclusion which is not distributed in the premisses.*

A valid argument is one whose premisses logically imply or entail its conclusion. The conclusion of a valid argument can not go beyond or assert any more than is (implicitly) contained in the premisses. If the conclusion does illegitimately "go beyond" what is asserted by the premisses, the argument is invalid. It is an "illicit process" for the conclusion to say more about its terms than the premisses do. A proposition which distributes one of its terms says more about the class designated by that term than it would if the term were undistributed by it. To refer to *all* members of a class is to say more about it (apart from questions of existence) than is said when only some of its members are referred to. Therefore when the conclusion of a syllogism distributes a term which was undistributed in the premisses, it says more about it than the premisses warrant, and the syllogism is invalid. Such an illicit process can occur in the case of either the major or the minor term. There are, then, two different ways in which Rule 3 may be broken. Special names have been given to the two fallacies involved.

When a syllogism contains its major term undistributed in the major premiss but distributed in the conclusion, the argument is said to commit the fallacy of *Illicit Process of the Major Term* (or, more briefly, the *Illicit Major*). An example of this fallacy is:

All dogs are mammals.
No cats are dogs.
―――――――――――――――
Therefore no cats are mammals.

The conclusion makes an assertion about *all* mammals, saying that all of them are excluded from the class of cats. But the premisses make no assertion about *all* mammals; so the conclusion illicitly goes beyond what the premisses assert. Since "mammals" is the major term, the fallacy here is an Illicit Major.

When a syllogism contains its minor term undistributed in its minor premiss but distributed in its conclusion, the argument commits the fallacy of *Illicit Process of the Minor Term* (more briefly called the *Illicit Minor*). An example of this fallacy is:

All communists are subversive elements.
All communists are critics of the present administration.
―――――――――――――――
Therefore all critics of the present administration are subversive elements.

The conclusion here makes an assertion about *all* critics of the present administration. But the premisses make no assertion about *all* such critics; so the conclusion illicitly goes beyond what the premisses warrant. Since it goes beyond the premisses in what it says about the minor term, the fallacy is an *Illicit Minor.*

The next two rules are called Rules of Quality because they refer to the ways in which the negative quality of one or both premisses restricts the kinds of conclusions which validly may be inferred.

> RULE 4: *No standard-form categorical syllogism is valid which has two negative premisses.*

We can see that this rule must be obeyed when we recall what negative propositions assert. Any negative proposition (***E*** or ***O***) denies class inclusion, asserting that all or some of one class is excluded from the whole of the other. Where *S, P,* and *M* are the minor, major, and middle terms, respectively, two negative premisses can assert only that *S* is wholly or partially excluded from all or part of *M,* and that *P* is wholly or partially excluded from all or part of *M*. But these conditions may very well obtain no matter how *S* and *P* are related, whether by inclusion or exclusion, partial or complete. Therefore from two negative premisses, no relationship whatever between *S* and *P* can validly be inferred. Any syllogism which breaks Rule 4 is said to commit the fallacy of *Exclusive Premisses.*

> RULE 5: *If either premiss of a valid standard-form categorical syllogism is negative, the conclusion must be negative.*

An affirmative conclusion asserts that one class is either wholly or partly contained in a second. This can be justified only by premisses which assert that there is a third class which contains the first and is itself contained in the second. In other words, to entail an affirmative conclusion, both premisses must assert class inclusion. But class inclusion can be expressed only by affirmative propositions. So an affirmative conclusion logically follows only from two affirmative premisses. Hence if either premiss is negative, the conclusion cannot be affirmative but must be negative also. Arguments breaking this rule are so implausible that they are very seldom encountered in serious discussions. Any syllogism which breaks Rule 5 may be said to commit the fallacy of *Drawing an Affirmative Conclusion from a Negative Premiss.* (Some lists of syllogistic rules also include the converse of Rule 5: "If the conclusion of a valid standard-form categorical syllogism is negative, at least one premiss must be negative." This additional rule is explained on much the same grounds that were appealed to in discussing Rule 5. If the conclusion is negative it *denies* inclusion. But affirmative premisses *assert* inclusion, hence they cannot entail a negative conclusion. This additional rule is both necessary and sufficient to complete the traditional or Aristotelian account of the Categorical Syllogism, which paid no attention to the problem of existential import. But on the Boolean interpretation, which pays particular attention to the problem of existential import, a separate syllogistic rule [Rule 6 below] is required. And the usual formulation of such a rule suffices—in the presence of the other rules—to prevent syllogisms with affirmative premisses and a negative conclusion. See Exercise 7 on page 206.)

Our sixth and final rule concerns existential import. It is:

RULE 6: *No valid standard-form categorical syllogism with a particular conclusion can have two universal premisses.*

To break this rule is to go from premisses which have no existential import to a conclusion which does. A particular proposition asserts the existence of objects of a specified kind, and to infer it from two universal premisses, which do not assert the existence of anything at all, is clearly to go beyond what is warranted by the premisses. An example of a syllogism which breaks this rule is:

All household pets are domestic animals.
No unicorns are domestic animals.
―――――――――――――――
Therefore some unicorns are not household pets.

On the traditional interpretation, which did attribute existential import to universal propositions, such arguments were said to have "weakened conclusions," because the "stronger" conclusion "No unicorns are household pets" might equally well have been inferred. But the latter is not stronger, it is simply different. The syllogism with the same premisses and the universal conclusion is perfectly valid. But the given syllogism is invalid, because its conclusion asserts that there are unicorns (a false proposition), whereas its premisses do not assert the existence of unicorns (or of anything at all). Being universal propositions, they are without existential import. The conclusion would follow validly if to the two universal premisses were added the additional premiss "There are unicorns." But the resulting argument, although perfectly valid, would have three premisses and would therefore not be a syllogism. Any syllogism which violates Rule 6 may be said to commit the *Existential Fallacy*.

The six rules here presented are intended to apply only to standard-form categorical syllogisms. Within this area they provide an adequate test for the validity of any argument. If a standard-form categorical syllogism violates any of these rules, it is invalid; whereas if it conforms to all of them it is valid.

EXERCISES

I. Name the fallacies committed and the rules broken by invalid syllogisms of the following forms:

★ 1. ***AAA*–2**	6. ***IAI*–2**	11. ***EAO*–1**
2. ***EAA*–1**	7. ***OAA*–4**	12. ***AII*–2**
3. ***IAO*–3**	8. ***EAO*–4**	13. ***EEE*–1**
4. ***OEO*–4**	9. ***OAI*–3**	14. ***OAO*–2**
★ 5. ***AAA*–3**	★ 10. ***IEO*–1**	15. ***IAA*–3**

II. Name the fallacies committed and the rules broken by any of the following syllogisms which are invalid:

★ 1. All textbooks are books intended for careful study.
Some reference books are books intended for careful study.
Therefore some reference books are textbooks.

2. All criminal actions are wicked deeds.
All prosecutions for murder are criminal actions.
Therefore all prosecutions for murder are wicked deeds.

3. No tragic actors are happy men.
Some comedians are not happy men.
Therefore some comedians are not tragic actors.

4. Some parrots are not pests.
All parrots are pets.
Therefore no pets are pests.

★ 5. All men who understand women are potentially perfect husbands.
All potentially perfect husbands are men of infinite patience.
Therefore some men of infinite patience are men who understand women.

6. Some good actors are not strong men.
All professional wrestlers are strong men.
Therefore all professional wrestlers are good actors.

7. Some diamonds are precious stones.
Some carbon compounds are not diamonds.
Therefore some carbon compounds are not precious stones.

8. Some diamonds are not precious stones.
Some carbon compounds are diamonds.
Therefore some carbon compounds are not precious stones.

9. All men who are most hungry are men who eat most.
All men who eat least are men who are most hungry.
Therefore all men who eat least are men who eat most.

10. Some spaniels are not good hunters.
All spaniels are gentle dogs.
Therefore no gentle dogs are good hunters.

III. Name the fallacies committed and the rules broken by any of the following syllogisms which are invalid:

★ 1. All chocolate eclairs are fattening foods, because all chocolate eclairs are rich desserts, and some fattening foods are not rich desserts.

2. All inventors are men who see new patterns in familiar things, so all inventors are eccentrics, since all eccentrics are men who see new patterns in familiar things.

3. Some snakes are not dangerous animals, but all snakes are reptiles, therefore some dangerous animals are not reptiles.

4. Some fishes are fur-bearing animals, for all fishes that are fur-bearing animals are fishes, and all fishes that are fur-bearing animls are fur-bearing animals.

★ 5. All advocates of basic economic and political changes are outspoken critics of the conservative leaders of Congress, and all communists are advocates of basic economic and political changes. It follows that all outspoken critics of the conservative leaders of Congress are communists.

6. No writers of lewd and sensational articles are honest and decent citizens, but some newspapermen are not writers of lewd and sensational articles, consequently some newspapermen are honest and decent citizens.

7. All supporters of popular government are democrats, so all supporters of popular government are opponents of the Republican Party, inasmuch as all Democrats are opponents of the Republican Party.

8. No coal-tar derivatives are nourishing foods, because all artificial dyes are coal-tar derivatives, and no artificial dyes are nourishing foods.

9. No coal-tar derivatives are nourishing foods, because no coal-tar derivatives are natural grain products, and all natural grain products are nourishing foods.

10. All people who live in London are people who drink tea, and all people who drink tea are people who like it. We may conclude, then, that all people who live in London are people who like it.

IV. Answer the following questions by appealing to the six rules. (Make sure you consider all possible cases.)

★ 1. Can any standard-form categorical syllogism be valid which contains exactly three terms, each of which is distributed in both of its occurrences?

2. In what mood or moods, if any, can a first-figure standard-form categorical syllogism with a particular conclusion be valid?

3. In what figure or figures, if any, can the premisses of a valid standard-form categorical syllogism distribute both major and minor terms?

4. In what figure or figures, if any, can a valid standard-form categorical syllogism have two particular premisses?

★ 5. In what figure or figures, if any, can a valid standard-form categorical syllogism have only one term distributed, and that one only once?

6. In what mood or moods, if any, can a valid standard-form categorical syllogism have just two terms distributed, each one twice?

7. In what mood or moods, if any, can a valid standard-form categorical syllogism have two affirmative premisses and a negative conclusion?

8. In what figure or figures, if any, can a valid standard-form categorical syllogism have a particular premiss and a universal conclusion?

9. In what mood or moods, if any, can a second-figure standard-form categorical syllogism with a universal conclusion be valid?

10. In what figure or figures, if any, can a valid standard-form categorical syllogism have its middle term distributed in both premisses?

11. Determine by a process of elimination which of the 256 forms of standard-form categorical syllogism are valid.

12. Can a valid standard-form categorical syllogism have a term distributed in a premiss that appears undistributed in the conclusion?

Chapter 7
Arguments in Ordinary Language

The value, therefore, of the syllogistic form and of the rules for using it correctly does not consist in their being the form and the rules according to which our reasonings are necessarily, or even usually, made, but in their furnishing us with a mode in which those reasonings may always be represented and which is admirably calculated, if they are inconclusive, to bring their inconclusiveness to light.

—*John Stuart Mill*

7.1 Reducing the Number of Terms in a Syllogistic Argument

In the preceding chapter two different tests were presented for distinguishing valid from invalid categorical syllogisms. These tests are applicable only to categorical syllogisms which are in *standard form.* A standard-form categorical syllogism may be thought of as being "chemically pure," free from all obscurities and irrelevancies. Needless to say, of course, arguments do not always occur thus refined in a "state of nature."

We introduce the term "syllogistic argument" to refer to any argument which either is a standard-form categorical syllogism or can be reformulated as a standard-form categorical syllogism without any loss or change of meaning. The process of reformulating a syllogistic argument as a standard-form categorical syllogism will be called translation or reduction to standard form, and the resulting standard-form categorical syllogism will be called a standard-form translation of the given syllogistic argument.

Syllogistic arguments are fairly common, but they usually appear in a guise far different from the stilted and artificial standard form to which the tests of the preceding chapter can be directly applied. They take on such varied shapes that to devise special logical tests for all of them would require a hopelessly complicated logical apparatus. The combined interests of logical simplicity and adequacy to arguments formulated in ordinary language require that we do two things. First, easily applicable tests must be devised by which we can distinguish valid from invalid standard-form categorical syllogisms. This has already been done. And second, the techniques of translating syllogistic arguments of *any* form into standard form must be understood and mastered. When these are both accomplished, *any* syllogistic argument may be tested: first, by translating it to standard form, and second, by applying to its standard form translation one of the tests described in the preceding chapter.

Apart from the relatively minor question of the order in which its premisses and conclusion happen to be stated, a syllogistic argument may deviate from standard form in either or both of two ways. Its component propositions may not all be standard-form categorical propositions. Or its component propositions may be standard-form categorical propositions which apparently involve more than three terms. In the latter case, the argument is not to be rejected out of hand as invalid through committing the Fallacy of Four Terms. It is frequently possible to translate such an argument into a logically equivalent standard-form syllogism which contains only three terms and is perfectly valid.

(1) Such translation often can be effected simply by eliminating synonyms. Thus, before attempting to apply Venn Diagrams or the Syllogistic Rules to the argument:

> No wealthy men are vagrants.
> All lawyers are rich men.
> ______________________
> Therefore no attorneys are tramps.

we should eliminate the synonymous terms occurring in it. When that is done, the argument translates into:

> No wealthy men are vagrants.
> All lawyers are wealthy men.
> ______________________
> Therefore no lawyers are vagrants.

In this standard form ***EAE*–1** the argument is easily seen to be valid.

Sometimes, however, the simple elimination of synonyms will not suffice. Consider the following argument, all of whose propositions are standard-form categorical propositions:

All mammals are warm-blooded animals.
No lizards are warm-blooded animals.
Therefore all lizards are nonmammals.

Were we to apply to this argument the six rules explained in Chapter 6, we should judge it to be invalid on more than one count. For one thing, it contains four terms: "mammals," "warm-blooded animals," "lizards," and "nonmammals." And for another, it has an affirmative conclusion drawn from a negative premiss. But it is nevertheless perfectly valid, as the reader can probably see for himself. Because it has four terms, it is not a standard-form categorical syllogism, and the rules are not directly applicable to it. To test it by the Syllogistic Rules presented in the preceding chapter, we must first translate it into standard form. To do so we reduce the number of its terms to three, which is easily accomplished by simply obverting the conclusion. Performing this obversion we obtain a standard-form translation of the original argument:

All mammals are warm-blooded animals.
No lizards are warm-blooded animals.
Therefore no lizards are mammals.

which is logically equivalent to it, having identically the same premisses and a logically equivalent conclusion. This standard-form translation conforms to all the Syllogistic Rules, and is thus known to be valid.

The latter is not the only standard-form translation of the given argument, although it is the most easily obtainable. A different (but logically equivalent) standard-form translation can be obtained by taking the contrapositive of the first premiss and obverting the second, leaving the conclusion unchanged. This would yield:

All non(warm-blooded animals) are nonmammals.
All lizards are non(warm-blooded animals).
Therefore all lizards are nonmammals.

which is also valid by the rules. There is no unique standard-form translation of a given syllogistic argument, but if any one is valid, all of the others must be valid also.

(2) Any syllogistic argument containing four terms can be reduced to standard form (or translated into a logically equivalent standard-form categorical syllogism) *if* one of its four terms is the complement of one of the other three. And any containing five (or six) terms can be reduced to standard form if two (or three) of its terms are the complements of two (or three) of the others. These reductions are all effected by means of valid immediate inferences: conversion, obversion, and contraposition.

Syllogistic arguments whose constituent propositions are all in standard form may contain as many as half a dozen different terms and may require the drawing of more than one immediate inference for their reduction to standard form. An example of a six-term syllogistic argument which is perfectly valid is the following:

No nonresidents are citizens.
All noncitizens are nonvoters.
Therefore all voters are residents.

There are alternative ways of reducing this argument to a standard-form syllogism. One method, perhaps the most natural and obvious, requires the use of all three types of immediate inference. Converting and then obverting the first premiss and taking the contrapositive of the second premiss yields the standard-form categorical syllogism:

All citizens are residents.
All voters are citizens.
Therefore all voters are residents.

which is easily proved valid by either of the methods set forth in the preceding chapter.

EXERCISES

Translate the following syllogistic arguments into standard form, and test their validity by one of the methods of Chapter Six:

★ 1. Some preachers are men of unfailing vigor. No preachers are nonintellectuals. Therefore some intellectuals are men of unfailing vigor.

2. Some metals are rare and costly substances, but no welder's materials are nonmetals, hence some welder's materials are rare and costly substances.

3. Some oriental nations are nonbelligerents, since all belligerents are

allies either of the U.S.A. or of the U.S.S.R., and some oriental nations are not allies either of the U.S.A. or of the U.S.S.R.

4. Some nondrinkers are athletes, because no drinkers are men in perfect physical condition, and some men in perfect physical condition are not nonathletes.

★ 5. All things inflammable are unsafe things, so all things that are safe are nonexplosives, since all explosives are flammable things.

6. All worldly goods are changeable things, for no worldly goods are things immaterial, and no material things are unchangeable things.

7. All those who are neither members nor guests of members are those who are excluded, therefore no nonconformists are either members or guests of members, for all those who are included are conformists.

8. All mortals are imperfect beings, and no humans are immortals, whence it follows that all perfect beings are nonhumans.

9. All things present are nonirritants, therefore no irritants are invisible objects, because all visible objects are absent things.

10. All useful things are objects no more than six feet long, since all difficult things to store are useless things, and no objects over six feet long are easy things to store.

7.2 Translating Categorical Propositions into Standard Form

The somewhat stilted ***A, E, I,*** and ***O*** forms are not the only ones in which categorical propositions may be expressed. Many syllogistic arguments contain nonstandard-form propositions. To reduce these arguments to standard form requires that their constituent propositions be translated into standard form. But ordinary language is too rich and multiform to permit a complete set of rules for such translation. In every case the crucial element is the ability to understand the given nonstandard-form proposition. We can, however, note a number of conventional techniques that are often useful. These must be regarded as guides rather than as rules, of course. Nine methods of dealing with various nonstandard-form propositions will be described in the present section.

(1) We ought first to mention singular propositions, such as "Socrates is a man," and "This table is not an antique." These do not affirm or deny the inclusion of one class in another, but rather affirm or deny that a specified individual or object belongs to a class. A singular proposition, however, can be interpreted as a proposition dealing with classes and their interrelations in the following way. To

every individual object there corresponds a unique *unit class* (one-membered class) whose only member is that object itself. Then to assert that an object *s* belongs to a class *P* is logically equivalent to asserting that the unit class *S* containing just that object *s* is wholly included in the class *P*. And to assert that an object *s* does *not* belong to a class *P* is logically equivalent to asserting that the unit class *S* containing just that object *s* is wholly excluded from the class *P*. It is customary to make this interpretation automatically without any notational adjustment. Thus we take any affirmative singular proposition of the form "*s* is *P*" as if it were already expressed as the logically equivalent ***A*** proposition "All *S* is *P*," and similarly understand any negative singular proposition "*s* is not *P*" as an alternative formulation of the logically equivalent ***E*** proposition "No *S* is *P*" . . . in each case understanding "*S*" to designate the unit class whose only member is the object *s*. Thus no explicit translations are needed for singular propositions; they are classified as ***A*** and ***E*** propositions as they stand.

(2) The first group of categorical propositions which require translation into standard form are those which have adjectives or adjectival phrases as predicates rather than substantives or class *terms*. For example, "Some flowers are beautiful" and "No warships are available for active duty" deviate from standard form only in that their predicates "beautiful" and "available for active duty" designate properties rather than classes. But every property *determines* a class, the class of things having that property; so to every such proposition corresponds a logically equivalent proposition which is in standard form. To the two examples cited correspond the ***I*** and ***E*** propositions "Some flowers are beauties" and "No warships are things available for active duty." Where a categorical proposition is in standard form except that it has an adjectival predicate instead of a predicate term, the translation into standard form is made by replacing the adjectival predicate with a term designating the class of all objects of which the adjective may truly be predicated.

(3) Next we turn to categorical propositions whose main verbs are other than the standard-form copula "to be." Examples of this type are "All men desire recognition" and "Some men drink." The usual method of translating such a statement into standard form is to regard all of it except the subject term and quantifier as naming a class-defining characteristic, and replace it by a standard copula and a term designating the class determined by that class-defining characteristic. Thus the two examples cited translate into the standard-form categorical propositions "All men are desirers of recognition" and "Some men are drinkers."

(4) Another type of statement easily put into standard form is that in which the standard-form ingredients are all present but not arranged in standard-form order. Two examples of this kind are: "Racehorses are all thoroughbreds" and "All is well that ends well." In such cases we must decide which is the subject term and then so rearrange the words as to express a standard-form categorical proposition. It is clear that the preceding two statements translate into the ***A*** propositions "All racehorses are thoroughbreds" and "All things that end well are things that are well."

(5) Many categorical propositions have their quantities indicated by words other than the standard-form quantifiers "all," "no," and "some." Statements involving the words "every" and "any" are very easily translated. The propositions "Every dog has his day" and "Any contribution will be appreciated" reduce to "All dogs are creatures which have their days" and "All contributions are things which are appreciated." Similar to "every" and "any" are "everything" and "anything." Paralleling these, but clearly restricted to classes of persons, are "everyone," "anyone," "whoever," "whoso," "who," "he who," and the like. These should occasion no difficulty. The grammatical particles "a," "an," and "the" can also serve to indicate quantity. The first two sometimes mean "all" and in other contexts mean "some." Thus "A bat is not a bird" and "An elephant is a pachyderm" are reasonably interpreted as meaning "All bats are nonbirds" (or "No bats are birds") and "All elephants are pachyderms." But "A bat flew in the window" and "An elephant escaped" quite clearly do not refer to all bats or all elephants, but are properly reduced to "Some bats are creatures which flew in the window" and "Some elephants are creatures which escaped." The word "the" may be used to refer either to a particular individual or to all the members of a class. But there is little or no danger of ambiguity here, for such a statement as "The whale is a mammal" translates in almost any context into the ***A*** proposition "All whales are mammals," whereas the singular proposition "The first president was a military hero" is already in standard form as an ***A*** proposition by the convention laid down in paragraph (1). (pages 211–212.)

(6) Categorical propositions involving the words "only" or "none but" are often called "exclusive" propositions, because in general they assert that the predicate applies exclusively to the subject named. Examples of such usages are "Only citizens can vote" and "None but the brave deserve the fair." The first translates into the standard-form categorical proposition "All those who can vote are citizens," and the second into the standard-form categorical proposition "All those who deserve the fair are those who are brave." So-called exclusive propositions, beginning with "only" or "none but,"

translate into *A* propositions whose subjects and predicate terms are the same, respectively, as the predicate and subject terms of the exclusive proposition. There are contexts in which "Only *S* is *P*" or "None but *S*'s are *P*'s" are intended not merely to express that "All *P* is *S*" but also to suggest either that "All *S* is *P*" or that "Some *S* is *P*." This is not always the case, however. Where context helps to determine meaning attention must be paid to it, of course. But in the absence of such additional information, the suggested translations are adequate.

(7) Some categorical propositions contain no words at all to indicate quantity, for example, "Dogs are carnivorous" and "Children are present." Where there is no quantifier, what the sentence is intended to express may be doubtful. We may be able to determine its meaning only by examining the context in which it occurs. The two examples cited are reasonably clear, however. In the first it is probable that *all* dogs are referred to, while in the second it is more likely that only *some* children are intended. The standard-form translation of the first is "All dogs are carnivores"; that of the second, "Some children are beings who are present."

(8) Next we may consider briefly some propositions which do not resemble standard-form categorical propositions at all, but which *can* be translated into standard form. Some examples are: "Not all children believe in Santa Claus," "There are white elephants," "There are no pink elephants," and "Nothing is both round and square." A moment's thought about the propositions expressed suffices to show that they are logically equivalent to, and therefore translate into, the following standard-form propositions: "Some children are not believers in Santa Claus," "Some elephants are white things," "No elephants are pink things," and "No round objects are square objects."

(9) It must be recognized that many propositions mention "quantity" more specifically than standard-form propositions do. This specification is accomplished by the use of numerical or quasinumerical quantifiers such as "one," "two," "three," . . . , "many," "a few," "most," and so on. But arguments which depend for their validity upon numerical or quasinumerical information are *asyllogistic,* and require a more penetrating analysis than is given in the simple theory of the categorical syllogism.

Some quasinumerical quantifiers, however, occur in arguments that lend themselves to syllogistic analysis. These include: "almost all," "not quite all," "all but a few," "almost everyone." Propositions in which these phrases appear as quantifiers are "exceptive" propositions, which make two assertions rather than one. They are of the same type as explicitly *exceptive* propositions like: "All except employees are eligible," "All but employees are eligible," and "Employees alone are not eligible." Each of these logically equivalent propositions asserts not merely that *all nonemployees are eligible,* but also (at least in the usual context) that *no employees are eligible.* Where "employees" is abbreviated by *S* and "eligible persons" by *P,* these two propositions can be written as "All non-*S* is *P*" and "No *S* is *P.*" These are clearly independent and together assert that *S* and *P* are complementary classes.

Each of these exceptive propositions is compound, and therefore cannot be translated into a single standard-form categorical proposition, but rather into an explicit conjunction of two standard-form categoricals. Thus the three propositions about eligibility translate identically into "All nonemployees are eligible persons and no employees are eligible persons." Also compound are the following exceptive propositions with quasinumerical quantifiers: "Almost all students were at the dance," "Not quite all students were at the dance," "All but a few students were at the dance," and "Only some students were at the dance." Each of these affirms that *some students were at the dance* and denies that *all students were at the dance.* The quasinumerical information they present is irrelevant from the point of view of syllogistic inference, and all are translated indifferently as "Some students are persons who were at the dance and some students are not persons who were at the dance."

Because exceptive propositions are not categorical propositions but conjunctions, arguments containing them are not syllogistic arguments as we are using that term. But they may nevertheless be susceptible to syllogistic analysis and appraisal. How an argument containing an exceptive proposition should be tested depends upon the exceptive proposition's position in the argument. If it is a premiss, then the argument may have to be given two separate tests. For example, consider the argument:

> Everyone who saw the game was at the dance.
> Not quite all the students were at the dance.
> ———
> So some students didn't see the game.

Its first premiss and its conclusion are categorical propositions, which are easily translated into standard form. But its second premiss is an exceptive proposition, not simple but compound. To discover whether or not its premisses imply its conclusion, one first tests the syllogism composed of the first premiss of the given argument, the first half of its second premiss, and its conclusion. In standard form, we have:

All persons who saw the game are persons who were at the dance.
Some students are persons who were at the dance.
____
Therefore some students are not persons who saw the game.

The standard-form categorical syllogism is of form ***AIO*–2** and violates Rule 2, committing the fallacy of the Undistributed Middle. But the original argument is not yet proved to be invalid, because the syllogism just tested contains only part of the premisses of the original argument. One now has the task of testing the categorical syllogism composed of the first premiss and the conclusion of the original argument together with the second half of the second premiss. In standard form we have:

All persons who saw the game are persons who were at the dance.
Some students are not persons who were at the dance.
____
Therefore some students are not persons who saw the game.

This standard-form categorical syllogism is of a different form, ***AOO*–2**, and is easily shown to be valid. Hence the original argument is valid, for the conclusion is the same, and the premisses of the original argument include the premisses of this valid standard-form syllogism. Thus to test the validity of an argument one of whose premisses is an exceptive proposition may require the testing of two different standard-form categorical syllogisms. If the premisses of an argument are both categorical propositions, and its conclusion is exceptive, then we know it to be invalid, for although the two categorical premisses may imply one or the other half of the compound conclusion, they cannot imply them both. Finally, if an argument contains exceptive propositions as both premisses and conclusion, all possible syllogisms constructable out of the original argument may have to be tested in order to determine its validity. Enough has been explained to enable the student to cope with such situations.

It is important to acquire facility at translating nonstandard-form propositions into standard form, for the tests of validity that we have developed can be applied directly only to standard-form categorical syllogisms.

EXERCISES

Translate the following into standard-form categorical propositions:

★ 1. Roses are fragrant.

2. Orchids are not fragrant.

3. Many a man has lived to regret a misspent youth.

4. Not everyone worth meeting is worth having as a friend.

★ 5. If it's a Junko, it's the best that money can buy.

6. If it isn't a real Havana, it isn't a Ropo.

7. Nothing is both safe and exciting.

8. Only brave men have ever won the Congressional Medal of Honor.

9. Good counselors are not universally appreciated.

★ 10. He sees not his shadow who faces the sun.

11. To hear him sing is an inspiration.

12. He who takes the sword shall perish by the sword.

13. Only members can use the front door.

14. Pledges can use only the side door.

★ 15. The Young Turks support no candidate of the Old Guard.

16. The party regulars support any candidate of the Old Guard.

17. They also serve who only stand and wait.

18. Happy indeed is the man who knows his own limitations.

19. A thing of beauty is a joy forever.

★ 20. He prayeth well who loveth well.

21. All that glitters is not gold.

22. None think the great unhappy but the great.

23. He jests at scars that never felt a wound.

24. Whatsoever a man soweth, that shall he also reap.

25. A soft answer turneth away wrath.

7.3 Uniform Translation

For a syllogistic argument to be tested, it must be expressed in propositions that together contain exactly three terms. Sometimes this aim is difficult to accomplish and requires a more subtle approach than that suggested in the preceding sections. Consider the proposition "The poor always ye have with you." It clearly does not assert that *all* the poor are with you, or even that *some* (particular) poor are *always* with you. There are alternative methods of reducing this proposition to standard form, but one perfectly natural route is by way of the key word "always." This word means "at all times" and suggests the standard-form categorical proposition "All times are times when ye have the poor with you." The word "times," which appears in both the subject and predicate terms, may be regarded as a *parameter,* that is, an auxiliary symbol which is of aid in expressing the original assertion in standard form.

Care should be taken not to introduce and use parameters in a mechanical, unthinking fashion. One must always be guided by an understanding of the proposition to be translated. Thus the proposition "Smith always wins at billiards" pretty clearly does not assert that Smith is incessantly, at all times, winning at billiards! It is more reasonable to interpret it as meaning that Smith wins at billiards whenever he plays. And so understood, it translates directly into "All times when Smith plays billiards are times when Smith wins at billiards." Not all parameters need be "temporal." To translate some propositions into standard form the words "places" and "cases" can be introduced as parameters. Thus "Where there is no vision the people perish" and "Jones loses a sale whenever he is late" translate into "All places where there is no vision are places where the people perish" and "All cases in which Jones is late are cases in which Jones loses a sale."

The introduction of parameters is often necessary for the *uniform translation* of all three constituent propositions of a syllogistic argument into standard form. Since a categorical syllogism contains exactly three terms, to test a syllogistic argument we must translate its constituent propositions into standard-form categorical propositions that contain just three terms. The elimination of synonyms and the applications of conversion, obversion, and contraposition were already discussed in Section 7.1. However, there are many syllogistic arguments which cannot have the number of their terms reduced to three either by eliminating synonyms or by applying conversion, obversion, or contraposition. Here uniform translation requires the introduction of a parameter—the same parameter—into all three of the constituent propositions. Consider the following argument:

> Soiled paper plates are scattered only where careless people have picnicked.
> There are soiled paper plates scattered about here.
> ____
> Therefore careless people must have been picnicking here.

This argument is perfectly valid, but before it can be proved valid by our diagrams or rules, its premisses and conclusion must be translated into standard-form categorical propositions involving only three terms. The second premiss and the conclusion might be translated most naturally into: "Some soiled paper plates are things which are scattered about here" and "Some careless people are those who have been picnicking here." But these two statements contain four different terms. To reduce the given argument to standard form we begin with the first premiss, which requires a parameter for its standard-form expression, and then use the same parameter in translating the second premiss and the conclusion into standard form. The word "where" in the first premiss suggests that the parameter "places" can be used. If this parameter is used to obtain uniform standard-form translations of all three propositions, the argument translates into:

> All places where soiled paper plates are scattered are places where careless people have picnicked.
> This place is a place where soiled paper plates are scattered.
> ___
> Therefore this place is a place where careless people have picnicked.

This standard-form categorical syllogism has mood and figure ***AAA*–1**, and has already been proved valid.

The notion of standardizing expressions through the use of a parameter is not an altogether easy one to grasp, but some syllogistic arguments cannot be translated into standard-form categorical syllogisms by any other method. Another example may help to make clear the technique involved. Let us take the argument:

> The hounds bay wherever a fox has passed, so the fox must have taken another path, since the hounds are quiet.

First of all, we must understand what is asserted in the given argument. We may take the statement that the hounds are quiet as asserting that the hounds are not baying here and now. This step is part of the necessary process of eliminating synonyms, since the first assertion makes explicit reference to the baying of hounds. And in the same manner we may understand the conclusion that the fox must have taken another path as asserting that the fox did not pass here. The word "wherever" in the first assertion should suggest that the parameter "places" can be used in its translation. The standard-form translation thus arrived at is:

> All places where a fox has passed are places where the hounds bay.

This place is not a place where the hounds bay.

Therefore this place is not a place where a fox has passed.

This standard-form categorical syllogism has mood and figure ***AEE*–2** and its validity is easy to establish.

EXERCISES

I. Translate the following propositions into standard form, using parameters where necessary:

★ 1. He groans whenever he is reminded of his loss.

2. She never drives her car to work.

3. He walks where he chooses.

4. She always orders the most expensive item on the menu.

★ 5. He does not give his opinion unless he is asked to do so.

6. He tries to sell life insurance wherever he may happen to be.

7. He gets red when he gets angry.

8. If he is asked to say a few words, he talks for hours.

9. Error of opinion may be tolerated where reason is left free to combat it.

10. Men are never so likely to settle a question rightly as when they discuss it freely.

II. Translate each of the following arguments into standard form, name the mood and figure of its standard-form translation, test its validity by a Venn Diagram, and if it is invalid, name the fallacy it commits:

★ 1. Bill didn't go to work this morning, because he wore a sweater, and he never wears a sweater to work.

2. Where there's smoke there's fire, so there's no fire in the basement, because there's no smoke there.

3. Henry must have spoken sharply to Louise, because she weeps whenever Henry speaks sharply to her, and she's weeping now.

4. All that glitters is not gold, so gold is not the only precious metal, since only precious metals glitter.

★ 5. There must be a strike at the factory, for there is a picket line there, and pickets are only present at strikes.

6. Only those who ignore the facts are likely to be mistaken. No one

who is truly objective in his approach is likely to be mistaken. Hence no one who ignores the facts is truly objective in his approach.

7. Not all who have jobs are temperate in their drinking. Only debtors drink to excess. So not all the unemployed are in debt.

8. Any argument worthy of logical recognition must be such as would occur in ordinary discourse. Now it will be found that no argument occurring in ordinary discourse is in the fourth figure. Hence, no argument in the fourth figure is worthy of logical recognition.

9. All valid syllogisms distribute their middle terms in at least one premiss, so this syllogism must be valid, for it distributes its middle term in at least one premiss.

★ 10. This syllogism is valid, for all invalid syllogisms commit an illicit process, and this syllogism commits no illicit process.

11. All invalid syllogisms commit an illicit process of their major terms, but this syllogism is valid, so this syllogism does not commit an illicit process of its major term.

12. No valid syllogisms have two negative premisses. No syllogisms on this page are invalid. Therefore no syllogisms on this page have two negative premisses.

13. All syllogisms having two negative premisses are invalid. Some valid syllogisms are sound. Therefore some unsound arguments are syllogisms having two negative premisses.

14. There are plants growing here, and since vegetation requires water, water must be present.

★ 15. No one present is out of work. No members are absent. Therefore all members are employed.

16. The competition is stiff, for there is a great deal of money involved, and there is never easy competition where much money is at stake.

17. All who were penniless were convicted. Some of the guilty were acquitted. Therefore some who had money were not innocent.

18. Although he complains whenever he is sick, his health is excellent, so he won't complain.

19. There are handsome men, but only man is vile, so it is false that nothing is both vile and handsome.

★ 20. The express train alone does not stop at this station, and as the last train did not stop, it must have been the express train.

21. It must have rained lately, because the fish are not biting, and fish never bite after a rain.

22. All buildings over three hundred feet tall are skyscrapers, but not all examples of modern architecture are buildings over three hundred feet tall, since skyscrapers are not the only examples of modern architecture.

23. It will be a good game tomorrow, for the conference title is at stake, and no title contest is ever dull.

24. Any two men who contradict each other cannot both be lying. Hence the first and third natives cannot both be lying, since they contradict each other.

★ 25. Not all is gold that glitters, for some base metals glitter, and gold is not a base metal.

26. All who are inebriated are undependable, so all who are dependable are nonalcoholics, since all alcoholics are ebriated.

27. And no man can be a rhapsode who does not understand the meaning of the poet. For the rhapsode ought to interpret the mind of the poet to his hearers, but how can he interpret him well unless he knows what he means?

—PLATO, *Ion*

28. It seems that mercy cannot be attributed to God. For mercy is a kind of sorrow, as Damascene says. But there is no sorrow in God; and therefore there is no mercy in Him.

—THOMAS AQUINAS, *Summa Theologica,* I, Question 21, Article 3, Objection I

29. . . . because intense heat is nothing else but a particular kind of painful sensation; and pain cannot exist but in a perceiving being; it follows that no intense heat can really exist in an unperceiving corporeal substance.

—GEORGE BERKELEY, *Three Dialogues Between Hylas and Philonous, In Opposition to Sceptics and Atheists*

★ 30. Since morals, therefore, have an influence on the actions and affections, it follows, that they cannot be deriv'd from reason; and that because reason alone, as we have already prov'd, can never have any such influence.

—DAVID HUME, *A Treatise of Human Nature*

31. All bridge players are people. All people think. Therefore all bridge players think.

—OSWALD and JAMES JACOBY, "Jacoby on Bridge," *Ann Arbor News,* November 5, 1966

32. Whenever I'm in trouble, I pray. And since I'm always in trouble, there is not a day when I don't pray.

—ISAAC BASHEVIS SINGER, Interview in the *New York Times*

33. The after-image is not in physical space. The brain-process is. So the after-image is not a brain-process.

—J. J. C. SMART, "Sensations and Brain Processes," *Philosophical Review,* April 1959

34. Also, what is simple cannot be separated from itself. The soul is simple; therefore, it cannot be separated from itself. . . .

—DUNS SCOTUS, *Oxford Commentary on the Sentences of Peter Lombard*

★ 35. . . . it is obvious that irrationals are uninteresting to an engineer, since he is concerned only with approximations, and all approximations are rational.

—G. H. HARDY, *A Mathematician's Apology*

36. All practice is theory; all surgery is practise; ergo, all surgery is theory.

—LANFRANC, *Chirurgia magna*

37. Since then to fight against neighbors is an evil, and to fight against the Thebans is to fight against neighbors, it is clear that to fight against the Thebans is an evil.

—ARISTOTLE, *Prior Analytics*

38. According to Aristotle, none of the products of Nature are due to chance. His proof is this: That which is due to chance does not reappear constantly nor frequently, but all products of Nature reappear either constantly or at least frequently.

—MOSES MAIMONIDES, *The Guide for the Perplexed*

39. She told me that she had a very simple attitude toward her students which was in fact no different from her feelings about people in general. That was, all her life she'd spoken only to people who were ladies and gentlemen. Since none of the students of 9D were ladies and gentlemen, she never spoke to them, never had, and never would.

—JAMES HERNDON, *The Way It Spozed to Be*

40. We . . . define a metaphysical sentence as a sentence which purports to express a genuine proposition, but does, in fact, express neither a tautology nor an empirical hypothesis. And as tautologies and empirical hypotheses form the entire class of significant propositions, we are justified in concluding that all metaphysical assertions are nonsensical.

—ALFRED J. AYER, *Language, Truth and Logic*

7.4 Enthymemes

Syllogistic arguments are often used, but it is the exception rather than the rule for conclusion and both premisses to be stated explicitly. More often than not, only part of the argument is expressed, the rest being "understood." Thus one may justify the conclusion that "Jones is a citizen" by mentioning only the one premiss: "Jones is a native-born American." As stated, the argument is incomplete, but the missing premiss is easily supplied from the Constitution of the United States. Were the missing premiss to be stated, the completed argument would appear as:

All native-born Americans are citizens.
Jones is a native-born American.
____
Therefore Jones is a citizen.

Fully stated, the argument is a categorical syllogism of form ***AAA*–1**, and perfectly valid. An argument which is stated incompletely, part being "understood" or only "in the mind," is called an "enthymeme." An incompletely stated argument is characterized as *enthymematic.*

In everyday discourse, and even in science, most inferences are expressed enthymematically. The reason is easy to understand. In most discussions, a large body of propositions can be presumed to be common knowledge. The majority of speakers and writers save themselves trouble by not repeating well-known and perhaps trivially true propositions which their hearers or readers can perfectly well be expected to supply for themselves. Moreover, it is not at all unusual for an argument to be *rhetorically* more powerful and persuasive when stated enthymematically than when enunciated in complete detail. With this rhetorical aspect, however, the logician is not concerned.

Because it is incomplete, an enthymeme must have its suppressed parts taken into account when the question arises of testing its validity. When a necessary premiss is missing, without that premiss the inference is invalid. But where the unexpressed premiss is easily supplied, in all fairness it ought to be included as part of the argument in appraising it. In such a case one assumes that the maker of the argument did have more "in mind" than he stated explicitly. In most cases there is no difficulty in supplying the tacit premiss that the speaker intended but did not express. A cardinal principle in supplying suppressed premisses is that the proposition must be one which the speaker can safely presume his hearers to accept as true. Thus it would be foolish to suggest taking the conclusion itself as a suppressed premiss, for if the arguer could have expected his auditors to accept that proposition as a premiss, without proof, it would have been idle for him to attempt to establish it as conclusion of an argument.

Any kind of argument can be expressed enthymematically, but the kinds of enthymemes that have been most extensively studied are incompletely expressed syllogistic arguments. We confine our attention to these in the remainder of this section. Enthymemes have traditionally been divided into different "orders," according to which part of the syllogism is left unexpressed. A *first-order* enthymeme is one in which the syllogism's major premiss is not stated. The preceding example is of the first order. A *second-order* enthymeme is one in which only the major premiss and the conclusion are stated, the minor premiss being suppressed. An example of this type is: "All students are opposed to the new regulations, so all coeds are opposed to them." Here the minor premiss is easily supplied, being the obviously true proposition "All coeds are students." A *third-order* enthymeme is one in which both premisses are stated, but the conclusion is left unexpressed. An example of this type is the argument: "No true Christian is vain, but some churchgoers are vain." If the context is such that the intended conclusion is "Some churchgoers are not true Christians," then the argument is valid. But if the speaker was intending to establish the conclusion that "Some true Christians are not churchgoers," then his enthymeme is invalid, committing the fallacy of Illicit Process of the Major Term. Here the context is decisive. But in other cases, a third-order enthymeme may be invalid regardless of context. Where both premisses are negative, or where both premisses are particular propositions, or where their common term is undistributed, no syllogistic conclusion follows validly, so such enthymemes are invalid in any context.

In testing an enthymeme for validity, two steps are involved. The first is to supply the missing parts of the argument; the second is to test the resulting syllogism. If one of the premisses is missing, it may be that only the addition of an implausible proposition as premiss will make the argument valid, while with any plausible proposition added the argument is invalid. Pointing this out is a legitimate criticim of an enthymematic argument. Of course, an even more crushing objection is to show that *no* additional premiss, no matter how implausible, can turn the enthymeme into a valid categorical syllogism.

It should be observed that no new logical principles need be introduced in dealing with enthymemes. They are ultimately tested by the same methods that apply to standard-form categorical syllogisms. The difference between enthymemes and syllogisms is rhetorical rather than logical.

EXERCISES

Name the order and discuss the correctness of each of the following enthymemes:

★ 1. Our ideas reach no farther than our experience: we have no experience of divine attributes and operations: I need not conclude my syllogism: you can draw the inference yourself.

—DAVID HUME, *Dialogues Concerning Natural Religion*

2. All physicians are college graduates, so all members of the American Medical Association must be college graduates.

3. It must have rained lately, because the fish just aren't biting.

4. Yond' Cassius has a lean and hungry look . . . such men are dangerous.

★ 5. Henry is interested only in making money, but you cannot serve both God and Mammon!

6. Adamson can't have a telephone, because his name isn't listed in the phone book.

7. No enthymemes are complete, so this argument is incomplete.

8. He would not take the crown
Therefore 'tis certain he was not ambitious.

9. Any reader who completes this argument is a good student, for it is difficult.

★ 10. He knows his own child, so he must be a wise father.

11. . . . we possess some immaterial knowledge. No sense knowledge, however, can be immaterial; therefore, etc.

—DUNS SCOTUS, *Oxford Commentary on the Sentences of Peter Lombard*

12. It could hardly be denied that a tax laid specifically on the exercise of these freedoms would be unconstitutional. Yet the license tax imposed by this ordinance is in substance just that.

—MR. JUSTICE DOUGLAS, for the Court, *Murdock* v. *Commonwealth of Pennsylvania* 319 US 105 (1943)

13. He who is without sin should cast the first stone. There is no one here who does not have a skeleton in his closet. I know, and I know them by name.

—REP. ADAM CLAYTON POWELL, Speech in the United States House of Representatives, 1967

14. Mary attended the opera, so her lamb must have attended the opera too.

★ 15. . . . I am an Idealist, since I believe that all that exists is spiritual.

—JOHN MCTAGGART ELLIS MCTAGGART, *Philosophical Studies*

16. Mr. Cole is well groomed, and we know what that implies because all successful men are well groomed.

17. However, the legal propriety of Manchester's book is at this writing before the courts and is accordingly not an appropriate subject for discussion.

—ARNOLD L. FAIN, "The Legal Right to Privacy,"
Saturday Review, January 21, 1967

18. I do not believe we can have any freedom at all in the philosophical sense, for we act not only under external compulsion but also by inner necessity.

—ALBERT EINSTEIN

19. I am an American and therefore what I do, however small, is of importance.

—STRUTHERS BURT

★ 20. Achilles is brave so he must be deserving of the fair.

21. Man tends to increase at a greater rate than his means of subsistence; consequently he is occasionally subject to a severe struggle for existence.

—CHARLES DARWIN, *The Descent of Man*

22. No internal combustion engines are free from pollution; but no internal combustion engine is completely efficient. You may draw your own conclusion.

23. A nation without a conscience is a nation without a soul. A nation without a soul is a nation that cannot live.

—WINSTON CHURCHILL

24. Liberty means responsibility. That is why most men dread it.

—GEORGE BERNARD SHAW, *Maxims for Revolutionists*

25. It is always possible to pretend to motives and abilities other than one's real ones, or to pretend to strengths of motives and levels of ability other than their real strengths and levels. The theatre could not exist, if it was not possible to make such pretences and to make them efficiently.

—GILBERT RYLE, *The Concept of Mind*

26. Only demonstrative proof should be able to make you abandon the theory of the Creation; but such a proof does not exist in Nature.

—MOSES MAIMONIDES, *The Guide for the Perplexed*

7.5 Sorites

There are occasions when a single categorical syllogism will not suffice for drawing a desired conclusion from a group of premisses. Thus from the premisses:

All diplomats are tactful.
Some government officials are diplomats.
All government officials are men in public life.

one cannot draw the conclusion:

Some men in public life are tactful.

by a single syllogistic inference. Yet the indicated conclusion is entailed by the stated premisses. To derive it requires two syllogisms rather than one. A stepwise process of argumentation must be resorted to, where each step is a separate categorical syllogism. When stated explicitly, the required argument will be:

All diplomats are tactful individuals.
Some government officials are diplomats.
―――――――――――――――――――――――――――――――
Therefore some government officials are tactful individuals.
All government officials are men in public life.
―――――――――――――――――――――――――――――――
Therefore some men in public life are tactful individuals.

The present argument is not a syllogism but a *chain* of categorical syllogisms, connected by the conclusion of the first, which is a premiss of the second. This chain has only two links, but more extended arguments may consist of a greater number. Since a chain is no stronger than its weakest link, an argument of this type is valid if, and only if, all of its constituent syllogisms are valid.

Where such an argument is expressed enthymematically, with only the premisses and the final conclusion stated, it is called a sorites. Sorites may have three, four, or *any* number of premisses. Some are very lengthy indeed. The following example is due to the philosopher Gottfried Leibniz:

> The human soul is a thing whose activity is thinking. A thing whose activity is thinking is one whose activity is immediately apprehended, and without any representation of parts therein. A thing whose activity is immediately apprehended without any representation of parts therein is a thing whose activity does not contain parts. A thing whose activity does not contain parts is one whose activity is not motion. A thing whose activity is not motion is not a body. What is not a body is not in space. What is not in space is insusceptible of

motion. What is insusceptible of motion is indissoluble (for dissolution is a movement of parts). What is indissoluble is incorruptible. What is incorruptible is immortal. Therefore the human soul is immortal.[1]

This sorites contains no less than ten premisses. Any sorites may be tested by making its intermediate conclusions or steps explicit and testing separately the various categorical syllogisms thus obtained. If we ignore the possibility that an equivocation is present, then the validity of Leibniz's sorites is easily verified.

It will be convenient, in connection with the exercises provided below, to say that a sorites is in standard form when all of its propositions are in standard form, when each term occurs exactly twice, and when every proposition (except the last) has a term in common with the proposition which immediately follows it. Thus one standard-form translation of Lewis Carroll's sorites:

(1) Every one who is sane can do Logic.
(2) No lunatics are fit to serve on a jury.
(3) None of your sons can do Logic.
Therefore none of your sons is fit to serve on a jury.

is

(2′) All persons fit to serve on a jury are sane persons.
(1′) All sane persons are persons who can do Logic.
(3′) No sons of yours are persons who can do Logic.
Therefore no sons of yours are persons fit to serve on a jury.

It can be tested by stating the suppressed subconclusions explicitly, and then testing the resulting categorical syllogisms.

EXERCISES[2]

I. Translate each of the following sorites into standard form, and test its validity:

★ 1. (1) Babies are illogical.
(2) Nobody is despised who can manage a crocodile.
(3) Illogical persons are despised.
Therefore babies cannot manage crocodiles.

[1] From *An Introduction to Logic* by H. W. B. Joseph, Oxford University Press, 1906, 1916.

[2] Practically all of the following exercises are taken, with little or no modification, from Lewis Carroll's *Symbolic Logic*.

2. (1) No experienced person is incompetent.
   (2) Jenkins is always blundering.
   (3) No competent person is always blundering.

   Therefore Jenkins is inexperienced.

3. (1) The only books in this library, that I do not recommend for reading, are unhealthy in tone.
   (2) The bound books are all well written.
   (3) All the romances are healthy in tone.
   (4) I do not recommend you to read any of the unbound books.

   Therefore all the romances in this library are well written.

4. (1) Only profound scholars can be dons at Oxford.
   (2) No insensitive souls are great lovers of music.
   (3) No one whose soul is not sensitive can be a Don Juan.
   (4) There are no profound scholars who are not great lovers of music.

   Therefore all Oxford dons are Don Juans.

5. (1) No interesting poems are unpopular among people of real taste.
   (2) No modern poetry is free from affectation.
   (3) All your poems are on the subject of soap bubbles.
   (4) No affected poetry is popular among people of real taste.
   (5) Only a modern poem would be on the subject of soap bubbles.

   Therefore all your poems are uninteresting.

6. (1) None but men of letters are poets.
   (2) Only military men are astronauts.
   (3) Whoever contributes to the new magazine is a poet.
   (4) Nobody is both a military man and a man of letters.

   Therefore not one astronaut is a contributor to the new magazine.

II. Each of the following sets of propositions can serve as premisses for a valid sorites. For each, find the conclusion and establish the argument as valid:

★ 1. (1) No one takes in the *Times* unless he is well educated.
   (2) No hedgehogs can read.
   (3) Those who cannot read are not well educated.

2. (1) All puddings are nice.
   (2) This dish is a pudding.
   (3) No nice things are wholesome.

3. (1) The only articles of food, that my doctor allows me, are such as are not very rich.
   (2) Nothing that agrees with me is unsuitable for supper.

(3) Wedding cake is always very rich.
(4) My doctor allows me all articles of food that are suitable for supper.

4. (1) All my sons are slim.
(2) No child of mine is healthy who takes no exercise.
(3) All gluttons, who are children of mine, are fat.
(4) No daughter of mine takes any exercise.

5. (1) When I work a Logic example without grumbling, you may be sure it is one that I can understand.
(2) These Sorites are not arranged in regular order, like the examples I am used to.
(3) No easy example ever makes my head ache.
(4) I can't understand examples that are not arranged in regular order, like those I am used to.
(5) I never grumble at an example, unless it gives me a headache.

7.6 Disjunctive and Hypothetical Syllogisms

A syllogism is a deductive argument consisting of two premisses and a conclusion. There are different kinds of syllogisms, taking their names from the kinds of propositions they contain. Thus the categorical syllogism is so called because it contains categorical propositions exclusively. Other kinds of propositions occur in other kinds of syllogisms.

We may think of categorical propositions as *simple,* in contrast to *compound* propositions which contain other propositions as components. The first kind of compound proposition to be considered is the *disjunctive* (or *alternative*) proposition, an example of which is "Either Fido ran away or Fido got hit by a car." Its two component propositions are "Fido ran away" and "Fido got hit by a car." The disjunctive proposition, or disjunction, contains two component propositions, which are its disjuncts. The disjunction does not categorically assert the truth of either one of its disjuncts, but says that at least one of them is true, allowing for the possibility that both may be true.

If we have a disjunction as one premiss, and as another premiss the denial or contradictory of one of its two disjuncts, then we can validly infer that the disjunction's other disjunct is true. Any argument of this form is a valid disjunctive syllogism, for example:

Either Fido ran away or Fido got hit by a car.
Fido did not run away.
Therefore Fido got hit by a car.

As we use the term in this section, not every disjunctive syllogism is valid. For example, the argument

> Either Fido ran away or Fido got hit by a car.
> Fido ran away.
> Therefore Fido did not get hit by a car.

may be classified as an invalid disjunctive syllogism. It bears a superficial resemblance to the preceding example, but is easily seen to be fallacious. Consistently with the premisses, Fido might have run away *and* got hit by a car. The truth of one disjunct of a disjunction does not imply the falsehood of the other disjunct, since both disjuncts of a disjunction can be true. Hence we have a valid disjunctive syllogism only where the categorical premiss contradicts one disjunct of the disjunctive premiss and the conclusion affirms the other disjunct of the disjunctive premiss.

An objection might be raised at this point, based on such an argument as the following:

> Either Smith is in New York or Smith is in Paris.
> Smith is in New York.
> Therefore Smith is not in Paris.

Here the categorical premiss affirms one disjunct of the stated disjunction, and the conclusion contradicts the other disjunct, yet the conclusion seems to follow validly. Closer analysis shows, however, that the stated disjunction plays no role in the argument. The conclusion follows enthymematically from the categorical premiss, with the unexpressed additional premiss being the obviously true proposition

> Either Smith is not in New York or Smith is not in Paris.

When this tacit premiss is supplied, and the superfluous original disjunction is discarded, the resulting argument is easily seen to be a valid disjunctive syllogism. The apparent exception is not really an exception, and the objection is groundless.

The second kind of compound proposition to be considered is the *conditional* (or *hypothetical*) proposition, an example of which is "If the first native is a politician then the first native lies." A conditional proposition contains two component propositions: the one following the "if" is the *antecedent,* and the one following the "then" is the *consequent.* A syllogism that contains conditional propositions exclusively is called a *pure hypothetical syllogism,* for example,

If the first native is a politician, then he lies.
If he lies, then he denies being a politician.
Therefore if the first native is a politician, then he denies being a politician.

In this argument it can be observed that the first premiss and the conclusion have the same antecedent, that the second premiss and the conclusion have the same consequent, and that the consequent of the first premiss is the same as the antecedent of the second premiss. It should be clear that any pure hypothetical syllogism whose premisses and conclusion have their component parts so related is a valid argument.

A syllogism having one conditional premiss and one categorical premiss is called a *mixed hypothetical syllogism.* There are two valid forms of the mixed hypothetical syllogism that have been given special names. The first is illustrated by

If the second native told the truth, then only one native is a politician.
The second native told the truth.
Therefore only one native is a politician.

Here the categorical premiss affirms the antecedent of the conditional premiss, and the conclusion affirms its consequent. Any argument of this form is valid, and is said to be in the *affirmative mood* or *modus ponens* (from the Latin *ponere,* meaning "to affirm"). One must not confuse the valid form *modus ponens* with the clearly invalid form displayed by the following argument

If Bacon wrote *Hamlet,* then Bacon was a great writer.
Bacon was a great writer.
Therefore Bacon wrote *Hamlet.*

This argument differs from *modus ponens* in that its categorical premiss affirms the consequent, rather than the antecedent, of the conditional premiss. Any argument of this form is said to commit the *Fallacy of Affirming the Consequent.*

The other valid form of mixed hypothetical syllogism is illustrated by

If the one-eyed prisoner saw two red hats, then he could tell the color of the hat on his own head.
The one-eyed prisoner could not tell the color of the hat on his own head.
Therefore the one-eyed prisoner did not see two red hats.

Here the categorical premiss denies the consequent of the conditional premiss, and the conclusion denies its antecedent. Any argument of this form is valid, and is said to be in the form *modus tollens* (from the Latin *tollere,* meaning "to deny"). One must not confuse the valid form *modus tollens* with the clearly invalid form displayed by the following argument

If Carl embezzled the college funds, then Carl is guilty of a felony.
Carl did not embezzle the college funds.
Therefore Carl is not guilty of a felony.

This argument differs from *modus tollens* in that its categorical premiss denies the antecedent, rather than the consequent, of the conditional premiss. Any argument of this form is said to commit the *Fallacy of Denying the Antecedent.*

EXERCISES

Identify the form and discuss the validity or invalidity of each of the following arguments:

★ 1. Smith is the fireman or Smith is the engineer. Smith is not the fireman. Therefore Smith is the engineer.

2. If the first native is a politician, then the first native denied being a politician. The first native denied being a politician. Therefore the first native is a politician.

3. If the first native denied being a politician, then the second native told the truth. If the second native told the truth, then the second native is not a politician. Therefore if the first native denied being a politician, then the second native is not a politician.

4. If Mr. Jones lives in Chicago, then Jones is the brakeman. Mr. Jones lives in Chicago. Therefore Jones is the brakeman.

★ 5. If the second native told the truth, then the first native denied being a politician. If the third native told the truth, then the first native denied being a politician. Therefore if the second native told the truth, then the third native told the truth.

6. If Robinson is the brakeman, then Mr. Robinson lives in Chicago. Mr. Robinson does not live in Chicago. Therefore Robinson is not the brakeman.

7. If Robinson is the brakeman, then Smith is the engineer. Robinson is not the brakeman. Therefore Smith is not the engineer.

8. The stranger is either a knave or a fool. He is a knave. Therefore the stranger is no fool.

9. If Mr. Jones is the brakeman's next-door neighbor, then 20,000 is exactly divisible by 3. But 20,000 is not exactly divisible by 3. Therefore Mr. Jones is not the brakeman's next-door neighbor.

★ 10. Mr. Smith is the brakeman's next-door neighbor or Mr. Robinson is the brakeman's next-door neighbor. Mr. Robinson is not the brakeman's next-door neighbor. Therefore Mr. Smith is the brakeman's next-door neighbor.

11. If this syllogism commits the Fallacy of Affirming the Consequent, then it is invalid. This syllogism does not commit the Fallacy of Affirming the Consequent. Therefore this syllogism is valid.

12. If the one-eyed prisoner does not know the color of the hat on his own head, then the blind prisoner cannot have on a red hat. The one-eyed prisoner does not know the color of the hat on his own head. Therefore the blind prisoner cannot have on a red hat.

13. If all three prisoners have on white hats, then the one-eyed man does not know the color of the hat on his own head. The one-eyed man does not know the color of the hat on his own head. Therefore all three prisoners have on white hats.

14. Mr. Robinson lives in Detroit or Mr. Robinson lives in Chicago. Mr. Robinson lives in Detroit. Therefore Mr. Robinson does not live in Chicago.

★ 15. If the first native is a politician, then the third native tells the truth. If the third native tells the truth, then the third native is not a politician. Therefore if the first native is a politician, then the third native is not a politician.

16. Mankind, he said, judging by their neglect of him, have never, as I think, at all understood the power of Love. For if they had understood him they would surely have built noble temples and altars, and offered solemn sacrifices in his honor; but this is not done. . . .

—PLATO, *Symposium*

17. I have already said that he must have gone to King's Pyland or to Capleton. He is not at King's Pyland, therefore he is at Capleton.

—A. CONAN DOYLE, *Silver Blaze*

18. If Pluto, according to Halliday's calculations, had a diameter of more than 4,200 miles, then an occultation would have occurred at McDonald [Observatory at Fort Davis, Texas], and the records clearly in-

dicated that it did not. Thus Pluto must be that size or smaller; it cannot be larger.

—THOMAS D. NICHOLSON, "The Enigma of Pluto," *Natural History,* Vol. LXXVI, March 1967, pp. 48–49

19. If then, it is agreed that things are either the result of coincidence or for an end, and these cannot be the result of coincidence or spontaneity, it follows that they must be for an end. . . .

—ARISTOTLE, *Physics*

★ 20. There is no case known (neither is it, indeed, possible) in which a thing is found to be the efficient cause of itself; for so it would be prior to itself, which is impossible.

—THOMAS AQUINAS, *Summa Theologica,* I, Question 2, Article 3

21. Either wealth is an evil or wealth is a good; but wealth is not an evil; therefore wealth is a good.

—SEXTUS EMPIRICUS, *Against the Logicians*

22. And certainly if its essence and power are infinite, its goodness must be infinite, since a thing whose essence is finite has finite goodness.

—ROGER BACON, *The Opus Majus*

23. I *do* know that this pencil exists; but I could not know this, if Hume's principles were true; *therefore,* Hume's principles, one or both of them, are false.

—GEORGE EDWARD MOORE, *Some Main Problems of Philosophy*

24. A theoryless position is possible only if there are no theories of evidence. But there are theories of evidence. Therefore, a theoryless position is impossible.

—HENRY W. JOHNSTONE, JR., "The Law of Non-Contradiction," *Logique et Analyse,* n.s. Vol. 3 (1960), p. 7

★ 25. It is clear that we mean something, and something different in each case, by such words [as *substance, cause, change,* etc.]. If we did not we could not use them consistently, and it is obvious that on the whole we do consistently apply and withhold such names.

—C. D. BROAD, *Scientific Thought*

26. If number were an idea, then arithmetic would be psychology. But arithmetic is no more psychology than, say, astronomy is. Astronomy is concerned, not with ideas of the planets, but with the planets themselves, and by the same token the objects of arithmetic are not ideas either.

—GOTTLOB FREGE, *The Foundations of Arithmetic*

27. If error were something positive, God would be its cause, and by Him it would continually be procreated (per Prop. 12). [All existing things are conserved by God's power alone.] But this is absurd (per Prop. 13). [God is never a deceiver, but in all things is perfectly true.] Therefore error is nothing positive. Q. E. D.

—BARUCH SPINOZA, *The Principles of Philosophy Demonstrated by the Method of Geometry*

28. . . . If a mental state is to be identical with a physical state, the two must share all properties in common. But there is one property, spatial localizability, that is not so shared; that is, physical states and events are located in space, whereas mental events and states are not. Hence, mental events and states are different from physical ones.

—JAEGWON KIM, "On the Psycho-Physical Identity Theory," *American Philosophical Quarterly*, 1966

29. When we regard a man as morally responsible for an act, we regard him as a legitimate object of moral praise or blame in respect of it. But it seems plain that a man cannot be a legitimate object of moral praise or blame for an act unless in willing the act he is in some important sense a "free" agent. Evidently free will in some sense, therefore, is a pre-condition of moral responsibility.

—C. ARTHUR CAMPBELL, *In Defence of Free Will*

30. Syllogism [is] not the great instrument of reason . . . if syllogisms must be taken for the only proper instrument and means of knowledge; it will follow, that before Aristotle there was not one man that did or could know anything by reason; and that since the invention of syllogisms there is not one of ten thousand that doth.

But God has not been so sparing to men to make them barely two-legged creatures, and left it to Aristotle to make them rational. . . .

—JOHN LOCKE, *An Essay Concerning Human Understanding*

7.7 The Dilemma

The dilemma, a common form of argument in ordinary language, is a legacy from older times when logic and rhetoric were more closely connected than they are today. From the strictly logical point of view, the dilemma is not of special interest or importance. But rhetorically, the dilemma is perhaps the most powerful instrument of persuasion ever devised. It is a devastating weapon in controversy.

Today one says somewhat loosely that a person is in a dilemma when he must choose between two alternatives, both of which are bad or unpleasant. More picturesquely such a person is described as being "impaled on the horns of a dilemma." Traditionally, a dilemma is an argument intended to put one's opponent in just that kind of position. In debate, one uses a dilemma to offer alternative positions to one's adversary, from which he must choose, and then to prove that no matter which choice he makes, he is committed to a conclusion that is distasteful to him. Thus in a debate on a proposed protective-tariff bill, an opponent of the measure may argue as follows:

> If the proposed tariff produces scarcity, it will be injurious; and if it does not produce scarcity, it will be useless. It will either produce scarcity or else it won't. Therefore the proposed tariff will either be injurious or useless.

Such an argument is designed to push the opponent (in this case the sponsor of the bill) into a corner and there annihilate him. The second premiss, which offers the alternatives, is a disjunction. The first premiss, which asserts that both of the alternatives have certain undesirable consequences, consists of two conditional propositions linked by a conjunction, e.g., "and," "but," or "though." The conclusion of a dilemma may be another disjunction, offering alternatives, or it may be a categorical proposition. In the former case the dilemma is said to be "complex," in the latter case "simple." A dilemma need not have an unpleasant conclusion. An example of one with a happy conclusion is provided by the following *simple* dilemma:

> If the blest in heaven have no desires, they will be perfectly content; so they will, if their desires are fully gratified; but either they will have no desires, or have them fully gratified; therefore they will be perfectly content.

Because of its importance in debate, a number of ways of evading or refuting the conclusion of a dilemma have been given special names. They are all picturesque, relating to the fact that a dilemma has two (or more) "horns." The three ways of defeating or refuting a dilemma are known as "going (or escaping) between the horns," "taking (or grasping) it by the horns," and "rebutting it by means of a counterdilemma." It should be borne in mind that these are not ways to prove the dilemma invalid, but are rather ways of avoiding its conclusion without challenging the formal validity of the argument.

One escapes between the horns of a dilemma by rejecting its disjunctive premiss. This method is often the easiest way to evade the conclusion of a dilemma, for unless one half of the disjunction is the explicit contradictory of the other, the disjunction may very well be false. One justification sometimes offered for giving grades to students is that recognizing good work will stimulate the student to study harder. A student may criticize this theory, using the following dilemma:

> If a student is fond of learning, he needs no stimulus, and if he dislikes learning, no stimulus will be of any avail. But any student is either fond of learning or dislikes it. Therefore a stimulus is either needless or of no avail.

This argument is formally valid, but we can evade its conclusion by *going between the horns*. The disjunctive premiss is false, for students have all kinds of attitudes toward learning: some may be fond of it, many dislike it, but a vast majority are indifferent. And for that vast majority a stimulus may be both needed and of some avail. It should be remembered that going between the horns does not prove the conclusion to be false but shows merely that the argument does not provide adequate grounds for accepting that conclusion.

Where the disjunctive premiss is unassailable, as when the alternatives exhaust the possibilities, it is impossible to escape between the horns. Another method of evading the conclusion must be sought. One such method is to *grasp the dilemma by the horns,* which involves rejecting the premiss which is a conjunction. To deny a conjunction we need only deny one of its parts. When we grasp the dilemma by the horns, we attempt to show that at least one of the conditionals is false. Consider again the dilemma attacking the protective tariff. The proponent of the tariff bill might grasp the dilemma by the horns and argue that even if the proposed tariff were to produce scarcity, it would not be injurious. After all, a scarcity would stimulate domestic production, thus giving the country increased employment and more highly developed industry. Were any scarcity produced, he might argue, it would be only temporary, and, far from being injurious, would be highly beneficial. Of course there may be more to be said, but the original dilemma has been grasped firmly by the horns.

Rebutting a dilemma by means of a counterdilemma is the most entertaining and ingenious method of all; but it is seldom cogent, for reasons that will appear presently. To rebut a given dilemma, one constructs another dilemma whose conclusion is opposed to the conclusion of the original. *Any* counterdilemma may be used in rebuttal, but ideally the counterdilemma should be built up out of the same ingredients (categorical propositions) that the original dilemma contained.

A classical example of this elegant kind of rebuttal concerns the following argument of an Athenian mother attempting to persuade her son not to enter politics:

> If you say what is just, men will hate you; and if you say what is unjust, the gods will hate you; but you must either say the one or the other; therefore you will be hated.

Her son rebutted the dilemma with the following one:

> If I say what is just, the gods will love me; and if I say what is unjust, men will love me. I must say either the one or the other. Therefore I shall be loved!

In public discussion, where the dilemma is the strongest of controversial weapons, a rebuttal like this, which derives an opposite conclusion from almost the same premisses, marks the absolute zenith of rhetorical skill. But if we examine the dilemma and rebutting counterdilemma more closely, we see that their conclusions are not as opposed as they might at first appear.

The conclusion of the first dilemma is that the son will be hated (by men or by the gods), whereas that of the rebutting dilemma is that the son will be loved (by the gods or by men). But these two conclusions are perfectly compatible. The rebutting counterdilemma serves merely to establish a conclusion different from that of the original. Both conclusions may very well be true together, so no refutation has been accomplished. But in the heat of controversy analysis is unwelcome; and if such a rebuttal occurred in a public debate, the average audience would overwhelmingly agree that the rebuttal completely demolished the original argument.

That this sort of rebuttal does not refute, but only directs attention to a different aspect of the same matter, is perhaps more clearly shown in the case of the following little dilemma, advanced by an "optimist."

> If I work, I earn money; and if I am idle, I enjoy myself. Either I work or I am idle. Therefore either I earn money or I enjoy myself.

A "pessimist" might offer the following counterdilemma:

> If I work, I don't enjoy myself; and if I am idle, I don't earn money. Either I work or I am idle. Therefore either I don't earn money or I don't enjoy myself.

These conclusions represent merely different ways of viewing the same facts; they do not constitute a disagreement over what the facts are.

No discussion of dilemmas would be complete unless it mentioned the celebrated lawsuit between Protagoras and Eulathus. Protagoras was a teacher who lived in Greece during the fifth century B.C. He taught many subjects but specialized in the art of pleading before juries. Eulathus wanted to become a lawyer, but, not being able to pay the required tuition, he made an arrangement according to which Protagoras would teach him but not receive payment until Eulathus won his first case. When Eulathus finished his course of study, he delayed going into practice. Tired of waiting for his money, Protagoras brought suit against his former pupil for the tuition money that was owed. Unmindful of the adage that the lawyer who tries his own case has a fool for a client, Eulathus decided to plead his own case in court. When the trial began, Protagoras presented his side of the case in a crushing dilemma:

> If Eulathus loses this case, then he must pay me (by the judgment of the court); if he wins this case, then he must pay me (by the terms of the contract). He must either lose or win this case. Therefore Eulathus must pay me.

The situation looked bad for Eulathus, but he had learned well the art of rhetoric. He offered the court the following counterdilemma in rebuttal:

> If I win this case, I shall not have to pay Protagoras (by the judgment of the court); if I lose this case, I shall not have to pay Protagoras (by the terms of the contract, for then I shall not yet have won my first case). I must either win or lose this case. Therefore I do not have to pay Protagoras!

Had you been the judge, how would you have decided?

It is to be noted that the conclusion of Eulathus' rebutting dilemma is *not* compatible with the conclusion of Protagoras' original dilemma. One conclusion is the explicit denial of the other. But it is a rare case in which a rebuttal stands in this relation to the dilemma against which it is directed. When it does so, the premisses involved are themselves inconsistent, and it is this implicit contradiction that the two dilemmas serve to make explicit.

EXERCISES

Discuss the various arguments which might be offered to refute each of the following:

★ 1. If we interfere with the publication of false and harmful doctrines, we shall be guilty of suppressing the liberties of others; while if we do not interfere with the publication of such doctrines, we run the risk of losing our own liberties. We must either interfere or not interfere with the publication of false and harmful doctrines. Hence we must either be guilty of suppressing the liberties of others or else run the risk of losing our own liberties.

2. If we are to have peace, we must not encourage the competitive spirit; while if we are to make progress, we must encourage the competitive spirit. We must either encourage or not encourage the competitive spirit. Therefore we shall either have no peace or make no progress.

3. If you tell me what I already understand, you do not enlarge my understanding; while if you tell me something which I do not understand, then your remarks are unintelligible to me. Whatever you tell me must be either something I already understand or something which I do not understand. Hence whatever you say either does not enlarge my understanding or else is unintelligible to me.

4. If what you say does not enlarge my understanding, then what you say is without value to me; and if what you say is unintelligible to me, then it is without value to me. Whatever you say either does not enlarge my understanding or else is unintelligible to me. Therefore nothing you say is of any value to me.

★ 5. If the conclusion of a deductive argument goes beyond the premisses, then the argument is invalid; while if the conclusion of a deductive argument does not go beyond the premisses, then the argument brings nothing new to light. The conclusion of a deductive argument must either go beyond the premisses or not go beyond them. Therefore deductive arguments are either invalid or else they bring nothing new to light.

6. If a deductive argument is invalid, it is without value; while a deductive argument which brings nothing new to light is also without value. Deductive arguments are either invalid or else they bring nothing new to light. Therefore deductive arguments are without value.

7. If the general was loyal, he would have obeyed his orders; and if he was intelligent, he would have understood them. The general either disobeyed his orders or else he did not understand them. Therefore the general must have been either disloyal or unintelligent.

8. If he was disloyal, then his dismissal was justified; and if he was unintelligent, then his dismissal was justified. He was either disloyal or unintelligent. Therefore his dismissal was justified.

9. If the several nations keep the peace, the United Nations Organization is unnecessary; while if the several nations go to war, the United Nations Organization will have been unsuccessful in its purpose of preventing war. Now either the several nations keep the peace or they go to war. Hence the United Nations Organization is unnecessary or unsuccessful.

★ 10. If men are good, laws are not needed to prevent wrongdoing; while if men are bad, laws will not succeed in preventing wrongdoing. Men are either good or bad. Therefore either laws are not needed to prevent wrongdoing or laws will not succeed in preventing wrongdoing.

11. Archbishop Morton, Chancellor under Henry VII, was famous for his method of extracting "contributions" to the king's purse. A person who lived extravagantly was forced to make a large contribution, because it was obvious that he could afford it. Someone who lived modestly was forced to make a large contribution because it was clear that he must have saved a lot of money on living expenses. Whichever way he turned he was said to be "caught on Morton's fork."

—DOROTHY HAYDEN, *Winning Declarer Play*

12. . . . a man cannot enquire either about that which he knows, or about that which he does not know; for if he knows, he has no need to enquire; and if not, he cannot; for he does not know the very subject about which he is to enquire.

—PLATO, *Meno*

13. There is a dilemma to which every opposition to successful iniquity must, in the nature of things, be liable. If you lie still, you are considered as an accomplice in the measures in which you silently acquiesce. If you resist, you are accused of provoking irritable power to new excesses. The conduct of a losing party never appears right. . . .

—EDMUND BURKE, *A Letter to a Member of the National Assembly*

14. And we seem unable to clear ourselves from the old dilemma, If you predicate what is different, you ascribe to the subject what it is *not;* and if you predicate what is *not* different, you say nothing at all.

—F. H. BRADLEY, *Appearance and Reality*

★ 15. All political action aims at either preservation or change. When desiring to preserve, we wish to prevent a change to the worse; when desiring to change, we wish to bring about something better. All political action is then guided by some thought of better and worse.

—LEO STRAUSS, *What Is Political Philosophy?*

16. If a thing moves, it moves either in the place where it is or in that where it is not; but it moves neither in the place where it is (for it re-

mains therein) nor in that where it is not (for it does not exist therein); therefore nothing moves.

—SEXTUS EMPIRICUS, *Against the Physicists*

17. And what a life should I lead, at my age, wandering from city to city, ever changing my place of exile, and always being driven out! For I am quite sure that wherever I go, there, as here, the young men will flock to me; and if I drive them away, their elders will drive me out at their request; and if I let them come, their fathers and friends will drive me out for their sakes.

—PLATO, *Apology*

18. If Socrates died, he died either when he was living or when he was dead. But he did not die while living; for assuredly he was living, and as living he had not died. Nor when he died; for then he would be twice dead. Therefore Socrates did not die.

—SEXTUS EMPIRICUS, *Against the Physicists*

19. The "paradox of analysis," which postulates the dilemma that an analysis is either a mere synonym and hence trivial, or more than a synonym and hence false, has its equivalent in Linguistic Philosophy: a neologism can either be accounted for in existing terms, in which case it is redundant, or it cannot, in which case it has not "been given sense."

—ERNEST GELLNER, *Words and Things*

20. If these books merely repeat what is in the Koran they are superfluous; and if they are in disagreement with the Koran they are pernicious. But they must either merely repeat what is in the Koran or they are in disagreement with it. Therefore they are either superfluous or pernicious, and so they should be burned.

—Attributed to the CALIPH OMAR when he burned the Alexandrian Library in 640 A.D.

Chapter 8
Symbolic Logic

. . . the woof and warp of all thought and all research is symbols, and the life of thought and science is the life inherent in symbols; so it is wrong to say that a good language is important *to good thought, merely; for it is the essence of it.*

—*Charles Sanders Peirce*

8.1 The Value of Special Symbols

Arguments formulated in English or any other natural language are often difficult to appraise because of the vague and equivocal nature of the words used, the amphiboly of their construction, the misleading idioms they may contain, their potentially confusing metaphorical style, and the distraction due to whatever emotive significance they may have. These topics were discussed at length in Part One. Even when these difficulties are resolved, there still remains the problem of deciding the validity or invalidity of the argument. To avoid these peripheral difficulties, it is convenient to set up an *artificial symbolic language,* free from these defects, in which statements and arguments can be expressed.

Some of the advantages of a technical vocabulary for a science have already been mentioned in Chapter 4. The use of a special logical notation is not peculiar to modern logic. Aristotle, the ancient founder of the subject, used variables to facilitate his own work. Although the difference in this respect between modern and classical logic is not one of kind but of degree, the difference in degree is tremendous. The greater extent to which modern logic has developed its own special technical language has made it immeasurably more powerful a tool for analysis and deduction. The special symbols of modern logic help us to exhibit with greater clarity the logical structures of propositions and arguments whose forms may tend to be obscured by the unwieldiness of ordinary language.

A further value of the logician's special symbols is the aid they give in the actual use and manipulation of statements and arguments. The situation here is comparable to that which led to the replacement of Roman numerals by the Arabic notation. We all know that Arabic numerals are clearer and more easily comprehended than the older Roman numerals which they displaced. But the real superiority of Arabic numerals is revealed only in computation. Any schoolboy can easily multiply 113 by 9. But to multiply CXIII by IX is a more difficult task, and the difficulty increases as larger and larger numbers are considered.[1] Similarly, the drawing of inferences and the evaluation of arguments is greatly facilitated by the adoption of a special logical notation. To quote Alfred North Whitehead, one of the great contributors to the advance of symbolic logic:

> . . . by the aid of symbolism, we can make transitions in reasoning almost mechanically by the eye, which otherwise would call into play the higher faculties of the brain.[2]

From this point of view, paradoxically enough, logic is not concerned with developing our powers of thought but with developing techniques that enable us to get along without thinking!

8.2 The Symbols for Conjunction, Negation, and Disjunction

In this chapter we shall be concerned with relatively simple arguments such as:

The blind man has a red hat or the blind man has a white hat.
The blind man does not have a red hat.

[1] There is much evidence that even the ancient Romans did not use their numerals in computation. Instead they utilized "counting boards," a Western version of the Oriental abacus. See *Number Words and Number Symbols* by Karl Menninger (Cambridge, Mass.: The MIT Press, 1969).

[2] *An Introduction to Mathematics* by A. N. Whitehead (New York: Oxford University Press, 1911).

Therefore the blind man has a white hat.

and

If Mr. Robinson is the brakeman's next-door neighbor, then Mr. Robinson lives halfway between Detroit and Chicago.
Mr. Robinson does not live halfway between Detroit and Chicago.
Therefore Mr. Robinson is not the brakeman's next-door neighbor.

Every argument of this general type contains at least one compound statement. It is customary in studying such arguments to divide all statements into two general categories, simple and compound. A *simple statement* is one which does not contain any other statement as a component. For example, "Charlie's neat" is a simple statement. A *compound statement* is one which does contain another statement as a component. For example, "Charlie's neat and Charlie's sweet" is a compound statement, for it contains two simple statements as components. Of course the components of a compound statement may themselves be compound.

The first type of compound statement to be considered is the *conjunction*. We can form the conjunction of two statements by placing the word "and" between them, and the two statements so combined are called *conjuncts*. Thus the compound statement "Charlie's neat and Charlie's sweet" is a conjunction, whose first conjunct is "Charlie's neat" and whose second conjunct is "Charlie's sweet."

The word "and" is a short and convenient word, but it has other uses besides that of connecting statements. For example, the statement "Lincoln and Grant were contemporaries" is *not* a conjunction but a simple statement expressing a relationship. To have a unique symbol whose only function is to connect statements conjunctively, we introduce the dot "•" as our symbol for conjunction. Thus the previous conjunction can be written as "Charlie's neat • Charlie's sweet." More generally, where p and q are any two statements whatever, their conjunction is written $p \cdot q$.

Since every statement is either true or false, every statement has a *truth value*—where the truth value of a true statement is *true* and the truth value of a false statement is *false*. We divide compound statements into two different categories, according to whether or not the truth value of the compound statement is completely determined by the truth values of its components. For example, the truth value of the compound statement "Othello believes that

Desdemona loves Cassio" is completely independent of the truth value of its component simple statement "Desdemona loves Cassio," for beliefs are sometimes mistaken. But there is a necessary connection between the truth value of a conjunction and the truth values of its conjuncts. A conjunction is true if both its conjuncts are true, but false otherwise. Any compound statement whose truth value is completely determined by the truth values of its components is said to be a *truth-functional* compound statement. Here we shall be concerned with truth-functional compound statements exclusively. In the remainder of this book, therefore, we shall use the term "simple statement" to refer to any statement that is not truth-functionally compound.

A conjunction is a truth-functional compound statement, so our dot symbol is a truth-functional connective. Given any two statements, p and q, there are only four possible sets of truth values they can have. These four possible cases, and the truth value of the conjunction in each, can be displayed as follows:

where p is true and q is true, $p \cdot q$ is true;
where p is true and q is false, $p \cdot q$ is false;
where p is false and q is true, $p \cdot q$ is false;
where p is false and q is false, $p \cdot q$ is false.

If we represent the truth values "true" and "false" by the capital letters **T** and **F**, the determination of the truth value of a conjunction by the truth values of its conjuncts can be represented more briefly by means of a truth table as:

p	q	$p \cdot q$
T	**T**	**T**
T	**F**	**F**
F	**T**	**F**
F	**F**	**F**

This truth table can be taken as defining the dot symbol, since it explains what truth values are assumed by $p \cdot q$ in every possible case.

We shall find it convenient to abbreviate simple statements by capital letters, generally using for this purpose a letter that will help us remember which statement it abbreviates. Thus we should abbreviate "Charlie's neat and Charlie's sweet" as $N \cdot S$. Some conjunctions both of whose conjuncts have the same subject term—for example, "Byron was a great poet and Byron was a great adventurer" —are more briefly and perhaps more naturally expressed in English by placing the "and" between the predicate terms and not repeating the subject term, as in "Byron was a great poet and a great adventurer." For our purposes we regard the latter as expressing the same statement as the former, and symbolize either one indifferently as $P \cdot A$. If both conjuncts of a conjunction have the same predicate term, as in "Lewis was a famous explorer and Clark was a famous explorer," again the conjunction would usually be expressed in English by placing the "and" between the subject terms and not repeating the predicate, as in "Lewis and Clark were famous explorers." Either formulation is symbolized as $L \cdot C$.

As shown by the truth table defining the dot symbol, a conjunction is true if and only if both of its conjuncts are true. But the word "and" has another use in which it signifies not *mere* (truth-functional) conjunction but has the sense of "and then," meaning temporal succession. Thus the statement "Jones entered the country at New York and went straight to Chicago" is significant and might be true, whereas "Jones went straight to Chicago and entered the country at New York" is hardly intelligible. And there is quite a difference between "He took off his shoes and got into bed" and "He got into bed and took off his shoes." Consideration of such examples emphasizes the desirability of having a special symbol with an exclusively truth-functional conjunctive use.

It should be remarked that the English words "but," "yet," "also," "still," "although," "however," "moreover," "nevertheless," and so on, and even the comma and the semicolon, can also be used to conjoin two statements into a single compound statement, and in their conjunctive sense they can all be represented by the dot symbol.

The *negation* (or contradictory or denial) of a statement in English is often formed by inserting a "not" into the original statement. Alternatively, one can express the negation of a statement in English by prefixing to it the phrase "it is false that" or "it is not the case that." It is customary to use the symbol "$\sim$" (called a *curl* or, less frequently, a *tilde)* to express the negation of a statement. Thus where M symbolizes the statement "All men are mortal," the various statements "Not all men are mortal," "Some men are not mortal," "It is false that all men are mortal," "It is not the case that all men are mortal," are all indifferently symbolized as $\sim M$. More generally, where p is any statement whatever, its negation is written $\sim p$. It is obvious that the curl is a truth-functional operator. The negation of any true statement is false, and the negation of any false statement is true. This fact can be expressed by means of a truth table very simply:

p	$\sim p$
T	**F**
F	**T**

This truth table may be regarded as the *definition* of the negation symbol "$\sim$."

The *disjunction* (or *alternation*) of two statements is formed in English by inserting the word "or" between them. The two component statements so combined are called *disjuncts* (or *alternatives*). The English word "or" is ambiguous, having two related but distinguishable meanings. One of them is exemplified in the statement "Premiums will be waived in the event of sickness or unemployment," for the intention here is obviously that premiums are waived not only for sick persons and for unemployed persons, but also for persons who are *both* sick *and* unemployed. This sense of the word "or" is called *weak* or *inclusive*. An inclusive disjunction is true in case one or the other or both disjuncts are true; only if both disjuncts are false is their inclusive disjunction false. The inclusive "or" has the sense of "either, possibly both." Where precision is at a premium, as in contracts and other legal documents, this sense is made explicit by use of the phrase "and/or."

The word "or" is also used in a *strong* or *exclusive* sense, in which the meaning is not "at least one" but "at least one and at most one." Where a restaurant lists "salad or dessert" on its table d'hôte menu, it is clearly meant that for the stated price of the meal, the diner may have one or the other *but not both*. When a mother succumbs to her child's teasing and gives permission to take "a cookie or a piece of cake," it would be a backward or disobedient child who helped himself to both. Where precision is at a premium and the exclusive sense of "or" is intended, the phrase "but not both" is usually added.

We interpret the inclusive disjunction of two statements as asserting that at least one of the statements is true, and their exclusive disjunction as asserting that at least one of the statements is true but not both are true. We observe here that the two kinds of disjunction have a part of their meanings in common. This partial common meaning, that at least one of the disjuncts is true, is the *whole* meaning of the inclusive "or" and a *part* of the meaning of the exclusive "or."

Although disjunctions are expressed ambiguously in English, they are unambiguous in Latin. The Latin language has two different words corresponding to the two different senses of the English word "or." The Latin word *vel* expresses weak or inclusive disjunction, and the Latin word *aut* corresponds to the word "or" in its strong or exclusive sense. It is customary to use the initial letter of the word *vel* to stand for "or" in its weak, inclusive sense. Where p and q are any two statements whatever, their weak or inclusive disjunction is written $p \vee q$. Our symbol for inclusive disjunction (called a *wedge*, or, less frequently, a *vee*) is also a truth-functional connective. A weak disjunction is false only in case both of its disjuncts are false. We may regard the wedge as being defined by the following truth table:

p	q	$p \vee q$
T	T	T
T	F	T
F	T	T
F	F	F

The first specimen argument presented in this section was a *Disjunctive Syllogism*:[3]

The blind man has a red hat or the blind man has a white hat.
The blind man does not have a red hat.
Therefore the blind man has a white hat.

Its form is characterized by saying that its first premiss is a disjunction, its second premiss is the negation of one disjunct of the first premiss, and its conclusion is the same as the other disjunct of the first premiss. It is evident that the Disjunctive Syllogism, so defined, is valid on either interpretation of the word "or," that is, regardless of whether an inclusive or exclusive disjunction is intended.[4] Since the typical valid argument that has a disjunction for a premiss is, like the Disjunctive Syllogism, valid on either interpretation of the word "or," a simplification may be effected by translating the English word "or" into our logical symbol "v"—*regardless of which meaning of the English word "or" is intended.* In general, only a close examination of the context or an explicit questioning of the speaker or writer can reveal which sense of "or" is intended. This problem, at best difficult and often impossible to resolve, can be avoided if we agree to treat *any* occurrence of the word "or" as in-

[3] A *syllogism* is a deductive argument consisting of two premisses and a conclusion.
[4] The student should note that the term "Disjunctive Syllogism" is being used in a narrower sense here than it was in the preceding chapter.

clusive. On the other hand, if it is explicitly stated that the disjunction is intended to be exclusive, by means of the added phrase "but not both," for example, we have the symbolic machinery for expressing that additional sense, as will be shown directly.

Where both disjuncts have either the same subject term or the same predicate term, it is often natural to compress the formulation of their disjunction in English by so placing the "or" that there is no need to repeat the common part of the two disjuncts. Thus "Either Smith is the owner or Smith is the manager" might equally well be expressed as "Smith is either the owner or the manager," and either is properly symbolized as O v M. And "Either Red is guilty or Butch is guilty" would often be expressed as "Either Red or Butch is guilty," either one being symbolized as R v B. It should be remarked that the word "unless" can also be used to form the disjunction of two statements. Thus "The picnic will be held unless it rains" and "Unless it rains the picnic will be held" can equally well be expressed as "Either the picnic will be held or it rains," and symbolized as P v R.

In English, punctuation is absolutely required if complicated statements are to be expressed clearly. A great many different punctuation marks are used, without which many sentences would be highly ambiguous. For example, quite different meanings attach to "The teacher says John is a fool," when it is given different punctuations. Other sentences require punctuation for their very intelligibility, as, for example, "John where James had had had had had had had had had had had the teacher's approval." Punctuation is equally necessary in mathematics. No number is uniquely denoted by the expression $2 \times 3 + 5$, although when it is made clear how its constituents are to be grouped, it denotes either 11 or 16: the first when punctuated $(2 \times 3) + 5$, the second when punctuated $2 \times (3 + 5)$. Punctuation is needed in both mathematics and English for ambiguity to be avoided and meaning made clear.

Punctuation is also required in the language of symbolic logic, for compound statements may themselves be compounded together into more complicated ones. The expression $p \cdot q$ v r is ambiguous: it might mean the conjunction of p with the disjunction of q with r, or it might mean the disjunction whose first disjunct is the conjunction of p and q and whose second disjunct is r. We distinguish between these two different senses by punctuating the given expression as $p \cdot (q$ v $r)$ or else as $(p \cdot q)$ v r. In symbolic logic parentheses, brackets, and braces are used as punctuation marks. That the different ways of punctuating the original expression do make a difference can be seen by considering the case in which p is false and q and r

are both true. In this case the second punctuated expression is true (since its second disjunct is true), whereas the first one is false (since its first conjunct is false). Here the difference in punctuation makes all the difference between truth and falsehood, for different punctuations can assign different truth values to the ambiguous expression $p \cdot q \vee r$.

The word "either" has a variety of different meanings and uses in English. It has conjunctive force in the sentence "There is danger on either side." More often it is used to introduce the first disjunct in a disjunction, as in "Either the blind man has a red hat or the blind man has a white hat." There it contributes to the rhetorical balance of the sentence but does not affect its meaning. Perhaps the most important use of the word "either" is to punctuate a compound statement. Thus the sentence

> The club will meet on Thursday and Al will be elected or the election will be postponed.

can have its ambiguity resolved in one direction by placing the word "either" at its beginning, or in the other direction by inserting the word "either" before the name "Al." Such punctuation is effected in our symbolic language by parentheses. The ambiguous formula $p \cdot q \vee r$ discussed in the preceding paragraph corresponds to the ambiguous sentence examined in this one. The two different punctuations of the formula correspond to the two different punctuations of the sentence effected by the two different insertions of the word "either."

The negation of a disjunction is often expressed using the phrase "neither-nor." Thus the disjunction "Either Fillmore or Harding was the greatest American President" would be denied by the statement "Neither Fillmore nor Harding was the greatest American President." The disjunction would be symbolized as $F \vee H$, and its negation as either $\sim(F \vee H)$ or as $(\sim F) \cdot (\sim H)$. (The logical equivalence of these two symbolic formulas will be discussed in Section 8.5.) It should be clear that to deny a disjunction stating that one or another statement is true requires that both be stated to be false.

The word "both" in English plays several roles. One is a matter of emphasis. To say that "Both Lewis and Clark were famous explorers" is merely to state more emphatically that "Lewis and Clark were famous explorers." But the word "both" also has a punctuational use, comparable to that of "either." We remarked in the preceding paragraph that "Both . . . and . . . are not . . ." can be used to make the same statement as "Neither . . . nor . . . is. . . ." The *order* of the words "both" and "not" is very important. There is considerable difference between

Dick and Ed will not both be elected.

and

Dick and Ed will both not be elected.

The first denies the conjunction $D \cdot E$ and is symbolized as $\sim(D \cdot E)$. The second says of each that he will not be elected. It might equally well be expressed as

Both Dick and Ed will not be elected.

and symbolized as $(\sim D) \cdot (\sim E)$.

In the interest of brevity, that is, to decrease the number of parentheses required, it is convenient to establish the convention that in any formula the negation symbol will be understood to apply to the smallest statement that the punctuation permits. Without this convention the formula $\sim p \vee q$ is ambiguous, meaning either $(\sim p) \vee q$ or $\sim(p \vee q)$. But by our convention we take it to mean the first of these alternatives, for the curl *can* (and therefore by our convention *does*) apply to the first component, p, rather than to the larger expression $p \vee q$.

Given a set of punctuation marks for our symbolic language, it is possible to formulate not merely conjunctions, negations, and weak disjunctions in it, but exclusive disjunctions as well. The exclusive disjunction of p and q asserts that at least one of them is true but not both are true, which is expressed quite simply as $(p \vee q) \cdot \sim(p \cdot q)$.

Any compound statement constructed from simple statements using only the truth-functional connectives dot, curl, and wedge, has its truth value completely determined by the truth or falsehood of its component simple statements. If we know the truth values of simple statements, the truth value of any truth-functional compound of them is easily calculated. In working with such compound statements we always begin with their inmost components and work outward. For example, if A and B are true and X and Y are false statements, we calculate the truth value of the compound statement $\sim[\sim(A \cdot X) \cdot (Y \vee \sim B)]$ as follows. Since X is false, the conjunction $A \cdot X$ is false, and so its negation $\sim(A \cdot X)$ is true. B is true; so its negation $\sim B$ is false, and since Y is false also, the disjunction of Y with $\sim B$, $Y \vee \sim B$ is false. The square-bracketed expression $[\sim(A \cdot X) \cdot (Y \vee \sim B)]$ is the conjunction of a true with a false statement and is therefore false. Hence its negation, which is the entire expression, is true. Such a stepwise procedure always enables us to determine the truth value of a compound statement from the truth values of its components.

EXERCISES

I. Which of the following statements are true?

★ 1. Washington was assassinated • Lincoln was assassinated

2. ∼(Lincoln was assassinated v Washington was assassinated)

3. ∼Lincoln was assassinated v ∼Washington was assassinated

4. ∼(Lincoln was assassinated • Washington was assassinated)

★ 5. ∼Lincoln was assassinated • ∼Washington was assassinated

6. Washington was assassinated v ∼Washington was assassinated

7. Lincoln was assassinated • ∼Lincoln was assassinated

8. (Washington was assassinated • Lincoln was assassinated) v (∼Washington was assassinated • ∼Lincoln was assassinated)

9. (Washington was assassinated v Lincoln was assassinated) • (∼Washington was assassinated • ∼Lincoln was assassinated)

★ 10. Lincoln was assassinated v ∼(Washington was assassinated • Lincoln was assassinated)

11. Washington was assassinated v ∼(Washington was assassinated v Lincoln was assassinated)

12. ∼(∼Washington was assassinated • ∼Lincoln was assassinated)

13. ∼[∼(∼Lincoln was assassinated v ∼Washington was assassinated) v ∼(∼Washington was assassinated v Lincoln was assassinated)]

14. ∼[∼(∼Washington was assassinated • Lincoln was assassinated) • ∼(Lincoln was assassinated • ∼Lincoln was assassinated)]

★ 15. ∼[∼(Washington was assassinated v Lincoln was assassinated) v ∼(∼Washington was assassinated • ∼Lincoln was assassinated)]

16. Washington was assassinated v (∼Lincoln was assassinated v New York is the largest city in America)

17. Lincoln was assassinated • ∼(Lincoln was assassinated • New York is the largest city in America)

18. (Washington was assassinated v ~Lincoln was assassinated) v ~(~Washington was assassinated • ~New York is the largest city in America)

19. ~[~(Lincoln was assassinated • New York is the largest city in America) v ~(~Washington was assassinated v ~New York is the largest city in America)]

20. ~[(~Lincoln was assassinated v New York is the largest city in America) • ~(~New York is the largest city in America v Chicago is the largest city in America)]

II. If *A, B,* and *C* are true statements, and *X, Y,* and *Z* are false statements, which of the following are true?

★ 1. $(C \vee Z) \cdot (Y \vee B)$

2. $(A \cdot B) \vee (X \cdot Y)$

3. $\sim(B \vee X) \cdot \sim(Y \vee Z)$

4. $\sim(C \vee B) \vee \sim(\sim X \cdot Y)$

★ 5. $\sim B \vee C$

6. $\sim B \vee X$

7. $\sim X \vee A$

8. $\sim X \vee Y$

9. $\sim[(\sim B \vee A) \vee (\sim A \vee B)]$

★ 10. $\sim[(\sim Y \vee Z) \vee (\sim Z \vee Y)]$

11. $\sim[(\sim C \vee Y) \vee (\sim Y \vee C)]$

12. $\sim[(\sim X \vee A) \vee (\sim A \vee X)]$

13. $\sim[A \vee (B \vee C)] \vee [(A \vee B) \vee C]$

14. $\sim[X \vee (Y \vee Z)] \vee [(X \vee Y) \vee Z]$

★ 15. $[A \cdot (B \vee C)] \cdot \sim[(A \cdot B) \vee (A \cdot C)]$

16. $\sim[X \cdot (\sim A \vee Z)] \vee [(X \cdot \sim A) \vee (X \cdot Z)]$

17. $\sim\{[(\sim A \vee B) \cdot (\sim B \vee A)] \cdot \sim[(A \cdot B) \vee (\sim A \cdot \sim B)]\}$

18. $\sim\{[(\sim C \vee Z) \cdot (\sim Z \vee C)] \cdot \sim[(C \cdot Z) \vee (\sim C \cdot \sim Z)]\}$

19. $[A \vee (B \cdot C)] \cdot \sim[(A \cdot B) \vee (A \cdot C)]$

20. $[B \vee (\sim X \cdot \sim A)] \cdot \sim[(B \vee \sim X) \cdot (B \vee \sim A)]$

III. Using the letters *A, B, C, D,* and *E* to abbreviate the simple statements: "Argentina mobilizes," "Brazil declares an embargo," "Cuba continues to send arms to South America," "The Dominican Republic appeals to the U.N.," and "Ecuador mobilizes," symbolize the following:

★ 1. Argentina mobilizes and either Brazil declares an embargo or Cuba continues to send arms to South America.

2. Either Argentina mobilizes and Brazil declares an embargo or Cuba continues to send arms to South America.

3. Argentina does not mobilize but Brazil declares an embargo.

4. Either Argentina mobilizes or Brazil does not declare an embargo.

★ 5. It is not the case that both Argentina mobilizes and Brazil declares an embargo.

6. It is not the case that either Argentina mobilizes or Brazil does not declare an embargo.

7. Either Argentina mobilizes and Brazil declares an embargo or it is not the case both that Cuba continues to send arms into South America and that the Dominican Republic appeals to the U.N.

8. Either Brazil declares an embargo and the Dominican Republic appeals to the U.N. or either Cuba continues to send arms to South America or Argentina mobilizes.

9. Argentina mobilizes and either Brazil declares an embargo or both Cuba continues to send arms to South America and the Dominican Republic appeals to the U.N.

★ 10. Either Cuba does not continue to send arms to South America or the Dominican Republic does not appeal to the U.N., and neither Argentina mobilizes nor does Brazil declare an embargo.

11. Argentina mobilizes and Brazil declares an embargo, and the Dominican Republic appeals to the U.N.

12. Argentina mobilizes; and Brazil declares an embargo and the Dominican Republic appeals to the U.N.

13. Both Argentina and Ecuador mobilize.

14. Either Argentina or Ecuador mobilizes.

★ 15. Neither Argentina nor Ecuador mobilizes.

16. Argentina and Ecuador both mobilize.

17. Argentina and Ecuador do not both mobilize.

18. Argentina and Ecuador both do not mobilize.

19. Argentina or Ecuador mobilizes but they do not both mobilize.

★ 20. Unless both Argentina and Ecuador mobilize neither Argentina nor Ecuador mobilizes.

21. Cuba continues to send arms to South America unless Argentina mobilizes.

22. Brazil declares an embargo unless both Argentina and Ecuador mobilize.

23. Unless Argentina mobilizes Brazil declares an embargo.

24. Brazil declares an embargo and the Dominican Republic appeals to the U.N., unless both Argentina and Ecuador do not mobilize.

25. It is not the case that neither Argentina nor Ecuador mobilizes.

8.3 Conditional Statements and Material Implication

Where two statements are combined by placing the word "if" before the first and inserting the word "then" between them, the resulting compound statement is a *conditional* (also called a *hypothetical*, an *implication*, or an *implicative statement*). In a conditional, the component statement between the "if" and the "then" is called the *antecedent* (or the *implicans* or—rarely—the *protasis*), and the component statement which follows the "then" is the *consequent* (or the *implicate* or—rarely—the *apodosis*). For example, "If Mr. Jones is the brakeman's next-door neighbor, then Mr. Jones earns exactly three times as much as the brakeman" is a conditional statement in which "Mr. Jones is the brakeman's next-door neighbor" is the antecedent, and "Mr. Jones earns exactly three times as much as the brakeman" is the consequent.

A conditional statement asserts that its antecedent implies its consequent. It does not assert that its antecedent is true, but only that if its antecedent is true then its consequent is true also. It does not assert that its consequent is true, but only that its consequent is true if its antecedent is true. The essential meaning of a conditional statement is the relation of implication asserted to hold between its antecedent and consequent, in that order. To understand the meaning of a conditional statement, then, we must understand what implication is.

The possibility suggests itself that perhaps "implication" has more than one meaning. We found it necessary to distinguish different senses of the word "or" before introducing a special logical symbol to correspond exactly to a single one of the meanings of the English word. Had we not done so, the ambiguity of the English would have infected our logical symbolism and prevented it from achieving the clarity and precision aimed at. It will be equally valuable to distinguish the different senses of "implies" or "if-then" before introducing a special logical symbol in this connection.

Let us begin by listing a number of different conditional statements, each of which seems to assert a different type of implication, and to each of which corresponds a different sense of "if-then."

A. If all men are mortal and Socrates is a man, then Socrates is mortal.

B. If Mr. Black is a bachelor, then Mr. Black is unmarried.

C. If blue litmus paper is placed in acid, then the litmus paper will turn red.

D. If State loses the Homecoming Game, then I'll eat my hat.

Even a casual inspection of these four conditional statements reveals that they are of quite different types. The consequent of *A* follows logically from its antecedent, whereas the consequent of *B* follows from its antecedent by the very definition of the term "bachelor," which means unmarried man. The consequent of *C* does not follow from its antecedent either by logic alone or by the definition of its terms; the connection must be discovered empirically, for the implication stated here is causal. Finally, the consequent of *D* does not follow from its antecedent either by logic or by definition, nor is there any causal law involved—in the usual sense of the term. Most causal laws, those discovered in physics and chemistry, for example, describe what happens in the world regardless of the hopes or desires of men. There is no such law connected with statement *D*, of course. That statement reports a decision of the speaker to behave in a certain way under certain circumstances.

The four conditional statements examined in the preceding paragraph are different in that each asserts a different type of implication between its antecedent and consequent. But they are not completely different; all assert types of implication. Is there any identifiable common meaning, any partial meaning that is common to these admittedly different types of implication, although perhaps not the whole or complete meaning of any one of them?

The search for a common partial meaning takes on an added significance when we recall our procedure in working out a symbolic representation for the English word "or." In that case we proceeded as follows. First: we emphasized the difference between the two senses of that word, contrasting inclusive with exclusive disjunction. The inclusive disjunction of two statements was observed to mean that at least one of the statements is true, and the exclusive disjunction of two statements was observed to mean that at least one of the statements is true but not both are true. Second: we noted that these two types of disjunction had a common *partial* meaning. This partial common meaning, that at least one of the disjuncts is true, was seen to be the *whole* meaning of the weak, inclusive "or," and a *part* of the meaning of the strong, exclusive "or." We then introduced the special symbol "v" to represent this common partial meaning (which was the entire meaning of "or" in its inclusive sense). Third: we noted that the symbol representing the common partial meaning was an adequate translation of either sense of the word "or" for the purpose of retaining the Disjunctive Syllogism as a valid form of argument. It was admitted that translating an exclusive "or" into the symbol "v" ignored and lost part of the word's meaning. But the part of its meaning that is preserved by this translation is all that is needed for the Disjunctive Syllogism to remain a valid form of argument. Since the Disjunctive Syllogism is typical of arguments involving disjunction with which we are here concerned, this partial translation of the word "or," which may abstract from its "full" or "complete" meaning in some cases, is wholly adequate for our present purposes.

Now we wish to follow the same pattern again, this time in connection with the English phrase "if-then." The first part is already accomplished: we have already emphasized the differences between some four senses of the "if-then" phrase, corresponding to four different types of implication. We are now ready for the second step, which is to discover a sense that is at least a part of the meaning of all four different types of implication.

One way of approaching this problem is to ask what circumstances would suffice to establish the falsehood of a given conditional statement. Let us consider another example. Under what circumstances should we agree that the conditional statement:

> If blue litmus paper is placed in this solution, then the litmus paper will turn red.

is false? There are, of course, many ways of investigating the truth of such a statement, and not all of them involve actually placing blue litmus paper in the solution. Some other chemical indicator might be used, and if it showed the solution to be acid, this would confirm the given conditional as true, since we know that blue litmus paper always turns red in acid. On the other hand, if it showed the solution to be alkaline, this would tend to show that the given conditional was false. It is important to realize that this conditional does not assert that any blue litmus paper is actually placed in the solution, or that any litmus paper actually turns red. It asserts merely that if blue litmus paper is placed in the solution, then the litmus paper will turn red. It is proved false in case blue litmus paper is actually placed in the solution and does not turn red. The acid test, so to speak, of the falsehood of a conditional statement is available when its antecedent is true, for if its consequent is false while its antecedent is true, the conditional itself is thereby proved false.

Any conditional statement "if p then q" is known to be false in case the conjunction $p \cdot \sim q$ is known to be true, that is, in case its antecedent is true and its consequent is false. For a conditional to be true, then, the indicated conjunction must be false, that is, its negation $\sim(p \cdot \sim q)$ must be true. In other words, for any conditional "If p then q" to be true, $\sim(p \cdot \sim q)$, the negation of the conjunction of its antecedent with the negation of its consequent, must also be true. We may, then, regard $\sim(p \cdot \sim q)$ as a part of the meaning of "If p then q."

Every conditional statement means to deny that its antecedent is true and its consequent false, but this need not be the whole of its meaning. A conditional such as *A* on p. 258 also asserts a logical connection between its antecedent and consequent, one like *B* asserts a definitional connection, *C* a causal connection, *D* a decisional connection. But no matter what type of implication is asserted by a conditional statement, part of its meaning is the negation of the conjunction of its antecedent with the negation of its consequent.

We now introduce a special symbol to represent this common partial meaning of the "if-then" phrase. We define the new symbol "$\supset$" (called a *horseshoe*) by taking $p \supset q$ as an abbreviation of $\sim(p \cdot \sim q)$. The exact significance of the "$\supset$" symbol can be indicated by means of a truth table:

p	q	$\sim q$	$p \cdot \sim q$	$\sim(p \cdot \sim q)$	$p \supset q$
T	**T**	**F**	**F**	**T**	**T**
T	**F**	**T**	**T**	**F**	**F**
F	**T**	**F**	**F**	**T**	**T**
F	**F**	**T**	**F**	**T**	**T**

Here the first two columns are the guide columns, the third is filled in by reference to the second, the fourth by reference to the first and third, the fifth by reference to the fourth, and the sixth is identically the same as the fifth by definition.

The symbol "$\supset$" is not to be regarded as denoting *the* meaning of "if-then," or standing for *the* relation of implication. That would be impossible, for there is no single meaning of "if-then"; there are several meanings. There is no unique relation of implication to be thus represented; there are several different implication relations. Nor is the symbol "$\supset$" to be regarded as somehow standing for *all* the meanings of "if-then." These are all different, and any attempt to abbreviate all of them by a single logical symbol would render that symbol multiply ambiguous—as ambiguous as the English phrase "if-then" or the English word "implication." The symbol "$\supset$" is completely unambiguous. What $p \supset q$ abbreviates is $\sim(p \cdot \sim q)$, whose meaning is included in the meanings of each of the various kinds of implications considered, but which does not constitute the entire meaning of any of them.

We can consider the symbol "$\supset$" as representing another kind of implication, and it will be expedient to do so, since convenient ways to read $p \supset q$ are "if p then q" or "p implies q." But it is not the same kind of implication as any of those mentioned earlier. It is called *material implication* by logicians, who in giving it a special name admit that it is a special notion, not to be confused with other, more usual, types of implication.

Not all conditional statements in English need assert one of the four types of implication previously considered. Material implication constitutes a fifth type that may be asserted in ordinary discourse. Consider the remark: "If Hitler was a military genius, then I'm a monkey's uncle." It is quite clear that it asserts neither logical, definitional, nor causal implication. It should also be apparent that it cannot represent a decisional implication, since it scarcely lies in the speaker's power to make the consequent true. No "real connection," either logical, definitional, or causal obtains between antecedent and consequent here. A conditional of this sort is often used as an emphatic or humorous method of denying its antecedent. The consequent of such a conditional is usually a statement which is obviously or ludicrously false. And since no true conditional can have both its antecedent true and its consequent false, to affirm such a conditional amounts to denying that its antecedent is true. The full meaning of the present conditional seems to be the denial that "Hitler was a military genius" is true when "I'm a monkey's uncle" is false. And since the latter is so obviously false, the conditional must be understood to deny the former.

No "real connection" between antecedent and consequent is suggested by a *material implication*. All that is asserted is that as a matter of fact it is not the case that the antecedent is true when the consequent is false. It should be noted that the material implication symbol is a truth-functional connective, just like the symbols for conjunction and disjunction. As such, it is defined by the truth table:

p	q	$p \supset q$
T	**T**	**T**
T	**F**	**F**
F	**T**	**T**
F	**F**	**T**

The strangeness that sometimes attaches to the horseshoe symbol "$\supset$" as defined by the given truth table can be dissipated at least in part by the following considerations. Because the number 2 is smaller than the number 4 (written symbolically as $2 < 4$) it follows that *any* number smaller than 2 is smaller than 4. The conditional formula

$$\text{If } x < 2 \quad \text{then} \quad x < 4$$

is true for any number x whatsoever. If we focus on the numbers 1, 3, and 4, and replace the number variable x in the preceding conditional formula by each of them in turn, we can make the following observations. In

$$\text{If } 1 < 2 \quad \text{then} \quad 1 < 4$$

both antecedent and consequent are true, and of course the conditional is true. In

$$\text{If } 3 < 2 \quad \text{then} \quad 3 < 4$$

the antecedent is false and the consequent is true, and of course the conditional is again true. In

$$\text{If } 4 < 2 \quad \text{then} \quad 4 < 4$$

both antecedent and consequent are false, but the conditional remains true. These three cases correspond to the first, third, and fourth rows of the table defining the horseshoe symbol "$\supset$." So there is nothing particularly remarkable or surprising that a conditional should be true where both antecedent and consequent are true, where the antecedent is false and the consequent is true, or where antecedent and consequent are both false. Of course there is no number which is smaller than 2 but not smaller than 4, that is, there is no true conditional statement with true antecedent and false consequent: this is exactly what the defining truth table for "$\supset$" lays down.

Now we propose to translate any occurrence of the "if-then" phrase into our logical symbol "$\supset$." This proposal means that in translating conditional statements into our symbolism we treat them all as merely material implications. Of course many, if not most, conditional statements assert more than a merely material implication to hold between their antecedents and consequents. So our proposal amounts to suggesting that we ignore, or throw away, or "abstract from" part of the meaning of a conditional statement when we translate it into our symbolic language. How can this proposal be justified?

The previous proposal to translate both inclusive and exclusive disjunctions by means of the "v" symbol was justified on the grounds that the validity of the Disjunctive Syllogism was preserved even if the additional meaning which attaches to the exclusive "or" was ignored. Our present proposal to translate all conditional statements into the merely material implications symbolized by "$\supset$" is to be justified in exactly the same way. Many arguments contain conditional statements of various different kinds, but the validity of all valid arguments of the general type with which we will be concerned is preserved even if the additional meanings of their conditional statements are ignored. This remains to be proved, of course, and will occupy our attention in the next section.

Conditional statements can be expressed in a variety of ways. The statement

If he has a good lawyer then he will be acquitted.

can equally well be expressed without using the word "then," as

If he has a good lawyer he will be acquitted.

Antecedent and consequent can have their order reversed, provided that the "if" still directly precedes the antecedent, as

He will be acquitted if he has a good lawyer.

It should be clear that in any of the above the word "if" can be replaced by such phrases as "in case," "provided that," "given that," or "on condition that" without any change in meaning. Minor adjustments in the phrasings of antecedent and consequent permit such alternative expressions of the same conditional as

That he has a good lawyer implies that he will be acquitted.

or

His having a good lawyer entails his acquittal.

A shift from active to passive voice accompanies a reversal of order of antecedent and consequent to yield the logically equivalent

His being acquitted is implied (or entailed) by his having a good lawyer.

Any of these is symbolized as $L \supset A$.

The notions of necessary and sufficient conditions provide other formulations of conditional statements. For any specified event there are many circumstances necessary for its occurrence. Thus for a car to run it is necessary that there be gas in its tank, its spark plugs properly gapped, its oil pump working, and so on. So if the event occurs every one of the conditions necessary for its occurrence must be fulfilled. Hence to say

> That there is gas in its tank is a necessary condition for the car to run.

can equally well be expressed as

> The car runs only if there is gas in its tank.

which is another way of saying that

> If the car runs then there is gas in its tank.

Any of these is symbolized as $R \supset G$, and in general, "q is a necessary condition for p" and "p only if q" are symbolized as $p \supset q$.

For a specified situation there are many alternative circumstances any one of which is sufficient to produce that situation. Thus for a purse to contain over a dollar it would be sufficient for it to contain one hundred one pennies, twenty-one nickels, eleven dimes, five quarters, and so on. If any one of these circumstances obtains, the specified situation will be realized. Hence to say: "That the purse contains five quarters is a sufficient condition for it to contain over a dollar" is to say the same as "If the purse contains five quarters then it contains over a dollar." In general, "p is a sufficient condition for q" is symbolized as $p \supset q$.

Not every statement containing the word "if" is a conditional. None of the following statements is a conditional: "There is food in the refrigerator if you want some," "Your table is ready, if you please," "There is a message for you if you're interested," "The meeting will be held even if no permit is obtained." The presence or absence of particular words is never decisive. In every case one must understand what a given sentence means and then re-express that meaning in a symbolic formula.

EXERCISES

I. If A, B, and C are true statements and X, Y, Z are false statements, determine which of the following are true:

★ 1. $A \supset (B \supset C)$

2. $A \supset (B \supset Z)$

3. $A \supset (Y \supset C)$

4. $A \supset (Y \supset Z)$

★ 5. $X \supset (B \supset C)$

6. $X \supset (B \supset Z)$

7. $X \supset (Y \supset C)$

8. $X \supset (Y \supset Z)$

9. $(A \supset B) \supset Z$

★ 10. $(X \supset Y) \supset Z$

11. $[(X \supset Y) \supset B] \supset Z$

12. $[(B \supset Z) \supset B] \supset Z$

13. $[(X \supset A) \supset X] \supset X$

14. $[X \supset (Y \supset Z)] \supset [(X \supset Y) \supset Z]$

★ 15. $\{[A \supset (B \supset C)] \supset \sim X\} \supset \{X \supset [(A \cdot B) \supset C]\}$

16. $[(A \supset Z) \cdot (Z \supset A)] \supset \sim[(A \cdot Z) \vee (\sim A \vee \sim Z)]$

17. $\{[X \supset (Y \supset Z)] \supset [(X \cdot Y) \supset Z]\} \supset [(X \supset A) \supset (B \supset Y)]$

18. $\{[A \supset (B \supset C)] \supset [(A \cdot B) \supset C]\} \supset [(A \supset B) \supset (C \supset Z)]$

19. $\{[(A \supset B) \cdot (B \supset A)] \supset [(A \cdot B) \vee (\sim A \cdot \sim B)]\} \supset$
$\{[(X \supset Y) \cdot (Y \supset X)] \supset [(\sim X \cdot \sim Y) \supset (X \cdot Y)]\}$

20. $\{[(X \supset Y) \cdot (Y \supset X)] \supset [(X \cdot Y) \vee (\sim X \cdot \sim Y)]\} \supset$
$\{[\sim(A \cdot B) \cdot \sim(A \cdot \sim B)] \supset [\sim(\sim A \cdot B) \supset (\sim A \cdot \sim B)]\}$

II. Symbolize the following, using capital letters to abbreviate the simple statements involved:

★ 1. If Edgar lodges a complaint, then Fulton will investigate and Greville will be disqualified.

2. If Edgar lodges a complaint then Fulton will investigate, and Greville will be disqualified.

3. If Edgar lodges a complaint then if Fulton will investigate then Greville will be disqualified.

4. If Edgar lodges a complaint then either Fulton will investigate or Greville will be disqualified.

★ 5. If Edgar lodges a complaint and Fulton investigates then Greville will be disqualified.

6. Either Edgar lodges a complaint or if Fulton investigates then Greville will not be disqualified.

7. If either Edgar lodges a complaint or Fulton investigates, then Greville will be disqualified.

8. If Edgar does not lodge a complaint then neither will Fulton investigate nor will Greville be disqualified.

9. If it is not the case that Edgar lodges a complaint then Fulton will investigate, and Greville will be disqualified.

★ 10. It is not the case that if Edgar lodges a complaint, then Fulton will investigate and Greville will not be disqualified.

11. Fulton will investigate if Edgar lodges a complaint.

12. Fulton will investigate only if Edgar lodges a complaint.

13. That Fulton investigates is a sufficient condition for Greville to be disqualified.

14. Edgar's lodging a complaint is a necessary condition for Greville to be disqualified.

★ 15. Fulton will not investigate unless Edgar lodges a complaint.

16. Greville will be disqualified unless Fulton investigates.

17. Fulton will investigate, but only if Edgar lodges a complaint.

18. Edgar's lodging a complaint is a necessary and sufficient condition for Greville to be disqualified.

19. Whenever Edgar lodges a complaint Fulton investigates.

20. Greville will be disqualified if and only if Edgar lodges a complaint.

8.4 Argument Forms and Arguments

In this section we specify more precisely what is meant by the term "valid." We relate our formal definition to more familiar and intuitive notions by considering the method of refutation by logical analogy.[5] Presented with the argument:

If Bacon wrote the plays attributed to Shakespeare, then Bacon was a great writer.
Bacon was a great writer.
Therefore Bacon wrote the plays attributed to Shakespeare.

we may agree with the premisses but disagree with the conclusion, judging the argument to be invalid. One way of proving its invalidity is by the method of logical analogy. "You might as well argue," we could retort, "that

If Washington was assassinated, then Washington is dead.
Washington is dead.
Therefore Washington was assassinated.

[5] Just as in discussing the categorical syllogism in Section 6.2.

And you cannot seriously defend this argument," we should continue, "because here the premisses are known to be true and the conclusion known to be false. This argument is obviously invalid; your argument is of the *same form;* so yours is invalid also." This type of refutation is very effective.

Let us examine more closely the technique of refutation by logical analogy, for it points the way to an excellent general method of testing arguments. To prove the invalidity of an argument it suffices to formulate another argument which: (a) has exactly the same form as the first, and (b) has true premisses and a false conclusion. This method is based upon the fact that validity and invalidity are purely *formal* characteristics of arguments, which is to say that any two arguments having exactly the same form are either both valid or both invalid, regardless of any differences in the subject matter with which they are concerned.[6]

A given argument exhibits its form very clearly when the simple statements which appear in it are abbreviated by capital letters. Thus we may abbreviate the statements "Bacon wrote the plays attributed to Shakespeare," "Bacon was a great writer," "Washington was assassinated," and "Washington is dead" by the letters *B, G, A,* and *D,* respectively, and symbolize the two preceding arguments as:

$B \supset G$		$A \supset D$
G	and	D
$\therefore B$		$\therefore A$

So written, their common form is easily seen.

If we are interested in discussing forms of arguments rather than particular arguments having those forms, we need some method of symbolizing argument forms themselves. To achieve such a method, we introduce the notion of a *variable.* In the preceding sections we used capital letters to symbolize particular simple statements. To avoid confusion, we use small, or lower-case letters from the middle part of the alphabet, $p, q, r, s, \ldots$ as *statement variables.* A statement variable, as we shall use the term, is simply a letter for which, or in place of which, a statement may be substituted. Com-

[6] Here we assume that the simple statements involved are neither logically true (for example, "All chairs are chairs") nor logically false (for example, "Some chairs are nonchairs"). We also assume that the only logical relations among the simple statements involved are those asserted or entailed by the premisses. The point of these restrictions is to limit our considerations in this chapter and the next to truth-functional arguments alone, and to exclude other kinds of arguments whose validity turns on more complex logical considerations not appropriately introduced at this place.

pound statements as well as simple statements may be substituted for statement variables.

We define an "argument form" as any array of symbols containing statement variables but no statements, such that when the statement variables are replaced by statements—the same statement replacing the same statement variable throughout—the result is an argument. For definiteness, we establish the convention that in any argument form p shall be the first statement variable that occurs in it, q shall be the second, r the third, and so on. Thus the expression

$$\begin{array}{l} p \supset q \\ q \\ \therefore p \end{array}$$

is an argument form, for when the statement variables p and q are replaced by the statements B and G, respectively, the result is the first argument of this section. If the variables p and q are replaced by the statements A and D, the result is the second argument. Any argument which results from the substitution of statements for statement variables in an argument form is called a *substitution instance* of that argument form. It is clear that any substitution instance of an argument form may be said to have that form, and that any argument which has a certain form is a substitution instance of that form.

We define *the specific form* of a given argument to be that argument form from which the argument results by replacing each different statement variable by a different *simple* statement. Thus the argument form above is *the specific form* of each of the two preceding arguments. Although both of those arguments are also substitution instances of the argument form

$$\begin{array}{l} p \\ q \\ \therefore r \end{array}$$

from which they result by replacing the statement variables p, q, and r by the statements $B \supset G$, G, and B, respectively, and by $A \supset D$, D, and A, respectively, this latter form is not *the specific form* of either of the two arguments, because the substitutions required to obtain them involve replacing a statement variable by a compound statement. For any given argument, there is a unique argument form which is *the specific form* of that argument.

The technique of refutation by logical analogy can now be described more precisely. If the specific form of a given argument has any substitution instance whose premisses are true and whose conclusion is false, then the given argument is invalid. We may define the term "invalid" as applied to argument forms as follows: an argument form is invalid if and only if it has a substitution instance with true premisses and a false conclusion. Refutation by logical analogy is based on the fact that any argument of which the specific form is an *invalid argument form* is an *invalid argument.* Any argument form which is not invalid must be valid. Hence an argument form is valid if and only if it has *no* substitution instances with true premisses and a false conclusion. And since validity is a formal notion, an argument is valid if and only if the specific form of that argument is a valid argument form.

A given argument is proved invalid if a refuting analogy for it can be found, but "thinking up" such refuting analogies may not always be easy. Happily, it is not necessary, because for arguments of this type there is a simpler, purely mechanical test based upon the same principle. Given any argument, we test the specific form of that argument, for its validity or invalidity determines the validity or invalidity of the argument.

To test an argument form, we examine all possible substitution instances of it to see if any of them have true premisses and false conclusions. Of course any argument form has infinitely many substitution instances, but we need not worry about having to examine them one at a time. Since we are interested only in the truth or falsehood of their premisses and conclusions, we need only consider the truth values involved. The arguments with which we are concerned here contain only simple statements and compound statements which are built up out of simple statements by means of the truth-functional connectives symbolized by the dot, curl, wedge, and horseshoe. Hence we obtain all possible substitution instances whose premisses and conclusions have different truth values by examining all possible different arrangements of truth values for the statements which can be substituted for the different statement variables in the argument form to be tested.

Where an argument form contains just two different statement variables p and q, all of its substitution instances are the result of either substituting true statements for both p and q, or a true statement for p and a false one for q, or a false one for p and a true one for q, or false statements for both p and q. These different cases are assembled most conveniently in the form of a truth table. To decide the validity of the argument form

$$p \supset q$$
$$q$$
$$\therefore p$$

we construct the following truth table:

p	q	$p \supset q$
T	**T**	**T**
T	**F**	**F**
F	**T**	**T**
F	**F**	**T**

Each row of this table represents a whole class of substitution instances. The **T**'s and **F**'s in the two initial or guide columns represent the truth values of the statements substituted for the variables p and q in the argument form. We fill in the third column by referring back to the initial or guide columns and the definition of the horseshoe symbol. The third column heading is the first "premiss" of the argument form, the second column is the second "premiss," and the first column is the "conclusion." In examining this truth table, we find that in the third row there are **T**'s under both premisses and an **F** under the conclusion, which means that there is at least one substitution instance of this argument form which has true premisses and a false conclusion. This row suffices to show that the argument form is invalid. Any argument of this specific form is said to commit the Fallacy of Affirming the Consequent, since its second premiss affirms the consequent of its conditional first premiss.

To show the validity of the Disjunctive Syllogism form

$$p \vee q$$
$$\sim p$$
$$\therefore q$$

we construct the following different truth table:

p	q	$p \vee q$	$\sim p$
T	**T**	**T**	**F**
T	**F**	**T**	**F**
F	**T**	**T**	**T**
F	**F**	**F**	**T**

Here too the initial or guide columns have written under them all possible different truth values of statements which may be substituted for the variables p and q. We fill in the third column by referring back to the first two, and the fourth by reference to the first alone. Now the third row is the only one in which a **T** appears under both premisses (the third and fourth columns) and there a **T** appears under the conclusion also (the second column). The truth table thus shows that the argument form has no substitution instance having true premisses and a false conclusion, and thereby proves the validity of the argument form being tested.

The truth table technique provides a completely mechanical method for testing the validity of any argument of the general type here considered. We are now in a position to justify our proposal to translate any occurrence of the "if-then" phrase into our material implication symbol "$\supset$." In the preceding section the claim was made that all valid arguments of the general type with which we are here concerned which involve "if-then" statements remain valid when those statements are interpreted as expressing merely material implications. Truth tables can be used to substantiate this claim, and will justify our translation of "if-then" into the horseshoe symbol.

The simplest type of intuitively valid argument involving a conditional statement is illustrated by the argument:

If the second native told the truth, then only one native is a politician.
The second native told the truth.
Therefore only one native is a politician.

The specific form of this argument, known as *modus ponens,* is

$$p \supset q$$
$$p$$
$$\therefore q$$

and is proved valid by the following truth table:

p	q	$p \supset q$
T	**T**	**T**
T	**F**	**F**
F	**T**	**T**
F	**F**	**T**

Here the two premisses are represented by the third and first columns, and the conclusion represented by the second. Only the first row represents substitution instances in which both premisses are true, and the **T** in the second column shows that in these arguments the conclusion is true also. This truth table establishes the validity of any argument of form *modus ponens.*

Another common type of intuitively valid argument contains

conditional statements exclusively and is called a Hypothetical Syllogism.[7] An example is:

If the first native is a politician, then he lies.
If he lies, then he denies being a politician.
Therefore if the first native is a politician then he denies being a politician.

The specific form of this argument is

$$p \supset q$$
$$q \supset r$$
$$\therefore p \supset r$$

Since it contains three distinct statement variables, the truth table here must have three initial or guide columns and will require eight rows for the listing of all possible substitution instances. Besides the initial columns, three additional columns are required, two for the premisses, the third for the conclusion. The table appears as

p	q	r	$p \supset q$	$q \supset r$	$p \supset r$
T	T	T	T	T	T
T	T	F	T	F	F
T	F	T	F	T	T
T	F	F	F	T	F
F	T	T	T	T	T
F	T	F	T	F	T
F	F	T	T	T	T
F	F	F	T	T	T

In constructing it, we fill in the fourth column by referring back to the first and second, the fifth by reference to the second and third, and the sixth by reference to the first and third. Examining the completed table, we observe that the premisses are true only in the first, fifth, seventh and eighth rows, and that in all of these the conclusion is true also. This truth table establishes the validity of the argument form, and proves that the Hypothetical Syllogism also remains valid when its conditional statements are translated by means of the horseshoe symbol.

Enough examples have been provided to illustrate the proper use of the truth-table technique for testing arguments. And perhaps

[7] Called a "pure Hypothetical Syllogism" in the preceding chapter.

enough have been given to show that the validity of any valid argument involving conditional statements is preserved when its conditionals are translated into merely material implications. Any doubts that remain can be allayed by the reader's providing, translating, and testing his own examples.

As more complicated argument forms are considered, larger truth tables are required to test them, for a separate initial or guide column is required for each different statement variable in the argument form. Only two are required for a form with just two variables, and that table will have four rows. But three initial columns are required for a form with three variables, like the Hypothetical Syllogism, and such truth tables will have eight rows. To test the validity of an argument form such as that of the Constructive Dilemma,

$$(p \supset q) \cdot (r \supset s)$$
$$p \vee r$$
$$\therefore q \vee s$$

which contains four distinct statement variables, a truth table with four initial columns and sixteen rows is required. In general, to test an argument form containing n distinct statement variables requires a truth table with n initial columns and 2^n rows.

The first argument form which we proved invalid,

$$p \supset q$$
$$q$$
$$\therefore p$$

bears a superficial resemblance to the valid argument form *modus ponens.* It has been called the Fallacy of Affirming the Consequent. Another invalid form which has been given a special name is

$$p \supset q$$
$$\sim p$$
$$\therefore \sim q$$

which is the Fallacy of Denying the Antecedent, and whose invalidity is readily established by means of truth tables. The latter fallacy bears a superficial resemblance to the valid argument form

$$p \supset q$$
$$\sim q$$
$$\therefore \sim p$$

called *modus tollens.*

It should be emphasized that although a valid argument form has only valid arguments as substitution instances, an invalid argument form can have both valid and invalid substitution instances. So to prove that a given argument is invalid we must prove that *the specific form* of that argument is invalid.

EXERCISES

I. For each of the following arguments, indicate which, if any, of the argument forms in Exercise II below have the given argument as a substitution instance, and indicate which, if any, is the specific form of the given argument:

★ a. $A \cdot B$
$\therefore A$

b. $C \supset D$
$\therefore C \supset (C \cdot D)$

c. E
$\therefore E \vee F$

d. $G \supset H$
$\sim H$
$\therefore \sim G$

★ e. I
J
$\therefore I \cdot J$

f. $(K \supset L) \cdot (M \supset N)$
$K \vee M$
$\therefore L \vee N$

g. $O \supset P$
$\sim O$
$\therefore \sim P$

h. $Q \supset R$
$Q \supset S$
$\therefore R \vee S$

i. $T \supset U$
$U \supset V$
$\therefore V \supset T$

★ j. $(W \cdot X) \supset (Y \cdot Z)$
$\therefore (W \cdot X) \supset [(W \cdot X) \cdot (Y \cdot Z)]$

k. $A \supset B$
$\therefore (A \supset B) \vee C$

l. $(D \vee E) \cdot \sim F$
$\therefore D \vee E$

m. $[G \supset (G \cdot H)] \cdot [H \supset (H \cdot G)]$
$\therefore G \supset (G \cdot H)$

n. $(I \vee J) \supset (I \cdot J)$
$\sim (I \vee J)$
$\therefore \sim (I \cdot J)$

o. $(K \supset L) \cdot (M \supset N)$
$\therefore K \supset L$

II. Use truth tables to prove the validity or invalidity of the following argument forms:

★ 1. $p \supset q$
$\therefore \sim q \supset \sim p$

2. $p \supset q$
$\therefore \sim p \supset \sim q$

3. $p \cdot q$
$\therefore p$

4. p
$\therefore p \vee q$

★ 5. p
$\therefore p \supset q$

6. $p \supset q$
$\therefore p \supset (p \cdot q)$

7. $(p \vee q) \supset (p \cdot q)$
$\therefore (p \supset q) \cdot (q \supset p)$

8. $p \supset q$
$\sim p$
$\therefore \sim q$

9. $p \supset q$
$\sim q$
$\therefore \sim p$

★ 10. p
q
$\therefore p \cdot q$

11. $p \supset q$
$p \supset r$
$\therefore q \vee r$

12. $p \supset q$
$q \supset r$
$\therefore r \supset p$

13. $p \supset (q \supset r)$
$p \supset q$
$\therefore p \supset r$

14. $p \supset (q \cdot r)$
$(q \vee r) \supset \sim p$
$\therefore \sim p$

★ 15. $p \supset (q \supset r)$
$q \supset (p \supset r)$
$\therefore (p \vee q) \supset r$

16. $(p \supset q) \cdot (r \supset s)$
$p \vee r$
$\therefore q \vee s$

17. $(p \supset q) \cdot (r \supset s)$
$\sim q \vee \sim s$
$\therefore \sim p \vee \sim r$

18. $p \supset (q \supset r)$
$q \supset (r \supset s)$
$\therefore p \supset s$

19. $p \supset (q \supset r)$
$(q \supset r) \supset s$
$\therefore p \supset s$

★ 20. $(p \supset q) \cdot [(p \cdot q) \supset r]$
$p \supset (r \supset s)$
$\therefore p \supset s$

21. $(p \vee q) \supset (p \cdot q)$
$\sim (p \vee q)$
$\therefore \sim (p \cdot q)$

22. $(p \vee q) \supset (p \cdot q)$
$p \cdot q$
$\therefore p \vee q$

23. $(p \cdot q) \supset (r \cdot s)$
$\therefore (p \cdot q) \supset [(p \cdot q) \cdot (r \cdot s)]$

24. $(p \supset q) \cdot (r \supset s)$
$\therefore p \supset q$

III. Use truth tables to determine the validity or invalidity of each of the following arguments:

★ 1. $(A \vee B) \supset (A \cdot B)$
$A \vee B$
$\therefore A \cdot B$

2. $(C \vee D) \supset (C \cdot D)$
$C \cdot D$
$\therefore C \vee D$

3. $E \supset F$
$F \supset E$
$\therefore E \vee F$

4. $(G \vee H) \supset (G \cdot H)$
$\sim (G \cdot H)$
$\therefore \sim (G \vee H)$

★ 5. $(I \vee J) \supset (I \cdot J)$
$\sim (I \vee J)$
$\therefore \sim (I \cdot J)$

6. $K \vee L$
K
$\therefore \sim L$

7. $M \vee (N \cdot \sim N)$
M
$\therefore \sim (N \cdot \sim N)$

8. $(O \vee P) \supset Q$
$Q \supset (O \cdot P)$
$\therefore (O \vee P) \supset (O \cdot P)$

9. $(R \vee S) \supset T$
$T \supset (R \cdot S)$
$\therefore (R \cdot S) \supset (R \vee S)$

10. $U \supset (V \vee W)$
$(V \cdot W) \supset \sim U$
$\therefore \sim U$

IV. Use truth tables to determine the validity or invalidity of each of the following arguments:

★ 1. If Allen withdraws from the contest, then either Brown will win the nomination or Clark will be disappointed. Brown will not win the nomination. Therefore if Allen withdraws from the contest, then Clark will be disappointed.

2. If the contract is awarded to Davis, then Edwards stands to earn a good deal of money next year. If the contract is awarded to Davis, then French will suffer financial reverses. Therefore if Edwards stands to earn a good deal of money next year, then French will suffer financial reverses.

3. If Graham is out on the golf course, then Harvey is on duty at the hospital and Ives must have changed his policy. Harvey is not on duty at the hospital. Therefore Graham is not out on the golf course.

4. If Jones discovers the plot, then if he values his life, then he will leave the country. He values his life. Therefore if Jones discovers the plot, then he will leave the country.

★ 5. If Kelly manages to borrow a car, then if he takes the expressway, then he will arrive before the deadline. Kelly will arrive before the deadline. Therefore if Kelly manages to borrow a car, then he takes the expressway.

6. If Lowell is ineligible, then either Monroe is the starting fullback or Norton is the starting fullback. Monroe is not the starting fullback. Therefore if Norton is not the starting fullback, then Lowell is not ineligible.

7. If Olson backs the incumbent, then Peterson jumps on the bandwagon. If Peterson jumps on the bandwagon, then Quackenbush leaves the party. If Quackenbush leaves the party, then Olson does not back the incumbent. Therefore Olson does not back the incumbent.

8. If Robinson is nominated for the presidency, then Smith will be nominated for the vice-presidency. If Thompson is nominated for the presidency, then Smith will be nominated for the vice-presidency. Either Robinson is nominated for the presidency or Thompson is nominated for the presidency. Therefore Smith will be nominated for the vice-presidency.

9. If Alice gets married, then either Betty is maid of honor or Caroline is maid of honor. If Betty is maid of honor and Caroline is maid of honor, then there will be a quarrel at the wedding. Therefore if Alice gets married, then there will be a quarrel at the wedding.

10. If Alice gets married, then Betty is maid of honor and Caroline is maid of honor. If either Betty is maid of honor or Caroline is maid of honor, then there will be a quarrel at the wedding. Therefore if Alice gets married, then there will be a quarrel at the wedding.

8.5 Statement Forms and Statements

We now make explicit a notion tacitly assumed in the preceding section, the notion of a *statement form*. There is an exact parallel between the relation of argument to argument form, on the one hand, and the relation of statement to statement form, on the other. The definition of "statement form" makes this evident: "a statement form is any sequence of symbols containing statement variables but no statements, such that when the statement variables are replaced by statements—the same statement replacing the same statement variable throughout—the result is a statement." Thus $p \vee q$ is a statement form, for when the variables p and q are replaced by statements, a statement results. Since the resulting statement is a disjunction, $p \vee q$ is a *disjunctive statement form*. Analogously, $p \cdot q$ and $p \supset q$ are *conjunctive* and *conditional statement forms*, and $\sim p$ is a *negation form* or *denial form*. Just as any argument of a certain form is said to be a substitution instance of that argument form, so any statement of a certain form is said to be a substitution instance of that statement form. And just as we distinguished *the specific form* of a given argument, so we distinguish *the specific form* of a given statement as that statement form from which the statement results by replacing each different statement variable by a different simple statement. Thus $p \vee q$ is *the specific form* of the statement "The blind man has a red hat or the blind man has a white hat."

It is perfectly natural to feel that although the statements "Lincoln was assassinated" (symbolized as L) and "Either Lincoln was assassinated or else he wasn't" (symbolized as $L \vee \sim L$) are both *true*, they are true "in different ways," or have "different kinds" of truth. Similarly, it is perfectly natural to feel that although the statements "Washington was assassinated" (symbolized as W) and "Washington was both assassinated and not assassinated" (symbolized as $W \cdot \sim W$) are both *false*, they are false "in different ways," or have "different kinds" of falsehood. While not pretending to give any kind of psychological explanation of these "feelings," we can nevertheless point out certain logical differences to which they are probably appropriate.

The statement L is true and the statement W is false; these are historical facts. There is no logical necessity about them. Events might have occurred differently, and the truth values of such statements as L and W must be discovered by an empirical study of history. But the statement $L \vee \sim L$, although true, is not a truth of history. There is logical necessity here, events could not have been such as to make it false, and its truth can be known independently of any particular empirical investigation. The statement $L \vee \sim L$ is a logical truth, a formal truth, true in virtue of its form alone. It is a substitution instance of a statement form *all* of whose substitution instances are true statements.

A statement form which has only true substitution instances is a *tautologous* statement form, or a *tautology*. To show that the statement form $p \vee \sim p$ is a tautology we construct the following truth table:

p	$\sim p$	$p \vee \sim p$
T	**F**	**T**
F	**T**	**T**

There is only one initial or guide column to this truth table, since the form under consideration contains only one statement variable. Consequently, there are only two rows, which represent all possible substitution instances. There are only **T**'s in the column under the statement form in question, and this fact shows that all of its substitution instances are true. Any statement which is a substitution instance of a tautologous statement form is true in virtue of its form and is itself said to be tautologous, or a tautology.

A statement form which has only false substitution instances is said to be *self-contradictory,* or a *contradiction,* and is logically false. The statement form $p \cdot \sim p$ is self-contradictory, for in its truth table only **F**'s occur under it, signifying that all of its substitution instances are false. Any statement, such as $W \cdot \sim W$, which is a substitution instance of a self-contradictory statement form, is false in virtue of its form and is itself said to be self-contradictory, or a contradiction.

Statement forms which have both true and false statements among their substitution instances are called *contingent* statement forms. Any statement whose specific form is contingent is called a contingent statement.[8] Thus p, $\sim p$, $p \cdot q$, $p \vee q$, and $p \supset q$ are all contingent statement forms. And such statements as L, $\sim L$, $L \cdot W$, L v W, and $L \supset W$ are contingent statements, since their truth values are dependent or contingent on their contents rather than on their forms alone.

[8] It will be recalled that we are assuming here that no simple statements are either logically true or logically false. Only contingent simple statements are admitted here. Cf. footnote 6 on page 268.

Not all statement forms are so obviously tautological or self-contradictory or contingent as the simple examples cited above. For example, the statement form $[(p \supset q) \supset p] \supset p$ is not at all obvious, though its truth table will show it to be a tautology. It even has a special name, "Peirce's Law."

Two statements are said to be *materially equivalent,* or *equivalent in truth value,* when they are either both true or both false. This notion is expressed by the symbol "$\equiv$." Material equivalence is a truth function and can be defined by the following truth table:

p	q	$p \equiv q$
T	**T**	**T**
T	**F**	**F**
F	**T**	**F**
F	**F**	**T**

Whenever two statements are materially equivalent they materially imply each other. This is easily verified by a truth table. Hence the symbol "$\equiv$" may be read either "is materially equivalent to" or "if and only if." A statement of form $p \equiv q$ is called a *biconditional,* and the form is also called a *biconditional.* The notion of "logical equivalence" is both more important and more complicated. In dealing with truth-functional compound statements we give the following definition: two statements are *logically equivalent* when the (biconditional) statement of their equivalence is a tautology. Thus the "principle of double negation," expressed as the biconditional $p \equiv \sim \sim p$, is proved to be tautologous by the following truth table:

p	$\sim p$	$\sim \sim p$	$p \equiv \sim \sim p$
T	**F**	**T**	**T**
F	**T**	**F**	**T**

There are two logical equivalences (i.e., logically true biconditionals) of some intrinsic interest and importance which express the interrelations between conjunction, disjunction, and negation. Since the disjunction $p \vee q$ asserts merely that *at least one* of its two disjuncts is *true,* it is not contradicted by asserting that *at least one is false,* but only by asserting that *both* are false. Thus asserting the negation of the disjunction $p \vee q$ is logically equivalent to asserting the conjunction of the negations of p and q. In symbols we have the biconditional $\sim(p \vee q) \equiv (\sim p \cdot \sim q)$, whose logical truth is established by the following truth table:

p	q	$p \vee q$	$\sim(p \vee q)$	$\sim p$	$\sim q$	$\sim p \cdot \sim q$	$\sim(p \vee q) \equiv (\sim p \cdot \sim q)$
T	T	T	F	F	F	F	T
T	F	T	F	F	T	F	T
F	T	T	F	T	F	F	T
F	F	F	T	T	T	T	T

Similarly, since the conjunction of p and q asserts that *both* are *true,* to contradict it we need merely assert that *at least one* is *false*. Thus asserting the negation of the conjunction $p \cdot q$ is logically equivalent to asserting the disjunction of the negations of p and q. In symbols we have the biconditional $\sim(p \cdot q) \equiv (\sim p \vee \sim q)$, which is easily proved to be a tautology. These two tautologous biconditionals are known as De Morgan's Theorems, having been stated by the mathematician and logician Augustus De Morgan (1806–1871). De Morgan's Theorems can be given a combined formulation in English as:

the negation of the $\left\{\begin{matrix}\text{disjunction}\\ \text{conjunction}\end{matrix}\right\}$ of two statements is logically equivalent to the $\left\{\begin{matrix}\text{conjunction}\\ \text{disjunction}\end{matrix}\right\}$ of the negations of the two statements.

Two statement forms are logically equivalent if no matter what statements are substituted for their statement variables—the same statements replacing the same statement variables in both statement forms—the resulting pairs of statements are equivalent. Since $\sim(p \cdot \sim q)$ and $\sim p \vee q$ are logically equivalent (by De Morgan's Theorem and the principle of double negation), there is no logical reason for defining $p \supset q$ as $\sim(p \cdot \sim q)$ rather than $\sim p \vee q$. And the latter is the more usual definition of the horseshoe symbol.

There is an important relationship between tautologies and valid arguments. To every argument there corresponds a conditional statement whose antecedent is the conjunction of the argument's premisses and whose consequent is the argument's conclusion. Thus to any argument of the form

$$\begin{array}{l} p \supset q \\ p \\ \therefore q \end{array}$$

corresponds a conditional statement of the form $[(p \supset q) \cdot p] \supset q$. It is clear that a truth table which proves an argument form valid will also show its corresponding conditional statement form to be tautologous. An argument form is valid if and only if its truth table has a **T** under the conclusion in every row in which there are **T**'s under all of its premisses. But an **F** can occur in the column headed by the corresponding conditional statement form only where there are **T**'s under all the premisses and an **F** under the conclusion. Hence only **T**'s will occur under a conditional which corresponds to a valid argument. Thus for every valid argument of the truth-functional variety discussed in the present chapter, the statement that its premisses imply its conclusion is a tautology.

EXERCISES

I. For each statement in the left-hand column indicate which, if any, of the statement forms in the right-hand column have the given statement as a substitution instance, and indicate which, if any, is the specific form of the given statement.

★ 1. $A \vee B$	a. $p \cdot q$
2. $C \cdot \sim D$	b. $p \supset q$
3. $\sim E \supset (F \cdot G)$	c. $p \vee q$
4. $H \supset (I \cdot J)$	d. $p \cdot \sim q$
★ 5. $(K \cdot L) \vee (M \cdot N)$	e. $p \equiv q$
6. $(O \vee P) \supset (P \cdot Q)$	f. $(p \supset q) \vee (r \cdot s)$
7. $(R \supset S) \vee (T \cdot \sim U)$	g. $[(p \supset q) \supset r] \supset s$
8. $V \supset (W \vee \sim W)$	h. $[(p \supset q) \supset p] \supset p$
9. $[(X \supset Y) \supset X] \supset X$	i. $(p \cdot q) \vee (r \cdot s)$
10. $Z \equiv \sim \sim Z$	j. $p \supset (q \vee \sim r)$

II. Use truth tables to characterize the following statement forms as tautologous, self-contradictory, or contingent:

★ 1. $[p \supset (p \supset q)] \supset q$

2. $p \supset [(p \supset q) \supset q]$

3. $(p \cdot q) \cdot (p \supset \sim q)$

4. $p \supset [\sim p \supset (q \vee \sim q)]$

★ 5. $p \supset [p \supset (q \cdot \sim q)]$

6. $(p \supset p) \supset (q \cdot \sim q)$

7. $[p \supset (q \supset r)] \supset [(p \supset q) \supset (p \supset r)]$

8. $[p \supset (q \supset p)] \supset [(q \supset q) \supset \sim (r \supset r)]$

9. $\{[(p \supset q) \cdot (r \supset s)] \cdot (p \vee r)\} \supset (q \vee s)$

10. $\{[(p \supset q) \cdot (r \supset s)] \cdot (q \vee s)\} \supset (p \vee r)$

III. Use truth tables to decide which of the following biconditionals are tautologies:

★ 1. $(p \supset q) \equiv (\sim q \supset \sim p)$

2. $(p \supset q) \equiv (\sim p \supset \sim q)$

3. $[(p \supset q) \supset r] \equiv [(q \supset p) \supset r]$

4. $[p \supset (q \supset r)] \equiv [q \supset (p \supset r)]$

★ 5. $p \equiv [p \cdot (p \vee q)]$

6. $p \equiv [p \vee (p \cdot q)]$

7. $p \equiv [p \cdot (p \supset q)]$

8. $p \equiv [p \cdot (q \supset p)]$

9. $p \equiv [p \vee (p \supset q)]$

10. $(p \supset q) \equiv [(p \vee q) \equiv q]$

8.6 The Paradoxes of Material Implication

There are two forms of statements, $p \supset (q \supset p)$ and $\sim p \supset (p \supset q)$, which are easily proved to be tautologies. Trivial as these statement forms may be in their symbolic formulation, when expressed in ordinary English they seem surprising and even paradoxical. The first may be expressed as "If a statement is true then it is implied by any statement whatever." Since it is true that the earth is round, it follows that "The moon is made of green cheese implies that the earth is round"; and this is very curious indeed, especially since it also follows that "The moon is *not* made of green cheese implies that the earth is round." The second tautology may be expressed as "If a statement is false then it implies any statement whatever." Since it is false that the moon is made of green cheese, it follows that "The moon is made of green cheese implies that the earth is round"; and this is all the more curious when we realize that it also follows that "The moon is made of green cheese implies that the earth is *not* round."

These seem paradoxical because we believe that the shape of the earth and the matter of the moon are utterly irrelevant to each other, and we believe further that no statement, true or false, can really imply any other statement, false or true, to which it is utterly irrelevant. And yet truth tables establish that a false statement implies any statement, and that a true statement is implied by any statement. This paradox is easily resolved, however, when we acknowledge the ambiguity of the word "implies." In several senses of the word "implies" it is perfectly true that no contingent statement can imply any other contingent statement with unrelated subject matter. It is true in the case of *logical* implication, and *definitional,* and *causal* implications. It may even be true of *decisional* implications, although here the notion of *relevance* may have to be construed more broadly.

But subject matter or *meaning* is strictly irrelevant to *material implication,* which is a truth function. Only truth and falsehood are relevant here. There is nothing paradoxical in stating that any disjunction is true which contains at least one true disjunct, and this fact is all that is asserted by statements of the forms $p \supset (\sim q \vee p)$ and $\sim p \supset (\sim p \vee q)$, which are logically equivalent to the "paradoxical" ones. We have already given a justification of treating material implication as *a* sense of "if-then," and of the logical expediency of translating *every* occurrence of "if-then" into the "$\supset$" notation. That justification was the fact that translating "if-then" into the "$\supset$" preserves the validity of all valid arguments of the type with which we are concerned in this part of our logical studies. There are other proposed symbolizations, adequate to other types of implication, but they belong to more advanced parts of logic, beyond the scope of this book.

8.7 The Three "Laws of Thought"

Those who have defined logic as the science of the laws of thought have often gone on to assert that there are exactly three fundamental or basic laws of thought necessary and sufficient for thinking to follow if it is to be "correct." These have traditionally been called the Principle of Identity, the Principle of Contradiction (sometimes the Principle of Noncontradiction), and the Principle of Excluded Middle. There are alternative formulations of these principles, appropriate to different contexts. The formulations appropriate here are the following:

The Principle of Identity asserts that *if any statement is true, then it is true.*
The Principle of Contradiction asserts that *no statement can be both true and false.*
The Principle of Excluded Middle asserts that *any statement is either true or false.*

In the terminology of the present chapter, we may rephrase them as follows. The Principle of Identity asserts that every statement of the form $p \supset p$ is true, that is, that every such statement is a tautology. The Principle of Contradiction asserts that every statement of the form $p \cdot \sim p$ is false, that is, that every such statement is self-contradictory. The Principle of Excluded Middle asserts that every statement of the form $p \vee \sim p$ is true, that is, that every such statement is a tautology.

Objections have been made to these principles from time to time, but for the most part the objections seem to be based upon misunderstandings. The Principle of Identity has been criticized on the grounds that things change, for what was true, say, of the United States when it consisted of the thirteen original tiny states is no longer true of the United States today with its fifty states. In one sense of the word "statement" this observation is correct; but that sense is not the one with which logic is concerned. Those "statements" whose truth values change with time are *elliptical* or incomplete formulations of propositions which do not change, and it is the latter with which logic deals. Thus the sentence "There are only thirteen states in the U.S.A." may be regarded as an elliptical or partial formulation of "There were only thirteen states in the U.S.A. *in 1790*," which is just as true in the twentieth century as it was in 1790. When we confine our attention to *complete* or *nonelliptical* formulations, the Principle of Identity is perfectly true and unobjectionable.

The Principle of Contradiction has been criticized by Hegelians, General Semanticists, and Marxists, on the grounds that there are contradictions, or situations in which contradictory or conflicting forces are at work. That there are situations containing conflicting forces must be admitted: this is as true in the realm of mechanics as in the social and economic spheres. But it is a loose and inconvenient terminology to call these conflicting forces "contradictory." The heat applied to a contained gas, which tends to make it expand, and the container, which tends to keep it from expanding, may be described as conflicting with each other, but neither is the negation or denial or contradictory of the other. The private owner of a large factory, which requires thousands of laborers working together for its operation, may oppose and be opposed by the labor union which could never have been organized if its members had not been brought together to work in that factory; but neither owner nor union is the negation or denial or contradictory of the other. When understood in the sense in which it is intended, the Principle of Contradiction is unobjectionable and perfectly true.

The Principle of Excluded Middle has been the object of more attacks than either of the other principles. It has been urged that its acceptance leads to a "two-valued orientation" which implies, among other things, that everything is either white or black, with any middle ground excluded. But although the statement "this is black" cannot be jointly true along with the statement "this is white" (where the word "this" refers to exactly the same thing in both statements), one is not the denial or contradictory of the other. Admittedly they cannot both be true, but they can both be false. They are contrary, but not contradictory. The negation or contradictory of "this is white," is "$\sim$ this is white," and one of these two statements must be true—if the word "white" is used in precisely the same sense in both statements. When restricted to statements containing completely unambiguous and perfectly precise terms, the Principle of Excluded Middle also is perfectly true.

Although the three principles are true, it may be doubted that they have the privileged and fundamental status traditionally assigned them. The first and third are not the only forms of tautologies, and the explicit contradiction $p \cdot \sim p$ is not the only contradictory form of statement. Yet the three Laws of Thought *can* be regarded as having a certain fundamental status in relation to truth tables. As we fill in subsequent columns by referring back to the initial columns, we are guided by the Principle of Identity: if a **T** has been placed under a symbol in a certain row, then in filling in other columns under expressions containing that symbol, when we come to that row we consider that symbol still to be assigned a **T**. In filling out the initial columns, in each row we put either a **T** or an **F**, being guided by the Principle of Excluded Middle; and nowhere do we put both **T** and **F** together, being guided by the Principle of Contradiction. The three Laws of Thought can be regarded as the basic principles governing the construction of truth tables.

Still, it should be remarked that when one attempts to set up logic as a system, the three laws are not merely no more "important" or "fruitful" than any others, but there are other tautologies which are more fruitful for purposes of deduction—and hence more important—than the three principles discussed. A treatment of this point, however, lies beyond the scope of this book.[9]

[9] For further discussion of these matters, the interested reader can consult Part Three of *Readings on Logic,* edited by I. M. Copi and J. A. Gould (New York: The Macmillan Company, 1964), and Part Nine of *Contemporary Readings in Logical Theory,* edited by I. M. Copi and J. A. Gould (New York: The Macmillan Company, 1967).

Chapter 9
The Method of Deduction

For as one may feel sure that a chain will hold when he is assured that each separate link is of good material and that it clasps the two neighboring links, viz., the one preceding and the one following it, so we may be sure of the accuracy of the reasoning when the matter is good, that is to say, when nothing doubtful enters into it, and when the form consists in a perpetual concatenation of truths which allows of no gap.

—*Gottfried Leibniz*

9.1 Formal Proof of Validity

In theory truth tables are adequate to test the validity of any argument of the general type here considered. But in practice they grow unwieldy as the number of component statements increases. A more efficient method of establishing the validity of an extended argument is to deduce its conclusion from its premisses by a sequence of elementary arguments each of which is known to be valid. This technique accords fairly well with ordinary methods of argumentation.

Consider, for example, the following argument:

If Anderson was nominated, then he went to Boston.
If he went to Boston, then he campaigned there.

If he campaigned there, he met Douglas.
Anderson did not meet Douglas.
Either Anderson was nominated or someone more eligible was selected.
Therefore someone more eligible was selected.

Its validity may be intuitively obvious, but let us consider the matter of proof. The discussion will be facilitated by translating the argument into our symbolism as:

$$\begin{array}{l} A \supset B \\ B \supset C \\ C \supset D \\ \sim D \\ A \vee E \\ \therefore E \end{array}$$

To establish the validity of this argument by means of a truth table would require one with thirty-two rows, since there are five different simple statements involved. But we can prove the given argument valid by deducing its conclusion from its premisses by a sequence of just four elementary valid arguments. From the first two premisses $A \supset B$ and $B \supset C$ we validly infer $A \supset C$ by a Hypothetical Syllogism. From $A \supset C$ and the third premiss $C \supset D$ we validly infer $A \supset D$ by another Hypothetical Syllogism. From $A \supset D$ and the fourth premiss $\sim D$ we validly infer $\sim A$ by *modus tollens*. And from $\sim A$ and the fifth premiss $A \vee E$, by a Disjunctive Syllogism, we validly infer E, the conclusion of the original argument. That the conclusion can be deduced from the five premisses of the original argument by four elementary valid arguments proves the original argument to be valid. Here the elementary valid argument forms Hypothetical Syllogism (H.S.), *modus tollens* (M.T.), and Disjunctive Syllogism (D.S.) are used as *rules of inference* in accordance with which conclusions are validly inferred or deduced from premisses.

A more formal proof of validity is given by writing the premisses and the statements which are deduced from them in a single column, and setting off in another column, to the right of each statement, its "justification," or the reason we can give for including it in the proof. It is convenient to list all the premisses first, and to write the conclusion slightly to one side, separated by a diagonal line from the premisses. The diagonal line automatically labels all statements above it as premisses. If all the statements in the column are numbered, the "justification" for each statement consists of the numbers of the preceding statements from which it is inferred, together with the abbreviation for the rule of inference by which it follows from them. The formal proof is written as:

1.	$A \supset B$	
2.	$B \supset C$	
3.	$C \supset D$	
4.	$\sim D$	
5.	$A \vee E \;/\therefore E$	
6.	$A \supset C$	1,2, H.S.
7.	$A \supset D$	6,3, H.S.
8.	$\sim A$	7,4, M.T.
9.	E	5,8, D.S.

We define a *formal proof* that a given argument is valid to be a sequence of statements each of which is either a premiss of that argument or follows from preceding statements of the sequence by an elementary valid argument, and the last statement in the sequence is the conclusion of the argument whose validity is being proved.

We define an *elementary valid argument* to be any argument which is a substitution instance of an elementary valid argument form. One matter to be emphasized is that *any* substitution instance of an elementary valid argument form is an elementary valid argument. Thus the argument

$$(A \cdot B) \supset [C \equiv (D \vee E)]$$
$$A \cdot B$$
$$\therefore C \equiv (D \vee E)$$

is an elementary valid argument because it is a substitution instance of the elementary valid argument form *modus ponens* (M.P.). It results from

$$p \supset q$$
$$p$$
$$\therefore q$$

by substituting $A \cdot B$ for p and $C \equiv (D \vee E)$ for q and is therefore of that form even though *modus ponens* is not *the specific form* of the given argument.

Modus ponens is a very elementary valid argument form indeed, but what *other* valid argument forms are to be included as Rules of Inference? We begin with a list of just nine Rules of Inference to be used in constructing formal proofs of validity:

Rules of Inference

1. *Modus Ponens* (M.P.)
   $p \supset q$
   p
   $\therefore q$

2. *Modus Tollens* (M.T.)
   $p \supset q$
   $\sim q$
   $\therefore \sim p$

3. *Hypothetical Syllogism* (H.S.)
   $p \supset q$
   $q \supset r$
   $\therefore p \supset r$

4. *Disjunctive Syllogism* (D.S.)
   $p \vee q$
   $\sim p$
   $\therefore q$

5. *Constructive Dilemma* (C.D.)
   $(p \supset q) \cdot (r \supset s)$
   $p \vee r$
   $\therefore q \vee s$

6. *Absorption* (Abs.)
   $p \supset q$
   $\therefore p \supset (p \cdot q)$

7. *Simplification* (Simp.)
   $p \cdot q$
   $\therefore p$

8. *Conjunction* (Conj.)
   p
   q
   $\therefore p \cdot q$

9. *Addition* (Add.)
   p
   $\therefore p \vee q$

These nine Rules of Inference correspond to elementary argument forms whose validity is easily established by truth tables. With their aid, formal proofs of validity can be constructed for a wide range of more complicated arguments. The names listed are for the most part standard, and the use of their abbreviations permits formal proofs to be set down with a minimum of writing.

EXERCISES

I. For each of the following arguments state the Rule of Inference by which its conclusion follows from its premiss or premisses:

★ 1. $(A \cdot B) \supset C$
   $\therefore (A \cdot B) \supset [(A \cdot B) \cdot C]$

2. $(D \vee E) \cdot (F \vee G)$
   $\therefore D \vee E$

3. $H \supset I$
   $\therefore (H \supset I) \vee (H \supset \sim I)$

4. $\sim(J \cdot K) \cdot (L \supset \sim M)$
   $\therefore \sim(J \cdot K)$

★ 5. $[N \supset (O \cdot P)] \cdot [Q \supset (O \cdot R)]$
   $N \vee Q$
   $\therefore (O \cdot P) \vee (O \cdot R)$

6. $(S \equiv T) \vee [(U \cdot V) \vee (U \cdot W)]$
   $\sim(S \equiv T)$
   $\therefore (U \cdot V) \vee (U \cdot W)$

7. $(X \vee Y) \supset \sim(Z \cdot \sim A)$
   $\sim\sim(Z \cdot \sim A)$
   $\therefore \sim(X \vee Y)$

8. $\sim(B \cdot C) \supset (D \vee E)$
   $\sim(B \cdot C)$
   $\therefore D \vee E$

9. $(F \equiv G) \supset \sim(G \cdot \sim F)$
   $\sim(G \cdot \sim F) \supset (G \supset F)$
   $\therefore (F \equiv G) \supset (G \supset F)$

★ 10. $\sim(H \cdot \sim I) \supset (H \supset I)$
   $(I \equiv H) \supset \sim(H \cdot \sim I)$
   $\therefore (I \equiv H) \supset (H \supset I)$

11. $(J \supset K) \cdot (K \supset L)$
   $L \supset M$
   $\therefore [(J \supset K) \cdot (K \supset L)] \cdot (L \supset M)$

12. $N \supset (O \vee P)$
   $Q \supset (O \vee R)$
   $\therefore [Q \supset (O \vee R)] \cdot [N \supset (O \vee P)]$

13. $(S \supset T) \supset (U \supset V)$
   $\therefore (S \supset T) \supset [(S \supset T) \cdot (U \supset V)]$

14. $(W \cdot \sim X) \equiv (Y \supset Z)$
   $\therefore [(W \cdot \sim X) \equiv (Y \supset Z)] \vee (X \equiv \sim Z)$

★ 15. $(A \supset B) \supset (C \vee D)$
   $A \supset B$
   $\therefore C \vee D$

16. $[E \supset (F \equiv \sim G)] \vee (C \vee D)$
   $\sim[E \supset (F \equiv \sim G)]$
   $\therefore C \vee D$

17. $[(H \cdot \sim I) \supset C] \cdot [(I \cdot \sim H) \supset D]$
   $(H \cdot \sim I) \vee (I \cdot \sim H)$
   $\therefore C \vee D$

18. $(C \vee D) \supset [(J \vee K) \supset (J \cdot K)]$
   $\sim[(J \vee K) \supset (J \cdot K)]$
   $\therefore \sim(C \vee D)$

19. $\sim[L \supset (M \supset N)] \supset \sim(C \vee D)$
   $\sim[L \supset (M \supset N)]$
   $\therefore \sim(C \vee D)$

20. $[(O \supset P) \supset Q] \supset \sim(C \vee D)$
   $(C \vee D) \supset [(O \supset P) \supset Q]$
   $\therefore (C \vee D) \supset \sim(C \vee D)$

II. Each of the following is a formal proof of validity for the indicated argument. State the "justification" for each line that is not a premiss:

★ 1.
1. $A \cdot B$
2. $(A \vee C) \supset D \;/\therefore A \cdot D$
3. A
4. $A \vee C$
5. D
6. $A \cdot D$

2.
1. $(E \vee F) \cdot (G \vee H)$
2. $(E \supset G) \cdot (F \supset H)$
3. $\sim G \;/\therefore H$
4. $E \vee F$
5. $G \vee H$
6. H

3.
1. $I \supset J$
2. $J \supset K$
3. $L \supset M$
4. $I \vee L \;/\therefore K \vee M$
5. $I \supset K$
6. $(I \supset K) \cdot (L \supset M)$
7. $K \vee M$

4.
1. $N \supset O$
2. $(N \cdot O) \supset P$
3. $\sim(N \cdot P) \;/\therefore \sim N$
4. $N \supset (N \cdot O)$
5. $N \supset P$
6. $N \supset (N \cdot P)$
7. $\sim N$

★ 5.
1. $Q \supset R$
2. $\sim S \supset (T \supset U)$
3. $S \vee (Q \vee T)$
4. $\sim S \;/\therefore R \vee U$
5. $T \supset U$
6. $(Q \supset R) \cdot (T \supset U)$
7. $Q \vee T$
8. $R \vee U$

6.
1. $W \supset X$
2. $(W \supset Y) \supset (Z \vee X)$
3. $(W \cdot X) \supset Y$
4. $\sim Z \;/\therefore X$
5. $W \supset (W \cdot X)$
6. $W \supset Y$
7. $Z \vee X$
8. X

7.
1. $(A \vee B) \supset C$
2. $(C \vee B) \supset [A \supset (D \equiv E)]$
3. $A \cdot D \;/\therefore D \equiv E$
4. A
5. $A \vee B$
6. C
7. $C \vee B$
8. $A \supset (D \equiv E)$
9. $D \equiv E$

8.
1. $F \supset \sim G$
2. $\sim F \supset (H \supset \sim G)$
3. $(\sim I \vee \sim H) \supset \sim\sim G$
4. $\sim I \;/\therefore \sim H$
5. $\sim I \vee \sim H$
6. $\sim\sim G$
7. $\sim F$
8. $H \supset \sim G$
9. $\sim H$

9.
1. $I \supset J$
2. $I \vee (\sim\sim K \cdot \sim\sim J)$
3. $L \supset \sim K$
4. $\sim(I \cdot J) \;/\therefore \sim L \vee \sim J$
5. $I \supset (I \cdot J)$
6. $\sim I$
7. $\sim\sim K \cdot \sim\sim J$
8. $\sim\sim K$
9. $\sim L$
10. $\sim L \vee \sim J$

10.
1. $(L \supset M) \supset (N \equiv O)$
2. $(P \supset \sim Q) \supset (M \equiv \sim Q)$

3. $\{[(P \supset \sim Q) \vee (R \equiv S)] \cdot (N \vee O)\} \supset [(R \equiv S) \supset (L \supset M)]$
4. $(P \supset \sim Q) \vee (R \equiv S)$
5. $N \vee O \; / \therefore (M \equiv \sim Q) \vee (N \equiv O)$
6. $[(P \supset \sim Q) \vee (R \equiv S)] \cdot (N \vee O)$
7. $(R \equiv S) \supset (L \supset M)$
8. $(R \equiv S) \supset (N \equiv O)$
9. $[(P \supset \sim Q) \supset (M \equiv \sim Q)] \cdot [(R \equiv S) \supset (N \equiv O)]$
10. $(M \equiv \sim Q) \vee (N \equiv O)$

III. Construct a formal proof of validity for each of the following arguments:

★ 1. $A \supset B$
$A \vee C$
$\sim B$
$\therefore C$

2. $D \supset E$
$F \vee \sim E$
$\sim F$
$\therefore \sim D$

3. $G \supset H$
$I \supset J$
$G \vee I$
$\therefore H \vee J$

4. $(K \vee L) \supset (M \vee N)$
$(M \vee N) \supset (O \cdot P)$
K
$\therefore O$

★ 5. $(Q \supset R) \cdot (S \supset T)$
$(U \supset V) \cdot (W \supset X)$
$Q \vee U$
$\therefore R \vee V$

6. $W \supset X$
$(W \cdot X) \supset Y$
$(W \cdot Y) \supset Z$
$\therefore W \supset Z$

7. $A \supset B$
$C \supset D$
$A \vee C$
$\therefore (A \cdot B) \vee (C \cdot D)$

8. $(E \vee F) \supset (G \cdot H)$
$(G \vee H) \supset I$
E
$\therefore I$

9. $J \supset K$
$K \vee L$
$(L \cdot \sim J) \supset (M \cdot \sim J)$
$\sim K$
$\therefore M$

10. $(N \vee O) \supset P$
$(P \vee Q) \supset R$
$Q \vee N$
$\sim Q$
$\therefore R$

IV. Construct a formal proof of validity for each of the following arguments, using the abbreviations suggested:

★ 1. If either George or Herbert wins, then both Jack and Kenneth lose. George wins. Therefore Jack loses. (*G*—George wins; *H*—Herbert wins; *J*—Jack loses; *K*—Kenneth loses.)

2. If Adams joins, then the club's social prestige will rise; and if Baker joins, then the club's financial position will be more secure. Either

Adams or Baker will join. If the club's social prestige rises, then Baker will join; and if the club's financial position becomes more secure, then Wilson will join. Therefore either Baker or Wilson will join. (*A*—Adams joins; *S*—The club's social prestige rises; *B*—Baker joins; *F*—The club's financial position is more secure; *W*—Wilson joins.)

3. If Brown received the wire, then he took the plane; and if he took the plane, then he will not be late for the meeting. If the telegram was incorrectly addressed, then Brown will be late for the meeting. Either Brown received the wire or the telegram was incorrectly addressed. Therefore either Brown took the plane or he will be late for the meeting. (*R*—Brown received the wire; *P*—Brown took the plane; *L*—Brown will be late for the meeting; *T*—The telegram was incorrectly addressed.)

4. If Neville buys the lot, then an office building will be constructed; whereas if Payton buys the lot, then it quickly will be sold again. If Rivers buys the lot, then a store will be constructed; and if a store is constructed, then Thompson will offer to lease it. Either Neville or Rivers will buy the lot. Therefore either an office building or a store will be constructed. (*N*—Neville buys the lot; *O*—An office building will be constructed; P—Payton buys the lot; *Q*—The lot quickly will be sold again; *R*—Rivers buys the lot; *S*—A store will be constructed; *T*—Thompson will offer to lease it.)

★ 5. If rain continues, then the river rises. If rain continues and the river rises, then the bridge will wash out. If continuation of rain will wash the bridge out, then a single road is not sufficient for the town. Either a single road is sufficient for the town or the traffic engineers have made a mistake. Therefore the traffic engineers have made a mistake. (*C*—Rain continues; *R*—The river rises; *B*—The bridge washes out; *S*—A single road is sufficient for the town; *M*—The traffic engineers have made a mistake.)

6. If Jacobson goes to the meeting, then a complete report will be made; but if Jacobson does not go to the meeting, then a special election will be required. If a complete report is made, then an investigation will be launched. If Jacobson's going to the meeting implies that a complete report will be made, and the making of a complete report implies that an investigation will be launched, then either Jacobson goes to the meeting and an investigation is launched or Jacobson does not go to the meeting and no investigation is launched. If Jacobson goes to the meeting and an investigation is launched, then some members will have to stand trial. But if Jacobson does not go to the meeting and no investigation is launched, then the organization will disintegrate very rapidly. Therefore either some members will have to stand trial or the

organization will disintegrate very rapidly. (*J*—Jacobson goes to the meeting; *R*—A complete report is made; *E*—A special election is required; *I*—An investigation is launched; *T*—Some members have to stand trial; *D*—The organization disintegrates very rapidly.)

7. If Ann is present, then Betty is present. If Ann and Betty are both present, then either Charlene or Doris will be elected. If either Charlene or Doris is elected, then Ethel does not really dominate the club. If Ann's presence implies that Ethel does not really dominate the club, then Florence will be the new president. So Florence will be the new president. (*A*—Ann is present; *B*—Betty is present; *C*—Charlene will be elected; *D*—Doris will be elected; *E*—Ethel really dominates the club; *F*—Florence will be the new president.)

8. If Mr. Jones is the brakeman's next-door neighbor, then Mr. Jones' annual earnings are exactly divisible by 3. If Mr. Jones' annual earnings are exactly divisible by 3, then $20,000 is exactly divisible by 3. But $20,000 is not exactly divisible by 3. If Mr. Robinson is the brakeman's next-door neighbor, then Mr. Robinson lives halfway between Detroit and Chicago. If Mr. Robinson lives in Detroit, then he does not live halfway between Detroit and Chicago. Mr. Robinson lives in Detroit. If Mr. Jones is not the brakeman's next-door neighbor, then either Mr. Robinson or Mr. Smith is the brakeman's next-door neighbor. Therefore Mr. Smith is the brakeman's next-door neighbor. (*J*—Mr. Jones is the brakeman's next-door neighbor; *E*—Mr. Jones' annual earnings are exactly divisible by 3; *T*—$20,000 is exactly divisible by 3; *R*—Mr. Robinson is the brakeman's next-door neighbor; *H*—Mr. Robinson lives halfway between Detroit and Chicago; *D*—Mr. Robinson lives in Detroit; *S*—Mr. Smith is the brakeman's next-door neighbor.)

9. If Mr. Smith is the brakeman's next-door neighbor, then Mr. Smith lives halfway between Detroit and Chicago. If Mr. Smith lives halfway between Detroit and Chicago, then he does not live in Chicago. Mr. Smith is the brakeman's next-door neighbor. If Mr. Robinson lives in Detroit, then he does not live in Chicago. Mr. Robinson lives in Detroit. Mr. Smith lives in Chicago or else either Mr. Robinson or Mr. Jones lives in Chicago. If Mr. Jones lives in Chicago, then the brakeman is Jones. Therefore the brakeman is Jones. (*S*—Mr. Smith is the brakeman's next-door neighbor; *W*—Mr. Smith lives halfway between Detroit and Chicago; *L*—Mr. Smith lives in Chicago; *D*—Mr. Robinson lives in Detroit; *I*—Mr. Robinson lives in Chicago; *C*—Mr. Jones lives in Chicago; *B*—The brakeman is Jones.)

10. If Smith once beat the fireman at billiards, then Smith is not the fireman. Smith once beat the fireman at billiards. If the brakeman is Jones, then Jones is not the fireman. The brakeman is Jones. If Smith is

not the fireman and Jones is not the fireman, then Robinson is the fireman. If the brakeman is Jones and Robinson is the fireman, then Smith is the engineer. Therefore Smith is the engineer. (*O*—Smith once beat the fireman at billiards; *M*—Smith is the fireman; *B*—The brakeman is Jones; *N*—Jones is the fireman; *F*—Robinson is the fireman; *G*—Smith is the engineer.)

9.2 The Rule of Replacement

There are many valid truth-functional arguments whose validity cannot be proved using only the nine Rules of Inference given thus far. For example, to construct a formal proof of validity for the obviously valid argument

$$A \supset B$$
$$C \supset \sim B$$
$$\therefore A \supset \sim C$$

additional rules are required.

In any truth-functional compound statement, if a component statement in it is replaced by another statement of the same truth value, the truth value of the compound statement will remain unchanged. But the only compound statements that concern us here are truth-functional compound statements. We may accept, therefore, as an additional principle of inference, the Rule of Replacement, which permits us to infer from any statement the result of replacing all or part of that statement by any other statement logically equivalent to the part replaced. Using the Principle of Double Negation (D.N.), which asserts that p is logically equivalent to $\sim\sim p$, we can infer from $A \supset \sim\sim B$ any of the following:

$$A \supset B, \quad \sim\sim A \supset \sim\sim B, \quad \sim\sim(A \supset \sim\sim B), \text{ or } A \supset \sim\sim\sim\sim B$$

by Replacement.

To make the new rule definite, we list a number of tautologous or logically true biconditionals with which it can be used, these biconditionals constituting the additional Rules of Inference we shall use in proving the validity of extended arguments. We number them consecutively after the first nine Rules already stated.

RULE OF REPLACEMENT: *Any of the following logically equivalent expressions may replace each other wherever they occur:*

10. De Morgan's Theorems (De M.): $\sim(p \cdot q) \equiv (\sim p \vee \sim q)$
    $\sim(p \vee q) \equiv (\sim p \cdot \sim q)$

11. Commutation (Com.): $(p \vee q) \equiv (q \vee p)$
$(p \cdot q) \equiv (q \cdot p)$

12. Association (Assoc.): $[p \vee (q \vee r)] \equiv [(p \vee q) \vee r]$
$[p \cdot (q \cdot r)] \equiv [(p \cdot q) \cdot r]$

13. Distribution (Dist.): $[p \cdot (q \vee r)] \equiv [(p \cdot q) \vee (p \cdot r)]$
$[p \vee (q \cdot r)] \equiv [(p \vee q) \cdot (p \vee r)]$

14. Double Negation (D.N.): $p \equiv \sim\sim p$

15. Transposition (Trans.): $(p \supset q) \equiv (\sim q \supset \sim p)$

16. Material Implication (Impl.): $(p \supset q) \equiv (\sim p \vee q)$

17. Material Equivalence (Equiv.): $(p \equiv q) \equiv [(p \supset q) \cdot (q \supset p)]$
$(p \equiv q) \equiv [(p \cdot q) \vee (\sim p \cdot \sim q)]$

18. Exportation (Exp.): $[(p \cdot q) \supset r] \equiv [p \supset (q \supset r)]$

19. Tautology (Taut.): $p \equiv (p \vee p)$
$p \equiv (p \cdot p)$

These nineteen Rules of Inference are somewhat redundant, in the sense that they do not constitute a bare minimum which would suffice for the construction of formal proofs of validity for extended arguments. For example, *modus tollens* could be dropped from the list without any real weakening of our proof apparatus, for any line depending upon *modus tollens* can be justified by appealing to other Rules in the list instead. Thus in the formal proof on page 289, line 8, $\sim A$, was deduced from lines 4 and 7, $\sim D$ and $A \supset D$, by *modus tollens*, but if *modus tollens* were eliminated as a Rule of Inference, we could still deduce $\sim A$ from $A \supset D$ and $\sim D$. This could be done by inserting the intermediate line $\sim D \supset \sim A$, which follows from $A \supset D$ by the Principle of Transposition (Trans.), and then obtaining $\sim A$ from $\sim D \supset \sim A$ and $\sim D$ by *modus ponens* (M.P.). But *modus tollens* is such a commonly used and intuitively obvious Rule of Inference that it has been included anyway. Others of the nineteen are also redundant in this same sense.

The list of nineteen Rules of Inference is characterized not only by redundancy, but also by a certain sort of deficiency. For example, although the argument

$A \vee B$
$\sim B$
$\therefore A$

is intuitively valid, its form

$$p \vee q$$
$$\sim q$$
$$\therefore p$$

is not included as a Rule of Inference. The conclusion A does not follow from the premisses $A \vee B$ and $\sim B$ by any single Rule of Inference, although it can be deduced from them by two Rules of Inference. A formal proof of validity for the given argument can be written as:

1. $A \vee B$
2. $\sim B$ / $\therefore A$
3. $B \vee A$ 1, Com.
4. A 3,2, D.S.

We could eliminate the indicated deficiency by adding another rule to our list, but if we made additions for all such cases we should end up with a list which was too long and therefore unmanageable.

The present list of nineteen Rules of Inference constitutes a *complete* system of truth-functional logic, in the sense that it permits the construction of a formal proof of validity for *any* valid truth-functional argument.[1]

The notion of *formal proof* is an *effective* notion, which means that it can be decided quite mechanically, in a finite number of steps, whether or not a given sequence of statements constitutes a formal proof (with reference to a given list of Rules of Inference). No thinking is required, either in the sense of thinking about what the statements in the sequence "mean," or in the sense of using logical intuition to check any step's validity. Only two things are required, of which the first is the ability to see that a statement occurring in one place is precisely the same as a statement occurring in another, for we must be able to check that some statements in the proof are premisses of the argument being proved valid, and that the last statement in the proof is the conclusion of that argument. The second thing required is the ability to see whether a given statement has a certain pattern or not, that is, to see if it is a substitution instance of a given statement form.

Thus any question about whether or not the preceding sequence

[1] A method of proving this kind of completeness for a set of rules of inference can be found in Chapter Seven of *Symbolic Logic,* Third Edition, by I. M. Copi (New York: The Macmillan Company, 1967). See also "The Completeness of Copi's System of Natural Deduction," by John A. Winnie, *Notre Dame Journal of Formal Logic,* Vol. XI, No. 3, July 1970, pp. 379–82.

of statements is a formal proof of validity can be settled in a completely mechanical fashion. That lines 1 and 2 are the premisses and line 4 is the conclusion of the given argument is obvious on inspection. That 3 follows from preceding lines by one of the given Rules of Inference can be decided in a finite number of steps—even where the notation "1, Com." is not written at the side. The explanatory notation in the second column is a help and should always be included, but it is not, strictly speaking, part of the proof itself. At every line, there are only a finite number of preceding lines and only a finite number of Rules of Inference or reference forms to be consulted. Although time-consuming, it can be verified by inspection and comparison of shapes that 3 does not follow from 1 and 2 by *modus ponens,* or by *modus tollens,* or by a Hypothetical Syllogism, . . . , and so on, until in following this procedure we come to the question of whether or not 3 follows from 1 by the Principle of Commutation, and there we see, simply by looking at the forms, that it does. In the same way the legitimacy of *any* statement in a formal proof can be tested in a finite number of steps, none of which involves anything more than comparing forms or shapes. It is to preserve this property of effectiveness that we lay down the rule that only one step should be taken at a time. One might be tempted to shorten a proof by combining steps, but the space and time saved are negligible. More important is the effectiveness we achieve by taking each step by means of one single Rule of Inference at a time.

Although a formal proof of validity is effective in the sense that it can be mechanically decided of any given sequence whether it is a proof, constructing a formal proof is not an effective procedure. In this respect formal proofs differ from truth tables. The use of truth tables is completely mechanical: given any argument of the sort with which we are now concerned, we can always construct a truth table to test its validity by following the simple rules of procedure set forth in the preceding chapter. But we have no effective or mechanical rules for the construction of formal proofs. Here we must think or "figure out" where to begin and how to proceed. Nevertheless, proving an argument valid by constructing a formal proof of its validity is much easier than the purely mechanical construction of a truth table with perhaps hundreds or even thousands of rows.

An important difference between the first nine and the last ten Rules of Inference must be understood. The first nine rules can be applied only to whole lines of a proof. Thus in a formal proof of validity the statement A can be inferred from the statement $A \cdot B$ by Simplification only if $A \cdot B$ constitutes a whole line. But the statement $A \supset C$ does not follow from the statement $(A \cdot B) \supset C$ by Simplification or by any other Rule of Inference. It does not follow at all, for if A is true and B and C are both false, $(A \cdot B) \supset C$ is true but $A \supset C$ is false. Again, although $A \vee B$ follows from A by Addition, we cannot infer $(A \vee B) \supset C$ from $A \supset C$ by Addition or by any other Rule of Inference. For if A and C are both false and B is true, $A \supset C$ is true but $(A \vee B) \supset C$ is false. On the other hand, any of the last ten Rules can be applied either to whole lines or to parts of lines. Not only can the statement $A \supset (B \supset C)$ be inferred from the whole line $(A \cdot B) \supset C$ by Exportation, but from the line $[(A \cdot B) \supset C] \vee D$ we can infer $[A \supset (B \supset C)] \vee D$ by Exportation. By Replacement, logically equivalent expressions can replace each other wherever they occur, even where they do not constitute whole lines of a proof. But the first nine Rules of Inference can be used only with whole lines of a proof serving as premisses.

Although we have no purely mechanical rules for constructing formal proofs, some rough-and-ready rules of thumb or hints on procedure may be suggested. The first is simply to begin deducing conclusions from the given premisses by the given Rules of Inference. As more and more of these subconclusions become available as premisses for further deductions, the greater is the likelihood of being able to see how to deduce the conclusion of the argument to be proved valid. Another hint is to try to eliminate statements that occur in the premisses but not in the conclusion. Such elimination can proceed, of course, only in accordance with the Rules of Inference. But the Rules contain many techniques for eliminating statements. Simplification is such a rule, whereby the right-hand conjunct can be dropped from a whole line that is a conjunction. And Commutation is a rule which permits switching the left-hand conjunct of a conjunction over to the right-hand side, from which it can be dropped by Simplification. The "middle" term q can be eliminated by a Hypothetical Syllogism given two statements of the patterns $p \supset q$ and $q \supset r$. Distribution is a useful rule for transforming a disjunction of the pattern $p \vee (q \cdot r)$ into the conjunction $(p \vee q) \cdot (p \vee r)$, whose right-hand conjunct can then be eliminated by Simplification. Another rule of thumb is to introduce by means of Addition a statement that occurs in the conclusion but not in any premiss. Another method is to work backward from the conclusion by looking for some statement or statements from which it can be deduced, and then trying to deduce those intermediate statements from the premisses. There is, however, no substitute for practice as a method of acquiring facility in constructing formal proofs.

EXERCISES

I. For each of the following arguments state the Rule of Inference by which its conclusion follows from its premiss:

★ 1. $(A \supset B) \cdot (C \supset D)$
$\therefore (A \supset B) \cdot (\sim D \supset \sim C)$

2. $(E \supset F) \cdot (G \supset \sim H)$
$\therefore (\sim E \vee F) \cdot (G \supset \sim H)$

3. $[I \supset (J \supset K)] \cdot (J \supset \sim I)$
$\therefore [(I \cdot J) \supset K] \cdot (J \supset \sim I)$

4. $[L \supset (M \vee N)] \vee [L \supset (M \vee N)]$
$\therefore L \supset (M \vee N)$

★ 5. $O \supset [(P \supset Q) \cdot (Q \supset P)]$
$\therefore O \supset (P \equiv Q)$

6. $\sim(R \vee S) \supset (\sim R \vee \sim S)$
$\therefore (\sim R \cdot \sim S) \supset (\sim R \vee \sim S)$

7. $(T \vee \sim U) \cdot [(W \cdot \sim V) \supset \sim T]$
$\therefore (T \vee \sim U) \cdot [W \supset (\sim V \supset \sim T)]$

8. $(X \vee Y) \cdot (\sim X \vee \sim Y)$
$\therefore [(X \vee Y) \cdot \sim X] \vee [(X \vee Y) \cdot \sim Y]$

9. $Z \supset (A \supset B)$
$\therefore Z \supset (\sim\sim A \supset B)$

★ 10. $[C \cdot (D \cdot \sim E)] \cdot [(C \cdot D) \cdot \sim E]$
$\therefore [(C \cdot D) \cdot \sim E] \cdot [(C \cdot D) \cdot \sim E]$

11. $(\sim F \vee G) \cdot (F \supset G)$
$\therefore (F \supset G) \cdot (F \supset G)$

12. $(H \supset \sim I) \supset (\sim I \supset \sim J)$
$\therefore (H \supset \sim I) \supset (J \supset I)$

13. $(\sim K \supset L) \supset (\sim M \vee \sim N)$
$\therefore (\sim K \supset L) \supset \sim(M \cdot N)$

14. $[(\sim O \vee P) \vee \sim Q] \cdot [\sim O \vee (P \vee \sim Q)]$
$\therefore [\sim O \vee (P \vee \sim Q)] \cdot [\sim O \vee (P \vee \sim Q)]$

★ 15. $[(R \vee \sim S) \cdot \sim T] \vee [(R \vee \sim S) \cdot U]$
$\therefore (R \vee \sim S) \cdot (\sim T \vee U)$

16. $[V \supset \sim(W \vee X)] \supset (Y \vee Z)$
$\therefore \{[V \supset \sim(W \vee X)] \cdot [V \supset \sim(W \vee X)]\} \supset (Y \vee Z)$

17. $[(\sim A \cdot B) \cdot (C \vee D)] \vee [\sim(\sim A \cdot B) \cdot \sim(C \vee D)]$
$\therefore (\sim A \cdot B) \equiv (C \vee D)$

18. $[\sim E \vee (\sim\sim F \supset G)] \cdot [\sim E \vee (F \supset G)]$
$\therefore [\sim E \vee (F \supset G)] \cdot [\sim E \vee (F \supset G)]$

19. $[H \cdot (I \vee J)] \vee [H \cdot (K \supset \sim L)]$
$\therefore H \cdot [(I \vee J) \vee (K \supset \sim L)]$

20. $(\sim M \vee \sim N) \supset (O \supset \sim\sim P)$
$\therefore \sim(M \cdot N) \supset (O \supset \sim\sim P)$

II. Each of the following is a formal proof of validity for the indicated argument. State the "justification" for each line which is not a premiss:

★ 1.
1. $A \supset B$
2. $C \supset \sim B \ / \therefore A \supset \sim C$
3. $\sim\sim B \supset \sim C$
4. $B \supset \sim C$
5. $A \supset \sim C$

2.
1. $(D \cdot E) \supset F$
2. $(D \supset F) \supset G \ / \therefore E \supset G$
3. $(E \cdot D) \supset F$
4. $E \supset (D \supset F)$
5. $E \supset G$

3.
1. $(H \vee I) \supset [J \cdot (K \cdot L)]$
2. $I \ / \therefore J \cdot K$
3. $I \vee H$
4. $H \vee I$
5. $J \cdot (K \cdot L)$
6. $(J \cdot K) \cdot L$
7. $J \cdot K$

4.
1. $(M \vee N) \supset (O \cdot P)$
2. $\sim O \ / \therefore \sim M$
3. $\sim O \vee \sim P$
4. $\sim(O \cdot P)$
5. $\sim(M \vee N)$
6. $\sim M \cdot \sim N$
7. $\sim M$

★ 5.
1. $(Q \vee \sim R) \vee S$
2. $\sim Q \vee (R \cdot \sim Q) \ / \therefore R \supset S$
3. $(\sim Q \vee R) \cdot (\sim Q \vee \sim Q)$
4. $(\sim Q \vee \sim Q) \cdot (\sim Q \vee R)$
5. $\sim Q \vee \sim Q$
6. $\sim Q$
7. $Q \vee (\sim R \vee S)$
8. $\sim R \vee S$
9. $R \supset S$

6.
1. $T \cdot (U \vee V)$
2. $T \supset [U \supset (W \cdot X)]$
3. $(T \cdot V) \supset \sim(W \vee X)$
   $/ \therefore W \equiv X$
4. $(T \cdot U) \supset (W \cdot X)$
5. $(T \cdot V) \supset (\sim W \cdot \sim X)$
6. $[(T \cdot U) \supset (W \cdot X)] \cdot$
   $[(T \cdot V) \supset (\sim W \cdot \sim X)]$
7. $(T \cdot U) \vee (T \cdot V)$
8. $(W \cdot X) \vee (\sim W \cdot \sim X)$
9. $W \equiv X$

7.
1. $Y \supset Z$
2. $Z \supset [Y \supset (R \vee S)]$
3. $R \equiv S$
4. $\sim(R \cdot S) \ / \therefore \sim Y$
5. $(R \cdot S) \vee (\sim R \cdot \sim S)$
6. $\sim R \cdot \sim S$
7. $\sim(R \vee S)$
8. $Y \supset [Y \supset (R \vee S)]$
9. $(Y \cdot Y) \supset (R \vee S)$
10. $Y \supset (R \vee S)$
11. $\sim Y$

8.
1. $A \supset B$
2. $B \supset C$
3. $C \supset A$
4. $A \supset \sim C \ / \therefore \sim A \cdot \sim C$
5. $A \supset C$
6. $(A \supset C) \cdot (C \supset A)$
7. $A \equiv C$
8. $(A \cdot C) \vee (\sim A \cdot \sim C)$
9. $\sim A \vee \sim C$
10. $\sim(A \cdot C)$
11. $\sim A \cdot \sim C$

9.
1. $(D \cdot E) \supset \sim F$
2. $F \vee (G \cdot H)$
3. $D \equiv E \ / \therefore D \supset G$
4. $(D \supset E) \cdot (E \supset D)$
5. $D \supset E$
6. $D \supset (D \cdot E)$
7. $D \supset \sim F$
8. $(F \vee G) \cdot (F \vee H)$
9. $F \vee G$
10. $\sim\sim F \vee G$
11. $\sim F \supset G$
12. $D \supset G$

10.
1. $(I \vee \sim\sim J) \cdot K$
2. $[\sim L \supset \sim(K \cdot J)] \cdot [K \supset (I \supset \sim M)]$ $/\therefore \sim(M \cdot \sim L)$
3. $[(K \cdot J) \supset L] \cdot [K \supset (I \supset \sim M)]$
4. $[(K \cdot J) \supset L] \cdot [(K \cdot I) \supset \sim M]$
5. $(I \vee J) \cdot K$
6. $K \cdot (I \vee J)$
7. $(K \cdot I) \vee (K \cdot J)$
8. $(K \cdot J) \vee (K \cdot I)$
9. $L \vee \sim M$
10. $\sim M \vee L$
11. $\sim M \vee \sim\sim L$
12. $\sim(M \cdot \sim L)$

III. Construct a formal proof of validity for each of the following arguments:

★ 1. $A \supset \sim B$
$C \supset B$
$\therefore A \supset \sim C$

2. $D \supset (E \vee F)$
$\sim E \cdot \sim F$
$\therefore \sim D$

3. $(G \supset \sim H) \supset I$
$\sim G \vee \sim H$
$\therefore I$

4. $(J \vee K) \supset \sim L$
L
$\therefore \sim J$

★ 5. $[(M \cdot N) \cdot O] \supset P$
$Q \supset [(O \cdot M) \cdot N]$
$\therefore \sim Q \vee P$

6. $R \vee (S \cdot \sim T)$
$(R \vee S) \supset (U \vee \sim T)$
$\therefore T \supset U$

7. $(\sim V \supset W) \cdot (X \supset W)$
$\sim(\sim X \cdot V)$
$\therefore W$

8. $[(Y \cdot Z) \supset A] \cdot [(Y \cdot B) \supset C]$
$(B \vee Z) \cdot Y$
$\therefore A \vee C$

9. $\sim D \supset (\sim E \supset \sim F)$
$\sim(F \cdot \sim D) \supset \sim G$
$\therefore G \supset E$

★ 10. $[H \vee (I \vee J)] \supset (K \supset J)$
$L \supset [I \vee (J \vee H)]$
$\therefore (L \cdot K) \supset J$

11. $M \supset N$
$M \supset (N \supset O)$
$\therefore M \supset O$

12. $(P \supset Q) \cdot (P \vee R)$
$(R \supset S) \cdot (R \vee P)$
$\therefore Q \vee S$

13. $T \supset (U \cdot V)$
$(U \vee V) \supset W$
$\therefore T \supset W$

14. $(X \vee Y) \supset (X \cdot Y)$
$\sim(X \vee Y)$
$\therefore \sim(X \cdot Y)$

★ 15. $(Z \supset Z) \supset (A \supset A)$
$(A \supset A) \supset (Z \supset Z)$
$\therefore A \supset A$

16. $\sim B \vee [(C \supset D) \cdot (E \supset D)]$
$B \cdot (C \vee E)$
$\therefore D$

17. $\sim F \vee \sim[\sim(G \cdot H) \cdot (G \vee H)]$
$(G \supset H) \supset [(H \supset G) \supset I]$
$\therefore F \supset (F \cdot I)$

18. $J \vee (\sim J \cdot K)$
$J \supset L$
$\therefore (L \cdot J) \equiv J$

19. $(M \supset N) \cdot (O \supset P)$
$\sim N \vee \sim P$
$\sim(M \cdot O) \supset Q$
$\therefore Q$

20. $(R \vee S) \supset (T \cdot U)$
$\sim R \supset (V \supset \sim V)$
$\sim T$
$\therefore \sim V$

IV. Construct a formal proof of validity for each of the following arguments, in each case using the suggested notation:

★ 1. Either the manager didn't notice the change or else he approves of it. He noticed it all right. So he must approve of it. (*N*, *A*)

2. The oxygen in the tube either combined with the filament to form an oxide or else it vanished completely. The oxygen in the tube could not have vanished completely. Therefore the oxygen in the tube combined with the filament to form an oxide. (*C*, *V*)

3. If a statesman who sees his former opinions to be wrong does not alter his course, he is guilty of deceit; and if he does alter his course, he is open to a charge of inconsistency. He either alters his course or he doesn't. Therefore he is either guilty of deceit or else he is open to a charge of inconsistency. (*A*, *D*, *I*)

4. It is not the case that he either forgot or wasn't able to finish. Therefore he was able to finish. (*F*, *A*)

★ 5. If the litmus paper turns red, then the solution is acid. Hence if the litmus paper turns red, then either the solution is acid or something is wrong somewhere. (*R*, *A*, *W*)

6. He can have many friends only if he respects them as individuals. If he respects them as individuals, then he cannot expect them all to behave alike. He does have many friends. Therefore he does not expect them all to behave alike. (*F*, *R*, *E*)

7. If the victim had money in his pockets, then robbery wasn't the motive for the crime. But robbery or vengeance was the motive for the crime. The victim had money in his pockets. Therefore vengeance must have been the motive for the crime. (*M*, *R*, *V*)

8. Napoleon is to be condemned if he usurped power that was not rightfully his own. Either Napoleon was a legitimate monarch or else he usurped power that was not rightfully his own. Napoleon was not a legitimate monarch. So Napoleon is to be condemned. (*C*, *U*, *L*)

9. If we extend further credit on the Wilkins account, they will have a moral obligation to accept our bid on their next project. We can figure a more generous margin of profit in preparing our estimates if they have a moral obligation to accept our bid on their next project. Figuring a more generous margin of profit in preparing our estimates will cause our general financial condition to improve considerably. Hence a considerable improvement in our general financial condition will follow from our extension of further credit on the Wilkins account. (*C*, *M*, *P*, *I*)

★ 10. If the laws are good and their enforcement is strict, then crime will diminish. If strict enforcement of laws will make crime diminish, then our problem is a practical one. The laws are good. Therefore our problem is a practical one. (*G, S, D, P*)

11. Had Roman citizenship guaranteed civil liberties, then Roman citizens would have enjoyed religious freedom. Had Roman citizens enjoyed religious freedom, there would have been no persecution of the early Christians. But the early Christians were persecuted. Hence Roman citizenship could not have guaranteed civil liberties. (*G, F, P*)

12. If the first disjunct of a disjunction is true, the disjunction as a whole is true. Therefore if both the first and second disjuncts of the disjunction are true, then the disjunction as a whole is true. (*F, W, S*)

13. If the new courthouse is to be conveniently located, it will have to be situated in the heart of the city; and if it is to be adequate to its function, it will have to be built large enough to house all the city offices. If the new courthouse is situated in the heart of the city and is built large enough to house all the city offices, then its cost will run to over a million dollars. Its costs cannot exceed a million dollars. Therefore either the new courthouse will have an inconvenient location or it will be inadequate to its function. (*C, H, A, L, O*)

14. Jones will come if he gets the message, provided that he is still interested. Although he didn't come, he is still interested. Therefore he didn't get the message. (*C, M, I*)

★ 15. If the Mosaic account of the cosmogony is strictly correct, the sun was not created till the fourth day. And if the sun was not created till the fourth day, it could not have been the cause of the alternation of day and night for the first three days. But either the word "day" is used in Scripture in a different sense from that in which it is commonly accepted now or else the sun must have been the cause of the alternation of day and night for the first three days. Hence it follows that either the Mosaic account of the cosmogony is not strictly correct or else the word "day" is used in Scripture in a different sense from that in which it is commonly accepted now. (*M, C, A, D*)

16. If the teller or the cashier had pushed the alarm button, the vault would have locked automatically and the police would have arrived within three minutes. Had the police arrived within three minutes, the robbers' car would have been overtaken. But the robbers' car was not overtaken. Therefore the teller did not push the alarm button. (*T, C, V, P, O*)

17. If a man is always guided by his sense of duty, he must forego the enjoyment of many pleasures; and if he is always guided by his

desire for pleasure, he must often neglect his duty. A man is either always guided by his sense of duty or always guided by his desire for pleasure. If a man is always guided by his sense of duty, he does not often neglect his duty; and if he is always guided by his desire for pleasure, he does not forego the enjoyment of many pleasures. Therefore a man must forego the enjoyment of many pleasures if and only if he does not often neglect his duty. (*D, F, P, N*)

18. The husband is wealthy and his bride is poor but honest. If a bride is poor and her husband is wealthy, then either she has made a good match, or else they will be childless or will have family trouble. She did not make a good match, yet they are neither quarrelsome nor have they any family trouble. Therefore they are childless. (*W, P, H, G, C, F, Q*)

19. Either the robber came in the door, or else the crime was an inside one and one of the servants is implicated. The robber could come in the door only if the latch had been raised from the inside; but one of the servants is surely implicated if the latch was raised from the inside. Therefore one of the servants is implicated. (*D, I, S, L*)

20. If I pay the tailor, I won't have any money left. I can take my girl to the dance only if I have money. She'll be unhappy unless I take her to the dance. But if I don't pay the tailor, he won't let me have my suit; and without the suit I certainly can't take my girl to the dance. I must either pay the tailor or not pay him. So my girl is bound to be unhappy! (*P, M, D, U, S*)

9.3 Proof of Invalidity

For an invalid argument there is, of course, no formal proof of validity. But if we fail to discover a formal proof of validity for a given argument, this failure does not prove that the argument is invalid and that no such proof can be constructed. It may mean only that we have not tried hard enough. Our inability to find a proof of validity may be caused by the fact that the argument is not valid, but it may be caused instead by our own lack of ingenuity—as a consequence of the noneffective character of the process of proof construction. Not being able to construct a formal proof of its validity does not prove an argument to be invalid. What does constitute a proof that a given argument is invalid?

The method about to be described is closely related to the truth-table method, although it is a great deal shorter. It will be helpful to recall how an invalid argument form is proved invalid by a truth table. If a single case (row) can be found in which truth values are assigned to the statement variables in such a way that the premisses are made true and the conclusion false, then the argument form is invalid. If we can somehow make an assignment of truth values to the simple component statements of an argument which will make its premisses true and its conclusion false, then making that assignment will suffice to prove the argument invalid. To make such an assignment is, in effect, what the truth table does. But if we can make such an assignment of truth values without actually constructing the whole truth table, a certain amount of work will be eliminated.

Consider the argument:

If the governor favors public housing, then he is in favor of restricting the scope of private enterprise.
If the governor were a communist, then he would be in favor of restricting the scope of private enterprise.
Therefore if the governor favors public housing, then he is a communist.

This is symbolized as:

$$P \supset R$$
$$C \supset R$$
$$\therefore P \supset C$$

and we can prove it invalid without having to construct a complete truth table. First we ask: what assignment of truth values is required to make the conclusion false? It is clear that a conditional is false only when its antecedent is true and its consequent false. Hence assigning the truth value "true" to P and "false" to C will make the conclusion $P \supset C$ false. Now if the truth value "true" is assigned to R, both premisses are made true, since a conditional is always true when its consequent is true. We can say, then, that if the truth value "true" is assigned to P and to R, and the truth value "false" is assigned to C, the argument will have true premisses and a false conclusion and is thus proved to be invalid.

This method of proving invalidity is an alternative to the truth-table method of proof. The two methods are closely related, however, and the essential connection between them should be realized. In effect, what we did when we made the indicated assignment of truth values was to construct one row of the given argument's truth table. The relationship can perhaps be seen more clearly when the truth-value assignments are written out horizontally, as

P	R	C	$P \supset R$	$C \supset R$	$P \supset C$
true	true	false	true	true	false

in which form they constitute one row of the truth table for the given argument. An argument is proved invalid if there is at least one row of its truth table in which all its premisses are true but its conclusion is false. Consequently we need not examine *all* rows of its truth table to discover an argument's invalidity: the discovery of a single row in which its premisses are all true and its conclusion false will suffice. The present method of proving invalidity is a method of constructing such a row without having to construct the entire truth table.

The present method is shorter than writing out a truth table, and the amount of time and work saved is proportionally greater for arguments involving a greater number of component simple statements. For arguments with a considerable number of premisses, or with premisses of considerable complexity, the needed assignment of truth values may not be so easy to make. It may be desirable to assign some truth values to make some premisses true before choosing an assignment to make the conclusion false. A certain amount of trial and error may be necessary. But it will generally be shorter and easier than writing out a complete truth table.

EXERCISES

Prove the invalidity of each of the following by the method of assigning truth values:

★ 1. $A \supset B$
$C \supset D$
$A \vee D$
$\therefore B \vee C$

2. $\sim(E \cdot F)$
$(\sim E \cdot \sim F) \supset (G \cdot H)$
$H \supset G$
$\therefore G$

3. $I \vee \sim J$
$\sim(\sim K \cdot L)$
$\sim(\sim I \cdot \sim L)$
$\therefore \sim J \supset K$

4. $M \supset (N \vee O)$
$N \supset (P \vee Q)$
$Q \supset R$
$\sim(R \vee P)$
$\therefore \sim M$

★ 5. $S \supset (T \supset U)$
$V \supset (W \supset X)$
$T \supset (V \cdot W)$
$\sim(T \cdot X)$
$\therefore S \equiv U$

6. $A \equiv (B \vee C)$
$B \equiv (C \vee A)$
$C \equiv (A \vee B)$
$\sim A$
$\therefore B \vee C$

7. $D \supset (E \vee F)$
$G \supset (H \vee I)$
$\sim E \supset (I \vee J)$
$(I \supset G) \cdot (\sim H \supset \sim G)$
$\sim J$
$\therefore D \supset (G \vee I)$

8. $K \supset (L \cdot M)$
$(L \supset N) \vee \sim K$
$O \supset (P \vee \sim N)$
$(\sim P \vee Q) \cdot \sim Q$
$(R \vee \sim P) \vee \sim M$
$\therefore K \supset R$

9. $(S \supset T) \cdot (T \supset S)$
$(U \cdot T) \vee (\sim T \cdot \sim U)$
$(U \vee V) \vee (S \vee T)$
$\sim U \supset (W \cdot X)$
$(V \supset \sim S) \cdot (\sim V \supset \sim Y)$
$X \supset (\sim Y \supset \sim X)$
$(U \vee S) \cdot (V \vee Z)$
$\therefore X \cdot Z$

10. $A \supset (B \supset \sim C)$ $\quad (I \supset G) \cdot (H \supset J)$
$(D \supset B) \cdot (E \supset A)$ $\quad I \equiv \sim D$
$F \vee C$ $\quad (B \supset H) \cdot (\sim H \supset D)$
$G \supset \sim H$ $\quad \therefore E \equiv F$

9.4 Inconsistency

If no truth value assignment can be given to the component simple statements of an argument which makes its premisses true and its conclusion false, then the argument must be valid. Although this follows from the definition of "validity," it has a curious consequence. Consider the following argument, whose premisses appear to be utterly irrelevant to its conclusion:

If the airplane had engine trouble, it would have landed at Bridgeport.
If the airplane did not have engine trouble, it would have landed at Cleveland.
The airplane did not land at either Bridgeport or Cleveland.
Therefore the airplane must have landed in Denver.

and its symbolic translation:

$$A \supset B$$
$$\sim A \supset C$$
$$\sim(B \vee C)$$
$$\therefore D$$

Any attempt to assign truth values to its component simple statements to make the conclusion false and the premisses all true is doomed to failure. If we ignore the conclusion and concentrate our attention upon the other objective, that of making all the premisses true by an assignment of truth values to their component simple statements, we are bound to fail even here, in this apparently less ambitious project.

The reason the premisses cannot be made true and the conclusion false is that the premisses cannot possibly be made true in any case by *any* truth value assignment. No truth value assignment can make the premisses true because they are inconsistent with each other. Their conjunction is *self-contradictory,* being a substitution instance of a self-contradictory statement form. Were we to construct a truth table for the given argument, we should find that in every row at least one of the premisses is false. There is no row in which the premisses are all true, hence there is no row in which the premisses are all true and the conclusion false. Hence the truth table for this argument would establish its validity. Its validity can also be established by the following formal proof:

1.	$A \supset B$	
2.	$\sim A \supset C$	
3.	$\sim(B \vee C) / \therefore D$	
4.	$\sim B \cdot \sim C$	3, De M.
5.	$\sim B$	4, Simp.
6.	$\sim A$	1,5, M.T.
7.	C	2,6, M.P.
8.	$\sim C \cdot \sim B$	4, Com.
9.	$\sim C$	8, Simp.
10.	$C \vee D$	7, Add.
11.	D	10,9, D.S.

In this proof the lines up through 9 are devoted to making explicit the inconsistency which was implicitly contained in the premisses. That inconsistency emerges in lines 7 and 9, which assert C and $\sim C$, respectively. Once this explicit contradiction is achieved, the conclusion follows swiftly by the Principle of Addition and the Disjunctive Syllogism.

Thus we see that if a set of premisses is inconsistent, those premisses will validly yield *any* conclusion, no matter how irrelevant. The essence of the matter is more simply shown in the case of the following argument, whose openly inconsistent premisses allow us validly to infer an irrelevant and fantastic conclusion.

Today is Sunday. Today is not Sunday.
Therefore the moon is made of green cheese.

In symbols, we have:

1. S
2. $\sim S / \therefore M$

The formal proof of its validity is almost immediately obvious:

3.	$S \vee M$	1, Add.
4.	M	3,2, D.S.

What is wrong here? How can such meager and even inconsistent premisses make any argument in which they occur valid? It should be noted first that if an argument is valid because of an inconsistency in its premisses, it cannot possibly be a sound argument. If they are inconsistent with each other, the premisses cannot possibly all be true. No conclusion can be established as true by an argument with inconsistent premisses, since its premisses are of necessity false themselves.

The present situation is closely related to the so-called paradox of material implication. In discussing the latter, we observed that the statement form $\sim p \supset (p \supset q)$ is a tautology, having all its substitution instances true. Its formulation in English asserts that "If a statement is false then it materially implies any statement whatever," which is easily proved by means of truth tables. What has been established in the present discussion is that the argument form

$$\begin{array}{l} p \\ \sim p \\ \therefore q \end{array}$$

is valid. We have proved that *any argument with inconsistent premisses is valid, regardless of what its conclusion may be.* It may be established either by a truth table or by the kind of formal proof given above.

The premisses of a valid argument imply its conclusion not merely in the sense of "material" implication, but *logically* or "strictly." In a valid argument, it is logically impossible for the premisses to be true when the conclusion is false. And this situation obtains whenever it is logically impossible for the premisses to be true, even when the question of the truth or falsehood of the conclusion is ignored. Its analogy with the corresponding property of material implication has led some writers on logic to call this a "paradox of strict implication." In view of the logician's technical definition of "validity," however, it does not seem to be especially paradoxical. The alleged paradox arises primarily from treating a technical term as if it were a term of ordinary, everyday language.

The foregoing discussion helps to explain why consistency is so highly prized. One reason, of course, is that inconsistent statements cannot both be true. This fact underlies the strategy of cross-examination, where an attorney may seek to maneuver a hostile witness into contradicting himself. If testimony contains incompatible or inconsistent assertions, it cannot all be true, and the witness's credibility is destroyed—or at least shaken. But another reason why inconsistency is so repugnant is that any and every conclusion follows logically from inconsistent statements taken as premisses. Inconsistent statements are not "meaningless," their trouble is just the opposite. They mean too much—they mean everything, in the sense of implying everything. And if *everything* is asserted, half of what is asserted is surely *false,* since every statement has a denial.

The preceding discussion incidentally provides us with an answer to the old riddle: What happens when an irresistible force meets an immovable object? The description involves a contradiction. For an irresistible force to meet an immovable object, both must exist. There must be an irresistible force and there must also be an immovable object. But if there is an irresistible force there can be no immovable object. Here is the contradiction made explicit: there is an immovable object, and there is no immovable object. Given these inconsistent premisses, *any* conclusion may validly be inferred. So the correct answer to the question, "What happens when an irresistible force meets an immovable object?" is "Everything!"

EXERCISES

I. For each of the following, either construct a formal proof of validity or prove invalidity by the method of assigning truth values to the simple statements involved.

★ 1. $(A \supset B) \cdot (C \supset D)$
$\therefore (A \cdot C) \supset (B \vee D)$

2. $(E \supset F) \cdot (G \supset H)$
$\therefore (E \vee G) \supset (F \cdot H)$

3. $I \supset (J \vee K)$
$(J \cdot K) \supset L$
$\therefore I \supset L$

4. $M \supset (N \cdot O)$
$(N \vee O) \supset P$
$\therefore M \supset P$

★ 5. $[(X \cdot Y) \cdot Z] \supset A$
$(Z \supset A) \supset (B \supset C)$
B
$\therefore X \supset C$

6. $[(D \vee E) \cdot F] \supset G$
$(F \supset G) \supset (H \supset I)$
H
$\therefore D \supset I$

7. $(J \cdot K) \supset (L \supset M)$
$N \supset \sim M$
$\sim(K \supset \sim N)$
$\sim(J \supset \sim L)$
$\therefore \sim J$

8. $(O \cdot P) \supset (Q \supset R)$
$S \supset \sim R$
$\sim(P \supset \sim S)$
$\sim(O \supset Q)$
$\therefore \sim O$

9. $T \supset (U \cdot V)$
$U \supset (W \cdot X)$
$(T \supset W) \supset (Y \equiv Z)$
$(T \supset U) \supset \sim Y$
$\sim Y \supset (\sim Z \supset X)$
$\therefore X$

10. $A \supset (B \cdot C)$
$B \supset (D \cdot E)$
$(A \supset D) \supset (F \equiv G)$
$A \supset (B \supset \sim F)$
$\sim F \supset (\sim G \supset E)$
$\therefore E$

II. For each of the following, either construct a formal proof of validity or prove invalidity by the method of assigning truth values to the simple statements involved.

★ 1. If the linguistics investigators are correct, then if more than one dialect was present in Ancient Greece, then different tribes came down at different times from the North. If different tribes came down at different times from the North, they must have come from the Danube River valley. But archeological excavations would have revealed traces of different tribes there if different tribes had come down at different times from the North, and archeological excavations have revealed no such traces there. Hence if more than one dialect was present in Ancient Greece, then the linguistics investigators are not correct. (*C, M, D, V, A*)

2. If there are the ordinary symptoms of a cold and the patient has a high temperature, then if there are tiny spots on his skin, he has measles. Of course the patient cannot have measles if his record shows that he has had them before. The patient does have a high temperature and his record shows that he has had measles before. Besides the ordinary symptoms of a cold, there are tiny spots on his skin. I conclude that the patient has a virus infection. (*O, T, S, M, R, V*)

3. If God were willing to prevent evil, but unable to do so, he would be impotent; if he were able to prevent evil, but unwilling to do so, he would be malevolent. Evil can exist only if God is either unwilling or unable to prevent it. There is evil. If God exists, he is neither impotent nor malevolent. Therefore God does not exist. (*W, A, I, M, E, G*)

4. If I buy a new car this spring or have my old car fixed, then I'll get up to Canada this summer and stop off in Duluth. I'll visit my parents if I stop off in Duluth. If I visit my parents, they'll insist upon my spending the summer with them. If they insist upon my spending the summer with them, I'll be there till autumn. But if I stay there till autumn, then I won't get to Canada after all! So I won't have my old car fixed. (*N, F, C, D, V, I, A*)

★ 5. If Smith is intelligent and studies hard, then he will get good grades and pass his courses. If Smith studies hard but lacks intelligence, then his efforts will be appreciated; and if his efforts are appreciated, then he will pass his courses. If Smith is intelligent, then he studies hard. Therefore Smith will pass his courses. (*I, S, G, P, A*)

6. If there is a single norm for greatness of poetry, then Milton and Edgar Guest cannot both be great poets. If either Pope or Dryden is regarded as a great poet, then Wordsworth is certainly no great poet; but if Wordsworth is no great poet, then neither is Keats nor Shelley. But

after all, even though Edgar Guest is not, Dryden and Keats are both great poets. Hence there is no single norm for greatness of poetry. (*N, M, G, P, D, W, K, S*)

7. If the butler was present, he would have been seen; and if he was seen, he would have been questioned. If he had been questioned, he would have replied; and if he had replied, he would have been heard. But the butler was not heard. If the butler was neither seen nor heard, then he must have been on duty; and if he was on duty, he must have been present. Therefore the butler was questioned. (*P, S, Q, R, H, D*)

8. If the butler told the truth, then the window was closed when he entered the room; and if the gardener told the truth, then the automatic sprinkler system was not operating on the evening of the murder. If the butler and the gardener are both lying, then a conspiracy must exist to protect someone in the house and there would have been a little pool of water on the floor just inside the window. We know that the window could not have been closed when the butler entered the room. There was a little pool of water on the floor just inside the window. So if there is a conspiracy to protect someone in the house, then the gardener did not tell the truth. (*B, W, G, S, C, P*)

9. Their chief would leave the country if he feared capture, and he would not leave the country unless he feared capture. If he feared capture and left the country, then the enemy's espionage network would be demoralized and powerless to harm us. If he did not fear capture and remained in the country, it would mean that he was ignorant of our own agents' work. If he is really ignorant of our agents' work, then our agents can consolidate their positions within the enemy's organization; and if our agents can consolidate their positions there, they will render the enemy's espionage network powerless to harm us. Therefore the enemy's espionage network will be powerless to harm us. (*L, F, D, P, I, C*)

★ 10. If the investigators of extrasensory perception are regarded as honest, then considerable evidence for extrasensory perception must be admitted; and the doctrine of clairvoyance must be considered seriously if extrasensory perception is tentatively accepted as a fact. If considerable evidence for extrasensory perception is admitted, then it must be tentatively accepted as a fact and an effort must be made to explain it. The doctrine of clairvoyance must be considered seriously if we are prepared to take seriously that class of phenomena called occult; and if we are prepared to take seriously that class of phenomena called occult, a new respect must be paid to mediums. If we pursue the matter further, then if a new respect must be paid to mediums, we must take seriously their claims to communicate with the dead. We do pursue the matter further, but still we are practically committed to believing in ghosts if we take seriously the mediums' claims to communicate with the dead. Hence if the investigators of extrasensory perception are regarded as honest, we are practically committed to believing in ghosts. (*H, A, C, F, E, O, M, P, D, G*)

11. If we buy a lot then we will build a house. If we buy a lot then if we build a house then we will buy furniture. If we build a house then if we buy furniture then we will buy dishes. Therefore if we buy a lot then we will buy dishes. (*L, H, F, D*)

12. If your prices are low then your sales will be high, and if you sell quality merchandise then your customers will be satisfied. So if your prices are low and you sell quality merchandise, then your sales will be high and your customers satisfied. (*L, H, Q, S*)

13. If your prices are low then your sales will be high, and if you sell quality merchandise then your customers will be satisfied. So if either your prices are low or you sell quality merchandise, then either your sales will be high or your customers will be satisfied. (*L, H, Q, S*)

14. If Jordan joins the alliance then either Algeria or Syria boycotts it. If Kuwait joins the alliance then either Syria or Iraq boycotts it. Syria does not boycott it. Therefore if neither Algeria nor Iraq boycotts it then neither Jordan nor Kuwait joins the alliance. (*J, A, S, K, I*)

15. If either Jordan or Algeria joins the alliance then if either Syria or Kuwait boycotts it then although Iraq does not boycott it Yemen boycotts it. If either Iraq or Morocco does not boycott it then Egypt will join the alliance. Therefore if Jordan joins the alliance then if Syria boycotts it then Egypt will join the alliance. (*J, A, S, K, I, Y, M, E*)

16. Weather predicting is an exact science. Therefore either it will rain tomorrow or it won't. (*W, R*)

Chapter 10
Quantification Theory

Because language is misleading, as well as because it is diffuse and inexact when applied to logic (for which it was never intended), logical symbolism is absolutely necessary to any exact or thorough treatment of our subject.

—*Bertrand Russell*

10.1 Singular Propositions

The logical techniques of the two preceding chapters permit us to discriminate between valid and invalid arguments of one certain type. Arguments of that type are roughly characterized as those whose validity depends only upon the ways in which simple statements are truth-functionally combined into compound statements. There are, however, other types of arguments to which the validity criteria of the two preceding chapters do not apply. An example of a different type is the obviously valid argument:

All humans are mortal.
Socrates is human.
Therefore Socrates is mortal.

Were we to apply to this argument the evaluation methods previously introduced, we would symbolize it as:

$$M$$
$$S$$
$$\therefore H$$

But in this notation it appears to be invalid. The techniques of symbolic logic presented thus far cannot be applied to arguments of this new type. The validity of the given argument does not depend upon the way in which simple statements are compounded, for no compound statements occur in it. Its validity depends rather upon the inner logical structure of the noncompound statements involved. To formulate methods for testing the validity of arguments of this new sort, techniques for describing and symbolizing noncompound statements by reference to their inner logical structure must be devised.[1]

The simplest kind of noncompound statement is illustrated by the second premiss of the preceding argument, "Socrates is human." Statements of this kind have traditionally been called *singular propositions.* An (affirmative) singular proposition asserts that a particular individual possesses a specified property. In the present example, ordinary grammar and traditional logic would agree in classifying "Socrates" as the *subject* term and "human" as the *predicate* term. The subject term denotes a particular individual and the predicate term designates some property the individual is asserted to have.

It is clear that one and the same subject term can occur in different singular propositions. Thus we have the term "Socrates" as subject term in each of the following: "Socrates is mortal," "Socrates is female," "Socrates is wise," and "Socrates is beautiful." Of these, some are true (the first and third) and some are false (the second and fourth).[2] It is also clear that one and the same predicate term can occur in different singular propositions Thus we have the term "human" as predicate term in each of the following: "Aristotle is human," "Brazil is human," "Chicago is human," and "Diogenes is human." Of these, some are true (the first and fourth) and some are false (the second and third).

It should be clear from the foregoing that the word "individual" is used to refer not only to persons, but to any *thing*—such as a

[1] It was to arguments of this type that the classical or Aristotelian logic was primarily devoted, as described in Chapters 5 and 6. The older methods, however, do not possess the generality or power of the newer symbolic logic and cannot be extended to cover asyllogistic inference.

[2] Here we shall follow the custom of ignoring the time factor, and will use the verb "is" in the tenseless sense of "is, will be, or has been." Where considerations of time change are crucial, the somewhat more complicated methods of the logic of relations permit an adequate treatment.

country, a city, or in fact to anything of which an attribute such as *human* or *mortal* can be meaningfully predicated. In all the examples given thus far the predicate term has been an *adjective*. From the point of view of grammar the distinction between adjective and noun is of considerable importance, but it is without significance from the point of view of logic. Thus there is logically no difference between "Socrates is mortal," and "Socrates is a mortal." Nor is there any difference between "Socrates is wise," and "Socrates is a wise individual." A predicate may be either an adjective or a noun, or even a verb, as in "Aristotle writes," which can alternatively be expressed as "Aristotle is a writer."

Assuming that we can distinguish between individuals which have properties and the properties they may have, we can introduce and use two different kinds of symbols for referring to them. In the following discussion we shall use small or lower case letters from a through w to denote individuals. These symbols are *individual constants*. In any particular context in which they occur, each will designate a single individual throughout the whole of that context. It will usually be convenient to denote an individual by the first letter of its (or his) name. Thus in the present context we should use the letters $s, a, b, c, d,$ to denote the individuals Socrates, Aristotle, Brazil, Chicago, and Diogenes, respectively. We shall use capital letters to symbolize properties, and it will be convenient to use the same guiding principle here, using the letters $H, M, F, W, B,$ to symbolize the properties of being human, of being mortal, of being female, of being wise, and of being beautiful, respectively.

Having two groups of symbols, one for individuals and one for properties of individuals, we adopt the convention that writing a property symbol immediately to the left of an individual symbol will be our symbolic formulation of the singular proposition asserting that the individual named has the property specified. Thus the singular proposition "Socrates is human," will be symbolized as Hs. The other singular propositions mentioned involving the predicate "human" are symbolized as Ha, Hb, Hc, and Hd. All of them, it will be observed, have a certain common pattern, not to be symbolized as H by itself, but rather as H—where the "—" indicates that to the right of the predicate symbol another symbol, an individual symbol, occurs. Instead of using the dash symbol ("—") as a place marker, it is customary to use the letter x (which is available since only the letters a through w are used as individual constants. We use Hx [sometimes written $H(x)$] to symbolize the common pattern of all singular propositions which assert an individual to have the property of being human. The letter x, called an individual variable, is a mere *place marker*, serving to indicate where the various letters *a* through *w*—our individual constants—may be written for singular propositions to result.

The various singular propositions *Ha, Hb, Hc, Hd,* are either true or false; but *Hx* is neither true nor false, not being a statement or proposition at all. The expression *Hx* is a propositional function, which may be defined as an expression which (1) contains an individual variable and (2) becomes a proposition when the individual variable is replaced by an individual constant.[3] Individual constants are to be thought of as proper names of individuals. Any singular proposition is a *substitution instance* of a propositional function, the result of substituting an individual constant for the individual variable in that propositional function. Ordinarily, a propositional function will have some true substitution instances and some false substitution instances. The propositional functions considered thus far, that is, *Hx, Mx, Fx,* and *Wx* are all of this kind. We shall call these propositional functions "simple predicates," to distinguish them from the more complex propositional functions introduced in the following sections.

10.2 Quantification

The substitution of individual constants for individual variables is not the only way for propositions to be obtained from propositional functions. Propositions may also be obtained by the process called generalization or quantification. Predicate terms occur frequently in propositions other than singular ones. Thus the propositions "Everything is mortal" and "Something is beautiful" contain predicate terms, but are not singular propositions since they do not contain the names of any particular individuals. Indeed, they do not refer specifically to *any* particular individuals, being *general* propositions.

The first may be expressed in various ways that are logically equivalent: either as "All things are mortal" or as

Given any individual thing whatever, it is mortal.

In the latter formulation, the word "it" is a relative pronoun, referring back to the word "thing" which precedes it in the statement. Using the letter *x,* our individual variable, in place of the pronoun "it" and its antecedent, we may rewrite the first general proposition as:

Given any *x*, *x* is mortal.

[3] Some writers have regarded "propositional functions" as the meanings of such expressions, but here we define them to be the expressions themselves.

Or, using the notation introduced in the preceding section, we may write:

Given any *x*, *Mx*.

Although the propositional function *Mx* is not a proposition, here we have an expression containing it which *is* a proposition. The phrase "Given any *x*" is customarily symbolized by (x), which is called the universal quantifier. Our first general proposition may be completely symbolized as:

$$(x)Mx$$

The second general proposition, "Something is beautiful," may also be expressed as:

There is at least one thing which is beautiful.

In the latter formulation, the word "which" is a relative pronoun referring back to the word "thing." Using our individual variable *x* in place of both the pronoun "which" and its antecedent, we may rewrite the second general proposition as:

There is at least one *x* such that *x* is beautiful.

Or, using the notation at hand, we may write:

There is at least one *x* such that *Bx*.

Just as before, although *Bx* is a propositional function, we have here an expression containing it which is a proposition. The phrase "there is at least one *x* such that" is customarily symbolized by "$(\exists x)$," which is called the existential quantifier. The second general proposition may be completely symbolized as:

$$(\exists x)Bx$$

Thus we see that propositions may be formed from propositional functions either by *instantiation,* that is, by substituting an individual constant for its individual variable, or by *generalization,* that is, by placing a universal or existential quantifier before it. It is clear that the universal quantification of a propositional function is true if and only if all of its substitution instances are true, and that the existential quantification of a propositional function is true if and only if it has at least one true substitution instance. If we grant that there is at least one individual, then every propositional function has at least one substitution instance. Under this assumption, if the universal quantification of a propositional function is true, then its existential quantification is true also.

All the propositional functions mentioned thus far have had only affirmative singular propositions as substitution instances. But not all propositions are affirmative. The denial of the affirmative singular proposition "Socrates is mortal," is the negative singular proposition "Socrates is not mortal." In symbols we have Ms and $\sim Ms$. The first is a substitution instance of the propositional function Mx. The second can be regarded as a substitution instance of the propositional function $\sim Mx$. Here we enlarge our conception of propositional functions beyond the simple predicates introduced in the preceding section to permit them to contain the negation symbol "$\sim$."

Now the further connections between universal and existential quantification can be illustrated. The (universal) general proposition "Everything is mortal" is denied by the (existential) general proposition "Something is not mortal." These are symbolized as $(x)Mx$ and $(\exists x)\sim Mx$, respectively. Since one is the denial of the other, the biconditionals:

$$[\sim(x)Mx] \equiv [(\exists x) \sim Mx] \quad \text{and} \quad [(x)Mx] \equiv [\sim(\exists x) \sim Mx]$$

are logically true. Similarly, the (universal) general proposition "Nothing is mortal" is denied by the (existential) general proposition "Something is mortal." These are symbolized as $(x)\sim Mx$ and $(\exists x)Mx$, respectively. Since one is the denial of the other, the further biconditionals:

$$[\sim(x) \sim Mx] \equiv [(\exists x)Mx] \quad \text{and} \quad [(x) \sim Mx] \equiv [\sim(\exists x)Mx]$$

are logically true also. If we use the Greek letter *phi* to represent any predicate whatsoever, the relations between universal and existential quantification can be set down as follows:

$$[(x)\phi x] \equiv [\sim(\exists x)\sim\phi x]$$

$$[(\exists x)\phi x] \equiv [\sim(x)\sim\phi x]$$

$$[(x)\sim\phi x] \equiv [\sim(\exists x)\phi x]$$

$$[(\exists x)\sim\phi x] \equiv [\sim(x)\phi x]$$

More graphically, the general connections between universal and existential quantification can be described in terms of the following square array:

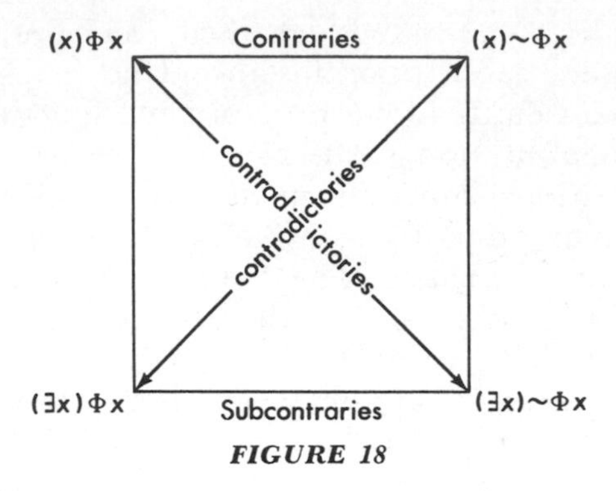

FIGURE 18

Continuing to assume the existence of at least one individual: we can say that the two top propositions are *contraries,* that is, they might both be false but cannot both be true; the two bottom propositions are *subcontraries,* that is, they can both be true but cannot both be false; propositions which are at opposite ends of the diagonals are *contradictories,* of which one must be true and the other false; and finally, on each side, the truth of the lower proposition is implied by the truth of the proposition directly above it.

10.3 Traditional Subject–Predicate Propositions

The four types of general propositions traditionally emphasized in the study of logic are illustrated by the following:

All humans are mortal.
No humans are mortal.
Some humans are mortal.
Some humans are not mortal.

These have been classified as "universal affirmative," "universal negative," "particular affirmative," and "particular negative," respectively, and their types abbreviated as ***A, E, I,*** and ***O,*** again respectively.[4]

In symbolizing these propositions by means of quantifiers, we are led to a further enlargement of our conception of a propositional function. Turning first to the ***A*** proposition, we proceed by means of successive paraphrasings, beginning with:

Given any individual thing whatever, if it is human then it is mortal.

[4] An account of their traditional analysis and nomenclature is presented in Chapter 5.

The two instances of the relative pronoun "it" clearly refer back to their common antecedent, the word "thing." As in the early part of the preceding section, since the three words have the same (indefinite) reference, they can be replaced by the letter "x," and the proposition rewritten as:

Given any x, if x is human then x is mortal.

Now using our previously introduced notation for "if-then," we can rewrite the preceding as:

Given any x, x is human $\supset$ x is mortal.

Finally, using our now familiar notation for propositional functions and quantifiers, the original *A* proposition is expressed as:

$$(x)[Hx \supset Mx]$$

Our symbolic translation of the *A* proposition appears as the universal quantification of a new kind of propositional function. The expression $Hx \supset Mx$ is a propositional function which has as its substitution instances neither affirmative nor negative singular propositions, but conditional statements whose antecedents and consequents are singular propositions having the same subject term. Among the substitution instances of the propositional function $Hx \supset Mx$ are the conditional statements $Ha \supset Ma$, $Hb \supset Mb$, $Hc \supset Mc$, $Hd \supset Md$, and so on. There are also propositional functions whose substitution instances are conjunctions of singular propositions having the same subject terms. Thus the conjunctions $Ha \cdot Ma$, $Hb \cdot Mb$, $Hc \cdot Mc$, $Hd \cdot Md$, and so on, are substitution instances of the propositional function $Hx \cdot Mx$. There are also proposition functions such as $Wx \vee Bx$, whose substitution instances are disjunctions such as $Wa \vee Ba$, and $Wb \vee Bb$. In fact, any truth-functionally compound statement whose ultimate simple component statements are singular propositions all having the same subject term can be regarded as a substitution instance of a propositional function containing some or all of the various truth-functional connectives dot, wedge, horseshoe, three-bar equivalence, and curl, in addition to the simple predicates Ax, Bx, Cx, Dx, . . . In our translation of the *A* proposition as $(x)[Hx \supset Mx]$ the square brackets serve as punctuation marks. They indicate that the universal quantifier (x) "applies to" or "has within its scope" the entire (complex) propositional function $Hx \supset Mx$.

Before going on to discuss the other traditional forms of categorical propositions, it should be observed that our symbolic formula $(x)[Hx \supset Mx]$ translates not only the standard-form proposition "All *H*'s are *M*'s," but any other English sentence having the same meaning. There are many ways in English of saying the same thing —a partial list of them may be set down as: "*H*'s are *M*'s," "An *H* is an *M*," "Every *H* is *M*," "Each *H* is *M*," "Any *H* is *M*," "No *H*'s are not *M*," "Everything which is *H* is *M*," "Anything which is *H* is *M*," "If anything is *H*, it is *M*," "If something is *H*, it is *M*," "Whatever is *H* is *M*," "*H*'s are all *M*'s," "Only *M*'s are *H*'s," "None but *M*'s are *H*'s," "Nothing is an *H* unless it is an *M*," and "Nothing is an *H* but not an *M*." Some English idioms are a little misleading in using a temporal term when no reference to time is intended. Thus the proposition "*H*'s are always *M*'s" is properly understood as meaning simply that *all* *H*'s are *M*'s. Again, the same meaning may be expressed by the use of abstract nouns: "Humanity implies (or entails) mortality" is correctly symbolized as an ***A*** proposition. That the language of symbolic logic has a singular expression for the common meaning of a considerable number of English sentences may be regarded as an advantage of symbolic logic over English for cognitive or informative purposes—although admittedly a disadvantage from the point of view of rhetorical power or poetic expressiveness.

The ***E*** proposition "No humans are mortal" may be successively paraphrased as:

Given any individual thing whatever, if it is human then it is not mortal.
Given any x, if x is human then x is not mortal.
Given any x, x is human $\supset$ x is not mortal.

and finally as:

$$(x)[Hx \supset {\sim}Mx]$$

The preceding symbolic translation expresses not only the traditional ***E*** form in English, but also such diverse ways of saying the same thing as: "There are no *H*'s which are *M*," "Nothing is both an *H* and an *M*," "*H*'s are never *M*," and so on.

Similarly, the ***I*** proposition "Some humans are mortal," may be successively paraphrased as:

There is at least one thing which is human and mortal.
There is at least one x such that x is human and x is mortal.
There is at least one x such that x is human $\cdot$ x is mortal.

and then as:

$$(\exists x)[Hx \cdot Mx]$$

Finally, the ***O*** proposition "Some humans are not mortal" is successively paraphrased as:

There is at least one thing which is human but not mortal.
There is at least one x such that x is human and x is not mortal.
There is at least one x such that x is human $\cdot \sim x$ is mortal.

and completely symbolized as:

$$(\exists x)[Hx \cdot \sim Mx]$$

Where the Greek letters *phi* and *psi* are used to represent any predicates whatever, the four general subject-predicate propositions of traditional logic may be represented in a square array as:

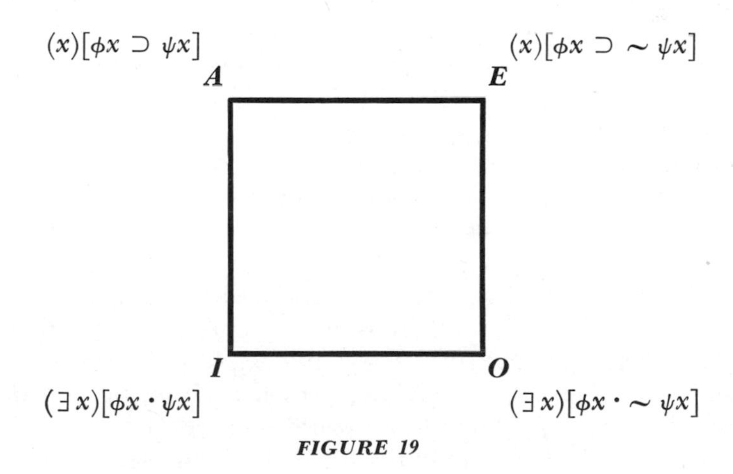

FIGURE 19

Of these, the ***A*** and the ***O*** are "contradictories," each being the denial of the other; ***E*** and ***I*** are also contradictories.

It might be thought that an ***I*** proposition follows from its corresponding ***A*** proposition, and an ***O*** from its corresponding ***E;*** but this is not so. An ***A*** proposition may very well be true while its corresponding ***I*** proposition is false. Where ϕx is a propositional function which has no true substitution instances, then no matter what kinds of substitution instances the propositional function ψx may have, the universal quantification of the (complex) propositional function $\phi x \supset \psi x$ will be true. For example, consider the propositional function "*x* is a centaur," which we abbreviate as *Cx*. Since there are no centaurs, every substitution instance of *Cx* is false, that is, *Ca, Cb, Cc*, . . . are all false. Hence every substitution instance of the complex propositional function $Cx \supset Bx$ will be a conditional statement whose antecedent is false. The substitution instances $Ca \supset Ba$, $Cb \supset Bb$, $Cc \supset Bc$, . . . are all true, since any conditional statement asserting a material implication must be true if its antecedent is false. Since all its substitution instances are true, the universal quantification of the propositional function $Cx \supset Bx$, which is the ***A*** proposition $(x)[Cx \supset Bx]$, is true. But the corresponding ***I*** proposition $(\exists x)[Cx \cdot Bx]$ is false, since the propositional function $Cx \cdot Bx$ has no true substitution instances. That $Cx \cdot Bx$ has no true substitution instances follows from the fact that *Cx* has no true substitution instances. The various substitution instances of $Cx \cdot Bx$ are: $Ca \cdot Ba$, $Cb \cdot Bb$, $Cc \cdot Bc$, . . . , each of which is a conjunction whose first conjunct is false, since *Ca, Cb, Cc*, . . . are all false. Because all its substitution instances are false, the existential quantification of the propositional function $Cx \cdot Bx$, which is the ***I*** proposition $(\exists x)[Cx \cdot Bx]$, is false. Hence an ***A*** proposition may be true while its corresponding ***I*** proposition is false. If the propositional function *Bx* is replaced by the propositional function $\sim Bx$ in the preceding discussion, it will then establish that an ***E*** proposition may be true while its corresponding ***O*** proposition is false.

If we make the general assumption that there is at least one individual, then $(x)[Cx \supset Bx]$ does imply $(\exists x)[Cx \supset Bx]$. But the latter is not an ***I*** proposition. The ***I*** proposition "Some centaurs are beautiful" is symbolized as $(\exists x)[Cx \cdot Bx]$, which asserts that there is at least one centaur. But what is symbolized as $(\exists x)[Cx \supset Bx]$ can be rendered in English as "there is at least one thing such that if it is a centaur then it is beautiful." It does not assert that there is a centaur, but only that there is an individual which is either not a centaur or is beautiful. And this proposition would be false in only two possible cases: first, if there were no individuals at all; and second, if all individuals were centaurs and none of them were beautiful. We rule out the first case by making the explicit (and obviously true) assumption that there is at least one individual in the universe. And the second case is so extremely unplausible that any proposition of the form $(\exists x)[\phi x \supset \psi x]$ is bound to be quite trivial—in contrast to the significant ***I*** form $(\exists x)[\phi x \cdot \psi x]$.

The foregoing should make clear that although in English the ***A*** and ***I*** propositions "All humans are mortal" and "Some humans are mortal" differ only in their initial words "all" and "some," their difference in meaning is not confined to the matter of universal versus existential quantification, but goes deeper than that. The propositional functions quantified to yield ***A*** and ***I*** propositions are not just differently quantified, they are different functions, one containing "$\supset$," the other "$\cdot$." In other words, ***A*** and ***I*** propositions are not so much alike as they appear in English. Their differences are brought out very clearly in the new notation of propositional functions and quantifiers.

Before turning to the topic of inferences involving noncompound statements, the reader should acquire some practice in translating noncompound statements from English into our logical symbolism. The English language has so many irregular or idiomatic constructions that there can be no simple rules for translating an English sentence into logical notation. What is required in each case is that the meaning of the sentence be understood and then re-expressed in terms of propositional functions and quantifiers.

EXERCISES

I. Translate each of the following into the logical notation of propositional functions and quantifiers, in each case using the abbreviations suggested, and having each formula begin with a quantifier, *not* with a negation symbol:

★ 1. Bats are mammals. (Bx: x is a bat; Mx: x is a mammal.)

2. Sparrows are not mammals. (Sx: x is a sparrow; Mx: x is a mammal.)

3. Ladies are present. (Lx: x is a lady; Px: x is present.)

4. Gentlemen are always considerate. (Gx: x is a gentleman; Cx: x is considerate.)

★ 5. Gentlemen are not always rich. (Gx: x is a gentleman; Rx: x is rich.)

6. Ambassadors are always dignified. (Ax: x is an ambassador; Dx: x is dignified.)

7. No boy scout ever cheats (Bx: x is a boy scout; Cx: x cheats.)

8. Only licensed physicians can charge for medical treatment. (Lx: x is a licensed physician; Cx: x can charge for medical treatment.)

9. Snake bites are sometimes fatal. (Sx: x is a snake bite; Fx: x is fatal.)

★ 10. The common cold is never fatal. (Cx: x is a common cold; Fx: x is fatal.)

11. A child pointed his finger at the emperor. (Cx: x is a child; Px: x pointed his finger at the emperor.)

12. Not all children pointed their fingers at the emperor. (*Cx: x* is a child; *Px: x* pointed his finger at the emperor.)

13. All that glitters is not gold. (*Gx: x* glitters; *Ax: x* is gold.)

14. None but the brave deserve the fair. (*Bx: x* is brave; *Dx: x* deserves the fair.)

★ 15. Only citizens of the United States can vote in United States elections. (*Cx: x* is a citizen of the United States; *Vx: x* can vote in United States elections.)

16. Citizens of the United States can vote only in United States elections. (*Ex: x* is an election in which citizens of the United States can vote; *Ux: x* is a United States election.)

17. There are honest politicians. (*Hx: x* is honest; *Px: x* is a politician.)

18. Not every applicant was hired. (*Ax: x* is an applicant; *Hx: x* was hired.)

19. Not any applicant was hired. (*Ax: x* is an applicant; *Hx: x* was hired.)

20. Nothing of importance was said. (*Ix: x* is of importance; *Sx: x* was said.)

II. Reformulate each of the following to make it begin with a quantifier instead of a negation symbol:

★ 1. $\sim(x)[Ax \supset Bx]$

2. $\sim(x)[Cx \supset \sim Dx]$

3. $\sim(\exists x)[Ex \cdot Fx]$

4. $\sim(\exists x)[Gx \cdot \sim Hx]$

★ 5. $\sim(x)[\sim Ix \vee Jx]$

6. $\sim(x)[\sim Kx \vee \sim Lx]$

7. $\sim(\exists x)[\sim(Mx \vee Nx)]$

8. $\sim(\exists x)[\sim(Ox \vee \sim Px)]$

9. $\sim(\exists x)[\sim(\sim Qx \vee Rx)]$

10. $\sim(x)[\sim(Sx \cdot \sim Tx)]$

11. $\sim(x)[\sim(\sim Ux \cdot \sim Vx)]$

12. $\sim(\exists x)[\sim(\sim Wx \vee \sim Xx)]$

10.4 Proving Validity

If we wish to construct formal proofs of validity for arguments whose validity turns upon the inner structures of noncompound statements occurring in them, we must expand our list of Rules of Inference. Only four additional rules are required, and they will be introduced in connection with arguments for which they are needed. Let us consider the first argument cited in the present chapter: "All humans are mortal. Socrates is human. Therefore Socrates is mortal." It is symbolized as:

$$(x)[Hx \supset Mx]$$
$$Hs$$
$$\therefore Ms$$

The first premiss affirms the truth of the universal quantification of the propositional function $Hx \supset Mx$. Since the universal quantification of a propositional function is true if and only if all of its substitution instances are true, from the first premiss we can infer any desired substitution instance of the propositional function $Hx \supset Mx$. In particular we can infer the substitution instance $Hs \supset Ms$. From that and the second premiss Hs, the conclusion Ms follows directly by *modus ponens*.

If we add to our list of Rules of Inference the principle that any substitution instance of a propositional function can validly be inferred from its universal quantification, then we can give a formal proof of the validity of the given argument by reference to the expanded list of elementary valid argument forms. This new Rule of Inference is the principle of Universal Instantiation[5] and is abbreviated as "**UI.**" Using the Greek letter *nu* to represent any individual symbol whatever, the new Rule is stated as:

UI: $\dfrac{(x)\phi x}{\therefore \phi \nu}$ (where ν is any individual symbol)

A formal proof of validity may now be written as:

1. $(x)[Hx \supset Mx]$
2. Hs $/\therefore Ms$
3. $Hs \supset Ms$ 1, **UI**
4. Ms 3,2, M.P.

The addition of **UI** strengthens our proof apparatus considerably, but more is required. The need for additional rules governing quantification arises in connection with arguments like: "All humans are mortal. All Greeks are human. Therefore all Greeks are mortal." The symbolic translation of this argument is

$$(x)[Hx \supset Mx]$$
$$(x)[Gx \supset Hx]$$
$$\therefore (x)[Gx \supset Mx]$$

[5] This rule and the three which follow are variants of rules for "natural deduction" which were devised independently by Gerhard Gentzen and Stanislaw Jaskowski in 1934.

Here both premisses and conclusions are general propositions rather than singular ones, universal quantifications of propositional functions rather than substitution instances of them. From the two premisses, by **UI,** we may validly infer the following pairs of conditional statements:

$$\begin{Bmatrix} Ga \supset Ha \\ Ha \supset Ma \end{Bmatrix}, \begin{Bmatrix} Gb \supset Hb \\ Hb \supset Mb \end{Bmatrix}, \begin{Bmatrix} Gc \supset Hc \\ Hc \supset Mc \end{Bmatrix}, \begin{Bmatrix} Gd \supset Hd \\ Hd \supset Md \end{Bmatrix}, \ldots$$

and by successive uses of the principle of the Hypothetical Syllogism we may validly infer the conclusions:

$$Ga \supset Ma, Gb \supset Mb, Gc \supset Mc, Gd \supset Md, \ldots$$

If $a, b, c, d, \ldots$ are all the individuals there are, it follows that from the truth of the premisses one can validly infer the truth of all substitution instances of the propositional function $Gx \supset Mx$. Since the universal quantification of a propositional function is true if and only if all of its substitution instances are true, we can go on to infer the truth of $(x)[Gx \supset Mx]$, which is the conclusion of the given argument.

The preceding paragraph may be thought of as containing an *informal* proof of the validity of the given argument, in which the principle of the Hypothetical Syllogism and two principles governing quantification are appealed to. But it describes indefinitely long sequences of statements: the lists of all substitution instances of the two propositional functions quantified universally in the premisses, and the list of all substitution instances of the propositional function whose universal quantification is the conclusion. A *formal* proof cannot contain such indefinitely, perhaps even infinitely long sequences of statements, so some method must be sought for expressing those indefinitely long sequences in some finite, definite fashion.

A method for doing this is suggested by a common technique of elementary mathematics. A geometer, seeking to prove that *all* triangles possess a certain property, may begin with the words "Let *ABC* be any arbitrarily selected triangle." Then the geometer begins to reason about the triangle *ABC,* and establishes that it has the property in question. From this he concludes that *all* triangles have that property. Now what justifies his final conclusion? Granted of the particular triangle *ABC* that *it* has the property, why does it follow that *all* triangles do? The answer to this question is easily given. If no assumption other than its triangularity is made about the triangle *ABC,* then the symbol "*ABC*" can be taken as denoting any triangle you please. Then the geometer's argument establishes that *any* triangle has the property in question, and if *any* triangle has it, then *all* triangles do. We wish now to introduce a notation analogous to the geometer's in talking about "any arbitrarily selected triangle ABC." This will avoid the pretense of listing an indefinite or infinite number of substitution instances of a propositional function, for instead we shall talk about *any* substitution instance of the propositional function.

We shall use the (hitherto unused) small letter y to denote *any arbitrarily selected* individual. We shall use it in a way similar to that in which the geometer used the letters ABC. Since the truth of *any* substitution instance of a propositional function follows from its universal quantification, we can infer the substitution instance which results from replacing x by y, where y denotes "any arbitrarily selected" individual. Thus we may begin our formal proof of the validity of the given argument as follows:

1. $(x)[Hx \supset Mx]$
2. $(x)[Gx \supset Hx] / \therefore (x)[Gx \supset Mx]$
3. $Hy \supset My$ 1, **UI**
4. $Gy \supset Hy$ 2, **UI**
5. $Gy \supset My$ 4,3, H.S.

From the premisses we have deduced the statement $Gy \supset My$, which in effect, since y denotes "any arbitrarily selected individual," asserts the truth of *any* substitution instance of the propositional function $Gx \supset Mx$. Since *any* substitution instance is true, all substitution instances must be true, and hence the universal quantification of that propositional function is true also. We may add this principle to our list of Rules of Inference, stating it as: From the substitution instance of a propositional function with respect to the name of *any arbitrarily selected* individual one can validly infer the universal quantification of that propositional function. Since this new principle permits us to *generalize*, that is, to go from a special substitution instance to a generalized or universally quantified expression, we may refer to it as the principle of Universal Generalization and abbreviate it as "**UG.**" It is stated as:

UG: $\dfrac{\phi y}{\therefore (x)\phi x}$ (Where y denotes "any arbitrarily selected individual")

The sixth and final line of the formal proof already begun may now be written (and justified) as:

6. $(x)[Gx \supset Mx]$ 5, **UG**

Let us review the preceding discussion. In the geometer's proof the only assumption made about *ABC* is that it is a triangle, hence what is proved true of *ABC* is proved true of *any* triangle. In our proof the only assumption made about *y* is that it is an individual. Hence what is proved true of *y* is proved true of *any* individual. The symbol *y* is an individual symbol, but it is a very special one. It can be introduced into a proof only by the use of **UI.** And only its presence permits the use of **UG.**

Another argument the demonstration of whose validity requires the use of **UG** as well as **UI** is: "No humans are perfect. All Greeks are humans. Therefore no Greeks are perfect." The formal proof of its validity is:

1.	$(x)[Hx \supset \sim Px]$	
2.	$(x)[Gx \supset Hx] / \therefore (x)[Gx \supset \sim Px]$	
3.	$Hy \supset \sim Py$	1, **UI**
4.	$Gy \supset Hy$	2, **UI**
5.	$Gy \supset \sim Py$	4,3, H.S.
6.	$(x)[Gx \supset \sim Px]$	5, **UG**

There may seem to be some artificiality about the foregoing. It may be urged that distinguishing carefully between $(x)\phi x$ and ϕy, so they are not identified but must be inferred from each other by **UI** and **UG,** is to insist upon a distinction without a difference. But there is certainly a *formal* difference between them. The statement $(x)[Hx \supset Mx]$ is a noncompound statement, whereas $Hy \supset My$ is compound, being a conditional. From the two noncompound statements $(x)[Gx \supset Hx]$ and $(x)[Hx \supset Mx]$ no relevant inference can be drawn by means of the original list of nineteen Rules of Inference. But from the compound statements $Gy \supset Hy$ and $Hy \supset My$ the indicated conclusion $Gy \supset My$ follows by a Hypothetical Syllogism. The principle of **UI** is used to get from noncompound statements, to which our earlier Rules of Inference do not apply, to compound statements, to which they can be applied. The quantification principles thus augment our logical apparatus to make it capable of validating arguments essentially involving noncompound (generalized) propositions as well as the other (simpler) kind of argument discussed in our earlier chapters. On the other hand, in spite of this formal difference, there must be a logical equivalence between $(x)\phi x$ and ϕy, or the rules **UI** and **UG** would not be valid. Both the difference and the logical equivalence are important for our purpose of validating arguments by reference to a list of Rules of Inference. The addition of **UI** and **UG** to our list strengthens it considerably.

The list must be further expanded when we turn to arguments

involving existential propositions. A convenient example with which to begin is: "All criminals are vicious. Some humans are criminals. Therefore some humans are vicious." It is symbolized as:

$$(x)[Cx \supset Vx]$$
$$(\exists x)[Hx \cdot Cx]$$
$$\therefore (\exists x)[Hx \cdot Vx]$$

The existential quantification of a propositional function is true if and only if it has at least one true substitution instance. Hence, whatever property may be designated by ϕ, $(\exists x)\phi x$ asserts that there is at least one individual which has the property ϕ. If an individual constant (other than the special symbol y) is used nowhere earlier in the context, we may use it to denote either the individual which has the property ϕ, or some one of the individuals which have ϕ, if there are several. Knowing that there is such an individual, say a, we know that ϕa is a true substitution instance of the propositional function ϕx. Hence we add to our list of Rules of Inference the principle that from the existential quantification of a propositional function we may infer the truth of its substitution instance with respect to an individual constant (other than y) which occurs nowhere earlier in that context. The new Rule of Inference is the principle of Existential Instantiation and is abbreviated as "**EI.**" It is stated as:

EI: $(\exists x)\phi x$ (Where ν is any individual constant (other than y)
$\therefore \phi\nu$ having no previous occurrence in the context)

Granted the additional Rule of Inference **EI**, we may begin a demonstration of the validity of the stated argument:

1. $(x)[Cx \supset Vx]$
2. $(\exists x)[Hx \cdot Cx]$ / $\therefore (\exists x)[Hx \cdot Vx]$
3. $Ha \cdot Ca$ 2, **EI**
4. $Ca \supset Va$ 1, **UI**
5. $Ca \cdot Ha$ 3, Com.
6. Ca 5, Simp.
7. Va 4,6, M.P.
8. Ha 3, Simp.
9. $Ha \cdot Va$ 8,7, Conj.

Thus far we have deduced $Ha \cdot Va$, which is a substitution instance of the propositional function whose existential quantification is asserted by the conclusion. Since the existential quantification of a propositional function is true if and only if it has at least one true substitution instance, we add to our list of Rules of Inference the principle that from any true substitution instance of a propositional function we may validly infer the existential quantification of that propositional function. This fourth and final Rule of Inference is the principle of Existential Generalization, abbreviated as "**EG**" and stated as:

$$\textbf{EG:}\quad \begin{array}{l} \phi\nu \\ \therefore (\exists x)\phi x \end{array} \quad \text{(where } \nu \text{ is any individual symbol)}$$

The tenth and final line of the demonstration already begun may now be written (and justified) as:

$$10.\ (\exists x)[Hx \cdot Vx] \qquad 9,\ \textbf{EG}$$

The need for the indicated restriction on the use of **EI** can be seen by considering the obviously invalid argument: "Some alligators are kept in captivity. Some birds are kept in captivity. Therefore some alligators are birds." If we failed to heed the restriction on **EI** that the substitution instance inferred by it from an existential quantification can contain only an individual symbol (other than y) having no previous occurrence in the context, then we might proceed to construct a "proof" of validity for this invalid argument. Such an erroneous "proof" might proceed:

1. $(\exists x)[Ax \cdot Cx]$
2. $(\exists x)[Bx \cdot Cx]$ $/\therefore (\exists x)[Ax \cdot Bx]$
3. $Aa \cdot Ca$ — 1, **EI**
4. $Ba \cdot Ca$ — 2, **EI** (wrong)
5. Aa — 3, Simp.
6. Ba — 4, Simp.
7. $Aa \cdot Ba$ — 5,6, Conj.
8. $(\exists x)[Ax \cdot Bx]$ — 7, **EG**

The error in this "proof" occurs at line 4. From the second premiss $(\exists x)[Bx \cdot Cx]$ we know that there is at least one thing which is both a bird and kept in captivity. *If* we were free to assign it the name *a* we could, of course, assert $Ba \cdot Ca$. But we are not free to make any such assignment of "*a*," for it has already been pre-empted in line 3 to serve as a name for an alligator which is kept in captivity. To avoid errors of this sort, we must obey the indicated restriction whenever we use **EI.** The preceding discussion should make clear that in any demonstration requiring the use of both **EI** and **UI**, **EI** should always be used first.

For more complicated modes of argumentation, especially those which involve relations, certain additional restrictions must be placed on our four quantification rules. But for arguments of the present sort, traditionally called Categorical Syllogisms, the present restrictions are sufficient to prevent mistakes.

EXERCISES

I. Construct a formal proof of validity for each of the following arguments:

★ 1. $(x)[Ax \supset \sim Bx]$
$(\exists x)[Cx \cdot Ax]$
$\therefore (\exists x)[Cx \cdot \sim Bx]$

2. $(x)[Dx \supset \sim Ex]$
$(x)[Fx \supset Ex]$
$\therefore (x)[Fx \supset \sim Dx]$

3. $(x)[Gx \supset Hx]$
$(x)[Ix \supset \sim Hx]$
$\therefore (x)[Ix \supset \sim Gx]$

4. $(\exists x)[Jx \cdot Kx]$
$(x)[Jx \supset Lx]$
$\therefore (\exists x)[Lx \cdot Kx]$

★ 5. $(x)[Mx \supset Nx]$
$(\exists x)[Mx \cdot Ox]$
$\therefore (\exists x)[Ox \cdot Nx]$

6. $(\exists x)[Px \cdot \sim Qx]$
$(x)[Px \supset Rx]$
$\therefore (\exists x)[Rx \cdot \sim Qx]$

7. $(x)[Sx \supset \sim Tx]$
$(\exists x)[Sx \cdot Ux]$
$\therefore (\exists x)[Ux \cdot \sim Tx]$

8. $(x)[Vx \supset Wx]$
$(x)[Wx \supset \sim Xx]$
$\therefore (x)[Xx \supset \sim Vx]$

9. $(\exists x)[Yx \cdot Zx]$
$(x)[Zx \supset Ax]$
$\therefore (\exists x)[Ax \cdot Yx]$

10. $(x)[Bx \supset \sim Cx]$
$(\exists x)[Cx \cdot Dx]$
$\therefore (\exists x)[Dx \cdot \sim Bx]$

II. Construct a formal proof of validity for each of the following arguments, in each case using the suggested notation:

★ 1. No athletes are bookworms. Carol is a bookworm. Therefore Carol is not an athlete. (Ax, Bx, c)

2. All dancers are effeminate. Some fencers are not effeminate. Therefore some fencers are not dancers. (Dx, Ex, Fx)

3. No gamblers are happy. Some idealists are happy. Therefore some idealists are not gamblers. (Gx, Hx, Ix)

4. All jesters are knaves. No knaves are lucky. Therefore no jesters are lucky. (Jx, Kx, Lx)

★ 5. All mountaineers are neighborly. Some outlaws are mountaineers. Therefore some outlaws are neighborly. (Mx, Nx, Ox)

6. Only pacifists are Quakers. There are religious Quakers. Therefore pacifists are sometimes religious. (Px, Qx, Rx)

7. To be a swindler is to be a thief. None but the underprivileged are thieves. Therefore swindlers are always underprivileged. (Sx, Tx, Ux)

8. No violinists are not wealthy. There are no wealthy xylophonists. Therefore violinists are never xylophonists. (Vx, Wx, Xx)

9. None but the brave deserve the fair. Only soldiers are brave. Therefore the fair are deserved only by soldiers. (Dx: x deserves the fair; Bx: x is brave; Sx: x is a soldier)

10. Everyone that asketh receiveth. Simon receiveth not. Therefore Simon asketh not. (Ax, Rx, s)

10.5 Proving Invalidity

To prove the invalidity of an argument involving quantifiers, we can use the method of refutation by logical analogy. For example, the argument "All communists are opponents of the Administration; some delegates are opponents of the Administration; therefore some delegates are communists" is proved invalid by the analogy "All cats are animals; some dogs are animals; therefore some dogs are cats"; which is obviously invalid since its premisses are known to be true and its conclusion known to be false. But such analogies are not always easy to devise. Some more nearly effective method of proving invalidity is desirable.

In the preceding chapter we developed a method of proving invalidity for arguments involving compound statements. That method consisted of making truth value assignments to the component simple statements of arguments in such a way as to make their premisses true and their conclusions false. That method can be adapted for arguments involving quantifiers. The adaptation involves our general assumption that there is at least one individual. For an argument involving quantifiers to be valid it must be impossible for its premisses to be true and its conclusion false as long as there is at least one individual.

The general assumption that there is at least one individual is satisfied if there is exactly one individual, or exactly two individuals, or exactly three individuals, or. . . . If any one of these assumptions about the exact number of individuals is made, there is an equivalence between general propositions and truth-functional compounds of singular propositions. If there is exactly one individual, say *a*, then:

$$(x)\phi x \equiv \phi a \equiv (\exists x)\phi x$$

If there are exactly two individuals, say *a* and *b*, then:

$$(x)\phi x \equiv [\phi a \cdot \phi b] \text{ and } (\exists x)\phi x \equiv [\phi a \vee \phi b]$$

If there are exactly three individuals, say *a, b,* and *c,* then:

$$(x)\phi x \equiv [\phi a \cdot \phi b \cdot \phi c] \text{ and } (\exists x)\phi x \equiv [\phi a \vee \phi b \vee \phi c]$$

In general, if there are exactly *n* individuals, say *a, b, c, . . . n,* then:

$$(x)\phi x \equiv [\phi a \cdot \phi b \cdot \phi c \cdot \ldots \cdot \phi n] \text{ and } (\exists x)\phi x \equiv [\phi a \vee \phi b \vee \phi c \vee \ldots \vee \phi n]$$

These biconditionals are true as a consequence of our definitions of the universal and existential quantifiers. No use is made here of the four quantification rules explained in the preceding section.

An argument involving quantifiers is valid *if and only if* it is valid no matter how many individuals there are, provided there is at least one. So an argument involving quantifiers is proved invalid if there is a possible universe or *model* containing at least one individual such that the argument's premisses are true and its conclusion false *of that model.* Consider the argument: "All mercenaries are undependable. No guerrillas are mercenaries. Therefore no guerrillas are undependable." It may be symbolized as:

$$(x)[Mx \supset Ux]$$
$$(x)[Gx \supset \sim Mx]$$
$$\therefore (x)[Gx \supset \sim Ux]$$

If there is exactly one individual, say *a*, this argument is logically equivalent to:

$$Ma \supset Ua$$
$$Ga \supset \sim Ma$$
$$\therefore Ga \supset \sim Ua$$

The latter can be proved invalid by assigning the truth value *true* to *Ga* and *Ua* and *false* to *Ma*. (This assignment of truth values is a shorthand way of describing the *model* in question as one which contains only the one individual *a* which is a guerrilla and undependable but is not a mercenary.) Hence the original argument is not valid for a model containing exactly one individual, and is therefore *invalid*. Similarly, we can prove the invalidity of the first argument mentioned in this section by describing a model containing exactly one individual *a* such that *Aa* and *Da* are assigned *truth* and *Ca* is assigned *falsehood*.[6]

Some arguments, for example,

$$(\exists x)Fx$$
$$\therefore (x)Fx$$

may be valid for any model in which there is exactly one individual, but invalid for a model containing two or more individuals. Such arguments must count as invalid also. Another example of this kind of argument is "All collies are affectionate. Some collies are watchdogs. Therefore all watchdogs are affectionate." Its symbolic translation is:

$$(x)[Cx \supset Ax]$$
$$(\exists x)[Cx \cdot Wx]$$
$$\therefore (x)[Wx \supset Ax]$$

For a model containing exactly one individual *a* it is logically equivalent to:

$$Ca \supset Aa$$
$$Ca \cdot Wa$$
$$\therefore Wa \supset Aa$$

which is valid. But for a model containing two individuals *a* and *b* it is logically equivalent to:

$$(Ca \supset Aa) \cdot (Cb \supset Ab)$$
$$(Ca \cdot Wa) \vee (Cb \cdot Wb)$$
$$\therefore (Wa \supset Aa) \cdot (Wb \supset Ab)$$

6 Here we assume that the simple predicates *Ax, Bx, Cx, Dx* . . . occurring in our propositions are neither necessary, that is, logically true of all individuals (for example, *x* is identical with itself), nor impossible, that is, logically false of all individuals (for example, *x* is different from itself). We also assume that the only logical relations among the simple predicates involved are those asserted or logically implied by the premisses. The point of these restrictions is to permit us to assign truth values arbitrarily to the substitution instances of these simple predicates without any inconsistency—for a model must of course be consistent.

which is proved invalid by assigning *truth* to *Ca, Aa, Wa, Wb,* and *falsehood* to *Cb,* and *Ab*. Hence the original argument is not valid for a model containing exactly two individuals, and is therefore *invalid.* For any invalid argument of this general type it is possible to describe a model containing some definite number of individuals for which its logically equivalent truth-functional argument can be proved invalid by the method of assigning truth values.

It should be emphasized again that in moving from a given argument involving general propositions to a truth-functional argument that for a specified model is logically equivalent to the given argument, no use is made of our four quantification rules. Instead, each statement of the truth-functional argument is logically equivalent to the corresponding general proposition of the given argument by way of biconditionals whose logical truth for the possible universe in question follows from the very definitions of the universal and existential quantifiers.

The procedure for proving the invalidity of an argument containing general propositions is the following. First consider a one-element model containing only the individual *a*. Then write out the logically equivalent truth-functional argument for that model, which is obtained by moving from each general proposition (quantified propositional function) of the original argument to the substitution instance of that propositional function with respect to *a*. If the truth-functional argument can be proved invalid by assigning truth values to its component simple statements, this suffices to prove the original argument invalid. If that cannot be done, next consider a two-element model containing the individuals *a* and *b*. To obtain the logically equivalent truth-functional argument for this larger model one can simply add on to each original substitution instance with respect to *a* a new substitution instance of the same propositional function with respect to *b*. This "adding on" must be in accord with the logical equivalence stated on page 337: that is, where the original argument contains a universally quantified propositional function $(x)[\phi x]$ the new substitution instance ϕb is combined with the first substitution instance ϕa by conjunction ("•"); but where the original argument contains an existentially quantified propositional function $(\exists x)[\phi x]$ the new substitution instance ϕb is combined with the first substitution instance ϕa by disjunction ("v"). The preceding example illustrates this procedure. If the new truth-functional argument can be proved invalid by assigning truth values to its component simple statements, this suffices to prove the original argument invalid. If that cannot be done, next consider a three-element model containing the individuals *a, b,* and *c*. And so on. None of the immediately following exercises requires a model containing more than two elements, but some of those on page 345 may require a three-element model. However, none of the exercises in this text requires a model containing more than three elements.

EXERCISES

I. Prove the invalidity of the following arguments:

★ 1. $(\exists x)[Ax \cdot Bx]$
$(\exists x)[Cx \cdot Bx]$
$\therefore (x)[Cx \supset \sim Ax]$

2. $(x)[Dx \supset \sim Ex]$
$(x)[Ex \supset Fx]$
$\therefore (x)[Fx \supset \sim Dx]$

3. $(x)[Gx \supset Hx]$
$(x)[Gx \supset Ix]$
$\therefore (x)[Ix \supset Hx]$

4. $(\exists x)[Jx \cdot Kx]$
$(\exists x)[Kx \cdot Lx]$
$\therefore (\exists x)[Lx \cdot Jx]$

★ 5. $(\exists x)[Mx \cdot Nx]$
$(\exists x)[Mx \cdot Ox]$
$\therefore (x)[Ox \supset Nx]$

6. $(x)[Px \supset \sim Qx]$
$(x)[Px \supset \sim Rx]$
$\therefore (x)[Rx \supset \sim Qx]$

7. $(x)[Sx \supset \sim Tx]$
$(x)[Tx \supset Ux]$
$\therefore (\exists x)[Ux \cdot \sim Sx]$

8. $(\exists x)[Vx \cdot \sim Wx]$
$(\exists x)[Wx \cdot \sim Xx]$
$\therefore (\exists x)[Xx \cdot \sim Vx]$

9. $(\exists x)[Yx \cdot Zx]$
$(\exists x)[Ax \cdot Zx]$
$\therefore (\exists x)[Ax \cdot \sim Yx]$

10. $(\exists x)[Bx \cdot \sim Cx]$
$(x)[Dx \supset \sim Cx]$
$\therefore (x)[Dx \supset Bx]$

II. Prove the invalidity of the following arguments, in each case using the suggested notation:

★ 1. All anarchists are bearded. All communists are bearded. Therefore all anarchists are communists. (Ax, Bx, Cx)

2. No diplomats are extremists. Some fanatics are extremists. Therefore some diplomats are not fanatics. (Dx, Ex, Fx)

3. All generals are handsome. Some intellectuals are handsome. Therefore some generals are intellectuals. (Gx, Hx, Ix)

4. Some journalists are not kibitzers. Some kibitzers are not lucky. Therefore some journalists are not lucky. (Jx, Kx, Lx)

★ 5. Some malcontents are noisy. Some officials are not noisy. Therefore no officials are malcontents. (Mx, Nx, Ox)

6. Some physicians are quacks. Some quacks are not responsible. Therefore some physicians are not responsible. (Px, Qx, Rx)

7. Some politicians are leaders. Some leaders are not orators. Therefore some orators are not politicians. (Px, Lx, Ox)

8. None but the brave deserve the fair. Every soldier is brave. Therefore none but soldiers deserve the fair. (*Dx: x* deserves the fair; *Bx: x* is brave; *Sx: x* is a soldier)

9. If anything is metallic, then it is breakable. There are breakable ornaments. Therefore there are metallic ornaments. (*Mx, Bx, Ox*)

10. Only students are members. Only members are welcome. Therefore all students are welcome. (*Sx, Mx, Wx*)

10.6 Asyllogistic Inference

All of the arguments considered in the preceding two sections were of the form traditionally called categorical syllogisms. These consist of two premisses and a conclusion, each of which is analyzable either as a singular proposition or as one of the ***A, E, I,*** or ***O*** varieties. We turn now to the problem of evaluating somewhat more complicated arguments. These require no greater logical apparatus than has already been developed. Yet they are *asyllogistic* arguments and require a more powerful logic than was traditionally used in testing categorical syllogisms.

In this section we are still concerned with general propositions formed by quantifying propositional functions that contain only a single individual variable. In the categorical syllogism, the only kinds of propositional functions quantified were of the forms $\phi x \supset \psi x$, $\phi x \supset \sim\psi x$, $\phi x \cdot \psi x$, and $\phi x \cdot \sim\psi x$. But now we shall be quantifying propositional functions which have more complicated internal structures. An example will help make this clear. Consider the argument:

> Hotels are both expensive and depressing.
> Some hotels are shabby.
> Therefore some expensive things are shabby.

This argument, for all obvious validity, is not amenable to the traditional sort of analysis. True enough, it could be expressed in terms of ***A*** and ***I*** propositions by using the symbols *Hx, Bx, Sx,* and *Ex* to abbreviate the propositional functions "*x* is a hotel," "*x* is both expensive and depressing," "*x* is shabby," and "*x* is expensive," respectively.[7] Using these abbreviations we might propose to symbolize the given argument as:

$$(x)[Hx \supset Bx]$$
$$(\exists x)[Hx \cdot Sx]$$
$$\therefore (\exists x)[Ex \cdot Sx]$$

[7] This would, however, violate the restriction stated in footnote 6 on page 338.

But forcing the argument into the straitjacket of the traditional ***A*** and ***I*** forms in this way obscures its validity. The argument in symbols is invalid, although the original argument is perfectly valid. The notation here obscures the logical connection between Bx and Ex. A more adequate analysis is obtained by using Hx, Sx, and Ex, as explained above, plus Dx as an abbreviation for "x is depressing." Using these symbols, the original argument can be translated as:

1. $(x)[Hx \supset (Ex \cdot Dx)]$
2. $(\exists x)[Hx \cdot Sx] / \therefore (\exists x)[Ex \cdot Sx]$

So formulated, a demonstration of its validity is easily constructed. One such demonstration proceeds:

3.	$Hw \cdot Sw$	2, **EI**
4.	$Hw \supset (Ew \cdot Dw)$	1,**UI**
5.	Hw	3, Simp.
6.	$Ew \cdot Dw$	4,5, M.P.
7.	Ew	6, Simp.
8.	$Sw \cdot Hw$	3, Com.
9.	Sw	8, Simp.
10.	$Ew \cdot Sw$	7,9, Conj.
11.	$(\exists x)[Ex \cdot Sx]$	10, **EG**

In symbolizing general propositions which result from quantifying more complicated propositional functions, care must be taken not to be misled by the deceptiveness of ordinary English. One cannot translate from English into our logical notation by following any formal or mechanical rules. In every case one must understand the meaning of the English sentence, and then re-express that meaning in terms of propositional functions and quantifiers. Three locutions of ordinary English which are sometimes troublesome to students are the following.

First, it should be observed that a statement like "All students at this school are either nonwhite or underprivileged" is *not* a disjunction, although it contains the connective "or." It definitely does *not* have the same meaning as "Either all students at this school are nonwhite or all students at this school are underprivileged." The former is properly symbolized—using obvious abbreviations, as:

$$(x)[Sx \supset (\sim Wx \vee Ux)]$$

whereas the latter is symbolized as:

$$\{(x)[Sx \supset \sim Wx]\} \vee \{(x)[Sx \supset Ux]\}$$

Second, it should be observed that a statement like "Oysters and clams are delicious," while it *can* be expressed as the conjunction of two general propositions, "Oysters are delicious and clams are delicious," can also be expressed as a single noncompound general proposition, in which case the word "and" is properly symbolized by the "v" rather than by the "•." The stated proposition is symbolized as:

$$(x)[(Ox \vee Cx) \supset Dx]$$

not as:

$$(x)[(Ox \cdot Cx) \supset Dx]$$

For to say that oysters and clams are delicious is to say that anything is delicious which is *either* an oyster *or* a clam, *not* to say that anything is delicious which is *both* an oyster *and* a clam.

Third, alternative ways of symbolizing *exceptive* propositions should be noted.[8] Such propositions as: "All except previous winners are eligible," "All but previous winners are eligible," "Previous winners alone are not eligible," are traditionally called exceptive propositions. Any proposition of this form may be translated as a conjunction of two general propositions, as, for example:

$$\{(x)[Px \supset \sim Ex]\} \cdot \{(x)[\sim Px \supset Ex]\}$$

It may also be translated as a noncompound general proposition which is the universal quantification of a propositional function containing the equivalence or biconditional symbol "≡." For the present example we have the translation:

$$(x)[Ex \equiv \sim Px]$$

which can alternatively be rendered in English as: "Anyone is eligible if and only if he is not a previous winner." In general, exceptive propositions are most conveniently regarded as quantified biconditionals. It is clear that exceptive propositions are compound in the sense explained, but it may not be clear whether or not a given sentence expresses an exceptive proposition. This question is one of interpreting or understanding the sentence, for which an examination of its context may be required.

We have seen that the expanded list of Rules of Inference which enabled us to demonstrate the validity of valid categorical syllogisms

[8] Cf. the earlier discussion of exceptive propositions on pages 214–216.

also suffices for the validation of asyllogistic arguments of the type described. The same method of describing possible nonempty universes or models which was used in proving syllogisms invalid also suffices to prove the invalidity of asyllogistic arguments of the present type. The following asyllogistic argument:

> Foremen and superintendents are either competent men or relatives of the owner.
> Anyone who dares to complain must be either a superintendent or a relative of the owner.
> Foremen and foremen alone are competent men.
> Someone did dare to complain.
> Therefore some superintendent is a relative of the owner.

may be symbolized as:

$$(x)[(Fx \vee Sx) \supset (Cx \vee Rx)]$$
$$(x)[Dx \supset (Sx \vee Rx)]$$
$$(x)[Fx \equiv Cx]$$
$$(\exists x)[Dx]$$
$$\therefore (\exists x)[Sx \cdot Rx]$$

and we can prove it invalid by describing a possible universe or model containing the single individual *a* and assigning the truth value *true* to *Ca, Da, Fa, Ra,* and the truth value *false* to *Sa.*

EXERCISES

I. Translate the following statements into logical symbolism, in each case using the abbreviations suggested:

★ 1. Apples and oranges are delicious and nutritious. (*Ax, Ox, Dx, Nx*)

2. Some foods are edible only if they are cooked. (*Fx, Ex, Cx*)

3. No car is safe unless it has good brakes. (*Cx, Sx, Bx*)

4. Any tall man is attractive if he is dark and handsome. (*Tx, Mx, Ax, Dx, Hx*)

★ 5. A man wins if and only if he is lucky. (*Mx, Wx, Lx*)

6. A man who wins if and only if he is lucky is not skillful. (*Mx, Wx, Lx, Sx*)

7. Not all men who are wealthy are both educated and cultured. (*Mx, Wx, Ex, Cx*)

8. Not all tools that are cheap are either soft or breakable. (Tx, Cx, Sx, Bx)

9. Any man is a coward who deserts. (Mx, Cx, Dx)

10. To achieve success, one must work hard if he goes into business, or study continuously if he enters a profession. (Ax: x achieves success; Wx: x works hard; Bx: x goes into business; Sx: x studies continuously; Px: x enters a profession.)

II. For each of the following arguments either construct a formal proof of validity or prove it invalid:

★ 1. $(x)[(Ax \vee Bx) \supset (Cx \cdot Dx)]$
$\therefore (x)[Bx \supset Cx]$

2. $(\exists x)\{(Ex \cdot Fx) \cdot [(Ex \vee Fx) \supset (Gx \cdot Hx)]\}$
$\therefore (x)[Ex \supset Hx]$

3. $(x)\{[Ix \supset (Jx \cdot \sim Kx)] \cdot [Jx \supset (Ix \supset Kx)]\}$
$(\exists x)[(Ix \cdot Jx) \cdot \sim Lx]$
$\therefore (\exists x)[Kx \cdot Lx]$

4. $(x)[(Mx \cdot Nx) \supset (Ox \vee Px)]$
$(x)[(Ox \cdot Px) \supset (Qx \vee Rx)]$
$\therefore (x)[(Mx \vee Ox) \supset Rx]$

★ 5. $(\exists x)[Sx \cdot Tx]$
$(\exists x)[Ux \cdot \sim Sx]$
$(\exists x)[Vx \cdot \sim Tx]$
$\therefore (\exists x)[Ux \cdot Vx]$

6. $(x)[Wx \supset (Xx \supset Yx)]$
$(\exists x)[Xx \cdot (Zx \cdot \sim Ax)]$
$(x)[(Wx \supset Yx) \supset (Bx \supset Ax)]$
$\therefore (\exists x)[Zx \cdot \sim Bx]$

7. $(\exists x)[Cx \cdot \sim (Dx \supset Ex)]$
$(x)[(Cx \cdot Dx) \supset Fx]$
$(\exists x)[Ex \cdot \sim (Dx \supset Cx)]$
$(x)[Gx \supset Cx]$
$\therefore (\exists x)[Gx \cdot \sim Fx]$

8. $(x)[Hx \supset Ix]$
$(x)[(Hx \cdot Ix) \supset Jx]$
$(x)[\sim Kx \supset (Hx \vee Ix)]$
$(x)[(Jx \vee \sim Jx) \supset (Ix \supset Hx)]$
$\therefore (x)[Jx \vee Kx]$

9. $(x)\{(Lx \vee Mx) \supset \{[(Nx \cdot Ox) \vee Px] \supset Qx\}\}$
$(\exists x)[Mx \cdot \sim Lx]$
$(x)\{[(Ox \supset Qx) \cdot \sim Rx] \supset Mx\}$
$(\exists x)[Lx \cdot \sim Mx]$
$\therefore (\exists x)[Nx \supset Rx]$

10. $(x)[(Sx \vee Tx) \supset \sim(Ux \vee Vx)]$
$(\exists x)[Sx \cdot \sim Wx]$
$(\exists x)[Tx \cdot \sim Xx]$
$(x)[\sim Wx \supset Xx]$
$\therefore (\exists x)[Ux \cdot \sim Vx]$

III. For each of the following arguments, either construct a formal proof of its validity or prove it invalid, in each case using the suggested notation:

★ 1. Acids and bases are chemicals. Vinegar is an acid. Therefore vinegar is a chemical. (*Ax, Bx, Cx, Vx*)

2. Teachers are either enthusiastic or unsuccessful. Teachers are not all unsuccessful. Therefore there are enthusiastic teachers. (*Tx, Ex, Ux*)

3. Argon compounds and sodium compounds are either oily or volatile. Not all sodium compounds are oily. Therefore some argon compounds are volatile. (*Ax, Sx, Ox, Vx*)

4. No employee who is either slovenly or discourteous can be promoted. Therefore no discourteous employee can be promoted. (*Ex, Sx, Dx, Px*)

★ 5. No employer who is either inconsiderate or tyrannical can be successful. Some employers are inconsiderate. There are tyrannical employers. Therefore no employer can be successful. (*Ex, Ix, Tx, Sx*)

6. There is nothing made of gold that is not expensive. No weapons are made of silver. Not all weapons are expensive. Therefore not everything is made of gold or silver. (*Gx, Ex, Wx, Sx*)

7. There is nothing made of tin that is not cheap. No rings are made of lead. Not everything is either tin or lead. Therefore not all rings are cheap. (*Tx, Cx, Rx, Lx*)

8. Some prize fighters are aggressive but not intelligent. All prize fighters wear gloves. Prize fighters are not all aggressive. Any slugger is aggressive. Therefore not every slugger wears gloves. (*Px, Ax, Ix, Gx, Sx*)

9. Some photographers are skillful but not imaginative. Only artists are photographers. Photographers are not all skillful. Any journeyman is skillful. Therefore not every artist is a journeyman. (*Px, Sx, Ix, Ax, Jx*)

10. A book is interesting only if it is well written. A book is well written only if it is interesting. Therefore any book is both interesting and well written if it is either interesting or well written. (Bx, Ix, Wx)

IV. Do the same for each of the following:

★ 1. All citizens who are not traitors are present. All officials are citizens. Some officials are not present. Therefore there are traitors. (Cx, Tx, Px, Ox)

2. Doctors and lawyers are professional men. Professional men and executives are respected. Therefore doctors are respected. (Dx, Lx, Px, Ex, Rx)

3. Only lawyers and politicians are members. Some members are not college graduates. Therefore some lawyers are not college graduates. (Lx, Px, Mx, Cx)

4. All cut-rate items are either shopworn or out of date. Nothing shopworn is worth buying. Some cut-rate items are worth buying. Therefore some cut-rate items are out of date. (Cx, Sx, Ox, Wx)

★ 5. Some diamonds are used for adornment. Only things worn as jewels or applied as cosmetics are used for adornment. Diamonds are never applied as cosmetics. Nothing worn as a jewel is properly used if it has an industrial application. Some diamonds have industrial applications. Therefore some diamonds are not properly used. (Dx, Ax, Jx, Cx, Px, Ix)

6. No candidate who is either endorsed by labor or opposed by the *Tribune* can carry the farm vote. No one can be elected who does not carry the farm vote. Therefore no candidate endorsed by labor can be elected. (Cx, Lx, Ox, Fx, Ex)

7. No metal is friable that has been properly tempered. No brass is properly tempered unless it is given an oil immersion. Some of the ash trays on the shelf are brass. Everything on the shelf is friable. Brass is a metal. Therefore some of the ash trays were not given an oil immersion. (Mx: x is metal; Fx: x is friable; Tx: x is properly tempered; Bx: x is brass; Ox: x is given an oil immersion; Ax: x is an ash tray; Sx: x is on the shelf.)

8. Anyone on the committee who knew the nominee would vote for him if he were free to do so. Everyone on the committee was free to vote for the nominee except those who were either instructed not to by the party caucus or had pledged support to someone else. Everyone on the committee knew the nominee. No one who knew the nominee had pledged support to anyone else. Not everyone on the committee voted

for the nominee. Therefore the party caucus had instructed some members of the committee not to vote for the nominee. (*Cx: x* is on the committee; *Kx: x* knows the nominee; *Vx: x* votes for the nominee; *Fx: x* is free to vote for the nominee; *Ix: x* is instructed by the party caucus not to vote for the nominee; *Px: x* had pledged support to someone else.)

9. All members of the Beta Omicron are good dancers and please their dates. To please his date one must buy her a corsage if he takes her dancing, or some ice cream if he takes her to a movie. No good dancer takes his date to a movie if he can afford to take her dancing. Some members of Beta Omicron buy their dates ice cream instead of corsages. Therefore not all the members of Beta Omicron can afford to take their dates dancing. (*Bx: x* is a member of Beta Omicron; *Gx: x* is a good dancer; *Px: x* pleases his date; *Cx: x* buys his date a corsage; *Dx: x* takes his date dancing; *Ix: x* buys his date ice cream; *Mx: x* takes his date to a movie; *Ax: x* can afford to take his date dancing.)

10. Some criminal robbed the Russell mansion. Whoever robbed the Russell mansion either had an accomplice among the servants or had to break in. To break in one would either have to smash the door or pick the lock. Only an expert locksmith could have picked the lock. Had anyone smashed the door, he would have been heard. Nobody was heard. If the criminal who robbed the Russell mansion managed to fool the guard, he must have been a convincing actor. No one could rob the Russell mansion unless he fooled the guard. No criminal could be both an expert locksmith and a convincing actor. Therefore some criminal had an accomplice among the servants. (*Cx: x* is a criminal; *Rx: x* robbed the Russell mansion; *Sx: x* had an accomplice among the servants; *Bx: x* broke in; *Dx: x* smashed the door; *Px: x* picked the lock; *Lx: x* is an expert locksmith; *Hx: x* was heard; *Fx: x* fooled the guard; *Ax: x* is a convincing actor.)

11. If anything is expensive it is both valuable and rare. Whatever is valuable is both desirable and expensive. Therefore if anything is either valuable or expensive then it must be both valuable and expensive. (*Ex: x* is expensive; *Vx: x* is valuable; *Rx: x* is rare; *Dx: x* is desirable.)

12. Figs and grapes are healthful. Nothing healthful is either illaudable or jejune. Some grapes are jejune and knurly. Some figs are not knurly. Therefore some figs are illaudable. (*Fx: x* is a fig; *Gx: x* is a grape; *Hx: x* is healthful; *Ix: x* is illaudable; *Jx: x* is jejune; *Kx: x* is knurly.)

13. Figs and grapes are healthful. Nothing healthful is both illaudable and jejune. Some grapes are jejune and knurly. Some figs are not knurly. Therefore some figs are not illaudable. (*Fx: x* is a fig; *Gx: x* is a grape; *Hx: x* is healthful; *Ix: x* is illaudable; *Jx: x* is jejune; *Kx: x* is knurly.)

Part Three Induction

Chapter 11
Analogy and Probable Inference

For when we determine a thing to be probably true, suppose that an event has or will come to pass, it is from the mind remarking in it a likeness to some other event, which we have observed has come to pass.

—*Joseph Butler*

11.1 Argument by Analogy

The preceding chapters have dealt with deductive arguments, which are valid if their premisses establish their conclusions demonstratively, but invalid otherwise. Not all arguments are deductive, however. A great many arguments are not designed to demonstrate the truth of their conclusions as following necessarily from their premisses, but are intended merely to establish them as probable, or probably true. Arguments of this latter kind are generally called *inductive*, and are radically different from the deductive variety. Of these nondeductive or inductive arguments, perhaps the type most commonly used is the argument by analogy. Two examples of analogical arguments are these:

1. . . . the first industrial revolution, the revolution of the "dark satanic mills," was the devaluation of the human arm by the competition of machinery. There is no rate of pay at which a United States pick-and-shovel laborer can live which is low enough to compete with the work of a steam shovel as an

excavator. The modern industrial revolution [high speed electronic computers, so-called "thinking machines"] is similarly bound to devalue the human brain at least in its simpler and more routine decisions. Of course, just as the skilled carpenter, the skilled mechanic, the skilled dressmaker have in some degree survived the first industrial revolution, so the skilled scientist and the skilled administrator may survive the second.[1]

2. We may observe a very great similitude between this earth which we inhabit, and the other planets, Saturn, Jupiter, Mars, Venus, and Mercury. They all revolve round the sun, as the earth does, although at different distances and in different periods. They borrow all their light from the sun, as the earth does. Several of them are known to revolve round their axis like the earth, and by that means, must have a like succession of day and night. Some of them have moons, that serve to give them light in the absence of the sun, as our moon does to us. They are all, in their motions, subject to the same law of gravitation, as the earth is. From all this similitude, it is not unreasonable to think that those planets may, like our earth, be the habitation of various orders of living creatures. There is some probability in this conclusion from analogy.[2]

Most of our own everyday inferences are by analogy. Thus I infer that a new pair of shoes will wear well on the grounds that I got good wear from other shoes previously purchased from the same store. If a new book by a certain author is called to my attention, I infer that I will enjoy reading it on the basis of having read and enjoyed other books by that author. Analogy is at the basis of most of our ordinary reasonings from past experience to what the future will hold. Not an explicitly formulated argument, of course, but something very much like analogical inference is presumably involved in the conduct of the burnt child who shuns the fire.

None of these arguments is certain, or demonstratively valid. None of their conclusions follow with "logical necessity" from their premisses. It is logically possible that what happened to skilled manual workers may not happen to skilled brain workers, that earth may be the only inhabited planet, that the new shoes may not wear well at all, and that I may find my favorite author's latest book to be intolerably dull. It is even logically possible that one fire may burn but not another. But then, no argument by analogy is *intended* to be mathematically certain. Analogical arguments are not to be classified as either valid or invalid. Probability is all that is claimed for them.

In addition to their frequent use in arguments, analogies are very often used nonargumentatively, and these different uses should not be confused. Since earliest times writers have made use of analogy for the purpose of lively description. The literary uses of analogy in

[1] Reprinted by permission from *Cybernetics* by N. Wiener, published jointly by The Technology Press, John Wiley & Sons, Inc., and Hermann et Cie, 1948.

[2] *Essays on the Intellectual Powers of Man,* by Thomas Reid (Essay I, Chapter 4).

metaphor and simile are tremendously helpful to the writer who strives to create a vivid picture in the reader's mind. Analogy is also used in explanation, where something unfamiliar is made intelligible through being compared to something else, presumably more familiar, to which it has certain similarities. The use of analogies in description and explanation is not the same as their use in argument, though in some cases it may not be easy to decide which use is intended.

Whether used argumentatively or otherwise, analogy is not difficult to define. To draw an analogy between two or more entities is to indicate one or more respects in which they are similar. This explains what an analogy is, but there is still the problem of characterizing an *argument by analogy*. We may approach this problem by examining a particular analogical argument and analyzing its structure. Let us take the simplest of the examples cited thus far, the argument that my new pair of shoes will wear well because my old shoes, which were purchased from the same store, have worn well. The two things said to be similar are the two pairs of shoes. There are three points of analogy involved: the respects in which the two entities are said to resemble each other are: first, in being shoes; second, in being purchased from the same store; and third, in wearing well. The three points of analogy do not play identical roles in the argument, however. The first two occur in the premisses, while the third occurs both in the premisses and in the conclusion. In quite general terms, the given argument may be described as having premisses which assert first, that two things are similar in two respects, and second, that one of those things has a further characteristic, from which the conclusion is drawn that the other thing also has that further characteristic.

Not every analogical argument need concern exactly two things or exactly three different characteristics, of course. Thus the argument quoted from Reid draws analogies among six things (the then known planets) in some eight respects. Apart from these numerical differences, however, all analogical arguments have the same general structure or pattern. Every analogical inference proceeds from the similarity of two or more things in one or more respects to the similarity of those things in some further respect. Schematically, where *a, b, c,* and *d* are any entities, and *P, Q,* and *R* are any properties or "respects," an analogical argument may be represented as having the form

a, b, c, d all have the properties *P* and *Q*.
a, b, c all have the property *R*.
Therefore *d* has the property *R*.

EXERCISES

All of the following passages contain analogies. Distinguish those which contain analogical arguments from those which make nonargumentatives uses of analogy.

★ 1. We have said that normal persons have little motivation to prompt special efforts at self-study. The same thing is true of arithmetic. If motivation were not supplied from parents and school pressure, there would be little learning of mathematics. By analogy, it seems possible that children could be motivated and trained to use their mental skills to solve *emotional* problems. They get almost no training in this important skill at the present time.

—JOHN DOLLARD and NEAL E. MILLER,
Personality and Psychotherapy[3]

2. Perhaps the most startling discovery made in astronomy this century is that the universe is populated by billions of galaxies and that they are systematically receding from one another, like raisins in an expanding pudding.

—MARTIN J. REES and JOSEPH SILK,
"The Origin of Galaxies"[4]

3. Suppose that someone tells me that he has had a tooth extracted without an anaesthetic, and I express my sympathy, and suppose that I am then asked, 'How do you know that it hurt him?' I might reasonably reply, 'Well, I know that it would hurt me. I have been to the dentist and know how painful it is to have a tooth stopped without an anaesthetic, let alone taken out. And he has the same sort of nervous system as I have. I infer, therefore, that in these conditions he felt considerable pain, just as I should myself.'

—ALFRED J. AYER, "One's Knowledge of Other Minds,"
Theoria, Vol. xix, 1953

4. Father was always a bit sceptical of this story, and of the new flying machines, otherwise he believed everything he read. Until 1909 no one in Lower Binfield believed that human beings would ever learn to fly. The official doctrine was that if God had meant us to fly He'd have given us wings. Uncle Ezekiel couldn't help retorting that if God had meant us to ride He'd have given us wheels, but even he didn't believe in the new flying machines.

—GEORGE ORWELL, *Coming Up for Air*

[3] By permission from *Personality and Psychotherapy,* by John Dollard and Neal E. Miller. Copyright, 1950. McGraw-Hill Book Company, Inc.

[4] Reprinted from "The Origin of Galaxies" by Martin J. Rees and Joseph Silk in *Scientific American,* Vol. 221, No. 2, August 1969.

★ 5. As one expert has explained it, forming a latent image on film is something like filling a leaky bucket with hot molasses. Pour in the thin molasses quickly and you can fill the bucket, but if you pour slowly, the thin fluid refuses to accumulate. If you switch to cold molasses, the thick fluid leaks at a much lower rate. You can fill the bucket with cold molasses by pouring at a much lower rate. The analogy applies to photographic emulsions. Some years ago it was discovered that if an emulsion is refrigerated during exposure, it will accumulate a latent image even under very dim light.

—C. L. STRONG, "The Amateur Scientist"[5]

6. In nearly all of the non-Communist world, socialism, meaning public ownership of industrial enterprises, in a spent slogan. Like promises to enforce the antitrust laws in the United States, it is no longer a political program but an overture to nostalgia.

—JOHN KENNETH GALBRAITH, *The New Industrial State*

7. The atomic model which emerged from the work of Rutherford and others resembled a planetary system, for the force which binds planets to the sun obeys the same general form of law as the force which binds electrons to the nucleus. Both gravity and electricity decrease in strength with the square of distance. From this it follows that the particle-electron, attracted by the positive electricity of the nucleus, should move around it in the same way that a planet moves around the sun.

—BARBARA LOVETT CLINE, *Men Who Made a New Physics*

8. One of the pleasures of science is to see two distant and apparently unrelated pieces of information suddenly come together. In a flash what one knows doubles or triples in size. It is like working on two large but separate sections of a jigsaw puzzle and, almost without realizing it until the moment it happens, finding that they fit into one.

—JOHN TYLER BONNER, "Hormones in Social Amoebae and Mammals"[6]

9. Before getting down to the main subject of this book, our own planet, let us make a brief survey of the other members of the solar system and compare their physical properties with those of the Earth. This "comparative planetology," as it may be called, will help us to understand the characteristics of our own planet, much in the same way as comparative anatomy gives biologists a better understanding of the human organism by comparing it with those of mosquitoes and elephants.

—GEORGE GAMOW, *Biography of the Earth*[7]

[5] Reprinted from "The Amateur Scientist" by C. L. Strong in *Scientific American*, Vol. 221, No. 2, August 1969.

[6] Reprinted from "Hormones in Social Amoebae and Mammals" by John Tyler Bonner in *Scientific American*, Vol. 221, No. 5, November 1969.

[7] George Gamow, *Biography of the Earth*, The Viking Press, Inc., New York, 1959.

★ 10. It seemed to us that the synchronous behavior of malaria parasites, all coming to cell division at the same time every 24 hours or a multiple thereof, was remarkably like the behavior of microfilariae, all entering or leaving the peripheral blood at the same time every 24 hours. Microfilariae are carried from one patient to another by mosquitoes, which suck blood mostly at night, and the swarming of the microfilariae in the peripheral blood is arranged to coincide with this time of sucking blood. The biological purpose of the cycle of the microfilariae is clearly to help them encounter mosquitoes and so get transmitted to new patients.

Since malaria is also carried from one person to another by mosquitoes, it seemed to us that the periodic behavior of the malaria parasites in the blood was similarly designed somehow or other to facilitate transmission by mosquitoes.

—FRANK HAWKING, "The Clock of the Malaria Parasite"[8]

11. Wittgenstein used to compare thinking with swimming: just as in swimming our bodies have a natural tendency to float on the surface so that it requires great physical exertion to plunge to the bottom, so in thinking it requires great mental exertion to force our minds away from the superficial, down into the depth of a philosophical problem.

—GEORGE PITCHER, *The Philosophy of Wittgenstein*

12. It is important that we make clear at this point what definition is and what can be attained by means of it. It seems frequently to be credited with a creative power; but all it accomplishes is that something is marked out in sharp relief and designated by a name. Just as the geographer does not create a sea when he draws boundary lines and says: the part of the ocean's surface bounded by these lines I am going to call the Yellow Sea, so too the mathematician cannot really create anything by his defining.

—GOTTLOB FREGE, *The Basic Laws of Arithmetic*

13. The matter stands on the same footing as the making of material tools, which might be argued about in a similar way. For, in order to work iron, a hammer is needed, and the hammer cannot be forthcoming unless it has been made; but, in order to make it, there was need of another hammer and other tools, and so on to infinity. We might thus vainly endeavor to prove that men have no power of working iron. But as men first made use of the instruments supplied by nature to accomplish very easy pieces of workmanship, laboriously and imperfectly, and then, when these were finished, wrought other things more difficult with less labor and greater perfection; and so gradually mounted from

[8] Reprinted from "The Clock of the Malaria Parasite" by Frank Hawking in *Scientific American,* Vol. 222, No. 6, June 1970.

the simplest operations of the making of tools, and from the making of tools to the making of more complex tools, and fresh feats of workmanship, till they arrived at making, with small expenditure of labor, the vast number of complicated mechanisms which they now possess. So, in like manner, the intellect, by its native strength, makes for itself intellectual instruments, whereby it acquires strength for performing other intellectual operations, and from these operations gets again fresh instruments, or the power of pushing its investigations further, and thus gradually proceeds till it reaches the summit of wisdom.

—BARUCH SPINOZA, *On the Improvement of the Understanding*

14. Children in school are like children at the doctor's. He can talk himself blue in the face about how much good his medicine is going to do them; all they think of is how much it will hurt or how bad it will taste. Given their own way, they would have none of it.

So the valiant and resolute band of travelers I thought I was leading toward a much-hoped-for destination turned out instead to be more like convicts in a chain gang, forced under threat of punishment to move along a rough path leading nobody knew where and down which they could see hardly more than a few steps ahead. School feels like this to children: it is a place where *they* make you go and where *they* tell you to do things and where *they* try to make your life unpleasant if you don't do them or don't do them right.

—JOHN HOLT, *How Children Fail*

15. Look round the world: contemplate the whole and every part of it: you will find it to be nothing but one great machine, subdivided into an infinite number of lesser machines, which again admit of subdivisions, to a degree beyond what human senses and faculties can trace and explain. All these various machines, and even their most minute parts, are adjusted to each other with an accuracy, which ravishes into admiration all men, who have ever contemplated them. The curious adapting of means to ends, throughout all nature, resembles exactly, though it much exceeds, the productions of human contrivance; of human design, thought, wisdom, and intelligence. Since therefore the effects resemble each other, we are led to infer, by all the rules of analogy, that the causes also resemble; and that the Author of Nature is somewhat similar to the mind of men; though possessed of much larger faculties, proportioned to the grandeur of the work, which he has executed. By this argument *a posteriori,* and by this argument alone, do we prove at once the existence of a Deity, and his similarity to human mind and intelligence.

—DAVID HUME, *Dialogues Concerning Natural Religion*

11.2 Appraising Analogical Arguments

Although no argument by analogy is ever valid, in the sense of having its conclusion follow from its premisses with logical necessity, some are more cogent than others. Analogical arguments may be appraised as establishing their conclusions as more or less probable. In this section we shall discuss some of the criteria which are applied to arguments of this type.

(1) The first criterion relevant to the appraisal of an analogical argument is the number of entities between which the analogies are said to hold. This principle is deeply rooted in common sense. If I advise you not to send your shirts to such and such a laundry because I sent one there once and it came back ruined, you might caution me against jumping to conclusions, and urge that they ought perhaps to be given another chance. On the other hand, if I give you the same advice and justify it by recounting four different occasions on which unsatisfactory work was done by them on my clothing, and report further that our mutual friends Jones and Smith have also patronized them repeatedly with unhappy results, these premisses serve to establish the conclusion with much higher probability than did the first argument which cited only a single instance. It should not be thought, however, that there is any simple numerical ratio between the number of instances and the probability of the conclusion. If I have known only one chow dog, and that one was ill-tempered, this gives some probability to the conclusion that the next one I meet will be ill-tempered also. On the other hand, if I have known ten chow dogs, all of them ill-tempered, this gives considerably higher probability to the conclusion that the next one will also be ill-tempered. But it by no means follows that the second argument's conclusion is *exactly ten times* as probable.

(2) A second criterion for appraising analogical arguments is the number of respects in which the things involved are said to be analogous. Take the example of the shoes again. That a new pair of shoes was purchased at the same store as an old pair that gave good wear is certainly a premiss from which it follows that the new shoes will probably give good wear also. But that same conclusion follows with greater probability if the premisses assert not only that the shoes were purchased from the same store, but that they were manufactured by the same company, that they were the highest priced shoes in the store, that they are the same style, and that I plan to wear them in the same circumstances and activities. Again, it should not be thought that there is any simple numerical ratio between the number of points of resemblance asserted in the premisses and the probability of the conclusion.

(3) A third criterion by which analogical arguments may be judged is the strength of their conclusions relative to their premisses. If Jones has a new car and gets twenty-three miles to the gallon, from this Smith can infer with some probability that his new car, of the same make and model as Jones', will also give good mileage. Smith can construct alternative arguments here, with the same premisses but different conclusions. If he draws the conclusion that his car will go over twenty miles to the gallon, that is very probable. If he infers that his car will go over twenty-one miles to the gallon, his argument is not so strong; that is, there is less likelihood or probability of his conclusion being true. If he concludes, however, that his own car will give exactly twenty-three miles to the gallon, he has a very much weaker argument.

(4) A fourth criterion used in appraising analogical arguments has to do with the number of *disanalogies* or points of difference between the instances mentioned in the premisses and the instance with which the conclusion is concerned. The conclusion of the preceding argument is made very doubtful if it is pointed out that Jones drives his car for the most part at a steady pace of about twenty-five miles per hour, while Smith habitually drives at speeds in excess of eighty miles per hour. This disanalogy between the instance in the premiss and that of the conclusion weakens the argument and greatly reduces the probability of its conclusion.

(5) Of course the larger the number of instances appealed to in the premisses, the less likely it is that they will *all* be disanalogous to the instance mentioned in the conclusion. To minimize disanalogies between the instances of the premisses and the instance of the conclusion, however, we need not enumerate more and more instances in the premisses. The same end can be achieved by taking instances in our premisses which are dissimilar to each other. The less similar the instances of the premisses are to each other, the less likely it is for *all* of them to be dissimilar to the conclusion's instance. Our fifth criterion for appraising arguments by analogy, then, is that the more dissimilar the instances mentioned in its premisses, the stronger is the argument.

This principle is just as often appealed to and just as commonly accepted as any of the others that have been mentioned. The conclusion that Johnny Jones, an entering freshman at State, will successfully finish his college education and receive a degree, can be established as highly probable on the grounds that ten other students who graduated from the same high school as Johnny Jones, and received grades there very similar to his, have entered State as freshmen and have successfully finished their college educations and received degrees. The argument is appreciably stronger if the ten other students mentioned in the premisses do not resemble each other too closely. The argument is strengthened by pointing out that those ten other students did not all come from the same economic backgrounds, that they differ from each other in racial stock, in religious affiliation, and so on. Incidentally, the fifth criterion explains the importance of the first. The greater the number of instances appealed to, the greater the number of disanalogies likely to obtain among them. None of these five criteria are new or in any way startling. They are constantly used by us in appraising analogical arguments.

(6) There is just one criterion for arguments by analogy that remains to be discussed. Although last, it is definitely not least, being the most important of them all. The examples presented thus far have all been fairly good arguments, because their analogies have all been *relevant*. Thus in support of the conclusion that Smith's new car will give good mileage, we adduced as evidence the fact that Jones' new car, which is known to give good mileage, is the same model; that is, it has the same number of cylinders, the same body weight, and the same horsepower as Smith's. These are all *relevant* considerations. Contrast this argument with one which draws the same conclusion from different premisses, from premisses which assert nothing about cylinders, body weight, or horsepower, but affirm instead that the two cars have the same color, the same number of gauges on their dashboards, and the same style of upholstery in their interiors. The latter is a much weaker argument. But it cannot be judged so by any of the first five criteria mentioned. The two arguments appeal to the same number of instances and the same number of analogies. The reason why the first is a good argument and the second ridiculously bad is that the factors in the first are relevant to mileage, while those of the second are completely irrelevant.

The question of relevance is all important. An argument based on a single *relevant* analogy connected with a single instance will be more cogent than one which points out a dozen *irrelevant* points of resemblance between its conclusion's instance and over a score of instances enumerated in its premisses. Thus a doctor's inference is sound when he reasons that Mr. Black will be helped by a specific drug on the grounds that Mr. White was helped by it when a blood test showed exactly the same type of germs in his system that are now in Mr. Black's. But it would be fantastic for him to draw the same conclusion from premisses which assert that Smith, Jones, and Robinson were all helped by it, and that they and Black all patronize the same tailor, drive the same make and model car, have the same number of children, had similar educations, and were all born under the same sign of the zodiac. The reason for the weakness of the second argument is that the points of resemblance cited are strictly irrelevant to the matter with which the conclusion is concerned.

Although there may be disagreement about what analogies are relevant for certain conclusions, that is, what properties are relevant for proving the presence of certain other properties in a given instance, it is doubtful that there is any disagreement about the *meaning* of relevance. An illustration given by Professor J. H. Wigmore in one of his important legal treatises is the following:

> To show that a certain boiler was not dangerously likely to explode at a certain pressure of steam, other instances of non-explosion of boilers at the same pressure would be relevant, provided the other boilers were substantially similar in type, age, and other circumstances affecting strength.[9]

Here we are given a criterion for relevance itself. An analogy is relevant to establishing the presence of a given property (strength, in Wigmore's illustration) provided it is drawn with respect to *other circumstances affecting it*. One property or circumstance is relevant to another, for purposes of analogical argument, if the first affects the second, that is, if it has a *causal* or determining effect on that other.

The factor of relevance is to be explained in terms of causality. In an argument by analogy, the relevant analogies are those which deal with causally related properties or circumstances. If my neighbor has his house insulated and his fuel bill goes down, then if I have my own house insulated, I can confidently expect my own fuel bill to decrease. The analogy is a good one, because insulation is relevant to the size of fuel bills, being causally connected with fuel consumption. Analogical arguments are highly probable whether they go from cause to effect or from effect to cause. They are even probable when the property in the premiss is neither cause nor effect of the conclusion's property, provided that both are effects of the same cause. Thus from the presence of some symptoms of a given disease a doctor can predict other symptoms—not that either symptom is the cause of the other, but because they are jointly caused by one and the same infection.

To evaluate analogical arguments, then, requires some knowledge of causal connections. These are discovered only empirically, by observation and experiment. The theory of empirical investigation is

[9] Reprinted from *Wigmore's Code of the Rules of Evidence in Trials at Law* by John H. Wigmore. Copyright, 1910, 1915, 1938, 1942 by John H. Wigmore. Published by Little, Brown and Company.

the central concern of inductive logic, and to this topic we turn in the following chapters.

EXERCISES

I. Each of the following arguments by analogy has six additional premisses suggested for it. For each of these alternative premisses, decide whether its addition would make the resulting argument more or less probable.

★ 1. An investor has purchased one hundred shares of oil stock every December for the past five years. In every case the value of the stock has appreciated about 3 per cent a year, and it has paid regular dividends of about 5 per cent a year on the price at which he bought it. This December he decides to buy another hundred shares of oil stock, reasoning that he will probably receive modest earnings while watching the value of his new purchase increase over the years.

a. Suppose he had always purchased stock in eastern oil companies before, and plans to purchase stock in an eastern oil company this year too.

b. Suppose he had purchased oil stocks every December for the past fifteen years instead of only five years.

c. Suppose the oil stocks previously purchased had gone up by 10 per cent a year instead of only 3 per cent.

d. Suppose his previous purchases of oil stock had been in foreign companies as well as in eastern, southern, and western American oil companies.

e. Suppose he learns that the federal government is considering the passage of a new law to regulate oil and gas companies more strictly.

f. Suppose he discovers that tobacco stocks have just raised their dividend payments.

2. A faithful alumnus, heartened by State's winning its last four football games, decides to bet his money that State will win its next game too.

a. Suppose that since the last game State's great triple-threat tailback was injured in practice and hospitalized for the remainder of the season.

b. Suppose that two of the last four games were played away and that two of them were home games.

c. Suppose that just before the game it is announced that a member of State's Chemistry Department has been awarded a Nobel Prize.

d. Suppose that State had won its last six games instead of only four of them.

e. Suppose it has rained hard during each of the four preceding games, and rain is forecast for next Saturday too.

f. Suppose that each of the last four games had been won by a margin of at least four touchdowns.

3. Although he was bored by the last few foreign films he saw, Charles agrees to go to see another one this evening, fully expecting to be bored again.

a. Suppose that Charles was also bored by the last few American movies he saw.

b. Suppose that the star of this evening's film has recently been accused of bigamy.

c. Suppose that the last few foreign films seen by Charles were Italian, and tonight's film is also Italian.

d. Suppose Charles was so bored by the other foreign films that he actually fell asleep during the performance.

e. Suppose the last few foreign films he saw included an Italian, a French, an English, and a Swedish film.

f. Suppose that tonight's film is in color, whereas all of those he saw before were in black and white.

4. Bill has taken three history courses and found them very stimulating and valuable. So he signs up for another one, confidently expecting that it too will be worthwhile.

a. Suppose that his previous history courses were in ancient history, modern European history, and American history.

b. Suppose that his previous history courses had all been taught by the same professor that is scheduled to teach the present one.

c. Suppose that his previous history courses had all been taught by Professor Smith, and the present one is taught by Professor Jones.

d. Suppose that Bill had found his three previous history courses the most exciting intellectual experiences of his life.

e. Suppose that his previous history courses had all met at 9 A.M., and the present one is scheduled to meet at 9 A.M. also.

f. Suppose in addition to the three history courses previously taken, Bill had also taken and enjoyed courses in anthropology, economics, political science, and sociology.

5. Dr. Brown has stayed at the Queen's Hotel every fall for the past six years on his annual visit to New York, and has been quite satisfied with his accommodations there. On his visit to New York this fall he goes again to the Queen's Hotel confidently expecting to enjoy his stay there again.

a. Suppose that when he stayed at the Queen's Hotel before he had occupied a single room twice, shared a double room twice, and twice occupied a suite.

b. Suppose that last spring a new manager had been put in charge of the Queen's Hotel.

c. Suppose he had occupied a suite on all of his previous trips and is assigned a suite this time too.

d. Suppose that on his previous trips he had come to New York by train, but this time he flew.

e. Suppose that when he stayed at the Queen's Hotel before, his quarters had been the most luxurious he had ever known.

f. Suppose he had stayed at the Queen's Hotel three times a year for the past six years.

II. Analyze the structures of the analogical arguments in the following passages and evaluate them in terms of the six criteria that have been explained:

★ 1. If you cut up a large diamond into little bits, it will entirely lose the value it had as a whole; and an army divided up into small bodies of soldiers, loses all its strength. So a great intellect sinks to the level of an ordinary one, as soon as it is interrupted and disturbed, its attention distracted and drawn off from the matter in hand: for its superiority depends upon its power of concentration—of bringing all its strength to bear upon one theme, in the same way as a concave mirror collects into one point all the rays of light that strike upon it.

—ARTHUR SCHOPENHAUER, "On Noise"

2. Every species of plant or animal is determined by a pool of germ plasm that has been most carefully selected over a period of hundreds of millions of years.

We can understand now why it is that mutations in these carefully selected organisms almost invariably are detrimental. The situation can be suggested by a statement made by Dr. J. B. S. Haldane: My clock is not keeping perfect time. It is conceivable that it will run better if I shoot a bullet through it; but it is much more probable that it will stop altogether. Professor George Beadle, in this connection, has asked: "What is the chance that a typographical error would improve *Hamlet?*"

—LINUS PAULING, *No More War!*[10]

3. And in truth, I am quite willing it should be known that the little I have hitherto learned is almost nothing in comparison with that of which I am ignorant, and to the knowledge of which I do not despair of being able to attain; for it is much the same with those who gradually discover truth in the sciences, as with those who when growing rich find

[10] Reprinted by permission of Dodd, Mead & Company from *No More War!* by Linus Pauling. © 1958 by Linus Pauling.

less difficulty in making great acquisitions, than they formerly experienced when poor in making acquisitions of much smaller amount. Or they may be compared to the commanders of armies, whose forces usually increase in proportion to their victories, and who need greater prudence to keep together the residue of their troops after a defeat than after a victory to take towns and provinces.

—RENÉ DESCARTES, *A Discourse on Method*

4. In the United States, especially, atom-smashing-equipment, such as the Van de Graaff generators and cyclotrons, had been constructed. These machines were already capable of accelerating certain particles used as 'projectiles' up to the enormous energy of nine million volts. Nevertheless, even they had only damaged, without breaking into, the protective walls with which Nature in her wisdom had encircled the atomic nucleus and the tremendous stores of energy it contained. The idea that neutrons, which carried no electrical charge at all, might have been able to accomplish what could not be done with such heavily charged projectiles, was too fantastic to be credited. It was as though one were to suggest to troops which had been vainly shelling an underground shelter with guns of the heaviest calibre for a long time that they should start trying their luck with ping-pong balls.

—ROBERT JUNGK, *Brighter Than a Thousand Suns*

★ 5. To the casual observer porpoises and sharks are kinds of fish. They are streamlined, good swimmers, and live in the sea. To the zoölogist who examines these animals more closely, the shark has gills, cold blood, and scales; the porpoise has lungs, warm blood, and hair. The porpoise is fundamentally more like man than like the shark and belongs, with man, to the mammals—a group that nurses its young with milk. Having decided that the porpoise is a mammal, the zoölogist can, without further examination, predict that the animal will have a four-chambered heart, bones of a particular type, and a certain general pattern of nerves and blood vessels. Without using a microscope he can say with reasonable confidence that the red blood cells in the blood of the porpoise will lack nuclei. This ability to generalize about animal structure depends upon a system for organizing the vast amount of knowledge about animals.

—RALPH BUCHSBAUM, *Animals Without Backbones*[11]

6. There is, however, a great difference between the measurement of time and the measurement of lengths; we can never find again an interval of time that has passed, whilst it is quite easy to find a length and to begin over again the operation of measuring it more carefully and more

[11] By permission from *Animals Without Backbones* by Ralph Buchsbaum, University of Chicago Press. Copyright 1938 by the University of Chicago.

accurately. This difference, however, is only apparent, for we never find again the *same* length, which has been displaced by the motion of the stars and put out of shape by the molecular motion which never ceases. It is, therefore, only the *approximate* length which we find again, and in an analogous manner we may say that *approximately* we find again the same interval of time. This is what happens when, in the course of several succeeding nights, an astronomer measures the time separating the passage of the meridian by two fixed stars. He finds that this interval of time is the same, just as we find that the dimensions of a solid body are the same today as they were yesterday. We know very well that the identity cannot be absolute, but the equality is very near, and it is sufficient for the requirements of our science.

—EMILE BOREL, *Space and Time*

7. In our study we should first start with the fundamental living unit, the cell. Following the fundamental method of physico-mathematical sciences, we do not attempt a mathematical description of a concrete cell, in all its complexity. We start with a study of highly idealized systems, which, at first, may even not have any counterpart in real nature. This point must be particularly emphasized. The objection may be raised against such an approach, because such systems have no connection with reality and therefore any conclusions drawn about such idealized systems cannot be applied to real ones. Yet this is exactly what has been, and always is, done in physics. The physicist goes on studying mathematically, in detail, such nonreal things as "material points," "absolutely rigid bodies," "ideal fluids," and so on. *There are no such things as those in nature.* Yet the physicist not only studies them but applies his conclusions to *real things.* And behold! Such an application leads to practical results—at least within certain limits.

—N. RASHEVSKY, *Mathematical Biophysics*

8. While he was attending a group of drug addicts at a sanitarium in Berlin in 1927, it occurred to Dr. Manfred Sakel to try insulin on them. This hormone promotes the utilization of sugar in the body, and on theoretical grounds he believed its effect should relieve the paradox by which a slave of the drug habit requires larger and larger doses of what is essentially a poison. He hoped that through the insulin he might free the victim of dependence on morphine.

. . . .

Some of the men reacted to the insulin with convulsions, but most of them broke into perspiration and lapsed into deep sleep. When they came out of their seizure, or were awakened after a few hours of coma, their conduct surprised the doctor. He noticed that the morbid fears and anxieties which habitually oppress addicts had diminished. Odd notions of persecution, jumpy nerves, and other psychotic symptoms were gone.

This unexpected outcome set Dr. Sakel to thinking. If insulin improved the mental climate of the drug-crazed men, what would it do for the frankly insane?

—GEORGE W. GRAY, *The Advancing Front of Medicine*

9. An electron is no more (and no less) hypothetical than a star. Nowadays we count electrons one by one in a Geiger counter, as we count the stars one by one on a photographic plate. In what sense can an electron be called more unobservable than a star? I am not sure whether I ought to say that I have seen an electron; but I have just the same doubt whether I have seen a star. If I have seen one, I have seen the other. I have seen a small disc of light surrounded by diffraction rings which has not the least resemblance to what a star is supposed to be; but the name "star" is given to the object in the physical world which some hundreds of years ago started a chain of causation which has resulted in this particular light-pattern. Similarly in a Wilson expansion chamber I have seen a trail not in the least resembling what an electron is supposed to be; but the name "electron" is given to the object in the physical world which has caused this trail to appear. How can it possibly be maintained that a hypothesis is introduced in one case and not in the other?

—SIR ARTHUR EDDINGTON, *New Pathways in Science*

★ 10. The discovery of this remarkable weapon against disease dates back to 1929. It was purely accidental. Dr. Alexander Fleming, in St. Mary's Hospital, London, was growing colonies of bacteria on glass plates for certain bacteriological researches. One morning he noticed that a spot of mold had germinated on one of the plates. Such contaminations are not unusual, but for some reason, instead of discarding the impurity and starting fresh, Dr. Fleming decided to allow it to remain. He continued to culture the plate, and soon an interesting drama unfolded beneath his eyes. The area occupied by the bacteria was decreasing, that occupied by the mold was increasing, and presently the bacteria had vanished.

Dr. Fleming now took up this fungus for study on its own account. He recognized it as of the penicillium genus, and by deliberately introducing a particle into culture mediums where bacteria were growing, he found that quite a number of species wouldn't grow in its presence. . . . In his laboratory, whenever he wanted to get rid of a growth of gram-positive bacteria, Fleming would implant a little penicillium, and after that the microbes disappeared. . . . So the medical scientists began to speculate. Since the mold destroyed gram-positive organisms on a culture plate, could it be used to destroy gram-positive disease germs in the living body?

—GEORGE W. GRAY, *Science at War*

11. One of woman's most natural attributes is the care of children. In fact, it is correct to say that groups in which men, rather than women, nurture small children are altogether exceptional. Since the ill and infirm resemble children in many ways, being not merely physically weak and helpless but also psychologically dependent and narcissistically regressed, it was fairly easy to assume that women are also especially qualified to care for the sick.

—GEORGE DEVEREUX and FLORENCE R. WEINER,
"The Occupational Status of Nurses,"
American Sociological Review,
Vol. 15, No. 5, October 1950

12. It is urged that motion pictures do not fall within the First Amendment's aegis because their production, distribution, and exhibition is a large-scale business conducted for private profit. We cannot agree. That books, newspapers, and magazines are published and sold for profit does not prevent them from being a form of expression whose liberty is safeguarded by the First Amendment. We fail to see why operation for profit should have any different effect in the case of motion pictures.

—MR. JUSTICE CLARK, for the Court. *Burstyn* v.
Wilson 343 US 495 (1952)

13. If a single cell, under appropriate conditions, becomes a man in the space of a few years, there can surely be no difficulty in understanding how, under appropriate conditions, a cell may, in the course of untold millions of years, give origin to the human race.

—HERBERT SPENCER, *Principles of Biology*

14. Now if we survey the universe, so far as it falls under our knowledge, it bears a great resemblance to an animal or organized body, and seems actuated with a like principle of life and motion. A continual circulation of matter in it produces no disorder: a continual waste in every part is incessantly repaired; the closest sympathy is perceived throughout the entire system: and each part or member, in performing its proper offices, operates both to its own preservation and to that of the whole. The world, therefore, I infer, is an animal, and the Deity is the *soul* of the world, actuating it, and actuated by it.

—DAVID HUME, *Dialogues Concerning*
Natural Religion

Chapter 12
Causal Connections: Mill's Methods of Experimental Inquiry

For the induction which proceeds by simple enumeration is childish; its conclusions are precarious, and exposed to peril from a contradictory instance; and it generally decides on too small a number of facts, and on those only which are at hand.

—*Francis Bacon*

12.1 The Meaning of "Cause"

To exercise any measure of control over our environment, we must have some knowledge of causal connections. A physican has more power to cure illnesses if he knows what *causes* them, and he should understand the *effects* of the drugs he administers. Since there are several different meanings of the word "cause," we begin by distinguishing them from one another.

It is a fundamental axiom in the study of nature that events do not just happen, but occur only under certain conditions. It is customary to distinguish between necessary and sufficient conditions for the occurrence of an event. A *necessary* condition for the occurrence of a specified event is a circumstance in whose absence the event cannot occur. For example, the presence of oxygen is a necessary condition for combustion to occur: if combustion occurs, then oxygen must have been present, for in the absence of oxygen there can be no combustion.

Although it is a necessary condition, the presence of oxygen is not a sufficient condition for combustion to occur. A *sufficient* condition for the occurrence of an event is a circumstance in whose presence the event must occur. The presence of oxygen is not a sufficient condition for combustion because oxygen can be present without combustion occurring. On the other hand, for almost any substance there is some range of temperature such that *being in that range of temperature in the presence of oxygen* is a sufficient condition for combustion of that substance. It is obvious that there may be several *necessary* conditions for the occurrence of an event, and that they must all be included in the sufficient condition.

The word "cause" is sometimes used in the sense of necessary condition and sometimes in the sense of sufficient condition. It is most often used in the sense of necessary condition when the problem at hand is the elimination of some undesirable phenomenon. To eliminate it, one need only find some condition which is necessary to its existence, and then eliminate that condition. Thus a physician seeks to discover what kind of germ is the "cause" of a certain illness in order to cure the illness by prescribing a drug that will destroy those germs. The germs are said to be the cause of the disease in the sense of a necessary condition for it, since in their absence the disease cannot occur.

The word "cause" is used in the sense of sufficient condition when we are interested not in the elimination of something undesirable but rather in the production of something desirable. Thus a metallurgist seeks to discover the cause of strength in alloys in order to create stronger metals. The process of mixing and heating and cooling is said to be the cause of the strengthening in the sense of a sufficient condition, since such processing suffices to produce a stronger alloy.

In certain practical situations, the word "cause" is used in still a different sense. An insurance company might send an investigator to determine the cause of a mysterious fire. If the investigator sent back a report that the fire was caused by the presence of oxygen in the atmosphere, he would not keep his job very long. And yet he would be right—in the sense of necessary condition—for had there been no oxygen present, there would have been no fire. But the insurance company did not have *that* sense in mind when they sent him to investigate. Nor is the company interested in the sufficient condition. If after several weeks the investigator reported that although he had proof that the fire was deliberately ignited by the policyholder, he hadn't as yet been able to learn *all* the necessary conditions, and so hadn't been able to determine the cause (in the sense of sufficient condition), the company would recall the investigator and tell him to stop wasting his time and their money. The insurance company was using the word "cause" in another sense—what they wanted to find out was the incident or action which, in the presence of those conditions that usually prevail, made the difference between the occurrence or nonoccurrence of the event.

We may distinguish between two different subdivisions of this third sense of cause. These are traditionally characterized as the *remote* and the *proximate* causes. Where there is a causal sequence or chain of several events, *A* causing *B, B* causing *C, C* causing *D,* and *D* causing *E,* we can regard *E* as effect of any or of all of the preceding events. The nearest of them, *D,* is the proximate cause of *E,* and the others are more and more remote causes, *A* more remote than *B,* and *B* more remote than *C*. In this case the proximate cause was the policyholder's lighting the fire. But his action, and thus the fire, may have been caused by his wife's nagging him for more money, and her nagging may have been caused by a neighbor's wife getting a new fur coat, which may have been caused by the neighbor's grain speculations turning out well because of rising food prices which were caused by a crop failure in India. The crop failure was a remote cause of the fire, but the insurance company would not have been interested in hearing that the mysterious fire was caused by an Indian crop failure.

There are several different senses of the term "cause," as we have seen. We can legitimately infer cause from effect only in the sense of necessary condition. And we can legitimately infer effect from cause only in the sense of sufficient condition. Where inferences are made both from cause to effect and from effect to cause, the term "cause" must be used in the sense of "necessary and sufficient condition." In this usage, cause is identified with sufficient condition, and sufficient condition is regarded as the conjunction of all necessary conditions. It should be clear that there is no single definition of "cause" that conforms to *all* of the different uses of that word.

On the conception of cause as necessary and sufficient condition there is a unique cause for any effect. This is not to say that the cause is simple: it may be extremely complex, involving a great many factors all of which must be present for the effect to occur. But there is only one such complex, on this view, that can produce the effect in question. This conception runs counter to the commonsense opinion that a given phenomenon may have been the result of alternative causes. If a man's death occurs, it may have been caused by heart failure, or by poisoning, by a bullet, by a traffic accident, or by any of the hundreds of other circumstances which are capable, as we say, of causing death. But the view that there may be a "plurality of causes" of a single kind of effect conflicts with the notion that a cause is a *necessary* and sufficient condition for its effect. If there can be a plurality of causes, then inferences from effects to their causes are not possible. The doctrine of plurality of causes is very widely accepted indeed. A crop failure may be caused either by drouth or by excessive rainfall, or by grasshoppers.

It should not be concluded, however, that interpreting cause as necessary and sufficient condition is mistaken and unfruitful. Any farmer would agree that there are different kinds of crop failures, and the kind produced by drouth could not possibly have been caused by excessive rainfall or grasshoppers. If an effect is specified with sufficient precision, the apparent plurality of causes tends to disappear. True enough, "death-in-general" may be caused by a plurality of alternative circumstances, but a specific kind of death, that induced, say, by strychnine poisoning, could not possibly have resulted from a coronary thrombosis. The unique cause of death is frequently discovered by post mortem examinations, where an autopsy reveals the particular kind of death with enough specificity to permit an inference that *the* cause of the death in question was one thing rather than any other. The doctrine of plurality of causes may be rejected, then, for in every case in which it is thought that alternative circumstances may have caused a given phenomenon, it is probable that a further specification or more precise description of that phenomenon would make the apparent plurality of causes disappear.

We need not rule out plurality of causes in an *a priori* fashion. We may regard the doctrine of uniqueness of cause as itself the result of an inductive generalization. In every case of alleged plurality of causes encountered thus far, the apparent plurality vanishes when the effect in question is more precisely specified. From this fact we can conclude with probability that in every case a more precise specification of the effect will decrease the number of alternative circumstances which might have caused that effect. And so we can accept, not as necessarily true *a priori,* but as highly probable on the evidence, the working hypothesis that every effect of a specific kind has a single and unique kind of cause.

An even stronger case can be made against the doctrine of plurality of causes. We may quote in this connection William James' dictum that *every difference must make a difference.* If two circumstances can result in the same kinds of effects, it is proper to regard them as being themselves of the same kind. If their effects are no different, then they are not really different from each other. Ordinarily we pay attention only to those differences which are important to us and ignore those in which we have no interest. Certainly their effects are of greatest moment in distinguishing circumstances as being of the same or of different kinds. If all their effects are the same—that is, do not differ in any "important" respects—then two circumstances are also "the same," whereas if their effects are significantly different, this difference is the basis on which we distinguish them as different circumstances. If we agree that *every difference must make a difference,* then we shall reject the doctrine of plurality of causes.

On the other hand, there is much to be said for the common sense view. If we consider certain types of effects, it seems plausible that alternative antecedent circumstances might equally well have produced them. Thus a solution of sugar in water would not be any different whether the sugar or the water was placed in the container first. To provide an adequate discussion of this issue, however, lies far beyond the scope of the present book.

Every use of the word "cause," whether in everyday life or in science, involves or presupposes the doctrine that cause and effect are *uniformly* connected. We admit that a particular circumstance caused a particular effect only if we agree that any other circumstance of that type will—if the attendant circumstances are sufficiently similar—cause another effect of the same kind as the first. In other words, similar causes produce similar effects. Part of the very meaning of the word "cause" as used today is that every occurrence of a cause producing an effect is an *instance* or *example* of the general causal law that such circumstances are *always* accompanied by such phenomena. Thus we are willing to relinquish a belief that circumstance *C* was the cause of effect *E* in one particular case if it can be shown that the same (type of) circumstance was present in another situation which was the same as the first except that the effect *E did not occur* in the latter.

Since a general causal law is implied by every assertion that a particular circumstance was the cause of a particular phenomenon, there is an element of generality in every such assertion. A causal law—as we shall use the term—is an assertion that such and such a circumstance is invariably attended by such and such a phenomenon, no matter when or where it occurs. Now how do we come to know such general truths? The causal relation is not a purely logical or deductive relationship; it cannot be discovered by any *a priori* reasoning. Causal laws can be discovered only *empirically,* by an appeal to experience. But our experiences are always of particular circumstances, particular phenomena, and particular sequences of them. We may observe several instances of a certain kind of circumstance (say *C*), and every instance *that we observe* may be accompanied by an instance of a certain kind of phenomenon (say *P*). These observations show us, of course, only that *some* cases of *C* are cases of *P*. How are we to get from this evidence to the general proposition that *all* cases of *C* are cases of *P*, which is involved in saying that *C causes P*?

The method of arriving at general or universal propositions from the particular facts of experience is called *inductive generalization*. From premisses which assert that three particular pieces of blue litmus paper turned red when dipped in acid, we may draw either a particular conclusion about what will happen to a particular fourth piece of blue litmus paper if it is dipped in acid, or a general conclusion about what happens to *all* blue litmus paper dipped in acid. If we draw the first, we have an argument by analogy; the second is an inductive generalization. The structure of these two types of arguments may be analyzed as follows. The premisses report a number of instances in which two properties (or circumstances or phenomena) occur together. By analogy we may infer that a different particular instance of one property will also exhibit the other property. By inductive generalization we may infer that *all* instances of the one property will also be instances of the other. An inductive generalization of the form:

Instance 1 of phenomenon *E* is accompanied by circumstance *C*.
Instance 2 of phenomenon *E* is accompanied by circumstance *C*.
Instance 3 of phenomenon *E* is accompanied by circumstance *C*.
. . . .

Therefore all instances of phenomenon *E* are accompanied by circumstance *C*.

is an induction by *simple enumeration*. An induction by simple enumeration is very similar to an argument by analogy, differing only in having a more general conclusion.

Simple enumeration is often used in establishing causal connections. Where a number of instances of a phenomenon are invariably accompanied by a certain type of circumstance, it is only natural to infer the existence of a causal relationship between them. Since the circumstance of dipping blue litmus paper in acid is accompanied in all observed instances by the phenomenon of the paper's turning red, we conclude that dipping blue litmus paper in acid is the *cause* of its turning red. Similarly, from the fact that a number of men have contracted yellow fever after being bitten by mosquitoes which had previously fed on yellow-fever patients, we may infer by simple enumeration that the bite of such a mosquito *causes* yellow-fever infection. The analogical character of such arguments is very apparent.

Because of the great similarity between argument by simple

enumeration and argument by analogy, it should be clear that the same types of criteria apply to both. Some arguments by simple enumeration may establish their conclusions with a higher degree of probability than others. The greater the number of instances appealed to, the higher the probability of the conclusion. The various instances or cases of phenomenon *E* accompanied by circumstance *C* are often called *confirming instances* of the causal law which asserts that *C* causes *E*. The greater the number of confirming instances, the higher the probability of the causal law—other things being equal. Thus the first criterion for analogical arguments applies directly to arguments by simple enumeration also.

Inductions by simple enumeration are frequently made, and are often very valuable and suggestive. But they are not very trustworthy. For example, consider the following argument:

Tom broke a mirror and cut his hand, which was bad luck.
Dick broke a mirror and then sprained his ankle, which was bad luck.
Harry broke a mirror and then lost his wallet, which was bad luck.

Therefore breaking a mirror *causes* bad luck.

Most of us would be inclined to put very little trust in such an argument. Yet it is an argument by simple enumeration, appealing to three "confirming instances." Nevertheless, we should probably say that the three instances reported were coincidences rather than cases of a causal law. This is the chief weakness of arguments by simple enumeration. Their very nature prevents them from distinguishing between confirming instances of genuine causal laws, on the one hand, and mere accidents or coincidences, on the other.

Our criticism of the method of simple enumeration can be put in this way. A single negative or disconfirming instance will overthrow an alleged causal law (any exception obviously *disproves* a rule), while the method of simple enumeration takes no account of such exceptions. For an exception or negative instance is either one where *C* is present without *E*, or where *E* is present without *C;* but the only legitimate premisses in an argument by simple enumeration are reports of instances in which both *C* and *E* are present. In other words, if we were to confine ourselves to simple enumeration arguments exclusively, we should look only for confirming instances and would tend to ignore any negative or disconfirming instances that might otherwise be found. For this reason, despite their fruitfulness and value in suggesting causal laws, inductions by simple enumeration are not at all suitable for *testing* causal laws. For the testing of causal laws, other types of inductive arguments have been devised, and to these we now turn.

12.2 Mill's Methods

His criticisms of induction by simple enumeration led the British philosopher Sir Francis Bacon (1561–1626) to recommend other types of inductive procedure. These were given their classic formulation by another British philosopher, John Stuart Mill (1806–1873), and have come to be called Mill's Methods of inductive inference. Mill formulated five of these "canons," as he called them, and they are known as the *Method of Agreement,* the *Method of Difference,* the *Joint Method of Agreement and Difference,* the *Method of Residues,* and the *Method of Concomitant Variation.* They will be presented here in that order.

1. ***Method of Agreement.*** The Method of Agreement is best introduced by way of an example. Suppose that some of the residents of a certain dormitory have become violently ill, suffering stomach distress and nausea, and it is desired to determine the cause of this illness. Half a dozen of the affected students are interviewed to find out what they ate the day on which the illness began. The first student ate soup, bread and butter, salad, vegetables, and canned pears; the second student ate soup, bread and butter, vegetables, and canned pears; the third student ate soup, a pork sandwich, salad, and canned pears; the fourth student ate bread and butter, salad, a pork sandwich, vegetables, and canned pears; the fifth student ate soup, salad, vegetables, and canned pears; and the sixth student ate bread and butter, vegetables, and canned pears. To make this information more readily available, we can set it down in the form of a table, using the capital letters *A, B, C, D, E, F* to denote the presence of the "antecedent circumstances" of having eaten soup, bread and butter, salad, pork sandwich, vegetables, and canned pears, respectively, and using the small letter *s* to denote the presence of the phenomenon of being sick. Where the six students are the six "instances" examined, our information can be represented as:

Instance	*Antecedent Circumstances*	*Phenomenon*
1	*A B C E F*	*s*
2	*A B E F*	*s*
3	*A C D F*	*s*
4	*B C D E F*	*s*
5	*A C E F*	*s*
6	*B E F*	*s*

From this data we should naturally infer that the circumstance *F* could have been the cause of the phenomenon *s*, that is, that the illness was probably due to eating the particular canned pears served in the dormitory. As in any other inductive argument, these premisses do not *prove* the conclusion, but they do establish it as probable. Any inference of this type is characterized as using the Method of Agreement. Mill's general formulation is this:

> If two or more instances of the phenomenon under investigation have only one circumstance in common, the circumstance in which alone all the instances agree, is the cause (or effect) of the given phenomenon.

Schematically, the Method of Agreement may be represented as follows, where capital letters represent circumstances and small letters denote phenomena:

A B C D occur together with *a b c d*.
A E F G occur together with *a e f g*.
Therefore *A* is the cause (or the effect) of *a*.

Another illustration of the use of the Method of Agreement can be drawn from a fairly recent innovation in dental hygiene. It was observed that the inhabitants of several cities enjoyed a much lower rate of dental decay than the national average, and some thought was given to discovering the cause of this happy phenomenon. It was found that the circumstances of these cities differed in many ways: in latitude and longitude, in elevation, in their types of economy, and so on. But one circumstance was common to all of them. This common circumstance was the presence of an unusually high percentage of fluorine in their water supplies, which meant that the diet of the inhabitants of these cities included an unusually large quantity of fluorine. It was inferred that the use of fluorine can cause a decrease in the incidence of dental decay, and acceptance of this conclusion has led to the adoption of fluorine treatments for this purpose in many other localities. Whenever we have found a single circumstance common to all instances of a given phenomenon, we believe ourselves to have discovered its cause.

A word should be said here about the limitations of the Method of Agreement. The available data in our first illustration of that method were remarkably well suited to the application of that method. But such convenient data may not always be available. For example, it might have been the case that all of the stricken students had eaten *both* salad and canned pears. In that case the Method of Agreement would have *eliminated* the soup, the bread and butter, the pork sandwiches, and the vegetables as possible causes of the illness, but would have left open the question as to whether it was the salad, the canned pears, or the combination of them which was responsible for the students' sickness. A different inductive method is required to establish the cause here, and it is provided by the second of Mill's Methods.

EXERCISES

Analyze each of the following arguments in terms of "circumstances" and "phenomena" to show that they follow the pattern of the Method of Agreement:

★ 1. Johnston compared the effects of smoking with those of hypodermically injected nicotine. The smokers almost invariably thought the sensation pleasant, although nonsmokers usually termed it "queer." Johnston, who gave himself 80 injections of 1.3 mg. of nicotine from three to four times a day, found that he preferred the hypodermic injections of nicotine to inhaling a cigarette. In his case, it would appear that nicotine was the major factor in the pleasant sensation due to smoking.

—*The Biologic Effects of Tobacco,* edited by ERNEST L. WYNDER, M.D.

2. It is interesting to note that one of the frequent symptoms of extreme combat anxiety cases is an interference with speech that may run from complete muteness to hesitation and stuttering. Similarly, the sufferer from acute stage fright is unable to speak. Many animals tend to stop vocalizing when frightened, and it is obvious that this tendency is adaptive in preventing them from attracting the attention of their enemies. In the light of this evidence one might suspect that the drive of fear has an innate tendency to elicit the response of stopping vocal behavior.

—JOHN DOLLARD and NEAL E. MILLER, *Personality and Psychotherapy*[1]

3. He [Edward] Jenner kept neatly detailed records of his work, noting how Sarah Portlock, Mary Barge and Elizabeth Wynne, and Simon Nichols, Joseph Merret and William Rodway, had "taken" cowpox and how they showed immunity when he inoculated them with smallpox. He repeated his observations on others, and years passed as he accumulated page upon page of records of cowpox and smallpox. Eventually he was satisfied. He was convinced that the people who had taken cowpox were without exception immune to smallpox.

[1] By permission from *Personality and Psychotherapy* by John Dollard and Neal E. Miller. Copyright, 1950, McGraw-Hill Book Company, Inc.

Jenner's crucial experiment was done in 1796. He took cowpox matter from the hands of Sarah Nelmes, dairymaid, and with it he vaccinated the arm of eight-year-old James Phipps. Two months later, Jenner inoculated Phipps with smallpox on both arms, and several months later he repeated the inoculation. There was neither fever nor pocks, only a trivial sore at the point of inoculation typical of immunity.

—A. L. BARON, *Man Against Germs*

4. A few years ago a small number of people living in various sections of the United States were inflicted with an identical disease. At about the same time the eyes of these individuals developed what the physician calls cataracts—small, irregular, opaque spots in the tissue of the lens. Cataracts interfere with the clear passage of light through the transparent medium of the eye lens. In severe cases they may block vision, visual acuity is lost and the lens must be removed. It turned out that all the individuals who developed these cataracts were physicists and that all of them had been connected with nuclear-energy projects during the war. While they worked with cyclotrons in atomic-energy laboratories they had been the targets of stray neutron rays. They were under medical supervision all during their work, but the density of the neutrons was thought to be entirely harmless. Several years later, however, they developed cataracts.

This case is one of the best examples of the insidiousness of nuclear radiation.

—HEINZ HABER, *Man in Space*[2]

5. We shall begin our consideration of this material with a fairly detailed examination of one of the more striking studies, that by Heilig and Hoff. This concerns the induction of herpetic blisters (cold-sores) by means of suggested hallucinations. Three psychopathic women were employed as subjects. The typical experimental procedure was as follows: The experimenter recalled to the subject's mind when in deep hypnotic state an extremely unpleasant emotional experience connected with her particular neurosis. Thereupon the patient showed signs of great excitement, such as flushing, tossing about, and groaning in fear. At this juncture the psychiatrist stroked the patient's lower lip and suggested a feeling of itchiness such as the patient had often felt when a cold-sore was starting. Calming suggestions were then given, after which the patient was dehypnotized. During the following twenty-four hours or so the patient reported an itching on the lower lip, at the end of which time there appeared a slight swelling on the lip in question. At the end of forty-eight hours numerous small herpetic blisters appeared, which gradually merged into a large blister. After a few days this dried up,

[2] From *Man in Space* by Heinz Haber, © 1953. Used by special permission of the publishers, The Bobbs-Merrill Company, Inc.

forming a scab, and finally healed. The contents of the fresh blister, when transmitted to the cornea of a rabbit, caused a herpes in the rabbit on the third day, thus providing the technical genuineness of the cold-sore. This picture, with unimportant variations, holds for all three patients.

—CLARK L. HULL, *Hypnosis and Suggestibility*

2. ***Method of Difference.*** The Method of Difference is often applicable to such cases as those described in our first illustration of the Method of Agreement, even where the data will not permit the use of the Method of Agreement. If on further investigation in the dormitory we found a student who, on the day that many had become ill, had eaten soup, bread and butter, salad, and vegetables only, and had *not* become ill, we could profitably compare his case with that of the first student described. Denoting this last student as "instance *n*," and using the same abbreviations as in our first table, we can set down a new table as:

Instance	*Antecedent Circumstances*	*Phenomenon*
1	*A B C E F*	*s*
n	*A B C E* —	–

From this new data we should again naturally infer that the circumstance *F* could have caused the phenomenon *s;* that is, the illness was probably due to eating the canned pears. Of course, the conclusion follows with probability rather than with certainty, but this is merely to say that the inference is inductive rather than deductive. Any inference of this type uses the Method of Difference, which was formulated by Mill in these words:

> If an instance in which the phenomenon under investigation occurs, and an instance in which it does not occur, have every circumstance in common save one, that one occurring only in the former; the circumstance in which alone the two instances differ, is the effect, or the cause, or an indispensable part of the cause, of the phenomenon.

Schematically, the Method of Difference may be represented as follows, where again capital letters represent circumstances, and small letters denote phenomena:

A B C D occur together with *a b c d;*
B C D occur together with *b c d;*

Therefore *A* is the cause, or the effect, or an indispensable part of the cause, of *a.*

Strictly speaking, we should have inferred not that eating the canned pears was *the* cause of sickness, but that eating the canned pears was "an indispensable part of the cause" of the sickness. This distinction is perhaps brought out more clearly in the case of a simpler example. We might have two cigarette lighters in exactly the same condition except that the flint has been removed from one but not the other. The presence of the flint is the only circumstance in which they differ, and the phenomenon of lighting occurs in the one instance but not in the other, yet we should not say that the presence of flint was *the* cause, but rather *an indispensable part of the cause* of the light. Where it is known that the phenomenon occurs later in time than the circumstance, as when eating the canned pears was an *antecedent* circumstance, there need be no doubt as to which is cause and which effect, for an effect can never precede its cause.

A more serious illustration of the Method of Difference is provided by the following:

> Experiments were devised to show that yellow fever was transmitted by the mosquito alone, all other reasonable opportunities for being infected being excluded. A small building was erected, all windows and doors and every other possible opening being absolutely mosquito-proof. A wire mosquito screen divided the room into two spaces. In one of these spaces fifteen mosquitoes, which had fed on yellow fever patients, were liberated. A non-immune volunteer entered the room with the mosquitoes and was bitten by seven mosquitoes. Four days later, he suffered an attack of yellow fever. Two other non immune men slept for thirteen nights in the mosquito-free room without disturbances of any sort.
>
> To show that the disease was transmitted by the mosquito and not through the excreta of yellow fever patients or anything which had come in contact with them, another house was constructed and made mosquito-proof. For 20 days, this house was occupied by three non-immunes, after the clothing, bedding and eating utensils and other vessels soiled with the discharge, blood and vomitus of yellow fever patients had been placed in it. The bed clothing which they used had been brought from the beds of the patients who had died of yellow fever, without being subjected to washing or any other treatment to remove anything with which it might have been soiled. The experiment was twice repeated by other non-immune volunteers. During the entire period all the men who occupied the house were strictly quarantined and protected from mosquitoes. None of those exposed to these experiments contracted yellow fever. That they were not immune was subsequently shown, since four of them became infected either by mosquito bites or the injection of blood from yellow fever patients.[3]

The preceding account contains three distinct uses of the Method of Difference. In the first paragraph, the reasoning involved may be schematized as follows, where *A* denotes the circumstance of being bitten by an infected mosquito, *a* denotes the phenomenon of

[3] Reprinted from *Exercises in Elementary Logic* by Paul Henle and W. K. Frankena. Copyright, 1940, by Paul Henle and W. K. Frankena.

suffering an attack of yellow fever, *B, C, D,* denote the circumstances of living in the small building described, and *b, c, d,* denote phenomena common to *all* the volunteers referred to:

A B C D——*a b c d*	first nonimmune man
B C D——*b c d*	second nonimmune man
B C D——*b c d*	third nonimmune man

Therefore *A* is the cause of *a*.

The second paragraph involves a refinement on the preceding, for the infected mosquitoes, presumably, did not merely bite the first nonimmune man but in lighting on him deposited some matter which they had picked up from the yellow-fever patients on whom they had previously fed. That it was the *bite* of the mosquito (*A*) which caused infection (*a*), rather than the circumstance (*M*) of coming into contact with matter which had been in contact with a yellow-fever patient, is established by the following pattern of argument:

B C D M——*b c d m*	nonimmune men in house
A B C D M——*a b c d m*	same nonimmune men when subsequently bitten.

Therefore *A* (rather than *M*) is the cause of *a*.

The third pattern of argument found in the preceding account emerges when the first and second paragraphs are considered together. Here we focus our attention on two instances: first, the nonimmune man who was both bitten by a mosquito *and* thus brought into contact with matter from a yellow-fever patient, and second, the nonimmune man who was not bitten but was nevertheless brought into contact with matter from a patient. Here the pattern emerges as:

A M——*a m*
M——*m*

Therefore *A* is the cause of *a*.

All these patterns exemplify the Method of Difference, which is thus seen to be a very pervasive type of experimental inference.

EXERCISES

Analyze each of the following arguments in terms of "circumstances" and "phenomena" to show that they follow the pattern of the Method of Difference:

★ 1. In 1861 Pasteur at last carried general conviction against spontaneous generation. He boiled meat broth in a flask with a very long thin neck until no bacteria were left. This was shown by the fact that he could now keep the broth in the flask for an indefinite period without change setting in, the narrow neck admitting nothing. Then he broke off the neck and in a few hours the liquid showed micro-organisms, and the meat was in full decay. That the air carried such organisms he proved by twice filtering it through sterile filters and showing that with the first filter, but not the second, he could set up putrefaction.

—H. T. PLEDGE, *Science Since 1500*

2. The primitive brain, as we saw it in the planaria, served chiefly as a sensory relay—a center for receiving stimuli from the sense organs and then sending impulses down the nerve cord. This is also true of the nereis, for, if the brain is removed, the animal can still move in a coordinated way—and, in fact, it moves about more than usual. If it meets some obstacle, it does not withdraw and go off in a new direction but persists in its unsuccessful forward movements. This very unadaptive kind of behavior shows that in the normal nereis the brain has an important function which it did not have in flatworms—that of *inhibition* of movement in response to certain stimuli.

—RALPH BUCHSBAUM, *Animals Without Backbones*[4]

3. It was assumed for a long time, by analogy with the mosquito and other blood-sucking vectors, that the virus of typhus was injected by the louse when sucking blood. But apparently this is not so. The infection is not in the saliva of the louse, as it probably is with the mosquito, but in the feces. The disease is thought to be spread through the feces coming into contact with scratches or abrasions in the skin, and scratching and louse infection are generally inseparable. This fact was first suggested in 1922 by the two workers who fed infected lice on a monkey, while taking great care that no feces from the lice should come into contact with the monkey's skin. They found that the monkey remained healthy.

—KENNETH M. SMITH, *Beyond the Microscope*

4. We have recently obtained conclusive experimental evidence that there can be no tooth decay without bacteria and a food supply for them. In germ-free laboratories at the University of Notre Dame and the University of Chicago, animals innocent of oral micro-organisms do not develop cavities. Where animals in normal circumstances average more than four cavities each, the germ-free rats show no signs of caries. At the Harvard School of Dental Medicine we have demonstrated the other

[4] By permission from *Animals Without Backbones* by Ralph Buchsbaum, University of Chicago Press. Copyright 1938 by The University of Chicago.

side of the coin: that food debris also must be present. Rats that have plenty of bacteria in their mouths but are fed by tube directly to the stomach do not develop cavities. In a pair of rats joined by surgery so that they share a common blood circulation, the one fed by mouth develops tooth decay, the one fed by tube does not.

—REIDER F. SOGNNAES, "Tooth Decay"[5]

5. There is a deep-red dye, well known to analytical chemists, which is used for the analysis of aluminum and to a lesser extent for beryllium and which, on paper, seemed to meet our requirements. This dye is known by the trade name "aluminon," and by the chemical name aurintricarboxylic acid, or simply ATA. In the first test of ATA we injected mice with enough beryllium salt to kill them within a few days. We then injected half the animals with a small dose of ATA and left the others untreated. The results were dramatic: virtually every animal treated with ATA survived and lived on normally, while all of the untreated animals died. We have repeated this experiment with hundreds of animals of different species, with the same high degree of protection.

—JACK SCHUBERT, "Beryllium and Berylliosis"[6]

3. ***Joint Method of Agreement and Difference.*** The Joint Method of Agreement and Difference can be explained simply as the use of both the Method of Agreement and the Method of Difference in the same investigation. Its pattern is:

$A\ B\ C$——$a\ b\ c$ $\qquad$ $A\ B\ C$——$a\ b\ c$
$A\ D\ E$——$a\ d\ e$ $\qquad$ $B\ C$——$b\ c$

Therefore A is the effect, or the cause, or an indispensable part of the cause, of a.

Since each Method, used separately, affords some probability to the conclusion, their joint use as illustrated above affords a higher probability to the conclusion. Although this interpretation would scarcely fit in with the view that the Joint Method is an additional and separate Method, it does reveal it as an extremely powerful pattern of inductive inference. Its use, in this form, is illustrated in Zeeman's report of his discovery of what has come to be known as the "Zeeman's Effect":

In consequence of my meaurements of Kerr's magneto-optical phenomena, the thought occurred to me whether the period of the light emitted by a flame

[5] Reprinted from "Tooth Decay" by Reider F. Sognnaes in *Scientific American,* Vol. 197, No. 6, December 1957.

[6] Reprinted from "Beryllium and Berylliosis" by Jack Schubert in *Scientific American,* Vol. 199, No. 2, August 1958.

might be altered when the flame was acted upon by magnetic force. It has turned out that such an action really occurs. I introduced into an oxyhydrogen flame, placed between the poles of a Ruhmkorff's electromagnet, a filament of asbestos soaked in common salt. The light of the flame was examined with a Rowland's grating. Whenever the circuit was closed both *D* lines were seen to widen.

Since one might attribute the widening to the known effects of the magnetic field upon the flame, which would cause an alteration in the density and temperature of the sodium vapour, I had resort to a method of experimentation which is much more free from objection.

Sodium was strongly heated in a tube of biscuit porcelain, such as Pringsheim used in his interesting investigations upon the radiation of gases. The tube was closed at both ends by plane parallel glass plates, whose effective area was 1 cm^2. The tube was placed horizontally between the poles, at right angles to the lines of force. The light of an arc lamp was sent through. The absorption spectrum showed both *D* lines. The tube was continuously rotated round its axis to avoid temperature variations. Excitation of the magnet caused immediate widening of the lines. It thus appears very probable that the period of sodium light is altered in the magnetic field.[7]

The pattern of Zeeman's inference may be schematized by using the following symbols: *A* denotes the presence of a magnetic field, *B* denotes the presence of an open oxyhydrogen flame, *C* denotes the arc lamp illumination described, *a* denotes the widening of the *D* lines of the sodium spectrum, *b* denotes the usual effects of an open oxyhydrogen flame, and *c* denotes the usual effects of arc lamp illumination. The inference is now symbolized as:

A B——*a b*	*A B*——*a b*	*A C*——*a c*
A C——*a c*	*B*——*b*	*C*——*c*

Therefore *A* is the cause, or an indispensable part of the cause, of *a*.

Here the left-hand pair of premisses yields the conclusion by the Method of Agreement, while the middle and right-hand pairs yield the conclusion by the Method of Difference, so the whole argument proceeds by the Joint Method.

EXERCISES

Analyze each of the following arguments in terms of "circumstances" and "phenomena" to show that they follow the pattern of the Joint Method of Agreement and Difference:

★ 1. Eijkman fed a group of chickens exclusively on white rice. They

[7] By permission from *A Source Book in Physics* by William Francis Magie. Copyright 1935. McGraw-Hill Book Company, Inc.

all developed polyneuritis and died. He fed another group of fowl unpolished rice. Not a single one of them contracted the disease. Then he gathered up the polishings from rice and fed them to other polyneuritic chickens, and in a short time the birds recovered. He had accurately traced the cause of polyneuritis to a faulty diet. For the first time in history, he had produced a food deficiency disease experimentally, and had actually cured it. It was a fine piece of work and resulted in some immediate remedial measures.

—BERNARD JAFFE, *Outposts of Science*[8]

2. An experiment by Greenspoon on the reinforcmement of a response (1950) provides another clear example of direct, automatic, or, in other words, unconscious learning. He had his subjects sit facing away from him so that they could not see him. He asked them to say all the words they could think of, pronouncing them individually without using any sentences or phrases, and he recorded their responses on a tape recorder. The response he was reinforcing was that of saying plural nouns; he did this by saying "Mmm-hmm" immediately after the subject said a plural noun. In this case the response was a highly generalized part of language habits and the reinforcing value of the stimulus "Mmm-hmm" must have been acquired as a part of social learning.

Greenspoon found that during the "training" period the experimental group, to whom he said "Mmm-hmm" after each plural noun, greatly increased the percentage of plural nouns spoken, while the control group, to whom nothing was said after plural nouns, showed no such increase. Furthermore this happened with subjects who on subsequent questioning showed that they had no idea what the purpose of the "Mmm-hmm" was and were completely unaware of the fact that they were increasing their percentage of plural nouns. This clearly demonstrates that the effect of a reinforcement can be entirely unconscious and automatic. Somewhat similar experiments have been performed by Thorndike (1932) and Thorndike and Rock (1934).A great deal of human learning seems to be of this direct, unconscious kind. Apparently many attitudes, prejudices, emotions, motor skills, and mannerisms are acquired in this way.

—JOHN DOLLARD and NEAL E. MILLER, *Personality and Psychotherapy*[9]

3. So Metchnikoff, with Roux always being careful and insisting upon good check experiments—so Metchnikoff, after all of his theorizing about why we are immune, performed one of the most profoundly practical of

[8] *Outposts of Science* by Bernard Jaffe. Copyright, 1935, by Bernard Jaffe. Reprinted by permission of Simon and Schuster, Publishers.

[9] By permission from *Personality and Psychotherapy,* by John Dollard and Neal E. Miller. Copyright, 1950. McGraw-Hill Book Company, Inc.

all the experiments of microbe hunting. He sat himself down and invented the famous calomel ointment—that now is chasing syphilis out of armies and navies the world over. He took two apes, inoculated them with the syphilitic virus fresh from a man, and then, one hour later, he rubbed the grayish ointment into that scratched spot on one of his apes. He watched the horrid signs of the disease appear on the unanointed beast, and saw all signs of the disease stay away from the one that had got the calomel.

Then for the last time Metchnikoff's strange insanity got hold of him. He forgot his vows and induced a young medical student, Maisonneuve, to volunteer to be scratched with syphilis from an infected man. Before a committee of the most distinguished medical men of France, this brave Maisonneuve stood up, and into six long scratches he watched the dangerous virus go. It was a more severe inoculation than any man would ever get in nature. The results of it might make him a thing for loathing, might send him, insane, to his death. . . . For one hour Maisonneuve waited, then Metchnikoff, full of confidence, rubbed the calomel ointment into the wounds—but not into those which had been made at the same time on a chimpanzee and a monkey. It was a superb success, for Maisonneuve showed never a sign of the ugly ulcer, while the simians, thirty days afterwards, developed the disease—there was no doubt about it.

—PAUL DE KRUIF, *Microbe Hunters*[10]

4. A variety of experimental results shows that alcohol produces a reduction in fear.

Conger . . . tested hungry rats in a simple approach-avoidance situation. He trained them to approach the distinctively lighted end of an alley to secure food and then threw them into an approach-avoidance conflict by giving them electric shocks at the goal. Five minutes after a control injection of water the rats would not approach the food-shock end of the alley; five minutes after one of alcohol (1.5 parts to 1,000 of body weight) they ran up to get the food.

Having determined that results could be secured in a simple situation, presumably not involving any complex habits, he performed a second experiment to determine whether the alcohol strengthened the approach habits based on hunger, weakened the avoidance habits based on fear, or modified both. He trained one group of rats to approach the lighted end of the alley for food and a *different* group to avoid the lighted end of the alley to escape shock. The strength of the tendencies to approach or avoid was measured by having the animal wear a little harness, tempo-

[10] Reprinted from *Microbe Hunters* by Paul de Kruif. Copyright, 1926, by Harcourt, Brace and Company, Inc.

rarily restraining it, and measuring how hard it pulled. Half the animals in each group were tested when mildly drunk and half when sober. The alcohol produced little if any decrease in the pull of the hungry animals toward food and a marked decrease in the pull of the frightened animals away from the place where they had been shocked on previous trials. Since the same responses of running and pulling were involved in both groups, it seems reasonable to interpret the difference as indicating that the alcohol reduced the strength of fear without markedly affecting hunger.

—JOHN DOLLARD and NEAL E. MILLER, *Personality and Psychotherapy*[11]

5. The discovery was made in this way. I had dissected and prepared a frog . . . and while I was attending to something else, I laid it on a table on which stood an electrical machine at some distance from its conductor and separated from it by a considerable space. Now when one of the persons who were present touched accidentally and lightly the inner crural nerves of the frog with the point of a scalpel all the muscles of the legs seemed to contract again and again as if they were affected by powerful cramps. Another one who was there, who was helping us in electrical researches, thought that he had noticed that the action was excited when a spark was discharged from the conductor of the machine. Being astonished by this new phenomenon he called my attention to it, who at that time had something else in mind and was deep in thought. Whereupon I was inflamed with an incredible zeal and eagerness to test the same and to bring to light what was concealed in it. I therefore myself touched one or the other nerve with the point of the knife and at the same time one of those present drew a spark. The phenomenon was always the same. Without fail there occurred lively contractions in every muscle of the leg at the same instant as that in which the spark jumped, as if the prepared animal was affected by tetanus.

With the thought that these motions might arise from the contact with the point of the knife, which perhaps caused the excited condition, rather than by the spark, I touched the same nerves again in the same way in other frogs with the point of the knife, and indeed with greater pressure, yet so that no one during this time drew off a spark. Now no motions could be detected. I therefore came to the conclusion that perhaps to excite the phenomenon there were needed both the contact of a body and the electric spark.

—Quoted in WILLIAM FRANCIS MAGIE, *A Sourcebook in Physics*[12]

[11] By permission from *Personality and Psychotherapy*, by John Dollard and Neal E. Miller. Copyright, 1950. McGraw-Hill Book Company, Inc.

[12] By permission from *A Source Book in Physics*, by William Francis Magie. Copyright, 1935. McGraw-Hill Book Company, Inc.

4. ***Method of Residues.*** In his statement of the Method of Residues, Mill varies his terminology slightly, referring not to *circumstances* and phenomena, but to *antecedents* and phenomena. Of course what he means is *antecedent circumstances.* Mill's formulation is:

> Subduct from any phenomenon such part as is known by previous inductions to be the effect of certain antecedents, and the residue of the phenomenon is the effect of the remaining antecedents.

An illustration of this method is provided by the discovery of the planet Neptune.

> In 1821, Bouvard of Paris published tables of the motions of a number of planets, including Uranus. In preparing the latter he had found great difficulty in making an orbit calculated on the basis of positions obtained in the years after 1800 agree with one calculated from observations taken in the years immediately following discovery. He finally disregarded the older observations entirely and based his tables on the newer observations. In a few years, however, the positions calculated from the tables disagreed with the observed positions of the planet and by 1844 the discrepancy amounted to 2 minutes of arc. Since all the other known planets agreed in their motions with those calculated for them, the discrepancy in the case of Uranus aroused much discussion.
>
> In 1845, Leverrier, then a young man, attacked the problem. He checked Bouvard's calculations and found them essentially correct. Thereupon he felt that the only satisfactory explanation of the trouble lay in the presence of a planet somewhere beyond Uranus which was disturbing its motion. By the middle of 1846 he had finished his calculations. In September he wrote to Galle at Berlin and requested the latter to look for a new planet in a certain region of the sky for which some new star charts had just been prepared in Germany but of which Leverrier apparently had not as yet obtained copies. On the twenty-third of September Galle started the search and in less than an hour he found an object which was not on the chart. By the next night it had moved appreciably and the new planet, subsequently named Neptune, was discovered within 1° of the predicted place. This discovery ranks among the greatest achievements of mathematical astronomy.[13]

Here the phenomenon being investigated was the movement of Uranus. The part of the phenomenon known by previous inductions to be the effect of certain antecedents was a certain calculated orbit known to be the effect of the gravitational influence of the sun and the interior planets. The residue of the phenomenon was the perturbation in the calculated orbit. The remaining antecedent was the (hypothesized) planet Neptune, which was inferred to be the *cause* of the residue of the phenomenon by the Method of Residues.

[13] By permission from *The Elements of Astronomy* by Edward Arthur Fath. Copyright, 1926, 1928, 1934. McGraw-Hill Book Company, Inc.

Schematically, the Method of Residues can be represented as follows:

A B C——*a b c*
B is known to be the cause of *b*.
C is known to be the cause of *c*.
———————————————
Therefore *A* is the cause of *a*.

A simpler illustration of the use of this method is in the weighing of various types of cargo, especially that of trucks. The truck is weighed when empty, and then weighed again when it has been loaded. The total phenomenon is the passage of the scale's pointer past the various numerals on its dial. The antecedents here are two: the truck and its cargo. The part of the phenomenon which consists of the scale's pointer moving up to the numeral which corresponds with the weight of the empty truck is known to be due to the truck alone. Then the residue of the phenomenon, the amount by which the scale's pointer moves beyond the numeral corresponding to the weight of the empty truck, is concluded to be the effect of the cargo, and therefore a measure of its weight.

The Method of Residues is sometimes said to be a strictly deductive pattern of inference and not inductive at all. It must be admitted that there are certainly differences between the other methods and the Method of Residues. Each of the other methods requires the examination of at least two instances, whereas the Method of Residues can be used with the examination of only one case. And none of the other Methods, as formulated by Mill, requires an appeal to any antecedently established causal laws, while the Method of Residues definitely does depend upon antecedently established causal laws. These differences are present, but they do not spell the difference between induction and deduction. For despite the presence of premisses which state causal laws, a conclusion inferred by the Method of Residues is only probable, and cannot be *validly deduced* from its premisses. Of course an additional premiss or two might serve to transform an inference by the Method of Residues into a valid deductive argument, but the same can be said for the other methods as well. There seems to be no basis for the claim that the Method of Residues is deductive rather than inductive.

EXERCISES

Analyze each of the following arguments in terms of "antecedents" and "phenomena" to show that they follow the pattern of the Method of Residues:

★ 1. Hoarders.

Is avarice a natural tendency or an acquired habit? Two Harvard psychologists have been investigating this question with rats. Louise C. Licklider and J. C. R. Licklider provided six rats with all the food they could eat and more. Their food after weaning consisted of pellets of Purina Laboratory Chow. Although none of the rats had ever experienced a food shortage, all immediately started hoarding pellets. Even after they had accumulated a hoard and the food-supply bin was empty, they kept coming back to hunt for more.

This behavior confirmed what previous investigators had found. But the Lickliders refined the experiment to try to unearth the rats' motives for hoarding. They covered half of the pellets with aluminum foil, thus eliminating their value as food. The experimenters discovered that four of the six avaricious rats actually preferred the worthless, inedible pellets in hoarding.

The rats were then put on short rations for six days. After this "deprivation period" they hoarded even more greedily and showed more interest in the plain food pellets, but some still hoarded foil-wrapped pellets and continued to prefer them.

The Lickliders conclude, in a report to the *Journal of Comparative and Clinical Psychology:* "The factors that lead to hoarding and that determine what is hoarded are by no means entirely alimentary. The initiation of hoarding seems to be for the rat, as for the human being, a complex motivational problem to which sensory and perceptual factors, rather than blood chemistry, hold the key."

—"Science and the Citizen," *Scientific American*[14]

2. The radioactivity of every pure uranium compound is proportional to its uranium content. The ores are, however, relatively four times as active. This fact led M. and Mme. Curie, just after 1896, to the discovery that the pitchblende residues, from which practically all of the uranium had been extracted, exhibited nevertheless considerable radioactivity. About a ton of the very complex residues having been separated laboriously into the components, it was found that a large part of the radioactivity remained with the sulphate of barium. From this a product free from barium, and at least one million times more active than uranium, was finally secured in the form of the bromide. The nature of the spectrum and the chemical relations of the element, now named radium, placed it with the metals of the alkaline earths. The ratio by weight of chlorine to radium in the chloride is 35.46 : 113, so that, on the assumption that the element is bivalent, its chloride is $RaCl_2$ and its atomic

14 Reprinted from "Science and the Citizen" in *Scientific American,* Vol. 183, No. 1, July 1950.

weight is 226. With this value it occupies a place formerly vacant in the periodic table.

—JAMES KENDALL, *Smith's College Chemistry*[15]

3. In H. Davies' experiments on the decomposition of water by galvanism, it was found that besides the two components of water, oxygen and hydrogen, an acid and an alkali were developed at opposite poles of the machine. Since the theory of the analysis of water did not give reason to expect these products, their presence constituted a problem. Some chemists thought that electricity had the power of producing these substances of itself. Davies conjectured that there might be some hidden cause for this part of the effect—the glass might suffer decomposition, or some foreign matter might be in the water. He then proceeded to investigate whether or not the diminution or total elimination of possible causes would change or eliminate the effect in question. Substituting gold vessels for glass ones, he found no change in the effect and concluded that glass was not the cause. Using distilled water, he found a decrease in the quantity of acid and alkali involved, yet enough remained to show that the cause was still in operation. He inferred that impurity of the water was not the sole cause, but was a concurrent cause. He then suspected that perspiration from the hands might be the cause, as it would contain salt which would decompose into acid and alkali under electricity. By avoiding such contact, he reduced the quantity of the effect still further, till only slight traces remained. These might be due to some impurity of the atmosphere decomposed by the electricity. An experiment determined this. The machine was put under an exhausted receiver and when it was thus secured from atmospheric influences, no acid or alkali was produced.

—G. GORE, *The Art of Scientific Discovery*[16]

4. The return of the comet predicted by Professor Encke a great many times in succession, and the general good agreement of its calculated with its observed place during any one of its periods of visibility, would lead us to say that its gravitation toward the sun and planets is the sole and sufficient cause of all the phenomena of its orbital motion; but when the effect of this cause is strictly calculated and subducted from the observed motion, there is found to remain behind a *residual phenomenon,* which would never have been otherwise ascertained to exist, which is a small anticipation of the time of its re-appearance, or a diminution of its periodic time, which cannot be accounted for by gravity, and whose cause is therefore to be inquired into. Such an anticipation would be caused

[15] Reprinted from *Smith's College Chemistry* by James Kendall. Copyright, 1905, 1906, 1908, 1916, 1923, 1929, by Appleton-Century-Crofts, Inc.

[16] Adapted from *The Art of Scientific Discovery* by G. Gore. Longmans, Green, and Company, 1878.

by the resistance of a medium disseminated through the celestial regions; and as there are other good reasons for believing this to be a *vera causa* (an actually existing antecedent), it has therefore been ascribed to such a resistance.

—SIR JOHN HERSCHEL, quoted by MILL in *A System of Logic*

5. It was not merely the amount of water in circulation which was influenced by temperature. . . . It was the total amount of haemoglobin. The mystery was: "Whence came this outpouring of haemoglobin?" It was not credible that the bone-marrow could have provided the body with new corpuscles at the rate required. Moreover, there was no evidence of increase of immature corpuscles in circulation. . . .

The question then was forced upon us: Has the body any considerable but hidden store of haemoglobin which can be drawn upon in case of emergency? . . . In searching for a locality which might fulfill such a condition one naturally seeks in the first instance for some place where the red blood corpuscles are outside the circulatory system—some backwater outside the arteries, capillaries, and veins. There is only one such place of any considerable size in the body—that place is the spleen.

—JOSEPH BARCROFT, *The Lancet,* February, 1925

5. ***Method of Concomitant Variation.*** At this point we may observe the common pattern which runs through all of the first four of Mill's Methods. In the Method of Agreement we eliminate as possible causes of a given phenomenon all those circumstances in whose absence the phenomenon can nevertheless occur, and the remaining circumstance is then inferred to be its cause. The essential character of that Method is thus seen to be eliminative. In the Method of Difference we exclude one of the circumstances which accompany a given phenomenon, while leaving the other circumstances the same. If the phenomenon is also removed thereby, we infer that the remaining circumstances can be eliminated as possible causes. Here we conclude that the one circumstance whose absence prevents the occurrence of the phenomenon in question is the cause of that phenomenon. The second Method also proceeds by elimination. The Joint Method of Agreement and Difference is easily shown to be essentially eliminative also, while the Method of Residues proceeds by eliminating as possible causes those antecedent circumstances whose effects have already been established by previous inductions.

There are situations, however, in which some circumstances cannot possibly be eliminated. Here none of the first four methods is applicable. One of Mill's own examples in discussing this problem concerns the cause of the phenomenon of the tides. We know that it is the gravitational attraction of the moon which causes the rise and fall of the tides, but this could not have been established by any of the first four Methods. The proximity of the moon at high tide is not the *only* circumstance present in all cases of high tide, for the fixed stars are also present, and cannot be eliminated. Nor can the moon be removed from the heavens for the sake of applying the Method of Difference. The Joint Method is inapplicable, as is the Method of Residues also. Of such situations, Mill writes:

> But we have still a resource. Though we can not exclude an antecedent altogether, we may be able to produce, or nature may produce for us some modification in it. By a modification is here meant, a change in it not amounting to its total removal. . . . We can not try an experiment in the absence of the moon, so as to observe what terrestrial phenomena her annihilation would put an end to; but when we find that all the variations in the *position* of the moon are followed by corresponding variations in the time and place of high water, the place being always either the part of the earth which is nearest to, or that which is most remote from, the moon, we have ample evidence that the moon is, wholly or partially, the cause which determines the tides.[17]

The argument here proceeds according to what Mill named the Method of Concomitant Variation. The general statement of this Method is:

> Whatever phenomenon varies in any manner whenever another phenomenon varies in some particular manner, is either a cause or an effect of that phenomenon, or is connected with it through some fact of causation.

If we use plus and minus signs to indicate the greater or lesser degree to which a varying phenomenon is present in a given situation, the Method of Concomitant Variation can be schematized as follows:

$$A\ B\ C \text{——} a\ b\ c$$
$$A^{+}\ B\ C \text{——} a^{+}\ b\ c$$
$$A^{-}\ B\ C \text{——} a^{-}\ b\ c$$

Therefore *A* and *a* are causally connected.

This method is very widely used. A farmer establishes that there is a causal connection between the application of fertilizer to his ground and the size of his crop by applying different amounts to different parts of his field and noting that the parts to which more fertilizer has been applied yield a more abundant harvest. A businessman verifies the efficacy of advertising by running larger and smaller advertisements at different intervals and noting that his business

[17] *A System of Logic* by John Stuart Mill. Book III, Chapter 8, § 6.

activity is increased during a period of intensive advertising. Here the phenomena are seen to vary *directly* with each other, that is, when one increases, the other increases also. However, the statement of the Method speaks of variation "in any manner," and in fact we infer a causal connection between phenomena which vary *inversely*, that is, phenomena such that when one increases the other *decreases*. Schematically, the Method of Concomitant Variation can also be represented as:

$A\ B\ C$——$a\ b\ c$
$A^+\ B\ C$——$a^-\ b\ c$
$A^-\ B\ C$——$a^+\ b\ c$

Therefore A and a are causally connected.

An example to illustrate this inverse variation is provided by economic phenomena: if the demand for a given type of goods remains constant, then any increase in the supply of those goods will be accompanied by a decrease in the price commanded by them. This concomitant variation is certainly part of the evidence for a causal connection between the supply and the price of a given commodity.

Mill's discussion of his own example is not altogether satisfactory. It may be objected that it is not the moon which is the cause of the tides, but the relative *position* of the moon. The moon itself is a circumstance which is never absent, but its occupation of this or that particular position is present only once every twenty-four hours, absent the rest of the time. Hence the Joint Method of Agreement and Difference is applicable to the situation and can perfectly well suffice to establish the causal connection between the position of the moon and the flow of the tides. The Method of Concomitant Variation is a new and important method, but its value was not adequately explained by Mill.

The other methods have an "all or nothing" character. Their use involves only the presence or absence of a given circumstance, the occurrence or nonoccurrence of a given phenomenon. Thus the first four methods permit only a limited kind of evidence to be adduced in favor of causal laws. The Method of Concomitant Variation utilizes our ability to observe changes in the degree to which circumstances and phenomena are present and admits a vastly greater amount of data as evidence for the presence of causal connections. Its chief virtue lies in admitting more evidence, for thereby the new method widens the range of inductive inference.

The Method of Concomitant Variation is important as the first *quantitative* method of inductive inference, the preceding ones having all been qualitative. Its use, therefore, presupposes the existence of some method of measuring or estimating—even if only roughly—the degrees to which phenomena vary.

EXERCISES

Analyze each of the following arguments in terms of the variation of "phenomena" to show that they follow the pattern of the Method of Concomitant Variation:

★ 1. In a *Harper's* article (October issue), the following observations on fuel-cancer relationships were attributed to Eugene J. Houdry, president of a firm that is developing a device for destroying harmful auto wastes: between 1940 and 1945 gasoline consumption in the United States dropped about 35 per cent because of wartime rationing, and in the same period lung cancer in U.S. white males dropped by approximately the same percentage; between 1914 and 1950 lung-cancer mortality increased nineteenfold and the rate of gasoline consumption also increased nineteenfold.

—*The New Yorker,* October 31, 1959

2. Careful studies have been made of the incidence of leukemia in the survivors of the atomic bomb burst over Hiroshima and Nagasaki. These survivors received exposures ranging from a few roentgens to 1000 roentgens or more.

They are divided into four groups. . . . The first group, A, consists of the estimated 1,870 survivors who were within 1 kilometer of the hypocenter (the point on the surface of the earth directly below the bomb when it exploded). There were very few survivors in this zone, and they received a large amount of radiation.

The second group, B, consists of the 13,730 survivors between 1.0 and 1.5 kilometers from the hypocenter, the third, C, of the 23,060 between 1.5 and 2.0 kilometers, and the fourth, D, of the 156,400 over 2.0 kilometers from the hypocenter.

The survivors of zones A, B, and C have been dying of leukemia during the period of careful study, the eight years from 1948 to 1955, at an average rate of about 9 per year . . . many more cases of leukemia occurred in the 15,600 survivors of zones A and B than in the 156,400 survivors of zone D, who received much less radiation. There is no doubt that the increased incidence is to be attributed to the exposure to radiation.

. . . The survivors of zone A received an estimated average of 650 roentgens, those of zone B, 250; those of zone C, 25, and of zone D, 2.5. . . . To within the reliability of the numbers, the incidence of leukemia in the three populations A, B, and C is proportional to the estimated dose of radiation, even for class C, in which the estimated dose is only 25 roentgens.

—LINUS PAULING, *No More War!*[18]

3. Effect of Moonlight on Insect Activity

It has been known to entomologists for many years that if a bright light is used for attracting insects at night, the catches are considerably higher near the period of new moon than near full moon. One of us (C. B. W.) showed that in three successive years, between May and October, the catches in a light trap, both of Lepidoptera alone and of all insects together (chiefly Diptera), reached a peak at, or shortly after, new moon, when the geometric mean catches were three to four times as great as those at full moon.

In spite of the fact that it is generally believed that other methods of catching are also poor at full moon, in the absence of any real evidence for this there was a distinct probability that the low catches in a light trap might be due to a lowered relative luminosity and hence a lowered attractiveness of the trap at full moon.

During the summer of 1950, we carried out continuous trapping of insects at night by means of a "suction-trap" which draws in the insects by a strong electric fan, and thus is in no way dependent on reaction to light. The insects so caught are mostly Diptera; but many other orders are present.

An analysis of five complete lunar cycles between July and November 1950 shows that the geometric mean catches in the four weeks, that is, three days on either side of (1) full moon, (2) last quarter, (3) new moon and (4) first quarter, were as follows:

204; 589; 1,259 and 562.

Each of these figures is the mean of thirty-five nights.

These results are slightly affected by accidental differences in temperature and wind on the different nights, and when a correction is made for these, the figures become:

240; 490; 1,175 and 589.

Thus the geometric mean catch in the new moon week is nearly five times that in the full moon week. As the records include nights with cloud as well as clear nights, the effect of full moon on a clear night must be greater than this.

Mr. Healy, of the Statistical Department at this station, informs me that the differences between full and new moon are significant at the 2 per cent level.

It appears, therefore, that the moonlight must have a definite effect on nocturnal insects, and that the low catches in a light trap at full

[18] Reprinted by permission of Dodd, Mead & Company from *No More War!* by Linus Pauling.

moon are not merely due to a physical reduction of the efficiency of the trap.

Further repetition and analysis will be carried out during the present year. In the meantime, we would be glad of any other evidence on this problem, particularly long series of night catches of insects by any technique not depending on attraction to light.

C. B. WILLIAMS
B. P. SINGH

Department of Entomology,
Rothamsted Experimental Station,
Harpenden.
Jan. 22.

—*Nature*[19]

4. Even as Banting was slaying dogs to save men, Evans was achieving a startling discovery in this field with another mysterious gland, *hypophysis cerebri,* commonly called the *pituitary*. This is a bit of an organ safely housed in a small pocket of bone attached to the base of the brain. Both Galen and Vesalius knew of this gland and thought it supplied the body with spit (in Latin, *sputus*). It is one of the most inaccessible glands in the living body. For many years, there appeared to be some connection between body growth and the functioning of this gland. In 1783 John Hunter had bargained with an undertaker for the body of an Irish giant of eight feet, four inches—Charles O'Brien, who had died at the age of twenty-two. The physician finally bought the body for twenty-five hundred dollars, and found a pituitary almost as large as a hen's egg. That of a normal adult man weighs hardly more than half a gram. A century later, *acromegaly,* an enlargement of the hands, feet, nose, lips, and jaw, was declared to be due to a tumor of the pituitary. The pituitary glands of dwarfs, some of them only eighteen inches high, all showed relatively small development or partial atrophy.

—BERNARD JAFFE, *Outposts of Science*[20]

5. First Douglass attempted to get records of rainfall of this district as far back as possible, to test the correlation of moisture and the thickness of tree rings. Fortunately, temperature and rainfall measurements had been made and recorded at Whipple Barracks to the south of Flagstaff since 1867, and they were made available for his study. Then, in January, 1904, he visited the lumber yards of the Arizona Lumber and Timber Company and spent hours in the snow measuring the rings of many of their oldest trees. The president of the company became interested in the singular pastime of this strange hybrid of astronomer and politician, and had sections cut from the ends of scores of logs and

[19] Reprinted from *Nature,* Vol. 167, No. 4256, May 26, 1951.

[20] *Outposts of Science* by Bernard Jaffe. Copyright, 1935, by Bernard Jaffe. Reprinted by permission of Simon and Schuster, Publishers.

stumps sent to Douglass for analysis. These pieces were carefully scraped with razor blades and brushed with kerosene for examination under the microscope. Every ring from the center of the tree to its bark was scrupulously scrutinized. To facilitate the dating of the rings, Douglass would make one pin prick to mark the last year of each decade, two to mark the middle year of each century, and three for the century year. Those cross sections which contained more than a thousand rings had an additional four pin pricks at the thousand-year tree-ring position. Douglass made tens of thousands of measurements, tabulated the data, drew curves and graphs, and as the average age of his trees was 348 years he was able to draw conclusions regarding the rainfall and tree-ring appearance of periods hundreds of years back.

Douglass found a striking correlation between tree growth and the recorded rainfall of the region. So accurate were his measurements and so apparently reliable his method that any marked peculiarity of any year could be identified with surprising ease and clarity in trees which often had grown more than four hundred miles apart. For example, the yellow pine ring of 1851 is small in trees which grew in regions between Santa Fe and Fresno because it represents a drought year. He could illustrate the accuracy of his technique in another way. He would pick out an old pine stump, study its rings, and then declare in what year the tree had been felled, much to the surprise of the owner of the land on which the tree had been cut. His tree time or "dendrochronology" was uncannily accurate.

—BERNARD JAFFE, *Outposts of Science*[21]

12.3 Criticisms of Mill's Methods

There are two general types of criticism that can be made of Mill's Methods. The first is that the Methods fail to fulfill the claims made for them by Bacon and Mill; the second is that the five Methods, as stated, do not constitute an adequate or complete account of scientific method. We shall discuss these criticisms separately. Before we can state and evaluate the first criticism, we must report the claims that have been made for these methods and explain the motivations for those claims.

It is a truism today that knowledge is power, that an understanding of natural laws and causal connections is needed for man to cope with his frequently hostile environment. Such understanding is not given to all men in the same degree. Beyond the more elementary cause-and-effect relations, such as those between fire and pain, or rainfall and harvest, the discovery of causal connections requires a

[21] Ibid.

rare and genuine insight. It is a sad truth, and like most sad truths, has often been denied. Devices have been sought which would permit *anyone* to discover causal connections, regardless of his natural aptitudes or lack of them. These Methods have been hailed as just such a device; Bacon himself wrote that:

> Our method of discovering the sciences is such as to leave little to the acuteness and strength of wit, and indeed rather to level wit and intellect. For as in the drawing of a straight line, or accurate circle by the hand, much depends on its steadiness and practice, but if a ruler or compass be employed there is little occasion for either; so it is with our method.[22]

This claim has certainly not been fulfilled. Scores of competent scientists have been working for decades to discover the cause of cancer (or the causes of the various types of cancer), and Bacon's "method"—Mill's Methods—have been used, but so far without success. There is no simple device or mechanical method for achieving scientific knowledge. In fact, the advance of empirical science has pushed the frontiers back so far that only those with the highest degree of "acuteness and strength of wit" can master enough of any field to approach the point from which new results can be sighted. Bacon's claim must be rejected as extravagant: his method simply cannot do what it is supposed to.

Mill himself made similar claims, regarding his Methods as adequate to serve two distinct functions. According to Mill, they are methods of *discovering* causal connections and also methods of *proving* or *demonstrating* the existence of particular causal connections. Mill's insistence upon the use of his Methods in discovering causals connections brought him into a long controversy with another nineteenth-century British philosopher, Dr. William Whewell, who minimized the value of Mill's Methods for discovery. In arguing against Whewell, Mill stated his view with great vigor, writing:

> . . . Dr. Whewell's argument, if good at all, is good against all inferences from experience. In saying that no discoveries were ever made by the . . . Methods, he affirms that none were ever made by observation and experiment; for assuredly if any were, it was by processes reducible to one or other of those methods.[23]

Mill was convinced further that his Methods permitted the *demonstration* of causal connections, writing that:

> The business of Inductive Logic is to provide rules and models (such as the Syllogism and its rules are for ratiocination) to which if inductive arguments

[22] *Novum Organum,* Vol. I, Section 61.
[23] *A System of Logic,* Book III, Chapter 9, § 6.

conform, those arguments are conclusive, and not otherwise. This is what the . . . Methods profess to be. . . .[24]

These are Mill's claims for his Methods: They are instruments for *discovery,* and they are rules for *proof.*

Let us examine first the doctrine that the Methods are instruments for discovery. We may begin with an example or two in which the scrupulous use of the Methods results in a more or less conspicuous failure to discover the cause of a given phenomenon. A favorite example used by critics of the Method of Agreement is the case of the Scientific Drinker, who was extremely fond of liquor and got drunk every night of the week. He was ruining his career and his health, and his few remaining friends pleaded with him to stop. Realizing himself that he could not go on, he resolved to conduct a careful experiment to discover the exact cause of his frequent inebriations. For five nights in a row he collected instances of the given phenomenon, the antecedent circumstances being respectively scotch and soda, bourdon and soda, brandy and soda, rum and soda, and gin and soda. Then using the Method of Agreement, he swore a solemn oath never to touch soda again!

Here is a case where the use of Mill's Method resulted in abysmal failure. The trouble here is not that the Method was not followed, for it was followed explicitly. The error, as we all can see, lay in a faulty analysis of the antecedent circumstances. Had the various liquors not been treated as so many different single circumstances but analyzed into their alcoholic contents plus their various other constituents, the Method of Agreement would have revealed, of course, that besides the soda, the alcohol too was a common circumstance, and then the Method of Difference would have sufficed to eliminate the soda and reveal the true cause. But how is one to know what kind of analysis to make of the antecedent circumstances? To make a correct analysis requires previous knowledge of causal laws, which must have been discovered by means other than Mill's Methods. Mill's Methods are not *sufficient* instruments for discovery, because their successful use requires a proper analysis of the factors of the antecedent circumstances, and the Methods themselves do not tell how to distinguish between a proper and an improper analysis.

Another objection to the use of Mill's Methods as sufficient instruments for discovery is illustrated by the following comment on an experiment which was interpreted as showing two things:

(a) frustration leads to aggression and (b) aggression which arises in a group with strong in-group feeling will be expressed against an out-group.

[24] Ibid.

> Thirty-one young men between the ages of eighteen and twenty years who worked in a camp were the subjects of this experiment. These young men looked forward to attending Bank Night in the theater in a nearby town, an event which was considered by them to be the most interesting one in the week. Interest in Bank Night was especially keen since one of them had won $200 the previous week. The conditions of the experiment were such, however, that the men missed this event. This then formed the frustrating circumstance. Instead of Bank Night there was "suddenly substituted" a "regime of testing." The tests were long and difficult.
>
> The 31 young men were called to the auditorium of the camp on the night in question. Without any forewarning as to what was in store for them, they were given a check list of twenty items pertaining to desirable and undesirable characteristics of two out-groups—Japanese and Mexicans. Half of the men rated the Japanese, the other half rated the Mexicans. The men were then given a series of tests which caused them to miss the truck to town. After the testing program, the half that rated the Japanese initially now rated the Mexicans, and likewise for the other half.
>
> The authors of the experiment concluded that the hypothesis that frustration leads to aggression was confirmed, because the young men became angry at the camp officials who ordered the tests and at the experimenters. With regard to the second hypothesis—that because of this aggression the men would rate the Japanese and Mexicans more unfavorably—the authors claim that the evidence pointed in the direction of confirming the hypothesis.
>
> From the point of view of the young men, the procedure of suddenly giving a series of long, difficult, and boring examinations when it was probably well known that the night in question was one of significance to them must have seemed unjust. Why not some other time? Do not their rights merit consideration by the camp officials in setting plans? The aggressiveness of these young men probably represents a reaction to an unfair situation rather than to the mere fact of a frustrating circumstance. In this case, aggression serves to maintain a sense of dignity or individuality.[25]

The structure of the argument criticized in the preceding passage is clearly that of the Method of Difference.[26] There are thirty-one instances *after* the truck to town had been missed, in which the antecedent circumstance was frustration and the phenomena were aggression and more unfavorable ratings given the out-groups. And there are thirty-one instances *before* the truck had left, in which the antecedent circumstances did not include frustration and the phenomena included neither aggression nor so unfavorable a rating for the out-groups. Schematically, with *A* denoting frustration, *B* denoting the presence of the thirty-one men taking the tests, *a* denoting the phenomena of aggression and more unfavorable ratings for the out-group, and *b* denoting the usual phenomena arising

[25] Reprinted from "A Neglected Factor in the Frustration-Aggression Hypothesis: A Comment" by Nicholas Pastore, in *The Journal of Psychology,* Volume 29 Second Half, April 1950.

[26] A more subtle analysis would show the Method of Concomitant Variation to be exemplified here also, but is not necessary for our purpose in this discussion.

when such tests are administered, the experiment can be represented as:

A B——*a b*
B——*b*

Therefore *A* causes *a*.

The criticism of this argument (regardless of whether one agrees or disagrees with the general point of view expressed) is perfectly straightforward. The preceding inference is unsound, according to the critic, because *a relevant factor was ignored*. The relevant factor which the experimenters ignored is characterized by their critic as *unfairness* or *injustice*. The suggestion seems implicit here that had the frustration been produced by natural or inevitable causes with which no human unfairness or injustice could be associated, neither aggression nor any lower ratings of out-groups would have occurred. Regardless of our own thoughts about the particular point at issue here, we should be able to see that the criticism is well taken. If a relevant circumstance is ignored, the Method of Difference is not properly applied; for according to its statement, that Method requires that the two or more instances "have every circumstance in common save one."

It should be realized that this criticism is different from the one leveled at the Method of Agreement. There the problem was the correct analysis of the instances into a proper set of distinct circumstances. Here the criticism turns on relevant factors or circumstances being *omitted* rather than improperly analyzed. The problem of relevance, to which our discussion of analogical argument had previously led, arises once again. The Methods cannot be used unless all relevant circumstances are taken into account. But circumstances do not come wearing neat little tags marked "relevant" and "irrelevant." Questions of relevance are questions about *causal connectedness*, and at least some of these must be answered *before* Mill's Methods can be used. Hence Mill's Methods cannot be *the* methods for discovering causal connections, for some causal connections must be known prior to any application of those Methods.

It may be objected that what Mill's Methods call for is a consideration of *all* circumstances, rather than just the relevant ones, so that questions of relevance need not arise in the use of the Methods. True enough, Mill's statements of his Methods read *all* rather than *all relevant* circumstances. But if Mill is taken quite literally here, the situation is made worse instead of better as far as the use of his Methods is concerned. Consider the Method of Agreement. In its application we must verify that two or more instances of a phenomenon have only *one* circumstance in common. But the number of circumstances common to any two physical objects is probably unlimited, no matter how different they may appear. In our earlier example, in which the instances were two students living in the same dormitory who suffered digestive disturbances on the same day, what circumstances might be common here? Presumably they both are students, each has two legs, both are over ten years old, each has a nose, both are over three feet tall, each weighs less than 400 pounds, and so on and on and on. It would be an unimaginative reasoner indeed who could ever stop and say that he had enumerated *all* common circumstances.

In the Method of Difference, two instances must "have every circumstance in common save one." Here the situation is even more hopeless, for it is extremely doubtful that *any* two things could differ in only one circumstance. Even of two peas in a pod, one must of necessity be either to the north or to the east or higher than the other, one must be closer to the stem, and it is highly probable that microscopic and chemical analysis would reveal many, many more differences between them. More devastating still is the fact that *all possible* circumstances in which they *might* differ must be examined to make sure that they do not differ in more than one of them before the Method of Difference can legitimately be applied. No, to interpret Mill literally here would make the Methods hopelessly inapplicable. The Methods must be understood as referring to *relevant* circumstances alone. When so understood, the previous criticism is inescapable, and we must conclude that Mill's Methods are not *the* methods for *discovering* causal laws.

So much for Mill's claim that the Methods are instruments for scientific discovery. Of his Methods Mill wrote:

> . . . but even if they were not methods of discovery, it would not be the less true that they are the sole methods of Proof. . . .[27]

Let us see whether or not this second claim is true. There are two reasons for denying that the Methods are *demonstrative.* In the first place, all of the Methods proceed on the basis of antecedent hypotheses about which circumstances are causally relevant to the phenomenon under investigation. Since not all circumstances can be considered, attention must be confined to those believed to be possible causes. This prior judgment is liable to error, and if it is mistaken, the conclusion inferred by Mill's Methods will be infected by that mistake. A variant of this same criticism has to do with

[27] Loc. cit.

the different ways in which even the relevant circumstances may be analyzed into separate factors. That analysis must be "correct" if the kind of mistake made by the Scientific Drinker is not to pervade all uses of Mill's Methods. Such analysis *must* be made prior to the use of the Methods, but since the analysis may be incorrect, the conclusion inferred may be incorrect also. This first criticism provides a strong reason for rejecting the claim that Mill's Methods are methods of proof or demonstration.

The second criticism is even more damaging. It applies most obviously, perhaps, to the Method of Concomitant Variation. It may well be the case that in a number—even a very large number—of observed instances of two phenomena they are seen to vary concomitantly. It might be the case, for example, that for a year or more the daily wind velocity in Chicago was found to vary with the birth rate in India. Such a correlation would generally be regarded as a mere coincidence rather than evidence of any causal connection between the two phenomena. Correlations, despite the great dependence of some of the social sciences upon them, are very often misleading. The danger of deception is attested by the common saying that there are three kinds of liars: liars, damn liars, and statistics. An observed correlation between two phenomena may be either a chance property peculiar to the *observed* instances, or it may be a regular, that is, lawful property of *all* instances of those phenomena. The greater the number of observed instances (and the greater the number of disanalogies among those instances), the higher the probability that the correlation is lawful rather than fortuitous. But no matter how great the number of observed instances, any inference from their properties to the properties of as yet unobserved instances will never be *certain*. It must be repeated that inductive inferences are never demonstrative.

This criticism applies with equal force to all of Mill's Methods. In the Method of Agreement, of all the circumstances explicitly taken into account, only one may accompany all the observed instances of the phenomenon under investigation. But the very next instance examined might *not* be accompanied by that circumstance. The greater the number of instances examined, the lower the probability of finding an exception; but so long as there are any unobserved instances, there is always the possibility that the inductive conclusion will be shown to be false by later investigation. The same remarks may be made of the Method of Difference, the Joint Method, and the Method of Residues. Moreover, since we rejected the possibility of a plurality of causes on the basis of arguments admitted to be at best merely probable, there is always the logical possibility that any particular phenomenon being investigated may have more than a single cause; if it has, none of the Methods will work. The plain fact is that there *is* a difference between deduction and induction. A valid deductive argument constitutes a proof or demonstration, but an inductive argument is at best highly probable. Therefore Mill's claim that his Methods are "methods of Proof" must be rejected along with his claim that they are "*the* methods of Discovery."

12.4 Vindication of Mill's Methods

The preceding criticisms are harsh; however, they were not directed against the Methods themselves, but rather against the too-extravagant claims made for them. Mill's Methods are more limited instruments than Bacon and Mill conceived them to be, but within those limits they are indispensable. This is shown by the following considerations.

Since it is absolutely impossible to take *all* circumstances into account, Mill's Methods can be used only in conjunction with the *hypothesis* that the circumstances mentioned are the only relevant ones. Such a hypothesis amounts to saying that the only possible causes are the circumstances listed. Every experimental investigation of the cause of a phenomenon begins with some such hypothesis. If we are investigating the cause of phenomenon *a,* we may begin with the hypothesis that either *A* or *B* or *C* or *D* or *E* or *F* or G is the cause of *a*. Then the following two instances:

A B C D——*a b c d*
A E F G——*a e f g*

which by the Method of Agreement yield the inductive conclusion that *A* is the cause of *a,* yield that conclusion *deductively,* that is, *validly, in the presence of the stated hypothesis as an additional premiss.* The way in which the deduction proceeds is very simple. If *G* is the cause of *a,* then *a* cannot occur in the absence of *G*. But the first instance is a case in which *a* does occur in the absence of *G*. Therefore G is not the cause of *a*. The first instance also shows that neither *E* nor *F* is the cause of *a,* while the second instance shows that neither *B* nor *C* nor *D* is the cause of *a*. From the two instances, then, we can infer that neither *B* nor *C* nor *D* nor *E* nor *F* nor *G* is the cause of *a,* and from this conclusion together with the original hypothesis, it follows validly that *A* is the cause of *a*. Although the Method of Agreement cannot be used without a hypothesis of the type indicated, in the presence of that hypothesis it provides us with a valid deductive argument.

Exactly similar remarks can be made with respect to the other Methods. If we are attempting to determine the cause of phenomenon *a* by the Method of Difference, we may begin with the hypothesis that either *A* or *B* is the cause of *a*. Our instances here may be:

$$A\ B\text{——}a\ b$$
$$B\text{——}b$$

from which the conclusion that *A* is the cause of *a* follows inductively by the Method of Difference. In the second instance, circumstance *B* occurs without phenomenon *a* being present, which shows that *B* is not the cause of *a*. But by hypothesis, either *A* is the cause of *a* or *B* is the cause of *a*, so it follows validly that *A* is the cause of *a*. In every case, Mill's Methods cannot be used unless some hypothesis is made about possible causes. But in every such case, where the hypothesis is explicitly added as a premiss, the use of the Methods provides a deductive, rather than a merely inductive, argument. The conclusion, however, is not deduced from the particular facts or instances alone but depends upon that additional premiss whose status is merely *hypothetical*. To gain a clearer insight into the type of argument which emerges here, we must examine the nature of these additional hypothetical premisses.

What was referred to in the preceding paragraph as *the* hypothesis that either *A* or *B* is the cause of *a* may with advantage be divided into *two* hypotheses: one, that *A* is the cause of *a*, the other, that *B* is the cause of *a*. Then we can apply the Method of Difference by setting up a situation in which circumstance *B* is present but not *A*. If the phenomenon *a* does not appear when this is done, we have refuted the second of the two hypotheses, and only the first remains. In Section 12.2 of the present chapter it was observed that Mill's Methods are essentially eliminative, for their applications serve in each case to show that some particular circumstance is *not* the cause of a given phenomenon. We can rephrase this account in terms of alternative hypotheses, where each hypothesis states that some different circumstance is the cause of the phenomenon under investigation. Mill's Methods now appear as instruments for testing hypotheses. Their statements describe the method of *controlled experiment,* which is an absolutely indispensable weapon in the arsenal of modern science. An example or two should suffice to make this fact clear.

In a famous experiment conducted in the spring of 1881, Pasteur put to the test his hypothesis that anthrax vaccination produces immunity to the disease. That hypothesis had been ridiculed by the veterinarians, and the experiment was performed publicly under the auspices of the Agricultural Society of Melun.[28] At the farm of Pouilly-le-Fort, twenty-four sheep, one goat, and several cattle were given Pasteur's vaccination against anthrax, while twenty-four other sheep, one goat, and several other cattle were left unvaccinated. These unvaccinated animals constituted the "control group," being instances which were assumed to differ from the first group in only the one circumstance *V* (vaccination). After the vaccinations had been properly administered,

> . . . on the fateful thirty-first of May all of the forty-eight sheep, two goats, and several cattle—those that were vaccinated and those to which nothing whatever had been done—all of these received a surely fatal dose of virulent anthrax bugs.[29]

Then on the second day of June, at two o'clock, when Pasteur and his assistants came to inspect the animals they found that:

> Not one of the twenty-four vaccinated sheep–though two days before millions of deadly germs had taken residence under their hides—not one of these sheep . . . had so much as a trace of fever. They ate and frisked about as if they had never been within a thousand miles of an anthrax bacillus.
>
> But the unprotected, the not vaccinated beasts—alas—there they lay in a tragic row, twenty-two out of twenty-four of them; and the remaining two were staggering about, at grips with that last inexorable, always victorious enemy of all living things. Ominous black blood oozed from their mouths and noses.
>
> "See! There goes another one of those sheep that Pasteur did not vaccinate!" shouted an awed horse doctor.[30]

The pattern of Pasteur's experiment is the Joint Method of Agreement and Difference, and may be analyzed as follows. Where the phenomenon in question is immunity to anthrax, the vaccinated animals constitute some thirty instances which agree in only the one relevant circumstance of having been vaccinated, although they all exhibit the phenomenon of immunity. From a consideration of these instances, the inference can be drawn that vaccination causes immunity, and this follows by the pattern of the Method of Agreement. The Method of Difference is also exemplified here. The infected animals which sickened and died constituted thirty-odd instances in which the phenomenon of immunity did *not* occur; the one respect in which they differed from the equal number of immune animals was the vaccination administered to the others but not to them. From these facts, by the Method of Difference, the

[28] As recounted by Paul de Kruif in *Microbe Hunters*. Copyright, 1926, by Harcourt, Brace and Company, Inc.

[29] Ibid., p. 161.

[30] Ibid., p. 162.

conclusion follows that Pasteur's vaccination does cause immunity. This account should make it clear that Mill's Methods do describe the general pattern of the modern scientific method of controlled experimentation.

It is obvious that the experiment *confirms* Pasteur's hypothesis. The newspaper reporter who was observing the experiment telegraphed his paper, the London *Times,* that "The experiment at Pouilly-le-Fort is a perfect, an unprecedented success."[31] The language used in his report was not too strong for the epoch-making event that it chronicled, but it was dangerously liable to misinterpretation. It must not be thought that the experiment was a "proof" or "demonstration" of the truth of Pasteur's hypothesis, in the sense of a valid deductive argument. It rendered it highly probable, but there still remains a possibility that what happened was fortuitous rather than a genuine instance of the causal law stated by Pasteur. This type of possibility is illustrated by another, somewhat simpler experiment in which Pasteur participated.

Several years prior to the experiment reported above, there had been

> . . . a great to-do about a cure for anthrax, invented by the horse doctor, Louvrier, in the Jura mountains in the east of France. Louvrier had cured hundreds of cows who were at death's door, said the influential men of the district: it was time that this treatment received scientific approval. . . .
>
> Pasteur arrived there, escorted by his young assistants, and found that this miraculous cure consisted first, in having several farm hands rub the sick cow violently to make her as hot as possible; then long gashes were cut in the poor beast's skin and into these cuts Louvrier poured turpentine; finally the now bellowing and deplorably maltreated cow was covered—excepting her face!—with an inch thick layer of unmentionable stuff soaked in hot vinegar. This ointment was kept on the animal—who now doubtless wished she were dead—by a cloth that covered her entire body.
>
> Pasteur said to Louvrier: "Let us make an experiment. All cows attacked by anthrax do not die, some of them just get better by themselves; there is only one way to find out, Doctor Louvrier, whether or no it is your treatment that saves them."
>
> So four good healthy cows were brought, and Pasteur in the presence of Louvrier and a solemn commission of farmers, shot a powerful dose of virulent anthrax microbes into the shoulder of each one of these beasts: this stuff would have surely killed a sheep, it was enough to do to death a few dozen guinea-pigs. The next day Pasteur and the commission and Louvrier returned, and all the cows had large feverish swellings on their shoulders, their breath came in snorts—they were in a bad way, that was very evident.
>
> "Now, Doctor," said Pasteur, "choose two of these sick cows—we'll call them A and B. Give them your new cure, and we'll leave cows C and D without any treatment at all." So Louvrier assaulted poor A and B with his villainous

[31] Ibid., p. 164.

treatment. The result was a terrible blow to the sincere would-be curer of cows, for one of the cows that Louvrier treated got better—but the other perished; and one of the creatures that had got no treatment at all, died—but the other got better.

"Even this experiment might have tricked us, Doctor," said Pasteur. "If you had given your treatment to cows A and D instead of A and B—we all would have thought you had really found a sovereign remedy for anthrax."[32]

This experiment involving four cows, two being given the alleged cure, the other two constituting the control group, served to refute the hypothesis that the horse doctor's treatment was a cure for anthrax. But Pasteur was right in remarking that had the cows been grouped differently, the experiment's results would have been deceptive. This remark emphasizes that the results of an experiment, even one which is carefully controlled and accords perfectly with Mill's Methods, are never demonstrative. A successful experiment (like Pasteur's own) *confirms* the hypothesis being tested, rendering it more probable, but never establishes its conclusion with *certainty*. Such qualifications are not intended to minimize the value of experimental investigation, but only to emphasize that its nature is inductive rather than deductive.

In concluding this chapter, we may summarize our discussion of Mill's Methods in these terms. Our need to control and understand the world in which we live leads us to search for causal connections between its various parts or aspects. Any assertion of a particular causal connection involves an element of generality, for to say that *C* is the cause of *E* is to say that *whenever* circumstance *C* occurs, *E* is sure to follow. Causal laws or general propositions are never *discovered* by Mill's Methods, nor are they ever established *demonstratively* by them. However, those Methods constitute the basic patterns for any attempt to confirm or disconfirm, by observation or experiment, a hypothesis asserting a causal connection. Experimental investigations cannot proceed without hypotheses, which are thus seen to play an all-important role in inductive logic. So important is the role of hypothesis in systematic empirical investigation that the formulation and testing of hypotheses can be regarded as *the* method of science. It is with science and hypothesis that our next chapter is concerned.

EXERCISES

Analyze each of the following arguments in terms of "circumstances" or "antecedents" and "phenomena," and indicate which of Mill's Methods are being used in each of them:

[32] Ibid., pp. 149–150.

★ 1. On August 23, 1948, individual tagged fruits of Rome Beauty apples and adjacent spur leaves were sprayed at the Plant Industry Station, Beltsville, Maryland, with aqueous solutions of 2, 4, 5–T at 10-, 100-, and 200-ppm concentrations. Fruits that received either the 100- or the 200-ppm spray concentration developed red coloration and were maturing rapidly by September 13. This same stage of maturity on unsprayed fruits was not attained until one month later, October 12, the usual harvest date for this variety. At 10-ppm concentration, the spray had no observable effect. Measurements on fruit softening were made on September 27 with the aid of a fruit pressure tester. At this time the untreated fruits showed an average pressure reading of 25.9 lb., whereas the fruits sprayed with 10-, 100-, and 200-ppm concentrations of 2, 4, 5–T tested 24.8, 19.8, and 18.9 lb., respectively.

—P. C. MARTH et al. in *Science*[33]

2. In the Spring of 1922, while the downy green of spring masked the discouragement of those Terra Ceia lands, Howell laid out his test plats: some with no tons of limestone; some with two tons to the acre; others with four; yet others with six—exactly as Hoffer had said. But he did more, did this Farmer Howell. Other little plats he laid out, with all the different amounts of limestone—from no tons to six tons per acre. But to each of *these* plats he added phosphate.

And to another set of little oblongs of ground, exactly like the first two, with more and more limestone, Howell added potash, crude sulphate of potash. . . .

Into all of them he sowed good seed of maize.

"I am testing the relative value of different fertilizer elements, both individually and collectively, in connection with lime and no lime," wrote Howell to Hoffer. Both individually and collectively—there he was at the very guts of science. . . .

Carefully Howell plowed each of these dozens of little plats of corn, the right number of times he cultivated them like the efficient farmer that he was; then he laid them by, and waited.

By late July he had the answer to his needs, the cure of the troubles of the tired Terra Ceia land. On the phosphate plats, and on the plats that had got phosphate and limestone, and on the land that had got limestone alone—even six tons to the acre of it!—there was sadness, there were broken-stalked, droop-shanked plants of maize with ears hanging down, chaffy, dejected.

But on every little plat where he'd put the potash, the corn trees shot up straight and strong. It was wonderful. Nearly as good these

[33] Reprinted from "Effect of 2,4,5-Trichlorophenoxyacetic Acid on Ripening of Apples and Peaches" by P. C. Marth, C. P. Harley, and A. L. Havis, in *Science,* Vol. III, No. 2883, March 31, 1950.

plants grew as if they were on the best black Iowa loam. It was potash that turned the trick—oh, no doubt of it. That stuck out like a sore thumb. "It has increased our yield from two hundred to three hundred percent," wrote Howell to Hoffer, in jubilation.

—PAUL DE KRUIF, *Hunger Fighters*[34]

3. About three years ago in the Carnegie Institution Laboratory at Cold Spring Harbor, N.Y., we were irradiating bacteria and the group of soil microorganisms known as the actinomycetes with ultraviolet light and X-rays. The purpose was to produce mutants with antibiotic activity. The radiation dose necessary to induce maximal mutation killed most of the cells (mutants were found among the few survivors). We noticed that when a culture of the actinomycete *Streptomyces griseus* was stored in the icebox for a few days after being irradiated with ultraviolet, the number of survivors would increase, sometimes as much as 10-fold. Some of the cells that had been thought "killed" had recovered.

Now a phenomenon similar to this had been observed a number of years before by Alexander Hollaender and Chester W. Emmons at the National Institute of Health. They had noticed that fungus spores irradiated with ultraviolet recovered after being stored in salt solution for several days. It was also known that X-rayed organisms sometimes partially recovered from radiation injury when they were kept cold after irradiation. It seemed to us that the phenomenon was eminently worth studying, because it might tell us something about the lethal and genetic effects of ultraviolet.

We set out to investigate more closely the possible role of temperature in the recovery of damaged cells. In an early experiment in this test we compared the survival rates of organisms (actinomycete spores) at icebox temperature and at room temperatures. After irradiation with large doses of ultraviolet, some suspensions of the spores were stored in the icebox at 5 degrees Centigrade and some in a glass bottle on a shelf in the laboratory. This produced a surprising result. While the organisms in the icebox showed the usual slight recovery (a 2- to 10-fold increase in survival), the survival rate of those stored at room temperatures increased 10,000 times!

Obviously cold *per se* had nothing to do with recovery. Indeed, it was a handicap. We began a systematic study of survival rates at various temperatures. There was considerable variation in the results of these experiments, even at the same temperature. We had stored some of the irradiated organisms in a thermostatically controlled water bath on a table in front of a window. The organisms in this bath consistently

34 Reprinted from *Hunger Fighters* by Paul de Kruif. Copyright, 1928, by Harcourt, Brace and Company, Inc.

showed high recovery rates. After a systematic study of various environmental factors that might be influencing recovery, we came to the conclusion that the recovery factor must be the light coming in the windows. We tested the light hypothesis by storing some irradiated spores in darkness and some in light. The result was clear-cut and conclusive. In the light there was a 10,000-fold increase in survival; in the dark there was none. The reason for the original observations—the recovery of organisms that had been stored in iceboxes or other places—was now plain: because of the extra handling they received, stored samples were generally exposed to more light than would otherwise have been the case.

—ALBERT KELNER, "Revival by Light"[35]

4. M. Arago, having suspended a magnetic needle by a silk thread, and set it in vibration, observed that it came much sooner to a state of rest when suspended over a plate of copper, than when no such plate was beneath it. Now, in both cases there were two *verae causae* (antecedents known to exist) why it *should* come at length to rest, viz., the resistance of the air, which opposes, and at length destroys, all motions performed in it; and the want of perfect mobility in the silk thread. But the effect of these causes being exactly known by the observation made in the absence of the copper, and being thus allowed for and subducted, a residual phenomenon appeared, in the fact that a retarding influence was exerted by the copper itself; and this fact, once ascertained, speedily led to the knowledge of an entirely new and unexpected class of relations.

—MILL, *A System of Logic,* Book III, Chapter 9, §5

★ 5. On the 31st of August, 1909, Paul Ehrlich and Hata stood before a cage in which sat an excellent buck rabbit. Flourishing in every way was this rabbit, excepting for the tender skin of his scrotum, which was disfigured with two terrible ulcers, each bigger than a twenty-five-cent piece. These sores were caused by the gnawing of the pale spirochete of the disease that is the reward of sin. They had been put under the skin of that rabbit by S. Hata a month before. Under the microscope—it was a special one built for spying just such a thin rogue as that pale microbe—under this lens Hata put a wee drop of the fluid from these ugly sores. Against the blackness of the dark field of this special microscope, gleaming in a powerful beam of light that hit them sidewise, shooting backwards and forwards like ten thousand silver drills and augers, played myriads of these pale spirochetes. It was a pretty picture, to hold you there for hours, but it was sinister—for what living things can bring worse plague and sorrow to men?

[35] Reprinted from "Revival by Light" by Albert Kelner in *Scientific American,* Vol. 184, No. 5, May 1951.

Hata leaned aside. Paul Ehrlich looked down the shiny tube. Then he looked at Hata, and then at the rabbit.

"Make the injection," said Paul Ehrlich. And into the ear-vein of that rabbit went the clear yellow fluid of the solution of 606, for the first time to do battle with the disease of the loathsome name.

Next day there was not one of those spiral devils to be found in the scrotum of that rabbit. His ulcers? They were drying already! Good clean scabs were forming on them. In less than a month there was nothing to be seen but tiny scabs—it was like a cure of Bible times—no less! And a little while after that Paul Ehrlich could write:

"It is evident from these experiments that, if a large enough dose is given, the spirochetes can be destroyed *absolutely and immediately with a single injection!*"

—PAUL DE KRUIF, *Microbe Hunters*[36]

6. It has long been assumed that a diet low in saturated fats (meaning mostly animal fats) can reduce the risk of cardiovascular disease. Direct evidence for this assumption, however, has been scarce. Such evidence is now provided by a study made at a veterans' hospital in Los Angeles. The study shows that the incidence of cardiovascular disease in a group of 424 veterans with a diet high in unsaturated fats for eight years was 31.3 percent, whereas a control group of 422 men with a normal diet high in saturated fats had a cardiovascular disease rate of 47.7 percent.

—"Science and the Citizen," *Scientific American*[37]

7. Experiments which demonstrate the sense of smell are similar to those on color vision. First, it is necessary to determine if the insects react to odors. Sugar water is placed in small boxes, and, after bees have found them and are making trips to and from the hive, the box is substituted by one just like it, also containing sugar water, but sprinkled inside with flower extract. After the bees have made sufficient trips to get used to the scent, several new unscented boxes are placed beside a new scented one. When the bees return for more sugar, they buzz about the openings of the boxes but finally go inside the scented one. Further, when they are trained to go to one odor—say rose—they will not go to another, such as lavender. That the sense organs are on the antennas is shown by removing parts or all of the antennas from bees trained to certain scented boxes. When the last eight segments are removed from each antenna, the bees cannot distinguish odors. That this result is not due to the shock of the operation is proved by a control experiment in which some bees are first trained to visit blue boxes for sugar water.

[36] Reprinted from *Microbe Hunters* by Paul de Kruif. Copyright, 1926, by Harcourt, Brace and Company, Inc.

[37] Reprinted from "Science and the Citizen" in *Scientic American,* Vol. 221, No. 3, September 1969.

Then their antennas are removed, and it is found that they still return to the correct boxes.

—RALPH BUCHSBAUM, *Animals Without Backbones*[38]

8. . . . McLarty had reasoned that these physiological disorders were most probably caused by some mineral deficiency or mineral unbalance within the trees. Following up this line of reasoning, he injected severely affected apple trees with some thirty different chemicals. In these experiments, the dry test material was packed in holes drilled into the trunks of the trees. The holes were about one-half inch in diameter and two inches deep. After having been filled the holes were sealed with a commercial grafting compound. The dry materials were used because of the convenience of handling and also because greater amounts could be used without injury to the foliage. The following year the crop of two of the injected trees was practically free of the disorders, and it was noted that one of these trees had been injected with boric acid and the other with manganese borate. The trees injected with manganese compounds, other than the borate, showed no change. Following up this lead, forty trees were injected with either boric acid or borax in the fall of 1934. In the summer of 1935 every tree that had been injected the previous fall showed none of the diseases or a very low incidence of them. Because of the great economic losses which many of the growers were suffering that year, the committee decided that it was well worthwhile to make an immediate recommendation that all affected trees be injected with boric acid crystals. . . .

—C. G. WOODBRIDGE, in *Scientific Monthly*[39]

9. Over in Denmark Johannes Fibiger, a pathologist of the University of Copenhagen, had been working thirteen years on the problem of tuberculosis among laboratory animals. During a series of postmortem examinations of tubercular rats, he found three had suffered from stomach cancers. Fibiger knew enough about cancer to realize that he had come across a singular phenomenon. Rats rarely suffered from tumors of the stomach.

Fibiger made a visit to the dealer who had been supplying him with these rats, and on questioning found that those sent to his laboratory had all come from a sugar refinery. Was there anything peculiar about this refinery which could account for the unusually large percentage of stomach-cancerous rats from this spot? He investigated the place

[38] By permission from *Animals Without Backbones* by Ralph Buchsbaum, University of Chicago Press. Copyright 1938 by the University of Chicago.

[39] Reprinted from "The Role of Boron in the Agricultural Regions of the Pacific Northwest" by C. G. Woodbridge, in *The Scientific Monthly,* Vol. LXX, No. 2, February 1950.

and found nothing unusual except a high infestation with cockroaches, which formed a fairly large part of the diet of its rats. Could he find some connection between roaches, rats, and cancer? Cancer as a disease of filth had been spoken about for years, and vermin were said to be responsible for the so-called "cancer houses," private homes from which emerged many a human cancer victim of the same family.

Fibiger planned a controlled experiment. He collected thousands of the refinery roaches and fed them to rats from another breeding establishment. The rats enjoyed this strange treatment, and for three years—that was the normal life span of his rodents—Fibiger remained skeptical. Then they died, and one by one he opened them up. To his astonishment, he found many stomach cancers. Fibiger made a careful microscopic study of the growths. He discovered that in every case they had formed around a parasitic worm, the same worm to which the roach had been host before it was fed to the rat. The larva of the worm coiled up in the muscles of the rat, later developing into an adult worm in the animal's stomach. Around this the tumorous growth had appeared. Fibiger had actually for the first time produced artificial cancer in a laboratory animal.

—BERNARD JAFFE, *Outposts of Science*[40]

★ 10. One of the procedures which showed a high correlation with ulcers involved training the monkeys to avoid an electric shock by pressing a lever. The animal received a brief shock on the feet at regular intervals, say, every 20 seconds. It could avoid the shock if it learned to press the lever at least once in every 20-second interval. It does not take a monkey very long to master this problem; within a short time it is pressing the lever far oftener than once in 20 seconds. Only occasionally does it slow down enough to receive a shock as a reminder.

One possibility, of course, was that the monkeys which had developed ulcers under this procedure had done so not because of the psychological stress involved but rather as a cumulative result of the shocks. To test this possibility we set up a controlled experiment, using two monkeys in "yoked chairs" in which both monkeys received shocks but only one monkey could prevent them. The experimental or "executive" monkey could prevent shocks to himself and his partner by pressing the lever; the control monkey's lever was a dummy. Thus both animals were subjected to the same physical stress (i.e., both received the same number of shocks at the same time), but only the "executive" monkey was under the psychological stress of having to press the lever.

We placed the monkeys on a continuous schedule of alternate periods

40 *Outposts of Science* by Bernard Jaffe. Copyright, 1935, by Bernard Jaffe. Reprinted by permission of Simon and Schuster, Publishers.

of shock-avoidance and rest, arbitrarily choosing an interval of six hours for each period. As a cue for the executive monkey we provided a red light which was turned on during the avoidance periods and turned off during the "off" hours. The animal soon learned to press its lever at a rate averaging between 15 and 20 times a minute during the avoidance periods, and to stop pressing the lever when the red light was turned off. These responses showed no change throughout the experiment. The control monkey at first pressed the lever sporadically during both the avoidance and rest sessions, but lost interest in the lever within a few days.

After 23 days of a continuous six-hours-on, six-hours-off schedule the executive monkey died during one of the avoidance sessions. Our only advance warning had been the animal's failure to eat on the preceding day. It had lost no weight during the experiment, and it pressed the lever at an unflagging rate through the first two hours of its last avoidance session. Then it suddenly collapsed and had to be sacrificed. An autopsy revealed a large perforation in the wall of the duodenum —the upper part of the small intestine near its junction with the stomach, and a common site of ulcers in man. Microscopic analysis revealed both acute and chronic inflammation around this lesion. The control monkey, sacrificed in good health a few hours later, showed no gastrointestinal abnormalities. A second experiment using precisely the same procedure produced much the same results. This time the executive monkey developed ulcers in both the stomach and the duodenum; the control animal was again unaffected.

—JOSEPH V. BRADY, "Ulcers in 'Executive' Monkeys"[41]

11. The commissioners are convinced that many more inmates should be paroled. For prison experience unquestionably boosts the chance that an offender will break the law again. In one experiment, conducted by The California Youth Authority, a group of convicted juvenile delinquents were given immediate parole and returned to their homes or foster homes, where they got intensive care from community parole officers. After five years, only 28% of this experimental group have had their paroles revoked, compared to 52% of a comparable group that was locked up after conviction.

—*Time* Essay: "Crime & The Great Society" *Time,* March 24, 1967, p. 21

12. It was Wolfgang Pauli who in 1930 postulated the existence of the neutrino in order to reconcile an apparent contradiction between

[41] Reprinted from "Ulcers in 'Executive' Monkeys" by Joseph V. Brady in *Scientific American,* Vol. 199, No. 4, October 1958.

the quantum-mechanical model of the phenomenon of nuclear beta decay and the observed products of this decay. (The term "beta decay" is used by physicists to describe the spontaneous transformation of a neutron in an unstable atomic nucleus into a proton and an electron; it is also applied to the transformation of a proton into a neutron and a positron, or positive electron.) When experimenters measured the total energy of the nuclear system both before and after beta decay, they invariably found a discrepancy in the energy budget. The observed products of the reaction not only varied in total energy from measurement to measurement: they were poorer in energy than the original nuclear system. Faced with the disturbing alternative of declaring a failure in the law of the conservation of energy, Pauli was moved to suggest a less radical solution, namely to postulate the existence of an unobserved particle that carries away the missing energy.[42]

13. A series of tests carried out by the Federal Aviation Agency has substantiated the common complaint of air travelers that swift transition through several time zones disturbs their bodily and even their mental functions. The tests may result in changes of schedule for the crews on certain types of international flight. Moreover, the tests have implications for the proposal to build supersonic airplanes that would travel even faster than today's jets.

The tests involved healthy male volunteers, who were carried by jet airplane from the U.S. to such cities as Tokyo, Manila and Rome, passing through as many as 10 time zones. As a control to make sure that the effects resulted from changes of times and not merely from jet travel, there was a flight from Washington, D.C., to Santiago, Chile; it covered a long distance but was all in the same time zone. On the outbound flights that crossed a number of time zones the passengers underwent physiological changes—in heart rate, temperature and perspiration—that persisted for several days. They also showed a deterioration, for about a day, in mental acuity as indicated by difficulty in doing simple problems in arithmetic and by slowed responses to sensory stimuli. Similar effects appeared on the return trips but did not last as long. In contrast, the flight to Chile produced only a sense of fatigue.

The F.A.A. plans to give the tests to some pilots on the New York–Rome run in March. Sheldon Freud, an Air Force psychologist who has worked on the testing, said that the reaction of the passengers made it important to test the crews. "These men are responsible for the lives of millions of passengers every year," he said. Freud also raised a question about supersonic flights, which will be at least twice as fast as today's jet

[42] Reprinted from "Neutrinos from the Atmosphere and Beyond" by Frederick Reines and J. P. F. Sellschop in *Scientific American,* Vol. 214, No. 2, February, 1966.

flights: "Will we have to rest twice as long afterward? Is it worthwhile getting over there in such a hurry?"[43]

14. Aristotle believed a moving object could continue in motion only as long as something moved it. In the case of a projectile, air displaced by compression in front of the object came around behind it and pushed it along. The new medieval theory of "impetus" insisted that a moving object continues to move until it is stopped by resistance: air has nothing to do with motion except insofar as it is a cause of friction. The anti-Aristotelian scientists of the 14th century used the rotary grindstone (a device that, as we have seen, was unknown to Aristotle) as a favorite nonspeculative proof of their position. The grindstone still turned for a time after the grinder's hand left the crank, but its motion, unlike the motion of a traveling projectile, displaced no air. Therefore the grindstone moved not by pressure of air but by impetus until the resistance of friction at the axle stopped it.

—LYNN WHITE, JR., "Medieval Uses of Air"[44]

15. It is not hard to demonstrate the key role that the love song plays in mating. Remove the male fly's wings and he will court with the same persistence as before, but his courtship is seldom successful. It is apparent that the male's wing display, at least, is a prerequisite to mating. Indeed, one species (D. obscura) sings no song and courts only by means of a silent wing display. This, however, is one of the few fruit fly species that will not mate in the dark. Since most species breed successfully at night, one must conclude that visual display alone is not enough to win female acceptance. The importance of sound to the female is also easy to demonstrate. Our colleague A. W. G. Manning has shown that when the antennae of a sexually responsive female are immobilized with glue, she ceases to be receptive.

—H. C. BENNET-CLARK and A. W. EWING,
"The Love Song of the Fruit Fly"[45]

16. Effectiveness in the prevention of dental decay by the use of fluoride is well accepted. However, in many parts of the world resistance to fluoridation of water supplies or the absence of a public water supply prevents the administration of this treatment. The addition of fluoride to a daily administered (by drop) solution of vitamins has been suggested as an alternate method.

[43] Reprinted from "Science and the Citizen" in *Scientific American,* Vol. 214, No. 2, February, 1966.

[44] Reprinted from "Medieval Uses of Air" by Lynn White, Jr., in *Scientific American,* Vol. 223, No. 2, August 1970.

[45] Reprinted from "The Love Song of the Fruit Fly" by H. C. Bennet-Clark and A. W. Ewing in *Scientific American,* Vol. 223, No. 1, July 1970.

Working in Stockholm through city child welfare centers, which are attended by about 85 percent of the city's children, Dr. Lennart Hamberg has conducted a study on the effectiveness of the addition of sodium fluoride to a solution of vitamin A and D drops. His findings are reported in the Feb. 27 LANCET. Of 705 children taking part in the experiment, 342 received the fluoride treatment and 363 were in a control group. All the children received yearly examinations from the time of their first birthday. After six years the fluoride group had up to 57 percent fewer decayed teeth.

Dr. Hamberg, of the department of pediatrics at the Karolinska Hospital in Stockholm, states that the simplicity, inexpensiveness and optional character of this method combine to make it far superior to all previous forms of fluoridation.

—*Science News,* Vol. 99, March 20, 1971

17. One of the arguments surrounding those weirdies of the botanical world, the carnivorous plants (such as the Venus flytrap), is whether in fact they digest their insect prey themselves. Digestion has seemed too "animal-like" to some botanists, who have proposed instead that, since the dead insects (or small animals) are quickly decomposed by bacteria and small fungi in any case, the plant itself is a mere parasite feeding on the products of microbes who really do the work of digesting the hapless insects.

The main purpose of the plant's carnivory is to obtain a source of nitrogen with which to make its protein. Such plants are usually found growing on soils that are poor in minerals, especially nitrogen, and the insects are a useful supplement to their diet. But before it can obtain nitrogen, in the useful form of amino acids all ready to build up again into the plant's own protein, the animal's protein must be broken down to amino acids by protein-digesting enzymes. To find out whether these enzymes come from the plant or from microbes, Dr. Ulich Lüttge . . . studied the carnivorous plant *Nepthenes,* or Pitcher leaf.

As its name implies, the insect-catching apparatus of the plant is a leaf rolled up to form a pitcher-like vessel. Animals are attracted by the mottled colour of the 'urn' and by the excretion of nectar from glands on its very smooth margin. They alight on this margin, slip and fall into a sap, containing digestive enzymes, in the base of the trap. They drown and are digested.

Dr. Lüttge took a young pitcher, still closed by a lid, and which could safely be said to be free of microbes. He removed some of the sap from within the pitcher with a syringe, introduced the sap into a protein solution and showed, by ultraviolet spectrophotometry, that the sap indeed contains protein-digesting enzymes.

Other enzymes were found in the sap from mature and open pitchers which did come from microbes, since they only occur in pitchers containing the remains of insects and small animals infested by microbes. They are absent in a sterile secretion and on sterile feeding. So although the plant does derive some benefit from microbes which help by a form of predigestion, this is only an additional aid, and the plant can quite well digest its prey without it.

—"Meat-Eating Plant Digests Unaided," *New Scientist,* April 27, 1967

Chapter 13
Science and Hypothesis

. . . every work of science great enough to be remembered for a few generations affords some exemplification of the defective state of the art of reasoning of the time when it was written; and each chief step in science has been a lesson in logic.

—*Charles Sanders Peirce*

13.1 The Values of Science

Modern science came into existence only a few hundred years ago. Yet it has profoundly changed almost every aspect of life in the Western world. Improvements in farming and manufacturing, in communication and transportation, in health and hygiene, and in our standard of living generally, have all resulted from the application of scientific knowledge. Steam and water power have been harnessed to run our machinery. Waterways have been diverted to turn deserts into vineyards. These are but a few of the beneficent uses of science as a tool for ameliorating a hostile environment.

Some of the practical results of science, of course, are not so cheerful. The tremendous increase in the destructive power of weapons has made the risk of nuclear war a menace to civilization itself. And the very habitability of our planet is increasingly threatened by industrial, chemical, and automotive pollution. Yet, despite these unhappy aspects of scientific achievement, on the whole the development of science and its applications have benefited mankind. Terrible as recent wars have been, their toll of human life would seem to be much less than that of the great plagues which formerly swept over Europe, decimating the population. And those plagues have been almost completely wiped out by modern medical science. The *practical* value of science lies in the easier and more abundant life made possible by technological advances based on scientific knowledge.

Its applications are not the only value of science, however. Science is knowledge and thus an end in itself. The laws and principles discovered in scientific investigation have a value apart from any narrow utility they may possess. This intrinsic value is the satisfaction of curiosity, the fulfillment of the desire to know. That human beings have such a desire has long been recognized. Aristotle wrote that: ". . . to be learning something is the greatest of pleasures not only to the philosopher but also to the rest of mankind, however small their capacity for it. . . ."[1] If we consult one of the most distinguished of modern scientists, Albert Einstein, we are told that: "There exists a passion for comprehension, just as there exists a passion for music. That passion is rather common in children, but gets lost in most people later on. Without this passion, there would be neither mathematics nor natural science."[2] Scientific knowledge does not merely give us power to satisfy our practical needs; it is itself a direct satisfaction of a particular desire, the desire to know.

Some philosophers, to be sure, have denied the second of these values. They have challenged the notion of a purely disinterested desire for knowledge. Men have only practical wants, they have said, and science is simply an instrument to be used for the control of nature. There can be no doubt that its utility has profoundly stimulated the development of science. But when the great contributors to scientific progress are consulted about their own motives for research, their answers seldom mention this pragmatic or engineering aspect. Most answers to such questions are like that of Einstein: "What, then, impels us to devise theory after theory? Why do we devise theories at all? The answer to the latter question is simply: because we enjoy 'comprehending,' i.e., reducing phenomena by the process of logic to something already known or (apparently) evident."[3] These remarks of Einstein suggest a very fruitful conception of the nature of science.

The job of science, we all know, is to discover facts; but a haphazard collection of facts cannot be said to constitute a science. To

[1] *Poetics,* 1448b 14.

[2] Reprinted from "On the Generalized Theory of Gravitation" by Albert Einstein, in *Scientific American,* Vol. 182, No. 4, April 1950.

[3] Ibid.

be sure, some parts of science may focus on this or that particular fact. A geographer, for example, may be interested in the exact configuration of a particular coastline, or a geologist in the rock strata in a particular locality. But in the more advanced sciences, bare descriptive knowledge of this or that particular fact is of little importance. The scientist is eager to search out more general truths, of which particular facts are instances and for which they constitute evidence. Isolated particular facts may be known—in a sense—by direct observation. That a particular released object falls, that this ball moves more slowly down an inclined plane than it did when dropped directly downwards, that the tides ebb and flow, all these are matters of fact open to direct inspection. But the scientist seeks more than a mere record of such phenomena; he strives to *understand* them. To this end he seeks to formulate general laws which state the patterns of all such occurrences and the systematic relationships between them. The scientist searches for natural laws governing particular events and the fundamental principles which underlie them.

This preliminary exposition of the theoretical aims of science can perhaps be made clearer by means of an example. By careful observation, and the application of geometrical reasoning to the data thus collected, the Italian physicist and astronomer Galileo (1564–1642) succeeded in formulating the laws of falling bodies, which gave a very general description of the behavior of bodies near the surface of the earth. At about the same time the German astronomer Kepler (1571–1630), basing his reasonings very largely on the astronomical data collected by Denmark's Tycho Brahe (1546–1601), formulated the laws of planetary motion describing the elliptical orbits traveled by the planets around the sun. Each of these two great scientists succeeded in unifying the various phenomena in his own field of investigation by formulating the interrelations between them: Kepler in celestial mechanics, Galileo in terrestrial mechanics. Their discoveries were great achievements, but they were, after all, separate and isolated. Just as separate particular facts challenge the scientist to unify and explain them by discovering their lawful connections, so a plurality of general laws challenges the scientist to unify and explain *them* by discovering a still more general principle which subsumes the several laws as special cases. In the case of Kepler's and Galileo's laws, this challenge was met by one of the greatest scientific geniuses of all time, Sir Isaac Newton (1642–1727). By his Theory of Gravitation and his three Laws of Motion, Newton unified and explained celestial and terrestrial mechanics, showing them both to be deducible within the framework of a single more fundamental *theory*. The scientist seeks not merely to know what the facts are, but to explain them, and to this end he devises *theories.* To understand exactly what is involved here, we must consider the general nature of explanation itself.

13.2 Explanations: Scientific and Unscientific

In everyday life it is the unusual or startling for which we demand explanations. An office boy may arrive at work on time every morning and no curiosity will be aroused. But let him come an hour late one day, and his employer will demand an *explanation.* What is it that is wanted when an explanation for something is requested? An example will help to answer this question. The office boy might reply that he had taken the seven-thirty bus to work as usual, but the bus had been involved in a traffic accident which entailed considerable delay. In the absence of any other transportation, the boy had had to wait a full hour for the bus to be repaired. This account would probably be accepted as a satisfactory explanation. It can be so regarded because from the statements which constitute the explanation the fact to be explained follows logically and no longer appears puzzling. An explanation is a group of statements or a story from which the thing to be explained can logically be inferred and whose assumption removes or diminishes its problematic or puzzling character. Of course the inference of the fact as conclusion from the explanation as premiss might have to be enthymematic, where the "understood" additional premisses may be generally accepted causal laws,[4] or the conclusion may follow with probability rather than deductively. It thus appears that explanation and inference are very closely related. They are, in fact, the same process regarded from opposite points of view. Given certain premisses, any conclusion which can logically be inferred from them can be regarded as being explained by them. And given a fact to be explained, we say that we have found an explanation for it when we have found a set of premisses from which it can logically be inferred. As was indicated in our first chapter,[5] *Q because P* can express either an argument or an explanation.

Of course some proposed explanations are better than others. The chief criterion for evaluating explanations is *relevance.* If the tardy office boy had offered as explanation for his late arrival the fact that there is a war in China or a famine in India, that would properly be regarded as a very poor explanation, or rather as "no explanation at all." Such a story would have "nothing to do with the case"; it would be *irrelevant,* because from it the fact to be explained *cannot*

[4] This complication will be considered further in Section VI, but for the present it can be ignored.

[5] Cf. pp. 19–20.

be inferred. The relevance of a proposed explanation, then, corresponds exactly to the cogency of the argument by which the fact to be explained is inferred from the proposed explanation. Any acceptable explanation must be relevant, but not all stories which are relevant in this sense are acceptable explanations. There are other criteria for deciding the worth or acceptability of proposed explanations.

The most obvious requirement to propose is that the explanation be *true*. In the example of the office boy's lateness, the crucial part of his explanation was a particular fact, the traffic accident, of which he was allegedly an eye witness. But the explanations of science are for the most part *general* rather than particular. The keystone of Newtonian Mechanics is the Law of Universal Gravitation, whose statement is:

> Every particle of matter in the universe attracts every other particle with a force which is directly proportional to the product of the masses of the particles and inversely proportional to the square of the distance between them.

Newton's law is not directly verifiable in the same way that a bus accident is at the time it occurs. There is simply no way in which we can inspect *all* particles of matter in the universe and observe that they do attract each other in precisely the way that Newton's law asserts. Few propositions of science are *directly* verifiable as true. In fact, none of the important ones are. For the most part they concern *unobservable* entities, such as molecules and atoms, electrons and protons, and the like. Hence the proposed requirement of truth is not *directly* applicable to most scientific explanations. Before considering more useful criteria for evaluating scientific theories, it will be helpful to compare scientific with unscientific explanations.

Science is supposed to be concerned with facts, and yet in its further reaches we find it apparently committed to highly speculative notions far removed from the possibility of direct experience. How then are scientific explanations to be distinguished from those which are frankly mythological or superstitious? An unscientific "explanation" of the regular motions of the planets was the doctrine that each heavenly body was the abode of an "Intelligence" or "Spirit" which controlled its movement. A certain humorous currency was achieved during World War II by the unscientific explanation of certain aircraft failures as being due to "gremlins," which were said to be invisible but mischievous little men who played pranks on aviators. The point to note here is that from the point of view of observability and direct verifiability, there is no great difference between modern scientific theories and the unscientific doctrines of mythology or theology. One can no more see or touch a Newtonian "particle," an atom, or electron, than an "intelligence" or a "gremlin." What, then, are the differences between scientific and unscientific explanations?

There are two important and closely related differences between the kind of explanation sought by science and the kind provided by superstitions of various sorts. The first significant difference lies in the attitudes taken toward the explanations in question. The typical attitude of one who really *accepts* an unscientific explanation is *dogmatic*. What he accepts is regarded as being absolutely true and beyond all possibility of improvement or correction. During the Middle Ages and the early modern period, the word of Aristotle was the ultimate authority to which scholars appealed for deciding questions of fact. However empirically and open-mindedly Aristotle himself may have arrived at his views, they were accepted by some schoolmen in a completely different and unscientific spirit. One of the schoolmen to whom Galileo offered his telescope to view the newly discovered moons of Jupiter declined to look, being convinced that none could possibly be seen because no mention of them could be found in Aristotle's treatise on astronomy! Because unscientific beliefs are absolute, ultimate, and final, within the framework of any such doctrine or dogma there can be no rational method of ever considering the question of its truth. The scientist's attitude toward his explanations is altogether different. Every explanation in science is put forward tentatively and provisionally. Any proposed explanation is regarded as a mere hypothesis, more or less probable on the basis of the available facts or relevant evidence. It must be admitted that the scientist's vocabulary is a little misleading on this point. When what was first suggested as a "hypothesis" becomes well confirmed, it is frequently elevated to the position of a "theory." And when, on the basis of a great mass of evidence, it achieves well-nigh universal acceptance, it is promoted to the lofty status of a "law." This terminology is not always strictly adhered to: Newton's discovery is still called the "Law of Gravitation," while Einstein's contribution, which supersedes or at least improves on Newton's, is referred to as the "Theory of Relativity." The vocabulary of "hypothesis," "theory," and "law" is unfortunate, since it obscures the important fact that *all* of the general propositions of science are regarded as hypotheses, never as dogmas.

Closely allied with the difference in the way they are regarded is the second and more fundamental difference between scientific and unscientific explanations or theories. This second difference lies in the basis for accepting or rejecting the view in question. Many unscientific views are mere prejudices, which their adherents could scarcely give any reason for holding. Since they are regarded as "certain," however, any challenge or question is likely to be regarded as an affront and met with abuse. If one who accepts an unscientific explanation *can* be persuaded to discuss the basis for its acceptance, there are only a few grounds on which he will attempt to "defend" it. It is true because "we've always believed it," or because "everyone knows it." These all too familiar phrases express appeals to tradition or popularity rather than evidence. Or a questioned dogma may be defended on the grounds of revelation or authority. The absolute truth of their religious creeds and the absolute falsehood of all others have been revealed from on high, at various times, to Moses, to Paul, to Mohammed, to Joseph Smith, and to many others. That there are rival traditions, conflicting authorities, and revelations which contradict one another does not seem disturbing to those who have embraced an absolute creed. In general, unscientific beliefs are held independently of anything we should regard as *evidence* in their favor. Because they are *absolute,* questions of evidence are regarded as having little or no importance.

The case is quite different in the realm of science. Since every scientific explanation is regarded as a hypothesis, it is regarded as worthy of acceptance only to the extent that there is evidence for it. As a hypothesis, the question of its truth or falsehood is open, and there is continual search for more and more evidence to decide that question. The term "evidence" as used here refers ultimately to experience; *sensible* evidence is the ultimate court of appeal in verifying scientific propositions. Science is *empirical* in holding that sense experience is the *test of truth* for all its pronouncements. Consequently, it is of the essence of a scientific proposition that it be capable of being tested by observation.

Some propositions can be tested directly. To decide the truth or falsehood of the proposition that it is now raining outside, we need only glance out the window. To tell whether a traffic light shows green or red, all we have to do is to look at it. But the propositions which scientists usually offer as explanatory hypotheses are not of this type. Such general propositions as Newton's Laws or Einstein's Theory are not directly testable in this fashion. They can, however, be tested indirectly. The indirect method of testing the truth of a proposition is familiar to all of us, though we may not be familiar with this name for it. For example, if his employer had been suspicious of the office boy's explanation of his tardiness, he might have checked up on it by telephoning the bus company to find out whether an accident had really happened to the seven-thirty bus. If the bus company's report checked with the boy's story, this would serve to dispel the employer's suspicions; whereas if the bus company denied that an accident had occurred, it would probably convince the employer that his office boy's story was false. This inquiry would constitute an indirect test of the office boy's explanation.

The pattern of indirect testing or indirect verification consists of two parts. First one deduces from the proposition to be tested one or more other propositions which are capable of being tested directly. Then these consequences are tested and found to be either true or false. If the consequences are false, any proposition which implies them must be false also. On the other hand, if the consequences are true, they are evidence for the truth of the proposition being tested, which is thus confirmed indirectly.

It should be noted that indirect testing is never demonstrative or certain. To deduce directly testable conclusions from a proposition usually requires additional premisses. The conclusion that the bus company will reply that the seven-thirty bus had an accident this morning does not follow validly from the proposition that the seven-thirty bus did have an accident. Additional premisses are needed, for example, that all accidents are reported to the company's office, that the reports are not mislaid or forgotten, and that the company does not make a policy of denying its accidents. So the bus company's denying that an accident occurred would not demonstrate the office boy's story to be false, for the discrepancy might be due to the falsehood of one of the other premisses mentioned. Those others, however, ordinarily have such a high degree of probability that a negative reply on the part of the bus company would render the office boy's story very doubtful indeed.

Similarly, establishing the truth of a conclusion does not demonstrate the truth of the premisses from which it was deduced. We know very well that a valid argument may have a true conclusion even though its premisses are not all true. In the present example, the bus company might confirm that an accident happened to the seven-thirty bus because of some mistake in their records, even though no accident had occurred. So the inferred consequent might be true even though the premisses from which it was deduced were not. In the usual case, though, that is highly unlikely; so a successful or affirmative direct testing of a conclusion serves to corroborate the premisses from which it was deduced.

It must be admitted that every proposition, scientific or unscientific, which is a relevant explanation for any observable fact, has *some* evidence in its favor, namely the fact to which it is relevant. Thus the regular motions of the planets must be conceded to constitute evidence for the (unscientific) theory that the planets are inhabited by "intelligences" which cause them to move in just the orbits which are observed. The motions themselves are as much evidence for that myth as they are for Newton's or Einstein's theories. The difference lies in the fact that that is the only evidence for the unscientific hypothesis. Absolutely no other directly testable propositions can be deduced from the myth. On the other hand, a very large number of directly testable propositions can be deduced from the scientific explanations mentioned. Here, then, is *the* difference between scientific and unscientific explanations. A scientific explanation for a given fact will have directly testable propositions deducible from it, other than the one asserting the fact to be explained. But an unscientic explanation will have no other directly testable propositions deducible from it. It is of the essence of a scientific proposition to be empirically verifiable.

It is clear that we have been using the term "scientific explanation" in a quite general sense. As here defined, an explanation may be scientific even though it is not a part of one of the various special sciences like physics or psychology. Thus the office boy's explanation of his tardiness would be classified as a scientific one, for it is testable, even if only indirectly. But had he offered as explanation the proposition that "God willed him to be late that morning, and God is omnipotent," the explanation would have been unscientific. For although his being late that morning is deducible from the proffered explanation, no other directly testable proposition is, and so the explanation is not even indirectly testable, and hence is unscientific.

13.3 Evaluating Scientific Explanations

The question naturally arises as to how scientific explanations are to be evaluated, that is, judged as good or bad, or at least as better or worse. This question is especially important because there is usually more than a single scientific explanation for one and the same fact. A man's abrupt behavior may be explained either by the hypothesis that he is shy or by the hypothesis that he is unfriendly. In a criminal investigation, two different and incompatible hypotheses about the identity of the criminal may equally well account for the known facts. In the realm of science proper, that an object expands when heated is explained by both the caloric theory of heat and the kinetic theory. The caloric theory regarded heat as an invisible weightless fluid, called "caloric," with the power of penetrating, expanding, and dissolving bodies, or dissipating them in vapor. The kinetic theory, on the other hand, regards the heat of a body as consisting of random motions of the molecules of which the body is composed. These are *alternative* scientific explanations which serve equally well to explain some of the phenomena of thermal expansion. They cannot both be true, however, and the problem is to evaluate or choose between them.

What is wanted here is a list of conditions that a good hypothesis can be expected to fulfill. It must not be thought that such a list of conditions will provide a *recipe* by whose means anyone at all can construct good hypotheses. No one has ever pretended to lay down a set of rules for the invention or discovery of hypotheses. It is likely that none could ever be laid down, for that is the *creative* side of the scientific enterprise. Ability to create is a function of a person's imagination and talent and cannot be reduced to a mechanical process. A great scientific hypothesis, with wide explanatory powers like those of Newton's or Einstein's, is as much the product of genius as a great work of art. There is no formula for discovering new hypotheses, but there are certain rules to which acceptable hypotheses can be expected to conform. These can be regarded as the criteria for evaluating hypotheses.

There are five criteria commonly used in judging the worth or acceptability of hypotheses. They may be listed as (1) relevance, (2) testability, (3) compatibility with previously well-established hypotheses, (4) predictive or explanatory power, and (5) simplicity. The first two have already been discussed, but we shall review them briefly here.

1. ***Relevance.*** No hypothesis is ever proposed for its own sake but is always intended as an explanation of some fact or other. Therefore it must be *relevant* to the fact which it is intended to explain, that is, the fact in question must be *deducible* from the proposed hypothesis—either from the hypothesis alone or from it together with certain causal laws which may be presumed to have already been established as highly probable, or from these together with certain assumptions about particular initial conditions. A hypothesis that is not relevant to the fact it is intended to explain simply fails to explain it and can only be regarded as having failed to fulfill its intended function. A good hypothesis must be *relevant.*

2. ***Testability.*** The chief distinguishing characteristic of scientific hypotheses (as contrasted with unscientific ones) is that they are testable. That is, there must be the possibility of making observations which tend to confirm or disprove any scientific hypothesis. It need not be directly testable, of course. As has already been observed, most of the really important scientific hypotheses are formulated in terms of such unobservable entities as electrons or electromagnetic waves. As one contemporary research scientist has written: "A physicist of this century, interested in the basic structure of matter, deals with radiation he cannot see, forces he cannot feel, particles he cannot

touch."[6] But there must be some way of getting from statements about such unobservables to statements about directly observable entities such as tables and chairs, or pointer readings, or lines on a photographic plate. In other words, there must be some connection between any scientific hypothesis and empirical data or facts of experience.

3. ***Compatibility with Previously Well-Established Hypotheses.*** The requirement that an acceptable hypothesis must be compatible or consistent with other hypotheses which have already been well confirmed is an eminently reasonable one. Science, in seeking to encompass more and more facts, aims at achieving a system of explanatory hypotheses. Of course such a system must be self-consistent, for no self-contradictory set of propositions could possibly be true—or even intelligible. Ideally, the way in which scientists hope to make progress is by gradually expanding their hypotheses to comprehend more and more facts. For such progress to be made, each new hypothesis must be consistent with those already confirmed. Thus Leverrier's hypothesis that there was an additional but not yet charted planet beyond the orbit of Uranus was perfectly consistent with the main body of accepted astronomical theory. A new theory must fit with older theories if there is to be orderly progress in scientific inquiry.

It is possible, of course, to overestimate the importance of the third criterion. Although the ideal of science may be the gradual growth of theoretical knowledge by the addition of one new hypothesis after another, the actual history of scientific progress has not always followed that pattern. Many of the most important new hypotheses have been inconsistent with older theories and have in fact replaced them rather than fitted in with them. Einstein's Relativity Theory was of that sort, shattering many of the preconceptions of the older Newtonian theory. The phenomenon of radioactivity, first observed during the last decade of the nineteenth century, led to the overthrow—or at least the modification—of many cherished theories which had almost achieved the status of absolutes. One of these was the Principle of the Conservation of Matter, which asserted that matter could be neither created nor destroyed. The hypothesis that radium atoms undergo spontaneous disintegration was inconsistent with that old, established principle—but it was the principle that was relinquished in favor of the newer hypothesis.

The foregoing is not intended to give the impression that scientific progress is a helter-skelter process in which theories are abandoned

[6] Reprinted from "The Bevatron" by Lloyd Smith in *Scientific American,* Vol. 184, No. 2, February 1951.

right and left in favor of newer and shinier ones. Older theories are not so much abandoned as corrected. Einstein himself always insisted that his own work was a modification rather than a rejection of Newton's. The Principle of the Conservation of Matter was modified by being absorbed into the more comprehensive Principle of the Conservation of Mass-Energy. Every established theory has been established through having proved adequate to explain a considerable mass of data, of observed facts. And it cannot be dethroned or discredited by any new hypothesis unless that new hypothesis can account for the same facts as well or even better. There is nothing capricious about the development of science. Every change represents an improvement, a more comprehensive and thus more adequate explanation of the way in which the world manifests itself in experience. Where inconsistencies occur between hypotheses, the greater age of one does not automatically prove it to be correct and the newer one wrong. The *presumption* is in favor of the older one if it has already been extensively confirmed. But if the new one in conflict with it *also* receives extensive confirmation, considerations of age or priority are definitely irrelevant. Where there is a conflict between two hypotheses, we must turn to the observable facts to decide between them. Ultimately our last court of appeal in deciding between rival hypotheses is experience. What our third criterion, compatibility with previous well-established hypotheses, comes to is this: the totality of hypotheses accepted at any time should be consistent with each other,[7] and—other things being equal—of two new hypotheses, the one which fits in better with the accepted body of scientific theory is to be preferred. The question of what is involved in "other things being equal" takes us directly to our fourth criterion.

4. ***Predictive or Explanatory Power.*** By the predictive or explanatory power of a hypothesis is meant the range of observable facts that can be deduced from it. This criterion is related to, but different from, that of testability. A hypothesis is testable if *some* observable fact is deducible from it. If one of two testable hypotheses has a greater number of observable facts deducible from it than from the other, then it is said to have greater predictive or explanatory power. For example, Newton's hypothesis of universal gravitation together with his three laws of motion had greater predictive power than either Kepler's or Galileo's hypotheses, because all observable consequences of the latter two were also consequences of the former, and the former had many more besides. An observable fact which can

[7] Scientists may, however, consider and even use inconsistent hypotheses for years while awaiting the resolution of that inconsistency. This situation obtains today with respect to the wave and the corpuscular theories of light.

be deduced from a given hypothesis is said to be explained by it and also can be said to be *predicted* by it. The greater the predictive power of a hypothesis, the more it explains, and the better it contributes to our understanding of the phenomena with which it is concerned.

Our fourth criterion has a negative side which is of crucial importance. If a hypothesis is inconsistent with any well-attested fact of observation, the hypothesis is false and must be rejected. Where two different hypotheses are both relevant to explaining some set of facts and both are testable, and both are compatible with the whole body of already established scientific theory, it may be possible to choose between them by deducing incompatible propositions from them which are directly testable. If H_1 and H_2, two different hypotheses, entail incompatible consequences, it may be possible to set up a *crucial experiment* to decide between them. Thus if H_1 entails that under circumstance C phenomenon P will occur, while H_2 entails that under circumstance C phenomenon P will *not* occur, then all we need do to decide between H_1 and H_2 is to realize circumstance C and observe the presence or absence of phenomenon P. If P occurs, this is evidence *for* H_1 and *against* H_2, while if P does not occur, this is evidence *against* H_1 and *for* H_2.

This kind of crucial experiment to decide between rival hypotheses may not always be easy to carry out, for the required circumstance C may be difficult or impossible to realize. Thus the decision between Newtonian Theory and Einstein's General Theory of Relativity had to await a total eclipse of the sun—a situation or circumstance clearly beyond the present powers of man to produce. In other cases the crucial experiment may have to await the development of new instruments, either for the production of the required *circumstances,* or for the observation or measurement of the predicted phenomenon. The proponents of rival astronomical hypotheses must frequently mark time while awaiting the construction of new and more powerful telescopes, for example. The topic of crucial experiments will be discussed further in Section 13.6.

5. *Simplicity.* It sometimes happens that two rival hypotheses satisfy the first four criteria equally well. Historically the most important pair of such hypotheses were those of Ptolemy (fl. 127–151) and Copernicus (1473–1543). Both were intended to explain all of the then known data of astronomy. According to the Ptolemaic theory, the earth is the center of the universe, and the heavenly bodies move about it in orbits which require a very complicated geometry of epicycles to describe. Ptolemy's theory was relevant, testable, and compatible with previously well-established hypotheses, satisfying the first three criteria perfectly. According to the Copernican theory, the sun rather than the earth is at the center, and the earth itself moves around the sun along with the other planets. Copernicus' theory too satisfied the first three criteria perfectly. And with respect to the fourth criterion, the two theories were almost exactly on a par. (True enough, the Copernican theory seemed to predict a stellar parallax which could not be observed, but this failure was easily accounted for by the auxiliary hypothesis that the fixed stars were too far away for any parallax to be noticed.) To all intents and purposes, the Ptolemaic and Copernican theories were of equal predictive or explanatory power. There was only one significant difference between the two rival hypotheses. Although both required the clumsy method of epicycles to account for the observed positions of the various heavenly bodies, *fewer* such epicycles were required within the Copernican theory. The Copernican system was therefore simpler, and on this basis it was accepted by all later astronomers, despite the greater age and equal predictive power of the Ptolemaic system, and in the teeth of persecution by the medieval Church!

The criterion of simplicity is a perfectly natural one to invoke. In ordinary life as well as in science, the simplest theory which fits all the available facts is the one we tend to accept. In court trials of criminal cases, the prosecution attempts to develop a hypothesis which includes the guilt of the accused and fits in with all the available evidence. Opposing him, the defense attorney seeks to set up a hypothesis which includes the innocence of the accused and also fits all the available evidence. Often both sides succeed, and then the case is usually decided—or *ought* to be decided—in favor of that hypothesis which is simpler or more "natural." Simplicity, however, is a very difficult term to define. Not all controversies are as straightforward as the Ptolemaic-Copernican one, in which the latter's greater simplicity consisted merely in requiring a smaller number of epicycles. And of course "naturalness" is an almost hopelessly deceptive term—for it seems much more "natural" to believe that the earth is still while the apparently moving sun really does move. The fifth and last criterion, simplicity, is an important and frequently decisive one, but it is vague and not always easy to apply.

13.4 The Detective as Scientist

Now that we have formulated and explained the criteria by which hypotheses are evaluated, we are in a position to describe the general pattern of scientific research. It will be helpful to begin by examining an illustration of that method. A perennial favorite in this connection is the detective, whose problem is not quite the same as that of the pure scientist, but whose approach and technique illustrate the method of science very clearly. The classical example of the astute detective who can solve even the most baffling mystery is A. Conan Doyle's immortal creation, Sherlock Holmes. Holmes, his stature undiminished by the passage of time, will be our hero in the following account.

1. ***The Problem.*** Some of our most vivid pictures of Holmes are those in which he is busy with magnifying glass and tape measure, searching out and finding essential clues which had escaped the attention of those stupid bunglers, the "experts" of Scotland Yard. Or those of us who are by temperament less vigorous may think back more fondly on Holmes the thinker, ". . . who, when he had an unsolved problem upon his mind, would go for days, and even for a week, without rest, turning it over, rearranging his facts, looking at it from every point of view until he had either fathomed it or convinced himself that his data were insufficient."[8] At one such time, according to Dr. Watson:

> He took off his coat and waistcoat, put on a large blue dressing-gown, and then wandered about the room collecting pillows from his bed and cushions from the sofa and armchairs. With these he constructed a sort of Eastern divan, upon which he perched himself cross-legged, with an ounce of shag tobacco and a box of matches laid out in front of him. In the dim light of the lamp I saw him sitting there, an old briar pipe between his lips, his eyes fixed vacantly upon the corner of the ceiling, the blue smoke curling up from him, silent, motionless, with the light shining upon his strong-set aquiline features. So he sat as I dropped off to sleep, and so he sat when a sudden ejaculation caused me to wake up, and I found the summer sun shining into the apartment. The pipe was still between his lips, the smoke still curled upward, and the room was full of a dense tobacco haze, but nothing remained of the heap of shag which I had seen upon the previous night.[9]

But such memories are incomplete. Holmes was not always searching for clues or pondering over solutions. We all remember those dark periods—especially in the earlier stories—when, much to the good Watson's annoyance, Holmes would drug himself with morphine or cocaine. That would happen, of course, between cases. For when there is no mystery to be unraveled, no man in his right mind would go out to look for clues. Clues, after all, must be clues for something. Nor could Holmes, or anyone else, for that matter, engage in profound thought unless he had something to think about. Sherlock Holmes was a genius at solving problems, but even a genius must have a problem before he can solve it. All reflective thinking, and this term includes criminal investigation as well as scientific

8 "The Man with the Twisted Lip."
9 Ibid.

research, is a problem-solving activity, as John Dewey and other pragmatists have rightly insisted. There must be a problem felt before either the detective or the scientist can go to work.

Of course the active mind sees problems where the dullard sees only familiar objects. One Christmas season Dr. Watson visited Holmes to find that the latter had been using a lens and forceps to examine ". . . a very seedy and disreputable hard-felt hat, much the worse for wear, and cracked in several places."[10] After they had greeted each other, Holmes said of it to Watson, "I beg that you will look upon it not as a battered billycock but as an intellectual problem."[11] It so happened that the hat led them into one of their most interesting adventures, but it could not have done so had Holmes not seen a problem in it from the start. A problem may be characterized as a fact or group of facts for which we have no acceptable explanation, which seem unusual, or which fail to fit in with our expectations or preconceptions. It should be obvious that *some* prior beliefs are required if anything is to appear problematic. If there are no expectations, there can be no surprises.

Sometimes, of course, problems come to Holmes already labeled. The very first adventure recounted by Dr. Watson began with the following message from Gregson of Scotland Yard:

> My Dear Mr. Sherlock Holmes:
>
> There has been a bad business during the night at 3, Lauriston Gardens, off the Brixton Road. Our man on the beat saw a light there about two in the morning, and as the house was an empty one, suspected that something was amiss. He found the door open, and in the front room, which is bare of furniture, discovered the body of a gentleman, well dressed, and having cards in his pocket bearing the name of 'Enoch J. Drebber, Cleveland, Ohio, USA.' There had been no robbery, nor is there any evidence as to how the man met his death. There are marks of blood in the room, but there is no wound upon his person. We are at a loss as to how he came into the empty house; indeed, the whole affair is a puzzler. If you can come round to the house any time before twelve, you will find me there. I have left everything in statu quo until I hear from you. If you are unable to come, I shall give you fuller details, and would esteem it a great kindness if you would favour me with your opinion.
>
> Yours faithfully,
>
> TOBIAS GREGSON[12]

Here was a problem indeed. A few minutes after receiving the message, Sherlock Holmes and Dr. Watson "were both in a hansom, driving furiously for the Brixton Road."

2. ***Preliminary Hypotheses.*** On their ride out Brixton way,

[10] "The Adventure of the Blue Carbuncle."

[11] Ibid.

[12] *A Study in Scarlet.*

Holmes "prattled away about Cremona fiddles and the difference between a Stradivarius and an Amati." Dr. Watson chided Holmes for not giving much thought to the matter at hand, and Holmes replied: "No data yet. . . . It is a capital mistake to theorize before you have all the evidence. It biases the judgment."[13] This point of view was expressed by Holmes again and again. On one occasion he admonished a younger detective that "The temptation to form premature theories upon insufficient data is the bane of our profession."[14] Yet for all of his confidence about the matter, on this one issue Holmes was completely mistaken. Of course one should not reach a *final judgment* until a great deal of evidence has been considered, but this procedure is quite different from *not theorizing*. As a matter of fact, it is strictly impossible to make any serious attempt to collect evidence unless one *has* theorized beforehand. As Charles Darwin, the great biologist and author of the modern theory of evolution, observed: ". . . all observation must be for or against some view, if it is to be of any service." The point is that there are too many particular facts, too many data in the world, for anyone to try to become acquainted with them all. Everyone, even the most patient and thorough investigator, must pick and choose, deciding which facts to study and which to pass over. He must have some working hypothesis for or against which to collect relevant data. It need not be a *complete* theory, but at least the rough outline must be there. Otherwise how could one decide what facts to select for consideration out of the totality of all facts, which is too vast even to begin to sift?

Holmes' actions were wiser than his words in this connection. After all, the words were spoken in a hansom speeding towards the scene of the crime. If Holmes really had no theory about the matter, why go to Brixton Road? If facts and data were all that he wanted, any old facts and any old data, with no hypotheses to guide him in their selection, why should he have left Baker Street at all? There were plenty of facts in the rooms at 221-B, Baker Street. Holmes might just as well have spent his time counting all the words on all the pages of all the books there, or perhaps making very accurate measurements of the distances between each separate pair of articles of furniture in the house. He could have gathered data to his heart's content and saved himself cab fare into the bargain!

It may be objected that the facts to be gathered at Baker Street have nothing to do with the case, whereas those which awaited Holmes at the scene of the crime were valuable clues for solving the problem. It was, of course, just this consideration which led Holmes to ignore the "data" at Baker Street and hurry away to collect those

[13] Ibid.

[14] *The Valley of Fear.*

off Brixton Road. It must be insisted, however, that the greater relevance of the latter could not be *known* beforehand but only conjectured on the basis of previous experience with crimes and clues. It was in fact a *hypothesis* which led Holmes to look in one place rather than another for his facts, the hypothesis that there was a murder, that the crime was committed at the place where the body was found, and that the murderer had left some trace or clue which could lead to his discovery. Some such hypothesis is always required to guide the investigator in his search for relevant data, for in the absence of any preliminary hypothesis, there are simply too many facts in this world to examine. The preliminary hypothesis ought to be highly tentative, and it must be based on previous knowledge. But a preliminary hypothesis is as necessary as the existence of a problem for any serious inquiry to begin.

It must be emphasized that a preliminary hypothesis, as here conceived, need not be a complete solution to the problem. The hypothesis that the man was murdered by someone who had left some clues to his identity on or near the body of his victim was what led Holmes to Brixton Road. This hypothesis is clearly incomplete: it does not say who committed the crime, or how it was done, or why. Such a preliminary hypothesis may be very different from the final solution to the problem. It will never be complete: it may be a tentative explanation of only part of the problem. But however partial and however tentative, a preliminary hypothesis is required for any investigation to proceed.

3. ***Collecting Additional Facts.*** Every serious investigation begins with some fact or group of facts which strike the investigator as problematic and which initiate the whole process of inquiry. The initial facts which constitute the problem are usually too meager to suggest a wholly satisfactory explanation for themselves, but they will suggest—to the competent investigator—some preliminary hypotheses which lead him to search out additional facts. These additional facts, it is hoped, will serve as clues to the final solution. The inexperienced or bungling investigator will overlook or ignore all but the most obvious of them; but the careful worker will aim at completeness in his examination of the additional facts to which his preliminary hypotheses lead him. Holmes, of course, was the most careful and painstaking of investigators.

Holmes insisted on dismounting from the hansom a hundred yards or so from their destination and approached the house on foot, looking carefully at its surroundings and especially at the pathway leading up to it. When Holmes and Watson entered the house, they were shown the body by the two Scotland Yard operatives, Gregson and Lestrade. ("There is no clue," said Gregson.

"None at all," chimed in Lestrade.) But Holmes had already started his own search for additional facts, looking first at the body:

> . . . his nimble fingers were flying here, there, and everywhere, feeling, pressing, unbuttoning, examining. . . . So swiftly was the examination made, that one would hardly have guessed the minuteness with which it was conducted. Finally, he sniffed the dead man's lips, and then glanced at the soles of his patent leather boots.[15]

Then turning his attention to the room itself,

> . . . he whipped a tape measure and a large round magnifying glass from his pocket. With these two implements he trotted noiselessly about the room, sometimes stopping, occasionally kneeling, and once lying flat upon his face. So engrossed was he with his occupation that he appeared to have forgotten our presence, for he chattered away to himself under his breath the whole time, keeping up a running fire of exclamations, groans, whistles and little cries suggestive of encouragement and of hope. As I watched him I was irresistibly reminded of a pure-blooded, well-trained foxhound as it dashes backward and forward through the covert, whining in its eagerness, until it comes across the lost scent. For twenty minutes or more he continued his researches, measuring with the most exact care the distance between marks which were entirely invisible to me, and occasionally applying his tape to the walls in an equally incomprehensible manner. In one place he gathered up very carefully a little pile of gray dust from the floor and packed it away in an envelope. Finally he examined with his glass the word upon the wall, going over every letter of it, with the most minute exactness. This done, he appeared to be satisfied, for he replaced his tape and his glass in his pocket.
>
> "They say that genius is an infinite capacity for taking pains," he remarked with a smile. "It's a very bad definition, but it does apply to detective work."[16]

One matter deserves to be emphasized very strongly. Steps 2 and 3 are not completely separable but are usually very intimately connected and interdependent. True enough, we require a preliminary hypothesis to begin any intelligent examination of facts, but the additional facts may themselves suggest new hypotheses, which may lead to new facts, which suggest still other hypotheses, which lead to still other additional facts, and so on. Thus having made his careful examination of the facts available in the house off Brixton Road, Holmes was led to formulate a further hypothesis which required the taking of testimony from the constable who found the body. The man was off duty at the moment, and Lestrade gave Holmes the constable's name and address.

> Holmes took a note of the address.
>
> "Come along, Doctor," he said: "we shall go and look him up. I'll tell you one thing which may help you in the case," he continued, turning to the

[15] *A Study in Scarlet.*
[16] Ibid.

two detectives. "There has been murder done, and the murderer was a man. He was more than six feet high, was in the prime of life, had small feet for his height, wore coarse, square-toed boots and smoked a Trichinopoly cigar. He came here with his victim in a four-wheeled cab, which was drawn by a horse with three old shoes and one new one on his off fore-leg. In all probability the murderer had a florid face, and the fingernails of his right hand were remarkably long. These are only a few indications, but they may assist you."

Lestrade and Gregson glanced at each other with an incredulous smile.

"If this man was murdered, how was it done?" asked the former.

"Poison," said Sherlock Holmes curtly, and strode off.[17]

4. ***Formulating the Hypothesis.*** At some stage or other of his investigation, any man—whether detective, scientist, or ordinary mortal—will get the feeling that he has all the facts needed for his solution. He has his "2 and 2," so to speak, but the task still remains of "putting them together." At such a time Sherlock Holmes might sit up all night, consuming pipe after pipe of tobacco, trying to think things through. The result or end product of such thinking, if it is successful, is a hypothesis which accounts for all the data, both the original set of facts which constituted the problem and the additional facts to which the preliminary hypotheses pointed. The actual discovery of such an explanatory hypothesis is a process of creation, in which imagination as well as knowledge is involved. Holmes, who was a genius at inventing hypotheses, described the process as reasoning "backward." As he put it,

> Most people if you describe a train of events to them, will tell you what the result would be. They can put those events together in their minds, and argue from them that something will come to pass. There are few people, however, who, if you told them a result, would be able to evolve from their own inner consciousness what the steps were which led up to that result.[18]

Here is Holmes' description of the process of formulating an explanatory hypothesis. However that may be, when a hypothesis has been proposed, its evaluation must be along the lines that were sketched in Section 13.3. Granted its relevance and testability, and its compatibility with other well-attested beliefs, the ultimate criterion for evaluating a hypothesis is its predictive power.

5. ***Deducing Further Consequences.*** A really fruitful hypothesis will not only explain the facts which originally inspired it, but will explain many others in addition. A good hypothesis will point beyond the initial facts in the direction of new ones whose existence might otherwise not have been suspected. And of course the verifica-

[17] Ibid.
[18] Ibid.

tion of those further consequences will tend to confirm the hypothesis which led to them. Holmes' hypothesis that the murdered man had been poisoned was soon put to such a test. A few days later the murdered man's secretary and traveling companion was also found murdered. Holmes asked Lestrade, who had discovered the second body, whether he had found anything in the room which could furnish a clue to the murderer. Lestrade answered, "Nothing," and went on to mention a few quite ordinary effects. Holmes was not satisfied and pressed him, asking, "And was there nothing else?" Lestrade answered, "Nothing of any importance," and named a few more details, the last of which was "a small chip ointment box containing a couple of pills." At this information,

> Sherlock Holmes sprang from his chair with an exclamation of delight.
> "The last link," he cried, exultantly. "My case is complete."
> The two detectives stared at him in amazement.
> "I have now in my hands," my companion said, confidently, "all the threads which have formed such a tangle. . . . I will give you a proof of my knowledge. Could you lay your hands upon those pills?"
> "I have them," said Lestrade, producing a small white box. . . .[19]

On the basis of his hypothesis about the original crime, Holmes was able to predict that the pills found at the scene of the second crime must contain poison. Here deduction has an essential role in the process of any scientific or inductive inquiry. The ultimate value of any hypothesis lies in its predictive or explanatory power, which means that additional facts must be deducible from an adequate hypothesis. From his theory that the first man was poisoned and that the second victim met his death at the hands of the same murderer, Holmes inferred that the pills found by Lestrade must be poison. His theory, however sure he may have felt about it, was only a theory and needed further confirmation. He obtained that confirmation by testing the consequences deduced from the hypothesis and finding them to be true. Having used deduction to make a prediction, his next step was to test it.

6. *Testing the Consequences.* The consequences of a hypothesis, that is, the predictions made on the basis of that hypothesis, may require various means for their testing. Some require only observation. In some cases, Holmes needed only to watch and wait—for the bank robbers to break into the vault, in the "Adventure of the Red-headed League," or for Dr. Roylott to slip a venomous snake through a dummy ventilator, in the "Adventure of the Speckled Band." In the present case, however, an experiment had to be performed.

[19] Ibid.

Holmes asked Dr. Watson to fetch the landlady's old and ailing terrier, which she had asked to have put out of its misery the day before. Holmes then cut one of the pills in two, dissolved it in a wineglass of water, added some milk, and

> . . . turned the contents of the wineglass into a saucer and placed it in front of the terrier, who speedily licked it dry. Sherlock Holmes's earnest demeanour had so far convinced us that we all sat in silence, watching the animal intently, and expecting some startling effect. None such appeared, however. The dog continued to lie stretched upon the cushion, breathing in a laboured way, but apparently neither the better nor the worse for its draught.
>
> Holmes had taken out his watch, and as minute followed minute without result, an expression of the utmost chagrin and disappointment appeared upon his features. He gnawed his lip, drummed his fingers upon the table, and showed every other symptom of acute impatience. So great was his emotion that I felt sincerely sorry for him, while the two detectives smiled derisively, by no means displeased at this check which he had met.
>
> "It can't be a coincidence," he cried, at last springing from his chair and pacing wildly up and down the room: "it is impossible that it should be a mere coincidence The very pills which I suspected in the case of Drebber are actually found after the death of Stangerson. And yet they are inert. What can it mean? Surely my whole chain of reasoning cannot have been false. It is impossible! And yet this wretched dog is none the worse. Ah, I have it! I have it!" With a perfect shriek of delight he rushed to the box, cut the other pill in two, dissolved it, added milk, and presented it to the terrier. The unfortunate creature's tongue seemed hardly to have been moistened in it before it gave a convulsive shiver in every limb, and lay as rigid and lifeless as if it had been struck by lightning.
>
> Sherlock Holmes drew a long breath, and wiped the perspiration from his forehead.[20]

By the favorable outcome of his experiment, Holmes' hypothesis had received dramatic and convincing confirmation.

7. ***Application.*** The detective's concern, after all, is a practical one. Given a crime to solve, he has not merely to explain the facts but to apprehend and arrest the criminal. The latter involves making application of his theory, using it to predict where the criminal can be found and how he may be caught. He must deduce still further consequences from the hypothesis, not for the sake of additional confirmation but for practical use. From his general hypothesis Holmes was able to infer that the murderer was acting the role of a cabman. We have already seen that Holmes had formed a pretty clear description of the man's appearance. He sent out his army of "Baker Street Irregulars," street urchins of the neighborhood, to search out and summon the cab driven by just that man. The successful "application" of this hypothesis can be described again in Dr. Watson's words. A few minutes after the terrier's death,

[20] Ibid.

. . . there was a tap at the door, and the spokesman of the street Arabs, young Wiggins, introduced his insignificant and unsavoury person.

"Please, sir" he said touching his forelock, "I have the cab downstairs."

"Good boy," said Holmes, blandly. "Why don't you introduce this pattern at Scotland Yard?" he continued, taking a pair of steel handcuffs from a drawer. "See how beautifully the spring works. They fasten in an instant."

"The old pattern is good enough," remarked Lestrade, "if we can only find the man to put them on."

"Very good, very good," said Holmes, smiling. "The cabman may as well help me with my boxes. Just ask him to step in, Wiggins."

I was surprised to find my companion speaking as though he were about to set out on a journey, since he had not said anything to me about it. There was a small portmanteau in the room, and this he pulled out and began to strap. He was busily engaged at it when the cabman entered the room.

"Just give me a help with this buckle, cabman," he said, kneeling over his task, and never turning his head.

The fellow came forward with a somewhat sullen, defiant air, and put down his hands to assist. At that instant there was a sharp click, the jangling of metal, and Sherlock Holmes sprang to his feet again.

"Gentlemen," he cried, with flashing eyes, "let me introduce you to Mr. Jefferson Hope, the murderer of Enoch Drebber and of Joseph Stangerson."[21]

Here we have a picture of the detective as scientist, reasoning from observed facts to a testable hypothesis which not only explains the facts but permits a practical application.

13.5 Scientists in Action: The Pattern of Scientific Investigation

As the term "scientific" is generally used today it refers to any reasoning which attempts to proceed from observable facts of experience to reasonable (that is, relevant and testable) explanations for those facts. The scientific method is not confined to professional scientists: anyone can be said to be proceeding scientifically who follows the general pattern of reasoning from evidence to conclusions which can be tested by experience. The skilled detective is a scientist in this sense, as are most of us—in our more rational moments, at least. The pervasive pattern of all scientific inquiry is expressible in terms of the steps illustrated in the preceding section.

Those seven steps will be explained further by analyzing an important example of scientific research.[22] During the eighteenth century, the caloric theory of heat became very widely accepted. Heat was believed to be a subtle, highly elastic fluid which could be added to or extracted from a body, thereby causing temperature

[21] Ibid.

[22] The following account is freely adapted from *Introduction to Modern Physics*, by F. K. Richtmyer. Copyright, 1928, 1934. McGraw-Hill Book Company, Inc.

changes in it. The hypothesized heat fluid was supposed to be indestructible; its particles were thought to be self-repellent but attracted by ordinary matter; and it was alleged to be all-pervading. The caloric theory of heat had considerable explanatory power. The expansion of bodies when heated was explained as the natural result of "swelling" caused by the heat fluid being forced into its pores. The production of heat by pounding on a body was explained as being due to the releasing or "jarring loose" of some of the caloric which had been condensed in the body, so that pounding increased the amount of free caloric heat in it. Even the conversion of fuel to power in the early steam engine could be explained on the caloric theory: a given quantity of caloric "falling" from a higher to a lower temperature was analogous to a given quantity of water falling from a higher to a lower level—each was capable of producing mechanical power. By the end of the eighteenth century the caloric theory of heat as a material substance was quite generally accepted.

It was against this background of accepted theory that Count Rumford (1753–1814) encountered the problem which guided much of his subsequent research. Rumford described the beginning in these words:

> Being engaged, lately, in superintending the boring of cannon, in the workshops of the military arsenal at Munich, I was struck with the very considerable degree of heat which a brass gun acquires, in a short time, in being bored; and with the still more intense heat (much greater than that of boiling water, as I found by experiment) of the metallic chips separated from it by the borer.
>
> The more I meditated on these phaenomena, the more they appeared to me to be curious and interesting.[23]

Here we have the first step in any inquiry: a problem is felt. It should be noted that in this case the felt problem arose from an apparent conflict between the data of experience and accepted scientific theories. The relevant theories were two: first, the caloric theory which asserted heat to be a material substance, and second, the principle of the conservation of matter, which asserted that material substance could neither be created nor destroyed. The observed fact, on the other hand, was that considerable amounts of heat were produced—without any apparent decrease in the amounts of any other material substances. The production of as much heat as Rumford observed was inexplicable on the basis of the science of his day. The situation was problematic, and demanded a solution. It

[23] By permission from *A Source Book in Physics,* by William Francis Magie. Copyright, 1935. McGraw-Hill Book Company, Inc.

should be clear that the problem would not be felt by anyone who was ignorant of the accepted theories. Nor would it be felt by an unobservant individual who took no notice of the facts before him. Finally, it would not be felt by anyone whose mind was not disturbed by gaps or inconsistencies between theory and observation. It may be remarked, then, that the requisite qualities a person must have to initiate any fruitful inquiry are three: one must be familiar with current theories, observant of new facts, and uncomfortable in the presence of any conflict or gap between fact and theory.

Judging by the various experiments he was subsequently led to perform, it seems reasonable to suppose that Count Rumford's preliminary hypothesis was something like the following. Since considerable heat was generated without appreciable diminution of any other material substances present, it might be possible to obtain an unlimited amount of heat without exhausting the supply of matter at hand. This conjecture was certainly suggested by the original data which posed the problem. Helpful in setting up an experiment to test this hypothesis, or to collect data suggested by it, was Rumford's previous knowledge that boring with dull tools generates more heat than is obtained by using sharp ones.

On the basis of this knowledge, and being guided by the preliminary hypothesis mentioned, Rumford went about collecting some additional relevant data, which he procured by the following experimental setup. He caused a blunt steel boring tool to rotate, under great pressure, against a piece of brass while both were immersed in water. The apparatus was powered by two horses. In just two and one half hours the water actually boiled, a process that continued as long as the horses kept the machinery in motion. Rumford thus arrived at the additional fact that there was no limit to the amount of heat which could be produced without any decrease in the amount of material substance in the vicinity. This fact was clearly incompatible with the caloric theory of heat, according to which there can be only a finite or limited amount of the heat fluid in any body.

Having gathered this additional data, Count Rumford addressed himself to the task of formulating a hypothesis which should explain all the facts encountered. It was with some reluctance that he abandoned the popular caloric theory. But the facts were stubborn, and not to be got around. Rumford wrote:

> . . . anything which any isolated body, or system of bodies, can continue to furnish without limitation cannot possibly be a material substance; and it appears to me to be extremely difficult, if not quite impossible, to form any distinct idea of anything capable of being excited and communicated in the

manner heat was excited and communicated in these experiments, except it be motion.[24]

Rumford's hypothesis that heat is a form of motion has come to be called the *mechanical* or *kinetic* theory of heat. On the basis of the facts at his disposal he rejected the *materialistic* or *caloric* theory.

But in science, as elsewhere, progress must struggle against inertia. The caloric theory had been accepted for a very long time, and Rumford's hypothesis was so revolutionary that its acceptance was very slow in coming. (Actually, it had been anticipated by Sir Isaac Newton in Query 18 of his *Opticks* almost one hundred years earlier, but Newton's authority had not been established in this field.) Before the kinetic theory could be widely accepted, further confirmation was necessary. That confirmation was supplied by other scientists.

Here we come to another important aspect of scientific thought. Science is *social,* an activity of the group rather than an isolated individual enterprise. A scientific structure can be built or created by many investigators, and the well-developed branches of science are all joint enterprises. The cooperative nature of scientific research accounts for the "objectivity" of science. The data with which scientists deal are public data, available to any qualified investigator who makes the appropriate observations. Scientists, in reporting their experiments, include a wealth of detail, not for its own intrinsic interest but to enable any other investigator to duplicate the experimental setup and thus see for himself whether the reported result really does occur. There are many cases in which individuals are mistaken in what they think they see. In a court of law witnesses will swear to conflicting versions of events at which both were present, with no intentional perjury on the part of either. Many times men will see what they expect, or what they want to see, rather than what actually occurs. Although the facts of experience are the ultimate court of appeal for scientists, they must be public facts which everyone can experience under appropriate conditions. When elaborate experiments are repeated by various different scientists again and again, it does not token suspicion or distrust of the other man's results, but universal agreement that to be decisive facts must be public and repeatable. Repetition and careful checking by qualified observers minimizes the intrusion of subjective factors and helps maintain the objectivity of science.

Sir Humphry Davy (1778–1829) was the next scientist of importance to interest himself in the kinetic theory of heat. From the

[24] By permission from *Introduction to Modern Physics* by F. K. Richtmyer. Copyright, 1928, 1934. McGraw-Hill Book Company, Inc.

two theories, Davy deduced testable consequences which were strictly incompatible with each other. He argued that *if* the caloric theory were true, then two pieces of ice which were initially below the melting point and were kept in a vacuum would not be melted by any amount of friction that could be produced between them.[25] On the other hand, with the kinetic theory of heat as premiss he deduced the conclusion that two pieces of ice which were rubbed together would melt no matter what their initial temperatures and regardless of whether or not the operation was performed in a vacuum. These deductions pointed the way to further experimentation.

The crucial experiment made possible by these deductions was then performed by Davy, who reported his procedures in great detail, specifying that he used "two parallelopipedons of ice, of the temperature of 29°, six inches long, two wide, and two-thirds of an inch thick. . . ."[26] It was experimentally verified that under the described conditions the ice *did melt*. That result convinced Sir Humphry Davy of the correctness of the kinetic theory of heat and of the untenability of the caloric theory. In Davy's own words:

> It has . . . been experimentally demonstrated that caloric, or the matter of heat, does not exist. . . . Since bodies become expanded by friction, it is evident that their corpuscles must move or separate from each other. Now a motion or vibration of the corpuscles of bodies must be necessarily generated by friction and percussion. Therefore we may reasonably conclude that this motion or vibration is heat, or the repulsive power.
>
> Heat, then, or that power which prevents the actual contact of the corpuscles of bodies, and which is the cause of our peculiar sensation of heat and cold, may be defined as a peculiar motion, probably a vibration, of the corpuscles of bodies, tending to separate them.[27]

Davy's experimental testing of his predictions resulted in the confirmation of Rumford's hypothesis. Perhaps more decisive even than Davy's experiments were those of the British physicist James Prescott Joule (1818–1889) who made the kinetic theory *quantitative* by experimentally establishing the mechanical equivalent of heat.

Especially in its quantitative form, the kinetic theory of heat has many applications. Some of these are theoretical: especially in connection with the kinetic theory of gases, it serves to unify mechanics

[25] His actual deduction involved considerations having to do with the theory of "heat capacity" and the phenomenon of oxidation and is too complex to reproduce here in detail. It can be found on pages 161–165 of W. F. Magie's *A Source Book in Physics.*

[26] Ibid.

[27] By permission from *A Source Book in Physics,* by William Francis Magie. Copyright, 1935. McGraw-Hill Book Company, Inc.

with the theory of heat phenomena. The almost independent science of thermodynamics has been one result of this unification. As for practical applications of the kinetic theory of heat, the most obvious is in the field of artificial refrigeration, which is only one of the technological results made possible by that theory.

EXERCISES

1. Take some detective story and analyze its structure in terms of the seven steps discussed in the preceding sections.

2. Find an account of some specific line of research in a popular or semipopular book on science, and analyze its structure in terms of the seven steps discussed in the preceding sections.

13.6 Crucial Experiments and Ad Hoc Hypotheses

From the foregoing account, a reader might form the opinion that scientific progress is ridiculously easy to make. It might appear that, given any problem, all one needs to do is to set down all relevant hypotheses and then perform a series of crucial experiments to eliminate all but one of them. The surviving hypothesis is then "the answer," and we are ready to go on to the next problem. But no opinion could possibly be more mistaken.

It has already been remarked that formulating or discovering relevant hypotheses is not a mechanical process but a creative one: some hypotheses require genius for their discovery. It has been observed further that crucial experiments may not always be possible, either because no different observable consequences are deducible from the alternative hypotheses or because we lack the power to arrange the experimental circumstances in which different consequences would manifest themselves. We wish at this time to point out a more pervasive theoretical difficulty with the program of deciding between rival hypotheses by means of crucial experiments. It may be well to illustrate our discussion by means of a fairly simple example. One that is familiar to all of us concerns the shape of the earth.

In ancient Greece, the philosophers Anaximenes and Empedocles had held that the earth is flat, and this view, close to common sense, still had adherents in the Middle Ages and the Renaissance. Christopher Columbus, however, insisted that the earth is round—or rather, spherical. One of Columbus' arguments was that as a ship sails away from shore, the upper portions of it remain visible to a watcher on land long after its lower parts have disappeared from view. A slightly different version of the same argument was included by Nikolaus Copernicus in his epoch-making treatise *On the Revolutions of the Heavenly Spheres.* In Section II of Book I of that work, entitled "That the Earth also is Spherical," he presented a number of arguments intended to establish the truth of that view. Of the many found there we quote the following:

> That the seas take a spherical form is perceived by navigators. For when land is still not discernible from a vessel's deck, it is from the masthead. And if, when a ship sails from land, a torch be fastened from the masthead, it appears to watchers on the land to go downward little by little until it entirely disappears, like a heavenly body setting.[28]

As between these two rival hypotheses about the earth's shape, we might regard the foregoing as a description of a crucial experiment. The general pattern is clear. From the hypothesis that the earth is flat, H_f, it follows that if a ship gradually recedes from view, then neither its masthead nor its decks should remain visible after the other has vanished. On the other hand, from the hypothesis that the earth is spherical, H_s, it follows that if a ship gradually recedes from view, its masthead should remain visible after its decks have vanished from sight. The rationale involved here is nicely represented by a diagram.

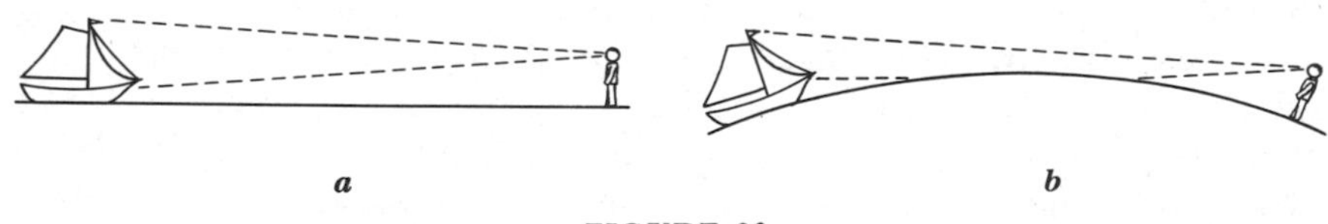

FIGURE 20

In the figure, *a* represents the situation which would obtain if H_f were true. It is clear that *if* the earth is flat there is no reason why any one portion of the ship should disappear from sight before any other portion. The figure *b* represents the situation corresponding to H_s. As the ship recedes, the curvature of the earth rises between the observer and the ship, blocking out his view of the decks while the masthead still remains visible. In each case the rays of light passing from ship to observer are represented by dotted lines. Now the experiment is performed, a receding ship is watched attentively, and the masthead *does* remain visible after the decks have disappeared. Our experiment may not have demonstrated the truth

[28] Reprinted from *On the Revolutions of the Heavenly Spheres* by Nikolaus Copernicus, as contained in *Masterworks of Science, Digests of 13 Great Classics,* edited by John Warren Knedler, Jr. Copyright, 1947, by Doubleday & Company, Inc.

of H_s, it can be admitted, but surely it has established the falsehood of H_f. We have as clear an example of a crucial experiment as it is possible to obtain.

But the experiment described is *not* crucial. It is entirely possible to accept the observed facts and still maintain that the earth is flat. The experiment has considerable value as evidence, but it is not decisive. It is not crucial because the various testable predictions were not inferred from the stated hypotheses H_f and H_s alone, but from them plus the additional hypothesis that "light travels in straight lines." The diagrams show clearly that this additional assumption is essential to the argument. That the decks disappear before the masthead does is not deducible from H_s alone but requires the additional premiss that light rays follow a rectilinear path (H_r). And that the decks do *not* disappear before the masthead does is not deducible from H_f alone but requires the same additional premiss: that light rays follow a rectilinear path (H_r). The latter argument may be formulated as:

> The earth is flat (H_f).
> Light rays follow a rectilinear path (H_r).
> Therefore the decks of a receding ship will *not* disappear from view before the masthead.

Here is a perfectly good argument whose conclusion is observed to be false. Its premisses cannot both be true; at least one of them must be false. But which one? We can maintain the truth of the first premiss, H_f, if we are willing to reject the second premiss, H_r. The second premiss, after all, is not a truth of logic but a contingent proposition that is easily conceived to be false. If we adopt the contrary hypothesis that light rays follow a curved path, concave upwards (H_c), what follows as conclusion now? Here we can infer the denial of the conclusion of the former argument. From H_f and H_c it follows that the decks of a receding ship will disappear before its masthead does. Figure 21 explains the reasoning involved here.

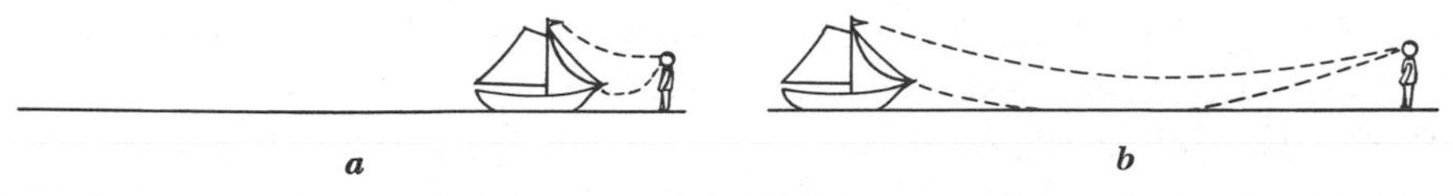

FIGURE 21

In that figure, *a* represents the situation when the ship is near the shore, while *b* shows that as the ship recedes, the earth (even though flat) blocks out the view of the decks while the masthead still remains visible. The light rays in this diagram too are represented by dotted lines, but in this case curved rather than rectilinear. The same experiment is performed, the decks do disappear before the masthead, and the observed fact is perfectly compatible with this group of hypotheses which includes H_f, the claim that the earth is flat. The experiment, therefore, is not *crucial* with respect to H_f, for that hypothesis can be maintained as true regardless of the experiment's outcome.[29]

The point is that where hypotheses of a fairly high level of abstractness or generality are involved, no observable or directly testable prediction can be deduced from just a single one of them. A whole group of hypotheses must be used as premisses, and if the observed facts are other than those predicted, *at least one* of the hypotheses in the group is shown to be false. But we have not established which one is in error. An experiment can be crucial in showing the untenability of a group of hypotheses. But such a group will usually contain a considerable number of separate hypotheses, the truth of any one of which can be maintained in the teeth of *any* experimental result, however "unfavorable," by the simple expedient of rejecting some *other* hypothesis of the group. A conclusion often drawn from these considerations is that no individual hypothesis can ever be subjected to a crucial experiment.

The preceding discussion may be objected to strenuously. It may be urged that the experiment in question "really does" refute the hypothesis that the earth is flat. It may be charged that the argument to the contrary is guilty of making an *ad hoc* hypothesis to obscure and get around the plain facts of the case. It may be felt that only the invention of *ad hoc* hypotheses right and left can prevent some experiments from being crucial and decisively refuting single hypotheses. This objection deserves careful attention.

The crux of the objection would seem to lie in the phrase *ad hoc,* which in this context is a highly charged term of abuse. Of its emotive significance there can be little doubt, but its literal meaning is somewhat ambiguous. There are three different senses in which the term *ad hoc* is often used. Its first and etymological meaning would seem to be that an *ad hoc* hypothesis is one which is specially made up to account for some fact *after* that fact had been established. In this sense, however, *all* hypotheses are *ad hoc,* since it makes no sense to speak of a hypothesis which has not been devised to account for *some* antecedently established fact or other. Hence the first sense

[29] This illustration was first suggested to me by my friend, Professor C. L. Stevenson.

does not fit in very well with the derogatory emotive significance of the term. We must consider its other meanings.

The term "ad hoc" is also used to characterize a hypothesis which accounts *only* for the particular fact or facts it was invented to explain and has no other explanatory power, that is, no other testable consequences. No *scientific* hypothesis is ad hoc in this second sense of the term, although *every* hypothesis is ad hoc in the first sense explained. A hypothesis which is ad hoc in the second sense is unscientific; since it is not testable, it has no place in the structure of science. The second sense of "ad hoc" fits in perfectly with the derogatory emotive meaning of the term. But it should be realized that the auxiliary hypothesis about light rays traveling in curved paths, which was sufficient to save the hypothesis that the earth is flat from being definitely refuted by the experiment described, is *ad hoc* only in the first sense, not the second. For it does have a considerable number of empirically testable consequences.

There is a third sense of the term "ad hoc," in which it is used to denote a mere descriptive generalization. Such a descriptive hypothesis will assert only that all facts of a particular sort occur in just some particular kinds of circumstances, and will have no explanatory power or theoretical scope. For example, limiting their diet to polished rice was found by Eijkman to cause polyneuritis in the small group of chickens with which he was working (as described in Exercise 1 on page 385 in the preceding chapter on Mill's Methods). Eijkman's hypothesis to account for this fact was *ad hoc* in the third sense: he simply drew the generalization that a diet limited to polished rice will cause polyneuritis in *any* group of chickens. His hypothesis accounts for more than just the particular facts observed; it is testable by controlling the diets of *other* groups of chickens. But it is descriptive rather than explanatory, *merely* empirical rather than theoretical. The science of nutrition has come a long way since Eijkman's contribution. The identification of vitamins and their analysis are required for a more adequate account of the facts first observed by Eijkman. Science seeks to explain rather than merely to describe, and hypotheses which consist of bare generalizations of the facts observed are said to be *ad hoc*.

The classical example of an *ad hoc* hypothesis in this third sense is the Fitzgerald Contraction Effect introduced to account for the results of the Michelson–Morley experiment on the velocity of light. By affirming that bodies moving at extremely high velocities contract, Fitzgerald accounted for the given data; his account was testable by repetitions of the experiment. But it was generally held to be ad hoc rather than explanatory, and not until Einstein's Special

Theory of Relativity were the anomalous results of the Michelson–Morley experiment given an adequate, that is, a theoretical, explanation. It should be noted that the auxiliary hypothesis about the curved path of light rays is not ad hoc in this third sense either, since it is not a mere generalization of observed facts. (It is, in fact, an essential ingredient in the General Theory of Relativity.)

The general situation seems to be that it is not necessary to invoke ad hoc hypotheses—in either the second or third senses of the term, which are the derogatory ones—to prevent experiments from being crucial. Even if we confine our attention to theoretically significant hypotheses, and never invoke any ad hoc hypotheses at all, no experiments are ever crucial for individual hypotheses, since hypotheses are testable only in groups.[30] Our limitation here serves to illuminate again the *systematic* character of science. Scientific progress consists in building ever more adequate theories to account for the facts of experience. True enough, it is of value to collect or verify isolated particular facts, for the ultimate basis of science is factual. But the theoretical structure of science grows in a more organic fashion. In the realm of theory, piecemeal progress, one-step-at-a-time advances, can be accomplished, but only within the framework of a generally accepted body of scientific theory. The notion that scientific hypotheses, theories, or laws are wholly discrete and independent is a naive and outdated view.

The term "crucial experiment" is not a useless one, however. Within the framework of accepted scientific theory which we are not concerned to question, a hypothesis *can* be subjected to a crucial experiment. If a negative result is obtained—that is, if some phenomenon fails to occur which had been predicted on the basis of the single dubious hypothesis together with accepted parts of scientific theory—then the experiment is crucial and the hypothesis is rejected. But there is nothing absolute about such a procedure, for even well-accepted scientific theories tend to be changed in the face of new and contrary evidence. Science is not monolithic, either in its practices or in its aims.

Perhaps the most significant lesson to be learned from the preceding discussion is the importance to scientific progress of dragging "hidden assumptions" into the open. That light travels in straight lines was assumed in the arguments of Columbus and Copernicus, but it was a hidden assumption. Because they are hidden, there is

[30] This view has been argued persuasively by P. Duhem in *The Aim and Structure of Physical Theory,* translated by P. P. Wiener, Princeton, 1954. A challenging objection to it can be found in "The Duhemian Argument" by Adolf Grünbaum, in *Philosophy of Science,* Vol. 27, No. 1, January, 1960.

no chance to examine such assumptions critically and to decide intelligently whether they are true or false. Progress is often achieved by formulating explicitly an assumption which had previously been hidden and then scrutinizing and rejecting it. An important and dramatic instance of this occurred when Einstein challenged the universally accepted assumption that it always makes sense to say of two events that they occurred *at the same time*. In considering how an observer could discover whether or not two distant events occurred "at the same time," Einstein was led to the conclusion that two events could be simultaneous for some observers but not for others, depending upon their locations and velocities relative to the events in question. Rejecting the assumption led to the Special Theory of Relativity, which constituted a tremendous step forward in explaining such phenomena as those revealed by the Michelson–Morley experiment. It is clear that an assumption must be recognized before it can be challenged. Hence it is enormously important in science to formulate explicitly all relevant assumptions in any hypothesis, allowing none of them to remain hidden.

13.7 Classification as Hypothesis

It might be objected that hypotheses play important roles only in the more advanced sciences, not in those which are relatively less advanced. It may be urged that although explanatory hypotheses may be central to such sciences as physics and chemistry, they play no such role—at least not yet—in the biological or social sciences. The latter are still in their descriptive phases, and it may be felt that the method of hypothesis is not relevant to the so-called descriptive sciences, such as botany or history. This objection is easily answered. An examination of the nature of description will show that description itself is based on or embodies hypotheses. Hypotheses are as basic to the various systems of taxonomy or classification in biology as they are in history or any of the other social sciences.

The importance of hypothesis in the science of history is easily shown and will be discussed first. Some historians believe that the study of history will reveal the existence of a single cosmic purpose or pattern, either religious or naturalistic, which accounts for or explains the entire course of recorded history. Others deny the existence of any such cosmic design but insist that the study of history will reveal certain historical laws which explain the actual sequence of past events and can be used to predict the future. On either of these views, explanations are to be sought by the historian which must account for and be confirmed by the recorded events of the past. On either of these views, therefore, history is a theoretical rather than a merely descriptive science, and the role of hypothesis must be admitted as central in the historian's enterprise.

There is, however, a third group of historians who set themselves what is apparently a more modest goal. According to them, the task of the historian is simply to chronicle the past, to set forth a bare description of past events in their chronological order. On this view, it might seem, the "scientific" historian has no need of hypotheses, since his concern is with the facts themselves, not with any theories about them.

But past events are not so easily chronicled as this view implies. The past itself is simply not available for this kind of description. What *is* available are present records and traces of the past. These range all the way from official government archives of the recent past to epic poems celebrating the exploits of half-legendary heroes, and from the writings of older historians to artifacts of bygone eras unearthed in the excavations of archeologists. These are the only facts available to the historian, and from them he must infer the nature of those past events it is his purpose to describe. Not *all* hypotheses are general; some are particular. The historian's description of the past is a particular hypothesis which is intended to account for his present data, and for which his present data constitute evidence.

The historian is a detective on a grand scale. Their methods are the same, and their difficulties too. The evidence is scanty, and much of it has been destroyed—if not by the bungling local constabulary, then by intervening wars and natural disasters. And just as the criminal may have left false or misleading clues to throw his pursuer off the scent, so many present "records" are falsifications of the past they purport to describe, either intentional, as in the case of such forged historical documents as the "Donation of Constantine," or unintentional, as in the writings of early uncritical historians. Just as the detective must use the method of science in formulating and testing his hypotheses, so the historian must make hypotheses too. Even those historians who seek to limit themselves to bare descriptions of past events must work with hypotheses: they are theorists in spite of themselves.

The biologist is in a somewhat more favorable position. The facts with which he deals are present and available for inspection. To describe the flora and fauna of a given region, he need not make elaborate inferences of the sort to which the historian is condemned. The data can be perceived directly. His description of these items is not casual, of course, but systematic. He is usually said to *classify* plants and animals, rather than merely to describe them. But classification and description are really the same process. To describe a given animal as carnivorous is to classify it as a carnivore; to classify it as a reptile is to describe it as reptilian. To describe any object as having a certain property is to classify it as a member of the class of objects having that property.

Classification, as generally understood, involves not merely a single division of objects into separate groups but further subdivision of each group into subgroups or subclasses, and so on. This pattern is familiar to most of us, if not from our various studies in school, then certainly from playing the old game of "Animal, Vegetable, or Mineral?" or its more recent version, "Twenty Questions." Apart from such games, there are many motives that have led men to classify objects. For primitive man to live, he was required to classify roots and berries as edible or poisonous, animals as dangerous or harmless, and other men as friend or foe. People tend to draw distinctions which are of practical importance to them and to neglect those that play a less immediate role in their affairs. A farmer will classify grains and vegetables carefully and in detail but may call all flowers "posies"; whereas a florist will classify his merchandise with the greatest of care but may lump all of the farmer's crops together as "produce." There are several motives that may lead us to classify things. One is practical, another theoretical. If one had only three or four books, he could know them all well and could easily take them all in at a glance, so there would be no need to classify them. But in a public or college library containing many thousands of volumes, the situation is different. If the books there were not classified, the librarian could not find the books that might be wanted, and the collection would be practically useless. The larger the number of objects, the greater is the need for classifying them. A practical purpose of classification is to make large collections accessible. This is especially apparent in the case of libraries, museums, and public records of one sort or another.

In considering the theoretical purpose of classification, we must realize that the adoption of this or that alternative classification scheme is not anything which can be true or false. Objects can be described in different ways, from different points of view. The scheme of classification adopted depends upon the purpose or interest of the classifier. Books, for example, would be classified differently by a librarian, a bookbinder, and a bibliophile. The librarian would classify them according to their contents or subject matter, the bookbinder according to their bindings, and a bibliophile according to their date of printing or perhaps their relative rarity. The possibilities are not thereby exhausted, of course: a book packer would divide books according to their shapes and sizes, and persons with still other interests will classify them differently in the light of those different interests.

Now what special interest or purpose does the scientist have which can lead him to prefer one scheme of classification to another? The scientist's aim is knowledge, not merely of this or that particular fact for its own sake, but knowledge of the general laws to which they conform and their causal interrelations. One classification scheme is better than another, from the scientist's point of view, to the extent that it is more fruitful in suggesting scientific laws and more helpful in the formulation of explanatory hypotheses.

The theoretical or scientific motive for classifying objects is the desire to increase our knowledge of them. Increased knowledge of things is further insight into their properties, their similarities and differences, and their interrelations. A classification scheme made for narrowly practical purposes may tend to obscure important similarities and differences. Thus a division of animals into dangerous and harmless will assign the wild boar and the rattlesnake to one class and the domestic pig and the grass snake to the other, calling attention away from what we should today regard as more profound similarities in order to emphasize superficial resemblances. A scientifically fruitful classification of objects requires considerable knowledge about them. A slight acquaintance with their more obvious properties would lead one to classify the bat with birds, as flying creatures, and the whale with fishes, as creatures that live in the sea. But a more extensive knowledge would lead us to classify both bats and whales as mammals, because being warm-blooded, bearing their young alive, and suckling them are more important characteristics on which to base a classificatory scheme.

A characteristic is important when it serves as a clue to the presence of other characteristics. An important characteristic, from the point of view of science, is one which is causally connected with many other characteristics, and hence relevant to the framing of a maximum number of causal laws and the formulation of very general explanatory hypotheses. That classification scheme is best, then, which is based on the most important characteristics of the objects to be classified. But we do not know in advance what causal laws obtain, and causal laws themselves partake of the nature of hypotheses, as was emphasized in the preceding chapter. Therefore any decision as to which classification scheme is best is itself a hypothesis, which subsequent investigations may lead us to reject. If later investigations revealed *other* characteristics to be more important, that is, involved in a greater number of causal laws and explanatory hypotheses, it would be reasonable to expect the earlier classification scheme to be rejected in favor of a newer one based upon the more important characteristics.

This view of classification schemes as hypotheses is borne out by the actual role such schemes play in the sciences. Thus taxonomy is a legitimate, important, and growing branch of biology, in which some classification schemes, like that of Linnaeus, have been adopted, used, and subsequently abandoned in favor of better ones, which are themselves in turn subject to modification in the light of new data. Classification is generally most important in the early or less developed stages of a science. It need not always diminish in importance as the science develops, however. For example, the standard classification scheme for the elements, as set forth in Mendeleeff's Table, is still an important tool for the investigator in the relatively far advanced science of chemistry.

In the light of the foregoing discussion, a further remark can be made on the role of hypothesis in the science of history. It has already been remarked that the historian's descriptions of past events are themselves hypotheses based on present data. There is an additional, equally significant role which hypotheses play in the descriptive historian's enterprise. It is obvious that no historical era or event of any magnitude can be described in *complete detail.* Even if all its details could be known, no historian could possibly include them all in his narrative. Life is too short to permit an exhaustive description of anything. The historian must therefore describe the past selectively, recording only some of its aspects. Upon what basis shall he make his selection? Clearly, the historian wants to include what is significant or important in his descriptions, and to ignore what is insignificant or trivial. The subjective bias of this or that historian may lead him to lay undue stress on the religious, the economic, the personal, or some other aspect of the historic process. But to the extent that he can make an objective or scientific appraisal, the historian will regard those aspects as important which enter into the formulation of causal laws and general explanatory hypotheses. Such appraisals are, of course, subject to correction in the light of further research.

The first Western historian, Herodotus, described a great many aspects of the events he chronicled, personal and cultural as well as political and military. The so-called first scientific historian, Thucydides, restricted himself much more to the political and the military. For a long period of time most historians followed Thucydides, but now the pendulum is swinging in another direction, and the economic and cultural aspects of the past are being given increased emphasis. Just as the biologist's classification scheme embodies his hypothesis as to which characteristics of living things are involved in a maximum number of causal laws, so the historian's decision to describe past events in terms of one rather than another set of properties embodies his hypothesis as to which properties are causally related to a maximum number of others. Some such hypothesis is required before the historian can even begin any systematic description of the past. It is this hypothetical character of classification and description, whether biological or historical, which leads us to regard hypothesis as the all-pervasive method of scientific inquiry.

EXERCISES

In each of the following passages:

a. What data are to be explained?

b. What hypotheses are proposed to explain them?

c. Evaluate the hypotheses in terms of the criteria presented in Section 13.3.

★ 1. Since Venus rotates so slowly, we might be tempted to conclude that Venus, like Mercury, keeps one face always toward the Sun. If this hypothesis were correct we should expect that the dark side would be exceedingly cold. Pettit and Nicholson have measured the temperature of the dark side of Venus. They find that the temperature is not low, its value being only −9°F., much warmer than our stratosphere in broad daylight. It is unlikely that atmospheric currents from the bright side of Venus could perpetually heat the dark side. The planet must rotate fairly often to keep the dark side from cooling excessively.

—FRED L. WHIPPLE, *Earth, Moon and Planets*

2. Toxin–antitoxin reactions were the first immunological processes to which experimental precision could be applied, and the discovery of principles of great importance resulted from such studies. . . . The simplest assumption to account for the manner in which an antitoxin renders a toxin innocuous would be that the antitoxin destroys the toxin. Roux and Buchner, however, advanced the opinion that the antitoxins did not act directly upon toxin, but affected it indirectly through the mediation of tissue cells. Ehrlich, on the other hand, conceived the reaction of toxin and antitoxin as a direct union, analogous to the chemical neutralization of an acid by a base.

The conception of toxin destruction was conclusively refuted by the experiments of Calmette. This observer, working with snake poison, found that the poison itself (unlike most other toxins) possessed the property of resisting heat to 100°C., while its specific antitoxin, like other antitoxins, was destroyed at or about 70°C. Nontoxic mixtures of the two substances, when subjected to heat, regained their toxic properties. The natural inference from these observations was that the toxin in the original mixture had not been destroyed, but had been merely inactivated by the presence of the antitoxin, and again set free after destruction of the antitoxin by heat.

—HANS ZINSSER and STANHOPE BAYNE-JONES, *A Textbook of Bacteriology*

3. Indeed, from the commencement of the period during which we possess historic accounts, that is, for a period of about 4000 years, the temperature of the earth has not sensibly diminished. From these old ages we have certainly no thermometric observations, but we have information regarding the distribution of certain cultivated plants, the vine, the olive tree, which are very sensitive to changes of the mean annual temperature, and we find that these plants at the present moment have the same limits of distribution that they had in the times of Abraham and Homer; from which we may infer backwards the constancy of the climate.

—HERMANN VON HELMHOLTZ, "The Conservation of Energy"

4. *The Migration of Angels*

With the advent of more powerful radar sets employing higher frequencies, radar operators have been bothered by "angels": clouds of dots that from time to time appear on the screen and sometimes become thick enough to obliterate what the operator is trying to see. Just what causes angels has been something of a mystery. Some scientists have suggested that various meteorological conditions may be responsible, but others have observed that this can hardly be the explanation, for angels usually move faster than the wind.

After independent studies, three British workers have concluded that angels are simply radar pictures of migrating birds, chiefly small songbirds. In *Proceedings of the Royal Society* they present their evidence:

Angel activity is at a peak near the end of March and again late in October. Small birds migrate over Britain at just these seasons. There are daily peaks in angel activity about 10 P.M. and 10 A.M. Most small migrating birds feed during the day and start flying soon after dark. Others, including crows and starlings, fly early in the day.

Angels are more prevalent on clear days, especially after a stretch of stormy weather. Migrating birds tend to weather storms by staying on the ground, then resume flying on the first good day.

If birds are indeed responsible for angels, there seems to be little that radar operators can do to keep their screens clear. On the other hand, radar can be an invaluable tool for ornithologists, who up to now have had no reliable way to observe nighttime migration.

The authors of the reports were J. G. Tedd of the R.A.F. Fighter

Command, David Lack of the Edward Grey Institute of Field Ornithology at Oxford and W. G. Harper of the British Meteorological Office.

—"Science and the Citizen," *Scientific American*[31]

★ 5. Dr. Konrad Buettner of the University of California at Los Angeles has recently advanced the hypothesis that, during the lifetime of the moon, the everlasting influx of cosmic rays has slowly ground the upper-surface layers of rocks into fine dust. That the moon's skin cannot consist of solid rocks has been demonstrated through temperature measurements during lunar eclipses. As soon as the shadow of the earth creeps over the measuring area the temperature drops steeply, and after half an hour it is over 200°F. lower than it was in the full sun. When the shadow has passed by, the temperature again rises at a similarly steep rate. No solid piece of rock can cool down and heat up so quickly. These drastic temperature changes can be explained only by the existence of a thick layer of heat-insulating dust as fine as face powder. The thickness of the layer must be at least several inches. The sandblasting of meteoric dust also grinds at the moon's surface, but cosmic rays can be expected to do a much better job.

—HEINZ HABER, *Man in Space*[32]

6. On the 7th of January 1610, at one o'clock in the morning, when he directed his telescope to Jupiter, he observed three stars near the body of the planet, two being to the east and one to the west of him. They were all in a straight line, and parallel to the ecliptic, and they appeared brighter than other stars of the same magnitude. Believing them to be fixed stars, he paid no great attention to their distances from Jupiter and from one another. On the 8th of January, however, when, from some cause or other, he had been led to observe the stars again, he found a very different arrangement of them: all the three were on the west side of Jupiter, *nearer one another than before,* and almost at equal distances. Though he had not turned his attention to the extraordinary fact of the mutual approach of the stars, yet he began to consider how Jupiter could be found to the east of the three stars, when but the day before he had been to the west of two of them. The only explanation which he could give of this fact was, that the motion of Jupiter was *direct,* contrary to astronomical calculations, and that he had got before these two stars by his own motion.

In this dilemma between the testimony of his senses and the results of calculation, he waited for the following night with the utmost anxiety; but his hopes were disappointed, for the heavens were wholly veiled in

[31] Reprinted from "Science and the Citizen" in *Scientific American,* Vol. 200, No. 3, March 1959.

[32] From *Man in Space* by Heinz Haber, © 1953. Used by special permission of the publishers, The Bobbs-Merrill Company, Inc.

clouds. On the 10th, two only of the stars appeared, and both on the east of the planet. As it was obviously impossible that Jupiter could have advanced from west to east on the 8th of January, and from east to west on the 10th, Galileo was forced to conclude that the phenomenon which he had observed arose from the motion of the stars, and he set himself to observe diligently their change of place. On the 11th, there were still only two stars, and both to the east of Jupiter; but the more eastern star was now *twice as large as the other one,* though on the preceding night they had been perfectly equal. This fact threw a new light upon Galileo's difficulties, and he immediately drew the conclusion, which he considered to be indubitable, '*that there were in the heaven three stars which revolved round Jupiter, in the same manner as Venus and Mercury revolved round the sun.*' On the 12th of January, he again observed them in new positions, and of different magnitudes; and, on the 13th, he discovered a fourth star, which completed the *four* secondary planets with which Jupiter is surrounded.

—SIR DAVID BREWSTER, *The Martyrs of Science*

7. Again however solid things are thought to be, you may yet learn from this that they are of rare body: in rocks and caverns the moisture of water oozes through and all things weep with abundant drops; food distributes itself through the whole body of living things; trees grow and yield fruit in season, because food is diffused through the whole from the very roots over the stem and all the boughs. Voices pass through walls and fly through houses shut, stiffening frost pierces to the bones. Now if there are no void parts, by what way can the bodies severally pass? You would see it to be quite impossible. Once more, why do we see one thing surpass another in weight though not larger in size? For if there is just as much body in a ball of wool as there is in a lump of lead, it is natural it should weigh the same, since the property of body is to weigh all things downwards, while on the contrary the nature of void is ever without weight. Therefore when a thing is just as large, yet is found to be lighter, it proves sure enough that it has more of void in it; while on the other hand that which is heavier shows that there is in it more of body and that it contains within it much less of void. Therefore that which we are seeking with keen reason exists sure enough, mixed up in things; and we call it void.

—LUCRETIUS, *On the Nature of Things,* Book I

8. . . . there was something wrong with the atomic model based on the discovery of the nucleus, the model that depicted the atom as a miniature solar system.

According to this model, the electron was attracted to the nucleus of opposite electrical charge. Therefore the electron would move; it would move, like the planets, in an elliptical orbit around the nucleus-sun. But a moving electron was impossible. Why? Because, according to the laws of electricity, a moving charge must produce electromagnetic radiation, light. The electron, always in motion, would produce radiation; all atoms would emit light at all times. But matter under ordinary circumstances does not glow with light.

—BARBARA LOVETT CLINE, *Men Who Made a New Physics*

9. While walking one night with Dr. Frink, we accidentally met a colleague, Dr. P., whom I had not seen for years, and of whose private life I knew nothing. We were naturally very pleased to meet again, and on my invitation, he accompanied us to a café, where we spent about two hours in pleasant conversation. To my question as to whether he was married, he gave a negative answer, and added, "Why should a man like me marry?"

On leaving the café, he suddenly turned to me and said: "I should like to know what you would do in a case like this: I know a nurse who was named as co-respondent in a divorce case. The wife sued the husband for divorce and named her as co-respondent, and *he* got the divorce." I interrupted him saying, "You mean *she* got the divorce." He immediately corrected himself saying, "Yes, she got the divorce," and continued to tell how the excitement of the trial had affected this nurse to such an extent that she became nervous and took to drink. He wanted me to advise him how to treat her.

As soon as I had corrected his mistake, I asked him to explain it, but, as is usually the case, he was surprised at my question. He wanted to know whether a person had no right to make mistakes in talking. I explained to him that there is a reason for every mistake, and that if he had not told me that he was unmarried, I should say that he was the hero of the divorce case in question, and that the mistake showed that he wished he had obtained the divorce instead of his wife, so as not to be obliged to pay alimony and to be permitted to marry again in New York State.

He stoutly denied my interpretation, but his emotional agitation, followed by loud laughter, only strengthened my suspicions. To my appeal that he should tell the truth "for science' sake," he said, "Unless you wish me to lie, you must believe that I was never married, and hence, your psychoanalytic interpretation is all wrong." He, however, added that it was dangerous to be with a person who paid attention to such little things. Then he suddenly remembered that he had another appointment and left us.

Both Dr. Frink and I were convinced that my interpretation of his *lapsus linguae* was correct, and I decided to corroborate or disprove it by further investigation. The next day, I found a neighbor and old friend of Dr. P., who confirmed my interpretation in every particular.

The divorce was granted to Dr. P's wife a few weeks before, and a nurse was named as co-respondent. A few weeks later, I met Dr. P., and he told me that he was thoroughly convinced of the Freudian mechanisms.

—A. A. BRILL, *Psychoanalysis: Its Theories and Practical Applications*[33]

★ 10. Nearly everyone has seen sleeping pets whimper, twitch their whiskers, and seemingly pump their legs in pursuit of dream rabbits. But are they really dreaming? Since animals can't wake up the next morning and describe their dreams, the question seemed unanswerable. But recently, Dr. Charles Vaughan of the University of Pittsburgh devised an ingenious experiment so animals could tell us, at last, that they were indeed dreaming. Rhesus monkeys were placed in booths in front of a screen and taught to press on a bar every time they saw an image on the screen. Then the monkeys were wired to an electroencephalograph machine and placed back in their special booths. Eventually they fell asleep. Soon the EEG was recording the special tracings produced by the dreaming brains of the monkeys. But most important—the sleeping monkeys were eagerly pressing the bars. Clearly they were seeing images on the screens of their minds—they were dreaming. Or so Dr. Vaughan believes.[34]

11. In the different excursions which he [Captain Vancouver] made, particularly about Port Discovery, the skulls, limbs, ribs, and backbones, or some other vestiges of the human body, were scattered promiscuously in great numbers; and, as no warlike scars were observed on the bodies of the remaining Indians, and no particular signs of fear and suspicion were noticed, the most probable conjecture seems to be that this depopulation must have been occasioned by pestilential disease.

—THOMAS ROBERT MALTHUS, *An Essay on Population*

12. . . . one of Rutherford's students, given the problem of measuring the ionizing property of the radioactive element thorium (which gave its degree of radioactivity), had run into difficulties. His electroscope gave a different intensity of ionization at different times; he could not arrive at a definite measurement. And curiously enough, the different intensities seemed to depend on whether the door to the laboratory was closed or open.

At this point Rutherford became very interested in the problem. Before long he had explained the capricious measurements with the

[33] Reprinted from *Psychoanalysis: Its Theories and Practical Applications* by A. A. Brill. Copyright, 1921, by W. B. Saunders Company.

[34] By permission from Bob Gaines, "You and Your Sleep," in *Ladies Home Journal,* March, 1967, page 56. Another short popular account of these experiments can be found in *Sleep,* by Gay Gaer Luce and Julius Segal, Coward-McCann, Inc., 1966, New York.

discovery that the element thorium emits a radioactive gas (now called "thoron"). When the laboratory door was closed, the gas hovered over the element, adding its radioactivity to that of thorium; but when the door was open, the gas was blown about the laboratory by air drafts.

—BARBARA LOVETT CLINE, *Men Who Made a New Physics*

13. Like multiple sclerosis, poliomyelitis in its paralytic form was a disease of the more advanced nations rather than of the less advanced ones, and of economically better-off people rather than of the poor. It occurred in northern Europe and North America much more frequently than in southern Europe or the countries of Africa, Asia or South America. Immigrants to South Africa from northern Europe ran twice the risk of contracting paralytic poliomyelitis than South-African-born whites ran, and the South-African-born whites ran a much greater risk than nonwhites. Among the Bantu of South Africa paralytic poliomyelitis was rarely an adult disease. During World War II in North Africa cases of paralytic poliomyelitis were commoner among officers in the British and American forces than among men in the other ranks. At the time various wild hypotheses for the difference were proposed; it was even suggested that it arose from the fact that the officers drank whisky whereas men in the other ranks drank beer!

We now understand very well the reason for the strange distribution of paralytic poliomyelitis. Until this century poliomyelitis was a universal infection of infancy and infants hardly ever suffered paralysis from it. The fact that they were occasionally so affected is what gave the disease the name "infantile paralysis." With the improvement of hygiene in the advancing countries of the world more and more people missed infection in early childhood and contracted the disease for the first time at a later age, when the risk that the infection will cause paralysis is much greater.

This explains why the first epidemics of poliomyelitis did not occur until this century and then only in the economically advanced countries.

—GEOFFREY DEAN, "The Multiple Sclerosis Problem"[35]

14. Two other theories assume that the Caribbean is basically oceanic. In one view, the sea opened when North and South America drifted apart; in the other, the Caribbean basin is a segment of Pacific crust that became wedged between the two large continents as they drifted westward. . . .

It was to test these hypotheses that scientists on Leg 15 of the Deep Sea Drilling Project went into the Caribbean for a two-month period ending Jan. 26. . . .

The findings were surprising. Each core, says Dr. Terence Edgar, co-

[35] Reprinted from "The Multiple Sclerosis Problem" by Geoffrey Dean in *Scientific American*, Vol. 223, No. 1, July 1970.

chief scientist for the cruise and now chief scientist for the entire project, is accurately dated by microorganisms entombed in the sediments. The oldest sediments turned out to be only 75 million to 85 million years old. In contrast, the oldest part of the Atlantic is about 180 million years old, dating from the time when the continents first split and the present phase of sea-floor spreading began. If the Caribbean were formed when the continents broke up, Dr. Edgar and Saunders point out, the Caribbean crust would be about the same age as the Atlantic. If it were a piece of Pacific crust, they say, it would be even older. The youth of the Caribbean basins, therefore, essentially eliminates these two hypotheses, the scientists conclude.

—LOUISE PURRETT, "The Birth of the Caribbean"[36]

15. A number of the Einsteinian gravitational effects, such as the bending of light rays by the gravity of a massive body or the existence of gravitational waves, have been tested experimentally, and proof is claimed for them.

In spite of its experimental successes, a number of physicists have been unhappy with Einstein's theory on philosophical grounds. In the late 19th century the physicist and philosopher Ernst Mach proposed that the strength of gravitational forces should depend on the distribution of matter in the universe. As the universe expands and the total mass in it is spread thinner, gravity should weaken, he said. That is, the force between two bodies of constant mass at a constant distance from each other should weaken as the universe expands.

Einstein rejected this suggestion. In his theory, as in Newton's, the strength of gravity remains constant. Other physicists, however, have put forth theories in which Mach's idea is accepted.

The latest of these theories, proposed by Drs. Carl H. Brans of Loyola University and Robert H. Dicke of Princeton University, has been the subject of a number of inconclusive tests in recent years. The latest, most stringent test, reported at California Institute of Technology last week by Dr. John D. Anderson of Caltech's Jet Propulsion Laboratory, claims definitely to support Einstein over Brans and Dicke.

The test involves the prediction, contained in both theories, that the speed of a light ray passing a massive body will be slowed by the body's gravitational effect. The prediction was first tested two years ago using the sun as the massive body and looking for the slowing of radar beams reflected from planets on the other side of it from the earth. The experiment showed that the slowing occurred, but was not accurate enough to distinguish between the rival theories, which predict slightly different amounts.

[36] Reprinted from "The Birth of the Caribbean" by Louise Purrett in *Science News*, Vol. 99, No. 10, March 6, 1971.

The experiment done by Dr. Anderson, with Dr. Duane O. Muhleman, Dr. Pasquale Esposito and Warren L. Martin, used radio signals reflected from Mariners 6 and 7 in the spring of 1970 as the spacecraft went behind the sun. The measured delay in the arrival of the signal at JPL's 210-foot antenna at Goldstone, Calif., was 204 microseconds in a maximum time of round-trip flight of 43 minutes. Einstein's theory predicts a delay of 200 microseconds, the Brans-Dicke theory 186 microseconds.

Dr. Anderson says the results are accurate to between 2 and 4 percent and claims they are a vindication of Einstein. So far Dr. Dicke is not giving up, although he concedes that later, more precise figures may force him to.

—"Space Age Support for Einstein," *Science News*[37]

[37] Reprinted with permission from *Science News*, the weekly news magazine of science and the applications of science, Vol. 98, No. 21, November 21, 1970. Copyright 1970 by Science Service, Inc.

Chapter 14
Probability

If we be, therefore, engaged by arguments to put trust in past experience, and make it the standard of our future judgment, these arguments must be probable only. . . .

—*David Hume*

14.1 Alternative Conceptions of Probability

The words "probable" and "probability" have been frequently used thus far in our discussion of inductive logic and scientific method. Even a hypothesis which fits all the available facts is not thereby established conclusively, it was said, but only *with probability*. And the most protracted and careful uses of Mill's Methods of experimental inquiry do not *demonstrate* the laws to which they lead as being certain, but only tend to confirm them as being highly *probable*. Even the best inductive arguments fall short of that certainty which attaches to valid deductive arguments.

The words "probable" and "probability" are used in various different ways. We say, for example, that the probability of a tossed coin showing *heads* is $\frac{1}{2}$; that the probability of a twenty-five-year-old man surviving his twenty-sixth birthday is .963; and that on the present evidence, it is highly probable that Einstein's Theory of Relativity is correct. There are other contexts in which the words "probable" and "probability" are used, as in speaking of "probable errors" of measurement, and so on. But the first three may be taken as the most important and typical uses of the terms. The third is the most significant for scientific hypotheses. It differs from the first two in not assigning any numerical coefficient of probability. *Degrees* of probability are assigned to scientific hypotheses only in terms of more and less. Thus the Darwinian theory is regarded as more probable than the account of creation given in the Book of Genesis, and the atomic theory has a higher degree of probability than any of the recent highly speculative hypotheses concerning the inner structures of nuclei.

The first two of our three examples assign numbers as measures of the probabilities they assert. The sources of these numbers seem fairly clear. Coins have two sides, heads and tails, and when they fall, one side or the other must face upward. One chance out of two will place heads up, and so the probability ½ is assigned to heads. To arrive at the probability coefficient mentioned in the second example, mortality statistics must be gathered and compared. Of perhaps 1,000 men who had celebrated their twenty-fifth birthday, it was found that 963 of them lived at least one additional year, and on the basis of these findings the figure .963 was assigned to the probability of a twenty-five-year-old man's surviving his twenty-sixth birthday. Such probability measurements as these are utilized by life insurance companies in fixing the size of premiums to be charged for their policies.

As the first two examples may suggest, studies of probability are bound up with gambling and mortality statistics; in fact, the modern study of probability had its beginnings in these two fields. The theory of probability is commonly regarded as having begun with the correspondence between Blaise Pascal (1623–1662) and Pierre de Fermat (1608–1665) over the proper division of the stakes in an interrupted game of chance. Another version had it begin with Pascal's advice to the Chevalier de Méré, a notorious seventeenth-century gambler, on how to wager in throwing dice. In connection with the study of mortality, in 1662 Captain John Graunt published a discussion of the mortality records which had been kept in London since 1592. Possibly as a consequence of its mixed ancestry, probability has been given two different interpretations.

The classical theory of the nature of probability, as formulated by Laplace, De Morgan, Keynes, and others, regards it as measuring degree of rational belief. When we are completely convinced of something, the measure of our belief may have the number 1 assigned it. And when we are utterly certain that a specified event cannot possibly happen, our belief that it *will* happen can be assigned the number 0. Thus a rational man's belief that a tossed coin will *either* show heads or not show heads is 1, and his belief that it will *both* show heads and not show heads is 0. Where he is not sure, the degree of his reasonable belief will fall somewhere between 0 and 1. Probability is predicated of an event according to the degree to which one rationally believes that it will occur. Or probability may be predicated of a statement or proposition according to the degree to which a completely rational man will believe it.

On the classical view, probability is always a result of partial knowledge and partial ignorance. If the exact motion of one's fingers in flipping a coin were known, together with the initial position, dimensions, and weight distribution of the coin, one could predict its trajectory and final resting position with complete confidence. But such complete information is not available. Only some information is known: that the coin has only two sides, that it will fall, and so on. Consequently our belief that it will show heads is measured by a consideration of the various possibilities, which are 2, of which heads is only 1. Therefore the probability $1/2$ is assigned to the event of the coin showing heads. Similarly, when a deck of cards is about to be dealt, the cards are in just the order that they are, and will come off the deck, in an honest deal, in exactly the sequence of spades and hearts and diamonds and clubs, aces and kings and queens and jacks, that is determined by their arrangement in the deck. But we do not know that arrangement. We know only that there are thirteen spades, out of fifty-two cards altogether, so the probability that the first card dealt will be a spade is exactly $13/52$ or $1/4$.

This view is known as the *a priori* theory of probability. It is so called because no trials need be run before the probability is assigned, no sample deals need be examined. All that is required is a knowledge of the antecedent conditions: that there are four aces only in the deck, that there are fifty-two cards altogether, and that it is an honest deal, so that one card has as much chance as any other of being dealt first. On the *a priori* view, all we need do to compute the probability of an event's occurring in given circumstances is to divide the number of ways in which it can occur by the total number of possible outcomes of those circumstances, provided there is no reason to believe that any one of those possible outcomes is more likely than any other.

An alternative to the *a priori* view is the theory which regards probability as a measure of "relative frequency." The relative-frequency theory seems especially suited to take account of probability judgments arising out of statistical investigations. Thus an actuary observes a number of men in order to determine what mortality rate they exhibit. Here we have a class and a property, the class being that of twenty-five-year-old men, the property that of surviving their twenty-sixth birthdays. The probability assigned is the measure of the relative frequency with which the members of the class exhibit the property in question. Of 1,000 twenty-five-year-old men, if 963 exhibit the property of surviving at least one additional year, the number .963 is assigned as the probability coefficient for the occurrence of this property in any such class. On the relative-frequency theory of probability, then, probability is not defined in terms of rational belief. Probability is defined as the relative frequency with which members of a class exhibit a specified property.

The relative-frequency theory, as its name implies, regards probability as relative. Thus if the question is raised as to the probability with which blondness of hair occurs, this varies with respect to the different reference classes relative to which the property may occur. For example, the probability of blondness is higher relative to the class of Scandinavians than it is relative to the total population of the world.

The *a priori* theory also regards probability as relative. In the language of the classical *a priori* theory, no event has any *intrinsic* probability. It can be assigned a probability only on the basis of the evidence available to the person making the assignment. This relativity is to be expected on a view which regards probability as a measure of rational belief, for the reasonable man's beliefs change according to the state of his knowledge. Suppose, for example, that two people are watching a deck of cards being shuffled. When the shuffle is finished, the dealer accidentally "flashes" the top card. One observer sees that the card is black, although he is not able to observe whether it is a spade or a club. But the second observer notices nothing. If the two observers are asked to estimate the probability of the first card's being a spade, the first observer will assign the probability ½, since there are only twenty-six black cards, of which half are spades. But the second observer will assign the probability ¼, since he knows only that there are thirteen spades in the deck of fifty-two cards. The two observers thus assign different probabilities to the same event. Has one of them made a mistake? Certainly not: each has assigned the correct probability *relative to the evidence at his disposal.* Both estimates are correct—even if the card turns out to be a club. No event has any probability *by itself,* which means that any prediction will have different probabilities in different contexts, that is, relative to different sets of evidence. It is important to notice that although the event has different probabilities relative to different amounts of evidence, it would be a mistake for anyone to use less than the total evidence available to him in judging probabilities.

Because of their agreement upon the relative nature of probability, adherents of both theories agree on the acceptability and utility of the probability calculus, of which an elementary presentation will be made in the following section.

14.2 The Probability Calculus

The probability calculus is a branch of pure mathematics which can be used in computing the probabilities of complex events from the probabilities of their component events. A complex event can be regarded as a whole of which its component events are parts. For example, the complex event of drawing two spades from a deck of playing cards is a whole of which the two parts are the event of drawing the first spade and the event of subsequently drawing another spade. Again, the complex event of a bride and groom living to celebrate their golden wedding is a whole of which the parts are the event of the bride's living an additional fifty years, the groom's living an additional fifty years, and no separation taking place. When it is known how the component events are related to each other, the probability of the complex event can be *calculated* from the probabilities of its components. Although the probability calculus has a much wider range of applications, it is most easily explained in terms of games of chance, so most of our examples and illustrations in this section will be drawn from the sphere of gambling. And the *a priori* theory will be used here, though it should be emphasized that all our results, with a minimum of reinterpretation, can be expressed and justified in terms of the relative-frequency theory.

1. ***Joint Occurrences.*** Let us first turn our attention to complex events which have as their component parts events which are *independent*. Two events are said to be *independent* if the occurrence or nonoccurrence of either of them has absolutely no effect on the occurrence or nonoccurrence of the other. For example, if two coins are tossed, whether one comes down heads or tails has no effect upon whether the other shows heads or tails. Let us pose as our first problem: what is the probability of getting two heads in tossing two coins? There are three possible outcomes to tossing two coins: we may get two heads, or we may get two tails, or we may get one head and one tail. *But these are not equipossible alternatives,* for there are two ways of getting one head and one tail, as contrasted with only one way of getting two heads. The first coin may be heads and the second tails, or the first coin may be tails and the second one heads; these are two distinct cases. There are four distinct possible events which may occur when two coins are tossed; they may be listed as follows:

First Coin	Second Coin
H	H
H	T
T	H
T	T

There is no reason for expecting any one of these cases to occur rather than any other, so we regard them as equipossible. The *favorable* case, that of getting two heads, is only one of four equipossible events, so the probability of getting two heads in tossing two coins is $1/4$. The probability for this complex event may be calculated from the probabilities of its two independent component events. The complex event of getting two heads is constituted by the joint occurrence of the event of getting a head on the first and the event of getting a head on the second. The probability of getting a head on the first is $1/2$, and the probability of getting a head on the second is also $1/2$. The events are presumed to be independent, so that the *product theorem* of the probability calculus can be used to compute the probability of their joint occurrence. The product theorem for independent events asserts that the probability of the joint occurrence of two independent events is equal to the product of their separate probabilities. The general formula may be written:

$$P(a \text{ and } b) = P(a) \times P(b)$$

where a and b designate the two independent events, $P(a)$ and $P(b)$ designate their separate probabilities, and $P(a \text{ and } b)$ designates the probability of their joint occurrence. In the present case, since a is the event of the first coin falling heads, and b is the event of the second coin falling heads, $P(a) = 1/2$ and $P(b) = 1/2$, so $P(a \text{ and } b) = 1/2 \times 1/2 = 1/4$.

Let us consider a second problem of the same sort. What is the probability of getting a 12 in rolling two dice? Two dice will show twelve points only if each of them shows six points. Each die has six sides, any one of which is as likely to be face up after a roll as any other. Where a is the event of the first die showing a 6, $P(a) = 1/6$. And where b is the event of the second die showing a 6, $P(b) = 1/6$. The complex event of the two dice showing a 12 is constituted by the joint occurrence of a and b. By the product theorem, then $P(a \text{ and } b) = 1/6 \times 1/6 = 1/36$, which is the probability of getting a 12 on one roll of two dice. We can arrive at the same result by taking the trouble to enumerate all the possible events which may occur when two dice are rolled. There are thirty-six equipossible events, which may be listed as follows, where of each pair of numbers the first stands for the number on the top face of the first die, the second for the number showing on the second one:

1–1	2–1	3–1	4–1	5–1	6–1
1–2	2–2	3–2	4–2	5–2	6–2
1–3	2–3	3–3	4–3	5–3	6–3
1–4	2–4	3–4	4–4	5–4	6–4
1–5	2–5	3–5	4–5	5–5	6–5
1–6	2–6	3–6	4–6	5–6	6–6

Of these thirty-six equipossible cases, only one is favorable (to getting a 12), so the probability is thus seen directly to be $\frac{1}{36}$.

The product theorem may be *generalized* to cover the joint occurrence of any number of independent events. Thus if we draw a card from a deck, replace it and draw again, and replace it and draw once more, the event of drawing three spades is the joint occurrence of the event of getting a spade on the first draw, the event of getting a spade on the second draw, and the event of getting a spade on the third draw. Where these three events are designated by a, b, and c, their joint probability $P(a \text{ and } b \text{ and } c)$ is equal to the product of the separate probabilities of the three events: $P(a) \times P(b) \times P(c)$. The probability is easily computed. A deck of cards contains fifty-two different cards of which thirteen are spades. There are fifty-two equipossible drawings, of which thirteen are favorable to the event of drawing a spade. The probability of getting a spade is $\frac{13}{52}$ or $\frac{1}{4}$. Since the card drawn is replaced before drawing again, the initial conditions for the second drawing are the same, so $P(a)$, $P(b)$, and $P(c)$ are all equal to $\frac{1}{4}$. Their joint occurrence has the probability $P(a \text{ and } b \text{ and } c) = \frac{1}{4} \times \frac{1}{4} \times \frac{1}{4} = \frac{1}{64}$. The *general product theorem* allows us to compute the probability of the joint occurrence of any number of independent events. Next we turn to events which are *not* independent.

It is frequently possible to compute the probability of the joint occurrence of several events even when they are not completely independent. In the previous example, if the card drawn is *not* replaced in the deck before the next drawing, the outcome of the earlier drawings *does* have an effect on the outcome of the later drawings. If the first card drawn is a spade, then for the second draw there are only twelve spades left among a total of fifty-one cards, whereas if the first card is *not* a spade, then there are thirteen spades left among fifty-one cards. Where a is the event of drawing a spade from the deck and not replacing it, and b is the event of drawing another spade from among the remaining cards, then the probability of b, $P(b \text{ if } a)$, is $^{12}/_{51}$ or $^{4}/_{17}$. And if both a and b occur, the third draw will be made from a deck of fifty cards containing only eleven spades. If c is this last event, then $P(c \text{ if both } a \text{ and } b)$ is $^{11}/_{50}$. Thus the probability that all three are spades if three cards are drawn from a deck and not replaced is, according to the product theorem, $^{13}/_{52} \times {}^{12}/_{51} \times {}^{11}/_{50}$, or $^{11}/_{850}$. This is *less* than the probability of getting three spades in three draws when the cards drawn are replaced before drawing again, which was to be expected, since replacing a spade enhances the probability of getting a spade on the next draw.

Let us consider another example involving the probability of the joint occurrence of dependent events. Suppose we have an urn containing two white balls and one black ball. If two balls are drawn in succession, the first one *not* being replaced before drawing the second, what is the probability that both balls drawn will be white? Let a be the event of drawing a white ball on the first draw. There are three equipossible draws, one for each ball. Of these, two are favorable, since two of the balls are white. The probability of getting a white ball on the first draw, $P(a)$, is therefore $^{2}/_{3}$. If a occurs, then there remain only two balls in the urn, one white and one black. The probability of getting a white ball on the second draw, which event we may call "b," is clearly $^{1}/_{2}$; that is, $P(b \text{ if } a) = {}^{1}/_{2}$. Now by the general product theorem, the probability of getting two white balls is the probability of the joint occurrence of a and b if a, which is the product of the probabilities of their separate occurrences, $^{2}/_{3} \times {}^{1}/_{2} = {}^{1}/_{3}$. The general formula here is

$$P(a \text{ and } b) = P(a) \times P(b \text{ if } a)$$

The probability of getting two white balls in two such successive draws can be reached, in this simple situation, by considering all possible cases. Where one white ball is designated by "W_1" and the other white ball by "W_2" and the black ball by "B," the following equipossible pairs of draws may be listed:

First Draw	Second Draw
W_1	W_2
W_1	B
W_2	W_1
W_2	B
B	W_1
B	W_2

Of these six equipossible events, two are favorable (the first and third), which gives $\frac{1}{3}$ directly as the probability of getting two white balls in two successive draws with no replacement made.

EXERCISES

★ 1. What is the probability of getting tails every time in three tosses of a coin?

2. What is the probability of getting three aces in three successive draws from a deck of cards: (a) if the card drawn is replaced before making the next drawing; (b) if the cards drawn are not replaced?

3. An urn contains twenty-seven white balls and forty black balls. What is the probability of getting four black balls in four successive drawings: (a) if each ball drawn is replaced before making the next drawing; (b) if the balls are not replaced?

4. What is the probability of rolling three dice so the total number of points which appear on their top faces is 3, three times in a row?

★ 5. Four men whose houses are built around a square spend an evening celebrating in the center of the square. At the end of the celebration each staggers off to one of the houses, no two going to the same house. What is the probability that each one reached his own house?

6. A dentist has his office in a building with five entrances, all equally accessible. Three patients arrive at his office at the same time. What is the probability that they all entered the building by the same door?

7. Suppose that the probability that a man of twenty-five will survive his fiftieth birthday is .742, and that the probability that a woman of twenty-two will survive her forty-seventh birthday is .801. Suppose further that the probability that a marriage contracted by such a couple will not end in divorce during the first twenty-five years is .902. What is the probability that such a couple will live to celebrate their silver wedding anniversary?

8. In each of two closets there are three cartons. Five of the cartons contain canned vegetables. The other carton contains canned fruits: ten cans of pears, eight cans of peaches, and six cans of fruit cocktail. Each can of fruit cocktail contains three hundred chunks of fruit of approximately equal size, of which three are cherries. If a child goes into one of the closets, unpacks one of the cartons, opens a can and eats two pieces of its contents, what is the probability that he will enjoy two cherries?

9. A player at draw poker holds the seven of spades and the eight, nine, ten, and ace of diamonds. Aware that all the other players are draw-

ing three cards, he figures that any hand he could win with a flush he could also win with a straight. For which should he draw? (A *straight* consists of five cards in numerical sequence; a *flush* consists of five cards all of the same suit.)

10. How would you distribute fifty white balls and fifty black balls in two urns to maximize the probability that a random drawing of one ball from each urn would yield two white balls?

2. ***Alternative Occurrences.*** The preceding discussion dealt with complex events constituted by the joint occurrence of two or more component events. Some events whose probability it may be desired to compute are of a different sort. These may be constituted by the occurrence of one or more of several alternative events. For example, in tossing two coins, we may be interested not in the event of getting two heads but in the event of getting *either* two heads or two tails. These component events, one of getting two heads, the other of getting two tails, are *exclusive* events, that is, they cannot both occur. The formula for computing the probability of a complex event which is said to occur when either of two *mutually exclusive* events occurs is:

$$P(a \text{ or } b) = P(a) + P(b)$$

That is, the probability that at least one of two mutually exclusive events occurs is the *sum* of their separate probabilities. Since the probability of getting two heads is $1/4$ and the probability of getting two tails is $1/4$, and since these are exclusive possibilities, the probability of getting *either* two heads or two tails is $1/4 + 1/4 = 1/2$. This result may also be obtained, in this simple case, by considering that the four equipossible events which could occur when two coins are tossed are *H–H, H–T, T–H, T–T,* of which two, the first and fourth, are favorable to the event of getting either two heads or two tails. Here direct inspection shows the probability to be $1/2$.

The *addition theorem* stated in the preceding paragraph obviously generalizes to the case of any number of exclusive alternative events. The product theorem and the addition theorem may be used together to compute the probabilities of complex events. Consider the problem of computing the probability of being dealt a flush in a poker game (a *flush* consists of five cards all of the same suit). There are four exclusive alternatives here: the event of getting five spades, the event of getting five hearts, the event of getting five diamonds, the event of getting five clubs. The probability of getting five spades, according to the product theorem for dependent probabilities, is $13/52 \times 12/51 \times 11/50 \times 10/49 \times 9/48 = 33/66{,}640$. Each of the other exclusive alternatives has the same probability, so the probability of getting a flush is $^{33}/_{66,640} + ^{33}/_{66,640} + ^{33}/_{66,640} + ^{33}/_{66,640} = ^{33}/_{16,660}$.

One more example will be considered. In drawing one ball from each of two urns, one containing two white balls and four black balls, the other containing three white balls and nine black balls, what is the probability of getting two balls of the same color? The event in whose probability we are interested is the alternative occurrence of two mutually exclusive events, one that of getting two white balls, the other that of getting two black balls. Their probabilities are to be computed separately and then added. The probability of getting two white balls is $2/6 \times 3/12 = 1/12$. And the probability of getting two black balls is $4/6 \times 9/12 = 1/2$. So the probability of getting two balls of the same color is $1/12 + 1/2 = 7/12$.

The addition theorem applies only when the alternative events are mutually exclusive. It may, however, be required to compute the probabilities of complex events which are constituted by the occurrence of at least one of two or more alternatives which are *not* mutually exclusive. For example, what is the probability of getting at least one head on two tosses of a coin? Here we know that the probability of getting a head on the first toss is $1/2$, and the probability of getting a head on the second toss is also $1/2$; but the sum of these separate probabilities is 1, or certainty, and it is *not* certain that at least one toss will yield a head, since both may yield tails. The point here is that the two events are *not exclusive;* both may occur. In computing the probability of the alternative occurrence of nonexclusive events, the addition theorem is *not directly applicable.* There are, however, two methods that can be used in computing probabilities of this type.

The first method of computing the probability that at least one of two nonexclusive events will occur requires that we break down or analyze the favorable cases into exclusive events. In the problem of finding the probability that at least one head will appear in two tosses of a coin, the equipossible cases are *H–H, H–T, T–H, T–T.* These are all mutually exclusive, and each of them has the probability $1/4$. The first three are favorable, that is, if any one of the first three occurs it will be true that at least one head appears in the two tosses. Hence the probability of getting at least one head is equal to the sum of the separate probabilities of all of the mutually exclusive favorable cases, which is $1/4 + 1/4 + 1/4 = 3/4$.

The other method of computing the probability that at least one of two nonexclusive events will occur depends upon the fact that *no case can be both favorable and unfavorable,* and the fact that *every case must be either favorable or unfavorable.* If "*a*" designates an event, say the event of getting at least one head on two tosses of a coin, then we shall use the notation "$\bar{a}$" to designate the event *unfavorable* to a, that is, the event of not getting any head at all on two tosses of the coin. Since no case can be both favorable and unfavorable, a and $\bar{a}$ are *mutually exclusive,* that is, a and $\bar{a}$ cannot possibly both occur. And since every case must be either favorable or unfavorable, it is certain that either a or $\bar{a}$ must occur. Since zero is the probability coefficient we assign to an event which cannot possibly occur, and 1 is the probability coefficient assigned to an event which is certain to occur, the following two equations are true:

$$P(a \text{ and } \bar{a}) = 0$$
$$P(a \text{ or } \bar{a}) = 1$$

where $P(a \text{ and } \bar{a})$ is the probability that a and $\bar{a}$ will both occur, and $P(a \text{ or } \bar{a})$ is the probability that either a or $\bar{a}$ will occur. Since a and $\bar{a}$ are mutually exclusive, the addition theorem is applicable, and we have

$$P(a \text{ or } \bar{a}) = P(a) + P(\bar{a})$$

The last two equations combine to give

$$P(a) + P(\bar{a}) = 1$$

which yields

$$P(a) = 1 - P(\bar{a})$$

Hence we can compute the probability of an event's occurrence by computing the probability that the event will *not* occur and subtracting that figure from 1. Applied to the event of tossing at least one head in two tosses of a coin, we can easily see that the only case in which the event does *not* occur is when both tosses result in tails. This is the unfavorable case, and by the product theorem, its probability is $\frac{1}{2} \times \frac{1}{2} = \frac{1}{4}$, whence the probability that the event of getting at least one head in two tosses *does* occur is $1 - \frac{1}{4} = \frac{3}{4}$.

Another illustration of an event composed of alternative but nonexclusive occurrences is the following. If one ball is drawn from each of two urns, the first containing two white balls and four black balls, the second containing three white balls and nine black balls, what is the probability of getting at least one white ball? This problem can be solved in either of the two ways discussed in the two previous paragraphs. We can divide the favorable cases into mutually exclusive alternatives. These are: a white ball from the first urn and a black ball from the second, a black ball from the first urn and a white ball from the second, and a white ball from both urns. The respective probabilities of these three are: $\frac{2}{6} \times \frac{9}{12} = \frac{1}{4}$, $\frac{4}{6} \times \frac{3}{12} = \frac{1}{6}$, and $\frac{2}{6} \times \frac{3}{12} = \frac{1}{12}$. Then the addition theorem for exclusive alternatives gives us $\frac{1}{4} + \frac{1}{6} + \frac{1}{12} = \frac{1}{2}$ as the probability of getting at least one white ball. The other method is somewhat simpler. The unfavorable case in which the draw does not result in at least one white ball is the event of getting two black balls. The probability of getting two black balls is $\frac{4}{6} \times \frac{9}{12} = \frac{1}{2}$, so the probability of getting at least one white ball is $1 - \frac{1}{2} = \frac{1}{2}$.

Let us now attempt to work out a moderately complicated problem in probability. The game of craps is played with two dice. The *shooter,* who rolls the dice, wins if a seven or an eleven turns up on his first roll, but loses if a 2, or 3, or 12 turn up on his first roll. If one of the remaining numbers, 4, 5, 6, 8, 9, or 10 turns up on his first roll, the shooter continues to roll the dice until either that same number turns up again, in which case he wins, or a 7 appears, in which case he loses. The problem can be posed: What is the probability that the shooter will win? First of all, let us obtain the probabilities that the various numbers will occur. There are thirty-six different equipossible ways for two dice to fall. Only one of these ways will show a 2, so the probability here is $\frac{1}{36}$. Only one of these ways will show a 12, so here the probability is also $\frac{1}{36}$. There are two ways to throw a 3, 1–2 and 2–1, so the probability of a 3 is $\frac{2}{36}$. Similarly, the probability of getting an 11 is $\frac{2}{36}$. There are three ways to throw a 4: 1–3, 2–2, and 3–1, so the probability of a 4 is $\frac{3}{36}$. Similarly, the probability of getting a 10 is $\frac{3}{36}$. Since there are four ways to roll a 5: 1–4, 2–3, 3–2, and 4–1, its probability is $\frac{4}{36}$, and this is also the probability of getting a 9. A 6 can be obtained in any one of five ways: 1–5, 2–4, 3–3, 4–2, and 5–1, so the probability of getting a 6 is $\frac{5}{36}$; and the same probability exists for an 8. There are six different combinations that yield 7: 1–6, 2–5, 3–4, 4–3, 5–2, and 6–1, so the probability of rolling a 7 is $\frac{6}{36}$.

The probability that the shooter will win on his first roll is the sum of the probability that he gets a 7 and the probability that he gets an 11, which is $\frac{6}{36} + \frac{2}{36} = \frac{8}{36}$ or $\frac{2}{9}$. The probability that he will lose on his first roll is the sum of the probabilities of getting a 2, a 3, and a 12, which is $\frac{1}{36} + \frac{2}{36} + \frac{1}{36} = \frac{4}{36}$ or $\frac{1}{9}$. The shooter is twice as likely to *win on his first roll* as to *lose on his first roll;* however, he is most likely not to do either on his first roll, but to get a 4, 5, 6, 8, 9, or 10. If he throws one of these six numbers, he is obliged to continue rolling the dice until he gets that number again, in which case he wins, or until he gets a 7, in which case he loses.

Those cases in which neither the number first thrown nor a 7 occurs can be ignored, for they are not decisive. Suppose the shooter gets a 4 on his first roll. The next *decisive* roll will show either a 4 or a 7. In a decisive roll, the equipossible cases are the three combinations that make up a 4 (1–3, 2–2, 3–1) and the six combinations that make up a 7. The probability of throwing a second 4 is therefore $3/9$. The probability of getting a 4 on his first roll was $3/36$, so the probability of winning by throwing a 4 on the first roll and then getting another 4 before a 7 occurs is $3/36 \times 3/9 = 1/36$. Similarly, the probability of the shooter winning by throwing a 10 on his first roll and then getting another 10 before a 7 occurs is also $3/36 \times 3/9 = 1/36$.

By the same line of reasoning, we can find the probability of the shooter winning by throwing a 5 on his first roll and then getting another before getting a 7. In this case, there are ten equipossible cases for the decisive roll: the four ways to make a 5 (1–4, 2–3, 3–2, 4–1), and the six ways to make a 7. The probability of winning with a 5 is therefore $4/36 \times 4/10 = 2/45$. The probability of winning with a 9 is also $2/45$. The number 6 is still more likely to occur on the first roll, its probability being $5/36$. And it is more likely than the others mentioned to occur a second time before a 7 appears, the probability here being $5/11$. So the probability of winning with a 6 is $5/36 \times 5/11 = 25/396$. And again similarly, the probability of winning with an 8 is $25/396$.

There are eight different ways for the shooter to win. If he throws a 7 or 11 on his first roll he wins. If he throws one of the six numbers 4, 5, 6, 8, 9, or 10 on his first roll *and* throws it again before getting a 7, then he wins also. These ways are all exclusive; so the total probability of the shooter's winning is the sum of the probabilities of the alternative ways in which he can win, and this is $6/36 + 2/36 + 1/36 + 2/45 + 25/396 + 25/396 + 2/45 + 1/36 = 244/495$. Expressed as a decimal fraction, this is .493 —, which shows that in a crap game the shooter has less than an even chance of winning—only slightly less, to be sure, but still less than .500.

EXERCISES

★ 1. Calculate the shooter's chances of winning in a crap game by the second method, that is, compute the chances of his losing, and subtract it from 1.

2. In drawing three cards in succession from a standard deck, what is the probability of getting at least one spade: (a) if each card is replaced before making the next drawing: (b) if the cards drawn are not replaced?

3. What is the probability of getting at least one head in three tosses of a coin?

4. If three balls are selected at random from an urn containing five red, ten white, and fifteen blue balls, what is the probability that they will all be the same color: (a) if each ball is replaced before the next one is withdrawn; (b) if the balls selected are not replaced?

★ 5. If someone offers to bet you even money that you will not throw an ace on any one of three successive throws of a die, should you accept the bet?

6. From a piggy bank containing three quarters, two dimes, five nickels, and eleven pennies, two coins are shaken out. What is the probability that their total value amounts to exactly:

(a) 50¢?	(b) 35¢?	(c) 30¢?	(d) 26¢?	(e) 20¢?
(f) 15¢?	(g) 11¢?	(h) 10¢?	(i) 6¢?	(j) only 2¢?

7. If the probability that a man of twenty-five will survive his fiftieth birthday is .742, and the probability that a woman of twenty-two will survive her forty-seventh birthday is .801, and such a man and woman marry, what is the probability: (a) that at least one of them lives at least another twenty-five years; (b) that only one of them lives at least another twenty-five years?

8. One partly filled case contains two bottles of root beer, four bottles of coke, and four bottles of beer; another partly filled case contains three bottles of root beer, seven cokes, and two beers. A case is opened at random and a bottle selected at random from it. What is the probability that it contains a soft drink? Had all the bottles been in one case, what is the probability that a bottle selected at random from it would contain a soft drink?

9. A player in a draw-poker game is dealt three jacks and two small odd cards. He discards the latter and draws two cards. What is the probability that he improves his hand on the draw? (One way to improve it is to draw another jack to make four-of-a-kind, the other way to improve it is to draw a pair to make a full house.)

10. Remove all cards except aces and kings from a deck, so that only eight cards remain, of which four are aces and four are kings. From this abbreviated deck, deal two cards to a friend. If he looks at his cards and announces (truthfully) that his hand contains an ace, what is the probability that both his cards are aces? If he announces instead that one of his cards is the ace of spades, what is the probability then that both his cards are aces? (These two probabilities are *not* the same!)

14.3 Expectation or Expected Value

In placing bets or in making investments, it is important to consider not only the probability of winning or receiving a return, but *how much* can be won on the bet or returned on the investment. The *safest* investment is not always the best one to make, nor is the one which promises the greatest return *if* it succeeds. To compare bets or investments, the notion of *expectation* or *expected value* has been introduced. An example or two will serve to illustrate how these terms are used.

If a coin is tossed and an even-money bet of, say, $1 is placed on heads, the dollar wagered may be thought of as a purchase price. What it purchases is a certain expectation, or *expected value*. If heads appears, then the bettor receives $2 (one is his own, the other is his winnings). If tails appears, then the bettor receives no return, or a return of $0. The two events (heads appearing, tails appearing) are the only two possible outcomes, and there is a specified *return* associated with each. The probability that heads will appear is $\frac{1}{2}$, and there is the same probability of $\frac{1}{2}$ that tails will appear. If we multiply the return yielded on each possible outcome by the probability of that outcome's being realized, the sum of all such products is the expectation or expected value of the bet or investment. The expected value of a dollar bet that heads will appear when a coin is tossed is thus equal to $(\frac{1}{2} \times \$2) + (\frac{1}{2} \times \$0)$, which is $1. In this case, as is well known, the odds are even, which means that the expected value of the purchase is equal to the purchase price.

The game of chuck-a-luck, often called crown and anchor, is a good illustration of the disparity between the price and the expected value of most purchases made in gambling casinos. The patron makes his bet by placing his money on one or more of six squares which are numbered 1 through 6. Three dice are tossed—usually inside an hour-glass-shaped cage—and the "house" pays off each bet according to how many dice show the number on which the bet was made. If all three dice show the number 4, then a $1 bet on 4 would win $3; if only two showed 4, a $1 on 4 would win $2; if only one of the dice showed 4, a dollar on 4 would win $1; whereas if none of the dice showed a 4, the $1 bet on 4 would be lost. These are the results associated with each outcome. A $1 bet on any single number is the purchase price of the expectation described. What is that expectation worth? There are four different possible outcomes, but they have very different probabilities. For definiteness, let us say that $1 is bet on 4. The probability that all three dice show the number 4 is $\frac{1}{6} \times \frac{1}{6} \times \frac{1}{6} = \frac{1}{216}$. The probability that exactly two dice show the number 4 is $(\frac{1}{6} \times \frac{1}{6} \times \frac{5}{6}) + (\frac{1}{6} \times \frac{5}{6} \times \frac{1}{6}) +$

$(5/6 \times 1/6 \times 1/6) = 15/216$. The probability that just a single one of the dice will show a 4 is $(1/6 \times 5/6 \times 5/6) + (5/6 \times 1/6 \times 5/6) + (5/6 \times 5/6 \times 1/6) = 75/216$. The probability that none of the dice will show a 4 is $5/6 \times 5/6 \times 5/6 = 125/216$. The returns to the bettor on each of these outcomes are \$4, \$3, \$2, and \$0, respectively. The expected value of his bet is then equal to the sum of the products of the return on each possible outcome and the probability of that outcome; in this case it is $(1/216 \times \$4) + (15/216 \times \$3) + (75/216 \times \$2) + (125/216 \times \$0) = \$199/216$ or approximately 92¢. This means that of every such dollar bet, almost 8¢ is a gift to the "house."

Some gamblers, in playing chuck-a-luck, try to beat the game by placing bets on more than one number, in the belief that this increases their chances of winning. Suppose you break your dollar and bet 50¢ each on the numbers 3 and 4. The greatest possible return is obtained when the dice show either two 3's and a 4 or two 4's and a 3; in either case you receive \$2.50—which includes your own dollar, of course. Each of these two cases has a probability of $3/216$. If all three dice show 4's, the return is only \$2, since the 50¢ bet on 3 is lost. The probability here is also $1/216$, as it is for three 3's, which yields the same return. Curiously enough, an equal return is obtained when one of the dice shows 3, a second shows 4, and the third some other number. The probability here is easily verified to be $24/216$. If exactly two of the dice show 3 and the other one some different number other than 4, the return is \$1.50; the probability that this will happen is $12/216$. The same return and the same probability attach to the event of two of the dice showing 4 and the other some different number other than 3. If a single 4 turns up, and no 3 at all, the return is \$1; the probability that this happens is $48/216$. The same return and the same probability attach to the event of a single 3 turning up, and no 4 at all. Since any other possible outcome results in a zero return, we need not bother to compute the probability here. What is the expectation purchased for a dollar spent on two 50¢ bets on different numbers at chuck-a-luck? It is the sum of the following products: $(3/216 \times \$2.50) + (3/216 \times \$2.50) + (1/216 \times \$2.00) + (1/216 \times \$2.00) + (24/216 \times \$2.00) + (12/216 \times \$1.50) + (12/216 \times \$1.50) + (48/216 \times \$1.00) + (48/216 \times \$1.00) = \$199/216$ or again approximately 92¢. True enough, there are more chances of winning by dividing a dollar bet between two numbers, but the *amounts* which can be won are sufficiently smaller to keep the expectation constant. In either case the expected value is almost 8¢ less than the purchase price, the difference being the patron's contribution to the casino's overhead—and profit.

It is sometimes argued that in a game in which there are even-money stakes to be awarded on the basis of approximately equiprobable alternatives, such as tossing a coin or betting black versus red on a roulette wheel, one can be *sure to win* by making the same bet consistently—always heads, or always black, say—and doubling the amount of money wagered after each loss. Thus if I bet $1 on heads, and tails show, then I should bet heads again to the tune of $2. If tails show again, my next bet—also on heads—should be $4, and so on. One cannot fail to win by following this procedure, because extended runs are highly improbable; the longest run must *sometimes* end—and when it does, the man who has pyramided or continued to double his bets will be money ahead!

What is wrong with this theory? Why need anyone work for a living, when we can all adopt this foolproof system of winning at the gaming table? We can ignore the fact that the usual gaming house has an upper limit on the size of the wager it will accept, and focus our attention on the real fallacy contained in the prescription. Although a long run of tails, say, is almost certain to end sooner or later, it may end later rather than sooner. An adverse run *may* last long enough to exhaust any finite amount of money the bettor may have to play. To be certain of being able to continue doubling his bet each time, no matter how long the adverse run may continue, the bettor would have to begin with an infinite amount of money. But of course a player with an infinite amount of money could not possibly win—in the sense of increasing his wealth. Such a case is too fanciful, anyway; let us confine our discussion to a player who has only a fixed, finite amount of money to lose. For definiteness, we may suppose that he has decided in advance how long he will play: if he is resolved to play until all his money is gone, then he is bound to lose all his money, sooner or later (provided that the house has sufficient funds to cover all of his bets, of course); whereas if he is resolved to play until he wins some antecedently specified amount, the game might go on forever with the player never either reaching his goal or going broke.

For the sake of simplicity, suppose a player begins with just $3, so that he is prepared to sustain just one loss: two in a row would wipe him out. Let him decide to bet just twice, and consider the different possible outcomes. The $3 is his purchase price; what is the expectation purchased? If two heads come up in a row, the player, winning $1 on each, will get a return of $5. If there is a head first and then a tail, the return will be just $3. If there is a tail first and then a head, having lost $1 on the first toss and having bet $2 on the second, which won, the player's return will be $4. Finally, two tails will wipe him out, yielding a return of $0. Each of these events has a probability of $\frac{1}{4}$, so the expected value is $(\frac{1}{4} \times \$5) + (\frac{1}{4} \times \$3) + (\frac{1}{4} \times \$4) = \$3$. The player's expectation is no greater when he uses the doubling technique than when he risks his entire capital on one toss of a coin.

Let us make a different supposition, that the same player decides to play three times (if his money holds out) so that with luck he can double his money. The eight possible outcomes can be listed in the form of a table:

First toss	*Second toss*	*Third toss*	*Return*	*Probability*
H	*H*	*H*	\$6	1/8
H	*H*	*T*	\$4	1/8
H	*T*	*H*	\$5	1/8
H	*T*	*T*	\$1	1/8
T	*H*	*H*	\$5	1/8
T	*H*	*T*	\$3	1/8
T	*T*	*H*	\$0	1/8
T	*T*	*T*	\$0	1/8

The expectation on this new strategy remains the same, still \$3.

Let us consider just one more aspect of the doubling technique. Suppose the same man wants to win just a single dollar, which means that he will play until he wins just once or else goes broke. With this more modest aim, what is the probable value of his investment? If heads appears on the first toss, the return is \$4 (the \$1 won and the original stake of \$3) and having won his dollar, the man stops playing. If tails appears on the first toss, \$2 is bet on the second. If heads appears, the return is \$4, and the player quits with his winnings. If tails appears, the return is \$0, and the player quits because he has lost all his money. There are only these three possible outcomes, the first of which has a probability of 1/2, the second 1/4, and the third 1/4. Such a player, following such a strategy, is three times as likely to win as to lose. But of course he can lose three times as much as he can win by this method. The expected value is: $(\frac{1}{2} \times \$4) + (\frac{1}{4} \times \$4) + (\frac{1}{4} \times \$0) = \$3$. The expectation is not increased at all by following the doubling technique. The *chances of winning* are increased, just as by betting on more numbers at chuck-a-luck or roulette, but the *amount* which can be won decreases rapidly enough to keep the *expected value constant.*

EXERCISES

★ 1. What is the expected value of a wager which consists of betting \$1 each on the numbers 1, 2, and 3 at chuck-a-luck?

2. What is the expected value of a wager which consists of betting \$1 each on all six numbers at chuck-a-luck?

3. At most crap tables in gambling houses, the house will give odds of six to one against rolling a 4 the "hard way," that is, with a pair of 2's as contrasted with a 3 and a 1, which is the "easy way." A bet made on a "hard way" 4 wins if a pair of 2's show before either a 7 is rolled or a 4 is made the "easy way," otherwise it loses. What is the expectation purchased by a $1 bet on a "hard way" 4?

4. If the odds are eight to one against rolling an 8 the "hard way" (that is, with two 4's), what is the expectation purchased by a $1 bet on a "hard way" 8?

★ 5. What expectation does a man with $15 have who bets on heads, beginning with a $1 bet, and uses the doubling technique, if he resolves to play just four times and quit?

6. On the basis of past performance, the probability that the favorite will win the Bellevue Handicap is .46, while there is a probability of only .1 that a certain dark horse will win. If the favorite pays even money and the odds offered are eight to one against the dark horse, which is the better bet?

7. If $100 invested in the preferred stock of a certain company will yield a return of $110 with a probability of .85, whereas the probability is only .67 that the same amount invested in common stock will yield a return of $140, which is the better investment?

8. A punchboard has a thousand holes, one containing a number which pays $5, five containing numbers which pay $2 each, and ten containing numbers which pay $1 each. What is the expected value of a punch which costs 5¢?

9. An investor satisfies himself that a certain region contains radioactive deposits, which may be either plutonium or uranium. For $500 he can obtain an option which will permit him to determine which element is present and to enjoy the proceeds from its extraction and sale. If only plutonium is present he will lose four fifths of his option money, whereas if uranium is present he will enjoy a return of $40,000. If there is only one chance in a hundred that uranium is present, what is the expected value of the option?

10. Before the last card is dealt in a stud poker game, a man who has the ace and king of spades and the six of diamonds showing bets the limit of $2. You are certain that he has an ace or a king in the hole, while your hand consists of the three and five of hearts and the four and six of clubs. No other player calls. If you are certain that your opponent will check and call a $2 bet after the last card is dealt, how much money must there be in the pot for your call to be worth $2?

Solutions to Selected Exercises

Exercises on pages 10–16

I. 1. PREMISS: Man wishes to live in society.
CONCLUSION: Man must forego a portion of his private good for the sake of public good.

5. PREMISS: Every art and every inquiry, and similarly every action and pursuit, is thought to aim at some good.
CONCLUSION: The good has rightly been declared to be that at which all things aim.

10. PREMISSES: (1) During the school period the student has been mentally bending over his desk. (2) At the University he should stand up and look around.
CONCLUSION: It is fatal if the first year at the University be frittered away in going over the old work in the old spirit.

15. PREMISS: No man who won't pull his weight in the boat has a right in the boat.
CONCLUSION: The conscientious objector . . . has no place in a republic like ours, and should be expelled from it.

20. PREMISSES: (1) Venus and Mercury never move far away from the sun. (2) Venus and Mercury are now seen beyond the sun and now on this side of it.
CONCLUSION: Venus and Mercury revolve around the sun.

II. 1. First argument:
PREMISS: Matter is activity.
CONCLUSION: A body is where it acts.

Second argument:
PREMISS: Every particle of matter acts (i.e., has an effect) all over the universe.
CONCLUSION: Every body is everywhere.

5. First argument:
PREMISS: A punishment which comes at the end of all things, when the world is over and done with, cannot have for its object either to improve or deter.
CONCLUSION: A punishment which comes at the end of all things, when the world is over and done with, is pure vengeance.
Second argument:
PREMISS: A punishment which comes at the end of all things, when the world is over and done with, is pure vengeance.
CONCLUSION: God, who prescribes forbearance and forgiveness of every fault, exercises none himself, but does the exact opposite.

10. First argument:
PREMISS: A journeyman who works by the piece derives a benefit by every exertion of his industry.
CONCLUSION: A journeyman who works by the piece is likely to be industrious.
Second argument:
PREMISS: An apprentice has no immediate interest to be otherwise than idle.
CONCLUSION: An apprentice is likely to be idle, and almost always is so.
Third argument:
PREMISS: An apprentice is likely to be idle, and almost always is so.
CONCLUSION: The institution of long apprenticeships has no tendency to form young people to industry.

15. First argument:
PREMISS: The right answer given to a teacher's question will tell him that his teaching is good and that he can go on to the next topic.
CONCLUSION: A teacher who asks a question is tuned to the right answer, ready to hear it, eager to hear it.
Second argument:
PREMISS: A teacher who asks a question is tuned to the right answer, ready to hear it, eager to hear it.
CONCLUSION: He will assume that anything that sounds close to the right answer is meant to be the right answer.
Third argument:
PREMISS: He (the teacher) will assume that anything that sounds close to the right answer is meant to be the right answer.
CONCLUSION: For a student who is not sure of the answer a mumble may be his best bet.

Exercises on pages 20–22

1. Argument: PREMISS: Friends have all things in common.
CONCLUSION: One of you can be no richer than the other, if you say truly that you are friends.

5. Not an argument, first because it is merely a conditional in form, and second because the consequent is a command rather than a statement or asserted proposition.

10. Arguments: First: PREMISSES: (1) The freshmen bring a little knowledge in to the University. (2) The seniors take no knowledge away from the University.
    CONCLUSION: Knowledge accumulates in the University.
    Second argument: PREMISS: Knowledge accumulates in the University.
    CONCLUSION: Universities are full of knowledge.

15. Argument: PREMISS: I can always get out of being mobilized in a war by suicide or by desertion.
    CONCLUSION: If I am mobilized in a war, this war is *my* war; it is in my image and I deserve it. For lack of getting out of it, I have *chosen* it.

Exercises on pages 26–31

1. Deductive argument:
   PREMISS: Tests proved that it took at least 2.3 seconds to operate the bolt on Oswald's rifle.
   CONCLUSION: Oswald obviously could not have fired three times—hitting Kennedy twice and Connally once—in 5.6 seconds or less.
   Although the premiss may have been established inductively, the present argument claims that *its* conclusion follows from the premiss "obviously," that Oswald *could not* have fired three times.

5. Deductive argument:
   PREMISS: A gardener who cultivates his own garden with his own hands, unites in his own person the three different characters of landlord, farmer, and labourer.
   CONCLUSION: The produce of a gardener who cultivates his own garden with his own hands should pay him the rent of the landlord, the profit of the farmer, and the wages of the labourer.
   The argument does not appeal to experience to establish what is probably the case, but appeals to principles of equity to *prove* what should be the case.

10. Inductive argument:
    The conclusion that *it is impracticable to raise any very considerable sums by direct taxation* is inferred on the basis of a good deal of experience with different tax laws, different methods of tax collecting, tax-evading habits of the people (our Founding Fathers!), disappointed public expectation, and empty state treasuries. No claim seems to be made, however, that the conclusion follows demonstratively from the premisses offered in its support.

15. Deductive argument:
    The first sentence expresses the premisses and the second sentence the conclusion. Although the premisses may themselves have been established inductively, the conclusion is inferred from them not as just likely or probable, but is claimed to be "always" found true.

20. There are two arguments here, one deductive, the other inductive.
    Deductive argument: PREMISS: The Philosopher speaks differently in different places and has different principles, from some of which one thing seems to follow whereas from others the very opposite can be inferred.
    CONCLUSION: It is doubtful what the Philosopher really held on this point.
    This conclusion does seem to follow demonstratively from the stated premiss.
    Inductive Argument: PREMISSES: These are both the premiss and the conclusion of the deductive argument already discussed.
    CONCLUSION: Stated in the second sentence.
    This conclusion is stated as being "probable" only, and is in fact a hypothesis offered to explain the inconsistent formulations of "the Philosopher." (See Chapter 13 for a discussion of the method of hypothesis.)

25. Inductive argument:
    The conclusion, expressed in the second sentence, is inferred from the premiss, expressed in the first sentence, only inductively in the light of experience that (aside from abuse, general deterioration, etc.) vacuum tubes chiefly go out of commission through the burning out of their filaments or heating elements. But the way is left completely open for a possible subsequent discovery that there is a natural maximum life span for transistors. If this *were* discovered it would leave the premiss true while making the conclusion false:

Exercises on pages 34–35

1. PREMISS: You are something more than property or speech.
   CONCLUSION: It is illogical . . . speech is superior to yours."
   Also each separate sentence between quotation marks formulates an argument whose premiss precedes and whose conclusion follows the word "therefore."

5. First argument:
   PREMISS: To be deceived about what I pronounce or conceive in my mind I must exist.
   CONCLUSION: When I think that I exist I cannot be deceived about that.
   Second argument:
   PREMISS: When I think that I exist I cannot be deceived about that.
   CONCLUSION: This proposition: "I am, I exist," is necessarily true every time that I pronounce it or conceive it in my mind.

Exercises on pages 37–40

1. If the first native is a politician, then he lies and denies being a politician. If the first native is not a politician, then he tells the truth and denies being a politician. In either case, then, the first native denies being a politician.

Since the second native reports that the first native denies being a politician, he tells the truth, and is, therefore, a nonpolitician.

The third native asserts that the first native is a politician. If the first native is a politician, then the third native speaks the truth and is, therefore, a nonpolitician. If the first native is a nonpolitician, then the third native lies and is, therefore, a politician. Hence only one of the first and third natives is a politician, and since the second is a nonpolitician, there is only one politician among the three natives.

5. Since Lefty said that Spike did it, Spike's first and third statements are equivalent in meaning and therefore either both true or both false. Since only one statement is false, they are both true.

   Dopey's third statement is, therefore, false, and so his first two are true. Therefore Butch's third statement is false and so his first two are true, of which the second reveals that Red is the guilty man.

   (An alternative method of solving this problem was communicated to me by Professor Peter M. Longley of the University of Alaska. All but Red both assert their innocence *and* accuse someone else. If their professions of innocence are false so are their accusations of other persons. But no one makes two false statements, so their statements that they are innocent must be true. Hence Red is the guilty one. This solution, however, presupposes that only one of the men is guilty.)

   (Still another method of solving this problem is due to James I. Campbell of Eisenhower College and Walter Charen of Rutgers College. Dopey's second statement and Butch's third statement are contradictory, so at least one must be false. But if Dopey's second statement were false his third statement would be true and Spike would be guilty. However, if Spike were guilty his first and third statements would both be false, so he cannot be guilty and hence Dopey's second statement cannot be false. Therefore Butch's third statement must be false, whence his second statement is true and Red is the guilty man.)

10. Green is an outfielder (i) and is married (o); but the right fielder and the center fielder are bachelors (c); so *Green is the left fielder* (p).

    Knight or Adams played outfield (f), but Adams played infield or battery (i) so Knight is an outfielder (q).

    White, Miller, and Brown are not outfielders (p and e), nor are Jones, Smith, and Adams (i), so Hunter is an outfielder (r).

    Hunter and Knight play right field and center field (p, q, and r), the right fielder is shorter than the center fielder (g), Knight is shorter than Hunter (b), so *Knight is the right fielder* (s) and *Hunter is the center fielder* (t).

    Brown is not the pitcher (a), nor the catcher (e and o), nor the shortstop (n), nor the second baseman (l), nor the third baseman (e and o), so *Brown is the first baseman* (u).

    The second baseman is a bachelor (k) so is either White, Miller, or Brown (e). But he is neither Brown (u) nor Miller (k), so *White is the second baseman* (v).

    The catcher is neither Jones, Brown, nor Hunter (l), neither Miller nor White (e and o), not Adams (m), neither Green (p) nor Knight (s), so *Smith is the catcher* (w).

    The third baseman is neither Green (p), nor Knight (s), nor Hunter

(t), nor Brown (u), nor White (v), nor Smith (w), nor Miller (e and o), nor Jones (c); so *Adams is the third baseman* (x).
And by elimination, *Miller is the shortstop*.

Exercises on pages 53–58

I. 1. Directive—avoid civil war, do not avoid foreign wars.
Expressive—to evoke antipathy towards civil war and approval of foreign wars.
Informative—civil war weakens a nation, foreign wars strengthen a nation.

5. Directive—do not depend upon language for complete communication.
Expressive—to evoke a feeling of distrust, perhaps even contempt, for language.
Informative—human language is not much more adequate and sometimes less adequate for communication than the sounds produced by animals.

10. Directive—let us stand fast together.
Expressive—to evoke strong feelings of solidarity.
Informative—if we do not stand together we shall all lose our lives.

15. Directive—be religious; and if you study philosophy at all, study it deeply.
Expressive—to evoke piety, and contempt for atheists as being shallow.
Informative—beginning students of philosophy tend towards atheism, advanced students of philosophy are religious.

20. Directive—do not oppose war.
Expressive—to evoke feelings of approval and moral enthusiasm for war.
Informative—if there were no war people would continue to have finite aims, become (in some obscure sense) "corrupt," and might lose their "ethical health" (a term not clearly defined in Hegel's context).

II. 1. Asserts that Disraeli achieved success by his own efforts, but that he is extremely conceited.
Intended to cause laughter at and scorn for Disraeli.
Provides evidence that the speaker scorns Disraeli and also that the speaker is witty.

5. Asserts that all who speak about constitutional rights, free speech, and the free press are Communists.
Intended to cause hostility toward those who defend constitutional rights, free speech, and a free press.
Provides evidence that the speaker is hostile toward constitutional rights, free speech, free press, Communists (and logic).

10. Asserts that there are three classes of citizens: rich—who are lazy and greedy; poor—who have nothing, are envious, hate the rich, and are susceptible to demagogy; and the middle class, who are law-abiding, law-enforcing, and make the state secure.

Intended to cause hostility toward the rich and (especially) toward the poor, and to produce approval of the middle class.
Provides evidence that the speaker is neither rich nor poor, or at least not poor.

15. Asserts (indirectly) that the speaker's country is wicked and deserving of punishment.
Intended to cause critical reappraisal of the country's goals, methods, and values.
Provides evidence that the speaker is sensitive to his country's shortcomings.

20. Asserts that the painting in question is overpriced and without aesthetic merit.
Intended to cause people to laugh—at Whistler, and not to buy and not to praise Whistler's paintings.
Provides evidence that the speaker is hostile toward Whistler, witty, bombastic, and not sensitive to Whistler's art.

Exercises on pages 66–67

1. Agreement in belief that Mrs. Blank is voluble.
Disagreement in attitude toward Mrs. Blank: *a* approves and *b* disapproves.

5. Disagreement in belief: *a* believes that Mrs. Roe served a small meal, and *b* believes that Mrs. Roe served a large meal. (It is possible that their words reveal no disagreement in belief about the exact size of the meal served by Mrs. Roe but only a difference in the amounts of food *a* and *b* are accustomed to see served at a meal.)
Agreement in attitude: both have an attitude of approval toward the meal served.

10. Agreement in belief that not all of Suzy's statements are literally true.
Disagreement in attitude toward Suzy and her assertions: *a* approves and *b* disapproves.

15. Agreement in belief that the functions of making history and of writing history are distinct, and that one is more important than the other. This may appear to be a merely verbal dispute in which the two writers are using the word "important" in different senses. See Section 4.2.
Disagreement in attitude: Bismarck esteems the maker and disesteems the writer, Wilde disesteems the maker and esteems the writer.

Exercises on pages 87–91

1. *Argumentum ad Hominem* (abusive).

5. False cause.

10. *Argumentum ad Hominem* (abusive).

15. *Ignoratio Elenchi* (irrelevant conclusion). Purporting to argue for the desirability of socialism, the speaker instead argues that it is inevitable. Perhaps also Converse Accident (hasty generalization) in generalizing from governmental operation of utilities and social security insurance programs to government operation of *all* productive activities.

20. *Argumentum ad Verecundiam* (appeal to authority).

25. *Ignoratio Elenchi* (irrelevant conclusion). Purporting to argue against hiring a skilled worker, the speaker instead argues against hiring someone who is "regarded as a skilled worker." Perhaps also Converse Accident (hasty generalization) in generalizing from many who are unskilled although regarded as skilled to the general conclusion that *no* worker regarded as skilled can be depended upon to be skilled.

30. *Argumentum ad Hominem* (circumstantial) can be seen to appear twice in this passage, as "You cannot be against something because you do not go where it is to oppose it." Also the *Argumentum ad Hominem* (abusive) appears in Phillips' more or less subtle way of telling his questioner to go to hell.

35. *Petitio Principii* (begging the question). Obviously a circular argument.

Exercises on pages 99–100

1. Composition: that the parts have functions does not imply that the whole has a function.

5. Accent.

10. Composition: what is good for each industry (such as a competitive advantage over other industries) need not be—and in some cases cannot be—good for the economy as a whole.

15. Composition again.

Exercises on pages 102–106

1. Converse Accident (hasty generalization).

5. *Argumentum ad Hominem* (circumstantial). "Poisoning the well."

10. *Argumentum ad Baculum* (appeal to force).

15. *Argumentum ad Hominem* (abusive). Also, that "interested men . . . are not to be trusted" may be regarded as an *Argumentum ad Hominem* (circumstantial).

20. Composition.

25. *Argumentum ad Ignorantiam* (argument from ignorance).

30. False Cause.

35. *Petitio Principii* (begging the question). Circular argument.

40. Converse Accident (hasty generalization).

45. *Petitio Principii* (begging the question).

Exercises on pages 114–116

1. An apparently verbal dispute that is really genuine. The ambiguous phrase "greatest hitter" is used by Black in the sense of *having the highest lifetime batting average* and by White in the sense of *hitting the largest number of home runs.* They really disagree in attitude toward Cobb and Ruth, Black having highest esteem for the former and White for the latter.

5. A merely verbal dispute. The ambiguous phrase "business . . . good" is used by Black in the sense of *increased sales* and by White in the sense of *increased profit.* There *may* be a disagreement in attitude toward the company in question, Black approving and White deploring, but this is not at all clear from their words.

10. An obviously genuine dispute, with Black affirming and White denying that *Dick bought himself a new car.*

15. Merely verbal, ambiguous word "unemployed" is used by Black in the (more usual) sense of "employable person who is ready and willing to work but not able to secure employment" and by White in the (somewhat odd) sense of "person who is not gainfully employed."

Exercise on page 128

I. 1. animal, vertebrate, mammal, feline, lynx, wildcat.

Exercises on page 132

I. 1. Richard Burton, John Gielgud, Lawrence Olivier.

5. Bromine, Chlorine, Iodine.

II. 1. Englishman.

5. Halogen.

Exercises on pages 135–136

I. 1. Ridiculous.

5. Vanity.

10. Danger.

15. Portent.

II.
1. Unmarried man.
5. Young offspring.
10. Very large man.
15. Very small man.
20. Very small meal.

Exercises on pages 140–143

II.
1. Too broad, since a coed must attend an educational institution in which students of both sexes are enrolled; and too narrow, since a coed need not be young (?). Violates Rule 3.
5. Too broad, since some odors are unpleasant whereas fragrances are pleasant odors. Violates Rule 3.
10. Circular, since "produces" is synonymous with "causes." Violates Rule 2.
15. Figurative language. Violates Rule 4.

III.
1. Figurative language. Violates Rule 4.
5. Too broad, since some prose records such moments; and too narrow, since some (great) poetry is tragic. Violates Rule 3. It may also be criticized as being phrased in figurative language, violating Rule 4, though this is not altogether obvious.
10. Too broad, since some persons with a very low opinion of themselves tend to behave this way; and too narrow, since some supremely conceited persons do not stoop to such vainglory or social climbing. Violates Rule 4. It may also be criticized for violating Rule 1 in not stating the essence, which is a trait of character rather than a tendency to overt behavior of the kinds specified.
15. Too narrow: not all political power is exercised "for the public good," certainly not "*only* for the public good." Violates Rule 3.

Exercises on page 151

1. S = historians, P = extremely gifted writers whose works read like first-rate novels. Form: particular affirmative.
5. S = members of families that are rich and famous, P = men of either wealth or distinction. Form: particular negative.

Exercises on page 155

1. Affirmative, particular. Subject and predicate both undistributed.
5. Negative, universal. Subject and predicate both distributed.

Exercises on page 159

1. If (a) is true: (b) is false, (c) is true, (d) is false.
   If (a) is false: (d) is true, (b) and (c) are undetermined.

Exercises on pages 165–169

I. 1. No reckless drivers who pay no attention to traffic regulations are men who are considerate of other people. Equivalent.

II. 1. Some college athletes are not nonprofessionals.

III. 1. All nonpessimists are nonjournalists. Equivalent.

IV. 1. False.
5. False.

V. 1. False.
5. Undetermined.

VI. 1. Undetermined.
5. True.
10. False.
15. False.
20. True.
25. Undetermined.

VII. 1. True.
5. False.
10. Undetermined.
15. False.
20. True.
25. Undetermined.

Exercise on page 172

I. Step (3) to (4) is invalid (conversion by limitation).

Exercises on pages 179–180

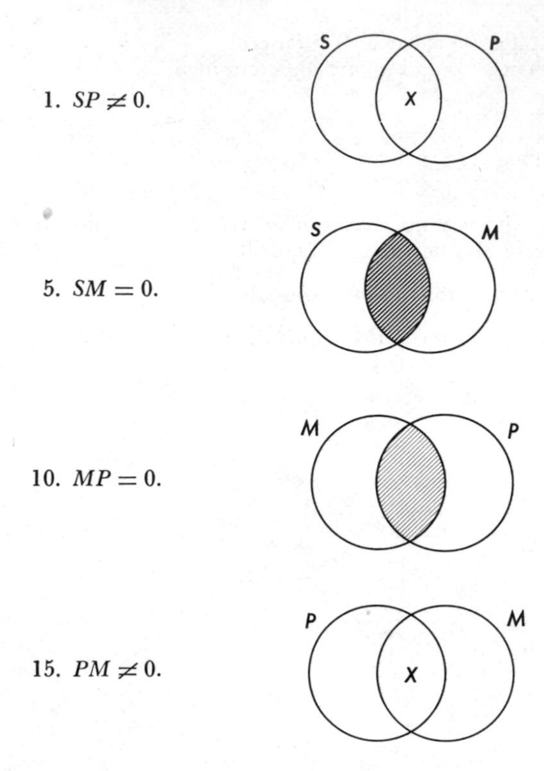

Exercises on page 184

1. No nuclear powered submarines are commercial vessels.
   All nuclear powered submarines are warships.
   Therefore no warships are commercial vessels.
   ***EAE*–3**

5. All advocates of high tariff rates are Republicans.
   Some Republicans are not conservatives.
   Therefore some conservatives are not advocates of high tariff rates.
   ***AOO*–4**

Exercises on page 187

1. All bipeds are astronauts, for all astronauts are men, and all men are bipeds.

5. All unicorns are mammals, so some mammals are not animals, since no animals are unicorns.

Exercises on pages 197–198

I. 1. All *M* is *P*.
No *S* is *M*.
∴ No *S* is *P*.

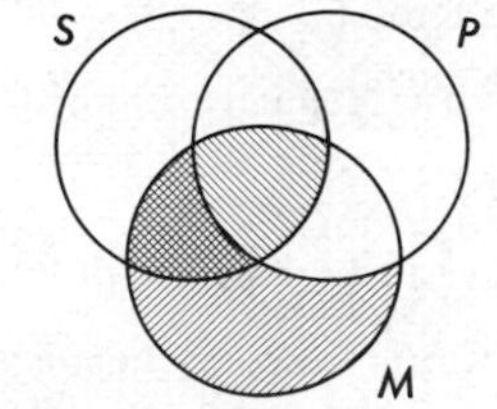

invalid.

5. No *P* is *M*.
Some *M* is *S*.
∴ Some *S* is not *P*.

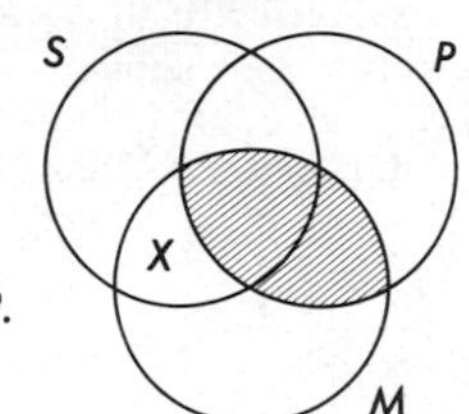

valid.

10. Some *P* is *M*.
All *M* is *S*.
∴ Some *S* is *P*.

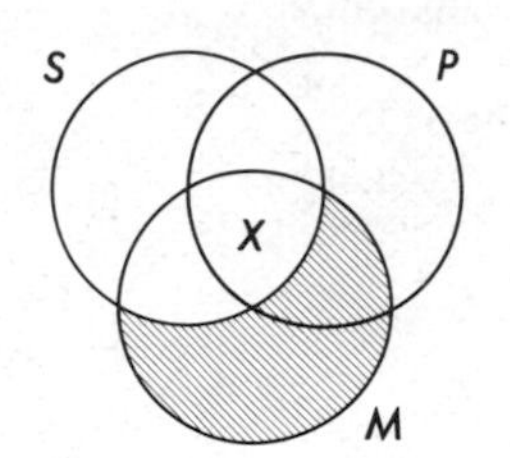

valid.

II. 1. Some reformers are fanatics.
All reformers are idealists.
∴ Some idealists are fanatics.

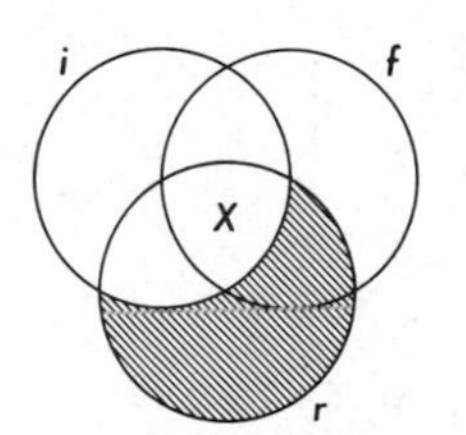

***IAI*–3**
valid.

5. No pleasure vessels are underwater craft.
All underwater craft are submarines.
∴ No submarines are pleasure vessels.

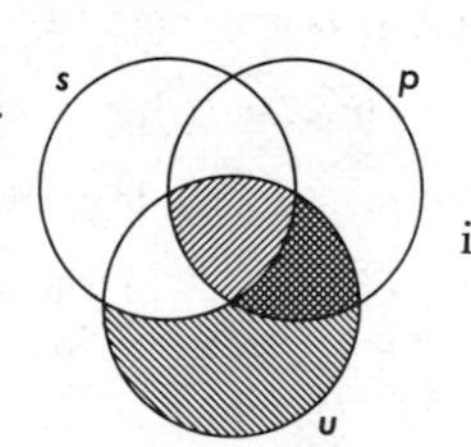

***EAE*–4**
invalid.

Exercises on pages 204–206

I. 1. Undistributed Middle. Breaks Rule 2.
5. Illicit Minor. Breaks Rule 3.
10. Illicit Major. Breaks Rule 3.

II. 1. Undistributed Middle. Breaks Rule 2.

5. Existential Fallacy. Breaks Rule 6.

III. 1. Affirmative Conclusion from a Negative Premiss. Breaks Rule 5.

5. Illicit Minor. Breaks Rule 3.

IV. 1. No, for its mood would have to be ***EEE*** in violation of Rule 4.

5. In Figure 2 one premiss would have to be negative to avoid violating Rule 2. But then by Rule 5 the conclusion would have to be negative and would distribute its predicate thus violating Rule 3. In all other figures (1, 3, 4) it is possible, as is shown by the fact that ***AII*–1**, ***AII*–3,** and ***IAI*–4** are all valid.

Exercises on pages 210–211

1. Some *P* is *M*.
   All *P* is *I*.
   ∴ Some *I* is *M*.

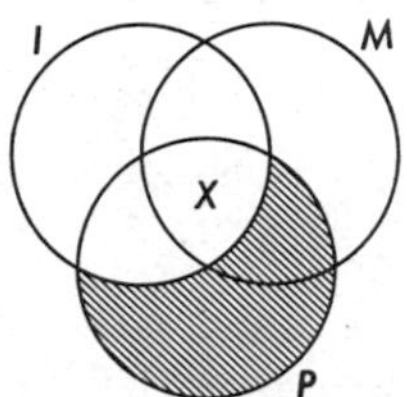

valid.

5. All *E* is *F*.
   No *F* is *S*.
   ∴ No *S* is *E*.

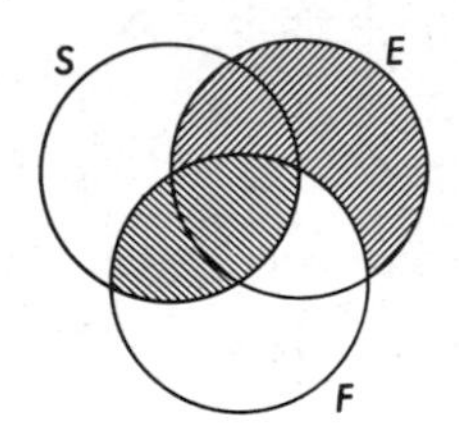

valid. ("Flammable" and "inflammable" are synonyms.)

Exercises on pages 216–217

1. All roses are fragrant things.
5. All Junkos are best things that money can buy.
10. No people who face the sun are people who see their own shadows.
15. No candidates of the Old Guard are persons supported by the Young Turks. (or) No Young Turks are supporters of candidates of the Old Guard.
20. All people who love well are people who pray well.

Exercises on pages 220–223

I. 1. All times when he is reminded of his loss are times when he groans.

5. All cases in which he gives his opinion are cases in which he is asked to give his opinion.

II. 1. No times that Bill goes to work are times that Bill wears a sweater.
This morning is a time that Bill wears a sweater.
∴ This morning is not a time that Bill goes to work.

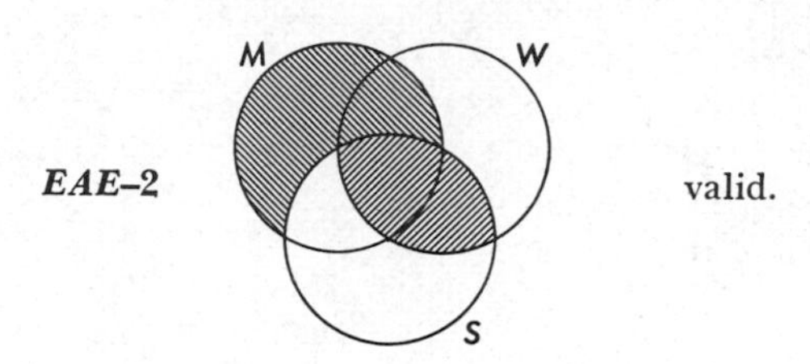

5. All places where pickets are present are places where there is a strike.
The factory is a place where pickets are present.
∴ The factory is a place where there is a strike.

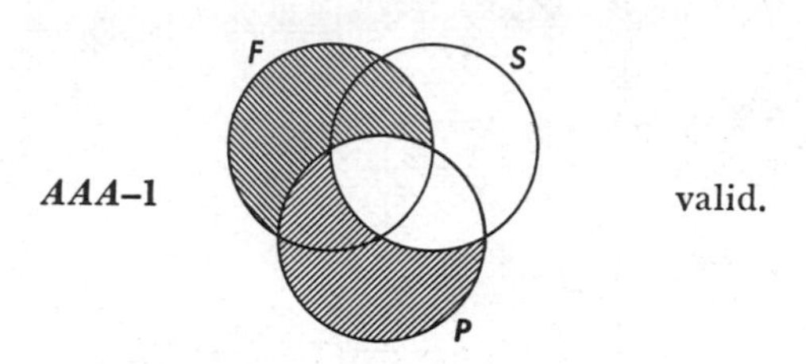

10. All invalid syllogisms are syllogisms that commit an illicit process.
This syllogism is not a syllogism that commits an illicit process.
∴ This syllogism is not an invalid syllogism.

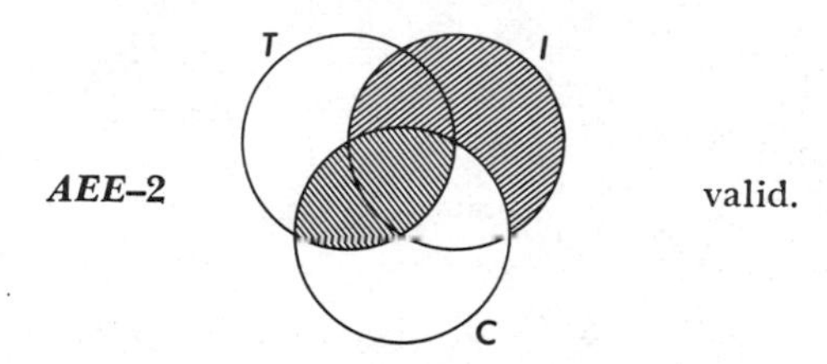

15. All persons present are employed persons.
All members are persons present.
∴ All members are employed persons.

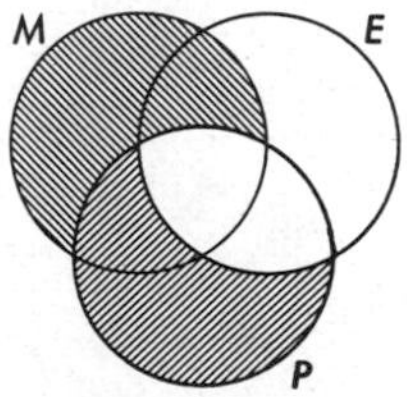

M E

AAA–1 valid.

P

20. All trains not stopping at this station are trains that are the express train.
The last train was a train not stopping at this station.
∴ The last train was a train that is the express train.

AAA–1 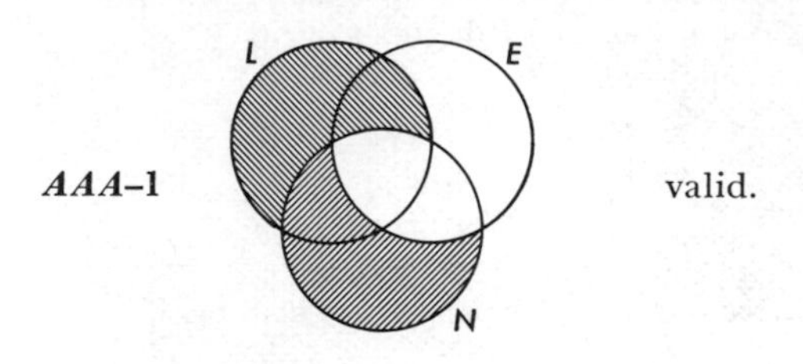

valid.

25. No gold is base metal.
Some base metals are things that glitter.
∴ Some things that glitter are not gold.

EIO–4 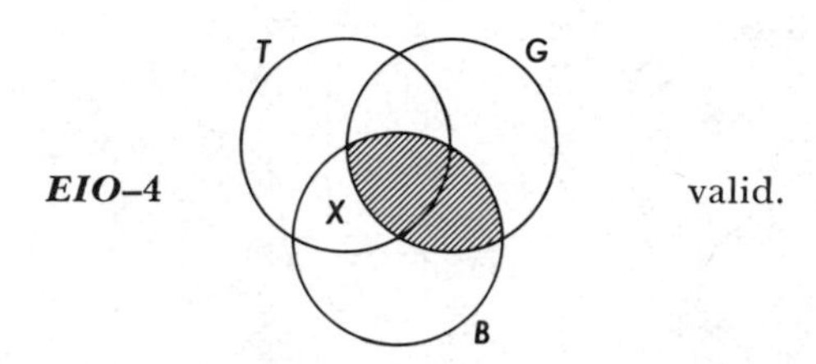

valid.

30. No things derived from reason are things that have an influence on the actions and affections.
All morals are things that have an influence on the actions and affections.
∴ No morals are things derived from reason.

EAE–2 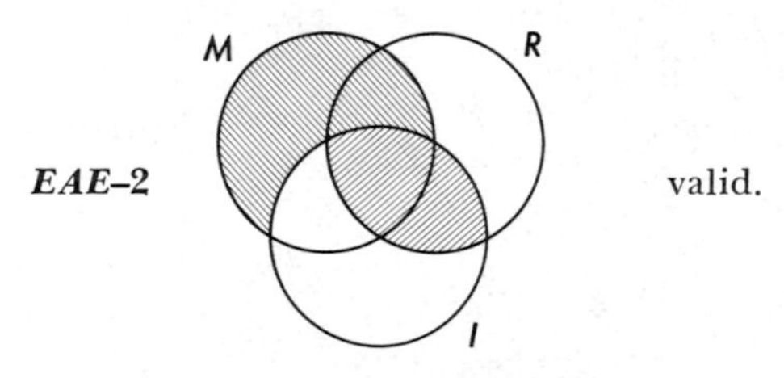

valid.

35. All things interesting to engineers are approximations.
No approximations are irrationals.
∴ No irrationals are things interesting to engineers.

AEE–4 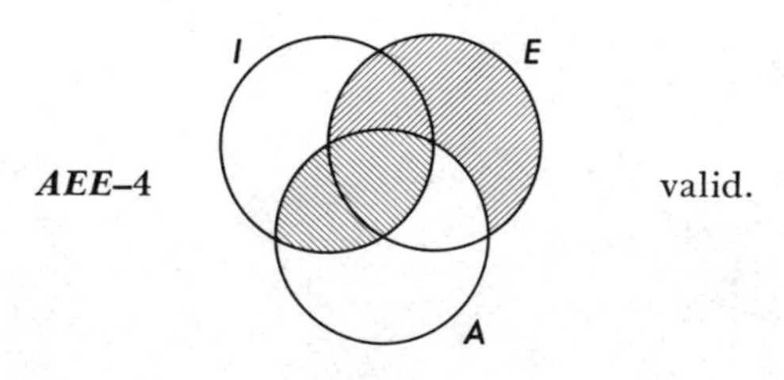

valid.

Exercises on pages 226–227

1. Third order.

All things of which we have ideas are things of which we have experience.
No divine attributes and operations are things of which we have experience.
∴ No divine attributes and operations are things of which we have ideas.

AEE–2 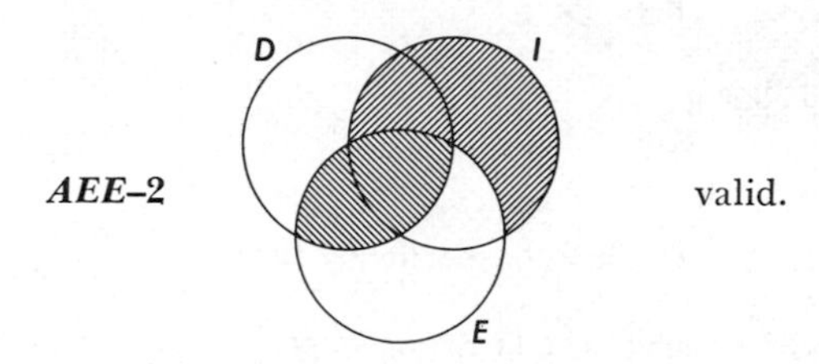

valid.

Valid enthymeme whose conclusion might be more colloquially expressed as, "We have no ideas of divine attributes and operations."

5. Third order.

No men who serve Mammon are men who serve God.
Henry is a man who serves Mammon.
∴ Henry is not a man who serves God.

EAE–1 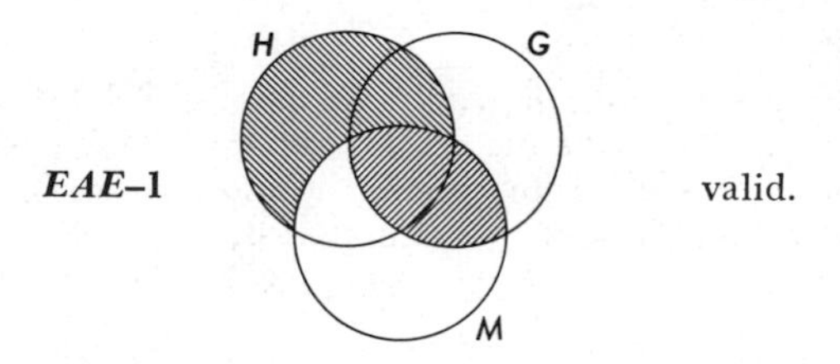

valid.

10. First order.

All fathers who know their own children are wise fathers.
He is a father who knows his own child.
∴ He is a wise father.

AAA–1 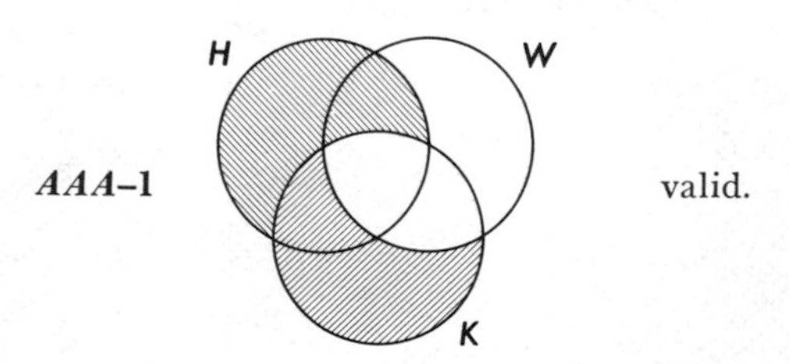

valid.

Here the missing major premiss was expressed in *The Merchant of Venice* as "It is a wise father that knows his own child."

15. First order.
    All who believe that all that exists is spiritual are Idealists.
    I am one who believes that all that exists is spiritual.
    ∴ I am an Idealist.

AAA–1

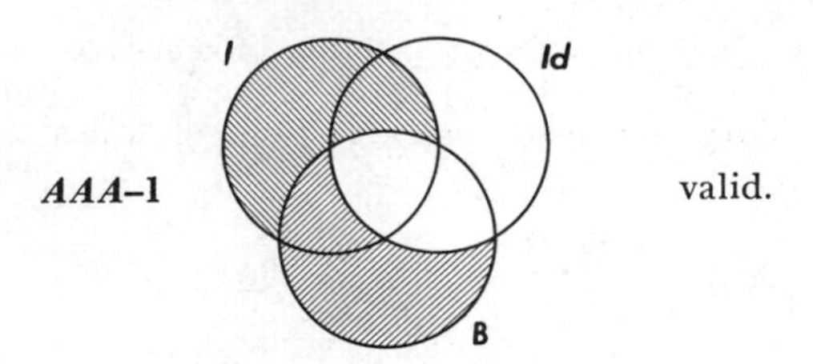

valid.

20. First order.
    All those who deserve the fair are those who are brave.
    Achilles is brave.
    ∴ Achilles is one who deserves the fair.

AAA–2

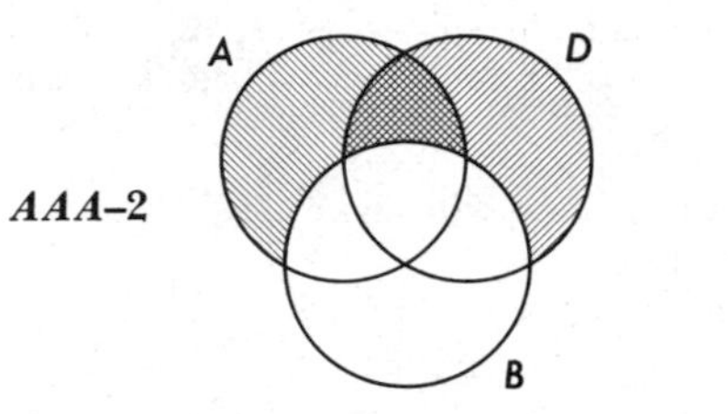

Invalid. (Undistributed Middle)

The missing major premiss was stated by Dryden as "None but the brave deserves the fair." To make the enthymeme into a valid syllogism the converse of the indicated missing premiss would have to be added. If it is, the result is a valid syllogism of form ***AAA*–1.**

Exercises on pages 229–231

I. 1. (1′) All babies are illogical persons.
(3′) All illogical persons are despised persons.
(2′) No persons who can manage crocodiles are despised persons.
∴ No babies are persons who can manage crocodiles.

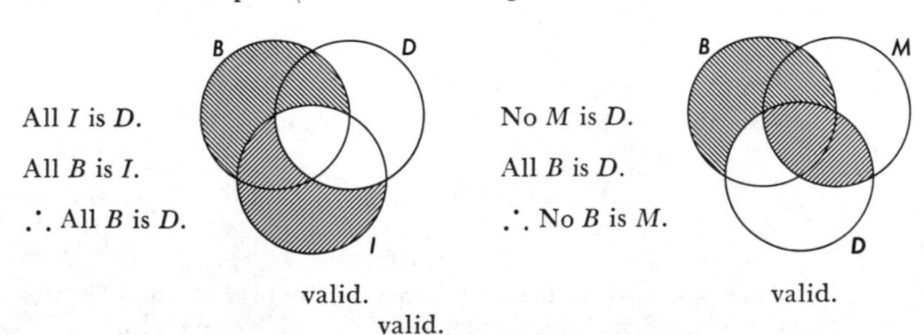

valid.

II. 1. (1′) All those who take in the *Times* are those who are well educated.
(3′) No creatures who cannot read are those who are well educated.
(2′) All hedgehogs are creatures who cannot read.
∴ No hedgehogs are those who take in the *Times*.

All *T* is *W*.
No *C* is *W*.
∴ No *C* is *T*.

valid.

No *C* is *T*.
All *H* is *C*.
∴ No *H* is *T*.

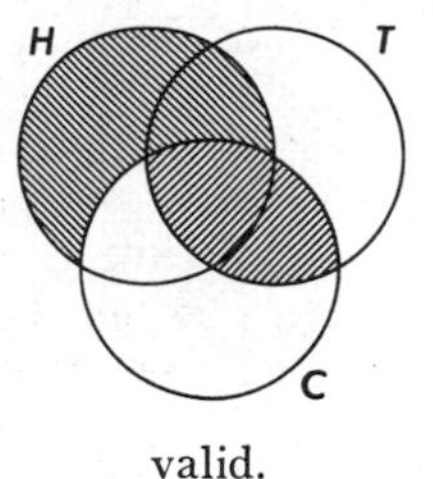

valid.

valid.

Exercises on pages 234–236

1. Disjunctive Syllogism. Valid.
5. Pure Hypothetical Syllogism. Invalid.
10. Disjunctive Syllogism. Valid.
15. Pure Hypothetical Syllogism. Valid.
20. Mixed Hypothetical Syllogism. *Modus Tollens.* Valid.
25. Mixed Hypothetical Syllogism. *Modus Tollens.* Valid.

Exercises on pages 241–243

1. Impossible to go between the horns. It would be plausible to grasp it by either horn, arguing either (a) that liberties do not properly include the right to publish false and harmful doctrines, or (b) that we run no risk of losing our own liberties if we vigorously oppose false and harmful doctrines with true and helpful ones. And it could be plausibly rebutted (but not refuted) by using its ingredients to prove that "we must either be guiltless of suppressing the liberties of others or else run no risk of losing our own liberties."

5. The key to refuting this dilemma lies in exposing the ambiguity of the key phrase "going beyond," which could mean "going logically beyond to what is not implied" or "going psychologically beyond to what is not suggested." When this is done it permits grasping it by one horn or the other depending upon which sense of "going beyond" is intended. And of course the usual plausible but nonrefuting rebuttal can be constructed here.

10. It is very easy to go between the horns here, because men lie on a continuum of virtue stretching from saints to sinners. It can plausibly be grasped by the second horn, arguing that even very bad men may be

deterred from wrongdoing by strictly enforced laws. And the usual plausible but nonrefuting rebuttal can be constructed here out of the ingredients of the given dilemma.

15. Impossible to go between the horns. It is plausible to grasp it by either horn, arguing either (a) that when desiring to preserve we may be motivated simply by inertia and seek to rest in the status quo even while admitting that a change would not be worse and might even be better —but just "not worth the trouble of changing," or (b) that when desiring to change we may be motivated simply by boredom with the status quo and seek a change even while admitting that a change might not be better and might even be worse—but "let's have a little variety." These are psychological rather than political or moral considerations, but the original dilemma appears to be itself psychological. The usual rebutting counterdilemma could be used here: When desiring to preserve, we do not wish to bring about something better; when desiring to change, we do not wish to prevent a change to the worse. It is a question, however, how plausible this is.

Exercises on pages 255–257

I. 1. False. 5. False. 10. True. 15. False.

II. 1. True. 5. True. 10. False. 15. False.

III. 1. $A \cdot (B \vee C)$ 5. $\sim(A \cdot B)$ 10. $(\sim C \vee \sim D) \cdot (\sim A \cdot \sim B)$

15. $(\sim A \cdot \sim E)$ 20. $(A \cdot E) \vee (\sim A \cdot \sim E)$

Exercises on pages 265–267

I. 1. True. 5. True. 10. False. 15. True.

II. 1. $E \supset (F \cdot G)$ 5. $(E \cdot F) \supset G$

10. $\sim[E \supset (F \cdot \sim G)]$ 15. $\sim F \vee E$

Exercises on pages 275–277

I. a. 3 is the specific form of a.
e. 10 is the specific form of e.
j. 6 has j as a substitution instance, and 23 is the specific form of j.

II. 1.

p	q	$p \supset q$	$\sim q$	$\sim p$	$\sim q \supset \sim p$
T	T	T	F	F	T
T	F	F	T	F	F
F	T	T	F	T	T
F	F	T	T	T	T

valid.

5.

p	q	$p \supset q$
T	**T**	**T**
T	**F**	**F**
F	**T**	**T**
F	**F**	**T**

invalid. (Shown by second row.)

10.

p	q	$p \cdot q$
T	**T**	**T**
T	**F**	**F**
F	**T**	**F**
F	**F**	**F**

valid.

15.

p	q	r	$q \supset r$	$p \supset (q \supset r)$	$p \supset r$	$q \supset (p \supset r)$	$p \vee q$	$(p \vee q) \supset r$
T	**T**	**T**	**T**	**T**	**T**	**T**	**T**	**T**
T	**T**	**F**	**F**	**F**	**F**	**F**	**T**	**F**
T	**F**	**T**	**T**	**T**	**T**	**T**	**T**	**T**
T	**F**	**F**	**T**	**T**	**F**	**T**	**T**	**F**
F	**T**	**T**	**T**	**T**	**T**	**T**	**T**	**T**
F	**T**	**F**	**F**	**T**	**T**	**T**	**T**	**F**
F	**F**	**T**	**T**	**T**	**T**	**T**	**F**	**T**
F	**F**	**F**	**T**	**T**	**T**	**T**	**F**	**T**

invalid. (Shown by fourth and sixth rows.)

20.

p	q	r	s	$p \cdot q$	$p \supset q$	$(p \cdot q) \supset r$	$r \supset s$	$p \supset (r \supset s)$	$(p \supset q) \cdot [(p \cdot q) \supset r]$	$p \supset s$
T	**T**	**T**	**T**	**T**	**T**	**T**	**T**	**T**	**T**	**T**
T	**T**	**T**	**F**	**T**	**T**	**T**	**F**	**F**	**T**	**F**
T	**T**	**F**	**T**	**T**	**T**	**F**	**T**	**T**	**F**	**T**
T	**T**	**F**	**F**	**T**	**T**	**F**	**T**	**T**	**F**	**F**
T	**F**	**T**	**T**	**F**	**F**	**T**	**T**	**T**	**F**	**T**
T	**F**	**T**	**F**	**F**	**F**	**T**	**F**	**F**	**F**	**F**
T	**F**	**F**	**T**	**F**	**F**	**T**	**T**	**T**	**F**	**T**
T	**F**	**F**	**F**	**F**	**F**	**T**	**T**	**T**	**F**	**F**
F	**T**	**T**	**T**	**F**	**T**	**T**	**T**	**T**	**T**	**T**
F	**T**	**T**	**F**	**F**	**T**	**T**	**F**	**T**	**T**	**T**
F	**T**	**F**	**T**	**F**	**T**	**T**	**T**	**T**	**T**	**T**
F	**T**	**F**	**F**	**F**	**T**	**T**	**T**	**T**	**T**	**T**
F	**F**	**T**	**T**	**F**	**T**	**T**	**T**	**T**	**T**	**T**
F	**F**	**T**	**F**	**F**	**T**	**T**	**F**	**T**	**T**	**T**
F	**F**	**F**	**T**	**F**	**T**	**T**	**T**	**T**	**T**	**T**
F	**F**	**F**	**F**	**F**	**T**	**T**	**T**	**T**	**T**	**T**

valid.

III. 1. $(A \vee B) \supset (A \cdot B)$
$A \vee B$
$\therefore A \cdot B$

has the specific form

$(p \vee q) \supset (p \cdot q)$
$p \vee q$
$\therefore p \cdot q$

p	q	$p \vee q$	$p \cdot q$	$(p \vee q) \supset (p \cdot q)$
T	**T**	**T**	**T**	**T**
T	**F**	**T**	**F**	**F**
F	**T**	**T**	**F**	**F**
F	**F**	**F**	**F**	**T**

valid.

5. $(I \vee J) \supset (I \cdot J)$ / $\sim(I \vee J)$ / $\therefore \sim(I \cdot J)$ has the specific form $(p \vee q) \supset (p \cdot q)$ / $\sim(p \vee q)$ / $\therefore \sim(p \cdot q)$

p	q	$p \vee q$	$p \cdot q$	$(p \vee q) \supset (p \cdot q)$	$\sim(p \vee q)$	$\sim(p \cdot q)$
T	T	T	T	T	F	F
T	F	T	F	F	F	T
F	T	T	F	F	F	T
F	F	F	F	T	T	T

valid.

IV. 1. $A \supset (B \vee C)$ / $\sim B$ / $\therefore A \supset C$ has the specific form $p \supset (q \vee r)$ / $\sim q$ / $\therefore p \supset r$

p	q	r	$q \vee r$	$p \supset (q \vee r)$	$\sim q$	$p \supset r$
T	T	T	T	T	F	T
T	T	F	T	T	F	F
T	F	T	T	T	T	T
T	F	F	F	F	T	F
F	T	T	T	T	F	T
F	T	F	T	T	F	T
F	F	T	T	T	T	T
F	F	F	F	T	T	T

valid.

5. $K \supset (E \supset A)$ / A / $\therefore K \supset E$ has the specific form $p \supset (q \supset r)$ / r / $\therefore p \supset q$

p	q	r	$q \supset r$	$p \supset (q \supset r)$	$p \supset q$
T	T	T	T	T	T
T	T	F	F	F	T
T	F	T	T	T	F
T	F	F	T	T	F
F	T	T	T	T	T
F	T	F	F	T	T
F	F	T	T	T	T
F	F	F	T	T	T

invalid. (shown by third row.)

Exercises on pages 282–283

I. 1. c is the specific form of 1.

5. c has 5 as a substitution instance, and i is the specific form of 5.

II. 1.

p	q	$p \supset q$	$p \supset (p \supset q)$	$[p \supset (p \supset q)] \supset q$
T	T	T	T	T
T	F	F	F	T
F	T	T	T	T
F	F	T	T	F

contingent.

5.

p	q	$\sim q$	$q \cdot \sim q$	$p \supset (q \cdot \sim q)$	$p \supset [p \supset (q \cdot \sim q)]$
T	T	F	F	F	F
T	F	T	F	F	F
F	T	F	F	T	T
F	F	T	F	T	T

contingent.

III. 1.

p	q	$p \supset q$	$\sim q$	$\sim p$	$\sim q \supset \sim p$	$(p \supset q) \equiv (\sim q \supset \sim p)$
T	T	T	F	F	T	T
T	F	F	T	F	F	T
F	T	T	F	T	T	T
F	F	T	T	T	T	T

tautology.

5.

p	q	$p \vee q$	$p \cdot (p \vee q)$	$p \equiv [p \cdot (p \vee q)]$
T	T	T	T	T
T	F	T	T	T
F	T	T	F	T
F	F	F	F	T

tautology.

Exercises on pages 290–294

I. 1. *Absorption* (Abs.)

5. Constructive Dilemma (C.D.)

10. *Hypothetical Syllogism* (H.S.)

15. *Modus Ponens* (M.P.)

II. 1.
3. 1, Simp.
4. 3, Add.
5. 2, 4, M.P.
6. 3, 5, Conj.

5.
5. 2, 4, M.P.
6. 1, 5, Conj.
7. 3, 4, D.S.
8. 6, 7, C.D.

III. 1.
1. $A \supset B$
2. $A \vee C$
3. $\sim B$ /∴ C
4. $\sim A$ 1, 3, M.T.
5. C 2, 4, D.S.

5.
1. $(Q \supset R) \cdot (S \supset T)$
2. $(U \supset V) \cdot (W \supset X)$
3. $Q \vee U$ /∴ $R \vee V$
4. $Q \supset R$ 1, Simp.
5. $U \supset V$ 2, Simp.
6. $(Q \supset R) \cdot (U \supset V)$ 4, 5, Conj.
7. $R \vee V$ 6, 3, C.D.

IV. 1.
1. $(G \vee H) \supset (J \cdot K)$
2. G /∴ J
3. $G \vee H$ 2, Add.
4. $J \cdot K$ 1, 3, M.P.
5. J 4, Simp.

5.
1. $C \supset R$
2. $(C \cdot R) \supset B$
3. $(C \supset B) \supset \sim S$
4. $S \vee M$ /∴ M
5. $C \supset (C \cdot R)$ 1, Abs.
6. $C \supset B$ 5, 2, H.S.
7. $\sim S$ 3, 6, M.P.
8. M 4, 7, D.S.

Exercises on pages 300–305

I. 1. *Transposition* (Trans.) 5. *Material Equivalence* (Equiv.)

10. *Association* (Assoc.) 15. *Distribution* (Dist.)

II. 1.
3. 2, Trans.
4. 3, D.N.
5. 1, 4, H.S.

5.
3. 2, Dist.
4. 3, Com.
5. 4, Simp.
6. 5, Taut.
7. 1, Assoc.
8. 7, 6, D.S.
9. 8, Impl.

III. 1.

1.	$A \supset \sim B$	
2.	$C \supset B$	$/ \therefore A \supset \sim C$
3.	$\sim B \supset \sim C$	2, Trans.
4.	$A \supset \sim C$	1, 3, H.S.

5.

1.	$[(M \cdot N) \cdot O] \supset P$	
2.	$Q \supset [(O \cdot M) \cdot N]$	$/ \therefore \sim Q \vee P$
3.	$[O \cdot (M \cdot N)] \supset P$	1, Com.
4.	$[(O \cdot M) \cdot N] \supset P$	3, Assoc.
5.	$Q \supset P$	2, 4, H.S.
6.	$\sim Q \vee P$	5, Impl.

10.

1.	$[H \vee (I \vee J)] \supset (K \supset J)$	
2.	$L \supset [I \vee (J \vee H)]$	$/ \therefore (L \cdot K) \supset J$
3.	$[(I \vee J) \vee H] \supset (K \supset J)$	1, Com.
4.	$[I \vee (J \vee H)] \supset (K \supset J)$	3, Assoc.
5.	$L \supset (K \supset J)$	2, 4, H.S.
6.	$(L \cdot K) \supset J$	5, Exp.

15.

1.	$(Z \supset Z) \supset (A \supset A)$	
2.	$(A \supset A) \supset (Z \supset Z)$	$/ \therefore A \supset A$
3.	$(A \supset A) \supset (A \supset A)$	2, 1, H.S.
4.	$\sim(A \supset A) \vee (A \supset A)$	3, Impl.
5.	$\sim(\sim A \vee A) \vee (A \supset A)$	4, Impl.
6.	$\sim(\sim A \vee A) \vee (\sim A \vee A)$	5, Impl.
7.	$(\sim \sim A \cdot \sim A) \vee (\sim A \vee A)$	6, De M.
8.	$(A \cdot \sim A) \vee (\sim A \vee A)$	7, D.N.
9.	$(\sim A \vee A) \vee (A \cdot \sim A)$	8, Com.
10.	$[(\sim A \vee A) \vee A] \cdot [(\sim A \vee A) \vee \sim A]$	9, Dist.
11.	$(\sim A \vee A) \vee A$	10, Simp.
12.	$\sim A \vee (A \vee A)$	11, Assoc.
13.	$\sim A \vee A$	12, Taut.
14.	$A \supset A$	13, Impl.

IV. 1.

1.	$\sim N \vee A$	
2.	N	$/ \therefore A$
3.	$N \supset A$	1, Impl.
4.	A	3, 2, M.P.

5.

1.	$R \supset A$	$/ \therefore R \supset (A \vee W)$
2.	$\sim R \vee A$	1, Impl.
3.	$(\sim R \vee A) \vee W$	2, Add.
4.	$\sim R \vee (A \vee W)$	3, Assoc.
5.	$R \supset (A \vee W)$	4, Impl.

10.
1. $(G \cdot S) \supset D$
2. $(S \supset D) \supset P$
3. G — $/\therefore P$
4. $G \supset (S \supset D)$ — 1, Exp.
5. $S \supset D$ — 4, 3, M.P.
6. P — 2, 5, M.P.

15.
1. $M \supset \sim C$
2. $\sim C \supset \sim A$
3. $D \vee A$ — $/\therefore \sim M \vee D$
4. $M \supset \sim A$ — 1, 2, H.S.
5. $A \vee D$ — 3, Com.
6. $\sim \sim A \vee D$ — 5, D.N.
7. $\sim A \supset D$ — 6, Impl.
8. $M \supset D$ — 4, 7, H.S.
9. $\sim M \vee D$ — 8, Impl.

Exercises on page 308

1.

A	*B*	*C*	*D*
f	f	f	t

5.

S	*T*	*U*	*V*	*W*	*X*
t	f	f	t	t	t

or any of thirteen other truth-value assignments.

Exercises on pages 312–315

I. 1.
1. $(A \supset B) \cdot (C \supset D)$ — $/\therefore (A \cdot C) \supset (B \vee D)$
2. $A \supset B$ — 1, Simp.
3. $\sim A \vee B$ — 2, Impl.
4. $(\sim A \vee B) \vee D$ — 3, Add.
5. $\sim A \vee (B \vee D)$ — 4, Assoc.
6. $[\sim A \vee (B \vee D)] \vee \sim C$ — 5, Add.
7. $\sim C \vee [\sim A \vee (B \vee D)]$ — 6, Com.
8. $(\sim C \vee \sim A) \vee (B \vee D)$ — 7, Assoc.
9. $(\sim A \vee \sim C) \vee (B \vee D)$ — 8, Com.
10. $\sim (A \cdot C) \vee (B \vee D)$ — 9, De M.
11. $(A \cdot C) \supset (B \vee D)$ — 10, Impl.

5.

X	*Y*	*Z*	*A*	*B*	*C*
t	f	t	f	t	f

II. 1.
1. $C \supset (M \supset D)$
2. $D \supset V$
3. $(D \supset A) \cdot \sim A$ — $/\therefore M \supset \sim C$
4. $D \supset A$ — 3, Simp.
5. $\sim A \cdot (D \supset A)$ — 3, Com.
6. $\sim A$ — 5, Simp.
7. $\sim D$ — 4, 6, M.T.
8. $(C \cdot M) \supset D$ — 1, Exp.
9. $\sim (C \cdot M)$ — 8, 7, M.T.
10. $\sim C \vee \sim M$ — 9, De M.
11. $\sim M \vee \sim C$ — 10, Com.
12. $M \supset \sim C$ — 11, Impl.

5. $(I \cdot S) \supset (G \cdot P)$
   $[(S \cdot \sim I) \supset A] \cdot (A \supset P)$
   $I \supset S$
   $\therefore P$

	I	S	G	P	A
proved invalid by	f	f	t	f	f
or	f	f	f	f	f

10. $(H \supset A) \cdot (F \supset C)$
    $A \supset (F \cdot E)$
    $(O \supset C) \cdot (O \supset M)$
    $P \supset (M \supset D)$
    $P \cdot (D \supset G)$
    $\therefore H \supset G$

	H	A	C	F	E	O	M	P	D	G
proved invalid by	t	t	t	t	t	f	f	t	f	f

Exercises on pages 327–328

I. 1. $(x)[Bx \supset Mx]$
5. $(\exists x)[Gx \cdot \sim Rx]$
10. $(x)[Cx \supset \sim Fx]$
15. $(x)[Vx \supset Cx]$

II. 1. $(\exists x)[Ax \cdot \sim Bx]$
5. $(\exists x)[Ix \cdot \sim Jx]$

Exercises on pages 335–336

I. 1.

1.	$(x)[Ax \supset \sim Bx]$	
2.	$(\exists x)[Cx \cdot Ax]$	$/\therefore (\exists x)[Cx \cdot \sim Bx]$
3.	$Ca \cdot Aa$	2, **EI**
4.	$Aa \supset \sim Ba$	1, **UI**
5.	$Aa \cdot Ca$	3, Com.
6.	Aa	5, Simp.
7.	$\sim Ba$	4, 6, M.P.
8.	Ca	3, Simp.
9.	$Ca \cdot \sim Ba$	8, 7, Conj.
10.	$(\exists x)[Cx \cdot \sim Bx]$	9, **EG**

5.

1.	$(x)[Mx \supset Nx]$	
2.	$(\exists x)[Mx \cdot Ox]$	$/\therefore (\exists x)[Ox \cdot Nx]$
3.	$Ma \cdot Oa$	2, **EI**
4.	$Ma \supset Na$	1, **UI**
5.	Ma	3, Simp.
6.	Na	4, 5, M.P.
7.	$Oa \cdot Ma$	3, Com.
8.	Oa	7, Simp.
9.	$Oa \cdot Na$	8, 6, Conj.
10.	$(\exists x)[Ox \cdot Nx]$	9, **EG**

II. 1.

1.	$(x)[Ax \supset \sim Bx]$	
2.	Bc	$/\therefore \sim Ac$
3.	$Ac \supset \sim Bc$	1, **UI**
4.	$\sim \sim Bc$	2, D.N.
5.	$\sim Ac$	3, 4, M.T.

5.

1.	$(x)[Mx \supset Nx]$	
2.	$(\exists x)[Ox \cdot Mx]$	$/\therefore (\exists x)[Ox \cdot Nx]$
3.	$Oa \cdot Ma$	2, **EI**
4.	$Ma \supset Na$	1, **UI**
5.	Oa	3, Simp.
6.	$Ma \cdot Oa$	3, Com.
7.	Ma	6, Simp.
8.	Na	4, 7, M.P.
9.	$Oa \cdot Na$	5, 8, Conj.
10.	$(\exists x)[Ox \cdot Nx]$	9, **EG**

Exercises on page 340

I. 1.

$(\exists x)[Ax \cdot Bx]$
$(\exists x)[Cx \cdot Bx]$
$\therefore (x)[Cx \supset \sim Ax]$

logically equivalent in $\boxed{a}$ to

$Aa \cdot Ba$
$Ca \cdot Ba$
$\therefore Ca \supset \sim Aa$

proved invalid by

Aa	Ba	Ca
t	**t**	**t**

5.

$(\exists x)[Mx \cdot Nx]$
$(\exists x)[Mx \cdot Ox]$
$\therefore (x)[Ox \supset Nx]$

logically equivalent in $\boxed{a, b}$ to

$(Ma \cdot Na) \vee (Mb \cdot Nb)$
$(Ma \cdot Oa) \vee (Mb \cdot Ob)$
$\therefore (Oa \supset Na) \cdot (Ob \supset Nb)$

proved invalid by

Ma	Mb	Na	Nb	Oa	Ob
t	**t**	**t**	**f**	**t**	**t**

or any of several other truth value assignments.

II. 1.

$(x)[Ax \supset Bx]$
$(x)[Cx \supset Bx]$
$\therefore (x)[Ax \supset Cx]$

logically equivalent in $\boxed{a}$ to

$Aa \supset Ba$
$Ca \supset Ba$
$\therefore Aa \supset Ca$

proved invalid by

Aa	Ba	Ca
t	**t**	**f**

5.

$(\exists x)[Mx \cdot Nx]$
$(\exists x)[Ox \cdot \sim Nx]$
$\therefore (x)[Ox \supset \sim Mx]$

logically equivalent in $\boxed{a, b}$ to

$(Ma \cdot Na) \vee (Mb \cdot Nb)$
$(Oa \cdot \sim Na) \vee (Ob \cdot \sim Nb)$
$\therefore (Oa \supset \sim Ma) \cdot (Ob \supset \sim Mb)$

proved invalid by

Ma	Mb	Na	Nb	Oa	Ob
t	**t**	**t**	**f**	**t**	**t**

or any of several other truth-value assignments.

Exercises on pages 344–347

I. 1. $(x)[(Ax \vee Ox) \supset (Dx \cdot Nx)]$ 5. $(x)[Mx \supset (Wx \equiv Lx)]$

II. 1.

1.	$(x)[(Ax \vee Bx) \supset (Cx \cdot Dx)]$	$/ \therefore (x)[Bx \supset Cx]$
2.	$(Ay \vee By) \supset (Cy \cdot Dy)$	1, UI
3.	$\sim(Ay \vee By) \vee (Cy \cdot Dy)$	2, Impl.
4.	$[\sim(Ay \vee By) \vee Cy] \cdot [\sim(Ay \vee By) \vee Dy]$	3, Dist.
5.	$\sim(Ay \vee By) \vee Cy$	4, Simp.
6.	$Cy \vee \sim(Ay \vee By)$	5, Com.
7.	$Cy \vee (\sim Ay \cdot \sim By)$	6, De M.
8.	$(Cy \vee \sim Ay) \cdot (Cy \vee \sim By)$	7, Dist.
9.	$(Cy \vee \sim By) \cdot (Cy \vee \sim Ay)$	8, Com.
10.	$Cy \vee \sim By$	9, Simp.
11.	$\sim By \vee Cy$	10, Com.
12.	$By \supset Cy$	11, Impl.
13.	$(x)[Bx \supset Cx]$	12, UG

5.
$(\exists x)[Sx \cdot Tx]$
$(\exists x)[Ux \cdot \sim Sx]$
$(\exists x)[Vx \cdot \sim Tx]$
$\therefore (\exists x)[Ux \cdot Vx]$

logically equivalent in $\boxed{a, b, c}$ to

$(Sa \cdot Ta) \vee (Sb \cdot Tb) \vee (Sc \cdot Tc)$
$(Va \cdot \sim Sa) \vee (Ub \cdot \sim Sb) \vee (Uc \cdot \sim Sc)$
$(Va \cdot \sim Ta) \vee (Vb \cdot \sim Tb) \vee (Vc \cdot \sim Tc)$
$\therefore (Ua \cdot Va) \vee (Ub \cdot Vb) \vee (Uc \cdot Vc)$

proved invalid by

Sa	*Sb*	*Sc*	*Ta*	*Tb*	*Tc*	*Ua*	*Ub*	*Uc*	*Va*	*Vb*	*Vc*
t	f	t	t	t	f	f	t	f	t	f	t

or any of several other truth value assignments.

III. 1.

1.	$(x)[(Ax \vee Bx) \supset Cx]$	
2.	$(x)[Vx \supset Ax]$	$/ \therefore (x)[Vx \supset Cx]$
3.	$(Ay \vee By) \supset Cy$	1, UI
4.	$Vy \supset Ay$	2, UI
5.	$\sim Vy \vee Ay$	4, Impl.
6.	$(\sim Vy \vee Ay) \vee By$	5, Add.
7.	$\sim Vy \vee (Ay \vee By)$	6, Assoc.
8.	$Vy \supset (Ay \vee By)$	7, Impl.
9.	$Vy \supset Cy$	8, 3, H.S.
10.	$(x)[Vx \supset Cx]$	9, UG

5. $(x)\{[Ex \cdot (Ix \vee Tx)] \supset \sim Sx\}$
$(\exists x)[Ex \cdot Ix]$
$(\exists x)[Ex \cdot Tx]$
$\therefore (x)[Ex \supset \sim Sx]$

This argument is logically equivalent in $\boxed{a, b}$ to

$\{[Ea \cdot (Ia \vee Ta)] \supset \sim Sa\} \cdot \{[Eb \cdot (Ib \vee Tb)] \supset \sim Sb\}$
$[Ea \cdot Ia] \vee [Eb \cdot Ib]$
$[Ea \cdot Ta] \vee [Eb \cdot Tb]$
$\therefore [Ea \supset \sim Sa] \cdot [Eb \supset \sim Sb]$

which is proved invalid by

	Ea	*Eb*	*Ia*	*Ib*	*Ta*	*Tb*	*Sa*	*Sb*
	t	t	t	f	t	f	f	t
or	t	t	f	t	f	t	t	f

IV. 1.

1.	$(x)[(Cx \cdot \sim Tx) \supset Px]$	
2.	$(x)[Ox \supset Cx]$	
3.	$(\exists x)[Ox \cdot \sim Px]$	$/ \therefore (\exists x)[Tx]$
4.	$Oa \cdot \sim Pa$	3, **EI**
5.	$Oa \supset Ca$	2, **UI**
6.	$(Ca \cdot \sim Ta) \supset Pa$	1, **UI**
7.	Oa	4, Simp.
8.	Ca	5, 7, M.P.
9.	$\sim Pa \cdot Oa$	4, Com.
10.	$\sim Pa$	9, Simp.
11.	$Ca \supset (\sim Ta \supset Pa)$	6, Exp.
12.	$\sim Ta \supset Pa$	11, 8, M.P.
13.	$\sim \sim Ta$	12, 10, M.T.
14.	Ta	13, D.N.
15.	$(\exists x)[Tx]$	14, **EG**

5. $(\exists x)[Dx \cdot Ax]$
$(x)[Ax \supset (Jx \vee Cx)]$
$(x)[Dx \supset \sim Cx]$
$(x)[(Jx \cdot Ix) \supset \sim Px]$
$(\exists x)[Dx \cdot Ix]$
$\therefore (\exists x)[Dx \cdot \sim Px]$
This argument is logically equivalent in $\boxed{a, b}$ to
$[Da \cdot Aa] \vee [Db \cdot Ab]$
$[Aa \supset (Ja \vee Ca)] \cdot [Ab \supset (Jb \vee Cb)]$
$[Da \supset \sim Ca] \cdot [Db \supset \sim Cb]$
$[(Ja \cdot Ia) \supset \sim Pa] \cdot [(Jb \cdot Ib) \supset \sim Pb]$
$[Da \cdot Ia] \vee [Db \cdot Ib]$
$\therefore [Da \cdot \sim Pa] \vee [Db \cdot \sim Pb]$
is proved invalid by

	Da	*Db*	*Aa*	*Ab*	*Ja*	*Jb*	*Ca*	*Cb*	*Ia*	*Ib*	*Pa*	*Pb*
	t	t	t	f	t	f	f	f	f	t	t	t
or	t	t	f	t	f	t	f	f	t	f	t	t

Exercises on pages 354–356

1. Analogical Argument.

5. Nonargumentative use of analogy.

10. Analogical Argument.

Exercises on pages 362–367

I. 1. (a) more, (b) more, (c) more, (d) more, (e) less, (f) neither.

II. 1. Large diamonds, armies, great intellects all have the properties of greatness [of value for diamonds, of military strength for armies, of mental superiority for intellects] and of divisibility [through cutting for diamonds, dispersion for armies, interruption, disturbance, and distraction for intellects].

Large diamonds and armies all have the property of having their greatness diminish when they are divided.

Therefore great intellects also have the property of having their greatness diminish when they are divided.

(1) There are only three kinds of instances among which the analogies are said to hold, which is not very many. On the other hand there are many, many instances of these kinds. By our first criterion the argument is fairly cogent.

(2) There are only three respects in which the things involved are said to be analogous. This is not many and the argument is accordingly rather weak.

(3) The conclusion states only that, when "divided," a great intellect will sink to the level of an ordinary one. This is not terribly strong a conclusion relative to the premisses, and so by our third criterion the argument is fairly cogent.

(4) The instances with which the conclusion deals are enormously, fantastically different from the instances mentioned in the premisses. There are so many disanalogies between intellects, on the one hand, and large diamonds and armies, on the other, that by our fourth criterion Schopenhauer's argument is almost totally lacking in probative force.

(5) There are but two kinds of instances in the premisses with which the conclusion's instances are compared. Armies and large diamonds are, however, quite dissimilar to each other, so from the point of view of our fifth criterion, the argument is moderately cogent.

(6) Schopenhauer recognizes that the question of relevance is important, for he introduces a separate little discussion on this point. He urges that the superiority (the "greatness") of a great intellect "depends upon" its concentration or undividedness. Here he invokes the illustrative or explanatory (nonargumentative) analogy of the concave mirror which focuses all its available light on one point. There is indeed some merit in this claim, and by our sixth criterion the argument has a fairly high degree of cogency.

Finally, however, it must be admitted that the whole passage might plausibly be analyzed as invoking large diamonds and armies for illustrative and explanatory rather than argumentative purposes. The plausibility of this alternative analysis, however, derives more from the weakness of the analogical argument than from what is explicitly stated in the passage in question.

5. This passage can be analyzed in two different ways. In both ways the analogical argument is presented primarily as an illustration of the biologist's reasoning.

(I) Porpoises and men all have lungs, warm blood, and hair.
Men are mammals.
Therefore porpoises are also mammals.

(1) There are many instances examined, which makes the conclusion probable.

(2) There are only three respects noted in the premisses in which porpoises and men resemble each other. In terms of their sheer

number, this is not many: not enough to make the argument plausible.

(3) The conclusion is enormously strong relative to the premisses, because so many properties are summarized in the term mammal (shown by the variety of other, specific properties confidently predicted by the zoologist). This tends, of course, to weaken the argument.

(4) There are many disanalogies between men and porpoises: porpoises are aquatic, men are terrestrial, porpoises have tails, men have not, porpoises do not have the well-developed, highly differentiated limbs characteristic of men, and so on. These tend to weaken the argument.

(5) There are very few dissimilarities among men—biologically speaking, and by our fifth criterion this tends to weaken the argument too.

(6) But in terms of relevance the argument is superlatively good, because biologists have found the three properties remarked in the premisses to be such remarkably dependable indicators of other mammalian characteristics.

(II) Porpoises and men all have lungs, warm blood, and hair.

Men also nurse their young with milk, have a four-chambered heart, bones of a particular type, a certain general pattern of nerves and blood vessels, and red blood cells that lack nuclei.

Therefore porpoises also nurse their young with milk, have a four-chambered heart, bones of the same particular type, the same general pattern of nerves and blood vessels, and red blood cells that lack nuclei.

This version of the analogical argument contained in the given passage is evaluated in much the same way as the first one discussed. It is somewhat stronger an argument than the first one according to the third criterion, because in spite of the apparently greater detail in the second version's conclusion, it is weaker than that of the first version because being a mammal entails all these details plus many more.

Nature has a way of reminding us that such arguments are only probable, however, and never demonstrative. For the platypus resembles all other mammals in having lungs, warm blood, hair, nursing their young with milk, and so on. Other mammals are viviparous (bearing their young alive). Therefore the platypus . . . ? No, the platypus lays eggs.

10. Gram-positive bacteria in culture mediums and gram-positive bacteria in the living body all have much the same properties: ways of growing, of reproducing, etc. Gram-positive bacteria in culture mediums have the property of being destroyed by the presence of penicillium. Therefore gram-positive bacteria in the living body also will be destroyed by the presence of penicillium.

(1) There are very many kinds and instances that have been examined, which makes the conclusion very probable.

(2) There are very many respects hidden in the "etc." in which gram-positive bacteria resemble each other whether in culture mediums or in the living body. These make the conclusion highly probable.

(3) The conclusion is strong relative to the premisses, though it could have been stronger. A weaker conclusion would have been that the presence of penicillium in the living body would have inhibited the growth of gram-positive bacteria there. A stronger conclusion would have stated that exactly that same amount of penicillium in the living body would destroy the gram-positive bacteria there in exactly the same time that it did in a culture medium. I think (especially in the light of subsequent knowledge!) that the conclusion could have been regarded at the time as highly probable.

(4) There are relatively few disanalogies between the living body and culture mediums *relative to the growth in them of bacteria.* (Of course this is a consequence of bacteriologists designing culture mediums to simulate the living body in the respects in which it is an acceptable habitat for bacteria.) So from this point of view also the conclusion is probable.

(5) There were many disanalogies among the instances mentioned in the premisses: Dr. Fleming "found that quite a number of species" were destroyed by penicillium. So here too the conclusion is highly probable.

(6) The analogy is very relevant because it was well known long before Dr. Fleming's discovery that a fungus subsists on organic matter. By this criterion also the conclusion is very probable.

Exercise on page 378

1. *A B C D* occur together with *a b c d*.
   A E F G occur together with *a e f g*.
   Therefore *A* is the cause ("the major factor") in *a*.

   Where *A* is the introduction of nicotine into the body; *B* is the introduction of hot carbon particles into the body; *C* is the introduction of assorted carcinogens into the body; *D* is the oral stimulation of the lips by cigarettes; *E* is the activity of preparing a hypodermic injection; *F* is the piercing of the skin with the hypodermic needle; *G* is the activity of cleaning the hypodermic equipment afterwards; *a* is a pleasant sensation; *b* is rawness of tongue, palate, and throat; *c* is gradual debilitation and increased susceptibility to emphysema, and so on; *d* is oral gratification; *e* is the satisfaction of preparing the injection; *f* is the slight pain at the site of the injection; and *g* is the bother of cleaning the hypodermic equipment afterward. WARNING: serious reflection on this example may be dangerous to your smoking habit.

Exercise on pages 382–383

1. Two arguments are present, both proceeding by the Method of Difference.

   (1) *A B* occur together with *a b*.
   B occurs together with *b*.
   Therefore *A* is the cause of *a*.

   Where *A* is air (containing micro-organisms), *B* is boiled meat broth, *a* is the presence of living micro-organisms in and putrefaction of the meat broth, *b* is the usual (other) phenomena connected with meat broth in a flask.

(2) *A B* occur together with *a b*.
B occurs together with *b*.
Therefore *A* is the cause of *a*.

Where *A* is ordinary, unfiltered air, *B* is a previously sterile filter, *a* is the presence of micro-organisms in the filter after *A* has been passed through *B* (proved by showing that it can set up putrefaction), *b* is the other physical phenomena common to filters whether or not they have been contaminated with micro-organisms. That *A* is absent in the second instance is the result of the second instance's *B* being the second filter through which air was passed. That *a* is absent in the second instance is proved by the fact that Pasteur could not set up putrefaction with it.

Exercise on pages 385–386

1. (1) *A B C* occur together with *a b c*.
A D E occur together with *a d e*.
A F G occur together with *a f g*.
. . . .
. . . .
. . . .
Therefore *A* is the cause of *a*.

Where the instances are the first group of chickens described; and *A* is the circumstance of feeding exclusively on white rice; *B, C, D, E, F, G*, . . . are other circumstances in which the chickens probably differed among themselves; *a* is the phenomenon of developing polyneuritis and dying; and b, c, d, e, f, g, . . . , are other phenomena attending the various chickens in this experiment. This is of course the Method of Agreement.

(2) *U B C* occur together with *u b c*.
U D E occur together with *u d e*.
U F G occur together with *u f g*.
. . . .
. . . .
. . . .
Therefore *U* is the cause of *u*.

Where the instances are the second group of chickens described; and *U* is the circumstance of being fed unpolished rice; *B, C, D, E, F, G*, . . . are other circumstances in which these chickens probably differed among themselves but resembled the various chickens in the first group; *u* is the phenomenon of remaining healthy (or *not* contracting polyneuritis); and *b, c, d, e, f, g*, . . . are other phenomena attending the various chickens in this (second) experiment. This too is the Method of Agreement.

(3) *A B C* occur together with *a b c*.
B C occur together with *b c*.
Therefore *A* is the cause of *a*.

Where the instances are the first chicken of the first group and the first chicken of the second group, and A, B, C, a, b, c are as described above (the *absence* of A and a correspond to the presence of U and u, respectively, so here the latter need not be symbolized explicitly). This is the Method of Difference, and there are as many uses of the Method of Difference here as there are "matching" pairs of chickens in the two groups.

(4) A B C occur together with a b c.
B C occur together with b c.
Therefore A is the cause of a.

Here is each instance of the polyneuritic chickens which recovered when fed polishings from rice. Here A is feeding the polishings from rice; B, C are other circumstances of the chicken in question; a is recovery from polyneuritis; and b and c are other phenomena attending the chicken in question. Here is the Method of Difference again.

Exercise on pages 390–391

1. A B occur together with a b.
B is known to be the cause of b.
Therefore A is the cause of a.

Where A is "sensory and perceptual factors" in rats, B is "alimentary factors" in rats (appetite, hunger, general need for and concern with food), a is rats hoarding "worthless inedible pellets" covered with aluminum foil, b is rats hoarding plain food pellets.

Exercise on page 396

1. A B C —— a b c.
$A-$ B C —— $a-$ b c.
$A+$ B C —— $a+$ b c.
Therefore A is a cause of or causally connected with a.

Where A is gasoline consumption (or automobile pollution of air), B, C are other circumstances roughly constant over the years, a is lung-cancer incidence in U.S. white males, and b and c are other phenomena roughly constant over the years. $A-$ is the 35 per cent drop in gasoline consumption between 1940 and 1945; $a-$ is the drop in incidence of lung cancer in U.S. white males "by approximately the same percentage" between 1940 and 1945; $A+$ is the nineteenfold increase in the rate of gasoline consumption between 1914 and 1950; $a+$ is the nineteenfold increase in lung cancer mortality between 1914 and 1950.

Exercises on pages 410–417

1. (1) A B C occur together with a b c.
A D E occur together with a d e.
Therefore A is the cause of a.

Here A is the circumstance of being sprayed with aqueous solutions of 2, 4, 5-T at 100- or 200-ppm. concentrations; *B, C, D, E* are other circumstances attending Rome Beauty apples; *a* is the phenomenon of ripening early; *b, c, d, e* are other phenomena attending ripening Rome Beauty apples. This is the Method of Agreement.

(2) *A B C* occur together with *a b c*.
B C occur together with *b c*.
Therefore *A* is the cause of *a*.

Here *A, B, C, a, b, c* are as above, where the first instance is a sprayed apple, the second is an unsprayed one that did not ripen early. This is the Method of Difference.

(3) *A* *B C* —— *a* *b c*.
A+ *B C* —— *a*+ *b c*.
A++ *B C* —— *a*++ *b c*.
A+++ *B C* —— *a*+++ *b c*.
Therefore *A* is the cause of *a*.

Here *A* is application of 0-, *A*+ application of 10-, *A*++ application of 100-, *A*+++ application of 200-ppm. concentrations of 2, 4, 5-T in aqueous solution; *a* is softness of fruit measured at 25.9 lb., *a*+ is softness of 24.8 lb., *a*++ softness of 19.8 lb., and *a*+++ softness of 18.9 lb. This is the Method of Concomitant Variation.

5. *A B C* occur together with *a b c*.
B C occur together with *b c*.
Therefore *A* is the cause of *a*.

The instance in the first line is the particular rabbit used by Ehrlich and Hata, first infected with syphilis and then injected with 606 solution. The instance in the second line is the same rabbit, after infection but before injection. Here *A* is the circumstance of injecting 606 solution, *B, C* are other circumstances attending the rabbit in question, *a* is the asbence of spirochetes and the remission of ulcers, *b, c* are other phenomena attending the rabbit in question. This is the Method of Difference.

10. *A B C* occur together with *a b c*.
A B D occur together with *a b d*.
Therefore *A B* is the cause of *a*.

The instances here are different monkeys undergoing stress, *A,* and suffering electric shock, *B,* with *C* and *D* being other circumstances attending each of the monkeys, respectively. Here *a* is the phenomenon of ulcers, *b* is the pain induced by the electric shock, and *c* and *d* other phenomena attending the two monkeys, respectively.

This use of the Method of Agreement establishes only that *A B* is the cause of ulcers, but not that *A* alone is the cause. The second experiment does that.

A B C occur together with *a b c*.
B C occur together with *b c*.
Therefore *A* is the cause of *a*.

The instance in the first line is the "executive" monkey who undergoes the stress *A* of having to prevent the electric shocks *B*. The other circumstances attending him are combined as *C*. The instance in the second line is the control monkey who undergoes the shock *B* but not the stress *A,* and also the other circumstances *C* of the rigid schedule arranged by the experimenters. They found ulcers *a* in the "executive" but not in the control, though they shared the other phenomena of pain *b* and miscellaneous *c*. This is the Method of Difference. The entire experiment proceeds by way of the Joint Method of Agreement and Difference.

Exercises on pages 460–465

1. The first datum to be explained is the apparent slowness of rotation of the planet Venus. The first hypothesis considered is that Venus, like Mercury, rotates at the same rate that it revolves about the sun, thus keeping the same side always toward the sun and the other side always dark.

   This hypothesis is surely relevant: if Venus does rotate slowly that would explain why it appears to rotate slowly. It is testable by various means, not all of which are as yet technically feasible. It is especially compatible with the previously established hypothesis that Mercury behaves the same way. It has predictive power, not only to explain the original datum, but other phenomena which can be used in testing it. And it is an admirably simple hypothesis.

   The first hypothesis leads to the prediction that the dark side of Venus must be exceedingly cold. But Pettit and Nicholson measured the temperature of the dark side of Venus and found it to be comparatively mild, −9°F. This disconfirms the first hypothesis, unless it can be salvaged by some other hypothesis that could explain the apparent discrepancy.

   The second hypothesis considered as a possible way to save the first one is that atmospheric currents from the warm and bright side of Venus could perpetually heat the cold and dark side. This second hypothesis could save the first one.

   The second hypothesis is clearly relevant. It is testable by various means, not all technically feasible at present. It has predictive power and is fairly simple. But it is not compatible with previously well-established hypotheses about the size of Venus and—especially—the behavior of atmospheric currents. So the second hypothesis is rejected, and with it the first.

   The third hypothesis intended to replace the first two is that Venus rotates "fairly often."

   This third hypothesis is relevant, for if Venus rotates only *fairly* often that would explain the original datum that Venus appears to rotate slowly, and if it rotates fairly *often* that would explain why the dark side does not cool excessively. This is of course very loose: the actual hypothesis in this case must ultimately be made quantitative to take account of the actual measurements that are made. And the third hypothesis also satisfies the several other criteria discussed in the text.

5. The data to be explained here are the steep rates at which the surface of the moon cools down and heats up during and after lunar eclipses.

   The hypothesis that the surface of the moon is solid rock, or composed of rocks of microscopic size, is rejected because it is incompatible with the previously well-established hypothesis that "no solid piece of rock can cool down and heat up so quickly."

The alternative hypothesis is that the upper surface of the moon is "a thick layer of heat-insulating dust as fine as face powder." This hypothesis is relevant, for it would certainly explain the extremely rapid changes of surface temperature: only the few inches of dust change temperature, the insulated substratum remains relatively constant in temperature. It is testable, though at the time it was proposed the techniques were not technically feasible. It is compatible with previously established hypotheses. It has predictive power: it could be used to predict what would happen if a meteorite should land on the surface of the moon. And it is fairly simple.

But there is the question: How did the surface of the moon become so minutely pulverized? Here Dr. Buettner proposed his hypothesis that the moon's rocks have been ground to dust not merely by "the sandblasting of meteoric dust" but by "the everlasting influx of cosmic rays."

This hypothesis is relevant, testable, compatible with previously well-established hypotheses, has predictive and explanatory power, and is simple.

And yet moon rocks brought back to earth by our Apollo flights show that the moon is not covered by "dust as fine as face powder." This should help emphasize the fact that scientific theories and hypotheses are continually subject to revision as new data are accumulated.

10. The data to be explained are the sleep movements of animals: whimpering, whisker twitching, and leg pumping. The hypothesis is that they are dreaming.

The hypothesis is certainly relevant even though it rests only on an analogy with human behavior, which has been tested through human subjects' reporting (on awakening) dreams which were earlier manifested by their sleep movements.

But the hypothesis applied to animal behavior is not testable in the same way, because animals cannot give postdreaming reports.

The experimenter devised two tests of the hypothesis based on deductions from it. The first test (not quite adequately reported in the brief excerpt) pertains to the electroencephalograph (EEG). Characteristic EEG tracings were associated with visual perceptions of rhesus monkeys while awake. It was further hypothesized that the same EEG tracings would accompany the hypothesized dream "visual perceptions" of the sleeping monkeys. Then it was predicted that during the sleep movements of the monkeys that suggest that they are dreaming, EEG tracings would occur. This test verified the prediction and thus tended to confirm the original hypothesis.

The second test of the original hypothesis involved conditioning monkeys to make a specific motor response to visual perceptions in their waking state. It was further hypothesized that the conditioning would be carried over from the waking to the sleeping state. Then it was predicted that during the sleep movements of the monkeys that suggest they are dreaming, the conditioned specific motor response would occur to the hypothesized dream "visual perceptions." This test verified the prediction and thus tended to confirm the original hypothesis also.

The hypothesis that animals dream is relevant, testable, compatible with previously well-established hypotheses, has predictive and explanatory power, and is simple.

Exercises on page 477

1. $1/2 \times 1/2 \times 1/2 = 1/8$
5. $1/4 \times 1/3 \times 1/2 \times 1/1 = 1/24$

Exercises on pages 482–483

1. Probability of losing with a 2, a 3, or a 12 is 4/36 or 1/9.
   Probability of throwing a 4, and then a 7 before another 4, is $3/36 \times 6/9 = 1/18$.
   Probability of throwing a 10, and then a 7 before another 10, is likewise 1/18.
   Probability of throwing a 5, and then a 7 before another 5, is $4/36 \times 6/10 = 1/15$.
   Probability of throwing a 9, and then a 7 before another 9, is likewise 1/15.
   Probability of throwing a 6, and then a 7 before another 6, is $5/36 \times 6/11 = 5/66$.
   Probability of throwing an 8, and then a 7 before another 8, is likewise 5/66.
   The sum of the probabilities of the exclusive ways of the shooter's losing is 251/495.
   So the shooter's chance of winning is $1 - 251/495 = 244/495$ or .493–.
5. No, for the probability of throwing an ace is $1 - 125/216 = 91/216$ or .421+.

Exercises on pages 487–488

1. $2.76
5. $15.00

Special Symbols

	Page
O	173
$=$	173
$\neq$	173
SP	174
$\bar{S}$	174
$\cdot$	247
$\sim$	249
v	251
$\supset$	261
$\equiv$	280
$/\therefore$	288f.
(x)	320
$(\exists x)$	320
ϕ	320
ψ	325
ν	329
$P(a)$	474
ā	480

Index